W9-ARX-111

A GUIDE TO
FORENSIC ACCOUNTING
INVESTIGATION

THOMAS W. GOLDEN, STEVEN L. SKALAK, AND MONA M. CLAYTON

WILEY

JOHN WILEY & SONS, INC.

This book is printed on acid-free paper. ∞

Copyright © 2006 by PricewaterhouseCoopers LLP. PricewaterhouseCoopers refers to the individual member firms of the worldwide PricewaterhouseCoopers organization. All rights reserved.

Published by John Wiley & Sons, Inc., Hoboken, New Jersey.

Published simultaneously in Canada.

No part of this publication may be reproduced, stored in a retrieval system, or transmitted in any form or by any means, electronic, mechanical, photocopying, recording, scanning, or otherwise, except as permitted under Section 107 or 108 of the 1976 United States Copyright Act, without either the prior written permission of the Publisher, or authorization through payment of the appropriate per-copy fee to the Copyright Clearance Center, Inc., 222 Rosewood Drive, Danvers, MA 01923, 978-750-8400, fax 978-646-8600, or on the Web at *www.copyright.com*. Requests to the Publisher for permission should be addressed to the Permissions Department, John Wiley & Sons, Inc., 111 River Street, Hoboken, NJ 07030, 201-748-6011, fax 201-748-6008, or online at *http://www.wiley.com/go/permissions*.

Limit of Liability/Disclaimer of Warranty: While the publisher and author have used their best efforts in preparing this book, they make no representations or warranties with respect to the accuracy or completeness of the contents of this book and specifically disclaim any implied warranties of merchantability or fitness for a particular purpose. No warranty may be created or extended by sales representatives or written sales materials. The advice and strategies contained herein may not be suitable for your situation. You should consult with a professional where appropriate. Neither the publisher nor author shall be liable for any loss of profit or any other commercial damages, including but not limited to special, incidental, consequential, or other damages.

For general information on our other products and services, or technical support, please contact our Customer Care Department within the United States at 800-762-2974, outside the United States at 317-572-3993 or fax 317-572-4002.

Wiley also publishes its books in a variety of electronic formats. Some content that appears in print may not be available in electronic books.

For more information about Wiley products, visit our Web site at *http://www.wiley.com*.

Library of Congress Cataloging-in-Publication Data

Golden, Thomas W.
  A guide to forensic accounting investigation / Thomas W. Golden, Steven L. Skalak, and Mona M. Clayton.
    p. cm.
  Includes index.
  ISBN-13: 978-0-471-46907-0 (cloth)
  ISBN-10: 0-471-46907-6 (cloth)
  1. Fraud investigation--Auditing. 2. Forensic accounting--Auditing. I. Golden, Thomas W. II. Skalak, Steven L. III. Clayton, Mona M. III. Title.
  HV8079.F4G65 2005
  363.25'963--dc22

                                          2004027090

Printed in the United States of America

10   9   8   7   6   5   4   3   2

CONTENTS

PREFACE

*T*he catastrophic business failures of this decade have been revealing on many levels. From my professional perspective as a forensic accounting investigator, I couldn't help but notice the need across much of the business community for a better grasp of the scope and skills of the forensic accounting investigator. Most people seemed to be struggling. How could these massive frauds have occurred? How can such events be deterred—if not wholly prevented—in the future? Who is responsible for deterrence, detection, and investigation? Is it a matter of systems, of attitudes, of aggressive internal policing, of more stringent regulatory oversight, of "all of the above" and more still? What methods are effective? What should an auditor, a corporate director, an executive look for? There were far more questions than answers, and all the questions were difficult. Forensic accounting investigation had become important to the larger business community and the public. They were relying on it to solve problems, deter new problems, and contribute to new, tougher standards of corporate behavior and reported information. But all concerned, from CEOs to financial statement auditors, still have much to learn about the relatively new discipline of forensic accounting investigation.

We live in the post-Enron era. The keynotes of the era are tough new legislation and regulation to strengthen corporate governance and new oversight of the auditors. Additionally, the Public Company Accounting Oversight Board (PCAOB) continues to review the need for a new fraud standard. All of these initiatives are intended to increase investor confidence in corporate information.

Pushing these trends relentlessly forward is the conviction of the concerned public that corporate fraud is unacceptable. It may well occur—this is an imperfect world—but everything must be done to deter, detect, investigate, and penalize it. Investors look to corporate directors and executives, internal and external auditors, and regulators to keep companies honest. They want to be able to trust securities analysts to report and recommend without concealed self-interest. And they expect lenders, business partners, and others who deal with a corporation to exercise and require sound business ethics.

Where fraud is concerned, there is no silver bullet. Clearly, a book would help to address the needs of three broad constituencies: management, corporate directors, and auditors (internal and external). Just as clearly, it shouldn't be a book that focused only on concepts and facts. It would need to look at practice. It would have to convey effective working attitudes and realistic perspectives on many issues, from the varied skills required of forensic accounting investigators to working with attorneys and reporting findings. It would have to offer case studies that reveal the thinking both of experienced investigators and of the fraudsters they pursue. In short, it would have to bring its readers into the complex and evolving culture of forensic accounting investigation while serving as a comprehensive, reliable, easily used reference source.

This was a tall order. Two close PricewaterhouseCoopers colleagues in our firm's forensic accounting investigation practice, Steven Skalak and Mona Clayton, accepted the challenge with me. We quickly realized that the topics worthy of inclusion needed a still larger team with diverse experience. With this in mind, we invited forensic accounting investigators within our global organization, as well as admired attorneys with whom we had worked in other organizations, to join us as chapter authors. We three necessarily remained at the center, questioning, revising, and applauding. We were also responsible for chapters of our own. The process took two years.

This is a book that some readers will explore page by page; others will use it as a reference. However it is approached, it will reveal the surprising complexity of fraud deterrence, detection, and investigation and offer a step-by-step method to understanding that complexity. The range of concerns is vast—from the tightly constructed guidelines of SAS 99 (the most recent *Statement on Auditing Standards* concerned with fraud detection) to the tough-minded skills required to conduct an admission-seeking interview with an alleged perpetrator of fraud. Some readers will seek in this book a broad appreciation for investigative techniques so that they can more effectively manage the process when and if needed. Others will want to commit the details to memory. For both types of reader, it is all here: common fraudulent schemes, the psychology of the fraudster, the need for professional skepticism, responding to whistle-blowers, working with lawyers and prosecutors, new technologies that facilitate detection, and much more.

A common theme running through all of the chapters is the need for change. External and internal auditors must train thoroughly in fraud-detection procedures and attitudes. The university education of the next generation of auditors should reflect the new emphasis on fraud deterrence, detection, and investigation. And executives and directors must be fully aware of the threat of fraud and do all they can to institute measures to deter it, ranging from robustly enforced codes of ethics to internal controls that make fraud less likely and easier to detect.

In practical reality, no one can guarantee that all frauds will be either prevented or detected in a timely manner. Yet the toolbox of those who safeguard the integrity of corporate information and investigate possible wrongdoing is well filled. This book will make that clear. It puts before the reader what is, to my mind, an extraordinary array of best practices, tools, and techniques for the deterrence, detection, and investigation of corporate fraud. The skills and knowledge of the forensic accounting investigator are evident in every page.

This is by no means a casual book, tossed off to meet an ephemeral need. We hope that the effort that has gone into it will make it substantively useful over the long term. With proper knowledge and diligence among all those who are responsible for providing financial information for the capital markets, financial fraud can be significantly deterred. As the suspicion and reality of fraud diminish across the corporate world, investors will regain confidence in the integrity of corporate information. The ultimate purpose of this book reaches past the audit profession—and the directors and managers who hire and work with auditors—to address the needs of the capital markets worldwide.

Thomas W. Golden
Partner
PricewaterhouseCoopers LLP

ACKNOWLEDGMENTS

A book of this scope is a collective endeavor. We want to take this opportunity to thank Dennis Nally, Juan Pujadas, Greg Bardnell, and Greg Garrison. We want also to identify those individuals who have contributed to a sustained effort of thinking, writing, fact-checking, editing, and project management.

There was a team around us from the beginning. We owe a particular debt of gratitude to Robbie Pound. This is a better book for his review and editorial suggestions. Mark Friedlich was indispensable as project manager, editor, and counselor. Hillary Ruben, serving as coproject manager, kept us focused on the next mountain to climb and ensured, thorough communication, as we progressed. If we remained of good cheer, it was largely her doing. Roger Lipsey's editorial skill is evident throughout the book. That we have achieved a consistent and clear voice has much to do with his efforts. We also benefited from the editorial contributions of Gene Zasadinski, David Evanson, Paula Plantier, and Michael Juhre. Wendy Amstutz kept us thinking about the audiences for this book and dazzled us with the possibility that we might someday actually complete and publish it. And Mark Starcher created and administered the enormously helpful Web site where we all could share in developments.

At John Wiley & Sons, we benefited from the patience and acumen—as they well know—of Robert Chiarelli, John DeRemigis, Julie Burden, and their colleagues.

We owe particular gratitude to our Chicago- and New York-based practice teams. The directors, managers, staff, and assistants with whom we work closely, as well as many other colleagues, performed research, checked exhibits, read chapters, chased facts, and provided insights. Their tireless effort and enthusiasm energized us each day in the conviction that this book will be useful to many people in these challenging times.

Our greatest thanks go to our fellow authors—practitioners in the United States and around the globe, and a number of attorneys with other firms or government, who drew on their time, experience, and wisdom to write many of the chapters. At the head of each chapter, readers will find these individuals clearly and gratefully identified. This is their book as much as it is ours.

The following roster names, with gratitude, the authors who created the original drafts of all chapters and approved their final form. All are partners or employees of PricewaterhouseCoopers apart from clearly identified exceptions.

1. Fraud: An Introduction
   Steven L. Skalak
   Manny A. Alas
   Gus Sellitto

The authors offer this book with the hope that it answers a very real need and will provide its readers with a new and compelling vision of the role of forensic accountants in the deterrence, detection, and investigation of corporate fraud. The views expressed in this book are those of the individual authors and are not necessarily the views of PricewaterhouseCoopers or any other Pricewaterhouse-Coopers partner or employee. Unless otherwise indicated, the authors are not attorneys and their comments are based on their personal experiences and do not represent legal advice.

Thomas W. Golden
Steven L. Skalak
Mona M. Clayton

CHAPTER 1

FRAUD: AN INTRODUCTION

Steven L. Skalak

Manny A. Alas

Gus Sellitto

Fraud evokes a visceral reaction in us. It is an abuse of our expectation of fair treatment by fellow human beings. Beyond that, it is a blow to our self-image as savvy managers capable of deterring or detecting a fraudulent scheme. Whether we react because of values or because of vanity, nobody likes to be duped. Many elements of modern society are focused on maintaining an environment of fair dealing. Laws are passed; agencies are established to enforce them; police are hired; ethics and morals are taught in schools and learned in businesses; and criminals are punished by the forfeiture of their ill-gotten gains and personal liberty—all with a view to deterring, detecting, and punishing fraud. The profession of auditing grew out of society's need to ensure fair and correct dealings in commerce and government.

One of the central outcomes of fraud is financial loss. Therefore, in the minds of the investing public, the accounting and auditing profession is inextricably linked with fraud deterrence, fraud detection, and fraud investigation. This is true to such an extent that there are those whose perception of what can be realistically accomplished in an audit frequently exceeds the services that any accountant or auditor can deliver and, in terms of cost, exceeds what any business might be willing to pay (see Chapter 2). In the past few years, public anger over occurrences of massive fraud in public corporations has spawned new legislation, new auditing standards, new oversight of the accounting profession, and greater penalties for those who conspire to commit or conceal financial fraud.

This book addresses the distinct roles of corporate directors, management, external auditors, internal auditors, and forensic accounting investigators with respect to fraud deterrence, fraud detection, and fraud investigation.[1] As will quickly become apparent later in this introductory chapter, these professionals are by no means the only ones concerned with combating fraud. However, each has a significant role in the larger effort to minimize fraud.

◆ FRAUD: WHAT IS IT?

Generally, all acts of fraud can be distilled into four basic elements:

1. A false representation of a material nature[2]
2. Scienter—knowledge that the representation is false, or reckless disregard for the truth
3. Reliance—the person receiving the representation reasonably and justifiably relied on it
4. Damages—financial damages resulting from all of the above

By way of illustration, consider the classic example of the purchase of a used car. The salesperson is likely to make representations about the quality of the car, its past history, and the quality of parts subject to wear and tear, ranging from the transmission to the paint job. The elements of fraud may or may not arise out of such statements. First, there is a distinction between hype and falsehood. The salesperson hypes when he claims that the 1977 Chevy Vega "runs like new." However, were he to turn back the odometer, he would be making a false representation. Second, the false statement must be material. If the odometer reading is accurate, the salesperson's representation that the car runs like new or was only driven infrequently, is, strictly speaking, mere hype: the purchaser need only look at the odometer to form a prudent view of the extent of use and the car's likely roadworthiness. Third, the fraudster must make the material false misrepresentation with *scienter,* that is, with actual knowledge that the statement is false or with a reckless disregard for the truth. For example, the car may or may not have new tires. But if the salesperson, after making reasonable inquiries, truly believes that the Vega has new tires, there is no knowing misrepresentation. There may be negligence, but there is no fraud. Fourth, the potential victim must justifiably rely on the false repre-

---

1. "Forensic accountants" are members of a broad group of professionals that *includes* those who perform financial investigations, but it is actually wider. The public often uses the term "forensic accountants" to refer to financial investigators, although many forensic accountants do not perform financial investigations. In Chapter 27 we discuss the many other services encompassed under the broader term "forensic accounting." A forensic accounting investigator is trained and experienced in investigating and resolving suspicions or allegations of fraud through document analysis to include both financial and nonfinancial information, interviewing, and third-party inquiries, including commercial databases. See Auditing and Investigation at end of this chapter. "Auditors" is used throughout this text to represent both internal and external auditors unless otherwise specified as pertaining to one group or the other.
2. The term "material" as used in this context is a legal standard whose definition varies from jurisdiction to jurisdiction; it should not be confused with the concept of materiality as used in auditing, in which one considers the effect of fraud and errors related to financial statement reporting.

sentation. A buyer who wants a blue car may actually believe the salesperson's representation that "it's really blue but looks red in this light." Reliance in that case is, at best, naive and certainly not justified. Finally, there must be some form of damage. The car must in fact prove to be a lemon when the purchaser drives off in it and realizes that he has been misled. Regardless of context, from Enron to WorldCom to Honest Abe's Used Car Lot, fraud is fraud, and it displays the four simple elements noted above.

◆ FRAUD: PREVALENCE, IMPACT, AND FORM

Fraud is a feature of every organized culture in the world. It affects many organizations, regardless of size, location, or industry. According to the ACFE survey, approximately $660 billion was lost by U.S. companies in 2004 due to occupational fraud and abuse, and nearly one in six cases cost the organization in excess of $1 million.[3] Thirty-two percent of all fraud is committed by males aged 41 to 50, while the greatest loss per fraudulent act is caused by males aged 60 and over.[4] In the area of material financial reporting fraud, in two studies conducted on the issue, both using information obtained from the SEC, it was determined that over 70 percent of all financial statement frauds are committed by the top executives of the organization.[5]

However, if one were to look at the FBI's statistics for white-collar crime, one would not reach this conclusion because those statistics are based upon prosecutions and, as discussed in Chapter 22, "Supporting a Criminal Prosecution," the overwhelming majority of frauds are not prosecuted. Based upon our own experience as well as on surveys conducted by PwC (PwC Economic Crime Survey) and the Association of Certified Fraud Examiners (ACFE), we believe that fraud is pervasive.

In Europe, according to the PwC Global Economic Crime Survey statistics for prior years, 42.5 percent of larger European companies fell victim to fraud in 2000 and 2001. Across all of the companies surveyed, the average cost of fraud was €6.7 million. Overall, approximately 40 percent of large European organizations believe that the risk of fraud in the future will be at least as high as it is now, while about one-third of them believe that it will be even higher.[6] While these statistics were gathered in 2001, if anything, the current climate in Europe suggests that higher percentages would prevail today in a resurvey of the same population.

---

3. Association of Certified Fraud Examiners, *2004 Report to the Nation on Occupational Fraud and Abuse* (Austin, Tex.: Association of Certified Fraud Examiners, 2004), ii, http://www.cfenet.com/pdfs/2004RttN.pdf.

4. Id.

5. Charles Cullinan and Steve Sutton, "Defrauding the Public Interest: A Critical Examination of Reengineered Audit Processes and the Likelihood of Detecting Fraud," *Critical Perspectives on Accounting*, 13 (2002), 297–310 (fix format). See also Mark S. Beasley, et al., *Fraudulent Financial Reporting 1987–1997: An Analysis of U.S. Public Companies* (New York: The Committee of Sponsoring Organizations of the Treadway Commission, 1999).

6. PricewaterhouseCoopers, *European Crime Survey 2001*, 1, http://www.pwcglobal.com/cz/eng/ins-sol/publ/Euro_fraudsurvey_2001.pdf.

◆ FRAUD IN HISTORICAL PERSPECTIVE

Fraud in one form or another has been a fact of business life for thousands of years. In Hammurabi's Babylonian Code of Laws, dating to approximately 1800 B.C.E., the problem of fraud is squarely faced: "If a herdsman, to whose care cattle or sheep have been entrusted, be guilty of fraud and make false returns of the natural increase, or sell them for money, then shall he be convicted and pay the owner ten times the loss."[7] The earliest lawmakers were also the earliest to recognize and combat fraud.

In the United States, frauds have been committed since the colonies were settled. A particularly well-known fraud of that era was perpetrated in 1616 in Jamestown, Virginia, by Captain Samuel Argall, the deputy governor. Captain Argall allegedly "fleeced investors in the Virginia Co. of every chicken and dry good that wasn't nailed down."[8] According to the book *Stealing from America*, within two years of Argall's assumption of leadership in Jamestown, the "whole estate of the public was gone and consumed. . . ."[9] When he returned to England with a boat stuffed with looted goods, residents and investors were left with only six goats.[10]

Later, during the American Civil War, certain frauds became so common that legislatures recognized the need for new laws. One of the most egregious frauds was to bill the United States government for defective or nonexistent supplies sold to the Union Army. The federal government's response was the False Claims Act, passed in March 1863, which assessed corrupt war profiteers double damages and a $2,000 civil fine for each false claim submitted. Remarkably enough, this law is still in force, though much amended.

Soon after the Civil War, another major fraud gained notoriety: the Crédit Mobilier scheme of 1872. Considered the most serious political scandal of its time, this fraud was perpetrated by executives of the Union Pacific Railroad Company, operating in conjunction with corrupt politicians. Crédit Mobilier of America was set up by railroad management and by Representative Oakes Ames of Massachusetts, ostensibly to oversee construction of the Union Pacific Railroad.[11] Crédit Mobilier charged Union Pacific (which was heavily subsidized by the government) nearly twice the actual cost of completed work and distributed the extra $50 million to company shareholders.[12] Shares in Crédit Mobilier were sold at half price, and at times offered gratis, to congressmen and prominent politicians in order to buy their support. Among the company's famous sharehold-

---

7. Hammurabi's Code of Laws (1780 BCE), L. W. King, trans.
8. Carol Emert, "A Rich History of Corporate Crime. Fraud Dates Back to America's Colonial Days," *The San Francisco Chronicle*, July 14, 2002.
9. Id.
10. Id.
11. Id.
12. Peter Carlson, "High and Mighty Crooked: Enron Is Merely the Latest Chapter in the History of American Scams," *The Washington Post*, February 10, 2002.

ers were Vice President Schuyler Colfax, Speaker of the House James Gillespie Blaine, future Vice Presidents Henry Wilson and Levi Parsons Morton, and future President James Garfield.[13]

◆ TYPES OF FRAUD

There are many different types of fraud, and many ways to characterize and catalog fraud; however, those of the greatest relevance to accountants and auditors are the following broad categories:

- *Employee Fraud*[14]*/Misappropriation of Assets.* This type of fraud involves the theft of cash or inventory, skimming revenues, payroll fraud, and embezzlement. Asset misappropriation is the most common type of fraud.[15] Primary examples of asset misappropriation are fraudulent disbursements such as billing schemes, payroll schemes, expense reimbursement schemes, check tampering, and cash register disbursement schemes. Sometimes employees collude with others to perpetrate frauds, such as aiding vendors intent on overbilling the company. An interesting distinction: Some employee misdeeds do not meet the definition of fraud because they are not schemes based on communicating a deceit to the employer. For example, theft of inventory is not necessarily a fraud—it may simply be a theft. False expense reporting, on the other hand, is a fraud because it involves a false representation of the expenses incurred. This fraud category also includes employees' aiding and abetting others outside the company to defraud third parties.

- *Financial Statement Fraud.* This type of fraud is characterized by intentional misstatements or omissions of amounts or disclosures in financial reporting to deceive financial statement users. More specifically, financial statement fraud involves manipulation, falsification, or alteration of accounting records or supporting documents from which financial statements are prepared. It also refers to the intentional misapplication of accounting principles to manipulate results. According to a study conducted by the Association of Certified Fraud Examiners, fraudulent financial statements, as compared with the other forms of fraud perpetrated by corporate employees, usually have a higher dollar impact on the victimized entity as well as a more negative impact on shareholders and the investing public.[16]

---

13. D. C. Shouter, "The Crédit Mobilier of America: A Scandal That Shook Washington," *Chronicles of American Wealth*, No. 4, November 30, 2001, http://www.raken.com/american_wealth/other/newsletter/chronicle301101.asp.
14. "Employee" here refers to all officers and employees who work for the organization.
15. Association of Certified Fraud Examiners, *2002 Report to the Nation on Occupational Fraud and Abuse* (Austin, Tex.: Association of Certified Fraud Examiners, 2002), 6.
16. Id.

As a broad classification, corruption straddles both misappropriation of assets and financial statement fraud. Transparency International, a widely respected not-for-profit think tank, defines corruption as "the abuse of entrusted power for private gain."[17] We would expand that definition to include corporate gain as well as private gain. Corruption takes many forms and ranges from executive compensation issues to payments made to domestic or foreign government officials and their family members. Corrupt activities are prohibited in the United States by federal and state laws. Beyond U.S. borders, contributions to foreign officials are prohibited by the Foreign Corrupt Practices Act.

This book is primarily concerned with fraud committed by employees and officers, some of which may lead to the material distortion of financial statement information, and the nature of activities designed to deter and investigate such frauds. Circumstances in which financial information is exchanged (generally in the form of financial statements) as the primary representation of a business transaction are fairly widespread. They include, for example, regular commercial relationships between a business and its customers or vendors, borrowing money from banks or other financial institutions, buying or selling companies or businesses, raising money in the public or private capital markets, and supporting the secondary market for trading in public company debt or equity securities. This book focuses primarily on two types of fraud: (1) frauds perpetrated by people within the organization that result in harm to the organization itself and (2) frauds committed by those responsible for financial reporting, who use financial information they know to be false in order to perpetrate a fraud on investors or other third parties, whereby the organization benefits.

◆ ROOT CAUSES OF FRAUD

As society has evolved from barter-based economies to e-commerce, so has fraud evolved into complex forms—Hammurabi's concern about trustworthy shepherds was just the beginning. Until just a few years ago, companies headquartered in the developed world took the view that their business risk was highest in emerging or Third World regions, where foreign business cultures and less-developed regulatory environments were believed to generate greater risk.[18] Gaining market access and operating in emerging or less-developed markets seemed often enough to invite business practices that were wholly unacceptable at home. Sharing this view, the governments of major industrial countries enacted legislation to combat the potential for corruption. The United States enacted the Foreign Corrupt Practices Act (FCPA); countries working together in the Organization for Economic Cooperation and Development (OECD) enacted the Convention on Combating Bribery of Foreign Public Officials in

---

17. Transparency International, "TI's Vision, Mission, Values, Approach and Strategy," http://www.transparency.org.

18. PricewaterhouseCoopers, "Financial Fraud—Understanding Root Causes," *Investigations & Forensic Services Report* (2002), 1.

International Business Transactions (known as the OECD Convention); and Canada enacted the Corruption of Foreign Public Officials Act.

However, this way of thinking about risk and markets and of combating corruption and fraud is no longer adequate. The new paradigm for understanding risk postulates that fraud risk factors are borderless and numerous. Fraud is now understood to be driven by concerns over corporate performance, financing pressures including access to financing, the competition to enter and dominate markets, legal requirements and exposure, and personal needs and agendas.[19] The need for this new paradigm has become increasingly clear in the past two years, when the greatest risk to investors has appeared to be participation in the seemingly well-regulated and well-established U.S. markets. More recently, events at several major European multinationals have shown that the risk of massive fraud knows no borders.

The recent spate of accounting and financial scandals has demonstrated that large-scale corporate improprieties can and do occur in sophisticated markets; they are by no means the exclusive province of "foreign" or "remote" markets. Capital market access and the related desire of listed companies to boost revenue growth, through whatever means necessary, are major factors contributing to corporate malfeasance worldwide.

◆ A HISTORICAL ACCOUNT OF THE AUDITOR'S ROLE

We have briefly examined the elements, forms, and evolution of fraud. We can now examine the role of one of the key players in the effort to detect fraud, the auditor.

AUDITING: ANCIENT HISTORY

Historians believe that recordkeeping originated about 4000 B.C.E., when ancient civilizations in the Near East began to establish organized governments and businesses.[20] Governments were concerned about accounting for receipts and disbursements and collecting taxes. An integral part of this concern was establishing controls, including audits, to reduce error and fraud on the part of incompetent or dishonest officials.[21] There are numerous examples in the ancient world of auditing and control procedures employed in the administration of public finance systems. The Shako dynasty of China (1122–256 B.C.E.), the Assembly in Classical Athens, and the Senate of the Roman Republic all exemplify early reliance on formal financial controls.[22]

Much later, in the twelfth and thirteenth centuries, records show that auditing work was performed in England, Scotland, Italy, and France. The audits in Great

---

19. Id.
20. Robert Hiester Montgomery, *Montgomery's Auditing*, 12th ed. (New York: John Wiley & Sons, 1998), 1–7.
21. Id.
22. Id.

Britain, performed before the seventeenth century, were directed primarily at ensuring the accountability of funds entrusted to public or private officials.[23] Those audits were not designed to test the quality of the accounts, except insofar as inaccuracies might point to the existence of fraud.

Economic changes between 1600 and 1800, which saw the beginning of widespread commerce, introduced new accounting concerns focused on the ownership of property and the calculation of profit and loss in a business sense. At the end of the seventeenth century, the first law prohibiting certain officials from serving as auditors of a town was enacted in Scotland, thus introducing the modern notion of auditor independence.[24]

GROWTH OF THE AUDITING PROFESSION IN THE NINETEENTH CENTURY

It was not until the nineteenth century, with the growth of railroads, insurance companies, banks, and other joint-stock companies, that the auditing profession became an important part of the business environment. In Great Britain, the passage of the Joint Stock Companies Act in 1844 and later the Companies Act in 1879 contributed greatly to the auditing field in general and to the development of external auditing in the United States.[25] The Joint Stock Companies Act required companies to make their books available for the critical analysis of shareholders at the annual meeting. The Companies Act in 1879 required all limited liability banks to submit to auditing, a requirement later expanded to include all such companies.[26] Until the beginning of the twentieth century, independent audits in the United States were modeled on British practice and were in fact conducted primarily by auditors from Britain, who were dispatched overseas by British investors in U.S. companies. British-style audits, dubbed "bookkeeper audits," consisted of detailed scrutiny of clerical data relating to the balance sheet. These audits were imperfect at best. J. R. Edwards, in Legal Regulation of British Company Accounts 1836–1900, cites the view of Sir George Jessel, a lawyer and judge famous in his day, on the quality of external auditing soon after passage of the Companies Act:

> The notion that any form of account will prevent fraud is quite delusive. Anybody who has had any experience of these things knows that a rogue will put false figures into an account, or cook as the phrase is, whatever form of account you prescribe. If anybody imagines that will protect the shareholders, it is simply a delusion in my opinion. . . . I have had the auditors examined before me, and I have said, "You audited these accounts?" "Yes." "Did

---

23. Id.
24. Id.
25. Id.
26. Dr. Sheri Markose, "Honest Disclosure, Corporate Fraud, Auditors and Stock Market Valuation," lecture from course EC247: "Financial Instruments and Capital Market Institutions," University of Essex (Essex, U.K., 2003).

you call for any vouchers?' "No, we did not; we were told it was all right, we supposed it was, and we signed it."[27]

Yet by the end of the nineteenth century, the most sophisticated minds in the auditing field were certain that auditors could do much better than this. Witness the incisive view of Lawrence R. Dicksee, author of a manual widely studied in its day (and still available today, many editions later):

> The detection of fraud is the most important portion of the Auditor's duties, and there will be no disputing the contention that the Auditor who is able to detect fraud is—other things being equal—a better man than the auditor who cannot. Auditor[s] should, therefore, assiduously cultivate this branch of their functions. . . .[28]

In response to the rapidly expanding American business scene, audits in the United States evolved from the more cumbersome British practice into "test audits." According to *Montgomery's Auditing*, the emergence of independent auditing was largely due to the demands of creditors, particularly banks, for reliable financial information on which to base credit decisions.[29] That demand evolved into a series of state and federal securities acts which significantly increased a company's burden to publicly disclose financial information and, accordingly, catapulted the auditor into a more demanding and visible role.

FEDERAL AND STATE SECURITIES REGULATION BEFORE 1934

Prior to the creation of the Securities and Exchange Commission (SEC) in 1934, financial markets in the United States were severely underregulated. Before the stock market crash of 1929, there was very little appetite for federal regulation of the securities market, and proposals that the government require financial disclosure and prevent the fraudulent sale of stock were not seriously pursued.[30] Investors were largely unconcerned about the dangers of investing in an unregulated market. In fact, many were seduced by the notion that they could make huge sums of money on the stock market. In the 1920s, approximately 20 million large and small shareholders took advantage of the postwar boom in the economy and tried to make their fortunes by investing in securities.[31]

Although there was little interest during the first decades of the century in instituting federal oversight of the securities industry, state legislatures had

---

27. J. R. Edwards, *Legal Regulation of British Company Accounts, 1836–1900* (New York: Garland, 1986), 17.
28. L. R. Dicksee, *Auditing: A Practical Manual for Auditors* (New York: Arno, 1976), 6. Reprint of the 1892 edition.
29. Id., 1–9.
30. U.S. Securities and Exchange Commission, "Introduction—The SEC: Who We Are, What We Do," http://www.sec.gov.
31. Id.

already begun to regulate the securities industry.[32] States in the Midwest and West were most active in pursuing securities regulation in response to citizens' complaints that unscrupulous salesmen and dishonest stock schemes were victimizing them.[33] The first comprehensive securities law of the era was enacted by Kansas in 1911. That law, the first of many known as "blue-sky laws," required the registration of both securities and those who sold them.[34] The intent was to prevent fraud in the sale of securities and also to prevent the sale of securities of companies whose organization, plan of business, or contracts included provisions that were "unfair, unjust, inequitable, or oppressive" or if the investment did not "promise a fair return." In the two years following the enactment of the securities laws in Kansas in 1911, 23 states passed some form of blue-sky legislation.[35]

It was only after the stock market crash in 1929 and the ensuing Great Depression that interest in enacting federal securities legislation became widespread. Congress passed the Securities Act of 1933, which had the basic objectives of requiring that investors receive financial and other significant information concerning securities offered for public sale, and prohibiting deceit, misrepresentations, and other fraud in the sale of securities. The primary means of accomplishing these goals was the disclosure of important financial information through the registration of securities.[36]

The second fundamental set of laws, the Securities Exchange Act of 1934, created the Securities and Exchange Commission and granted it broad authority over all aspects of the securities industry, including registering, regulating, and overseeing brokerage firms, transfer agents, and clearing agencies. The Act addressed the need for regulation of the securities industry, as well as the need to address the potential for fraud inherent within it. Several sections of the Act deal with fraud, including Section 9 (Manipulation of Security Prices), Section 10 (Manipulative and Deceptive Devices), Section 18 (Liability for Misleading Statements), Section 20 (Liability of Controlling Persons and Persons Who Aid and Abet Violations), and Section 20A (Liability to Contemporaneous Traders for Insider Trading).

CURRENT ENVIRONMENT

The recent financial scandals at major corporations and conflict of interest issues in the financial services industry have caused investor confidence in the stock market to decline dramatically. In response to the wave of corporate malfeasance, the U.S. Congress passed the Sarbanes-Oxley Act of 2002, intended to

---

32. Wisconsin Department of Financial Institutions, "A Brief History of Securities Regulation," http://www.wdfi.org/fi/securities/regexemp/history.htm.
33. Id.
34. Id.
35. Id.
36. U.S. Securities and Exchange Commission, "Introduction—The SEC: Who We Are, What We Do."

"protect investors by improving the accuracy and reliability of corporate disclosures made pursuant to the securities laws, and for other purposes."[37]

Sarbanes-Oxley prohibits accounting firms from providing many consulting services for the companies they audit, requires audit committees to select and essentially oversee the external auditor, and generally strengthens the requirement that auditors must be independent from their clients. Section 101 of the Sarbanes-Oxley Act established the Public Company Accounting Oversight Board (PCAOB) to oversee the audit of public companies that are subject to the securities laws and related matters. The purpose of the PCAOB is to protect the interests of investors and to further the public interest.[38] The PCAOB was authorized to establish auditing and related professional practice standards, and Rule 3100 requires the auditor to comply with these standards.[39] The Sarbanes-Oxley Act begat an extensive and still evolving series of audit rule changes, prompting the issuance of three audit standards as of the writing of this book.

In October 2002, the AICPA issued *Statement on Auditing Standards (SAS) No. 99*, "Consideration of Fraud in a Financial Statement Audit." Effective for audits of financial statements for periods beginning on or after December 15, 2002, SAS 99 seeks to improve auditing practice, especially as it relates to the auditor's role in detecting fraud, if it exists, in the course of the audit. According to the AICPA President and CEO, the new "standard will substantially change auditor performance, thereby improving the likelihood that auditors will detect material misstatements due to fraud. … It puts fraud in the forefront of the auditor's mind."[40] Further, according to the AICPA's own assessment, the new standard is the "cornerstone of a multifaceted effort by the AICPA to help restore investor confidence in U.S. capital markets and to reestablish audited financial statements as a clear picture window into Corporate America."[41] The standard, however, does not increase or alter the auditor's fundamental responsibility, which is to plan and conduct an audit such that if there is a fraud or error causing a material misstatement of a company's financial statements, it may be detected. While this seems an unambiguous mandate, there still remains a difference between the public perception that audits should detect all fraud and the actual standards governing the conduct of audits. There is a significant and legitimate difference between *performing an audit* and *conducting a financial fraud investigation*. That difference is explored throughout this book.

---

37. *Sarbanes-Oxley Act of 2002*, Public Law 107–204, 107th Cong., 2d sess. (January 23, 2002), 1 (from statute's official title: "An Act to protect investors by improving the accuracy and reliability of corporate disclosures made pursuant to the securities laws, and for other purposes").

38. Public Company Accounting Oversight Board, *Sarbanes–Oxley Act of 2002*, http://www.pcaobus.org/rules/Sarbanes_Oxley_Act_of_2002.pdf.

39. Public Company Accounting Oversight Board, *Rules of the Board*, 127, http://www.pcaobus.org/documents/rules_of_the_board/Standards%20-%20AS1.pdf.

40. American Institute of Certified Public Accountants, "AICPA Issues New Audit Standard for Detecting Fraud, Cornerstone of Institute's New Anti-Fraud Program," October 15, 2002, http://www.aicpa.org/news/2002/p021015.htm.

41. Id.

In November 2003, the SEC approved the final versions of corporate governance listing standards proposed by the NYSE and NASDAQ Stock Market. Both standards expand upon the Sarbanes-Oxley Act of 2002 and SEC rules to impose significant new requirements on listed companies. These sweeping reforms mandate independence of directors, increased transparency, and new standards for corporate accountability. These and other governance standards emphasize the importance of enhancing governance, ethics, risk, and compliance oversight capabilities.

In 2004, the Committee of Sponsoring Organizations of the Treadway Commission (COSO) issued its new Enterprise Risk Management framework. The new COSO framework identifies key elements of an effective enterprise risk management approach for achieving financial, operational, compliance, and reporting objectives. The new COSO framework emphasizes the critical role played by governance, ethics, risk, and compliance in enterprise management.

On November 1, 2004, the United States Organizational Sentencing Guidelines (the "Guidelines") were amended to provide expanded guidance regarding the criteria for effective compliance programs. The Guidelines emphasize the importance of creating a "culture of compliance" within the organization; establish the governance and oversight responsibilities of the board and senior management; and frame the need for dedicating appropriate resources and authority. The Guidelines also focus on the relationship between governance, ethics, risk management, and compliance.

◆ AUDITORS ARE NOT ALONE

Although auditors have long been recognized to have an important role in detecting fraud, it is well recognized that they do not operate in a vacuum. Management, boards of directors, standard setters, and market regulators are key participants in corporate governance, each charged with specific responsibilities in the process of ensuring that financial markets, investors, and other users of corporate financial reports are well served. They are, in effect, links in a Corporate Reporting Supply Chain (CRSC) that includes several additional participants (see Exhibit 1.1).

The concept of the Corporate Reporting Supply Chain makes clear that auditors are only one of several interconnected participants having a role in delivering accurate, timely, and relevant financial reports into the public domain.[42] While many may consider the internal, external, and regulatory auditors as the first lines of defense against fraud, in fact they are all in secondary positions. The first line of defense is a properly constructed system of corporate governance, risk management, and internal controls, for which management is responsible. The board, in turn, and its audit committee are responsible for overseeing

---

42. Samuel A. DiPiazza and Robert G. Eccles, *Building Public Trust: The Future of Corporate Reporting* (New York: John Wiley & Sons, 2002), 10–11.

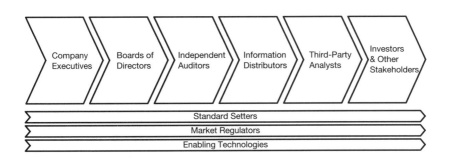

EXHIBIT 1.1 THE CORPORATE REPORTING SUPPLY CHAIN

management on behalf of shareholders, and so the board too has its share of responsibility for defending against fraud.

Management and the board share responsibility for certain critical aspects of deterring fraud in financial reporting:

- Setting a "tone at the top" that communicates the expectation of transparent and accurate financial reporting
- Responding quickly, equitably, and proportionately to violations of corporate policy and procedure
- Maintaining internal and external auditing processes independent of management's influence
- Ensuring a proper flow of critical information to the board and external parties
- Establishing an adequate system of internal accounting control that will satisfy the requirements of Section 404 of the Sarbanes-Oxley Act
- Investigating and remediating problems when they arise

These duties are far-reaching. They incorporate responsibilities from every component of the Fraud Deterrence Cycle discussed in the next section. And they represent the first line of defense against fraud. While an audit responds to the risk of fraud, the forensic accounting investigation responds to suspicions, allegations, or evidence of fraud. The forensic accounting investigator can assist the auditor in formulating a plan to respond to outside influences such as whistleblower allegations.

◆ DETERRENCE, AUDITING, AND INVESTIGATION

The increased size and impact of financial reporting scandals and the related loss of billions of dollars of shareholder value have rightly focused both public and regulatory attention on all aspects of financial reporting fraud and corporate governance. Some of the issues upsetting investors and regulators—for example, executive pay that could be considered by some to be excessive—are in the nature of questionable judgments, but do not necessarily constitute fraud. On the

EXHIBIT 1.2   THE FRAUD DETERRENCE CYCLE

other end of the spectrum, there have been more than a few examples of willful deception directed toward the investing community via fabricated financial statements, and many of these actions are gradually being identified and punished. The investing public may not always make a fine distinction between the outrageous and the fraudulent—between bad judgment and wrongdoing. However, for professionals charged with the deterrence, discovery, investigation, and remediation of these situations, a systematic and rigorous approach is essential.

The remainder of this chapter discusses various elements of what we call the Fraud Deterrence Cycle (Exhibit 1.2) many of which will be the topics of chapters to come. Without an effective regimen of this kind, fraud is much more likely to occur. Yet even with a fraud deterrence regimen effectively in place, there remains a chance that fraud will occur. Absolute fraud prevention is a laudable but unobtainable goal. No one can create an absolutely insurmountable barrier against fraud, but many sensible precautionary steps can and should be taken by organizations to deter fraudsters and would-be fraudsters. While fraud cannot be completely prevented, it can and should be deterred.

◆ CONCEPTUAL OVERVIEW OF THE FRAUD DETERRENCE CYCLE

The Fraud Deterrence Cycle occurs over time, and it is an interactive process. Broadly speaking, it has four main elements:

1. Establishment of corporate governance
2. Implementation of transaction-level control processes, often referred to as the system of internal accounting controls

3. Retrospective examination of governance and control processes through audit examinations

4. Investigation and remediation of suspected or alleged problems

CORPORATE GOVERNANCE

An appropriate system of governance should be born with the company itself, and grow in complexity and reach as the company grows. It should predate any possible opportunity for fraud. Corporate governance is about setting and monitoring objectives, tone, policies, risk appetite, accountability, and performance. Embodied in this definition it is also a set of attitudes, policies, procedures, delegations of authority, and controls that communicate to all constituencies, including senior management, that fraud will not be tolerated. It further communicates that compliance with laws, ethical business practices, accounting principles, and corporate policies is expected, and that any attempted or actual fraud is expected to be disclosed by those who know or suspect that fraud has occurred. There is substantial legal guidance concerning standards for corporate governance, but generally, the substance and also the vigorous communication of governance policies and controls need to make clear that fraud will be detected and punished. While prevention would be a desirable outcome for corporate governance programs, complete prevention is impossible. Deterrence, therefore, offers a more realistic view. In short, corporate governance is an entire culture that sets and monitors behavioral expectations intended to deter the fraudster.

Today, changes in business are being driven by increased stakeholder demands, heightened public scrutiny, and new performance expectations. Critical issues related to governance reform are surfacing in the marketplace on a daily basis. These issues include:

- Protecting corporate reputation and brand value
- Meeting increased demands and expectations of investors, legislators, regulators, customers, employees, analysts, consumers, and other stakeholders
- Driving value and managing performance expectations for governance, ethics, risk management, and compliance
- Managing crisis and remediation while defending the organization and its executives and board members against the increased scope of legal enforcement and the rising impact of fines, penalties and business disruption

In order to execute effective governance, boards and management must effectively oversee a number of key business processes, including the following:

- Strategy and operation planning
- Risk management
- Ethics and compliance (tone at the top)
- Performance measurement and monitoring

- Mergers, acquisitions, and other transformational transactions
- Management evaluation, compensation, and succession planning
- Communication and reporting
- Governance dynamics

All the preceding elements are critical to a good governance process.

TRANSACTION-LEVEL CONTROLS[43]

Transaction-level controls are next in the cycle. They are accounting and financial controls designed to help ensure that only valid, authorized, and legitimate transactions occur and to safeguard corporate assets from loss due to theft or other fraudulent activity. These procedures are preventive because they may actively block or prevent a fraudulent transaction from occurring. Such systems, however, are not foolproof, and fraudsters frequently take advantage of loopholes, inconsistencies, or vulnerable employees. As well, they may engage in a variety of deceptive practices to defeat or deceive such controls. Anti–money-laundering procedures employed by financial institutions are an excellent example of a proactive process designed to deter fraudulent transactions from taking place through a financial institution. Another familiar example is policy relating to the review and approval of documentation in support of disbursements.

RETROSPECTIVE EXAMINATION

The first two elements of the Fraud Deterrence Cycle are the first lines of defense against fraud and are designed to deter fraud from occurring in the first place. Next in the cycle are the retrospective procedures designed to help detect fraud before it becomes large and, therefore, harmful to the organization. Retrospective procedures, such as those performed by auditors and forensic accounting investigators, do not prevent fraud in the same way that front-end transaction controls do, but they form a key link in communicating intolerance for fraud and discovering problems before they grow to a size that could threaten the welfare of the organization. Further, with the benefit of hindsight, the cumulative impact of what may have appeared as innocent individual transactions at the time of execution may prove to be problematic in the aggregate. Although auditing cannot truly "prevent" fraud in the sense of stopping it before it happens, it can be an important part of an overall fraud deterrence regime.

INVESTIGATION AND REMEDIATION

Positioned last in the Fraud Deterrence Cycle is forensic accounting investigation of suspected, alleged, or actual frauds. Entities that suspect or experience a fraud should undertake a series of steps to credibly maintain and support the other elements of the Fraud Deterrence Cycle. Investigative findings often form the basis for both internal actions such as suspension or dismissal and external

---

43. Principal focus of PCAOB Auditing Standard No. 2 (AS2).

actions[44] against the guilty parties or restatement of previously issued financial statements. An investigation also should form the basis for remediating control procedures. Investigations should lead to actions commensurate with the size and seriousness of the impropriety or fraud, no matter whether it is found to be a minor infraction of corporate policy or a major scheme to create fraudulent financial statements or misappropriate significant assets.

All elements of the cycle are interactive. Policies are constantly reinforced and revised, controls are continually improved, audits are regularly conducted, and investigations are completed and acted upon as necessary. Without the commitment to each element of the Fraud Deterrence Cycle, the overall deterrent effect is substantially diminished.

◆ FIRST LOOK INSIDE THE FRAUD DETERRENCE CYCLE

We have seen that the Fraud Deterrence Cycle involves four elements: corporate governance, transaction-level controls, retrospective examination, and investigation and remediation. Here we want to take a first look inside each of the elements to identify some of their main features.

CORPORATE GOVERNANCE

In our experience, the key elements of corporate governance are:

- An independent board composed of a majority of directors who have no material relationship with the company
- An independent chairperson of the board *or* an independent lead director
- An audit committee that actively maintains relationships with internal and external auditors
- An audit committee that includes at least one member who has financial expertise, with all members being financially literate
- An audit committee that has the authority to retain its own advisers and launch investigations as it deems necessary
- Nominating and compensation committees composed of independent directors
- A compensation committee that understands whether it provides particularly lucrative incentives that may encourage improper financial reporting practices or other behavior that goes near or over the line
- Board and committee meetings regularly held without management and CEO present
- Explicit ethical commitment ("walking the talk") and a tone at the top that reflects integrity in all respects
- Prompt and appropriate investigation of alleged improprieties

---

44. See Chapter 22 for considerations surrounding a referral of matters for prosecution.

- Internally publicized enforcement of policies on a "no exception" or "zero tolerance" basis
- The board and/or audit committee's reinforcement of the importance of consistent disciplinary action of individuals found to have committed fraud
- Timely and balanced disclosure of material events concerning the company
- A properly administered hotline or other reporting channels, independent of management
- An internal audit function that reports directly to the audit committee without fear of being "edited" by management (CEO, CFO, controller, et al.)
- Budgeting and forecasting controls
- Clear and formal policies and procedures, updated in a timely manner as needed
- Well-defined financial approval authorities and limits
- Timely and complete information flow to the board

TRANSACTION-LEVEL CONTROLS

Systems of internal accounting control are also key elements in the Fraud Deterrence Cycle. Literature on this topic is extensive, but one manual in particular is widely recognized as authoritative: *Internal Control: Integrated Framework*, prepared by the Committee of Sponsoring Organizations of the Treadway Commission (COSO) and published by the AICPA. This manual lays out a comprehensive framework for internal control. Any entity undertaking fraud deterrence will want to be conversant with the elements and procedures covered in this book. Briefly, the critical elements highlighted in the COSO framework are:

- *The Control Environment.* This is the foundation for all other components of internal control, providing discipline and structure, and influencing the control awareness of the organization's personnel. Control environment factors include the integrity, ethical values, and competence of the organization's people; management's philosophy and operating style; management's approach to assigning authority and responsibility; and how personnel are organized and developed.[45]
- *Risk Assessment.* Effectively assessing risk requires the identification and analysis of risks relevant to the achievement of the entity's objectives, as a basis for determining how those risks should be managed and controlled. Because economic, industry, regulatory, and operating conditions continually change, mechanisms are needed to identify and deal with risks on an ongoing basis.[46]

---

45. Committee of Sponsoring Organizations of the Treadway Commission (COSO), *Internal Control—Integrated Framework* (New York: Committee of Sponsoring Organizations of the Treadway Commission, 1994), 23. *Note:* Commonly referred to as the COSO Report.
46. Id., 33.

- *Control Activities.* Control activities occur throughout an organization at all levels and in all functions, helping to ensure that policies, procedures, and other management directives are carried out. They help, as well, to ensure that necessary actions are taken to address risks that may prevent the achievement of the organization's objectives. Control activities are diverse, but certainly may include approvals, authorizations, verifications, reconciliations, operating performance reviews, security procedures over facilities and personnel, and segregation of duties.[47]

- *Information and Communication.* Successfully operating and controlling a business usually requires the preparation and communication of relevant and timely information. This function relies in part on information systems that produce reports containing operational, financial, and compliance-related data necessary for informed decision making. Communication should also occur in the broader sense, flowing down, up, and across the organization, so that employees understand their own roles and how they relate to others. Further, there must be robust communication with external parties such as customers, suppliers, regulators, and investors and other stakeholders.[48]

- *Monitoring.* COSO recognizes that no system can be both successful and static. It should be monitored and evaluated for improvements and changes made necessary by changing conditions. The scope and frequency of evaluations of the internal control structure depend on risk assessments and the overall perceived effectiveness of internal controls. However, under the Sarbanes-Oxley requirements, management and the external auditors are each charged with performing an evaluation at least annually.[49]

To serve the needs of a thorough Fraud Deterrence Cycle, several aspects of control processes are of particular importance. Among them are the following:

- Additions/changes/deletions to master data files of customers, vendors, and employees
- Disbursement approval processes
- Write-off approval processes (in accounts such as bad debt, inventory, etc.)
- Revenue recognition procedures
- Inventory controls
- Processes for signing contracts and other agreements
- Segregation of duties
- Information systems access and security controls
- Proper employment screening procedures, including background checks
- Timely reconciliation of accounts to subsidiary ledgers or underlying records

47. Id., 49.
48. Id., 59.
49. Id., 69.

- Cash management controls
- Safeguarding of intellectual assets such as formulas, product specifications, customer lists, pricing, and so forth
- Top-level reviews of actual performance versus budgets, forecasts, prior periods, and competitors

◆ AUDITING AND INVESTIGATION

The remaining two elements of the Fraud Deterrence Cycle are retrospective examination, that is, auditing and investigation, and remediation of any discovered problems. As discussed later in detail, there are differences between auditing and investigating.

	GAAS Audit	Forensic Accounting Investigation
Objective	Form an opinion on the overall financial statements taken as a whole	Determine the likelihood and/or magnitude of fraud occurring[a]
Purpose	Usually required by third-party users of financial statements	Sufficient predication that a fraud has or may have occurred
Value	Adds credibility to reported financial information	Resolves suspicions and accusations; determines the facts
Sources of evidence	Inquiry, observation, examination, and reperformance of accounting transactions to support financial statement assertions	Review detailed financial and nonfinancial data, search public records, conduct fact-finding as well as admission-seeking interviews, including third-party inquiries
Sufficiency of evidence	Reasonable assurance	Establish facts to support or refute suspicions or accusations

[a] Ultimately the trier of fact concludes whether fraud has occurred. The focus of a fraud investigation is fact finding, based on the investigator's knowledge of the elements of fraud that a trier of fact considers.

Source: Adapted from Association of Certified Fraud Examiners

These differences make clear that audits and investigations are not the same. During the course of an audit, an auditor seeks to detect errors or improprieties, absent any specific information that such improprieties exist. During an investigation, a forensic accounting investigator seeks to discover the full methods and extent of improprieties that are suspected or known. Both are important features of the Fraud Deterrence Cycle, but they are, and should be, separate. They involve different procedures and they are performed by professionals with different skills, training, education, knowledge, and experience. This is an important distinction in the current environment, when some commentators have suggested that the spate of corporate scandals cries out for the conversion of the standard audit into something resembling an investigation. If the audit in the future were to take this path, the cost of performing the audit may increase.

CHAPTER 2

THE ROLES OF THE AUDITOR AND THE FORENSIC ACCOUNTING INVESTIGATOR

James S. Gerson

John P. Brolly

Steven L. Skalak

To understand the forensic accounting investigator's role in deterring, detecting, and investigating fraud—as distinct from the independent auditor's role as a financial statement examiner—we need to first recall the differences between what auditors do and what forensic accounting investigators do and why. In addition, their professional worlds have changed in recent years, in ways that bear close examination.

The auditor's concern is that the financial statements of an entity be stated fairly in all material respects. Accordingly, the auditor's responsibility is to design and implement audit procedures of sufficient scope and depth to detect material deficiencies in the financial statements—essentially, without regard to the source or origin of the deficiency. Auditors are charged with (1) making appropriate, reasonable efforts to detect material misstatements in financial statements and (2) causing management to correct material misstatements or misrepresentations before the financial statements are shared with the user community or, alternatively, alerting investors not to place reliance on the statements through qualification of their professional opinion issued as part of the company's public filings. Even this seemingly simple statement of the auditor's mission brings into play a series of interrelated and complex concepts, including:

- Reasonable assurance
- Material misstatement
- Detection, as distinct from deterrence and investigation
- Expectations about the efficacy of the auditing process

The forensic accounting investigator has a largely separate set of concerns based on a different role that calls for different tools, different thought processes, and different attitudes. The forensic accounting investigator's concern is not with reaching a general opinion on financial statements taken as a whole, derived from reasonable efforts within a reasonable materiality boundary. Instead, the forensic accounting investigator's concern is, at a much more granular level, with the detailed development of factual information—derived from both documentary evidence and testimonial evidence—about the who, what, when, where, how, and why of a suspected or known impropriety. Sampling and materiality concepts are generally not used in determining the scope of forensic accounting procedures. Instead, all relevant evidence is sought and examined. Based on the investigative findings, the forensic accounting investigator assesses and measures losses or other forms of damage to the organization and recommends and implements corrective actions, often including changes in accounting processes and policies and/or personnel actions. In addition, the forensic accounting investigator takes preventive actions to eliminate recurrence of the problem. The forensic accounting investigator's findings and recommendations may form the basis of testimony in litigation proceedings or criminal actions against the perpetrators. They may also be used in testimony to government agencies such as the Securities and Exchange Commission in the United States or the Serious Fraud Office in the United Kingdom. Accordingly, the scope of the investigation and the evidence gathered and documented must be capable of withstanding challenges that may be brought by adversely affected parties or skeptical regulators.

Clearly, there are many commonalities between auditing and forensic accounting. Both rely on:

- Knowledge of the industry and the company, including its business practices and processes
- Knowledge of the generally accepted accounting principles of the jurisdiction in question
- Interpretation of business documents and records
- Independence and objectivity—perhaps the most important commonality

Another commonality is that both the auditor and the forensic accounting investigator must function effectively in the complex and ever-changing business environment. However, despite many common bases, audits are not the same as forensic accounting investigations. Two simple analogies will help convey the differences.

◆ THE PATROLMAN AND THE DETECTIVE

Neither auditors nor forensic accounting investigators are law enforcement officers; however, while imperfect, a simplified analogy to patrolmen and detectives can help illustrate the auditor's challenge to detect material misstatements in financial statements in contrast to the forensic accounting investigator's mission to fully investigate allegations of a suspected impropriety.

A patrolman, working a particular shift, circulates through the community inspecting and observing its visible elements for signs of improper behavior ranging from minor infractions of municipal ordinances to evidence that a major crime may have been committed. The patrolman selects his route based on past experience, the time of day, and the length of his shift, and adjusts it for any particular observations during his patrol. He knows these judgments and adjustments to the patrol are necessary because no matter how much he might like to be continuously present at every location in the community, it is impossible to do so. So, too, with the auditor, who examines a selected sample of transactions to support the opinion on the financial statements and, based on those results, decides whether to examine more, whether to change the audit technique or test, or whether to conclude on the basis of procedures already completed. These decisions are based in large part on his or her assessment of the risk of material misstatement based on both past experience and current evidence. Auditors might like to go everywhere in a company and examine every transaction but, because, like the patrolman, they cannot be every place at all times, they must determine when and where to concentrate their procedures.

The analogy of detective work is similarly instructive of the forensic accounting investigator's mission. As compared to patrol officers, who circulate throughout the community concentrating on high-risk areas, detectives are not on patrol. They are called in once a crime is suspected or observed. These related but differing activities—routine patrolling and criminal investigation—can be balanced with relative ease. If greater deterrence is needed, more patrol officers covering more territory more often is a solution. Similarly, if there are many crimes or if there is a highly complex situation to investigate, then assigning more detectives, or in the financial context, more forensic accounting investigators, is a solution.

While it is clear that forensic accounting and detective work are roughly analogous, the analogies between issues confronting the auditor and the patrol officer—namely, how detailed should observations be in varying circumstances—are less obvious. Take the example of a garage—the customary storage location for a reasonably valuable asset: a car. A patrol officer who drives by in the middle of the night might observe any of the following circumstances:

- Garage door closed, light off
- Garage door closed, light on
- Garage door open, light off
- Garage door open, light on, car visible
- Garage door open, light on, no car

In each case, the officer has choices, informed by knowledge of the community, past experience on patrol, knowledge of the homeowner, if any, and overall security conditions in the community. If the door is closed, the light is off, and the officer drives by without stopping, few would argue neglect of duty. If the door is closed and the light on, the likely explanation is that the owner just got home and the garage door light has not gone out yet or was left on by accident. If the officer comes into the yard, looks in the garage window, sees the car and no other activity, and then leaves, almost everyone would agree that the officer has performed a careful, thorough patrol. Even if the officer drives by without looking more closely—on the assumption that the light was left on by accident—few would conclude that the officer was remiss in his or her duty. And even if a crime were silently in progress in a back room of the house, no one would fault the officer for failing to detect it from the visible evidence.

Conversely, if you were that homeowner and the officer rang your doorbell, woke you from a sound sleep, told you your car was safe and sound in the garage but the garage light needed to be turned off, you'd almost certainly consider the officer overly zealous and inconsiderate, even if you agreed in principle that the light should not burn through the night.

Contrast this scenario with another. The officer spots the garage light on and the door open, comes up your driveway for a better look, sees that everything is in order, and leaves. An hour later, someone steals the entire contents of your garage. If you were to find out that the officer had been on the scene an hour beforehand and did not wake you to suggest closing the garage door, you might well be disappointed with the officer's judgment, although, truth be told, you would have been annoyed had the officer awakened you and urged you to close the door and turn off the light. Complaining loudly about the inconvenience and offering the helpful thought that there must be better things for police officers to do with their time, you would nonetheless have risen, turned off the light, and closed the door.

We all can imagine a wide range of scenarios related to patrol officers and their choices, and there will be a spectrum of views about how much investigation is appropriate. Some risk-averse residents would no doubt prefer that the officer check on whether their car is still there, even if the light is off and the door closed. Others would take the view that checking is too costly for the minimal risk evident in that circumstance. And still others would assert a right to privacy, perhaps saying that even if the light is on and the door open, stay away unless a crime is obviously in progress.

Like the patrol officer, the auditor sits outside the client company, looking in at its operations with a less-than-complete view of everything that is going on. Like the patrol officer, the auditor cannot be in all places in the company at once, cannot visit every location in each period, and can sample transactions only at visited locations rather than examining every transaction. Further, before going out on an audit, the auditor must select the timing, location, and nature of the transactions or controls to be examined—that is, make judgments about the scope of the audit work. Finally, in examining the items sampled—like the patrol officer observing the garage—the auditor has to balance risk and expectations to decide the correct scope of any further examination. An auditor who finds a potential issue must decide whether to expand the audit, for example by further inquiry, or decide to conclude on the basis of the available evidence that nothing improper is indicated. Choices and judgments, large and small, abound throughout the audit process.

In contrast, the forensic accounting investigators could be compared to the detectives called in to investigate a crime, like the theft of the car. The detectives will examine the scene of the crime, question everyone who might be able to shed light on the theft, and bring to bear a host of specialized forensic resources to gather any and all clues that might exist. This is a specialized, time-consuming, and costly mission not directly connected with the original mission of patrolling the community to ascertain that everything is substantially in order. After all of their effort, the detectives may find out only that your child—a newly licensed teenage driver—decided to take the car down by the river to practice guitar without disturbing you. On the other hand, they may uncover a car theft ring. It might make sense to call upon the detectives more frequently, but consideration must be given to the ratio of detectives to patrol officers (there just are not as many) and to the cost of detectives, which is typically higher than that of patrol officers. Judgments are made that balance the community's desire for safety with the cost it is willing to pay for such comfort.

The fundamental challenge is to integrate the greater depth of investigation by the forensic accounting investigator into the audit when it is appropriate to do so—either by calling in forensic accounting investigators to investigate or by adapting some of their own procedures to an appropriate extent in order to continue to meet the requirements of the profession, the client, and the public and to restore or enhance confidence in the accuracy of the conclusions of an audit. We understand that both the PCAOB and the AICPA are considering the role of a forensic accountant in the conduct of an audit and may address this issue in future auditing standards.

The problems, judgments, and expectations illustrated in this analogy permeate the environment in which auditors conduct audits and forensic accounting investigators conduct investigations. But that environment is characterized by a greater degree of complexity than can be illustrated through simple analogies. These complexities and their impact should be neither overlooked nor underestimated.

◆ COMPLEXITY AND CHANGE

The worlds of the auditor and the forensic accounting investigator are complex, fast paced, constantly changing, and diverse. Complexity and change are important considerations for both because, separately and together, they create uncertainty about the outcome of business affairs. The quest for certainty in business affairs motivates businesses and businesspeople the world over to take charge, exercise control, hedge risks, and secure the bottom line (see Exhibit 2.1). In some cases, this basic desire for control will give rise to improper activities in the conduct of business—for example, unfair competitive practices, false advertising, price fixing, breach of contract, and circumvention of regulations. In other cases, in which control is desired but cannot be obtained or when efforts are unsuccessful or not yet successful, false reports of success may be issued (see Chapter 4). While

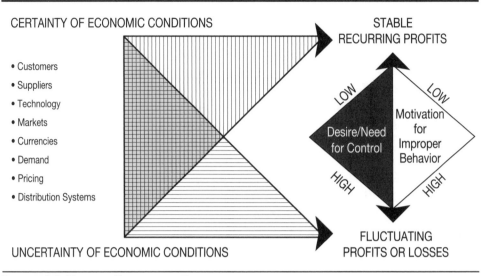

EXHIBIT 2.1 TYPES OF PRESSURE ON EXECUTIVES

complexity and change are not in and of themselves negative, business failures have time and time again shown that the combination of the two creates uncertainties that may motivate improper business behavior on the part of employees and executives. Auditors and forensic accounting investigators must appreciate this dynamic to carry out their respective roles effectively.

Today's business world is complex. Global competition, instantaneous global communications, advances in science and technology, risks unknown even 10 years ago, and many other factors define today's business life. We are working harder and longer and dealing with high levels of rapid and frequent change that few could have expected or predicted.

Open that most basic of corporate communications—the annual report—and it will be evident how much has changed. Companies are offering an astounding number and diversity of products and services. Old models that distinguished one industry from another have blurred, as industrial companies can look in some respects like banks, while banks can look like investment banks, security dealers, and insurers. Management's Discussion and Analysis in virtually any annual report will probably reveal many different complexities and changes confronting the business, some of which are inventoried in Exhibit 2.2.

Among the factors in Exhibit 2.2, some are more critical than others:

- *Ever-increasing globalization adds greatly to the complexity of today's business world.* Controlling diverse organizations around the world and ensuring that they understand and meet the company's business objectives while operating ethically require thorough understanding of local economic and political conditions as well as customs, laws, and regulations at each key location.
- *Information technology, while adding enormously to business productivity, has intrinsic challenges.* As companies exchange information internally

Business Structure

- More than one industry within the company—for instance, automotive manufacture and financial services under one roof
- Global scope of customers, vendors, and operations
- Interdependence between the company and its suppliers, customers, and competitors through:
  - Outsourcing arrangements
  - Joint ventures
  - R&D contracts
  - Marketing agreements
  - Cross ownership and board membership
  - Shared facilities
  - Industry standardization of technical or documentary requirements
- No two companies exactly alike

Business Methods

- Information technology that's automating business processes from the factory floor to headquarters
- Instantaneous global communications
- Internet-enabled business systems for dealing with external parties
- Paperless business processes updated in real time
- Complex financial, insurance, and hedging arrangements to control risks

Rules and Regulations

- Voluminous rules governing all aspects of business life
- Complex accounting and reporting requirements in separate jurisdictions worldwide
- Complex judgments requiring a mix of information about the past, present, and future
- Aggressive enforcement and low public tolerance for error or failure

Social Trends

- Increased employee mobility and decreased loyalty
- Reduced security over data and intellectual property
- Demands for short-term success
- Economic disparity among countries and/or markets
- Economic disparity among people within countries and/or markets
- Cultural diversity within the business world
- Differences in transparency and objectivity of press or other reports about a particular location or subject
- Public health crises, food and water shortages, HIV/AIDS, severe acute respiratory syndrome
- Speed of medical and technological changes
- Political change such as events in the Middle East and periodic turmoil in South America
- The threat and reality of terrorist attacks and efforts geared toward extensive homeland security

EXHIBIT 2.2 TWENTY-FIRST-CENTURY BUSINESS COMPLEXITY

and with their suppliers and customers on a real-time basis via the Internet and struggle to keep up with technological advances, the challenge to keep corporate information relevant, reliable, secure, and private is very real. Outsourcing is becoming more and more common as companies recognize the complexity and cost of meeting these requirements.

Very important to companies and their auditors is the complexity of today's financial reporting rules and regulations. To operate effectively in an increasingly complex world, companies and their auditors must be capable of continuous learning, interpretation, and application of complex and ever-changing rules.

- *And as if these complexities were not enough, the pace of change continues to accelerate, challenging companies as never before to keep up.* In the past few years, trillions of dollars in new wealth among millions of investors have evaporated—in many cases, just as quickly as that wealth had accumulated in the course of the dot-com bubble. Success is often fleeting, and failure to meet expectations rarely escapes punishment by the capital markets.

◆ AUDITOR ROLES IN PERSPECTIVE

While both management and the auditor address some of the same issues, their roles are vastly different. There has been some confusion on this point, especially within the general public, which tends to attribute to the auditor certain responsibilities that actually rest with management. The professional standards of the American Institute of Certified Public Accountants (AICPA) have long made clear that the financial statements and the decisions shaping the financials are the responsibility of management.

The financial statements are management's responsibility. The auditor's responsibility is to express an opinion on the financial statements. Management is responsible for adopting sound accounting policies and for establishing and maintaining internal control that will, among other things, record, process, summarize, and report transactions (as well as events and conditions) consistent with management's assertions embodied in the financial statements. The entity's transactions and the related assets, liabilities, and equity are within the direct knowledge and control of management. The auditor's knowledge of these matters and internal control is limited to that acquired through the audit. Thus, the fair presentation of financial statements in conformity with generally accepted accounting principles is an implicit and integral part of management's responsibility.[1]

---

1. American Institute of Certified Public Accountants, Statement on Auditing Standards (SAS) No. 1 (§ 110), *Codification of Auditing Standards and Procedures*, revised, April 1989, to reflect conforming changes necessary due to the issuance of SAS 53 through 62. As amended, effective for audits of financial statements for periods beginning on or after January 1, 1997, by SAS 78. Paragraph renumbered by the issuance of SAS 82, February 1997. Revised, April 2002, to reflect conforming changes necessary due to the issuance of SAS 94. (Codified in AICPA Professional Standards—U.S. Auditing Standards—AU § 110, par. 3).

Enlarging on these concepts in a much-cited court opinion, the judge in *Bily v. Arthur Young*[2] memorably stated:

> An auditor is a watchdog, not a bloodhound.... As a matter of commercial reality, audits are performed in a client-controlled environment. The client typically prepares its own financial statements; it has direct control over and assumes primary responsibility for their contents.... The client engages the auditor, pays for the audit, and communicates with audit personnel throughout the engagement. Because the auditor cannot in the time available become an expert in the client's business and record-keeping systems, the client necessarily furnishes the information base for the audit. Thus, regardless of the efforts of the auditor, the client retains effective primary control of the financial reporting process.[3]

◆ NOT ALL GOOD PEOPLE

The overwhelming majority of corporate managements do the right thing when it comes to financial reporting.[4] Still, there are some who do not. Complicating matters is the fact, according to the SEC, that the majority of large and complex corporate frauds are perpetrated by top management—the very people charged with responsibility for the quality of the company's financial reporting. A recent SEC staff report confirmed this observation. A review of the commission's enforcement actions filed during the period July 31, 1997, through July 30, 2002, concerning improper financial reporting, found that 157 of the 227 enforcement matters involved charges against at least one senior manager. In these matters, charges were brought against 75 board chairpersons, 111 chief executive officers, 111 presidents, 105 chief financial officers, 21 chief operating officers, 16 chief accounting officers, and 27 vice presidents of finance.[5] As the Public Oversight Board (predecessor of today's Public Company Accounting Oversight Board [PCAOB]) pointed out:

> On the one hand, to accomplish the audit requires the cooperation of management; on the other hand, management is in a position to mislead the auditors in their quest for valid evidence.[6]

2. *Bily v. Arthur Young & Co.*, 3 Cal. 4th 370, 11 *Cal. Rptr.* 2d 51, 834 P.2d 745 (1992).
3. Id.
4. PricewaterhouseCoopers, *PricewaterhouseCoopers LLP 2002 Securities Litigation Study*, 7, http://www.pwcglobal.com/us/eng/about/svcs/fas/ 2002%20Securities%20Litigation%20Study.pdf.
5. U.S. Securities and Exchange Commission, *Report Pursuant to Section 704 of the Sarbanes-Oxley Act of 2002*, 2–3, http://www.sec.gov/news/studies/sox704report.pdf.
6. Public Oversight Board, Panel on Audit Effectiveness, *Report and Recommendations* (2000), Chap. 3, § 3.45, 86, http://www.pobauditpanel.org/downloads/chapter3.pdf.

◆ EACH COMPANY IS UNIQUE

Auditors and forensic accounting investigators know that each company is unique and that they must understand and respond to those unique characteristics if they are to be effective. While the list is virtually endless, the ways in which companies can be highly distinct from one another include corporate governance; ownership and organizational structure; industry; products and services; size and geographic reach; business objectives and risks; key business processes and systems; relationships with customers, suppliers, and other business partners; management style and attitudes; management experience and competence; internal control; and accounting policies.

◆ ROLE OF COMPANY CULTURE

A company's culture consists of its shared history, values, beliefs, and goals. To this must be added the shared operating style—at all levels and in all parts of the organization—through which behavior in keeping with the culture is encouraged and rewarded, while conduct that disregards or defies the culture is deterred, detected, and eliminated or, if need be, penalized.

Appearances can deceive. The need to discern the substance of a company's culture and not be swayed by form or appearance is key for both forensic accounting investigators and auditors. Codes of conduct, ethics statements, and conflict-of-interest policies are important, but unfortunately, some companies have all those documents in place yet fall far short of honoring them. Essential to fostering a healthy and widely shared corporate culture are the commitment and attitudes of top management, vigilantly monitored by an engaged board of directors. The lofty phrase *tone at the top* is often heard in discussions of these matters, but a rough proverb is more to the point: "A fish rots from the head."

The CPA's Handbook of Fraud and Commercial Crime Prevention[7] compares the environment and culture of entities with a high potential for fraud with entities that are far less likely to experience or generate fraud.

The factors listed in Exhibit 2.3 are only representative or directional indicators of what may likely be encountered within a business and should be supplemented by the knowledge of the individuals experienced on the engagement. There will frequently be exceptions to these general characteristics; there is no substitute for good judgment. In one matter, a senior executive of a subsidiary would annually participate in the planning process and include in the budget the amount of money he intended to steal. In this way, his expenses never exceeded the plan. He escaped detection for more than 10 years.

---

7. T. Avey, T. Baskerville, and A. Brill, *The CPA's Handbook of Fraud and Commercial Crime Prevention* (New York: American Institute of Certified Public Accountants, 2002).

Variable	High Fraud Potential	Low Fraud Potential
1. Management style	a. Autocratic	a. Participative
2. Management orientation	a. Low trust b. Power driven	a. High trust b. Achievement driven
3. Distribution of authority	a. Centralized, reserved by top managment	a. Decentralized, dispersed to all levels, delegated
4. Planning	a. Centralized b. Short range	a. Decentralized b. Long range
5. Performance	a. Measured quantitatively and on a short-term basis	a. Measured both quantitatively and qualitatively and on a long-term basis
6. Business focus	a. Profit focused	a. Customer focused
7. Management strategy	a. Management by crisis	a. Management by objective
8. Reporting	a. Reporting by routine	a. Reporting by exception
9. Policies and rules	a. Rigid and inflexible, strongly policied	a. Reasonable, enforced fairly
10. Primary management concern	a. Capital assets	a. Human, then capital and technological assets
11. Reward system	a. Punitive b. Penurious c. Politically administered	a. Generous b. Reinforcing c. Administered fairly
12. Feedback on performance	a. Critical b. Negative	a. Positive b. Stroking
13. Interaction mode	a. Issues and personal differences skirted or repressed	a. Issues and personal differences confronted and addressed openly
14. Payoffs for good behavior	a. Mainly monetary	a. Recognition, promotion, added responsibility, choice assignments, plus money
15. Business ethics	a. Ambivalent, rides the tide	a. Clearly defined and regularly followed
16. Internal relationships	a. Highly competitive, hostile	a. Friendly, competitive, supportive
17. Values and beliefs	a. Economic, political, self-centered	a. Social, spiritual, group centered
18. Success formula	a. Works harder	a. Works smarter
19. Human resources	a. Burnout b. High turnover c. Grievances	a. Not enough promotional opportunities for all the talent b. Low turnover c. Job satisfaction
20. Company loyalty	a. Low	a. High

EXHIBIT 2.3   ENVIRONMENTAL AND CULTURAL COMPARISON OF THOSE ORGANIZATIONS WITH HIGH FRAUD POTENTIAL AND THOSE WITH LOW FRAUD POTENTIAL

Source: The CPA's Handbook of Fraud and Commercial Crime Prevention, copyright © 2000, 2001 by American Institute of Certified Public Accountants

Variable	High Fraud Potential	Low Fraud Potential
21. Major financial concern	a. Cash flow shortage	a. Opportunities for new investments
22. Growth pattern	a. Sporadic	a. Consistent
23. Relationship with competitors	a. Hostile	a. Professional
24. Innovativeness	a. Copycat, reactive	a. Leader, proactive
25. CEO characteristics	a. Swinger, braggart, self-interested, driver, insensitive to people, feared, insecure, gambler, impulsive, tightfisted, numbers and things oriented, profit seeker, vain, bombastic, highly emotional, partial, pretend to be more than they are	a. Professional, decisive, fast paced, respected by peers, secure risk-taker, thoughtful, generous with personal time, and money, people, products, and market oriented, builder helper, self-confident, composed, calm, deliberate, even disposition, fair, know who they are, know what they are, and know where they are going
26. Management structure, systems and controls	a. Bureaucratic b. Regimented c. Inflexible d. Imposed controls e. Many-tiered structure, vertical f. Everything documented, a rule for everything	a. Collegial b. Systematic c. Open to change d. Self-controlled e. Flat structure, horizontal f. Documentation adequate but not burdensome, some discretion afforded
27. Internal communication	a. Formal, written, stiff, pompous, ambiguous	a. Informal, oral, clear, friendly, open, candid
28. Peer relationships	a. Hostile, aggressive, rivalrous	a. Cooperative, friendly, trusting

EXHIBIT 2.3 *(CONTINUED)* ENVIRONMENTAL AND CULTURAL COMPARISON OF THOSE ORGANIZATIONS WITH HIGH FRAUD POTENTIAL AND THOSE WITH LOW FRAUD POTENTIAL

Source: The CPA's Handbook of Fraud and Commercial Crime Prevention, copyright © 2000, 2001 by American Institute of Certified Public Accountants

◆ ESTIMATES

Another area that often causes complexity in financial reporting, as well as confusion among users, is the pervasive need for estimates. Estimates appear in financial statements due to the continuous nature of business. Unlike a footrace that ends at the finish line or an athletic contest that ends with the final buzzer, a business and its transactions are continually in varying stages of completion. There are many items in a financial statement for which the final outcome is not known with precision.

Given the complexity and continuity of business, it is difficult to capture a clear snapshot of a company's financial position and performance at a point in time. As a general matter, estimates are most commonly made concerning the final amounts of cash that will be received or paid once assets or liabilities are finally converted into cash. Such estimates can encompass, for example, allowances for uncollectible customer receivables, estimates of liabilities for claims or lawsuits brought against a company, the amount of profit or loss on a long-term contract, and the salability of inventory that is past its prime. Most estimates are based on three types of information: past performance of the same or similar items, what is currently occurring, and what management perceives as the probable outcome. Further complicating matters, the weight to assign each type of information varies depending on the particular circumstances. But no matter how determined, unlike the score of a sporting contest, an estimate in financial statements is a prediction of what will happen, not the objective tally of what has already taken place.

Estimates can create difficult challenges for auditors. The following Public Oversight Board report addresses the significance of estimates and their implications to auditors.

> ...the amounts involve subjective estimation and judgment. Unlike most third-party transactions, the amounts involved are not fixed. They may be based on a range of potential results, and reasonable people may disagree on the most likely outcome or amount.

> ...activity in reserves may be driven principally by management's intentions and decisions rather than by external events or transactions. (For example, management has the ability to determine whether it will offer to settle outstanding litigation.) Indeed, determining just when management's intentions create a liability has vexed accountants and auditors for decades, and, for example, has been a significant factor in the uncertainties surrounding the accounting for restructuring and similar reserves.[8]

All of these features could have an impact on a forensic accounting investigation into the propriety of an estimate that turns out to be incorrect. A legitimate assertion of managerial confidence in the business's ability to achieve certain estimated results is one thing. A deceptive misinterpretation that is intended to generate a favorable estimate is another thing altogether and may pose a substantial investigative challenge. The forensic accounting investigator is often vexed by the myriad complexities and alternative rationales that may be offered to explain the difference between an estimate and an actual result. Given that estimates often constitute the cause of material differences in financial statement presentations, the ability to distinguish between the manipulatively self-serving and the merely incorrect is a critical element of many investigations.

◆ CHOICES

In addition to judgments about estimates, there are many other areas in which management uses judgment and makes choices that affect the company's reported financial results. Obviously, management is paid to make judgments

---

8. Public Oversight Board, Panel on Audit Effectiveness, *Report and Recommendations* (2000), Chap. 2, §§ 2.148–2.150, 50, http://www.pobauditpanel.org/downloads/chapter2.pdf.

and develop strategies that affect the results of the business over time—in both the short and long terms. The challenge for accountants is to reflect objectively and properly the impact of those decisions—without regard to the underlying motivation. However, when the motivation for a transaction is solely to obtain the accounting impact of its recognition, then the business merits of the transaction may be questionable. While some of these so-called earnings management decisions must be recorded because they have in fact taken place, others often have features or terms that require careful evaluation of their legitimacy. Complicating this is the fact that there is often no bright line differentiating the acceptable from the unacceptable, so that management and the auditor may spend a great deal of time focusing on the large expanse of gray areas in which management's decisions can significantly affect reported earnings.

Some earnings management activities involve legitimate discretionary choices of when to enter into transactions that require accounting recognition, not unlike legitimate year-end tax-planning decisions made to accelerate deductions or defer taxable income. For example, advertising expenditures, which generally should be expensed when incurred, may be accelerated in the fourth quarter if the entity is exceeding its earnings target or deferred if it is failing to meet that target. This would generally be an appropriate earnings management technique. Other earnings management activities involve legitimate choices of how to account for transactions and other events and circumstances—particularly those involving accounting estimates and judgments—in conformity with *generally accepted accounting principles* (GAAP). For example, implementation of a decision to enhance the entity's credit and collection activities may legitimately support reducing the estimate of bad debt expense.[9]

Unfortunately, as the Public Oversight Board has pointed out, earnings management may also involve intentionally recognizing or measuring transactions and other events and circumstances in the wrong accounting period or recording fictitious transactions, both of which constitute fraud. The Public Oversight Board provides the following example of the potential for improper earnings management in one of the most difficult areas: revenue recognition.

Assume that an entity announces that—either in response to higher costs, to meet current-period sales targets, or for any other reason—it will increase prices at the beginning of the next quarter, thereby stimulating some customers to purchase unusually high quantities before the end of the current quarter. If the sales meet all the criteria for revenue recognition, the entity should recognize the sales when the product is shipped, possibly resulting in an effective and legitimate management of earnings. If, however, there is an unusual right-of-return privilege and there is no basis for estimating the returns that will take place, the transaction essentially becomes a conditional sale, and recognizing the revenue when the product is shipped violates GAAP and misstates the financial statements. If the right-of-return privilege has been concealed from the auditor as part of a

---

9. Id., Chap. 3, § 3.15, 78, http://www.pobauditpanel.org/downloads/chapter3.pdf.

scheme to increase reported earnings, the financial statement misstatement involves fraudulent financial reporting.[10]

◆ WHAT AUDITORS DO

Why is it unrealistic to assume that all material financial statement frauds can be detected? This can be answered by the Statement on Auditing Standards (SAS) No. 1, which sets out the auditor's fundamental responsibility:

> The auditor has a responsibility to plan and perform the audit to obtain reasonable assurance about whether the financial statements are free of material misstatement, whether caused by error or fraud. This Statement establishes standards and provides guidance to auditors in fulfilling that responsibility, as it relates to fraud, in an audit of financial statements conducted in accordance with generally accepted auditing standards.[11]

To further understand this answer, three fundamental concepts must be examined. They are (1) the difference between error and fraud as it relates to the auditor's responsibility, (2) the meaning of reasonable assurance, and (3) materiality.

FRAUD VERSUS ERROR

U.S. auditing standards state that the main difference between fraud and error is intent. Errors are *unintentional* misstatements or omissions of amounts or disclosures in financial statements.[12] Errors may involve:

- Mistakes in gathering or processing data from which financial statements are prepared
- Unreasonable accounting estimates arising from oversight or misinterpretation of facts
- Mistakes in the application of accounting principles related to amount, classification, manner of presentation, or disclosure[13]

Fraud, on the other hand, is defined in SAS 99 as an *intentional* act that results in a material misstatement.[14] The motive or intent of an individual in

---

10. Id., Chap. 3, § 3.16, 78.
11. American Institute of Certified Public Accountants, Statement on Auditing Standards (SAS) No. 1 (§ 110), 78, and 82, paragraph added, effective for audits of financial statements for periods ending on or after December 15, 2002, by SAS 99. (Codified in AICPA Professional Standards—U.S. Auditing Standards—AU § 110, par. 2.).
12. American Institute of Certified Public Accountants, AICPA Professional Standards—U.S. Auditing Standards—AU § 312, *Audit Risk and Materiality in Conducting an Audit*, par. 7.
13. Id., par. 6.
14. American Institute of Certified Public Accountants, Statement on Auditing Standards (SAS) No. 99, *Consideration of Fraud in a Financial Statement Audit* (codified in AICPA Professional Standards—U.S. Auditing Standards—AU § 316), par. 5.

making accounting entries is not the primary focus of the auditor's procedures. Auditors direct their efforts toward determining objectively measurable criteria regarding account balances and transactions by asking: Do the assets exist? How much was paid? What is the basis of the estimate? Is it reasonable? How much was collected? Were the goods shipped to the customer? By asking questions such as these and obtaining evidence to support the estimate where appropriate, auditors can be better positioned to ascertain that the amounts in the books are correct. If by all of these criteria, transactions have been recorded and reflected correctly in the financial results, then the intent of management in initiating and completing the transactions is irrelevant to the auditor. It is reasonable to presume that the transactions have been undertaken for appropriate corporate purposes, generally making profits in the current period or preparing to do so in the future. Thus, given the focus of the auditor, intent is not uniformly relevant; evaluation of intent is a subjective as opposed to an objective evaluation, and ascertaining intent is a difficult exercise. SAS 99 comments directly on the question of intent:

> Intent is often difficult to determine, particularly in matters involving accounting estimates and the application of accounting principles. For example, unreasonable accounting estimates may be unintentional or may be the result of an intentional attempt to misstate the financial statements. Although an audit is not designed to determine intent, the auditor has a responsibility to plan and perform the audit to obtain reasonable assurance about whether the financial statements are free of material misstatement, whether the misstatement is intentional or not.[15]

REASONABLE ASSURANCE

Why is it that auditors cannot provide better than reasonable assurance? Why not provide absolute insurance?

Professional auditing standards explain that the auditor cannot guarantee that the financial statements are entirely free of material misstatement and cannot provide absolute assurance for two reasons: the nature of audit evidence and the characteristics of fraud. The first reason audits cannot provide absolute assurance—the nature of audit evidence—springs in part from the fact that auditors test only selectively the data being audited. They do not audit all subsidiaries and divisions, all accounts, or all transactions. There are not enough auditors in the world to audit everything, and even if there were, a company's operations would grind to a halt, timely audited financial statements would be an impossibility, and the cost of an audit in strictly financial terms—that is, the auditor's fee—would be prohibitive. Auditors, by necessity, make judgments about the areas to be audited and the nature, timing, and extent of the tests to be performed. In addition, auditors use their judgment in interpreting the results of their work and in evaluating

---

15. American Institute of Certified Public Accountants, Statement on Auditing Standards (SAS) No. 82, *Consideration of Fraud in a Financial Statement Audit* (superseded by SAS 99 and codified in AICPA Professional Standards—U.S. Auditing Standards—AU § 316), fn 3.

audit evidence, especially with regard to areas dependent on management's judgments, such as significant accounting estimates. As a result of these factors, the auditor often has to rely on evidence that is persuasive rather than conclusive. This distinction is important when it comes to the subjective areas of an audit such as estimates and as discussed later, in certain situations in which a fraud is being concealed. The distinction is explicitly cited in auditing standards concerning audit evidence.[16]

The second reason audits cannot provide absolute assurance involves the characteristics of fraud, particularly fraud based on collusion among management or falsified documentation, including forgery that serves to inhibit or prevent the auditor from detecting the related misstatements. Fraud, by nature, is hidden. It is buried in financial statement accounts and hidden in transactions in subledgers and account reconciliations. If buried in an account that rolls up with hundreds of others into one line item on the income statement, it then gets transferred to retained earnings and becomes hidden from sight in future periods. AU 230, *Due Professional Care in the Performance of Work,* states in this regard:

> Because of the characteristics of fraud, a properly planned and performed audit may not detect a material misstatement. Characteristics of fraud include (a) concealment through collusion among management, employees, or third parties; (b) withheld, misrepresented, or falsified documentation; and (c) the ability of management to override or instruct others to override what otherwise appears to be effective controls. For example, auditing procedures may be ineffective for detecting an intentional misstatement that is

---

16. American Institute of Certified Public Accountants, AICPA Professional Standards—U.S. Auditing Standards—AU § 326, *Evidential Matter*, par. 22 and 23. These paragraphs explain that the auditor must typically rely on evidence that is persuasive as opposed to convincing because of the time and cost parameters under which an audit necessarily takes place to retain its usefulness. Specifically:

"(22) The independent auditor's objective is to obtain sufficient competent evidential matter to provide him or her with a reasonable basis for forming an opinion. The amount and kinds of evidential matter required to support an informed opinion are matters for the auditor to determine in the exercise of his or her professional judgment after a careful study of the circumstances in the particular case. However, in the great majority of cases, the auditor has to rely on evidence that is persuasive rather than convincing. Both the individual assertions in financial statements, and the overall proposition that the financial statements as a whole are fairly presented, are of such a nature that even an experienced auditor is seldom convinced beyond all doubt with respect to all aspects of the statements being audited. [Paragraph renumbered by the issuance of Statement on Auditing Standards No. 48, July 1984. Paragraph subsequently renumbered and amended, effective for engagements beginning on or after January 1, 1997, by the issuance of Statement on Auditing Standards No. 80.]

(23) An auditor typically works within economic limits; the auditor's opinion, to be economically useful, must be formed within a reasonable length of time and at reasonable cost. The auditor must decide, again exercising professional judgment, whether the evidential matter available to him or her within the limits of time and cost is sufficient to justify expression of an opinion. [Paragraph renumbered by the issuance of Statement on Auditing Standards No. 48, July 1984. Paragraph subsequently renumbered by the issuance of Statement on Auditing Standards No. 80, December 1996.]."

concealed through collusion among personnel within the entity and third parties or among management or employees of the entity. Collusion may cause the auditor who has properly performed the audit to conclude that evidence provided is persuasive when it is, in fact, false. In addition, an audit conducted in accordance with generally accepted auditing standards rarely involves authentication of documentation; nor are auditors trained as or expected to be experts in such authentication. Furthermore, an auditor may not discover the existence of a modification of documentation through a side agreement that management or a third party has not disclosed. Finally, management has the ability to directly or indirectly manipulate accounting records and present fraudulent financial information by overriding controls in unpredictable ways.[17]

Most people would agree that auditors cannot provide absolute assurance that material misstatements do not exist. This is so despite the best efforts of auditors and despite the desire and the unrealistic expectation on the part of the user and regulatory communities that auditors will provide that assurance. Because of the matters noted above, there exists a difference between what auditors actually do and what the public may expect them to do.

MATERIALITY

The standard auditor's report includes the following expression or its equivalent: "In our opinion, the accompanying financial statements present fairly, *in all material respects ...*" [emphasis *added*]. In other words, auditors are responsible for providing reasonable assurance that the financial statements are stated fairly—but only with regard to material matters.

The Financial Accounting Standards Board describes the concept of materiality as follows:

> The omission or misstatement of an item in a financial report is material if, in light of surrounding circumstances, the magnitude of the item is such that it is probable that the judgment of a reasonable person relying upon the report would have been changed or influenced by the inclusion or correction of the item.[18]

This formulation is in substance equivalent to the holding of the U.S. Supreme Court that a fact is material if there is "a substantial likelihood that the

---

17. American Institute of Certified Public Accountants, AICPA Professional Standards—U.S. Auditing Standards—AU § 230, *Due Professional Care in the Performance of Work*, par. 12. [Paragraph added, effective for audits of financial statements for periods ending on or after December 15, 1997, by Statement on Auditing Standards No. 82. As amended, effective for audits of financial statements for periods beginning on or after December 15, 2002, by Statement on Auditing Standards (SAS) No. 99.].

18. American Institute of Certified Public Accountants, Statement of Financial Accounting Concepts No. 2, *Qualitative Characteristics of Accounting Information,* par. 132.

. . . fact would have been viewed by the reasonable investor as having significantly altered the 'total mix' of information made available."[19] The concept of materiality recognizes that some matters, either individually or in the aggregate, are important to the fair presentation of financial statements in accordance with GAAP, while other matters are not important.

The SEC addresses the issue of materiality in Staff Accounting Bulletin (SAB) 99, *Materiality*, in the following terms:

> The omission or misstatement of an item in a financial report is material if, in the light of surrounding circumstances, the magnitude of the item is such that it is probable that the judgment of a reasonable person relying upon the report would have been changed or influenced by the inclusion or correction of the item.[20]

Historically, many auditors may have focused on a standard of 5 percent of pretax income (loss) or after-tax income (loss) from continuing operations as the benchmark for materiality. However, based upon the nature and circumstances of the company being audited, other elements of the financial statements might be considered to be more appropriate measurements of what is of greatest significance to financial statement users. Such measures include operating earnings, gross profit, current assets, net working capital, total assets, total revenues, total equity, and cash flows from operations. Further, SAB 99 cautions the auditor not to place exclusive emphasis on amounts, per se: ". . . misstatements are not immaterial simply because they fall beneath a numerical threshold."[21]

The guidance provided for auditors in SAS 99, *Consideration of Fraud in a Financial Statement Audit*, warns auditors that their procedures cannot be driven by materiality concerns alone, and they must take a view toward the nature of the error and by whose hand it was committed.[22] Judgments about materiality are among the most difficult auditors are required to make. The auditor—as well as the company—considers materiality from both quantitative and qualitative standpoints. In quantitative terms, there are no hard-and-fast rules; the auditor looks at the impact of identified misstatements—both separately and in the aggregate—and considers whether in relation to individual amounts, subtotals, or totals in the financial statements, they materially misstate the financial statements taken as a whole. From a qualitative standpoint, misstatements of relatively small amounts that come to the auditor's attention could have a material effect on the financial statements. For example, an illegal payment of an immaterial amount could be material if there is a reasonable possibility that it could lead to a material contingent liability or a material loss of revenue.

---

19. *Basic, Inc. v. Levinson*, 485 U.S. 224 (1988).
20. U.S. Securities and Exchange Commission, *SEC Staff Accounting Bulletin: No. 99—Materiality*, 17 CFR Part 211 [Release No. SAB 99], http://www.sec.gov/interps/account/sab99.htm.
21. Id.
22. American Institute of Certified Public Accountants, Statement on Auditing Standards (SAS) No. 99, par. 76.

◆ BEDROCK OF AN EFFECTIVE AUDIT

The auditing profession and regulatory authorities—CPA firms, industry standard setters like the AICPA, and regulators including Congress, the SEC, and the Public Company Accounting Oversight Board (PCAOB)—are all working to restore investor confidence in financial reporting. This is manifest in SAS 99 and in the requirements of the Sarbanes-Oxley Act and in the ongoing work of the PCAOB to revise auditing standards. Despite these changes, the bedrock of an effective and high-quality audit process still consists of competence and the professional attitude of individual auditors. These attributes consist primarily of (1) professional skepticism, (2) knowledge and experience, and (3) independence and objectivity. These form the bedrock of an effective audit.

PROFESSIONAL SKEPTICISM

SAS 99 summarizes the importance of professional skepticism in the auditor's approach to possible fraud:

> Because of the characteristics of fraud, the auditor's exercise of professional skepticism is important when considering the risk of material misstatement due to fraud. Professional skepticism is an attitude that includes a questioning mind and a critical assessment of audit evidence. The auditor should conduct the engagement with a mindset that recognizes the possibility that a material misstatement due to fraud could be present, regardless of any past experience with the entity and regardless of the auditor's belief about management's honesty and integrity. Furthermore, professional skepticism requires an ongoing questioning of whether the information and evidence obtained suggest that a material misstatement due to fraud has occurred. In exercising professional skepticism in gathering and evaluating evidence, the auditor should not be satisfied with less-than-persuasive evidence because of a belief that management is honest.[23]

Professional skepticism requires an objective attitude toward the availability of evidence to sustain management's assertions—especially in areas that are more subjective, such as estimates of loss contingencies. The auditing standards have always required professional skepticism in the performance of an audit; however, in light of catastrophic business failures such as Enron and WorldCom, auditors are continuing to focus their efforts in this important area. The increased effort comports with SAS 99. Sarbanes-Oxley has much the same effect on management and boards: they, too, are called upon to exercise greater skepticism. (Professional skepticism is explored in more depth in Chapter 6.)

KNOWLEDGE AND EXPERIENCE

Auditors must deploy professionals with the necessary skills to perform an effective audit. Auditors should have a thorough understanding of the company and its industry or industries, and companies today often participate in widely

---

23. Id., par. 13.

different industries. For instance, a major retailer may have operations that include manufacturing and distribution and that also maintain a large portfolio of credit cards, which may require auditors to have skills in each of those three distinct businesses. Because every company is unique, auditors need to understand the important features of a company. Knowledge of a company and its complex and varied transactions is a cumulative endeavor. Forcing on companies a change of auditor in an effort to improve independence could run counter to this important ongoing need.

In addition to knowledge of the company and its industries, the audit team should have on hand individuals with the particular skills and expertise necessary to address a myriad of technical audit areas. Some of these are broad areas in which all auditors are knowledgeable, including auditing, internal control, and financial reporting. Others require specialized knowledge of forensic accounting, taxation, information technology, complex accounting, and financial reporting in such areas as derivatives and valuation and actuarial techniques.

INDEPENDENCE AND OBJECTIVITY

Professional auditing standards require the auditor to maintain independence:

> It is of utmost importance to the profession that the general public maintains confidence in the independence of independent auditors. Public confidence would be impaired by evidence that independence was actually lacking, and it might also be impaired by the existence of circumstances which reasonable people might believe likely to influence independence. To be independent, the auditor must be intellectually honest; to be recognized as independent, he must be free from any obligation to or interest in the client, its management, or its owners.[24]

In January 2003, as required by the Sarbanes-Oxley Act of 2002, the SEC established independence rules governing auditors of SEC registrants. In those rules, the commission stated three basic principles of independence with respect to services provided by auditors, violations of which would impair the auditor's independence: (1) auditors are not permitted to function in the role of management, (2) auditors are not permitted to audit their own work, and (3) auditors are not permitted to serve in an advocacy role for their client. (For a more detailed discussion of these rules, see Chapter 6.)

These general principles and the specific rules for carrying them out were established to enhance both the fact and the appearance of auditor independence. The critical reason for *being* independent is to help ensure that the auditor will think and act with objectivity; the critical reason for *appearing to be* independent is to inspire public trust with no ambiguity whatever.

---

24. American Institute of Certified Public Accountants, AICPA Professional Standards—U.S. Auditing Standards—AU § 220, *Independence*, par. 3.

◆ SPADE

A framework that auditors may want to consider incorporates professional skepticism and several other elements that should be considered in the auditor's assessment of the risk of material misstatement caused by error or fraud:

S—Skepticism
P—Probing Communication
A—Analytics
D—Documentation
E—Evaluation

Skepticism stresses that the auditor must critically evaluate audit evidence and maintain a questioning mind, as described above. Probing communication involves inquiry and discussion with the audit team, company personnel, and the audit committee. While inquiry and discussion are not the only tools available to help the auditor obtain evidence, when inquiries are probing and incorporated with skepticism, the auditor is more likely to obtain the desired evidence. Analytics can provide excellent audit evidence in initial planning, scoping, validating, and audit completion. There are numerous types of analytics that can be performed, as well as tools that can be used to perform the analytics, and the auditor must be aware of these in order to use them most effectively. Documentation, which allows the auditor to describe the work performed and the basis for it, is a required duty of the auditor. It is the best means of allowing the proper assessment as to the execution of an audit response to risk and further, to determine if additional risk was identified during execution. Evaluation is essential in all phases of the audit, as it is the act of assessing the evidence obtained when taking into consideration other factors surrounding the company, such as the economy, industry, and internal controls.

Each of these elements is a powerful tool that the auditor should consider using throughout the audit.

◆ AUDITING STANDARDS TAKE A RISK-BASED APPROACH TO FRAUD

Auditors are exposed to what is called engagement risk, which is the risk taken on by their professional practice due to its relationship with an engagement client. This risk might take the form of litigation, adverse publicity, lack of payment for the services performed, loss of professional reputation, and/or the loss of other clients. In addition, engagement risk is increased when the auditor has reservations about the integrity of management. Conversely, "engagement risk may exist even if there are no misstatements in the financial statements and the audit is conducted according to professional standards." For example, a client in poor financial condition presents engagement risk to the auditor based upon its likelihood of nonpayment or bankruptcy.[25] Engagement risk is usually assessed

---

25. Larry E. Rittenberg and Bradley J. Schwieger, *Auditing: Concepts for a Changing Environment*, 4th ed. (Mason, Ohio: Thomson South-Western, 2003), 94.

as part of the audit firm's client acceptance or continuance procedures. An auditor may decide that the risk of association with a client is so great that the engagement should not be undertaken, or the auditor may make the assessment that the engagement risk is within fully acceptable bounds and that the audit can, as a consequence, be planned and undertaken. Having decided to accept or continue the engagement, the auditor will then adopt a risk-based approach to planning and performing the audit.

The nature and characteristics of fraud have been discussed in the previous chapter, including the types of fraud relevant to the auditor and the conditions generally present when fraud occurs. (See also Chapters 10 and 11 on fraudulent schemes.) SAS 99 provides guidance for auditors concerning how to apply a risk-based approach to the possibility of fraud. The key guidelines are the following:

- *Discussion among engagement personnel regarding the risks of material misstatement due to fraud.* As part of planning the audit, there needs to be discussion among audit team members concerning how and where the entity's financial statements might be susceptible to material misstatement due to fraud. The discussion should reinforce the importance of adopting the mind-set of professional skepticism.

- *Obtaining the information needed to identify risks of material misstatement due to fraud.* The auditor must gather information needed to identify risks of material misstatement due to fraud. This is done by:
  - Inquiring of management and others within the entity about the risks of fraud: This inquiry encompasses information about alleged or suspected fraud, knowledge of actual fraud, and management's views on the risk of fraud in the entity as well as about the programs and controls the company has established to mitigate specific, identified fraud risks.
  - Considering the results of the analytic procedures performed in planning the audit: Here the auditor's focus is on identifying unusual transactions and events as well as amounts, ratios, and trends that might indicate heightened risk of material misstatement due to fraudulent financial reporting.
  - Considering fraud risk factors: Here the auditor considers events or conditions that indicate incentives/pressures to perpetrate fraud, opportunities to carry out and conceal it, or attitudes/rationalizations that a fraudster might have in mind.
  - Considering certain other information, including results of the engagement team's fraud discussion, the auditor's client acceptance and continuance procedures, and information gained as a result of reviews of interim financial statements.

- *Identifying risks that may result in a material misstatement due to fraud.* The auditor uses the information gathered as described in the foregoing to identify risks that may result in a material misstatement due to fraud.

- *Assessing the identified risks after taking into account an evaluation of the entity's programs and controls.* The auditor evaluates the entity's programs and controls that address the identified risks of material misstatement due to fraud and assesses the risks in light of this evaluation.

- *Responding to the results of the assessment.* The auditor's response to the risks of material misstatement due to fraud involves the application of professional skepticism when gathering and evaluating audit evidence. The auditor considers responding to the results of the risk assessment in three ways:

  o A response that has an overall effect on how the audit is conducted—that is, a response involving general considerations apart from the specific procedures otherwise planned: This might involve the assignment of additional staff with specialized knowledge and skills to the engagement. Another example would be the decision to incorporate greater unpredictability in the selection of auditing procedures and locations to be audited from year to year.

  o A response to identified risks in terms of the nature, timing, and extent of the auditing procedures to be performed: Such procedures will vary depending on the types of risks identified and the account balances, classes of transactions, and related financial statement assertions that may be affected. The auditor may test the entity's controls designed to prevent and detect fraud, perform substantive auditing procedures, or use a combination of both.

  o A response involving the performance of certain procedures to further address the risk of material misstatement due to fraud involving management override of controls, as discussed in the next section.

- *Evaluating audit evidence.* Throughout the audit, the auditor must assess the risks of material misstatement due to fraud and must evaluate at the completion of the audit whether the accumulated results of auditing procedures and other observations affect the assessment. Further, the auditor has to first consider whether identified misstatements may be indicative of fraud and then, if so, evaluate their implications.

◆ MANAGEMENT OVERRIDE

The previous chapter discussed the importance of management in the overall framework for fraud deterrence. Most often, management is part of the solution, but sometimes it is not just part of the problem but the source of the problem. Auditors face a dilemma with regard to their reliance on management: while they need management's cooperation to do the audit, management is in a position to mislead them in their gathering of evidence. Regarding controls over the quality of financial reporting and deterrence of fraud, this potential dilemma is particularly acute. On one hand, top management is responsible for fostering effective internal control throughout the organization. On the other hand, top management is in a unique position to perpetrate fraud because of its ability directly or indirectly to override established controls and enlist others in its efforts to do so.

Auditing standards have long recognized the possibility of management override as one of the limitations on the auditor's ability to rely on internal controls to prevent or detect misstatements. As a result, no matter how effective the auditor assesses the company's internal controls to be, the auditor generally performs substantive tests on significant account balances and classes of transactions. With regard to fraud, SAS 99 sets out three areas that require substantive procedures that specifically address the risk of management override: (1) journal entries and other adjustments, (2) accounting estimates, and (3) significant unusual transactions.

Massive financial statement fraud often involves manipulation of the financial reporting process by the recording of inappropriate or unauthorized journal entries or by the adjusting of amounts reported in the financial statements that are not reflected in formal journal entries—for example, through consolidating adjustments, report combinations, and reclassifications. To specifically address this risk, SAS 99 requires the auditor to design procedures to test the appropriateness of journal entries recorded in the general ledger and of other adjustments made in the preparation of the financial statements.

As noted earlier in this chapter, significant estimates requiring management judgment have often been used as vehicles for committing fraud. To address this risk, SAS 99 instructs auditors to perform a retrospective review of past accounting estimates for biases that could result in material misstatement due to fraud. Such reviews are intended to afford auditors a look at management's past estimates, with the benefit of hindsight, so that they can identify management biases, if any, that might call into question the reasonableness of current estimates.

Fraud often involves the use of fictitious transactions or transactions whose sole or main purpose is to generate a particular financial result. Recognizing this, SAS 99 instructs auditors to gain an understanding of the business rationale for all significant transactions that fall outside the normal course of business or otherwise appear to be unusual, given the auditor's understanding of the entity and its environment.

◆ REGULATORY REACTION TO FRAUD

Sarbanes-Oxley does not emphasize fraud per se, even though the act originated out of recent corporate fraud scandals. Rather, it addresses the root of the problem by addressing the framework for *effective* controls over financial reporting and other public disclosures. Section 302 requires the CEO and chief financial officer (CFO) to certify quarterly that the auditors and the audit committee have received notice of any fraud—*whether or not material*—involving management or others with a significant role in internal controls.

Signing officers—in addition to those within the organization who certify lower-level financial statements, thereby providing support for the CEO and

CFO—are urged to fully understand the U.S. government's reasoning for the 302 provision. In previous frauds, the Department of Justice (DOJ) often became frustrated because it could not prove a nexus between the company's officers and the fraud. The officers would shrug their shoulders upon learning of the defalcation and claim that they had no knowledge of it. Since the enactment of 302, those days are gone: Section 302 specifically requires the CEO and CFO to take certain steps before they sign that one-page statement. Failure to do so now could land them in prison.

◆ FINANCIAL BENEFITS OF EFFECTIVE FRAUD MANAGEMENT

Sarbanes-Oxley and SAS 99 demand that management, boards, and auditors pay closer attention to fraud. The good news is that effective fraud management is good for business. The Association of Certified Fraud Examiners reports that the average U.S. company loses the equivalent of *6 percent of revenue* to fraud and abuse. Consider the impact of an additional 6 percent of revenue dropping to the bottom line. This amount corresponds closely to the aggregate net income of all of the Fortune 500 companies listed in the year 2003. Most management teams would be very pleased with that degree of profit improvement.

◆ CONCLUSION

For the foreseeable future, corporate fraud is likely to present substantial challenges to both auditors and forensic accounting investigators. Remembering the analogy of the patrol officer, we can recognize that auditing cannot realistically prevent financial reporting fraud or prevent employees from looting corporate assets. It may deter some fraud and detect others, but it is unlikely that auditors using the traditional audit concepts of selective testing (sampling) to obtain reasonable—not absolute—assurance that financial statements are fairly presented—not necessarily 100 percent accurate—will always identify material misstatements caused by fraud. As contemplated by SAS 99, auditing techniques and procedures can and will be improved, and future standards will likely institute further improvements. However, it must be recognized that the complexities of the business world and the ingenuity of highly educated, white-collar criminals will always manage to produce schemes that unfortunately go undetected until they reach significant proportions. Forensic accounting investigators will investigate, prosecutors will convict, and regulators will react with new and more requirements. However, fraud will always persist.

CHAPTER 3

PSYCHOLOGY OF THE FRAUDSTER

Thomas W. Golden

Start with the pleasant assumption that most people are honest. It's a nice way to look at the world, and it summons up childhood memories about learning that honesty is the best policy and George Washington telling his father, "I cannot tell a lie."

Sad to say, human history and human nature tell a different story, and so do the statistics that examine them. While most societies explicitly abhor violent crime and bodily harm, many societies hold financial fraud, whatever its scale, as a less reprehensible wrongdoing. Charles Ponzi, creator of the Ponzi scheme, was celebrated in some quarters as a folk hero and cheered by many of the people he helped defraud. Financiers and executives, whose frauds can disrupt thousands or tens of thousands of lives, have historically been "punished" with relatively light sentences or serve their time at a low-security federal "tennis camp." Some scholars have called this attitude toward white-collar crime "a perversion of our general societal admiration for intelligence."[1] With the advent of the Sarbanes-Oxley Act and recent increases in prison terms for certain financial crimes, there is the expectation that this perception will change as white-collar criminals begin to endure what many would deem just punishment for their crimes.

During much of the past century, psychologists and sociologists struggled to understand the inner workings of people who commit white-collar crime. Edwin Sutherland's *White Collar Crime*,[2] the most influential work in the field, argued in 1939 that an individual's personality has no relevance to a propensity to commit such crimes. Rather, he said, economic crimes originate from the situations and social bonds within an organization, not from the biological and psychological characteristics of the individual.[3] Sutherland also made the useful, if apparent, observation that criminality is not confined to the lower classes and to social misfits but extends, especially where financial fraud is concerned, to upper-class, socially well-adjusted people. Later authors

---

1. Ezra Stotland, "White Collar Criminals," *Journal of Social Issues* 33, No. 4 (1977), 179–196. The author offers a detailed discussion of society's ambivalent attitude toward certain white-collar criminals.
2. Edwin H. Sutherland, *White Collar Crime* (New Haven, Conn.: Yale University Press, 1983), 7.
3. Id.

introduced quite different ideas—for example, suggesting that financial fraud is an inevitable feature of capitalism, in which the culture of competition promotes and justifies the pursuit of material self-interest, often at the expense of others and even in violation of the law.[4]

Over the many decades since *White Collar Crime* was published, persuasive studies have argued that two factors should be considered in analyzing the psychology and personality of the fraudster:

- The biological qualities of an individual, which vary widely and influence behavior, including social behavior
- The social qualities that are derived from and in turn shape how the individual deals with other people[5]

From these studies of psychology, two general types of financial fraudster have been observed:

- Calculating criminals who want to compete and to assert themselves
- Situation-dependent criminals who are desperate to save themselves, their families, or their companies from a catastrophe[6]

Since these studies were published, a third type of criminal has emerged out of catastrophic business failures and embarrassments. We will call them *power brokers.*

◆ CALCULATING CRIMINALS

Calculating criminals are predators. They tend to be repeat offenders, they have higher-than-average intelligence, and they're relatively well educated. They usually begin their careers in crime later in life than other criminals.[7] These predators are generally inclined to risk taking—no surprise there—and they lack feelings of anxiety and empathy.[8] A related view, somewhat different in its emphasis, was offered in a 1993 study of Wall Street's insider-trading scandals by a team of psychologists who suggested that individuals willing to commit such crimes had an "external locus of control"—that is, they lacked inner direction, self-confidence, and self-esteem and were motivated by their desire to fit in and be accepted. Furthermore, the study found that they define success by others' standards.[9]

---

4. James E. Coleman, "Toward an Integrated Theory of White-Collar Crime," *American Journal of Sociology*, Vol. 93, 1987, 406-439.
5. R. Lazarus, *Personality* (Stockholm: Whalstrom & Widstrand, 1973), 12–13.
6. These categories and the research supporting them are discussed in detail by Tage Alalehto, "Economic Crime: Does Personality Matter?" *International Journal of Offender Therapy and Comparative Criminology* 47, No. 3 (2003), 335–355.
7. David Weisbrod, Ellen F. Chayet, and Eljin J. Waring, "White-Collar Crime and Criminal Careers: Some Preliminary Findings," *Crime and Delinquency* 36, No. 3 (1990), 342–355.
8. Georges Kellens, "Sociological and Psychological Aspects," *Criminological Aspects of Economic Crime*, Vol. 15 (Strasbourg, France: European Committee on Crime Problems, 1977).
9. D. E. Terpstra, E. J. Rozel, and P. K. Robinson, "The Influence of Personality and Demographic Variables on Ethical Decisions Related to Insider Trading," *Journal of Psychology* 127, No. 4 (1993), 375–389.

CASE 1: "IT CAN'T BE BOB"

Bob Davies (not his real name) seemed to be a terrific employee as vice president of operations at a billion-dollar company that he had joined six years before. His résumé listed academic and business successes. He was well liked and a hard worker, always willing to pitch in and help break a logjam. When needed, he worked nights or weekends—whatever it took to get the job done. He remembered employees' names, used them when giving out praise, and, even remembering their children's names, would often ask about their children. Then, one day, Davies wired $10 million of his company's money to a bank in Germany and took off after it, bringing along his secretary and abandoning his wife of 12 years and their three children.

"There must be some mistake. It can't be Bob," echoed through the office. To Davies's friends and colleagues, this episode was a nightmare. To the forensic accounting investigators called in to investigate, the incident was in its main features unsurprising. Appearances notwithstanding, Davies was a predator—a con man whose life's work was to steal for personal gain. Predators develop considerable skills and make a career of deceiving people, as though it were just another career track to follow. Predators are dangerous and cause great harm. And once in place, they're hard to detect. The chances are good that a predator who wants access to company assets will accomplish that goal regardless of the controls established to prevent intrusion. Fraud deterrence and detection controls are often robust enough to stop other types of white-collar criminals, but they may not stop the predator. The best defense against predators—somewhat sadly and disturbingly—is a thorough background check *before hiring*. This is a key element of an antifraud program. The company that employed Davies could have discovered his four prior felony convictions during the hiring process. If it had, he wouldn't have been hired.

◆ SITUATION-DEPENDENT CRIMINALS

But the vast majority of corporate criminals are not predators at all. They are situation-dependent criminals: seemingly ordinary people who commit crimes without the intent to harm others. This is a key to understanding white-collar crime, because almost all news coverage and much of the scholarly literature in the area focuses on "egregious, highly publicized, and largely atypical cases" and ignores "the more common, run-of-the-mill, garden-variety" offenders and offenses that account for most white-collar crimes.[10]

This category of financial fraudster—run-of-the-mill, garden-variety, but still capable of doing great harm—is the focus of the balance of this chapter.

The white-collar criminals profiled in Exhibit 3.1 don't stand out. Many employees share these characteristics.

---

10. Michael L. Benson and Elizabeth Moore, "Are White-Collar and Common Offenders the Same? An Empirical and Theoretical Critique of a Recently Proposed General Theory of Crime," *Journal of Research in Crime and Delinquency* 29, No. 3 (1992), 251–272.

Typical White-Collar Criminal

- Older (30+ years)
- 55% male, 45% female
- An appearance of a stable family situation
- Above-average (postgraduate) education
- Less likely to have criminal record
- Good psychological health
- Position of trust
- Detailed knowledge of accounting systems and their weaknesses
- Prior accounting experience

Source: ACFE

EXHIBIT 3.1 CHARACTERISTICS OF THE TYPICAL WHITE-COLLAR CRIMINAL

At the start of an investigation, the forensic accounting investigator often sits down with the client and goes over the organizational chart. The forensic accounting investigator and the client talk about each employee one by one, about each employee's work, and about what is known of the lifestyle of each.

"What about Anne?" the forensic accounting investigator might say, pointing to an employee on the chart. "Oh, no, it couldn't be Anne. She's been with us for 20 years," the client responds. "She's always assisting others with their duties. She's pleasant and rarely takes time off. My wife and I have been to her home. Our daughters are on the same soccer team." The client may believe that what he knows, or thinks he knows, about Anne's character eliminates her from the list of suspects of fraud. In fact, an experienced forensic accounting investigator will understand that Anne fits the profile of a white-collar criminal. This is not to suggest that all nice people are criminals but, rather, that most white-collar criminals give the appearance of being nice people, thereby fitting the exact profile of Anne.

◆ POWER BROKERS

Many of today's once highly placed corporate criminals show characteristics of each of the previous two categories, but they are different enough in their methods and motives to deserve a category all their own: power brokers. Like many of us, you have read about their excesses and asked yourself how respected business leaders could have been so deluded as to believe that they could usurp the financial and human resources of their companies to line their own pockets and deceive a wide range of stakeholders, including their own employees.

Did the U.S. corporate leaders now facing criminal charges begin their careers with the intention of creating a company that would enrich themselves while eventually destroying the dreams and plans of thousands of innocent victims—employees and investors alike? Were all of them predators? Probably not. But a combination of predator characteristics and the circumstances of their positions led them to commit financial crimes.

◆ FRAUDSTERS DO NOT INTEND TO HARM

Generally speaking, situation-dependent criminals carry out their frauds with no intention to do any harm. A high-ranking executive of Westinghouse Electric Co. who was accused of price-fixing in 1961 was asked whether he thought his behavior was illegal. He responded: "Illegal? Yes, but not criminal. Criminal action means hurting someone, and we did not do that."[11]

It is critical to an understanding of the psychology of such people to accept this key point: most of them carry out their frauds with no intention of doing harm, and they believe—they are able to convince themselves—that what they're doing is not wrong. These people may even convince themselves that what they're doing is for the good of the company and everyone associated with it, including employees, investors, creditors, and other constituencies. Or they may believe that they deserve the spoils they seize because they rationalize their crimes as immaterial, innocent, or deserved—but not *wrong*. In most cases, they start small, but in time the fraud grows in size, usually encompassing more than one scheme.

CASE 2: "FOR THE GOOD OF THE COMPANY"

The duping effect of rationalization can be carried to an extreme. In an investigation of a public company's chief financial officer (CFO), placed on administrative leave during the investigation, the independent counsel hired by the company said, "He was trying to help the company, but his misguided efforts just ended up getting him as well as the company in trouble." When asked exactly what he meant by good intentions, the counsel said, "What he did he did for the good of the company." The CFO was found guilty of participating in a fraud, and the company paid a fine of $8 million. Thus, rather than "helping out the company," the CFO caused the company to incur significant penalties. The CFO's motivation: getting great discounts from the vendor for his company.

CASE 3: PERSONAL CATASTROPHES

White-collar criminals are difficult to spot. A 45-year-old middle manager at a textile manufacturer, making $85,000 a year, gets laid off after his company has become weakened by global competition. He held no one responsible; his only concern was to find another suitable job quickly, before his savings ran out. But he couldn't find one for 14 months, and when he did, it wasn't what he had hoped for. Still, he didn't have to relocate his family, and he did have a managerial position with some prospects for promotion in the next several years. Then the dreadful news began piling up.

His little girl hadn't seen the jagged sidewalk that her bicycle wheel slammed into, throwing her over the handlebars. At the hospital, the doctor assured him that his daughter was in no danger and that a good plastic surgeon could restore

---

11. Gilbert Geis, "Toward a Delineation of White Collar Offense," *Sociological Inquiry* 32 (1962), 160–171.

her features. But the family's HMO ruled that the procedures were cosmetic and that a substantial portion of the expense would not be covered. Then his mother-in-law had a stroke and needed full-time care. The family had no money for this, so she would have to move in with them. But where? His wife was pregnant with their second child. No extra bedroom was available for her mother; they would have to build an addition.

The pressure mounted daily. In these circumstances, this harried middle manager was the perfect candidate to become a white-collar criminal. He had a *need* and could probably find the *opportunity* to convert some company assets for personal use. All he needed was a way to *rationalize* his actions.

Such circumstances happen every day. Industries contract, high-flying companies taper off, wages and benefits get cut. Surveys have found that for the first time in decades, parents no longer expect their children to have a better life than they do. Under this duress, many people may find that their customary ethical behavior may seem beside the point when criminal opportunities seemingly provide solutions to complex personal problems.[12]

CASE 4: AN EDUCATED, UPSTANDING CITIZEN

We present this case at some length because it touches on many elements in the psychology of the fraudster: the profile of good citizenship, even professional engagement in good works and church affairs, combined with hidden wrongdoing. The case also offers a first example of the forensic accounting investigative team at work.

The board of a Midwestern foundation dedicated to helping East European and Russian children in need of medical assistance asked for a review of its controls over receipts and expenses. A forensic team examining the executive director's expenses noticed that some personal expenses had been charged to the foundation, including $315 for schoolbooks recently purchased for her children. The team expanded the review to an entire year and found evidence that car repairs, groceries, liquor, theater tickets, and a flight to Miami by the director and her family had been paid for by the foundation. The forensic accounting investigators showed the evidence to the board chairman, who was puzzled and who assured the team that the board had not authorized these expenditures. The board then authorized a broader investigation. The question on everyone's mind was: Were these simply clerical errors, misunderstandings—or the work of a dishonest executive director?

Throughout the investigation, the forensic accounting investigators stayed in continual contact with the executive director to give her the impression that she was leading the investigation and had nothing to fear. The forensic accounting investigators were surprised that she might be a fraudster; she did not fit the preconceived profile of the white-collar criminal they had in their heads.

Eventually, the investigation determined that the foundation had been paying the private school tuition of the executive director's children, bringing the total

---

12. Benson and Moore, 262.

of unauthorized expenses to at least $90,000. With no remaining doubt that it had identified a fraudster in the organization, the team now needed to determine whether there might be other fraudulent schemes or coconspirators. Only more investigative work would provide the answers. The Association of Certified Fraud Examiners (ACFE) fraud manual[13] instructs that once a fraudster has been identified, forensic accounting investigators should:

- Look for additional schemes
- Look for coconspirators
- Look to see what the targets have touched and test those areas[14]

Having thoroughly examined the director's expenses, the forensic accounting investigators thought about what other possibilities for fraud existed. They learned that the director had been directly involved in conducting fund-raising, and so they needed to track the donations received. This search for possibly unrecognized revenue would prove to be an especially challenging task. The director could easily have converted contributions to the foundation for her personal use without anyone's knowing about it. It would be very difficult indeed to confirm revenue from donors known only to her.

Knowing where to look is greatly facilitated by understanding the operations of the organization and the scope of transactions that a suspect has generated or approved. The forensic team knew that the director favored churches as targets for fund-raising. A good place to start was with a study of her travel around the country, based on her expense report vouchers and correlated with churches near the hotels where she stayed. Each time that the forensic accounting investigators identified a church where she had conducted an appeal, they looked for a deposit in the foundation's bank account. They then began calling each church to track donations. They did not disclose that they were investigating suspected criminal behavior—only that they were auditing the foundation's books and confirming donations. If the response was that a donation had not been made and in fact no such appeal had taken place, the forensic accounting investigators simply apologized for troubling that church.

Before long, they found what they were looking for. At a Presbyterian church in Dallas, the minister told the forensic accounting investigators that the executive director had addressed the congregation one Sunday morning and was handed a check for $10,000: a combination of donations from worshippers and a contribution from the church's discretionary fund authorized by the minister himself. The forensic accounting investigators requested a copy of the check,

---

13. Association of Certified Fraud Examiners, *Fraud Examiners Manual* (Austin, Tex.: Association of Certified Fraud Examiners, 1998).

14. For the auditors of this organization, findings of this type present the complex issue of continued reliance on the representations of the executive director. A review of the working papers would likely find specific representations by the executive director, obtained in the course of the audit, as well as her signature on the management representation letter provided to the auditors at or near completion of their work. While another officer might be able to step in and provide the necessary representations, this is often a difficulty cured only through a combination of additional procedures.

front and back, and the minister faxed it promptly. They noted the absence of any endorsement—only the handwritten account number of an account different from the foundation's but matching the executive director's personal account number. Here was another fraud scheme in addition to the false reporting of expenses. There was no firm means of determining how many appeals the director had made in the three years of her directorship or how much she had stolen. Without a court order, the forensic accounting investigators could not obtain her personal banking records, although a good investigative procedure in determining possible theft is to determine valid sources for all deposits on a bank statement. The minister mentioned that the appeal had been videotaped, and he provided the team with a copy.

The team now brought its findings to the foundation's board:

- The executive director had stolen at least $90,000 through expense reimbursement and fraudulent payments for personal expenses.
- She had diverted to her own use checks made payable to the foundation and intended for support of its programs.
- The team had been unable to determine how many foundation donations she had diverted.
- The target was not aware that forensic accounting investigators knew of her frauds.

Board members were stunned and not yet ready to take the matter to the prosecutor. "There has to be a reasonable explanation for these allegations," some board members said. Others were worried about the adverse publicity that a criminal prosecution would bring in addition to its effect on their reputations and the future of the foundation.

As the next step, the forensic accounting investigators prepared for an admission-seeking interview (see Chapter 18) in an attempt to get the executive director to admit to the thefts. During that interview, they would also attempt to get the suspect to admit to other frauds or to provide access to her banking records. Eventually, she confessed. Her explanation? "I only borrowed the money and had every intention of paying it back." She rationalized her actions by reasoning that if she could circulate in high society, she'd be in a better position to solicit large donations for the foundation. To fit in with wealthy donors, she believed that her children had to attend the best private schools and that she needed to travel and dress appropriately. She honestly believed that she was doing nothing wrong in taking "only a little" to meet these "needs."

It is critical that auditors understand how rationalizations of this kind underlie white-collar crime. This executive director, an educated and upstanding citizen, fits the profile of most people they will encounter in an audit—yet there was a difference. Rationalization cuts right to the heart of the psychology of the fraudster: the ability of fraudsters to convince themselves that what they are doing is acceptable enables otherwise good people to do stupid things. Most people engage in rationalization daily, whether deciding to have a second portion of dessert, skip the last set of exercises, or play golf instead of mowing the lawn.

But few people act as the executive director did, rationalizing fraud as ultimately in the best interest of the charitable foundation she served.

Looking back after the investigation had run its course, team members agreed that studying the executive director's actions and her deceits was the best training they had ever received about the value of professional skepticism (see Chapter 6).

◆ KINDS OF RATIONALIZATION

In many admission-seeking interviews, suspects confess to their crimes, but rarely do they say, "I stole the money." Instead, they bring up their rationalization for the crime. Such rationalizations can be of many kinds:

- "It was a loan, and I had every intention of paying it back. See (*pulling out a spreadsheet*), I kept track of all my loans so that I could pay it all back one day."
- "That accounting rule is confusing and subjective. Accounting for the transactions in the manner I chose is entirely acceptable."
- "My boss has been cheating on his taxes for years. I'm just getting my share."
- "Everyone in this industry takes kickbacks. I'm sure my employer is aware of it, and that's why they don't pay me very much. They expect me to supplement my income with 'gifts' from our suppliers."
- "I'm the hardest-working employee here, and I know my boss would give me a substantial raise if he could do it without other people knowing. Instead, I take a little bit, but I'm actually saving the company money because only I get the 'raise.'"
- "What do you expect me to do? You give me no health insurance coverage, and I need to provide for my children and my parents. They depend on me, and I can't let them down."
- "There are a lot of good people here. If I didn't make up a few entries to give the appearance to corporate that we were making budgeted income, they would close our division and put 50 people out of work. I did it to save their jobs."

In sum, rationalization enables a person to take that final step toward crime.

◆ AUDITORS' NEED TO UNDERSTAND THE MIND OF THE FRAUDSTER

In the introduction to *Why Smart People Do Dumb Things*, Mortimer Feinberg and John J. Tarrant begin:

> If you are of above average intelligence—and if you have mastered the use of high intelligence to solve problems and achieve goals—it is the premise of

this book that you are at risk [of perpetrating a fraud] because of the strength of your cognitive equipment.[15]

The book recounts tale after tale of successful professionals and politicians who did something dumb and ruined their lives. It is also a book that can help auditors understand the mind of the white-collar criminal. Because auditors, within the time at their disposal, cannot verify every transaction, they must make assumptions based on audit evidence gathered until the point of the decision. The more auditors understand about why criminals do what they do, the better prepared they may be to determine the nature, timing, and extent of audit procedures relative to the risks identified during the planning stage and modified, as may be warranted, on the basis of the audit evidence found. Professional skepticism is the attitude that must drive the financial statement audit. If we lived in a perfect world in which no one made mistakes, or lied, or cheated, or stole, audits would be unnecessary. But we don't, and so audits are required. Even with effective auditing, at the end of every audit and forensic accounting investigation, uncertainty will remain.

As auditors continue to focus on the fact that smart people do dumb things and on the conditions under which white-collar criminals may act, auditors may be able to better select transactions worthy of expanded testing and know also how to evaluate the results of those tests. The so-called fraud triangle, shown in Exhibit 3.2, offers three conditions that tend to be present when frauds occur:

- Incentive or pressure
- Opportunity
- Rationalization and attitude

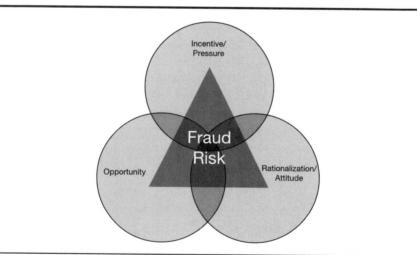

EXHIBIT 3.2 THE FRAUD TRIANGLE

---

15. Mortimer Feinberg and John J. Tarrant, *Why Smart People Do Dumb Things* (New York: Simon & Schuster, 1995), 11.

The fraud triangle is discussed in further detail in Chapter 8, but for now, it is sufficient to know that it takes all three conditions for a fraud to occur. The first two parts of the triangle, incentive and opportunity, are usually observable. The third condition, rationalization, is usually the toughest of the three to identify. This is why auditors need to be ever vigilant to the possibility of fraud. A more informed understanding of the psychology of the fraudster usually makes for a better auditor.

◆ CONCLUSION

As auditors focus on the number of people they encounter in the course of an audit, they would probably agree that a great many of those people would no doubt have opportunities to commit fraud. How many others also have the undisclosed incentive and ability to rationalize that are demonstrably part of the fraud triangle? There is no easy way to judge this.

In the design of controls to prevent financial crime and in the performance of audit procedures, it is important to keep in mind the expression, "Locks on doors keep out honest people." Predators, as noted earlier, have a good chance of circumventing most of the controls a company puts in place. Fraud deterrence and detection controls are designed, theoretically, to stop everyone else, but they won't, because it is unrealistic to expect controls that can be designed to stop everyone. Collusion, for example, may well defeat a well-designed control and may not be detected in a timely manner by individuals performing daily control activities.

The best fraud deterrence mechanism is simple: create the expectation in your organization that wrongdoers will be caught and that punishment will be swift and commensurate with the offense. The emphasis on expectation is important. It can be brought about in a number of ways. Effective training and education on the importance of ethical conduct, background checks on all employees, regular fraud audits by forensic accounting investigators, and a strong internal control system are among the means. To create that perception, employees must also be well aware that their activities are being monitored, and all employees with access to financial assets and transactions must have a healthy respect for the robustness of the control system. If employees believe they will be caught and punished for wrongdoing, that belief may be enough to keep them from adding rationalization to incentive and opportunity.

Some experts have suggested that attention to the institutional level rather than the individual level can be fruitful. For example, Susan P. Shapiro wrote in *American Sociological Review,* "I suggest we begin sampling from settings of trust—legislatures, pension funds, hospitals, labor unions, probate or surrogates' courts, charities, law enforcement agencies, wire services, purchasing departments, universities—and examine how these fiduciaries define and enforce trust norms, the structural opportunities for abuse, the patterns of misconduct that ensue, and the social control pressures that respond."[16] This would provide

---

16. Susan P. Shapiro, "Collaring the Crime, Not the Criminal: Reconsidering the Concept of White-Collar Crime," *American Sociological Review* 55 (1990), 346–365.

greater understanding, she says, of the conditions that allow the individual to rationalize.

Be that as it may, auditors—working as necessary with forensic accounting investigators—realize that there could be a fraudster somewhere in the organization they're auditing. The fraudster may be a predator—an individual who works there to steal—or may be a seemingly upstanding citizen with a secret incentive such as a problem at home, a "golden" opportunity such as knowledge of a weakness in the control system, and a rationalization such as, "It doesn't really harm anyone." There is another possibility: outright greed.

CHAPTER 4

FINANCIAL REPORTING FRAUD AND THE CAPITAL MARKETS

Daniel V. Dooley

Steven L. Skalak

The world's major capital markets are informed and fueled by accurate, complete, and timely financial information of all types. While other types of information—commercial, scientific, political, weather, and demographic data—are also relevant to capital market activity, no other kind of information is as sought or as relied on in the normal course of the capital markets' operations as is financial information. This is the case whether you define *capital market* as individual investors trading a company's shares on a stock exchange or as sophisticated private equity firms investing in emerging companies. In fact, to discuss fraud comprehensively, a relatively broad definition of capital markets should include all forums in which consumers of capital contract with suppliers of capital to fulfill their requirements. Wherever money is involved, that is where you will likely find the fraudsters.

There are many types of capital markets. They include both debt and equity markets for the issuance of publicly traded securities, implemented by organized exchanges and also by special types of markets, as in the case of certain debt instruments such as U.S. Treasury securities. Similarly important are credit markets, in which companies, governments, and individuals can borrow funds for both short- and long-term use from lenders ranging from traditional banks and commercial paper markets to credit card issuers. Also figuring in this inventory are organized exchange markets such as the commodities exchanges in Chicago and London; the Chicago Board of Trade, where agricultural commodities are traded; and the London Metal Exchange, where both base and precious metals are traded. Managed investment funds ranging from public mutual fund complexes to private hedge funds open to only a few selected investors also represent an important sector of the capital markets. Foreign exchange markets must be considered: billions of dollars of currencies are traded every day in spot and forward markets around the world. Finally, the secondary markets—in which individuals and the world's largest investors, such as pension and mutual funds, trade in the debt and equity securities of public companies—must be included.

Participants in all of these markets rely on financial information of one type or another to direct the flow of their funds and determine their trading strategies. At the most fundamental level, capital markets are about the flow of money from one party to another, and to a fraudster they represent an opportunity to redirect the flow of funds, often by deceiving transaction parties with false financial information.

◆ TARGETS OF CAPITAL MARKET FRAUD

Experience has shown that anyone in a position to lend money to or invest money in the business venture of another is likely at some point to be the target or—as the fraudster hopes—the victim of fraud. All capital market participants can be victimized in one way or another; none is exempt. For example, banks can be duped into making loans to fraudulent enterprises, or by becoming indirect participants in fraudulent schemes such as money-laundering operations in which the services of the bank are used for improper purposes.

The primary participants in the capital markets are:

- Banks, including commercial banks, money center banks, national or central banks, savings and loans, credit unions, and mortgage bankers
- Investment banks—the primary underwriters of newly issued securities in both the debt and equity markets
- Broker/dealers—that is, stock and bond brokers for both institutional and retail (individual) customers, foreign exchange traders, primary dealers in U.S. Treasury securities, online or Internet stockbrokers, and commodities brokers and traders
- Insurance companies
- Mutual funds and their advisers and sponsors
- Individual investors

Excluding individual investors for the moment, all of the other participants may become victims of fraudulent schemes in three fundamental ways: by being (1) attacked from within, generally by a rogue employee exceeding the scope of his or her authority for personal gain; (2) attacked from the outside through a wide variety of schemes to obtain funds under false pretenses; or (3) used as an unwitting participant to facilitate a fraudulent scheme perpetrated on others or for the benefit of others. Money laundering is the classic example of the third category.

Some simple examples of the first two categories would be the loan officer who approves bogus loan applications and disburses the money to entities he secretly controls and the currency, bond, or commodities trader who hides losses and then tries to trade his way out of the losses through transactions that exceed approved limits.

Financial institutions such as broker/dealers in securities, commodities brokers, investment banks, investment management firms, and mutual fund complexes can also perpetrate fraud. Generally, this occurs when institutions use for their own advantage their greater access to key information about investment values and prospects instead of sharing the information with their clients. Many investment banking houses earned lucrative fees for bringing new stock and bond issues to market for corporate giants like Enron and WorldCom, as well as for untried dot-com initial public offerings (IPOs). This activity was supported in part by their analysts pumping out research reports touting the companies' stock. Only after the fact have investors learned of internal e-mails showing that the analysts and investment bankers had long before concluded that the business prospects of these companies—clients of the banks—were not at all as rosy as their reports had portrayed.

This is the latest revival of the long-running melodrama "Wall Street versus Main Street." The state of Kansas, in 1911, initiated the blue-sky laws, later emulated by many other states. There followed in later decades the Depression-era revolution in investor protection and market regulation with establishment of the U.S. Securities and Exchange Commission (SEC) in 1934; the Investment Company Act of 1940; and the Security Investors Protection Corp., initiated in 1970, which introduced stringent rules covering suitability, churning, time stamping, trade reporting, and program trading. More recently, there has been vigorous litigation concerning the use of derivative instruments by Gibson Greetings and Procter & Gamble, imposition of the fair disclosure regulations, and the Sarbanes-Oxley Act of 2002.

Although this body of legislation, institutions, and rules is powerful, sophisticated insiders have occasionally taken advantage of less-informed investors since the dawn of modern capitalism. Nonetheless, the model of securities investing based on financial information is a central feature of modern economies, and the task of all ethical participants in the corporate reporting supply chain is to do all they can to ensure that the information is reliable, complete, clear, and timely.

◆ SECURITIES INVESTMENT MODEL

Investors purchase equity securities in the expectation that their investments will generate a satisfactory return in at least one of two ways—or, ideally, in both ways: through dividends and through appreciation in the market value of the securities. Market value can be influenced by many factors, but for the most part, the value of equity securities is based on the profitability of the enterprise. Value may be measured and predicted by consideration of past (i.e., historical) performance, by assessment of the current results of operations and financial condition, and by evaluation of likely future results. Some of the metrics of corporate performance—past, present, and future—are accounting measures, such as:

- Revenues and revenue trends
- Profit margins
- Earnings and earnings trends
- Cash flows from operations and expected future cash flows

Other indicators of potential value may include known or anticipated market success of existing or anticipated products and services; market share; competitive factors such as intellectual property rights, management quality, customer base, superior distribution, or effectiveness of supply chain and manufacturing resources; and technological advantage. These value indicators are proxies for operating results, in that they are expected to result in increased value of equity securities because of their inherent ability to create revenue growth, control costs and expenses, achieve attractive profit margins, and, ultimately, obtain increased profitability.

Risk is a factor in all equity investments. The most basic risk is that future outcomes—in terms of results of operations, profitability, and share value—will not meet expectations. Risk also may be associated with volatility of revenues or any other accounting metric, changes in underlying stock value, and uncertainties regarding many variables such as exogenous economic factors; markets, market share, and competitive behavior; liquidity and the ability to produce and sustain necessary cash flows and to obtain necessary financing; management judgment; and changes in technology or customer preferences.

Investors use financial information principally to assess operating results, make judgments about probable future performance, and evaluate nonaccounting factors within the framework of a microeconomic and financial model of the enterprise in which an investment might be made. Thus, one of the greatest risks to investors is the risk that the financial information upon which they rely is materially misstated. Financial information may be misstated either erroneously or intentionally. Further, financial information may be misstated by means of the inclusion of incorrect information or by excluding information. When financial information is misstated by any scheme, artifice, or device with the intent to mislead investors, it is a form of financial fraud.

OVERVIEW OF FINANCIAL INFORMATION AND THE REQUIREMENT TO PRESENT FAIRLY

In U.S. capital markets, financial information reporting takes the basic form of either a general purpose financial statement—which includes balance sheets—or a statement of financial position; a profit-and-loss statement, also known as P&L or statement of operations; a statement of changes in equity; a statement of cash flows; and footnotes that provide additional information concerning accounting policies and procedures used in preparing the financial information contained in a financial statement, the nature and composition of balances shown in a financial statement, and other significant matters requiring disclosure in order for a financial statement to present fairly the results of operations and the financial condition of the reporting entity. Most U.S. securities registrants are required to file certain financial information with the SEC in various annual, quarterly, and periodic filings, including annual reports, on Form 10-K, and quarterly interim reports, on Form 10-Q. A company's annual report on Form 10-K also is required, by SEC rules and regulations, to include additional and supplemental information in the nature of certain statistical information; descriptions of the company's business, products and services, plant and properties, major operating units and their locations, and significant risk factors; management's discussion and analysis of operations, also known as MD&A; an assessment of liquidity and liquidity risks; and certain supplementary schedules such as a schedule of valuation reserves and loss accruals.

Quarterly interim information filed on Form 10-Q contains condensed financial information and abbreviated footnote disclosure to be used in conjunction with the more detailed disclosure set forth in an entity's annual report. Any other material financial disclosures—typically those that might occur during periods between annual and quarterly reporting dates—may be reported in the form of press releases such as preliminary earnings releases or, depending on their significance, in a Form 8-K filing. As a general matter, if any of these required reports contain false statements or omit significant information, they may be in violation of U.S. laws and regulations.[1]

Generally accepted accounting principles (GAAP) represent a body of authoritative guidance, promulgated by one or more of the following:

- Financial Accounting Standards Board (FASB)
- Accounting Principles Board (APB), predecessor of the FASB
- American Institute of Certified Public Accountants (AICPA), usually through its Accounting Standards Executive Committee (AcSEC)
- Emerging Issues Task Force (EITF) of the FASB

Such authoritative guidance may be in the form of FASB Statements of Financial Accounting Standards (SFASs), APB Opinions (APBs), AICPA Statements of Position (SOPs), EITF Issues (EITFs), APB Interpretations (AINs), FASB Interpretations (FINs), FASB Technical Bulletins (FTBs), or FASB Statements of Financial Accounting Concepts (CONs). SEC guidance, usually in the form of Staff Accounting Bulletins (SABs), provides insights on the SEC staff's interpretation of GAAP.

With this background in mind—much of it common knowledge among working auditors—we can turn to the question of what it means to present fairly the financial statements of an entity. AICPA Statement on Auditing Standard No. 69, *The Meaning of* Present Fairly *in Conformity with Generally Accepted*

---

1. Some of the most commonly cited provisions of U.S. law and regulation are Section 10(b) of the Securities Exchange Act of 1934 and corresponding Rule 10b-5, "Employment of Manipulative & Deceptive Devices," of the Securities Exchange Act of 1934 [Public Law 73-291, 73rd Cong., 2d sess., 13 (1934)]: "It shall be unlawful for any person, directly or indirectly, by the use of any means or instrumentality of interstate commerce, or of the mails or of any facility of any national securities exchange,

   a. To employ any device, scheme, or artifice to defraud,

   b. To make any untrue statement of a material fact or to omit to state a material fact necessary in order to make the statements made, in the light of the circumstances under which they were made, not misleading, or

   c. To engage in any act, practice, or course of business, which operates or would operate as a fraud or deceit upon any person, in connection with the purchase or sale of any security."

Accounting Principles in the Independent Auditor's Report, correlates as follows the concept of *present fairly,* in financial statements, with GAAP:

> Judgment concerning the "fairness" of the overall presentation of the financial statements should be applied within the framework of generally accepted accounting principles. Without this framework, the auditor would have no uniform standard for judging the presentation of financial position, results of operations, and cash flows in financial statements.

SEC Financial Reporting Practices (FRP) Section 101 (Accounting Series Release, or ASR 4, April 25, 1938) states:

> In cases where financial statements filed with the Commission pursuant to its rules and regulations under the Securities Act or the Exchange Act are prepared in accordance with accounting principles for which there is *no substantial authoritative support,* such financial statements will be *presumed to be misleading or inaccurate* despite disclosures contained in the certificate of the accountant or the footnotes to the statements, provided the matters involved are material. [*emphasis added*]

And SEC FRP Section 150 (ASR 150, December 20, 1973) states:

> In the exercise of its statutory authority with respect to the form and content of filings under the Acts, the Commission has the responsibility to ensure that investors are provided with adequate information. *A significant portion of the necessary information is provided by a set of basic financial statements (including the notes thereto), which conform to generally accepted accounting principles.* [*emphasis added*]

Thus, by definitions of both the AICPA and the SEC, financial statements that do not conform to GAAP are not presented fairly and are presumed to be misleading or inaccurate. When investors perceive that financial statements are misleading, a class-action lawsuit is often the result. Such lawsuits typically alleged that false statements were made or material information was omitted. (See box Elements of a Securities Class-Action Complaint, p. 65.)

OVERVIEW OF FRAUD IN FINANCIAL STATEMENTS

Fraudulent financial information typically takes the form of material misstatements made either intentionally or recklessly in one or more of the foregoing types of reports. The most-common vehicles are the annual and quarterly financial statements. Such misstatements generally involve overstatement of revenues; understatement of expenses; overstatement of assets; omission of liabilities; mischaracterization of, or failure to disclose, transactions, accounting events, or other information material to a fair presentation of the reported results of operations; and materially misleading disclosures in respect of MD&A;

ELEMENTS OF A SECURITIES CLASS-ACTION COMPLAINT

1. The defendants made misleading statements and material omissions during the class period.
2. Company X securities traded on the New York Stock Exchange, which is an efficient market.
3. Company X stock price effectively reflected new information and announcements concerning the company that entered the market.
4. Company X is a regulated issuer and, as such, filed periodic public reports with the SEC.
5. Trading volume of the company's stock was substantial during the class period.
6. During the class period, Company X was followed by and regularly communicated with securities analysts employed by brokerage and research firms, who wrote reports that were distributed to the sales force and certain customers of such firms and that were available via various automated data retrieval services.
7. Misrepresentations and material omissions alleged in this complaint would tend to induce a reasonable investor to misjudge the value of the company's stock.
8. Plaintiff and other members of the class bought the company's securities—either at or after the time the misleading statements and material omissions were made—without knowledge of the misrepresented and omitted facts. *(This last point could alternatively be made in the context of shareholders who are selling.)*

---

liquidity and liquidity risks; products and services and their efficacy, market success, and so on; and supplemental information.

Financial statements that are intentionally or recklessly misstated, so that they are misleading or inaccurate and do not conform to GAAP, represent a fraud upon investors. The most common type of financial statement fraud involves overstatements of revenues and earnings and understatement of costs and expenses so as to inflate the profitability or minimize the losses of an entity. Concurrently, such misstatements of the P&L also result in overstatements of assets and understatements of liabilities. Such fraud also is known as an *inclusive* fraud because the financial statements *include* transactions or values that are incorrect. Alternatively, a fraud may involve the intentional omission of liabilities and obligations from the financial statements of a company. Such a fraud is known as an *exclusive* fraud because transactions that *should be included* are not. Most typically, *inclusive* frauds involve the combinations of misstatements arrayed in Exhibit 4.1.

The types of *inclusive* frauds reflected in Exhibit 4.1 may involve either the creation of fictitious assets, or the omission of actual liabilities, or both, or they may involve the timing of transactions so as to improperly reflect, for example:

- Revenues and receivables prematurely recognized before they are earned and realized or realizable
- Costs of goods sold deferred beyond when such costs should have been accrued, either by improperly overstating the value of inventories or by

Assets or Liabilities	Income Statement Effect
Accounts Receivable [Overstated]	Revenue [Overstated]
Allowance for Sales Returns [Understated]	Revenue [Overstated]
Doubtful Accounts Allowance [Understated]	Bad Debt Expense [Understated]
Inventory [Overstated]	Cost of Goods Sold [Understated]
Inventory Reserves (for Lower-of-Cost-or-Market Impairment) [Understated]	Cost of Goods Sold [Understated]
Inventory [Overstated]	Direct Expenses [Understated]
Prepaid or Deferred Assets [Overstated]	Direct, Indirect or Selling, General and Administrative Expenses[Understated]
Accounts Payable, or Accrued Liabilities, or Other Obligations [Understated]	Expenses [Understated]

EXHIBIT 4.1   COMBINATIONS OF MISSTATEMENTS IN TYPICAL INCLUSIVE FRAUDS

deferring the recognition of purchases or costs (materials, labor, and/or supplies) or of indirect expenses and overhead expenses

- Contingencies—in the form of doubtful accounts allowances, sales returns allowances, warranty and product liability reserves, litigation reserves, and the like—not recognized in a timely manner (when they were first *probable* and *estimable*), thus resulting in delayed recognition of associated provision expenses

- Accruals of accounts payable and other liabilities not recognized in a timely manner when the obligations actually were incurred, thereby deferring recognition of the related expenses

In the case of the creation of fictitious assets, the two most common frauds involve recording fictitious revenues and associated fictitious receivables and recording fictitious inventory and thus understating cost of goods sold or other expense. However, any balance sheet account for which a fictitious debit can be created can be used to create an equal and inapposite fictitious credit to post to either a revenue or an expense account in the P&L, thus overstating earnings.

Exclusive frauds typically involve the exclusion of liabilities or other obligations—such as commitments, guarantees, or contingencies—from a company's balance sheet. The effects of such exclusions can include:

- Associated understatement of an expense, such as:
  - Environmental cleanup expenses and related litigation expense provisions, associated with a failure to properly record environmental liabilities
  - Litigation expense provisions, associated with a failure to properly record litigation reserves and judgment liabilities

- ○ Losses associated with debts and other long-term liability obligations that inure to a company as a result of undisclosed guarantees, commitments, or other debt-related contingencies
- ○ Reserves or direct charge-offs associated with impairments of unconsolidated assets such as equity investments, joint ventures, and partnerships, with the failure to record such also resulting in understatement of investment losses or impairment charges to earnings
- ○ Allowances or loss accruals related, among other possibilities, to doubtful account allowances, loan loss allowances, inventory reserves, warranty and product liability reserves, or self-insurance reserves that are intentionally excluded and thus result in understatement of the associated expense provisions
- Associated overstatement of liquidity measures—such as debt to equity or current ratios—and understatement of the true balance of a company's total liabilities
- Associated understatement of interest expense

Some frauds involve the intentional mischaracterization of the nature of transactions and misleading disclosures dealing with the accounting policies and procedures used to account for such transactions or events, the effects of accounting changes, the classification of transactions, or how such transactions affect reported results of operations. Among the most common examples are:

- Failure to properly disclose the effects—on both current and, possibly, future operations—of material changes in accounting estimates
- Misclassification of operating expenses and costs or losses as nonrecurring, when in fact such expenses should be reflected as operating
- Creation of reserves—most typically associated with preacquisition liabilities, restructuring charges, and other so-called onetime charges—intentionally exceeding probable and estimable liabilities expected to be incurred as well as subsequent release of such reserves in order to offset expenses or increase revenues for which such reserves were not provided. In many cases, the provisions of such reserves are reflected as nonoperating charges, while their subsequent release, in whole or in part, is reflected improperly as results of continuing operations incurred in the ordinary course of business.
- Misstatement of—or failure to include—key accounting policies and/or their effect upon reported results of operations

Another type of financial fraud involves the intentional creation of "cookie jar" reserves—that is, general reserves of the kind that are prohibited under SFAS No. 5, *Accounting for Contingencies*. This usually occurs in times when a company is enjoying excess earnings—meaning, earnings that exceed the company's profit plan and analysts' consensus on earnings expectations. The "excess" is kept for a "rainy day," when release of such reserves helps the company achieve earnings targets, absent which the company's results of operations would not meet market expectations. Just about any allowance, loss accrual, or reserve account will do as a cookie jar. The only common denominator is the intentional provision and/or maintenance of reserves in excess of contingent liabilities that are specifically identifiable and are both *probable* and *estimable* under the criteria set forth in SFAS No. 5.

ACCOUNTING IRREGULARITIES AS AN ELEMENT OF FINANCIAL FRAUD

SAS No. 99, *Consideration of Fraud in a Financial Statement Audit,* defines financial fraud, involving accounting irregularities, as follows:

> Misstatements arising from fraudulent financial reporting are intentional misstatements or omissions of amounts or disclosures in financial statements to deceive financial statement users. Fraudulent financial reporting may involve acts such as the following:
> - Manipulation, falsification, or alteration of accounting records or supporting documents from which financial statements are prepared
> - Misrepresentation in, or intentional omission from, the financial statements of events, transactions, or other significant information
> - Intentional misapplication of accounting principles relating to amounts, classification, manner of presentation, or disclosure[2]

Generally, badges of financial fraud include:

- Reported results that do not comport with GAAP (although GAAP violations alone do not necessarily mean fraud).
- Pressures or incentives to commit fraud, including pressure to achieve unrealistic operating results and incentives in the form of performance-based compensation such as stock options, bonuses, or other forms of performance-based compensation, the value of which is tied to achieving such unrealistic operating results.
- Opportunities to commit fraud, resulting from lack of adequate controls, insufficient segregation of duties, or dominance by one or more individuals over critical elements of the accounting and reporting process.
- Concealment through falsification, alteration, destruction, or the hiding of documents and other accounting evidence.
- Collusion, owing to the fact that just one person alone rarely perpetrates major financial frauds: instead, major financial frauds typically involve and require acts, by commission or omission, by a number of individuals.
- Misrepresentations about a wide variety of factors: saying control activities have been performed properly, when in fact they have not; the true

---

2. American Institute of Certified Public Accountants, Statement on Auditing Standards (SAS) No. 99, *Consideration of Fraud in a Financial Statement Audit* (codified in AICPA Professional Standards—U.S. Auditing Standards—AU § 316), par 6.

nature of transactions or accounting events; management's true intent in respect of transactions being entered into; the reasonableness and support for management's judgments and estimates, when such are in fact known to be unreasonable or lacking in valid support; or false evidence, misrepresented to be true and valid, again regarding a wide variety of possible factors: absence of side letters; authenticity of documents known to have been falsified or otherwise altered; relationships with counterparties, including concealment of related party arrangements; the dating of documents—such as back dating—and actual timing of transactions; and the true nature of arrangements such as those concerning rights of return, contingent arrangements, consignment arrangements represented to be completed sales, and undisclosed rebates and other price concessions.

Ponzi Schemes

In 1919 and 1920, Charles Ponzi operated an investment scheme through his business, Securities Exchange Co., which promised investors returns of up to 50 percent, purportedly to be earned from investing in and arbitraging International Postal Union reply coupons. In reality, after some initial success in his venture, Ponzi sustained losses and to keep the scheme going, began repaying old investors with funds provided by new investors. Although Ponzi was exposed, jailed, and eventually exiled back to Italy, where he died penniless, his name lives on to identify a kind of financial fraud that depends on claims of astonishing profits to investors in the form of rates of return, on attracting more and more new investors to provide the funds repaid to old investors, and on a pyramid structure in which only the initial investors and the sponsor of the scheme recover their investments and earn profits thereon. Modern versions of Ponzi schemes may involve multiple pledging of assets claimed to be security for the investors' loans or other investments, commingling of funds and diversion of cash collateral, and fraud in the inducement to invest by:

- Mischaracterizing the nature of, and risks associated with, the investment
- Overstating anticipated returns and misstating the security backing up the investment
- Misstating financial statements by overstating investment returns and operating results and/or understating losses
- Misrepresenting the success of the product, service, or financial scheme upon which the investment is to be based
- Concealing losses and the failure of the scheme—at least for a time—by paying out later investors' monies to earlier investors

Bank Frauds

Although they are not usually investors in equity securities, banks invest in loans to entities that are based at least in part on reliance upon the financial statements and other financial information provided by the borrower. Thus, fraudulent financial statements may be used to defraud lenders just as they defraud equity investors: usually by overstating a company's financial condition and results of operations. Several additional forms of fraud may also affect lenders. Typically, they involve overstating the value of collateral, pledging fictitious collateral, multiple pledging of assets as security, and fraudulently conveying assets—against which loans were made—to related parties, third parties, or other lending institutions.

In the special case of so-called floor-plan loans, a fraud can be committed by manipulation of asset identification records, misrepresentation of improperly converted assets as in transit, and the kiting of cash collateral to use proceeds from borrowing on new, securitized assets to pay off loans made against old assets—another form of the Ponzi scheme.

Fraud on Auditors

The purpose of an independent audit is to determine whether financial statements do in fact present fairly the financial condition and results of operations of a company in accordance with GAAP. If reported results contain accounting irregularities and do not comply with GAAP, any intentional failure to disclose such a condition represents a fraud perpetrated on the auditors. This type of fraud has as its purposes obtaining from the auditors an unqualified audit opinion and keeping the auditors from knowing about and disclosing the accounting irregularities. Fraud on auditors typically includes some combination of the following elements:

- Misrepresentations by management and/or employees concerning the nature of transactions, the accounting applied, the absence of accounting irregularities—when in fact such accounting irregularities exist—and adequacy of disclosure

- Concealment of fraudulent transactions by means of falsification, alteration, and manipulation of documents and accounting records or in some cases, by keeping a separate set of books and records

- Subornation of collusion to defraud from among management and/or employees, taking the form of silence when in fact these persons have knowledge of the fraudulent activities but do not disclose their knowledge to the auditors, active participation in the fraud by corroborating misrepresentations and/or assisting in the falsification of books and records, and assistance in the circumvention of internal controls designed to prevent or detect fraud

- Collusion with third parties or other employees of the victim company, in which such parties are aware of irregular transactions but do nothing to prevent them and/or nothing to bring them to the attention of either their auditors or the counterparty's auditors

- Deceptions, including planning the fraud to take advantage of known or anticipated patterns of auditing—such as scope of testing or audit locations—and furnishing false information to auditors in response to their audit inquiries

- Destruction of evidential matter and/or withholding key documents such as side letters

Lying to an auditor can also result in criminal sanctions. According to the U.S. Department of Justice, lying to auditors or a forensic accounting investigator can be considered obstruction of justice. Also, lying to any member of an audit team may trigger penalties under Sarbanes-Oxley (misleading an auditor).

◆ SOME OBSERVATIONS ON FINANCIAL FRAUD

Based on statistics for private securities class actions and SEC investigations from 1991 through 2001, the incidence of allegations of financial fraud among SEC registrants was found to be less than 3 percent in any year. However, as recent events have demonstrated, even as few as some 220 financial frauds per year—among more than 14,000 SEC registrants—is shocking to U.S. capital markets and to investors. However, financial fraud may be minimized and reduced in its effects on capital markets and investors if it is sought out and recognized in its early stages. Most financial frauds start small and then grow bigger and bigger until they cause significant harm. The application of sufficient vigilance and professional skepticism may serve as deterrents to financial fraud and the attendant financial losses suffered by investors and other users of financial information. Experience has shown that adequate internal controls, proper tone at the top, effective auditing, and alertness to fraudulent activities can make a real difference.

FRAUD FROM WITHIN

At the beginning of this chapter, we said certain capital market participants—generally, financial institutions such as banks, insurance companies, broker/dealers, and investment banks—are sometimes defrauded by their own employees. Some of these instances are relatively straightforward thefts of an employer's assets or of customer assets in the custody of the institution. For example, a loan officer might create false borrowing requests to draw on borrowing facilities and then circumvent confirmation and statement delivery procedures to keep the customer from learning of the misappropriation. Alternatively, more complex trading schemes are sometimes developed—normally, from a desire to hide losses incurred in trading activities that exceeded the limits of the employee's authority. This type of fraud can be extremely harmful to the institution because huge debts can quickly mount beyond the financial capacity of the institution to repay.

◆ SUMMARY

In the current financial accounting and reporting environment, the temptations to commit accounting irregularities can be great. The value of performance-based compensation—especially the value of options, bonuses, and other variable compensation awards for CEOs, CFOs, and other senior management—often acts as a strong lure to manage earnings, set unrealistic revenue and profit targets, and manipulate accounting to achieve results in line with market expectations. Especially in certain sectors—such as software, electronics, and high technology—the pressures of competition, technology change, and the need for capital sometimes cause some people to do dumb things, including perpetration of financial fraud. Further, because of the waves of lucrative IPOs in the 1990s and the significant growth of middle-market firms, the accounting bench of properly trained, suitably experienced, and ethically aware financial officers became lean. The traditionally rigorous system of training, developing, supervising, and promoting accountants gave way in some companies to instant accountancy among inexperienced accountants, younger MBAs, and others who lacked the appropriate knowledge, experience, and professional discipline to perceive properly the difference between what is right and what is wrong in accounting judgments. Some of these people were swayed by senior management to act in ways that put company performance before ethical values.

Sweeping changes are under way in the entire area of financial accounting and reporting. The changes under consideration by regulators and the accounting profession include:

- Less complex, more understandable, and more commonsensical accounting rules and GAAP authoritative pronouncements: As this book went to press, GAAP includes 154 FASBs, 47 FINs, 31 APBs, and 7 CONs, as well as myriad AINs, EITFs, FTBs, and SEC SABs. Much of this literature is difficult to read and complex even for sophisticated professionals. Less would be better; less formulaic would be preferable.

- New auditing standards, including those recently promulgated or under review and consideration by the PCAOB

- Improved effectiveness of audit committees, especially with respect to accounting and auditing literacy and basic knowledge; independence from management both de jure and in fact; more activism in terms of number of meetings held and consideration and understanding of key accounting policies, procedures, and practices, as well as inquiry into the propriety of significant transactions; better oversight of management; and more emphasis on the establishment and monitoring of internal controls designed to prevent fraud

- Corporate policies and management actions that establish and maintain a proper tone at the top, making clear that there is no tolerance for accounting irregularities or violations of established accounting and internal control policies

The SEC and the Justice Department, as well as many state regulatory agencies and judicial departments, have increased their focus on, and activities involving, financial fraud. The penalties, both civil and criminal, for financial fraud are severe, and recent investigations and prosecutions of alleged financial frauds have been tenacious and thorough. Likewise, the auditing profession has experienced a wake-up call regarding financial fraud and has become even more sensitive to, and vigilant for, any instances that suggest irregularities or improper accounting. Although it will always be true that some people think the rules apply only to others and not to themselves, the message is clear: Many financial frauds are caught and the perpetrators punished. Increased vigilance will push those statistics even higher.

However, even one financial fraud that is spectacular in terms of size, audacity, and harm can do enormous damage to investor confidence in financial markets, the strength of financial institutions, and the reliability of financial statements. Even though the incidence of financial statement fraud is low relative to the total number of companies with shares traded on U.S. and foreign exchanges, the economic losses associated with a small number of recent financial frauds have been enormous and shocking to investors, financial analysts, accounting professionals, and regulators. More needs to be done to deter, detect, and expose such financial frauds in order to sustain confidence in the system of financial reporting and audit assurance that underpins U.S. capital markets.

CHAPTER 5

AUDITOR RESPONSIBILITIES AND THE LAW

Geoffrey Aronow

Andrew Karron

James Thomas

The pressure to establish increased auditor responsibility has been stronger in some decades and weaker in others. The Sarbanes-Oxley Act of 2002 and its implementation are the latest steps in seeking to enhance the role of auditors in detecting and helping prevent financial fraud. There are lessons to be learned from a review of the past eight decades—lessons that can help identify potential future risks to auditors and strategies for minimizing those risks.

Nearly 75 years ago, Judge (later Justice) Benjamin Cardozo recognized in the important *Ultramares* decision the danger of exposing auditors to "a liability in an indeterminate amount for an indeterminate time to an indeterminate class" for "failure to detect a theft or forgery beneath the cover of deceptive entries"— in other words, management fraud.[1] Cardozo held that under the rule of privity of contract (the relationship between contracting parties), only the audit client could sue accountants for negligent auditing and failing to detect a fraud. To allow other parties to sue on such grounds, Cardozo warned, would make the "hazards of a business conducted on these terms . . . so extreme as to enkindle doubt whether a flaw may not exist in the implication of a duty that exposes to these consequences."

Since then, with each wave of corporate scandals reformers have pushed, often with some success, to enhance the safeguards for investors, and implementation of those safeguards has fallen principally on the shoulders of the accounting profession. From one perspective, many of those measures aimed at closing

---

1. *Ultramares Corp. v. Touche, Niven & Co.*, 255 N.Y. 170, 179; 174 N.E. 441, 444 (1931). The fraud in this case involved posting to the general ledger a fictitious entry of more than $700,000 in accounts receivable, thereby more than doubling the true amount of accounts receivable. See id., 443.

the so-called expectations gap[2] between the auditor's legal responsibilities and the widespread public belief that the audit process should provide absolute assurance against financial fraud and misstatement. Through the years, new rules have sought to redefine the auditor's role and make it easier in certain instances for people to seek recovery from auditors for alleged injuries resulting from failures to detect management fraud or financial misstatement.

The modern practice of external auditing through selective testing dates to the early twentieth century. These early test audits examined not only internal company records of selected transactions but also evidence from outside sources about such transactions. The American Institute of Certified Public Accountants (AICPA) published the first authoritative auditing pronouncement in 1917 and revised it in 1929. Lenders increasingly began demanding audited financial statements as a basis for making credit decisions, and investors also began seeking audited financial data.

In that environment, *Ultramares* was decided in 1931. That landmark decision can be understood as judicial recognition that audited financial statements have social value. Because audited financial statements are more reliable than unaudited financial statements, lenders and others are more willing to rely on them and to risk capital, which encourages investment. The lower risk associated with audited financial statements is reflected in a lower cost of capital. Cardozo implicitly recognized that the cost of exposing auditors to "a liability in an indeterminate amount for an indeterminate time to an indeterminate class" might lead to abandonment of the field of auditing or to prohibitive audit fees that would reduce the frequency—and, as a consequence, the social utility—of audits. Thus, he found, any benefit to the plaintiff from a broad rule of liability would be vastly outweighed by the social costs of the loss of affordable financial statement audits.

Shortly after *Ultramares*, Congress recognized the social value of audits in the Securities Act of 1933 and the Securities Exchange Act of 1934. These laws, and the implementing regulations of the new Securities and Exchange Commission (SEC), required every public company to submit annual audited financial statements. Subsequently, government regulators of banks and other financial institutions followed suit.

The widespread adoption of requirements concerning audited financial statements led to the dramatic development of the profession. During the next 40 years, the AICPA published more than four dozen statements on auditing standards. Public accounting firms grew in size and scope and developed sophisticated training procedures and auditing systems. As audited financial statements became ubiquitous, public expectations about the effectiveness and significance of audits also grew.

---

2. The notion of an expectations gap, frequently cited in this chapter, has in recent years acquired a corollary concept: restoring investor confidence. We write here of the expectations gap because the term remains an effective label for the issues under discussion.

Even the U.S. Supreme Court, in its important decision of 1984—*United States v. Arthur Young & Co.*—placed heavy emphasis on public responsibility and public trust in its discussion of audit responsibility:

> By certifying the public reports that collectively depict a corporation's financial status, the independent auditor assumes a public responsibility transcending any employment relationship with the client. The independent public accountant performing this special function owes ultimate allegiance to the corporation's creditors and stockholders, as well as to the investing public. This "public watchdog" function demands that the accountant maintain total independence from the client at all times and requires complete fidelity to the public trust.[3]

Notwithstanding that the accounting profession and its authoritative literature continued to prescribe selective testing and concepts of "reasonable assurance"—implicit recognition that an audit might not detect all errors or fraud—users of financial statements increasingly treated audited financial statements as providing something more. Many in the public came to presume that audits should provide a virtual guarantee against fraud.

The National Commission on Fraudulent Financial Reporting, better known as the Treadway Commission, said in 1987 that users of audited financial statements "expect auditors to search for and detect material misstatements, whether intentional or unintentional, and to prevent the issuance of misleading financial statements." A survey in Canada from around the same time reported: "The public at large and even some quite sophisticated members of the financial community have only a vague understanding of the responsibilities undertaken and the work done by the auditor. To the public it is the end result, the financial disclosure, that is important. The auditor is quite likely to be the first to be blamed for errors or inadequacies in financial disclosure almost without regard to his or her audit responsibility."[4]

The accounting profession has taken steps over the years to close the expectations gap by clarifying the respective responsibilities of management and auditors for financial statements. The standard audit opinion report was revised to state that the "financial statements are the responsibility of the Company's management" and that the auditors "express an opinion on these financial statements based on our audit."[5] Other participants in the corporate reporting process have sought to improve management's compliance with its obligations. For example, the Treadway Commission focused attention on best practices for corporate governance to improve financial reporting. The commission reiterated that the "public company has the initial and the final responsibility for its financial

---

3. *United States v. Arthur Young & Co.*, 465 U.S. 805, 817-118 (1984).

4. Canadian Institute of Chartered Accountants (CICA), *Report of the Commission to Study the Public's Expectations of Audits* (Toronto: 1988), 11.

5. American Institute of Certified Public Accountants (AICPA), AICPA Professional Standards—U.S. Auditing Standards—AU § 508, *Reports on Audited Financial Statements*, par. 8.

statements. Within the company lies the greatest potential for reducing fraudulent financial reporting."[6] Management controls the environment in which financial reporting takes place; notably, it develops and implements the internal controls over financial reporting. It will always be the case that company personnel in general and management in particular will have greater access to information and greater insights into the operations of the company than the outside auditor. Sarbanes-Oxley reinforced the role of corporate management by requiring that CEOs and chief financial officers of public companies certify the accuracy of their financial statements and other financial information in their companies' annual and quarterly reports.

But the accounting profession knew that it had further work to do in clarifying its role. The profession addressed the expectations gap by revisiting the standards for detection of fraud. Reexamining the auditor's role in detecting fraud and reporting suspected illegal acts has been a recurrent theme in virtually all of the profession's periodic self-examinations in the past quarter century—from the Cohen Commission in 1977[7] through the Treadway Commission in 1987, the Special Report of the Public Oversight Board in 1993,[8] the report of the AICPA Special Committee on Financial Reporting in 1994,[9] and the Report of the Public Oversight Board Panel on Audit Effectiveness in 2000.[10]

The standard setters followed suit. In 1988, the Auditing Standards Board issued what came to be known as the expectations gap standards, which consisted of two standards that addressed auditors' responsibilities with regard to the detection of fraud and the reporting of illegal acts: Statement on Auditing Standards (SAS) Nos. 53 and 54. SAS 53, *The Auditor's Responsibility to Detect and Report Errors and Irregularities*, defined the auditor's responsibilities for detecting material misstatements in a financial statement audit, with the emphasis on factors indicating fraud. SAS 54, *Illegal Acts by Clients*, required heightened awareness of the possibility of illegal acts and required the auditor to report to the audit committee certain illegal acts that came to the auditor's attention in the course of the audit.

In 1997, SAS 82, *Consideration of Fraud in a Financial Statement Audit*, superseded SAS 53 and clarified the auditor's role in detecting client fraud by identifying certain fraud risk factors that the auditor should consider and assess in the course of an audit. SAS 82 has, in turn, been superseded by SAS 99, *Con-*

---

6. The Committee of Sponsoring Organizations of the Treadway Commission (COSO), *Report of the National Commission on Fraudulent Financial Reporting*, 1987, Chap. 2, p. 31, http://www.coso.org/publications.

7. American Institute of Certified Public Accountants (AICPA), Commission on Auditors' Responsibilities (Manuel F. Cohen, chairman), *Report, Conclusions and Recommendations*, 1977.

8. Public Oversight Board, *In the Public Interest—A Special Report*, 1993.

9. American Institute of Certified Public Accountants (AICPA), AICPA Special Committee on Financial Reporting, *Improving Business Reporting—A Customer Focus*, 1994.

10. Public Oversight Board, Panel on Audit Effectiveness, *Report and Recommendations*, 2000, http://www.pobauditpanel.org/download.html.

sideration of Fraud in a Financial Statement Audit, which further refines the auditor's responsibility to assess the risk of financial statement fraud.

Each of these standards made clear that auditors must take certain steps designed to enhance the likelihood of detecting fraud. At the same time, the standards carefully reiterated that the auditor seeks only to obtain "reasonable assurance" as to whether fraud has occurred and that, given the nature of fraudulent conduct and the inherently limited nature of audit procedures, a proper audit may not detect fraud. This topic is currently under review by the Public Company Accounting Oversight Board (PCAOB).

In the courts, rulings in auditor liability cases have, at various times in various circumstances (and jurisdictions), reflected:

- An emphasis on the public responsibilities of the auditors of public companies
- A tendency on the part of some courts to view the auditor's report as verification of the health and stability of a company
- The search for a source of funds to make whole the victims of financial fraud

Legislators and the courts, reflecting the concerns first voiced in *Ultramares*, have periodically enhanced protections for auditors against liability claims. In other circumstances, however, courts have issued decisions threatening more exposure and more risk for auditors, particularly for alleged failure to detect fraud.

One of the U.S. Supreme Court's seminal decisions in this area, *Ernst & Ernst v. Hochfelder*,[11] reflects these competing considerations. The Court addressed the question of whether there was liability under Section 10(b) of the Securities Exchange Act of 1934 and SEC Rule 10b-5 governing negligent conduct or whether a plaintiff needed to prove *scienter*, "a mental state embracing intent to deceive, manipulate, or defraud." On one hand, the Court held that proof of negligence was insufficient to impose liability. Rather, the Court held that a violation required *scienter*. But on the other hand, the Court also said that in "certain areas of the law, recklessness is considered to be a form of intentional conduct for purposes of imposing liability." The Court explicitly declined to address whether proof of "recklessness" could suffice to support liability under Section 10(b) and Rule 10b-5 and since then has never directly addressed the issue.

Since that ruling, courts have uniformly accepted recklessness as sufficient to support auditor liability.[12] While various rulings have emphasized that recklessness should be understood as a "lesser form of intent," not a "heightened form of ordinary negligence,"[13] it is nonetheless true that more cases now survive dismissal than would be the case if liability were confined to truly intentional conduct. And once a case goes before a jury, anything can happen.

---

11. *Ernst & Ernst v. Hochfelder*, 425 U.S. 185 (1976).
12. See, e.g., *Greebel v. FTP Software, Inc.*, 194 F.3d 185, 198-200 (1st Cir. 1999); *Press v. Chemical Inv. Servs. Corp.*, 166 F.3d 529, 538 (2d Cir. 1999); *Helwig v. Vencor*, 251 F.3d 540 (6th Cir. 2001); *City of Philadelphia v. Fleming Cos.*, 264 F.3d 1245, 1259 (3d Cir. 2001).
13. See, e.g., *SEC v. Steadman*, 967 F.2d 636, 641-42 (D.C. Cir. 1992); *Greebel*, 194 F.3d, at § 199.

At the same time, the law in certain jurisdictions governing negligence claims under state or common law has evolved to expose the auditor to substantially greater risk of liability than under the strict privity standard that New York State's highest court articulated in *Ultramares*. The high-water mark of expansive liability was probably reached in 1983 with the New Jersey Supreme Court's decision in *H. Rosenblum, Inc. v. Adler*.[14] There the court rushed past *Ultramares* and held that auditors could be liable to any user of the financial statements for reasonably foreseeable negligence.

The bases for that decision provide important insights into the perceptions some have of the auditor's role, which underlie much of the persistent pressure toward imposing greater responsibility—and therefore greater liability when things go wrong. In reaching its conclusion, the *Rosenblum* court asserted that "accountability has clearly been the social and organizational backbone of accounting for centuries. . . . Accountability is what distinguishes accounting from other information systems in an organization or in a society." On the issue of fraud detection, the court conceded that the auditors will not "always be able to discover material fraud" but asserted that "the independent auditor should be expected to detect illegal or improper acts that would be uncovered in the exercise of normal professional skill and care." Almost wistfully, the court declared that "the audit, particularly when it uncovers fraud, dishonesty, or some other illegal act, serves an undeniably beneficial public purpose." The New Jersey court also dismissed practical concerns about the potential for "financial catastrophe" that had motivated the court in *Ultramares*, suggesting that accounting firms would be able to "purchase malpractice insurance policies that cover their negligent acts" and that increasing their liabilities would "cause accounting firms to engage in more thorough reviews."

Nine years later, in *Bily v. Arthur Young & Co.*,[15] the California Supreme Court expressly rejected the *Rosenblum* "foreseeability" standard, stating that it subjected auditors to unreasonable exposure. Rather, the court concluded, "an auditor owes no general duty of care regarding the conduct of an audit to persons other than the client."[16] The court held that an auditor could be liable to those "who act in reliance upon those misrepresentations in a transaction which the auditor intended to influence," which the court said was consistent with the standard set forth in the Restatement (Second) of Torts.[17] In reaching that decision, the court said that an audit requires "a high degree of professional skill and judgment" and is "a professional opinion based on numerous and complex factors. . . . The report is based on the auditor's interpretation and application of hundreds of professional standards, many of which are broadly phrased and readily subject to different constructions. . . . Using different initial assumptions and approaches, different sam-

14. *H. Rosenblum, Inc. v. Adler*, 93 N.J. 324, 461 A.2d 138, (1983).461 A.2d 138 (N.J. 1983).
15. *Bily v. Arthur Young & Co.*, 3 Cal. 4th 370, 11 Cal. Rptr. 2d 51, 834 P.2d 745 (1992). 834 P.2d 745 (Cal. 1992).
16. Id., § 747.
17. Id., § 770.

pling techniques and the wisdom of 20-20 hindsight, few CPA audits would be immune from criticism."[18]

That ruling, in what has become a renowned phrase, asserted that an "auditor is a watchdog, not a bloodhound."[19] Yet, in a way seldom duplicated in recent years, the ruling recognized and took account of the reality of the dynamics of litigation:

> Although the auditor's role in the financial reporting process is secondary and the subject of complex professional judgment, the liability it faces in a negligence suit by a third party is primary and personal and can be massive. The client, its promoters, and its managers have generally left the scene, headed in most cases for government-supervised liquidation or the bankruptcy court. The auditor has now assumed center stage as the remaining solvent defendant and is faced with a claim for all sums of money ever loaned to or invested in the client . . . Although hindsight suggests [the plaintiffs] misjudged a number of major factors (including, at a minimum, the product, the market, the competition, and the company's manufacturing capacity), plaintiffs' litigation-focused attention is now exclusively on the auditor and its report.[20]

Taking a different tack, the court reasoned that responsibility is more properly allocated in a much different manner:

> As a matter of economic and social policy, third parties should be encouraged to rely on their own prudence, diligence, and contracting power, as well as other informational tools. . . . If, instead, third parties are simply permitted to recover from the auditor for mistakes in the client's financial statements, the auditor becomes, in effect, an insurer of not only the financial statements, but of bad loans and investments in general.[21]

Finally, the court rejected the notion of the New Jersey Supreme Court in *Rosenblum* that imposing liability on auditors would create an incentive to do better work.

Since then, most jurisdictions have rejected—by court decision or by statute—New Jersey's broad foreseeability approach, including New Jersey itself, which enacted a statute overturning the *Rosenblum* decision.[22] Most states that have addressed the issue have adopted some form of the rule set forth in the Restatement (Second) of Torts. The Restatement standard essentially provides

---

18. Id., § 763.
19. Id.
20. Id., § 764.
21. Id., § 765.
22. See Carl Pacini et al., "At the Interface of Law and Accounting," *American Business Law Journal* 37 (Academy of Legal Studies in Business, 2000), 171, 175-179; see also *Dickerson & Son, Inc. v. Ernst & Young, LLP,* 2004 WL 963944 (N.J. May 6, 2004) (construing New Jersey statute to bar a claim against an accounting firm).

that "a supplier of information is liable for negligence to a third party only if he or she intends to supply the information for the benefit of one or more third parties in a specific transaction or type of transaction identified to the supplier."[23]

The most recent spate of public scandals involving alleged and proven accounting improprieties may be the harbinger of heightened exposure. Recently, some courts have been less attuned to limiting auditor liability and have taken an approach that focuses once again on such themes as the importance of audited financial statements in modern society and the gravity of the duty assumed by auditors of those financial statements. For example, in reversing the dismissal of a fraud claim by a lower court, the Appellate Division of the New York Supreme Court wrote:

> Keeping in mind the difficulty of establishing in a pleading exactly what the accounting firm knew when certifying its client's financial statements, it should be sufficient that the complaint contains *some rational basis* for inferring that the alleged misrepresentation was knowingly made. *Indeed, to require anything beyond that would be particularly undesirable at this time,* when it has been widely acknowledged that our society is experiencing a proliferation of frauds perpetrated by officers of large corporations, for their own personal gain, unchecked by the "impartial" auditors they hired.[24] (*emphasis added*)

In another case, a United States district judge suggested that an auditor may be liable for a client's accounting that is technically compliant with generally accepted accounting principles (GAAP) but fails to comply with "GAAP's ultimate goal of fairness and accuracy in reporting."[25]

Quite apart from varying legal standards, efforts by the profession to close the expectations gap and even the enactment of the Private Securities Litigation Reform Act of 1995 (PSLRA)[26]—which enhanced protection for auditors by adopting new procedures to weed out baseless litigation—have increased the pressure on auditors to detect fraud.[27]

Notwithstanding the enactment of the PSLRA, the number of securities fraud cases involving auditors continues apace. Even putting aside the spate of initial-public-offering allocation and stock analyst cases, the number of securities

---

23. *Bily v. Arthur Young & Co.*, 758.
24. *Houbigant, Inc. v. Deloitte & Touche LLP*, 753 N.Y.S.2d 493, 498 (N.Y. App. Div. 2003).
25. In re *Global Crossing Secs. Litig.*, 02 CIV 910 (GEL), slip op. at 28-30 (S.D.N.Y. March 23, 2004). Other reported examples that demonstrate the reluctance of some courts to dismiss claims of negligence or fraud before trial include In re *Reliance Securities Litigation*, 135 F. Supp.2d 480, 509-510 (D. Del. 2001); In re *Visionamerica, Inc. Securities Litigation*, 2002 WL 31619079, (M.D. Tenn. Oct. 2, 2002), *4; *Lumbermens Mut. Cas. Co. v. Grant Thornton, et al.*, 92 S.W.3d 259 (Mo. Ct. App. 2002).
26. Public Law No. 104-67, 109 Stat. 737 (1995).
27. Sarbanes-Oxley counteracted some of the protections for accountants provided in the PSLRA by lengthening the statute of limitations for fraud claims from one to two years and the statute of repose from three to five years. See 28 U.S.C. § 1658.

class-action suits filed in 2002 was 31 percent higher than in 2001.[28] Auditors were named in 7 percent of the cases in 2002.[29] These trends abated a bit in 2003—a year in which securities fraud class-action filings dipped by 22 percent—but they still were at a higher level than 2001 and auditors were named in 5 percent of the cases.[30]

Although actual losses associated with allegations of securities fraud are difficult to measure, figures tied to market capitalization losses show that the average and median losses have grown enormously in the past few years.[31] Median settlements in cases in which the auditor has been named as a defendant have been significantly larger than when the auditor is not a defendant, and they are larger when the case involves allegations of departures from GAAP and restatements.[32] About one-third of the settlements in 2002 were for $10 million or greater.[33] The average settlement in accounting-related cases from 1996 through 2000 was approximately $18.6 million.[34] The median settlement in accounting-related cases in 2001 was $8.4 million—up 10 percent more than the median from the previous five years.[35] Eighteen of the top 20 settlements in 2001 were in accounting cases.[36]

Those averages and medians tend to obscure the degree of risk: the exposure in these cases can be staggering. Auditors who failed to detect alleged management fraud have faced extraordinary potential financial liability and have paid large settlements in several recent cases: $335 million to settle claims arising from audits of Cendant Corporation; $125 million to settle claims arising from

---

28. Cornerstone Research, *Securities Class Action Case Filings, 2002: A Year in Review* (New York: Cornerstone Research, 2003), 3.

29. Id., 17. According to the PricewaterhouseCoopers *2002 Securities Litigation Study*, independent auditors were named in 16 percent of private securities class actions and 23 percent of accounting-related private securities class actions filed in 2002 (PricewaterhouseCoopers, *2002 Securities Litigation Study*, 8).

30. Cornerstone Research, *Securities Class Action Case Filings, 2003: A Year in Review* (New York: Cornerstone Research, 2004), 2, 15.

31. Cornerstone Research, *Securities Class Action Case Filings, 2002: A Year in Review* (New York: Cornerstone Research, 2003), id., 5-10. (Alleged median "maximum dollar loss" rose from $0.7 billion in 2001 to $1.5 billion in 2002 versus a $0.4 billion average from 1996 to 2001; alleged median market capitalization loss at the end of the class period, when presumably the "bad news" was disclosed to the marketplace, went from $92 million in 2001 to $152 million in 2002 against an average of $85 million from 1996 to 2001.) In the same publication for the year 2003, along with the reduction in total number of securities cases filed, the size of the alleged median "maximum dollar loss" decreased in cases filed in 2003 to $0.5 billion, as did the alleged median market capitalization loss upon disclosure to approximately $58 million. At the time of this writing, it is too early to tell whether 2003 was an aberration.

32. Cornerstone Research, *Post-Reform Act Securities Lawsuits: Cases Reported through December 2003* (New York: Cornerstone Research, 2004), 7.

33. PricewaterhouseCoopers, *2001 Securities Litigation Study*, 2.

34. Id., 3.

35. Id.

36. Id., 7.

audits of Rite-Aid Corporation; and $110 million to settle claims arising from audits of Sunbeam Corporation.[37]

The profession and the courts have not been the only ones to address the auditor's role in detecting and reporting fraud and illegal acts. In response to a wave of financial failures in the 1980s, Congress considered legislation that would increase auditor responsibility to detect and disclose fraud, with many of the efforts led by Representative Ron Wyden, a Democrat from Oregon. While many of Wyden's proposals failed to win congressional approval, in 1995 Congress adopted the PSLRA, which was enacted into law over President Bill Clinton's veto.[38] Section 301 of the PSLRA amended the Securities and Exchange Act to add a new Section 10A, which requires that audits of public company financial statements include "procedures designed to provide reasonable assurance of detecting illegal acts that would have a direct and material effect on the determination of financial statement amounts."

Section 10A requires that an auditor who comes across information about an illegal act or strongly suggestive of it must "determine whether it is likely that an illegal act has occurred" and if so, "determine and consider the possible effect of the illegal act on the financial statements of the issuer." The auditor must then inform management and the audit committee of the illegal act. If the company's board fails to take remedial action, the auditor is required to take additional steps, up to and including resignation from the engagement and reporting the matter to the SEC.

The SEC has relied on Section 10A as a basis for enforcement actions against independent auditors.[39] Several aspects of those enforcement efforts reflect an expansive approach to holding auditors liable for failing to detect and report fraud.

---

37. Auditors face increased pressure from regulators as well. In early 2004, an SEC administrative law judge imposed on Ernst & Young LLP a six-month bar from accepting new public company audit clients as a sanction for violations of the independence requirements—even though there was no allegation or proof of any audit failure or financial statement misstatement by Ernst & Young's client. See *In the Matter of Ernst & Young LLP*, Administrative Proceeding File No. 3-10933 (ALJ Apr. 16, 2004).

38. U.S. Congress, House, 104th Cong., 2d sess., *Congressional Record* 141, H15,224 (daily ed. Dec. 20, 1995); *Congressional Record* 141 S19,146 (daily ed. Dec. 22, 1995).

39. *Grant Thornton LLP, et al.*, Admin. Proc. File No. 3-11377 (Jan. 20, 2004); *In the Matter of Jeffrey M. Yonkers, CPA*, Admin. Proc. File No. 3-10354, AAER No. 1428 (July 27, 2001); *SEC v. Solucorp Indus. Ltd.*, 197 F. Supp.2d 4 (S.D.N.Y. 2002); *In the Matter of Charles K. Springer, CPA, Robert S. Haugen, CPA, Haugen, Springer & Co., PC*, Admin. Proc. File No. 3-10589, AAER No. 14*56 (Sept. 27, 2001); *In the Matter of Aaron Chaitovsky, CPA, and Robert Glass, CPA*, Admin. Proc. File No. 3-10917, AAER No. 1652 (Oct. 21, 2002); *In the Matter of David Decker, CPA, and Theodore Fricke, CPA*, Admin. Proc. File No. 3-11091, AAER No. 1762 (Apr. 24, 2003); *In the Matter of Pat A. Rosetti*, Admin. Proc. File No. 3-10354 (May 2, 2001). See also *SEC v. KPMG, et al.*, Civ. Act. No. 03-CV-0671 (DLC) S.D.N.Y. (Complaint, Second Claim) (Jan. 29, 2003); *SEC v. Chancellor Corp.*, 1:03-CV-10762, D. Mass. (Complaint, Twelfth Claim) (April 24, 2003).

In *SEC v. Solucorp Indus. Ltd.*,[40] for example, the court held that unlike Section 10(b) (the antifraud provision of the Securities Exchange Act), Section 10A does not contain a *scienter* requirement, and the SEC need not prove that an auditor acted knowingly or recklessly to establish a Section 10A violation. *In the Matter of David Decker, CPA, and Theodore Fricke, CPA*,[41] the SEC brought administrative proceedings under Exchange Act Section 21C and SEC Rule of Practice 102(e) against not only an audit partner but also an audit manager for failing to discharge their responsibilities under Section 10A. In a December 2000 speech to the AICPA, the SEC's then director of enforcement Richard H. Walker asserted that an auditor's Section 10A responsibilities extend not only to illegal acts learned of in connection with year-end audit procedures but also to acts learned of by the auditor in connection with interim quarterly reviews of unaudited financial statements.

Yogi Berra once said, "It's tough to make predictions, especially about the future." Nonetheless, it seems safe to predict that many among the investing public and government officials will continue to view auditors as responsible for detecting and preventing fraud and will seek to impose high standards of accountability for perceived failures to do so. Ironically, efforts to respond to those expectations by enhancing audit procedures risk raising expectations—and the accompanying risk of litigation—even higher.

One likely result of the additional requirements imposed by Sarbanes-Oxley and the Public Company Accounting Oversight Board (PCAOB) is that financial statement audits will become more expensive—perhaps substantially so. This appears to have already begun to happen in 2004, particularly as a result of Sarbanes-Oxley's and the PCAOB's new requirement for reports by companies and attestation reports by auditors on the internal controls of public companies.[42] As the major firms are effectively self-insured because the cost of insurance is prohibitive, the risks associated with audits of new and innovative businesses may be viewed as creating unacceptable risks to those firms that can afford to pick and choose their clients. The result may be that such companies will not be able to retain the most sophisticated and most experienced accounting firms. There is some indication that this has begun to happen, in part due to the resources needed to comply with the new requirement for reports on internal

---

40. *SEC v. Solucorp Indus. Ltd.*, 197 F. Supp.2d 4 (S.D.N.Y. 2002).

41. *In the Matter of David Decker, CPA, and Theodore Fricke, CPA*, Admin. Proc. File No. 3-11091, AAER No. 1762 (April 24, 2003).

42. See, e.g., Deborah Solomon and Cassell Bryan-Low, "Companies Complain about Cost of Corporate-Governance Rules," *New York Times*, February 10, 2004 (noting 30 percent increase in audit costs); see also "Auditing Standard No. 2—An Audit of Internal Control over Financial Reporting Performed in Conjunction with an Audit of Financial Statements" (Public Company Accounting Oversight Board, March 9, 2004), http://www.pcaobus.com/Rules_of_the_Board/Documents/Rules_of_the_Board/Auditing_Standard_2.pdf.

controls.[43] Thus, in attempting to preserve the social utility of financial statement audits, the new regulatory framework ultimately may have the opposite effect—at least in some parts of the economy.

But the adoption of enhanced fraud detection procedures may not inevitably lead to increased risks of liability. The PCAOB is likely to continue to press the profession to take additional responsibility for designing audits to detect fraud and for identifying and eliminating the reasons audits may fail to detect fraud.[44] Well-designed and well-implemented fraud detection procedures may reduce liability by increasing the likelihood that fraud will be detected and remedied promptly. At the same time, the inevitable risk that enhanced auditing for fraud might create unreasonable expectations on the part of clients, the investing public, and the government may be mitigated through careful delineation of the scope of the auditor's efforts and the level of assurance that can be provided on that basis. Clear communication and a constructive dialogue with the audit committee and the board of directors about such matters should help avoid misunderstanding.

Fraud auditors cannot become guarantors of corporate integrity, which remains the responsibility of the company and its board. But to the extent that enhanced fraud-auditing procedures may assist corporate management and boards in discharging their duties, the benefits are likely to be wide-ranging: Clients should benefit from financial statements that have been subject to such enhanced procedures. The capital markets should have greater confidence in the reliability of such financial statements. And, finally, to the extent that fraud is reduced, auditors should benefit from reduced liability by avoiding the enormous burdens that extended litigation can impose on a firm and its professionals.

---

43. See "Auditing Standard No. 2," *supra.* Sarbanes-Oxley's and the PCAOB's requirements relating to the documentation of audits may also spur this trend. See Auditing Standard No. 3 (AS3)—*Audit Documentation* (PCAOB: June 9, 2004), http://www.pcaobus.com/Rules_of_the_Board/Documents/Rules_of_the_Board/Auditing_Standard_3.pdf.

44. See, e.g., the remarks of Douglas R. Carmichael, chief auditor of the PCAOB, made to the AICPA National Conference on December 12, 2003, http://www.pcaobus.org/transcripts/Carmichael_12-12-03.asp. (Audits are to be conducted "in a manner that makes it probable that fraud will be detected," and where a fraud is missed and later discovered, auditors should not "invoke the tired litany that an auditor is not responsible for detecting fraud" but instead, should investigate to determine why they missed it.)

CHAPTER 6

INDEPENDENCE, OBJECTIVITY, SKEPTICISM

Steven L. Skalak

Thomas W. Golden

*T*his chapter divides at the center. On this side of the divide is a necessary account of legislation, codes, and rules that now govern the critical issues of auditor independence, objectivity, and professional skepticism. On the other side are case studies illustrating independence, objectivity, and professional skepticism in action during the course of forensic accounting investigations.

The wave of financial scandals at major corporations in the past few years has prompted lawmakers to pass new laws governing the accounting industry and the public companies they audit. The Sarbanes-Oxley Act of 2002 was enacted in part to remedy the perceived weaknesses in corporate governance and oversight of the auditing profession and to eliminate potential conflicts of interest. Among the areas that the act addresses is auditor independence.

Independence rules have been designed to avoid the appearance as well as the reality of impaired independence. In addition, the independence rules of the Securities and Exchange Commission (SEC), the Public Company Accounting Oversight Board (PCAOB) and the American Institute of Certified Public Accountants (AICPA) Professional Code of Ethics set forth independence rules governing relationships with companies for which CPAs provide attest and certain other services. The range of proscribed relationships covered by those rules is both wide and carefully defined. The rules are quite stringent, and adhering to them has become a matter of course at accounting firms serving companies registered with the SEC.

One of the dominant perceptions driving the enactment of the Sarbanes-Oxley Act was that accountants had, at times, sacrificed auditor *independence* to obtain and maintain lucrative consulting and other business relationships with audit clients. Many lawmakers and their constituents took the view that if auditors are anything less than stringently independent, they will lack *objectivity* in evaluating audit evidence and fall short of the rigorous *professional skepticism* so central to their function as independent examiners of a company's financial statements. When investors and other stakeholders do not believe the auditor to be independent, objective, and skeptical, they may lack confidence in the truthfulness of information disseminated by management. The three linked topics of this chapter are auditor independence, objectivity, and professional skepticism.

◆ SEC FINAL RULES FOR STRENGTHENING AUDITOR INDEPENDENCE

On January 22, 2003, the SEC voted to adopt rules that would fulfill the mandate of Title II of the act, which called on the SEC to strengthen auditor independence. Section 201(a) of the Sarbanes-Oxley Act, implemented by the SEC under Section 10A(g) of the Securities Exchange Act of 1934, sets out 10 nonaudit services that registered public accounting firms are prohibited from providing to issuers for whom they perform financial statement audits:

1. Bookkeeping or other services related to accounting records or financial statements
2. Financial information systems design and implementation
3. Appraisal or valuation services, fairness opinions, or contribution-in-kind reports
4. Actuarial services
5. Internal audit outsourcing services
6. Management functions
7. Human resources services
8. Broker or dealer, investment adviser, or investment banking services
9. Legal services and expert services unrelated to the audit
10. Any other service the PCAOB determines, by regulation, is impermissible.[1] For example, the PCAOB recently proposed rules that would limit auditors from providing certain tax services for registered audit clients.[2]

◆ SEC REGULATION OF FORENSIC ACCOUNTING SERVICES

There was much speculation in advance of the final rules published by the SEC about the types of services that would fall under the ninth category: legal services and expert services unrelated to the audit. As the now published rules read, in an effort to shore up the independence requirement of auditors, Rule 2-01(c)(4)(x) of Regulation S-X and Exchange Act Rule 10A-2 deem it unlawful for an accountant to provide "expert opinions or other services to an audit client, or a legal representative of an audit client, for the purpose of advocating that

---

1. U.S. Securities and Exchange Commission, *Final Rule: Strengthening the Commission's Requirements regarding Auditor Independence* (as required by *Sarbanes-Oxley Act of 2002* and effective March 31, 2003), 9, http://www.sec.gov/rules/final/33-8183.htm.
2. Public Company Accounting Oversight Board, PCAOB Release No. 2004-015 (December 14, 2004), Rulemaking Docket Matter No. 017, *Proposed Ethics and Independence Rules concerning Independence, Tax Services, and Contingent Fees*, http://www.pcaobus.org/Rules_of_the_ Board/Documents/Docket_017/Release2004-015.pdf.

audit client's interests in litigation or regulatory, or administrative investigations or proceedings."[3] The rule goes on to explain that this prohibition extends to working behind the scenes to provide assistance and expertise that educate the audit client's legal counsel in connection with a litigation, proceeding, or investigation.[4] Because auditors have legal obligations in their capacity as auditors, this does not, however, preclude the auditing firm from enlisting its own forensic accounting investigators to (1) extend their audit procedures, in essence conducting a separate investigation into the allegations; (2) "shadow" the audit client's independent legal counsel and retained outside forensic accounting investigators, if engaged; or (3) perform some combination of the two.

Because the SEC recognizes the difference between "expert services" provided during litigation and forensic accounting investigative procedures performed either at the request of the audit committee (provided litigation or regulatory investigations are not under way) or in support of the audit when suspicions of illegal acts arise, it has permitted certain forensic accounting services under its new rule. In particular, the commission has provided that auditors can investigate suspected illegal acts at the request of the audit committee in situations *not* involving litigation or regulatory proceedings. If such proceedings begin during the course of the work, auditors may continue the service so long as they remain in control of their work. An excerpt from the SEC's ruling in this regard is as follows:

> We recognize that auditors have obligations under Section 10A of the Exchange Act and GAAS [generally accepted auditing standards] to search for fraud that is material to an issuer's financial statements and to make sure the audit committee and others are informed of their findings. Auditors should conduct these procedures whether they become aware of a potential illegal act as a result of audit, review or attestation procedures they have performed or as a result of the audit committee expressing concerns about a part of the company's operations or compliance with the company's financial reporting system. In these situations, we believe that the auditor may conduct the procedures, with the approval of the audit committee, and provide the reports that the auditor deems appropriate. . . . Should litigation arise or an investigation commence during the time period that the auditors are conducting such procedures, it is permitted for the auditor to complete the procedures under way, so long as the auditor remains in control of his or her work and that work does not become subject to the direction or influence of legal counsel for the issuer. Furthermore, . . . an accountant's independence will not be deemed to be impaired if, in an investigation or proceeding, an accountant provides factual accounts or testimony describing work it performed. Further, an accountant's independence will not be deemed to be impaired if an accountant explains the positions taken or conclusions

---

3. U.S. Securities and Exchange Commission, *Final Rule: Strengthening the Commission's Requirements regarding Auditor Independence*, 19.
4. Id., 20 and fn. 98.

reached during the performance of any service provided by the accountant for the audit client.[5]

The passage illustrates that although expert services are deemed to be advocacy in nature and are prohibited under the act and the rules adopted by the SEC, forensic accounting investigative services performed either in aid of the audit committee's or management's carrying out of its corporate governance responsibilities or in aid of the audit team's satisfying its responsibilities pursuant to GAAS and Section 10A of the Exchange Act (Section 10A) are still permitted under the new rules. Furthermore, the rules do not penalize a proactive management team or board for involving an investigative team; an auditing firm can continue to provide forensic accounting investigative services for an audit client if those services were already under way when a government investigation commenced so long as the auditor controls its work. In addition, forensic accounting investigative services related to a violation of internal policy or procedures are appropriate; so, too, is investigation of whistleblower allegations. Further, the auditors may already be performing investigative procedures if they were the first to detect a suspected fraud and are therefore well placed to conduct forensic accounting investigative work in the event of an investigation, assuming that they utilize professionals specially trained for such work. The auditing team in place may enable a forensic services team to be deployed more quickly and effectively.

The commission's rules governing the provision of expert services now prohibit an independent auditor from being engaged to provide forensic accounting services for the audit client's legal representative in connection with the defense of an investigation by the SEC's Division of Enforcement, a litigation proceeding, or other type of government investigation[6] such as investigations conducted by the Department of Justice (DOJ) or the Environmental Protection Agency.[7] This ruling is due to a direct conflict between legal and accounting ethical requirements: lawyers are required to be advocates for their clients, while accountants performing audit functions are required to act independently. Were an auditor to be engaged by a lawyer on behalf of an audit client, the auditor[8] would enter into a relationship that is incompatible with the SEC's independence rules. It is not difficult to trigger this prohibition. Once there is an "inquiry" of a regulatory body there can be no forensic accounting services provided for the company by the auditor because such services may be perceived to be expert services, unless of course the services were begun before the inquiry occurred.

---

5. Id.

6. For the purposes of its Final Rule, the SEC defines an *investigation* as "an inquiry by a regulatory body, including by its staff."

7. U.S. Securities and Exchange Commission, *Final Rule: Strengthening the Commission's Requirements regarding Auditor Independence*, 20.

8. It's important to recognize that *the auditor* is considered to mean the auditing firm and includes all staff working for that firm. Therefore, a forensic accountant of the auditing firm is covered with this prohibition just as the auditor is.

While the company is busy hiring lawyers and outside forensic accounting investigators to perform an independent investigation and provide for its own defense, the proactive audit firm will not be sitting by, patiently waiting for the findings. The audit engagement partner—working together with a risk management partner, other partners, and the firm's lawyers—is usually planning a strategy for learning the structure and execution of the client's investigation to efficiently and effectively evaluate the ultimate findings of the investigation and the company's remedial action plan as required by Section 10A. As time is typically of the essence due to SEC filing requirements, it usually is best for the audit firm to establish its own plan early in an investigation.

While by no means required to do so, the auditing firm may consider the value of deploying its own forensic accounting investigators. Its forensic accounting investigators would work under the existing audit engagement letter as an extension of the audit scope. The forensic accounting investigators may neither take direction from client's counsel nor aid client's counsel in any manner typical of consultants or expert witnesses working on behalf of the company. Auditors and their forensic accounting investigators are precluded from an advocacy role on behalf of clients—however minimal the role might be. On the other hand, they may share their planned investigative and other audit procedures, as well as their findings, with the client and client's counsel at the direction of the Audit Committee or Special Committee charged with overseeing the investigation. Nonetheless, the auditing firm's forensic accounting investigators must be careful not to cross the line between the permitted, expanded audit scope and the prohibited expert services listed earlier.

The introduction of the auditing firm's forensic accountants to the audit when fraud concerns arise may be likened to calling upon tax or pension specialists. The regulations recognize that audit committees, or companies, find it beneficial to engage the auditing firm to perform internal investigations or fact-finding engagements (understood to include forensic accounting investigative work), provided that no expert role in litigation is expected. This is consistent with the overall mission of Sarbanes-Oxley to improve corporate governance. The SEC permits this activity on the part of auditors because it recognizes the positive role that forensic accounting plays in the conduct of a comprehensive audit. It specifically commented that " . . . performing such procedures is consistent with the role of the independent auditor and should improve audit quality."[9] Further, auditors are obligated under Section 10A and under GAAS to assess the risk of fraud that is material to an issuer's financial statements and to plan procedures to address that risk and ensure that the audit committee and others are informed of their findings. Not surprisingly, the audit firm, recognizing the differences between auditors and forensic accounting investigators, may prefer that these extended-scope procedures include the significant involvement of their own forensic accounting investigators who actually become part of the audit team.

---

9. U.S. Securities and Exchange Commission, *Final Rule: Strengthening the Commission's Requirements regarding Auditor Independence*, 20.

	Services Rendered in Defense of Enforcement Agency Investigation	Services Provided as an Extension of Audit Scope to Assist Current Auditors	Providing Expert or Consulting Services under a Legal Privilege	Assisting Audit Committee with Internal Investigation of Potential Accounting Impropriety[a]
Nonaudit Client	Allowed	Allowed	Allowed	Allowed
Audit Client	Prohibited	Allowed	Prohibited	Allowed

[a]It is not permitted for this assistance to include defending or helping to defend the audit committee, or the company generally, in a shareholder class action or derivative lawsuit, or an investigation commenced by a governmental enforcement agency whether criminal (U.S. Department of Justice) or civil (SEC), unless begun prior to an enforcement proceeding. Fact witness services are permitted.

EXHIBIT 6.1 FORENSIC ACCOUNTING SERVICES: PROHIBITED AND ALLOWED

Exhibit 6.1 summarizes which forensic accounting services and fact-finding engagements are prohibited under Sarbanes-Oxley and which are allowed.

♦ CONSULTING VERSUS ATTEST SERVICES

Even before Sarbanes-Oxley was enacted, the accounting profession had clear independence standards in place. Professionals at public accounting firms who provide attest services such as financial statement audits and financial statement reviews[10] as defined in the Statements on Standards for Attestation Engagements[11] are required to be independent of the parties they audit. Auditors were understood to have an obligation to provide unbiased, objective opinions—in view of the fact that their reports are relied upon by third parties, such as the investing public and creditors, who cannot independently verify the results or assess the scope of the auditor's work. Independence in this context is a specifically defined attribute pursuant to AICPA Rule of Professional Ethics 101 (ET Rule 101), which appears in the adjoining box. The categories of direct financial interest covered by ET Rule 101 represent only one element in the relationship between auditors and their clients that raised concerns in the wake of the corporate scandals at Enron and WorldCom.

---

10. In addition to *audit* and other *attestation* services, *compilations* and *reviews* are considered assurance services and are conducted in accordance, respectively, with GAAS and the AICPA Standards for Compilation and Review Services as adopted by the PCAOB.

11. For private companies, the Auditing Standards Board (ASB) remains the senior technical committee of the AICPA designated to issue auditing, attestation, and quality-control standards and guidance. The ASB develops and issues standards in the form of Statements on Auditing Standards, Statements on Standards for Attestation Engagements, and Statements on Quality Control Standards (together, "ASB Statements").

ET RULE 101

According to ET Rule 101, independence is considered to be impaired during an attestation engagement if:[12]

A. During the period of the professional engagement, a covered member:

1. Had or was committed to acquire any direct or material indirect financial interest in the client

2. Was a trustee of any trust or executor or administrator of any estate if such trust or estate had or was committed to acquire any direct or material indirect financial interest in the client and (i) the covered member (individually or with others) had the authority to make investment decisions for the trust or estate, or (ii) the trust or estate owned or was committed to acquire more than 10 percent of the client's outstanding equity securities or other ownership interests, or (iii) the value of the trust's or estate's holdings in the client exceeded 10 percent of the total assets of the trust or estate

3. Had a joint closely held investment that was material to the covered member

4. Except as specifically permitted in interpretation 101-5,[a] had any loan to or from the client, any officer or director of the client, or any individual owning 10 percent or more of the client's outstanding equity securities or other ownership interests

B. During the period of the professional engagement, a partner or professional employee of the firm, his or her immediate family, or any group of such persons acting together owned more than 5 percent of a client's outstanding equity securities or other ownership interests.

C. During the period covered by the financial statements or during the period of the professional engagement, a firm or a partner or a professional employee of the firm was simultaneously associated with the client as a:

1. Director, officer, or employee or in any capacity equivalent to that of a member of management

2. Promoter, underwriter, or voting trustee

3. Trustee for any pension or profit-sharing trust of the client

---
[a] Consider also ET Section 101, Rule 101.07.

◆ INTEGRITY AND OBJECTIVITY

In addition to requirements about independence, ET Section 100 of the AICPA Code of Professional Conduct addresses the issues of integrity and objectivity. ET Rule 102 on integrity and objectivity states, "In the performance of any professional service, a member shall maintain objectivity and integrity, shall be free of conflicts of interest, and shall not knowingly misrepresent facts or subordinate his or her judgment to others."[13] In the eyes of the AICPA and the accounting profession generally, ET Rules 101 and 102 are separate and distinct from one another. Independence is defined narrowly and codified by ET Rule 101. Integrity and objectivity are also specifically defined and codified by a separate list of rules

---

12. American Institute of Certified Public Accountants, Code of Professional Conduct, ET Section 101, *Independence*, Rule 101, http://www.aicpa.org/about/code/index.html.

13. American Institute of Certified Public Accountants, Code of Professional Conduct, ET Section 102, *Integrity and Objectivity*, Rule 102, http://www.aicpa.org/about/code/index.html.

(ET Rule 102). The wave of corporate scandals demonstrated the critical importance of all three concepts: independence, integrity, and objectivity.

INDEPENDENCE STANDARDS FOR NONATTEST SERVICES

Rule 101 recognizes that the independence of auditors engaged in attestation services is impaired if they do not meet the requirements noted in the aforementioned sidebar. In contrast, accountants at public accounting firms who provide nonaudit services (practitioners), such as litigation or forensic accounting services, remain independent pursuant to ET Rule 101—and in particular pursuant to Rule 101-3—without considering the requirements in the sidebar. The role of the practitioner who delivers attest services is quite different from the role of the practitioner who provides litigation and forensic accounting services. In attest services, the auditor assesses the fairness of the assertions of others—such as in financial statements—whereas in litigation engagements, the practitioner renders an expert opinion or provides other consulting services based on expert analysis, judgment, experience, education, and so on. Moreover, the results of attestation engagements are relied upon by third parties who cannot investigate the validity of the opinion expressed, while in litigation engagements, the opposing party has the opportunity to closely question the expert's findings, methods and procedures, education, and experience.

Sarbanes-Oxley does not change the applicability of ET Rule 101 to practitioners performing litigation services engagements.[14] The AICPA has published a Consulting Services Special Report—03-1—*Litigation Services and Applicable Professional Standards*, written to provide "practitioners with additional guidance on the existing professional standards and the related responsibilities that affect the litigation services practitioner."[15] According to the 03-1 report, independence is "ordinarily not required when performing litigation service engagements. As a result of the act, the practitioner should be aware that in some instances, if the practitioner provides audit services, they may be precluded from providing litigation services."[16]

In a similar vein, previous AICPA literature also stated that independence was not required in the performance of a litigation services engagement without a related attestation service.[17] According to an AICPA Special Report published in 1993, "Independence as an ethical issue is limited to attestation engagements as required by the attestation standards, which also address the question of the appearance of independence."[18]

---

14. American Institute of Certified Public Accountants, *Litigation Services and Applicable Professional Standards* (Consulting Services Practice Aid 03-1), 2003, 3. Currently, the AICPA is reconsidering the interpretations of ET Rule 101 as applied to litigation services and is developing new guidance to better define litigation and forensic accounting services.
15. Id., 1.
16. Id., 3.
17. American Institute of Certified Public Accountants, Consulting Services Special Report 93-2, *Conflicts of Interest in Litigation Services Engagements* (1993), 72, 100-102. The AICPA is currently considering an amendment.
18. Id.

The 03-1 report emphasizes that while the independence standards for providing litigation services differ from those for providing attestation services, the practitioner is not exempt from professional standards. The point is simply that the standards are somewhat different.

◆ PROFESSIONAL SKEPTICISM

The AICPA Code of Professional Ethics requires member auditors to address professional skepticism as follows:

> Professional skepticism is an attitude that includes a questioning mind and a critical assessment of audit evidence. The auditor should conduct the engagement with a mindset that recognizes the possibility that a material misstatement due to fraud could be present, regardless of any past experience with the entity and regardless of the auditor's belief about management's honesty and integrity.[19]

Throughout this book are examples where the appropriate level of professional skepticism was absent from the minds of the auditors. Imagine how certain corporate scandals might have been different had the auditors brought a greater degree of objectivity and professional skepticism to bear on gathering and evaluating sufficient competent audit evidence to ensure that the accounts were stated fairly and in accordance with the professional standards applicable at the time (both the AICPA and the Institute of Internal Auditors) governing reasonable assurance.

Being hit by fraud is much like being hit by lightning. While we all know that people get hit by lightning, it is an unlikely event for any particular person. Most of us take precautions—but in reality, we do not dwell on the possibility that we may get hit by a lightning bolt. However, those who have been struck by lightning and survive are certain in the future to take every reasonable precaution. So it is with victims of fraud. An auditor and the auditor's client are likely never to have been defrauded at all or to a significant extent. They take standard precautions against fraud because they know that fraud can occur; they follow the relevant professional standards. Even though the rate of incidence of material financial statement fraud is only 2 percent, auditors' professional standards require auditors to practice professional skepticism at all times.

In organizational life, few things are more distressing than witnessing the painful aftermath when a trusted employee is shown to have perpetrated a fraud. For example, a not-for-profit organization recently learned that one of its trusted employees, who had joined the organization immediately after high school and stayed for 30 years, was responsible for a whole series of scams to defraud the organization. The investigation identified three distinct scams totaling $1.4 million. (See Chapters 10 and 11 on fraudulent schemes.) Unfortunately, the employee fled the area, and the organization is unlikely to make any recovery.

---

19. American Institute of Certified Public Accountants, Statement on Auditing Standards (SAS) No. 99, Consideration of Fraud in a Financial Statement Audit (codified in AICPA Professional Standards—U.S. Auditing Standards—AU § 316), par. 13.

Understandably, the organization's executive director was beside himself with anger and filled with a sense of betrayal. When forensic accounting investigators first met with him, they could see that his attitude was undergoing radical change as he attempted to come to grips with this violation of trust. Lightning will not strike him twice. He is a changed man. He will trust—but he will verify for the rest of his days.

◆ TRUST BUT VERIFY: A CASE STUDY

Many forensic accounting investigators have had an episode in their careers that changed forever their perspective on trust. The following narrative recalls that moment of truth for a young auditor confronted for the first time with material fraud.

In the early years of his career as an auditor, before becoming a forensic accounting investigator, he liked to say that he followed his mother's advice to trust others unless there was good reason to mistrust. He had no notion that a criminal would ever cross his path or do serious financial harm to a company he was auditing. He was naive: one of his audit clients was destroyed by fraud, and the overall experience converted a competent young auditor into the founder of a specialized forensic accounting investigations practice.

In the mid-1980s, he was assigned to participate in the audit of a public company in the high-tech industry, which had gone public two years earlier. This particular year was the third audit cycle. As he went about his work, the young auditor encountered an anomaly in the lease-contracts receivable[20] (LCR) accounts he was examining. While wrapping up his audit procedures in the LCR area, he was having a conversation with an accounts receivable clerk in the office—and happened to notice on that individual's desk a fairly thick file labeled *Complaints*. Walking back to his desk, he found himself thinking about that file. Why, he asked himself, would there be a file like that in a company that is growing at an industry-leading rate and highly regarded by the capital markets and the financial press?

That evening, he took a closer look at that file.[21] What he found was shocking. The file was filled with what amounted to hate letters—at least a hundred letters from angry customers stating that the company's products were inferior and demanding that the company's alarm system product be pulled and their contracts canceled. Recovering his mental poise, the young auditor began asking himself how it could be that when he had recently circularized a population of 15,000 leases and selected several hundred of them for positive confirmation, he

20. Lease contracts receivable is the asset created when a lease is capitalized as required by Statement of Financial Accounting Standards No. 13, *Accounting for Leases* (Norwalk, Conn.: Financial Accounting Standards Board, 1976), http://www.fasb.org/pdf/fas13.pdf. Similar to an accounts receivable, the asset is decreased by monthly lease payments.
21. The company had previously given the auditors access to such files in recognition of the fact that the auditors worked late and, in the interest of efficiency, did not wish to require them to wait until company staff returned the following day. Hence, the company staff was requested by the company to make accessible to the auditors all files pertaining to the accounts.

had not randomly selected even one of these unhappy customers. The odds seemed reasonable that he would have selected at least one irate customer. Even if the odds were not all that good, there was something here worth looking into.

The following day, he took it upon himself to extend his audit procedures to determine whether there were other customers upset with the company.[22] Besides the newly discovered Complaints file, there was nothing in the testing results that warranted such an audit step—except his intuition. He went forward with the additional testing. From the Complaints file, he randomly selected five letters demanding that the company's equipment system be pulled and the contract canceled. All were dated prior to year-end. Giving the list of five names and addresses to an LCR clerk, he asked the clerk to furnish a phone number for each customer, because he wanted to speak directly with these customers to confirm their issues with the company. He did this without explanation as to why the audit scope had just been expanded.

He had, in the normal course, already sent out several hundred confirmations to customers but had not received back any exceptions. This, too, seemed odd, particularly because this newly minted public company was growing rapidly and systems and controls were straining to keep up with the pace of growth. The company appeared to be managing well enough, but it still seemed strange that not one customer took exception to any contract information or complained in any way during the standard confirmation procedure. Until seeing the Complaints file, he had not given this situation a second thought.

Within an hour, the young auditor received copies of the customer names and telephone numbers, as he had requested. Oddly, the information had been photocopied from the precise pages in the LCR subsidiary ledger that had been his control copy supporting the asset balance for LCR accounts as of the audit date. He reread all of the information about the assets and unearned balances relative to each lease—and abruptly realized that if the customer's letter requested cancellation of the contract and removal of the system *prior to year-end*, then the proper accounting procedure would have been to remove the asset from the balance sheet and write off the remaining balances. There was no evidence this had been done for the five customers picked at random from the Complaints file, nor did there appear to be any reserve account serving the same purpose. The LCR subsidiary ledger was reconciled to the general ledger—proving to him that the net asset balances for those five customers were recorded in the financial statements. This was wrong. They should have been written off.

Now the young auditor became anxious. Not wanting to leave until he had resolved the situation, he continued his examination. Adding to his concern, none of the five customers had been selected for positive confirmation. Because they were part of a population of about 15,000 leases, this was not too worrisome;

---

22. This matter predated both SAS 82 and SAS 99 and, of course, enactment of the Sarbanes-Oxley Act. The auditor's actions today would be different, given the new standards and regulations as well as subsequently improved training on specific protocols to follow when fraud is suspected.

nonetheless, it was a fact. The thing to do next was to call these "former" customers and verbally confirm the details in their letters.

What better time to do this than that very evening? The company was planning to release earnings in three days, and the audit process was all but complete. A voice inside the young auditor insisted, "There is a reasonable explanation for all this. You are missing something and wasting time." In spite of that internal message, he continued investigating.

One by one, each of the five customers confirmed the details in their letters. Each had had the company's equipment system pulled and the contract canceled prior to year-end. Then why, the auditor asked himself, was the asset still listed at year-end? There was no write-off, no reserve, no reconciling item between the general ledger and the financial statements. His attention was drawn back to his circularization procedures, and he decided to reperform the selection process manually. An audit intern had looked after these procedures in the first round, but now the auditor had to see for himself. Knowing the random start and the interval used for the positive confirmation selection process, he began counting manually. He began counting his way through the subsidiary listing of 15,000 customers. Hours passed. He continued manually counting the interval of every fiftieth customer. Then, at about 3 A.M., he hit the fiftieth count on one particular customer and noted that it was not selected for confirmation. The selection process was computer automated. Computers do not make these kinds of mistakes.

Feeling that fatigue was causing him to make mistakes, he recounted and got the same result. He copied the name and other relevant balance information on this fiftieth customer who was mysteriously not selected for positive confirmation and proceeded to leaf through the Complaints file in search of the name. The letters in the file were in no particular order. It took a while to find the name, but find it he did: a letter dated in August from a lease customer requesting that the equipment system be pulled and the lease contract canceled. As of December 31, the asset representing this customer and lease was still included on the LCR listing and, accordingly, included in the company's financial statements.

He had found just this one. From the perspective of materiality, it was valued at only about $3,500 net of the unearned revenue portion and deferred monitoring costs. On a balance sheet of about $50 million, this was certainly no show-stopper—but then, he was just getting started.

He continued his count and soon found others with the same characteristics. By 8:30 A.M., when the company's staff began arriving for their day's work, he had found a total of seven for which there was a complaint letter demanding that the company remove their equipment system and cancel the contract, yet the asset was still listed in the year-end LCR asset listing. This manual review had covered less than 10 percent of 15,000 leases, but the auditor had learned enough to go on to the next step. He asked one of the company's information technology (IT) staff members to print out every column in the electronic file for each of these seven customers. Examining that printout, he noticed there were some 15 fields detailing customer information such as customer number, name, phone number, and asset and liability balances. This was the same information listed in the LCR subsidiary ledger. However, on this new listing, in the far right column, there was a Z for each of the seven.[23] No caption at the head of the column made clear what Z signified. It was the only common characteristic among the seven. The auditor asked the IT staffer to perform a query on the entire LCR master file: he wanted all customers listed out who had that Z in their customer file history at December 31.

Hours passed. Once the staffer had brought the report, it seemed clear to the auditor that the staffer must have misinterpreted the request, because the report was very long. Upon closer examination, it became evident that the query, correctly conducted, had captured nearly 4,000 customers with an aggregate net LCR balance of just under $11 million. For a company with $7 million in pretax net income, the $11 million was obviously material to the financial statements and promised to be a highly significant discovery.

The auditor still refused to believe the result of his examination. He went home, rested, and mentally reviewed every step of the procedures performed in the past few days. He could not find a procedural flaw, and he could not argue away the ominous implication of the findings. He got in touch with his engagement partner and reported the findings. After several internal conversations and review, the partner relayed the findings to senior company executives and the board of directors. This set in motion a seven-week investigation, led by the young auditor, to determine the extent of the fraud he had single-handedly uncovered. Who was involved? How large in dollar terms was the accounting fraud? What years were affected? How did it escape detection? What effects would these discoveries have on the company and on the auditing firm?

After completing this thorough investigation, the audit firm withdrew its prior-year opinions. Not surprisingly, the SEC Division of Enforcement took notice and rapidly issued subpoenas directed at both documents and persons, including the young auditor. As the consequences of the fraud played out, the company stock was delisted and the company eventually filed for bankruptcy.

The young auditor had experienced his moment of truth and learned the meaning of professional skepticism. However, the moral of the story is not to withhold trust. It is to trust—but verify.

TRUST BUT VERIFY: EXPLORING FURTHER

We owe the expression *trust but verify* to President Ronald Reagan, who used it during the Cold War to define the U.S. position on missile systems inspection. *Trust but verify* should be the credo of all auditors as they perform their duty of ensuring that the information disseminated by management properly depicts the financial condition of the company being audited. We all know what *trust* means, but the word *verify* may need clarification.

---

23. Later, it was determined that someone at the company had changed the program of the tape used to select customers for confirmation. Essentially, when the fiftieth item selected had a Z in the record, the program change permitted that customer to be skipped over, selecting instead the fifty-first customer for confirmation.

We can start with its definition. Merriam-Webster defines *verify* as a verb that means *to confirm or substantiate; to establish the truth, accuracy, or reality of.* Defined in this way, the word is not a specific term of art in the world of auditing. Instead, we refer to the process of verification in terms of ascertaining the completeness, accuracy and validity of a transaction, of groups of transactions, or of balances.

- *Completeness.* Whether all transactions and other events and circumstances that occurred in a specific period and should have been recognized in that period have in fact been recorded.[24]

- *Accuracy.* The correctness and appropriateness of a statement, account, set of accounts, or document—such as a voucher—in portraying facts or opinions whose degree of accuracy is measured by the relative correspondence of a statement, account, or document to the facts. Accuracy is a close cousin to *validation*.[25]

- *Validity.* Involves the actual occurrence and approval of transactions, as well as relevancy, truth, correctness, and enforceability. *Validation* is the determination of whether a test yields desired results with the necessary elements of accuracy, precision, reliability, and relevance.[26]

Verification is the means by which an auditor gathers sufficient auditor evidence. Yet auditors cannot in all reasonableness mistrust their clients. If clients were not trusted, they would not be clients for very long. However, the auditor's trust should be supported by whatever processes of verification are appropriate under given circumstances. An auditor who adheres to the practice of trusting but verifying should not rely on the presumed character of any individual who creates a transaction or has responsibility for an important control function without ascertaining, on an independent and objective basis, the accuracy, validity, and completeness of the matter under review. Paragraph 13 of Statement on Auditing Standards (SAS) No. 99 addresses the issue of trust and honesty:

> Professional skepticism is an attitude that includes a questioning mind and a critical assessment of audit evidence. The auditor should conduct the engagement with a mindset that recognizes the possibility that a material misstatement due to fraud could be present, regardless of any past experience with the entity and regardless of the auditor's belief about management's honesty and integrity. Furthermore, professional skepticism requires an ongoing questioning of whether the information and evidence obtained suggests that a material misstatement due to fraud has occurred. In exercising professional skepticism in gathering and evaluating evidence, the auditor should not be satisfied with less-than-persuasive evidence because of a belief that management is honest.

---

24. Robert Hiester Montgomery, *Montgomery's Auditing*, 12th ed. (New York: John Wiley & Sons, 1998), 6–1.

25. Eric Louis Kohler, *Kohler's Dictionary for Accountants*, 6th ed. (Englewood Cliffs, N.J.: Prentice Hall, 1983), 18.

26. Id., 528.

The basis for trust must be verification of the underlying financial data and not any prior experience with management. Even seemingly honest people can defraud, depending on current-year incentives, opportunities, and the ability to rationalize one's actions.

Paragraph 15 of SAS 99 requires for the first time that any prior impressions of management's integrity should have no bearing on the current-year audit. In a parallel to the concept of zero-based budgeting, the auditor must reassess the environment for fraud each year:

> The discussion among the audit team members about the susceptibility of the entity's financial statements to material misstatement due to fraud should include a consideration of the known external and internal factors affecting the entity that might (a) create incentives/pressures for management and others to commit fraud, (b) provide the opportunity for fraud to be perpetrated, and (c) indicate a culture or environment that enables management to rationalize committing fraud. The discussion should occur with an attitude that includes a questioning mind as described in paragraph 16 and, for this purpose, *setting aside any prior beliefs the audit team members may have that management is honest and has integrity.* In this regard, the discussion should include a consideration of the risk of management override of controls. [*emphasis added*]

While determination of the appropriate audit procedures is usually a facts-and-circumstances undertaking, the following examples of the practice of trust but verify can shed useful light on making that determination.

Example 1

AUDITOR OBSERVATION

Several significant accounts receivable have been re-aged, there is no valid documentation supporting such a practice, and the practice of re-aging is not permitted by company policy. The auditor presents the issue to the client for explanation.

CLIENT RESPONSE

We noticed this problem several weeks ago in preparing for the audit, and we are in the process of correcting it. The amounts are not material. During a system implementation, there were some glitches in the accounts receivable program, but now they are fixed.

POTENTIAL AUDITOR RESPONSES

The auditor who trusts but verifies may consider performing the following steps:

- Interview the employee who first noted the problem.
- Interview the IT technician who worked on the fix, and confirm the company's message about the nature of the problem.

- Extend testing in the aging of accounts receivable to verify that the matter is (1) immaterial as indicated and (2) corrected, with all appropriate adjustments made.

- Reevaluate bad debt reserve, which may have been understated due to re-aging of the invoices.

Example 2

AUDITOR OBSERVATION

While performing sales cutoff testing procedures during year-end audit proce-dures, the auditor discovers a large number of invoices marked *Bill, but do not ship. See George.*

CLIENT RESPONSE

These invoices belong to our largest client in Germany. Given that storing costs are astronomical in Germany and that the client is able to obtain inventory from our independent warehouse facility within one day, we believe that the arrange-ment and recognition of these sales are appropriate.

POTENTIAL AUDITOR RESPONSES

Upon receiving this verbal response, the auditor may consider requesting sup-porting documentation, such as purchase orders, sales agreements, and bills of lading. The auditor keeps in mind that a sale should be recognized only once the risk and rewards of the transaction have been transferred, the amount of the sale is determinable, and the collectibility of such sale is not in doubt. In addition to items that may not be mentioned below, the auditor may consider performing all or a portion of:[27]

- Make inquiries of management and employees who are approving and generating these transactions.

- Select a sample of recorded sales, review their terms to assess reasonable-ness, and confirm such with your customers.

- Examine and assess for validity the existence and appropriateness of sup-porting documentation for each selection.

- Select a sample of shipping documents, and trace back to the open-accounts-receivable report.

---

27. Please note that this roster of audit steps is not exhaustive; other steps might also be needed in an actual situation. The applicable SEC guidance is Staff Accounting Bulletin 101, also referred to as Topic 13-A, which addresses revenue recognition under the following criteria, cited verbatim:
    - The staff believes that revenue generally is realized or realizable and earned when all of the fol-lowing criteria are met:
      ○ Persuasive evidence of an arrangement exists,
      ○ Delivery has occurred or services have been rendered,
      ○ The seller's price to the buyer is fixed or determinable, and
      ○ Collectibility is reasonably assured.

- Review prior- and current-year January journal entries, specifically for sales reversals related to bill-and-hold invoices.
- Make inquiries of management regarding the agreement between management and the warehouse facility.
- Independently confirm your understanding of the client's arrangement with the warehouse facility by specifically asking the following of the warehouse manager:
  - Who is in control of the inventory while staged at the warehouse facility?
  - Does your customer (the audit client) ever inform you that the buyer has canceled the order and request that you refrain from shipping?
  - How often is inventory returned?

If everything checks out, you would normally move on in your audit program. If there are discrepancies to the extent that you question the truthfulness of the client representative who initially explained the problem and its solution, it is often wise to consult with a forensic accounting investigator before confronting that representative: it usually is a tactical error to confront client personnel with suspicions before consulting with an expert on fraud and deceit. (See Chapter 14 on common missteps.) All too often, a fraudster may play the auditor by simply calling the matter a misunderstanding or brushing it off with: "I'm sorry. I must have misspoken."

◆ LOOSE-THREAD THEORY OF AUDITING

The loose-thread theory postulates that in most frauds there are indications of the defalcation that could reveal the *nature* of the offense, although not its *total impact*. If such indications—or, in the technical language of the field, *indicia*—are recognized on a timely basis and investigated in an appropriate manner, they may identify an even larger fraud, perhaps material to the financial statements taken as a whole. By definition, loose threads are usually small and easily overlooked. As discussed in Chapter 8, on warning signs, they are ignored at grave peril.

An illustrative example will be helpful. An audit firm was completing a rotational audit of a small division of a large apparel manufacturer. With $28 million in total assets and $23 million in annual sales, the division was one of 60 such divisions around the world. The most recent external audit procedures had been performed at this division four years earlier. The parent company was a long-term client of the audit firm and had never been found to have noteworthy problems in its financial statements. The division CEO paid close attention to his unit's operations, scrutinized all financial reports, and tracked both revenue and expenses to budget on a monthly basis. In all of these respects, the division was much like thousands of other divisions of global companies.

On a consolidated basis, the parent company had $750 million in total assets, with annual sales stabilizing at $300 million after a nearly five-year slide from $650 million. The company had taken some huge expense charges in the prior two years to downsize operations and improve the bottom line. In the current year, consolidated pretax net income was $21 million after a loss of $44 million the previous year. All things considered, it looked like a reasonably good year for the company, and management was ready to take its bows at the upcoming shareholders' meeting.

The audit team at that modest division came across a customer confirmation that took exception to its accounts receivable balance as reflected in the accounts receivable subledger at December 31. This subsidiary ledger was the source used for selecting customers for confirmation of amounts owed to the company. In the confirmation, the customer disputed an invoice for $22,000, claiming it had been paid several months earlier. The staff auditor called the customer and received confirmation that the invoice had been paid; a faxed copy of the canceled check dispelled any remaining doubt. The auditor suspected that a small oversight had obviously occurred, but there was no reason for concern. He would simply mention it to Fran, the controller and top financial person at the division. It was just a loose thread.

Fran had been at the division for 26 years. Fran was well liked, trusted, and married to the division's IT manager. They had two children. The family lived in the home she had been raised in, the couple was happily married, and the two of them obviously enjoyed and valued their jobs at the company. The auditor was confident that Fran could set things right in short order.

This was the staff auditor's second year on the audit. The audit manager communicated to the staff auditor that he had worked with Fran four years ago and found her to be competent, helpful, and pleasant. When the staff auditor approached Fran with the confirmation exception and asked her to resolve it, she said she would get right on it. The next day, she met with the staff auditor and explained that the discrepancy had occurred in April, a month during which the system had crashed and several resulting problems later came to light. She said she would scrub the entire accounts receivable subledger to ensure that there were no other problems and would report back in a day or two. That timing put resolution of the matter on the last day of fieldwork, but the staff auditor was confident that Fran would follow through because according to the audit manager, she had always done so in the past.

True to her word, Fran returned to the staff auditor on the last day of fieldwork with four similar discrepancies totaling $53,000 in customer payments that should have been credited off but had not been. The original credits actually went to the cost-of-goods-sold account. Fran reported with a surprised smile, "I have no idea how that happened." She assured the staff auditor that the credits would be reclassified as of December 31 and apologized for the oversight. The total income statement effect was immaterial on both division and consolidated bases. Reviewing the additional payment misclassifications, the staff auditor noted that none of them was selected for confirmation. He discussed the matter with the engagement manager, who in turn consulted with the engagement partner. All agreed that the matter was immaterial, but they had less comfort than before and decided that additional work would need to be performed before they could sign off on the accounts.

While all this was occurring, the audit manager was also winding up her work at the division by completing a review of accounts payable and accrued liabilities—and she noted some concerns. Although the accrued expense balances appeared to be in line with prior periods and other measurements, there were a few unfamiliar accounts designated as "retailer allowances." The audit manager questioned Fran directly about these entries, and Fran both minimized the issue and complained that she was short staffed and already working on resolving the accounts receivable issue brought to her attention a few days earlier. She said she would get to the accrued-expenses questions—but probably not until next week. However, "next week" was close to the audit committee meeting and the parent's intended earnings release date. The manager was uncomfortable with that plan and said as much to the company's regional controller. He agreed that speed was of the essence and sent his assistant at once to help Fran resolve this and any other problems that required attention before the auditors could leave.

Fran's accounts were receiving a lot of attention. This did not make her happy, and she was not shy about expressing her displeasure. The Fran whom the auditors had known for years had become a very different person. She wanted the auditors out. But the closer the auditors looked, the more issues and questions surfaced. The audit engagement partner, becoming suspicious, got in touch with a forensic accounting investigator, who sent two forensic accounting investigators to the division on the following day. Examining four electronic files—Payments, Employee Master, Vendor Master File, and Journal Entries—with the use of forensic software applications, they identified many questionable transactions.

The audit engagement partner had seen enough. He recommended to the parent company's chief financial officer (CFO) that he should strongly consider postponing the company's earnings release. Not surprisingly, this was the last thing the CFO wanted to hear. Only a day or two earlier, he had been told everything appeared to be fine for the planned earnings release date.

What transpired from that point was an avalanche of discoveries and events. Two additional auditors and two additional forensic accounting investigators arrived on the scene. Management's jubilation over its comeback year was quickly dissipating, as the income statement impact of this relatively small division began to become apparent. At the end of that first week of forensic investigation, the total hit to income amounted to $6 million pretax. At the end of the investigation two weeks later, the final tally was $11 million—just over half of the company's consolidated pretax net income. This was material by any measure.

Although the numbers were now sound, the auditors had not yet completed their work. The forensic accounting investigator had informed the audit team that Fran was a fraudster, and the task at hand was to look at everything within her reach and formal span of responsibility. Were there additional schemes extending beyond the books and records—for example, bribery or kickback schemes? The fact that Fran's husband was the IT manager also made his activities fall under additional scrutiny. The last thing the parent's CFO wanted was to extend the investigation, but he realized he had no choice in the matter if he wanted the auditors to sign off. In due course, the forensic team conducted an admission-seeking interview with Fran and determined that she had not engaged in any additional schemes, but it became clear to them that she was withholding information likely to incriminate the division CEO. He in turn became a suspect, and the same process was repeated: examination of everything he touched followed by an admission-seeking interview.

It was critically important to follow up on leads and identify every culpable employee. If this fraud could be isolated to the division, then the team had completed its work, but if, for example, investigation of the division CEO revealed that he had conspired with someone at corporate headquarters, then the investigation would have to continue until all culpable parties were identified and the fraud contained and quantified.

The auditors completed their procedures, including an assessment of previously performed procedures at corporate and other divisions. Once the company had assessed that it had identified the total extent of the fraud, corporate management issued a press release. Its share price dropped 20 percent on the news, and SEC Enforcement immediately began an informal inquiry. As of this writing, the stock has not recovered. The two miscreants were terminated and the government's investigation is proceeding.

Recognition of a loose thread had led to discovery of a high-impact, multimillion-dollar fraud. Who was defrauded? Many individuals along the line were fooled by the numbers, but ultimately, it was the investors from whom accurate information about the company's revenues had been concealed.

◆ FURTHER THOUGHTS ON THE LOOSE-THREAD THEORY

The preceding case study demonstrates—as would many, many others—that a small anomaly may be a sign of fraud. The loose-thread theory could not be more appropriately named. Fraud is usually hidden, and the discovery of fraud usually is unlikely, at least at the beginning, to involve a huge revelation.

Financial fraud occurs in manipulated accounts, but it has some points in common with a crime scene. You suspect a crime has been committed, and there is a room you believe the crime occurred in. Picture yourself walking into it. You slowly pan the room for clues. You would certainly not expect to see someone sitting in a chair in a corner of the room holding a sign saying: "I stole $2 million. Just ask me, and I'll tell you how I did it." Ultimately, that admission is your objective, but there is much work to do before scheduling an admission-seeking interview (see Chapter 18). Like loose threads on clothing, the clues you need are easily overlooked.

An audit does not presume that those you interview and the documents you examine have something sinister about them. The overwhelming majority of audits are conducted in companies in which material fraud does not exist. However, the auditor is always aware that material fraud could be present. In some respects, steady maintenance of professional skepticism is a more difficult challenge than responding to a crime you know has occurred. Imagine walking down a dark alley into which you know a suspect has entered just before you. You do not know where the suspect is, but as you walk down that alley, you are acutely aware of and attuned to your surroundings. Your senses are at their highest level. You know beyond the shadow of a doubt that danger lurks nearby.

Audits are not like that. Audits are more like walking through a busy mall and watching normal people go about their daily activities. In the back of your mind, you know that among all the shoppers are a few—a very few—shoplifters. They look just like everyone else. You know they are there because statistical studies and past experience have shown they are there, but you do not know exactly where or who they are or when you will encounter them, if at all. If you were engaged to find them, you would have to design procedures to increase the likelihood of discovery without annoying the great majority of honest shoppers. So it is with an audit. If an audit firm *knew* that management was engaged in fraud, it would not accept the audit engagement in the first place or would withdraw while complying with all applicable standards of performance and regulations. Professional skepticism is a key practice in a context in which the auditor has reason to trust—but also reason to verify.

As noted earlier, many perpetrators of fraud have no desire to harm others. When apprehended, most white-collar criminals are typically—and sincerely— regretful that the frauds they've perpetrated cause others to lose security, careers, investments, or savings. That most financial fraudsters execute their devious strategies without intent to harm actually complicates the task of the auditor in discerning the validity, completeness, and accuracy of the information provided to them in the normal course of an audit. The auditor's guard must always be up. If there is a hidden fraud operating in a company, the path to its discovery often will be littered with tiny loose threads rather than large neon signs. Professional skepticism is the attitude most likely to detect those loose threads, understand their meaning, and, when appropriate, set in motion a forensic investigation performed by competent forensic accounting investigators.

CHAPTER 7

FORENSIC INVESTIGATIONS AND FINANCIAL AUDITS: COMPARE AND CONTRAST

Lawrence F. Ranallo

While their roles sometimes overlap, financial statement auditors and forensic accounting investigators tackle financial fraud issues from different perspectives, usually using different information that is documented in different ways for different purposes. Subsequent to Statement on Auditing Standards (SAS) No. 99 and the standards currently being promulgated by the Public Company Accounting Oversight Board (PCAOB), there is a pressing need for financial statement auditors and forensic accounting investigators to work closely in an effort to detect and deter material financial statement fraud. Auditors work diligently to develop new techniques of uncovering more indicia of fraud. When indicia of fraud surface, they may consider calling upon trained and experienced forensic accounting investigators to aid in developing and implementing investigative procedures that will help resolve the concerns or allegations. Chapter 13 discusses at length how auditors may make use of forensic accounting investigators. This chapter seeks only to identify the primary differences, as well as some similarities, between the two disciplines of financial statement auditing and forensic accounting investigation.

We should add that this is the only chapter in this book that does not offer headings as the text moves from topic to topic. Virtually every paragraph offers a comparison and a contrast between the two fields. The approach is appropriate and well detailed, but more like phyllo dough—with innumerable layers—than like a club sandwich!

The common ground between financial auditors and forensic accounting investigators is considerable. Practitioners in each area have a broad understanding of business and industry trends; a thorough understanding of the issues, timing, and concerns of the auditing process; an understanding of the types of financial records and documents that should exist to support recorded amounts; and a shared concern about the impact of fraud on company operations. Forensic accounting investigators and auditors also share a common goal: corporate financial reporting that complies fully with the law.

They diverge in that financial auditors are charged with performing an examination of a company's financial statements in accordance with generally accepted auditing standards (GAAS), while forensic accounting investigators principally tackle two broad categories of financial fraud: (1) fraudulent accounting and reporting and (2) misappropriation of assets. Much of the forensic accounting investigator's work involves the retrieval, interrogation, and analysis of relevant information to answer specific questions about what, why, when, how, and by whom allegedly improper behavior may have occurred.

Demand for forensic accounting investigation and curiosity about it have never been at higher levels. This reflects the growing complexity of financial fraud schemes, the increased pressure to resolve any accusations of improper financial reporting in a timely fashion, and the widespread publicity and public awareness of whistleblowers and financial fraud that have surrounded the corporate scandals of the past few years.

Much of the recent pressure for forensic accounting derives from the Sarbanes-Oxley Act of 2002, which requires the management of public companies to certify both the accuracy of financial statements and the nature and effectiveness of internal controls they have in place. This obligation adds more scope to quarterly and annual filings without providing more time for them to be completed. To the contrary, Sarbanes-Oxley significantly shortens the timing of filing requirements, which many fear will cause a rash of restatements owing to the interpretation and implementation of new and complex rules.

Because fraud is usually hidden, investigating it is time-consuming, typically involving document review, interviews, and evaluation of electronic media. It is by its very nature often an inefficient process. The assessment of misappropriated assets, false financial reporting, or employee violations of laws should be completed in such a way as to lay to rest any speculation and to determine the nature of remedial action if deemed necessary.

The U.S. Securities and Exchange Commission (SEC) requires that independent accountants review quarterly financial information before a filing is considered compliant. While a short filing delay may be allowed based on a properly filed extension request,[1] the financial markets do not welcome the news that a company will not be filing its form 10-Q on time, and the impact on share price can be severe. Not surprisingly, issuers do everything in their power to avoid such delays. SAS 99, *Consideration of Fraud in a Financial Statement Audit*, which took effect for audits for periods beginning on or after December 15, 2002, specifies, "The auditor should ordinarily presume that there is a risk of material misstatement due to fraud relating to revenue recognition."[2] No longer can the auditor evaluate the current-year audit risk of fraud based solely on the favorable results of prior years' work.

---

1. See SEC Rule 12b-25, Notification of Inability to Timely File All or Any Required Portion of a Form 10-K, 10-KSB, 20-F, 11-K, N-SAR, Form 10-Q, or 10-QSB, http://www.sec.gov/divisions/corpfin/forms/reg12b.htm. A separate statement is required if the subject report or portion thereof cannot be filed because a person other than the registrant is unable to furnish a required opinion, report, or certification. The filing must also state an intent to file the required form within 15 calendar days from the due date for annual filings and within 5 calendar days for quarterly filings.

2. American Institute of Certified Public Accountants, Statement on Auditing Standards (SAS) No. 99, *Consideration of Fraud in a Financial Statement Audit* (codified in AICPA Professional Standards—U.S. Auditing Standards—AU § 316), par. 41.

Even so, while financial auditors are required to perform audit procedures in response to the risk of material fraud, it is acknowledged that those procedures may not detect material fraud. SAS 1 as amended acknowledges that

> . . . collusion may cause the auditor who has properly performed the audit to conclude that evidence provided is persuasive when it is, in fact, false. In addition, an audit conducted in accordance with generally accepted auditing standards rarely involves authentication of documentation, nor are auditors trained as or expected to be experts in such authentication. Furthermore, an auditor may not discover the existence of a modification of documentation through a side agreement that management or a third party has not disclosed. Finally, management has the ability to directly or indirectly manipulate accounting records and present fraudulent financial information by overriding controls in unpredictable ways.[3]

Forensic investigations, in contrast, usually begin with a heightened concern that a specific irregularity exists and that it needs to be evaluated, its size determined, and the problem corrected. Additionally, a forensic investigation typically includes a goal to discover evidence that may be instructive as to the intent of those participating in the irregularity. (Of course, an investigation may also determine that no wrongdoing has occurred.)

On one hand, the primary objective of a financial audit is to render an opinion on the financial statements as a whole. The relative significance of transactions, trends, or disclosures is evaluated in the context of the financial statements taken as a whole and is not necessarily based on just one or a small number of transactions. Forensic accounting investigation, on the other hand, explicitly does *not* involve financial statements taken as a whole but, rather, focuses on evaluation of transactions, people, or business units to determine whether there are perceived problems that require further action. The focus of forensic accounting investigation on specific transactions or their components generally results in more attention being directed to these elements than is directed to them in the financial statement audit.

But perhaps it is in the audience for the work that the difference is greatest. The financial auditor's work serves the public interest: specifically, investors and other stakeholders, including the regulatory community. The auditor's work stands on its own; the auditor has no need or responsibility to develop a consensus with other professionals. In contrast, forensic accounting investigators serve the broad or narrow interests of the party that engaged them. The overall focus of their activity may be set by a committee of a company's board of directors, by counsel, or by senior management. Yet forensic accounting investigators are expected to be unbiased and objective about the entity and the issues being investigated.

While the audit report, or opinion, will stand on its own, the forensic accounting investigator's work does not stand on its own. In most cases, it is but one discovery device used by counsel or a company to resolve an allegation. The

---

3. American Institute of Certified Public Accountants, Statement on Auditing Standards (SAS) No. 1, *Codification of Auditing Standards and Procedures* (as amended, codified in AICPA Professional Standards—U.S. Auditing Standards—AU § 230), par. 12.

forensic accounting investigator's work typically becomes either a catalyst for action against an accused or the basis for exoneration, depending on the results. Typically, outside legal counsel or the board engages the forensic accounting investigator to assist in the evaluation of financial-reporting allegations. The forensic accounting investigator develops a sufficient base of information and analysis that enables consensus to be reached by counsel, the independent auditors, management, and the board on what to do next.

To express the matter somewhat differently, auditors provide an opinion on financial statements for general or limited use, while forensic accounting investigators seek to confirm or deny the existence of a particular problem and to determine its extent and likely cause. Forensic accounting investigators may also seek to recover misappropriated assets and may recommend changes to deter future irregularities. The recommended changes are likely to represent just a small part of the company's overall compliance program in establishing controls for the detection and deterrence of fraud. (See Chapter 20.)

Forensic accounting investigators are deeply concerned with differentiating between errors in execution or judgment and deliberate misrepresentations. On one hand, motivation for behavior different from that established by policy is evaluated closely. Auditors, on the other hand, do not focus initially on the motivation of individuals involved in transactions unless there is a basis for closer scrutiny. The auditors' primary focus is on the validity, accuracy, and completeness of the financial accounting and reporting on which they opine. The audit concludes, and is essentially complete, with the issuance of an opinion. A forensic accounting investigator's work is typically part of a larger project to evaluate allegations. The forensic accounting investigator is expected to participate in meetings and activities, often on a daily basis, throughout the investigation and thereafter. And there may well be follow-up with regulatory agencies, insurance carriers, or parties to litigation.

Because the auditor's work is conducted in the open, it is typically known and understood by client personnel. The auditor seeks to minimize disruption of the operations of the enterprise. The contrast here with the forensic accounting investigator's work is sharp. Company personnel may not know of the forensic investigation, its purpose, or its full scope, and while forensic accounting investigators seek to minimize disruption, they recognize that disruptions will occur. They usually discuss with the party who engaged them any trade-off between access to information and disruption of business activities. Depending on the degree of needed secrecy, forensic investigations range from those that come and go with little notice and those that turn the organization upside down.

Forensic accounting investigators normally have few predetermined boundaries. They often develop the scope of an inquiry with input from various sources—including counsel, the responsible committee of the board of directors, management, the independent auditors, and the company's internal audit group. On this basis, they propose a plan and generally seek agreement that its proposed scope address the issues of concern. As the inquiry begins and findings come to light, the investigation is often shaped by instinct and judgment calls, and the initial plan evolves. Rarely is there a relevant base of prior work to draw upon.

Auditors, in contrast, set the scope of the audit, based on risk factors determined after consideration of relevant information, including books and records, management input, and other data such as industry norms. The auditors benefit from cumulative knowledge based on prior work and advance planning. While the auditor places at least some reliance on management representations, the forensic accounting investigator usually places little or no specific reliance on management representations.[4] Indeed, the task of the forensic accounting investigator is often to evaluate the reasonableness of management positions.

A financial audit is usually more consistently executed and documented than a forensic investigation. The audit is coordinated and efficient, with the aggregate of procedures performed to provide a basis for attestation. Work that does not directly link to evaluation of a management assertion would not be performed. A forensic investigation is not so often that neat or efficient. Work may be based on a hypothesis or a suspicion, and multiple hypotheses may be evaluated. The sum of the efforts is likely to include work that went down blind alleys. While the audit advances toward providing a sound basis for the auditor to deliver an opinion, the forensic accounting investigation engagement may generate several different, equally probable outcomes. As wise forensic accounting investigators tell their clients, "You pay us to look, not to find."

The relative orderliness of the processes is reflected in their communications.[5] The auditor customarily meets with the audit committee at regularly scheduled times and with executive management on an as-needed basis. The forensic accounting investigator, on the other hand, may have frequent, irregular contacts by telephone or in person over a short period to keep an audit committee or counsel informed of

---

4. American Institute of Certified Public Accountants, AICPA Professional Standards—U.S. Auditing Standards—AU § 333, *Management Representations* (Source—SAS 85 and SAS 89: "The auditor obtains written representations from management to complement other auditing procedures.").

5. American Institute of Certified Public Accountants, AICPA Professional Standards—U.S. Auditing Standards—AU § 325, *Communication of Internal Control Related Matters Noted in an Audit* (Source—SAS 60, SAS 78, and SAS 87):

> During the course of an audit, the auditor may become aware of matters relating to internal control that may be of interest to the audit committee. The matters that this section requires for reporting to the audit committee are referred to as reportable conditions. Specifically, these are matters coming to the auditor's attention that, in his judgment, should be communicated to the audit committee because they represent significant deficiencies in the design or operation of internal control, which could adversely affect the organization's ability to record, process, summarize, and report financial data consistent with the assertions of management in the financial statements.
>
> Conditions noted by the auditor that are considered reportable under this section or that are the result of agreement with the client should be reported, preferably in writing.

American Institute of Certified Public Accountants, AICPA Professional Standards—U.S. Auditing Standards—AU § 380, *Communication with Audit Committees* (Source—SAS 61, SAS 89, and SAS 90):

> This section instructs the auditor to ensure that the audit committee receives additional information regarding the scope and results of the audit that may assist the audit committee in overseeing the financial reporting and disclosure process for which management is responsible.

status and progress. Throughout the investigation, the forensic accounting investigator usually has ready and continual access to executive management.

Staffing and executing an audit is necessarily different from staffing and executing a forensic investigation. On one hand, most financial audits delegate work among staff, based on the complexity of the tasks. On the other hand, it is more typical than not in forensic accounting investigation that the more senior, more experienced personnel both direct and execute substantial portions of the scope. This results in a narrower staffing mix that causes a higher cost per billed hour for the overall project. Some phases of forensic investigations can make use of more junior staff—for example, when there is a need for extensive e-mail review or account analysis. However, due to the nature of financial crime investigation, there is no substitute for experience, and more senior players are very active throughout.

A sharp contrast exists in how sampling is used for accomplishing various goals in the two related but distinct disciplines. On one hand, auditors may use attributes sampling to test compliance with internal control procedures or may use variables sampling to test the dollar amount of errors or estimate a population value from sampling techniques. They may test all large transactions for certain accounts. Forensic accounting investigators, however, are more likely to use discovery-sampling techniques, which allow for quantification of the likelihood of finding one specified condition in a population. They may use sampling in proportion to size—also called *dollar-interval sampling*—to estimate the upper limit of a population value. And they may examine all transactions in a relevant period that meet a particular profile, such as all transactions approved by a certain responsible person; all transactions with a specific third party; or all transactions of an unusual dollar amount. Data mining, including e-mail review, can examine the entirety of a vast set of transactions and communications. Much comfort can be derived by electronically searching for key terms and conditions through hundreds of thousands of transactions and e-mails, in search of that potential smoking gun that can redirect and accelerate the investigation. If this exhaustive process turns up nothing remarkable, that too is a finding: it is very likely that no crime was committed.

On one hand, a financial auditor does not ordinarily create work product under an attorney privilege or report findings to a lawyer; audit working papers are, on the whole, not privileged. On the other hand, most forensic work is customarily structured to be performed in a privileged environment because of the likelihood of related litigation.[6] Auditors must work without indemnification protection: the SEC prohibits such arrangements. Forensic accounting investigators, however, usually have both indemnification and hold-harmless protections because of the use made of third-party information, the contentiousness of the issues covered by the forensic report, and the fact that they do not control the scope of their work.

---

6. Chapters 6 and 13 discuss situations in which forensic accountants are called upon by their audit colleagues when suspicions of fraud arise. In those situations, the forensic accountant works under the existing audit engagement letter as an expansion of the audit scope and, accordingly, the work is typically not privileged. Working under the audit engagement letter, forensic accounting investigators serve in the role of auditors with all of the attendant rules that apply to auditors.

The scope issue merits further exploration. In audits conducted under GAAS, the auditor determines the scope, nature, and timing of the procedures. To the extent that the auditor's scope is limited in any matter by the company's being audited or by a third party, the auditor may qualify his or her report or resign if the scope restriction is unacceptable. In most forensic accounting investigation engagements, the forensic accounting investigator uses knowledge, skills, education, training, and experience to advise the client as to a menu of recommended forensic procedures. After a discussion that may include input from various parties involved in the investigation, the client determines the scope, nature, and timing of the forensic procedures to be performed. Because the client sets the scope, it is appropriate for the forensic accounting investigator to receive indemnification and liability protection from the client.

In their findings and opinions, further differences between the professions are evident. Financial auditors may offer an opinion (qualified, unqualified, disclaimer of) in an audit, negative assurance in a review, or no assurance in a compilation or application of agreed-upon procedures. Using established criteria under GAAS, the auditor, on one hand, evaluates whether the client must restate prior periods. A forensic accounting investigator, in contrast, when assisting the audit team, would offer no view on whether a restatement is necessary or how it should be done. Forensic accounting investigators are rarely asked for opinions; they are primarily fact finders. When an opinion is provided, it is not in the context of GAAS or attestation services,[7] and forensic accounting investigators would be held responsible neither for information not reviewed by them nor for work done by others. The type of conclusion reached in a forensic investigation involving financial reporting is often that the information obtained and the analyses performed are (1) consistent, (2) not consistent, or (3) not related to a particular accounting treatment or other standards, such as contractual standards.

When requesting information, the financial auditor seeks from clients and others specific documentation, including accounting records, contracts, and source documents. The focus is on information drawn from company records, company employees, third-party confirmation, independent observations, and tests of recorded amounts or disclosures. A forensic accounting investigator's requests, on the other hand, are more along the lines of discovery requests in litigation, with no limiting conditions on particular information.[8] A request may be made, for example, for all contracts executed by a certain individual rather than a request for certain specific customer contracts. A forensic inquiry may also

---

7. American Institute of Certified Public Accountants, AICPA Professional Standards—U.S. Auditing Standards—AU § 625, *Reports on the Application of Accounting Principles* (Source—SAS 50 and SAS 97).

8. Limitations on auditors' requests no doubt may be deemed a scope restriction, and therefore all such requests are usually honored; however, auditors typically put forth a good reason for a request for information and have in mind a definite purpose for it. The forensic accountant may not yet have solidified a good reason for an information request but, nonetheless, wants it. The client rarely refuses such requests.

search public records databases and company e-mail and may draw on interviews with people inside and outside the company, as well as on information provided by counsel and company accounting records.

One of the sharp contrasts, as noted earlier, is that the auditor presumes the validity of documents and information unless contrary information is known or suspected. The forensic accounting investigator is more skeptical and commonly assesses documents for alteration or falsification, thereby independently assessing their validity.

An auditor's interviews with personnel are generally straightforward, with explanations of the purpose of an inquiry when it is not self-evident. Counsel is typically not present during discussions about routine accounting and reporting issues. A forensic accounting investigator, on the other hand, explains the purpose of the inquiry but may solicit responses in confidence as part of the fact-gathering process. The extent to which confidences will be kept also may be conveyed. The outside counsel involved with the forensic investigation may be present, and interviewees may have their own counsel present.

An auditor's interest in evidence is to support the opinion toward which the work is moving. In contrast, a forensic accounting investigator, like a law enforcement officer, obtains and preserves evidence so that a chain of custody exists. The documentation and communications that grow out of each of these activities differ in several ways. On one hand, financial auditors have specific documentation requirements under GAAS.[9] The documentation retained depends on professional standards and firm policies and is typically organized by financial statement categories. Forensic accounting investigators, on the other hand, generally have far greater flexibility in the amount and nature of documentation they accumulate—both financial and nonfinancial. Interviews get documented in notes or memorandums. Summary memorandums may be developed from the interviews and other analyses for each issue or transaction examined, with cross-references back to individual interview memorandums. If working directly for outside counsel, they may advise on documentation retention requests, and various legal requirements may also influence document retention. As of this writing, the PCAOB has adopted Auditing Standard No. 3, *Audit Documentation* and an amendment to AU Section 543 of the Interim Auditing

---

9. American Institute of Certified Public Accountants, Statement on Auditing Standards (SAS) No. 96, *Audit Documentation*:

   1. The auditor should prepare and maintain audit documentation, the form and content of which should be designed to meet the circumstances of the particular audit engagement. Audit documentation is the principal record of auditing procedures applied, evidence obtained, and conclusions reached by the auditor in the engagement. The quantity, type, and content of audit documentation are matters of the auditor's professional judgment.

   2. Other Statements on Auditing Standards contain specific documentation requirements . . . Additionally, specific documentation requirements may be included in other standards (for example, government auditing standards), laws, and regulations applicable to the engagement.

Standards, outlining new requirements concerning auditors' documentation of their procedures and findings.

While it is rare for an auditor to be asked to present any findings orally, forensic accounting investigators usually are expected to be very good at presenting their work and findings orally to the various and numerous constituents of the investigation, including counsel, management, board committees, and regulatory authorities. They may also testify in the course of litigation.

The success of any investigation lies in part in recognizing the considerable noise in the data. The challenge is to determine what among the available evidence is relevant and reliable in the evaluation of an accusation or a suspicion of wrongdoing. Most often, a thorough investigation and timely remedial action constitute the best demonstration of both corporate legal compliance and management's willingness to find and fix wrongful behavior. This requires, of course, differentiating efficiently between noise and pertinent evidence.

At the close of a financial audit there is reasonable assurance that the related financial statements are free of material misstatement. At the close of a forensic investigation there are findings based on accumulated information related to focused issues. Neither service can be expected to conclude beyond the shadow of a doubt; neither the auditor nor the forensic accounting investigator is an insurer, and their reports are not guarantees. Each ends with a high degree of professional judgment based on the procedures undertaken, what has become evident as a result of those procedures, and what appears to be reasonable. Yet each acknowledges that information not known and scope not covered could materially affect the appropriateness of the judgments reached.

But it is inappropriate to end this chapter with a caveat. Both forensic accounting and financial auditing are remarkable disciplines and of immense service to the capital markets, to investors and all stakeholders in the integrity of companies, and to management. This chapter, an exercise in compare and contrast, will have served well if it elicits an appreciation from both forensic and financial accountants of some of the intricacies of their professions and if it promotes their knowledgeable cooperation.

CHAPTER 8

POTENTIAL RED FLAGS AND FRAUD DETECTION TECHNIQUES

Will Kenyon

Patricia D. Tilton

As noted in earlier chapters, management is responsible for the quality of financial statements and an organization's internal control structure. Statement of Auditing Standards (SAS) No. 1 states this: "Management is responsible for adopting sound accounting policies and for establishing and maintaining internal control that will initiate, record, process, and report transactions consistent with management's assertions embodied in the financial statements." Sections 302 and 404 of the Sarbanes-Oxley Act of 2002 require certifications by members of management as to the completeness and accuracy of financial reports and the nature and effectiveness of internal controls.

The accounting literature about the auditor's role in fraud detection is extensive. SAS 1 states, "The auditor has a responsibility to plan and perform the audit to obtain reasonable assurance about whether the financial statements are free of material misstatement, whether caused by error or fraud." Subsequently issued standards reiterate this responsibility, including SAS 53, which was superseded and supplemented by SAS 82 and, in turn, superseded by SAS 99, *Consideration of Fraud in a Financial Statement Audit*. The guidance in SAS 99 is discussed throughout this chapter. Related guidance includes SAS 54, regarding illegal acts (partially superseded and partially supplemented by SAS 82, which was superseded by SAS 99), and SAS Nos. 60 and 71, addressing reportable conditions related to internal control defects. Other relevant guidance includes SAS 22 (Planning and Supervision), SAS 31 (Evidential Matter), SAS 47 (Audit Risk and Materiality), SAS 56 (Analytical Procedures), SAS 57 (Accounting Estimates), and Public Company Accounting Oversight Board (PCAOB) Auditing Standard 2 (AS2). Additionally, the report by the Treadway Commission's Committee of Sponsoring Organizations (COSO) provides a framework for internal control that forms the basis for the rules of the PCAOB.[1]

---

1. Committee of Sponsoring Organizations of the Treadway Commission (COSO), *Internal Control—Integrated Framework* (New York: COSO, 1994).

Federal legislation also addresses the issue of auditor responsibility. Title III of the Private Securities Litigation Reform Act of 1995 indicates that each audit shall include procedures designed to provide reasonable assurance of (1) detecting illegal acts that would have a direct and material effect on the determination of financial statement amounts and (2) detecting material related-party transactions. Sarbanes-Oxley requires that auditors attest to management's report regarding internal controls and procedures for financial reporting.

Without attempting to convert financial statement auditors into forensic accounting investigators—the previous chapter emphasized their different roles and methods—this chapter discusses potential red flags and available detection techniques that financial statement auditors might use, consistent with professional standards, when appropriate, in their judgment.

◆ TYPES OF FRAUD REVISITED

Fraud schemes can be frauds *by* the corporation or frauds *against* the corporation. Frauds committed by the corporation carry legal risk—potentially civil, regulatory, and criminal in nature. Frauds committed against the corporation carry the risk of loss of income or assets for the corporation—and the risk of discovery and prosecution for the perpetrator.

This chapter and those that follow consider four broad categories of fraud that may significantly affect financial statements. They are:

1. Fraudulent financial-reporting schemes
2. Misappropriation of assets—by far the most common fraud against the corporation
3. Revenues and assets obtained by fraud
4. Expenditures and liabilities for an improper purpose

SAS 99 instructs auditors to focus on two areas of fraud—fraudulent financial-reporting schemes and misappropriation of assets—each of them encompassing many other types of schemes. We will be more concerned here with these two types of fraud than with the second pair in the preceding list, although these, too, can be significant. Corruption—the use of official authority for private gain—straddles all of these categories. Corruption in the traditional sense generally involves government officials' profiting from their public office. What might be thought of as private corruption—a breach of fiduciary duty—also exists; for example, corporate officers' abusing their authority for personal gain. The recipients must obtain a gain without the knowledge or consent of their employer and in contradiction to their duty of loyalty to their employer. The most common corruption mechanisms are bribes and kickbacks. Bribes are *paid;* kickbacks are *received.* While it may appear that the entity involved is unharmed by the illegal payment to its employee, ultimately, most kickback schemes result in overbillings to an entity. Even though corruption is less common in the United States than other types of fraud, it can be costly and is among the hardest schemes to detect because it is typically off the books. (See Chapters 10 and 11 on common fraudulent schemes.)

Financial-reporting fraud, as previously noted, can be *inclusive,* meaning that false entries are made to the company's books and records and, therefore, to the financial statements, or it can be *exclusive,* meaning that entries required for the fair presentation of financial statements are omitted. In either case, fraud is distinguished from error by the intent of the action. Fraudulent misstatements, often perpetrated by managers, include such acts as manipulation or falsification of financial or accounting records, such as recording fictitious sales; financial statement misrepresentation of events or transactions, such as incorrect inventory valuation; and intentional misapplication of accounting principles with respect to amounts, classification, and manner of presentation or disclosure, such as classification of short-term debt as long-term debt or refraining from disclosing a contingency that may represent future losses for the company.

In addition to financial statement frauds, auditors are concerned with frauds involving material misappropriation of assets. Asset misappropriation is by far the most common type of fraud,[2] although the size of the loss from an individual asset misappropriation scheme is typically smaller than that from other fraud schemes.[3] Misappropriation of assets involves theft of an entity's assets. These acts usually involve one or more individuals among management, employees, or third parties. Misstatements occur when the effect of the theft causes the financial statements not to be presented in conformity with generally accepted accounting principles or when adjustments are intentionally made to hide the theft. Misappropriation of assets can be accomplished in various ways—for example, stealing assets such as cash or inventory or making an entity pay for goods or services it did not receive (in other words, fraudulent disbursements).

◆ FRAUD DETECTION: OVERVIEW

Detecting fraud is difficult, especially frauds involving material financial statement misstatements, which occur only in about 2 percent of all financial statements. Fraud is generally concealed and often occurs through collusion. Normally, the documents supporting omitted transactions are not kept in company files. False documentation is often created or legitimate documents are altered to support fictitious transactions. While fraud detection techniques will not identify all fraud, the use of sound techniques can increase the likelihood that misstatements or defalcations will be discovered on a timely basis.

---

2. PricewaterhouseCoopers, *Global Economic Crime Survey 2003,* 7, which cites this fraud at an incidence rate of approximately 60 percent.
3. Association of Certified Fraud Examiners, *2002 Report to the Nation on Occupational Fraud and Abuse* (Austin, Tex.: Association of Certified Fraud Examiners, 2002). Based on survey responses from 663 certified fraud examiners: 85.7 percent of fraud schemes involved asset misappropriation, 12.8 percent involved corruption, and 5.1 percent involved fraudulent financial statements. (The total percentage exceeds 100 because some of the fraud involved more than one scheme.) The median losses, respectively, were $80,000, $530,000, and $4.25 million.

Knowing where to look is the first step in fraud detection. Understanding the motivations of those committing fraud and knowing in which accounts fraud is more likely to exist based on a risk assessment helps identify the areas that might be subject to greatest scrutiny. Similarly, being aware of the types of transactions that warrant further review, as well as other potential red flag indicators, may alert auditors to areas that might require a closer look. Specific detection techniques discussed in this chapter include carrying out analytic procedures, using unpredictable audit tests, observing and inspecting, making inquiries, and conducting interviews. While these techniques may be performed routinely in the course of a financial statement audit, approaching them with the mind-set of professional skepticism (Chapter 6) and with better knowledge of the various types of fraudulent schemes (Chapters 10 and 11) may make the difference between detecting and not detecting fraud. This chapter also discusses the importance of continually bringing together all of the information obtained through the application of these detection techniques and evaluating the risk of fraud on the basis of such information.

The detection techniques discussed in this chapter—including techniques performed as a routine part of audits—rely on certain procedures and attitudes to achieve the desired result of detecting fraud. These key procedures and attitudes include the following:

- Perform all procedures with an attitude of professional skepticism.
- Consider deception techniques during the review of documents, including the possibility of falsified documents.
- Thoroughly understand and be alert to potential red flags that are possible indicators of irregularities and likely indicators of areas requiring further analysis.
- Request more documentation in fulfilling audit responsibilities. Trust but verify.

Most audits do not result in the detection of material misstatements owing to fraud by management or others, for the simple reason that most audited financial statements are free of such misstatements. On the face of it, this is good news and it is important not to lose sight of this fact in any discussion of fraud risk. But the fact that material misstatements due to fraud are relatively rare does not diminish the grave consequences for companies, auditors, and stakeholders when such cases arise. No one in the corporate reporting chain can become complacent about the honesty and integrity of management.

When a material misstatement due to fraud arises, the actions or omissions that give rise to the misstatement often occur over an extended period. The initial financial accounting impact may be relatively insignificant but can accumulate over time. Management may seek, for example, to mask a revenue shortfall in one period by accelerating recognition of certain transactions that belong in the subsequent period. The impact at the initial stage may not be material, and the intention may not be consciously fraudulent.

Management may have persuaded itself—that is, may have rationalized—that its actions are justified to smooth over a short-term dip in sales and that the long-term effect will be negligible when business recovers. Should business fail to pick up in the next period, however, management is faced with a double problem: it has contributed to unrealistic revenue expectations, and the shortfall is now compounded by the fact that revenues that should have been booked in the current period were recognized in the previous period. Should management choose to persevere in plugging the gap, it may need to be even more aggressive in its revenue recognition—to the extent that at some point it may create fictitious transactions to make the numbers.

The challenge for the auditor is to recognize early any signs that a material misstatement may have occurred or might occur if the same policies and practices are continued. SAS 99[4] envisages a series of steps, as follows, which are designed to assist the auditor in identifying, evaluating, and responding to the risk of material misstatement due to fraud:

- Holding discussions among the audit team concerning fraud risk
- Obtaining information relevant to the identification of fraud risk
- Identifying the risk of material misstatement due to fraud
- Assessing the identified risks, taking into account the internal controls designed to address those risks
- Responding to the results of the assessment
- Evaluating audit evidence

We will look at each of these steps in turn.

While SAS 99 presents the approach of identifying and addressing fraud risk factors as a series of discrete and sequential steps, the reality is likely to be more fluid. The collation and interpretation of evidence that may indicate the presence of fraud risk factors require a holistic, iterative approach that is unlikely to be achieved simply by adhering to a set of procedures or applying a checklist. The steps set out in SAS 99 are means to an end, not an end in themselves. This holistic, iterative approach is reflected in SAS 99; for example, paragraph 75 instructs the auditor to consider whether audit test results identifying misstatements may be indicative of fraud. SAS 99, paragraph 76, expands on that requirement.

---

4. American Institute of Certified Public Accountants, Statement on Auditing Standards (SAS) No. 99, *Consideration of Fraud in a Financial Statement Audit* (codified in AICPA Professional Standards—U.S. Auditing Standards—AU § 316), October 2002. SAS 99 supersedes SAS 82 (having the same title) and is applicable to all audits required to be conducted in accordance with U.S. Generally Accepted Auditing Standards (GAAS) and is effective for audits of financial statements for periods beginning on or after December 15, 2002. Readers based outside the United States will want to know that International Standard on Auditing (ISA) 240, *The Auditor's Responsibility to Consider Fraud and Error in an Audit of Financial Statements*, issued by the International Auditing and Assurance Standards Board of the International Federation of Accountants, may be applicable.

If the auditor believes that misstatements are or may be the result of fraud but the effect of the misstatements is not material to the financial statements, then the auditor nevertheless should evaluate the implications, especially those dealing with the organizational position of the persons involved.[5]

There are two reasons for this. First, even immaterial frauds can prove embarrassing to the company and the auditor, thereby diminishing investor confidence in the quality of the audit and the reliability of management's representations. In addition, frauds often occur gradually, starting small and growing over time. Finding a small fraud may be the window to an even larger one not yet discovered. (See the discussion of the loose-thread theory in Chapter 6.)

The discovery of material misstatements in a set of financial statements, resulting from deliberate acts or omissions on the part of management or others, commonly prompts questions as to how such a situation could have arisen, whether it could have been discovered sooner, and if so, why it was not. With hindsight, it is all too easy to see facts and circumstances that, had they been identified earlier and interpreted differently, might have enabled the auditor to uncover the fraud and make appropriate disclosure.

The attempt to convert some of this hindsight into foresight has become an increasing focus of auditors, standard setters, and regulators alike. Their approach is to try to distill from past experience those events or circumstances related to any business, its management, and its environment that are commonly associated in one way or another with fraudulent acts or omissions. These are referred to as fraud risk factors or, more informally, potential red flags.

◆ LAYING A FOUNDATION FOR DETECTION

An auditor's ability to detect fraud may be significantly enhanced by personal understanding of an enterprise and the environment in which it operates. With this knowledge, the auditor may be better able to identify anomalies or other potential red flags such as nonsensical analytic relationships, control weaknesses, transactions that have no apparent business purpose, related parties, and unexpected financial performance. It is important to understand the business, the control procedures in place, the budgeting process, the accounting policies, the industry, and the general economic climate affecting the company.

To understand the business, and how it makes money, it is important to identify the key business partners (customers, vendors, and so forth) and understand the corporate culture and organizational structure. To understand the industry, auditors might identify competitors or comparable companies, determine how the competitors and comparable companies perform, consider changes in the competitive structure such as mergers and new entrants to the market, changes in the company's market share, and trends and overall issues affecting the industry. SAS 22 offers additional guidance on obtaining knowledge about an entity's business and its relevant industry. Such information provides a critical founda-

---

5. Id., pars. 75, 76.

tion for the evaluation of the information obtained through the techniques discussed later.

ASSESSING THE RISK OF FRAUD

Some level of uncertainty and risk exists in any financial statement audit. For example, there may be uncertainty about the competence of management and the accounting staff, about the effectiveness of internal controls, about the quality of evidence, and so on. These uncertainties or risks are commonly classified as inherent risks, control risks, or detection risks.

Assessing the degree of risk present and identifying the areas of highest risk are critical initial steps in detecting financial statement fraud. The auditor specifically evaluates fraud risk factors when assessing the degree of risk and as noted in previous chapters, approaches this risk assessment with a high level of professional skepticism, setting aside any prior beliefs about management's integrity. Knowing the circumstances that can increase the likelihood of fraud, as well as other risk factors, should aid in this assessment.

FRAUD RISK FACTORS

SAS 99 identifies fraud risk categories that auditors may evaluate in assessing the risk of fraud. The three main categories of fraud risk factors related to fraudulent financial reporting are management characteristics, industry characteristics, and operating characteristics including financial stability.

- *Management characteristics* pertain to management's abilities, pressures, style, and attitude as they have to do with internal control and the financial-reporting process. These characteristics include management's motivation to engage in fraudulent financial reporting—for instance, compensation contingent on achieving aggressive financial targets; excessive involvement of nonfinancial management in the selection of accounting principles or estimates; high turnover of senior management, counsel, or board members; strained relationship between management and external auditors; and any known history of securities violations.

- *Industry characteristics* pertain to the economic and regulatory environment in which the entity operates, ranging from stable features of that environment to changing features such as new accounting or regulatory requirements, increased competition, market saturation, or adoption by the company of more aggressive accounting policies to keep pace with the industry.

- *Operating characteristics and financial stability* encompass items such as the nature and complexity of the entity and its transactions, the geographic areas in which it operates, the number of locations where transactions are recorded and disbursements made, the entity's financial condition, and its profitability. Again, the auditor would look for potential risk factors such as significant pressure on the company to obtain additional capital, threats of bankruptcy, or hostile takeover.

The two primary categories of fraud risk factors related to asset misappropriation are susceptibility of assets to misappropriation and adequacy of controls.

- *Susceptibility of assets to misappropriation* refers to the nature or type of an entity's assets and the degree to which they are subject to theft or a fraudulent scheme. A company with inventories or fixed assets that include items of small size, high value, or high demand often is more susceptible, as is a company with easily convertible assets such as diamonds, computer chips, or large amounts of cash receipts or cash on hand. Cash misappropriation is also included in this category through fraudulent schemes such as vendor fraud. (See Chapter 20.)
- *Adequacy of controls* refers to the ability of controls to prevent or detect misappropriations of assets, owing to the design, implementation, and monitoring of such controls.

SAS 99 discusses fraud risk factors in the context of the fraud triangle, a concept first discussed in Chapter 3. Additionally, SAS 99, paragraph 40, suggests considering the following attributes of risk:

- Type of risk that may be present—that is, fraudulent financial reporting, asset misappropriation, and/or corruption
- Significance of the risk—that is, whether it could result in a material misstatement
- Likelihood of the risk
- Pervasiveness of the risk—that is, whether it relates to the financial statements as a whole or to particular accounts, transactions, or assertions

Additionally, management's selection and application of accounting principles are important factors to consider.

A WORD ON INFORMATION TECHNOLOGY

The effective use of information systems and technology pervades all five COSO framework components (discussed in Chapter 9) and is integral to an effective antifraud program. From an information technology (IT) perspective, the more complex a company's system environment is, the more susceptible the organization may be to fraud. With regard to determining the "ability to commit fraud," IT security controls are examined with particular emphasis on the way security is administered in an organization. Security systems are one way that organizations accomplish segregation of duties, a cornerstone of good internal controls. Historically, most large and complex organizations are not good at this. Poor administration controls—over who should or should not have access to data—inevitably lead to inappropriate access. Once that happens, the vehicle to commit the fraud comes into being, providing the opportunity for other motivational factors to kick in. (See discussion of the fraud triangle, Chapter 3.) Moreover, if other problems exist within IT—for example, problems in change control and ease of system access—disguising fraud could be relatively easy.

◆ INTERPRETING POTENTIAL RED FLAGS

It is not, of course, as easy as it sounds to identify and interpret potential red flags. First, *flags* is a bit of a misnomer and creates a false impression of plainly visible warning signs. While this is true of some frauds, it is important to remember that fraud is fundamentally a crime of deception and deceit. Calling to mind a mental picture of a scarcely visible red thread waving in the wind is more accurate than picturing a bold red flag. Some of the difficulties inherent in identifying and interpreting potential red flags are summarized in the following:

1. *Fraud risk factors are not the same as evidence of fraud.* Risk factors are not evidence of fraud. To the extent that risk factors are evidence of anything, they point to an environment or situation in which there is an increased risk that material misstatement due to fraud might occur either generally or in a specific functional or geographic sector of the entity's operations.

    Individuals may be motivated by the prospect of bonuses and other incentives to manipulate results to their advantage and in a manner that may amount to fraud. Several high-profile instances of financial statement fraud have been motivated in part by bonus and incentive arrangements. As an example, a chairman and CEO was accused of earning substantial bonuses and profiting on the sale of shares in the company on the basis of fraudulent financial reporting that misrepresented the company's results. This does not mean, of course, that the presence of bonus and other incentive schemes is prima facie evidence of fraudulent financial reporting, but it may be considered in the overall risk assessment.

    Another example of a fraud risk factor is the so-called dominant CEO. Over the years—in a number of notorious cases, including the collapse of the Robert Maxwell empire—a larger-than-life individual apparently held sway over a cowed and ineffectual board and senior management, which enabled him to perpetrate or preside unchecked over a material financial-reporting fraud. Even absent a dominant CEO, similar risks can emerge whenever corporate governance is weak—for example, when power is concentrated in the hands of senior management without an effective counterbalance from the board. No one would seriously suggest, however, that the existence of a CEO with a forceful personality and a strong sense of mission is indicative of fraud. It is simply a risk factor.

2. *Fraud risk factors may indicate the existence of risks other than fraud.* Many risk factors are not exclusively indicative of fraud risk. They may also suggest a heightened risk of material misstatements due to human or process error. For example, deficiencies in internal controls may be regarded as fraud risk factors, but they also pose the risk that errors may occur and go undetected without any intent to commit fraud. Sometimes, weak internal controls simply fail to limit or identify accounting or reporting mistakes. The auditor should not discount either possibility without reasonable grounds for doing so.

3. *Fraud risk factors can be ambiguous.* Many fraud risk factors are susceptible to both innocent and sinister interpretations. The fact that a company
has a complex structure with a large number of overseas subsidiaries and
significant intracompany trading may indicate an increased fraud risk, or
it may simply be a legitimate characteristic of that business. On one hand,
that a ledger clerk drives a car he appears to be unable to afford may indicate a risk that he has misappropriated company assets. On the other hand,
he and his wife may have a two-income household that allows them certain luxuries. The focus must be on fact-finding and critical assessment of
cumulative evidence.

4. *There is no linear relationship between the number of fraud risk factors
and the level of fraud risk.* It may be that, in general, the more risk factors
the auditor identifies in a client, the greater the overall risk of fraud. But
even a few risk factors in key areas may be grounds for concern. A sim-
plistic attempt to quantify fraud risk by a count of risk factors is misguided. The objective is not to estimate how likely it is that a material
misstatement due to fraud will occur but, rather, to identify where and in
what manner that might happen.

5. *Fraud risk factors are of limited significance in isolation.* In general, individual risk factors are of limited significance in isolation. Rather, they
need to be considered as a whole. The point about the dominant CEO factor, for example, is that it may actually contain a number of separate risk
factors that when looked at together, create a risk situation: a bullying
CEO, lack of counterweight among other senior executives, and apparent
absence of an effective audit committee, supervisory board, or similar
corporate governance function. The auditor attempts to interpret evidence
of potential risk factors within the wider context of other observations
about the company, its management, and the business environment in
which it operates. Nonetheless, the identification of an anomaly or loose
thread can lead to the identification of multiple risk factors and control
weaknesses or actual instances of financial statement fraud or misappropriation of assets. The auditor considers whether one particular risk factor
may, in fact, be linked to one or more other factors.

6. *Some fraud risk factors are very difficult to observe.* Certain fraud risk
factors are essentially states of mind or related to an individual's private
life or personal financial affairs. They may be impossible to observe
directly. The auditor might nonetheless become aware of indirect signs
that relevant states of mind or private-life factors may exist.

All of these issues increase the challenge faced by the auditor in trying to
identify indications of the existence of fraud risk within the substantial body of
information available from the audit process.

SAS 99 distinguishes between risk factors relevant to the risk of material misstatement due to fraudulent financial reporting and those relevant to the risk of
material misstatement arising out of the misappropriation of assets. In practice,

as the standard acknowledges, many risk factors are potentially common to both kinds of misstatement. Risk factors related to weaknesses in control or supervision may, for example, be equally applicable to either type of fraud.

◆ IMPORTANCE OF PROFESSIONAL SKEPTICISM

According to SAS 1, *Codification of Auditing Standards and Procedures,* adequate professional care means that the auditor exercises professional skepticism. This attitude has always been a cornerstone of auditing standards, and the current environment, characterized by increased complexities and risks, creates a heightened sense of its importance. As discussed in Chapter 6, professional skepticism is a key attribute of an effective auditor. SAS 99 and other standards emphasize the importance of professional skepticism in the consideration of fraud risk. SAS 99 offers examples of skepticism at work: "Thoroughly probe the issues, acquire additional evidence as necessary, and consult with other team members and, if appropriate, experts in the firm, rather than rationalize or dismiss information or other conditions that indicate a material misstatement due to fraud may have occurred."[6]

By definition, fraud involves the use of deception. This may take the form of manipulated or falsified accounting records and vouchers, improper accounting or disclosure, or false, inaccurate, or incomplete explanations. While auditors are not required to assume that they are being lied to or that documents provided for them are false[7]—absent indications that such may be the case—they challenge explanation or documentary evidence that is inconsistent with information from other credible sources inside or outside the client organization or with their well-founded expectations based on prior experience or knowledge. When such inconsistencies arise, SAS 99 is explicit[8]—and experience suggests that auditors will not simply accept the evidence offered because they believe the individual concerned, or management generally, to be honest.

Professional skepticism has several aspects: keeping an open mind, developing a heightened awareness, making a critical assessment of evidence, and seeking corroboration.

Auditors keep an open mind and avoid preconceived notions about the entity or its management.[9] This approach in no way undermines the importance of cumulative audit knowledge in relation to a client or familiarity with the people responsible for management; both are important elements in the identification

---

6. Id., par. 16.
7. Id., par. 9, "An audit conducted in accordance with GAAS rarely involves the authentication of such documentation, nor are auditors trained as or expected to be experts in such authentication."
8. Id., par. 13.
9. American Institute of Certified Public Accountants, Statement on Auditing Standards (SAS) No. 99, par. 13, states: "The auditor should conduct the engagement with a mindset that recognizes the possibility that a material misstatement due to fraud could be present, *regardless of any past experience* with the entity and regardless of the auditor's belief about management's honesty and integrity." [*emphasis added*]

and evaluation of risk factors. How an entity has operated and how management has behaved in previous periods may be good indicators of what the auditor may expect in the period currently subject to audit.

Or they may not be. Circumstances change, and so does the way people behave. The auditor is alert to this possibility and is able to identify warning signs as they arise. While the auditor is not required to assume that management is dishonest—in the absence of any evidence to that effect—such a possibility may not be altogether discounted; neither should positive indicators of dishonesty—or the risk thereof—be ignored because of a prior belief that So-and-So would not commit fraud. Naturally, the converse also applies. The auditor should not rush to judgment in situations in which risk factors are identified. Further analysis, fact-finding, and testing often lead to the conclusion that despite the presence of certain risk factors, no material misstatement resulting from fraud has arisen.

Developing a heightened awareness of fraud risk helps the auditor maintain professional skepticism. Knowing the kinds of things that can go wrong—based on, among other things, analysis of the corporate scandals of recent years—and relating that knowledge to a specific client can be an important tool in detecting fraud.

The auditor should assess critically the evidence gathered at all stages of the audit by using professional judgment to determine whether sufficient appropriate audit evidence has been obtained upon which to draw conclusions. In addressing an area in which factors indicating a risk of material misstatement due to fraud have been identified, the auditor carefully considers whether circumstances demand a greater quantity or quality of audit evidence to obtain a reasonable level of assurance as to the completeness or accuracy of a particular balance, transaction, or other item. To do this, the auditor assesses all of the available evidence and considers whether, taken together, it provides the appropriate level of assurance.

It is important to corroborate management's explanations with evidence from other credible sources, including third parties, when appropriate and possible. This is consistent with existing auditing standards, which recognize that third-party evidence is generally more reliable than evidence created by the entity itself.

The auditor's attitude is one of professional skepticism. It is worth recalling here several key formulations in SAS 99: "The auditor should conduct the engagement with a mind-set that recognizes the possibility that a material misstatement due to fraud could be present, regardless of any past experience with the entity and regardless of the auditor's belief about management's honesty and integrity."[10] This is particularly important in light of the fact that "management has a unique ability to perpetrate fraud because it is frequently in a position to directly or indirectly manipulate accounting records. . . . Fraudulent financial reporting often involves management's override of controls that otherwise may appear to be operating effectively. Management can either direct employees to

---

10. Id.

perpetrate fraud or solicit their help in carrying it out."[11] SAS 99 specifically calls for an auditor mind-set of neutrality in conducting audit procedures, recognizing that the perceived character of the client should never be a substitute for obtaining objective evidence.

Probing and explicit questions about fraud risks and the possibility of fraud are contemplated by SAS 99. They may be asked during interviews with management and key financial staff. For example, to probe the fraud risk factor of pressure to meet budget,[12] such questions might include the following:

Sample Questions for Management

- How were goals and/or budgets achieved during a down economy?
- What did your company do differently from its competitors to obtain revenue or earnings-per-share goals when the rest of the industry was not meeting expectations?
- Were any changes implemented during the quarter so that goals and/or budgets could be achieved? For example, were new customers obtained or were cost-cutting measures implemented?
- What specifically caused the company to meet goals and/or budgets?

Sample Questions for Financial Staff

- Do you ever feel pressured to maintain the books and records with an eye toward managing actual expenses or revenues to be in line with budgeted expenses or revenues?
- Can you give an example of instructions from management that may have made you feel uncomfortable?[13]

It is also generally advisable to probe management and other financial staff regarding the overall ethical environment of the organization. Does a written code of ethics exist? Are top managers and employees required to periodically confirm that they are in compliance with the code of ethics? Do top managers and employees receive training in the code of ethics? Have disciplinary actions been taken related to violations of the code? All of these are legitimate and pertinent questions.

A mind-set of professional skepticism may result in taking additional steps while performing analytic procedures and detail testing to corroborate management's

---

11. Id., par. 8.
12. Comparing budget with actual is an important analytic procedure discussed later in this chapter. From a fraud perspective, such a comparison is important for several reasons. A common fraudulent financial statement scheme involves falsification of revenues to meet budget. A common asset misappropriation scheme involves stealing up to a budgeted amount. In both cases, just because a reported amount for a budgeted line item appears to be in line with the expected amounts for that line item does not ensure the absence of fraudulent activity.
13. Recognize that a question of this type is provocative and anticipates that something inappropriate may have occurred. Interviewing techniques are discussed briefly later in this chapter but are addressed in detail in Chapter 18 of this book. Such provocative questions may not be used in all circumstances.

assertions. Analytic procedures discussed later in this chapter identify testing or analysis that could assist the auditor in evaluating the reasonableness of management's assertions and could provide corroborating or contradictory information. Additional corroboration could come from interviews of personnel from different departments, including nonaccounting personnel. Critically assessing all evidence and seeking verifications of assertions are standard procedures in the effort to detect a fraudulent transaction.

◆ REVISITING THE FRAUD TRIANGLE

In the context of this discussion of potential red flags, it is worthwhile to revisit the concept of the fraud triangle. As you will recall, SAS 99 identifies three categories of risk—the fraud triangle—and views them as key conditions that tend to be present when fraud occurs.[14]

- Incentive and pressure—that is, need
- Opportunity
- Rationalization and attitude

Within each of these broad risk categories, many different and specific potential red flags may be visible within a company.

INCENTIVE AND PRESSURE

Management or other employees may find themselves offered incentives or placed under pressure to commit fraud. When, for example, remuneration or advancement is significantly affected by individual, divisional, or company performance, individuals may have an incentive to manipulate results or to put pressure on others to do so. Pressure may also come from the unrealistic expectations of investors, banks, or other sources of finance.

Certain risk factors are usefully considered in the evaluation of whether or not the organization is at a greater or lesser degree of risk, owing to incentives or pressures that could potentially lead to material misstatements. These risk factors include:

- Circumstances that threaten the profitability or financial stability of the business
- Excessive pressure on management to meet or exceed the expectations of third parties, including investors and lenders

---

14. ISA 240 (see footnote 4) identifies a broadly similar range of risk factors but categorizes them differently. Risk factors concerning the risk of material misstatements resulting from fraudulent financial reporting are arranged under the headings "Management's Characteristics and Influence over the Control Environment," "Industry Conditions," and "Operating Characteristics and Financial Stability." Risk factors concerning the risk of material misstatements resulting from misappropriation of assets are grouped under "Susceptibility of Assets to Misappropriation" and "Controls." These headings were used in the old SAS 82 [ISA 240, Appendix 1].

- Significant threats to the personal wealth of management as a result of the performance of the business
- Excessive internal pressures on divisional or departmental management imposed by the board of directors or senior management
- A struggle to retain the company's listing on a stock exchange or debt rating
- Inability to meet debt covenants or satisfy conditions in merger or acquisition agreements

Incentive and pressure can take a variety of forms within an organization: bonuses or incentive pay representing a large portion of an employee or group's compensation; triggers built into debt covenants tied to share price targets and levels; significant stock option awards throughout the organization but particularly to top management; and aggressive earnings-per-share and revenue targets set by top management and communicated to analysts, investment bankers, and other market participants, with resultant pressure from these groups.

With regard to the risk of material misstatement due to misappropriation of assets, the risk factors are:

- Personal financial problems that might motivate an individual to misappropriate assets
- Adverse relationships between the entity and one or more of its employees, which might create feelings of resentment or disloyalty

Personal pressures have increased significantly in recent decades as stock options became a common means of compensating and motivating management. Many managers today have a large portion of their compensation and even their net worth tied to the performance of the company and, specifically, the performance of the company's stock. As a result of compensation and retirement contributions in the form of stock grants and as a result of stock ownership and personal debt secured by stock, the financial position of many managers is inextricably tied to the financial performance of their employer.[15] Fear of losing one's position or of delivering bad news, the desire to be promoted, personal financial obligations, or simply greed[16] can also be the driving forces behind fraudulent activity.

Determining the presence and degree of these pressures or incentives is part of the auditor's goal in evaluating the risk that misstatements due to fraud may have occurred. Keep in mind that some people will go to extraordinary lengths to satisfy their needs. The ability to satisfy those needs through inappropriate measures is increased if the other components of the fraud triangle are present.

---

15. In one example, key officers of a publicly traded company were pressured to make significant purchases of company stock to signal to Wall Street their confidence in the company's prospects. These stock purchases were financed with loans collateralized by the stock. The loans were callable if stock prices fell below a certain point. This was strong incentive to maintain the stock prices.
16. Some people, regardless of their income level, live beyond their means. Maintaining their standard of living becomes a need they may seek to fulfill regardless of methods.

OPPORTUNITY

Circumstances may exist that create opportunities for management or other staff to commit fraud. When such opportunities arise, those who might not otherwise be inclined to behave dishonestly may be tempted to do so. Even individuals under pressure and susceptible to incentives to perpetrate a fraud are not a grave threat to an organization unless an opportunity exists for them to act on their need. An opportunity must exist to commit fraud, and the fraudster must believe the fraud can be committed with impunity. Absent or ineffective controls, lack of supervision, or inadequate segregation of duties may provide such opportunities. Opportunities may also be inherent in the nature, size, or structure of the business. Certain types of transactions lend themselves more than others to falsification or manipulation, as do certain kinds of balances or accounts. Certain corporate and group structures may be more opaque and susceptible to misuse. And certain types of asset are more prone to misappropriation.

Risk factors indicative of opportunities that could lead to material misstatements as a result of fraudulent financial reporting include:

- Factors related to the nature of the industry in which the entity operates, the nature of the entity's business and the transactions it enters into, and the manner in which they are recorded in the profit-and-loss account or balance sheet.
- The nature of the entity's relationships with customers and suppliers and its position in its markets: the ability to dominate or dictate terms may create the opportunity for inappropriate or non–arm's-length transactions.
- The degree of judgment involved in determining the level of income or expenditure or the valuation of assets or liabilities: Generally, a higher degree of judgment will give rise to a greater opportunity for deliberate manipulation.
- The extent and effectiveness of supervision of senior management by independent corporate governance functions such as the audit committee, nonexecutive directors, and supervisory boards.
- The degree of complexity and stability of the entity or group.
- The overall control environment, including the continuity and effectiveness of internal audit, information technology, and accounting personnel as well as the effectiveness of accounting and reporting systems.

In several large financial statement fraud cases, opportunity existed by virtue of management's role in the internal control structure and its ability to override or avoid existing controls. With regard to the risk of material misstatement resulting from misappropriation of assets, the risk factors best categorized as related to opportunity can be summarized as follows:

- Susceptibility of fixed assets, inventories, or other assets to misappropriation, depending on such variables as value, demand, portability, and convertibility

- Weaknesses in the controls designed to safeguard assets, such as supervision, segregation of duties, employee screening, physical controls, reconciliations, and other accounting controls

RATIONALIZATION AND ATTITUDE

Some individuals are more prone than others to commit fraud. Other things being equal, the propensity to commit fraud depends on people's ethical values as well as on their personal circumstances. Ethical behavior is motivated both by a person's character and by external factors. External factors may include job insecurity, such as during a downsizing, or a work environment that inspires resentment, such as being passed over for promotion. The external environment also includes the tone at the top—the attitude of management toward fraud risk and management's responses to actual instances of fraud. When fraud has occurred in the past and management has not responded appropriately, others may conclude that the issue is not taken seriously and they can get away with it.

Risk factors that fall into this category of rationalization and attitude are typically the least tangible or measurable, and many are by nature difficult for an auditor to observe or otherwise ascertain. Fundamentally, rationalization and attitude are functions of the culture of an organization, the psychology of those who work in it, and the interaction between the two—for example, the level of employee loyalty to the company. The wider business environment must also be considered: hard times in an industry or in the overall economy may make it easier for some individuals to rationalize fraud. Risk factors to look for, in this somewhat intangible but critically important category, include:

- Lack of clarity or communication about corporate ethical values or infrequent communication and reinforcement of such values
- Disregard for the risk of fraud—or ineffective measures when fraud rises
- Lack of realism in budgeting and forecasting and in communicating expectations to third parties
- Recurring attempts by management to justify inappropriate accounting or disclosure policies and practices on grounds of materiality or other grounds
- Difficult relationships with the entity's auditors: a bullying attitude, imposition of unreasonable time pressure, or constraints on access to relevant audit evidence

Most frauds begin small and build over time. Many people can easily rationalize small infractions such as using the office phone for personal long-distance phone calls or stocking their home office with supplies from the company supply cabinet—and the auditor will come into contact with individuals who are, of course, capable of these rationalizations. These rationalizations can be simple, even for a complex financial crime. Some of the most common rationalizations prove to be the following:

- *It is just temporary.*
  - The company will do better next quarter and the act can be reversed. No one will ever know.

○ It is not really fraud, right, if I book this entry one month and then reverse it the next? In the end, it washes and no one's harmed. The company stays in compliance with debt covenants, and we make our dividend payments.

- *Management does not care.*
  ○ Management does not seriously monitor internal controls.
  ○ Management does not correct known deficiencies in controls.
  ○ Management does not discipline this kind of behavior.
- *Management participates in, expects, and rewards this kind of behavior.*
  ○ Management has entered into certain transactions purely for the purpose of meeting specific reporting objectives.
  ○ Management traditionally uses aggressive accounting policies, and we need to remain consistent with prior periods.
  ○ The people being promoted helped the company achieve its objectives without regard to the means of getting there.
  ○ Risk taking is rewarded. We are cowboys—but nobody is allowed to say that anymore.
- *No one is hurt and the company is helped.*
  ○ It is not material to the company as a whole. But it makes a huge difference to our proceeds from the public offering.
- *I deserve this.*
  ○ I was passed over for the promotion I deserved.
  ○ I'm paid at less than the market rate for my services and the value I provide.
  ○ The company has no loyalty to its employees; I'm likely to be laid off soon.
  ○ This will make up for the benefits the company just eliminated.

Determining whether a basis exists to rationalize a fraudulent act is a key part of the evaluation of the risk that misstatements due to fraud may have occurred.

Typically, all three conditions of the fraud triangle will be present in varying degrees when fraud occurs. They are closely related. When the incentive to commit fraud is strong, it is likely to be easier for perpetrators to rationalize their actions. Easy opportunity may have a similar effect: when internal controls are absent or ineffective, an employee may conclude that management is indifferent to fraud—that "nobody cares." The greater the extent to which all three conditions are present, the greater the likelihood that fraud will occur. Cultivating an environment that minimizes these conditions is vital to avoiding or limiting fraud risk. However, even if one or more conditions are absent, fraud risk is not eliminated. The incentive or pressure may be such as to drive an individual or group to commit fraud despite the absence of easy opportunities to do so. Similarly, predators (see Chapter 3) may not need to rationalize their depredations on a firm: it just comes naturally.

◆ IDENTIFYING AND EVALUATING RISK FACTORS

As noted earlier, fraud risk factors need to be evaluated in context. That context can be defined as an understanding of the business of the entity and the general economic and market environment in which it operates; the presence of other fraud risk factors, if any; and the existence and effectiveness of mitigating controls. Facts or circumstances that may constitute fraud risk factors in one context may have less significance in another. For example, a small owner-managed entity is likely to have in place less-sophisticated corporate governance structures and systems of internal control than is a large multinational organization. Basic elements such as independent supervision of management—such as by way of an effective audit committee—and segregation of duties between key operational and accounting functions may not be as well developed and may not even be practical in a smaller entity. Such matters might be cause for concern in a larger organization, but in a smaller one, their potential impact on fraud risk may be at least partially offset by the closer involvement of the owner-manager and perhaps by cultural differences.

An adequate understanding of the entity's business and its relationship with business partners, suppliers, and customers is crucial to the proper evaluation of fraud risk factors. The ability to identify unusual or suspicious transactions, questionable financial ratios, and implausible explanations by management or others clearly implies an awareness and understanding of what is normal and expected in the context of the entity, the industry sector, and the general business and economic environment in which the entity operates.

The auditor also considers the accumulation of fraud risk factors. For example, that a significant portion of management's remuneration is in the form of bonuses or stock options linked to so-called aggressive targets of one kind or another is listed as a fraud risk factor in SAS 99. Yet such arrangements are common in publicly listed companies and often viewed as effective ways of aligning the interests of management with those of stockholders. Further, the aggressiveness of targets may not be easy to judge. Therefore, in isolation, this risk factor may not immediately set alarm bells ringing. But if the auditor were to conclude that the audit committee was insufficiently robust in its stance vis-à-vis management decisions and that management—including nonfinancial management—appeared to be exerting undue influence over accounting policies in a manner likely to distort key financial measures in their favor, then the cumulative effect of these circumstances might be more persuasive of the existence of a risk of material misstatement due to fraud.

In the immediately preceding example, the observed fraud risk factors exemplify the first two conditions of the fraud triangle: incentive and opportunity. While the presence of all three conditions is not a prerequisite to the existence of a significant risk of material misstatement due to fraud, the example illustrates that the presence of even two conditions tends to create more persuasive grounds for concern.

The evaluation of the impact of fraud risk factors on the level of audit risk also involves consideration of any internal controls that might mitigate the risk of material misstatement due to fraud. Knowledge of controls will be drawn both from the auditor's cumulative audit knowledge and experience and from the results of the examination and testing of controls during the current audit. The additional internal control focus required by Sarbanes-Oxley will provide a further source of information on the internal control environment and may highlight gaps in the internal control structure that need to be considered from a fraud risk perspective.

In placing reliance on a control to mitigate the risk of fraud, auditors may satisfy themselves that the control would, if operated properly, mitigate the risk in question and that the control has operated effectively during the period subject to audit. Even if auditors can obtain reasonable assurance on these counts, they should not discount the possibility that management or others may override controls or otherwise circumvent normal processes to manipulate results or balances.

The identification and evaluation of fraud risk factors should not be seen as a one-time-only process carried out and completed at the planning stage. Rather, it is a cumulative process that continues through the audit. Auditors remain alert to the risk of material misstatement resulting from fraud at all stages of the audit so that their assessment may be updated in light of new information. Such information may emerge:

- During planning and risk assessment
- In discussions with management or other employees
- As a result of controls testing or substantive analytic or detailed testing at the review or audit completion stage

The audit engagement leader ensures that a mechanism is in place within the audit team for the sharing of information concerning potential fraud risk factors—or evidence of fraud—so that any such information is brought forward and can be considered in a broader context. This helps ensure that the existing assessment of fraud risk is reevaluated regularly in light of new evidence. To achieve these goals, the audit team holds discussions about the risk of material misstatement due to fraud and the need to apply healthy professional skepticism at all times. As noted earlier, this step is actually set out under SAS 99. On larger audit assignments, in particular those whose audit team is divided among different locations or operating units, it may be advisable to establish procedures for channeling information about potential fraud risk factors, so that the information is readily available to the audit engagement leader and those assisting in the management of the audit. The team might also establish a formal step during audit completion to discuss the cumulative evidence.

DISCUSSION AMONG AUDIT TEAM MEMBERS

Because discussion within the audit team is now a required part of the audit process, it bears a closer look. SAS 99 instructs that such a discussion take place and include an exchange of ideas about how the entity's financial statements "might be susceptible to material misstatement due to fraud, how management could perpetrate and conceal fraudulent financial reporting, and how assets of the entity could be misappropriated."[17] SAS 99 also calls on the audit team to emphasize how to maintain "the proper state of mind throughout the audit regarding the potential for material misstatement due to fraud."

The discussion of the entity's susceptibility to material misstatement due to fraud is expected to encompass consideration of fraud risk factors discussed in this chapter and exemplified in SAS 99. In addition, it is intended to cover the risk that management might override controls and set aside any previously held views concerning management's integrity. The discussion should also address how the audit team proposes to respond—such as with additional or alternative procedures—to any fraud risk factors identified at this stage.

While SAS 99 does not prescribe the manner in which the importance of professional skepticism is to be conveyed to the audit team in the course of the discussion, a reasonable approach might involve touching on each of the following issues, perhaps with the help of illustrative examples:

- Impact of any issues emerging from the client acceptance or client continuance assessment
- Past experience: any frauds or accounting errors uncovered previously
- Assessment of the quality of accounting and reporting personnel or client employees involved in the internal control structure
- Fraud risk factors set out in the relevant guidance: Attendees might consider these factors in advance to allow for informed discussion during the meeting.
- The information needed for assessing the risk of material misstatement due to fraud and how it will be gathered. Options include:
  - Inquiries of management
  - Analytic procedures
  - Consideration of any fraud risk factors identified
  - Other sources
- Additional steps required:
  - Using information obtained to identify fraud risk
  - Assessing fraud risks identified, taking into account an evaluation of relevant controls, including the risk of management override of controls
  - Responding to the results of the assessment through additional procedures or other responses, as appropriate
  - Evaluating audit evidence
- Indicators to look out for, and what to do about them

17. American Institute of Certified Public Accountants, Statement on Auditing Standards (SAS) No. 99, pars. 14–18.

- The audit engagement leader's reaffirmation of the importance of professional skepticism at all stages of the audit
- How to document audit work in relation to the consideration of fraud risk
- Points to take from the team meeting and incorporate into the audit-planning process

Not all of these points will be relevant in every case. The auditor has discretion to decide whether to deal with the points in one or more separate meetings or as part of a larger meeting.

◆ INFORMATION GATHERING

SAS 99 suggests that the key sources for the identification of fraud risk factors are inquiries of management and others, analytic procedures, consideration of fraud risks, and other information available within or about a specific company.[18] The expression *management and others* encompasses executive management, the audit committee, and internal audit, as well as others within the organization who might be expected to have relevant views, including those involved in operational matters rather than directly involved in the financial reporting process.

SAS 99 has the effect of amending the requirements of SAS 85 concerning the nature of representations that the auditor obtains from executive management.[19] Among the questions the auditor might well raise with management, the following would be among the most important:

- Does management have knowledge of any fraud—whether related to financial reporting or to asset misappropriation—perpetrated, alleged, or suspected that could result in a material misstatement of the entity's financial statements?
- Regardless of materiality, does management have knowledge of any fraud perpetrated, alleged, or suspected?
- Has management received any letters or communications from employees, former employees, analysts, short sellers, or others concerning allegations of fraud?
- What is management's understanding of the risks of fraud in the company?
- Are there any specific fraud risks the company has identified or any account balances or classes of transactions for which a risk of fraud may be more likely to exist, and why?
- What programs and controls has management established to mitigate specific fraud risks that have been identified or to help prevent, deter, and detect fraud of other kinds? How does management monitor those programs or controls?

---

18. Id., pars. 19–34.
19. Id., Appendix, Amendment to SAS 85, *Management Representations* (codified in AICPA Professional Standards—U.S. Auditing Standards—AU § 333), par. 6, and Appendix A.

- How does management communicate its views on business practices and ethical behavior?
- How does management demonstrate behavior consistent with its views?
- What procedures are in place to monitor the operating locations or business segments of the business? Are there any particular subsidiary locations or business segments in which the risk of fraud is more likely?
- Has management reported to the audit committee—or to others with equivalent authority and responsibility for the entity's internal control—concerning how management believes the internal control framework serves to prevent, deter, or detect material misstatements due to fraud? The report would be likely to include the entity's control environment, risk assessment process, control activities, information and communication systems, and monitoring activities.
- Has anyone asked a member of management or others within the company to withhold information from the auditor, alter documents, or make fictitious entries in the books?

When appropriate, the auditor should ask management either to provide corroborative evidence for its answers to these questions or to indicate where and how such evidence might be obtained. When answers are given in general terms, the auditor may ask for specific examples. The auditor should also be alert to answers that appear evasive or otherwise indicate that management does not take the risk of material misstatement due to fraud as seriously as might be expected. These signs do not necessarily indicate a lack of honesty or integrity on the part of the respondent—or they may indicate precisely that. At the very least, they may raise the concern that management underestimates the risk and, as a consequence, the auditor may find that important areas of corporate governance or control are less than wholly effective.

Inquiries of management and others in the context of identifying potential fraud risk factors are not interviews conducted in the style of a forensic accounting investigator (see Chapter 18). However, application of some of the same basic principles may not be out of place. In particular, the auditor may ask a combination of open and closed questions, the former to elicit a broad answer and the latter to focus on particular aspects or to confirm or clarify specific matters. The auditor listens carefully to answers and responds to them with follow-up questions. A checklist approach to such discussions is unlikely to be as useful or effective as this more searching, iterative approach.

The auditor should keep in mind that the views of management concerning fraud risk may vary with the level of management. For example, divisional management, responsible for divisional results that contribute to the overall profit-and-loss account and balance sheet, may provide the auditor with a different perspective from that of senior management. Divisional management may be subject to different incentives or pressures and may have a different attitude toward fraud risk yet may be a valuable source of information in the context of a review of adjusted journal entries at the corporate level whether by providing satisfactory explanations of what it is that particular adjustments represent or by an inability to provide such explanations.

To the audit committee, the auditor might pose these questions:

- What are the audit committee's views regarding the risk of fraud?
- Is the audit committee aware of any fraud perpetrated, alleged, or suspected?
- How does the audit committee exercise oversight over activities concerned with the risks of fraud and the programs and controls established to mitigate risks?
- What is the audit committee's assessment of management's performance in this regard?

As with management, the auditor may seek to corroborate answers, when appropriate, and bear in mind that the answers are likely to provide not just information but also an indication of the audit committee's awareness and effectiveness. In the aftermath of recent corporate scandals, the composition and responsiveness of audit committees have changed. Audit committees are becoming increasingly sensitized to issues of financial misstatement and impropriety, although there are always exceptions. The auditor should be mindful of situations in which the audit committee attempts to steer the auditor to accept a certain outcome.

A similar approach can be taken with the organization's internal audit function. Internal audit personnel were key in identifying financial statement errors at WorldCom. However, a company with a large staff of internal auditors may not be particularly skilled in risk assessment or in conducting an investigation into financial accounting irregularities or other fraud. Some internal auditors use sophisticated tools and techniques and adopt an active approach to risk assessment. Others, including those at many major companies, may be considerably less sophisticated.

It is important to gain a comprehensive understanding of where the internal auditors spend their time. In the case of multinational entities, the external auditor may gain an understanding of what internal audit is doing in each location. Questions designed both to bring to light specific instances of fraud and to assist the auditor in assessing the effectiveness and independence of internal audit might include:

- What are internal audit's views regarding the risk of fraud?
- What specific internal audit procedures have been performed to prevent, deter, or detect fraud?
- What were the results of this work?
- Is internal audit aware of any instances of fraud perpetrated, alleged, or suspected?
- Has management responded satisfactorily to internal audit findings throughout the year?
- Have there been any limitations with respect to what internal audit can review or when the review can take place?

Questions to be asked of others within the organization will be tailored to their areas of knowledge and their positions in the company. While people lower in the hierarchy may not have the same overview as senior management, their views should not be disregarded or discounted. They may have a more detailed understanding about the operation of particular controls, perhaps because they're directly involved with them. In instances in which management is the perpetrator of the fraud, lower-level personnel may know what is going on or can direct the audit team to relevant documents or transactions.

The auditor may consider the possibility that the company's general counsel may have relevant information or views. If frauds or other reportable events have occurred in the past, it is likely that in-house counsel will be aware of this. Indeed, they're likely to have been involved in any remedial or other steps taken. In-house counsel may also be aware of any regulatory or other proceedings involving the entity that may have a bearing on the financial statements. Legal counsel, a compliance officer, or human resources may have details of investigations and ethics violations. And there may be instances of suspected embezzlement that were handled through these channels. Others in management, especially new management, may not be aware of such ethics violations.

OTHER SOURCES

In specific cases, other potentially relevant sources of information or procedures may also be available to the auditor, such as:

- General press and media reports that indicate the existence of concerns about matters directly or indirectly related to the entity's financial statements
- Specialist industry publications and trade journals
- Analysts' reports
- Legal and litigation data
- Data mining (see Chapter 20), which may be useful in identifying transactions for further review, especially when fraud risk may be high: Data mining can identify high-dollar round numbers that could be journal entries booked at the end of a period. In selecting such journal entries for testing, the auditor may encounter a lack of support or an explanation revealing between the lines that the purpose of the entries was to make the numbers for the period.
- Public records searches and background checks (see Chapter 17) for verifying the existence of a customer, supplier, or employee: They may identify undisclosed conflicts of interests, ownership of real estate, judgments, liens, and more. Many free and fee-based databases contain public records and information, but searching them and interpreting the results can be an art. The skilled professional knows which databases to access in a cost-efficient and cost-effective manner.

The extent to which the auditor incorporates such sources into the audit approach will be a matter of professional judgment, taking into account what is practical and reasonable in the circumstances.

Information gathering and identification of fraud risk factors may be inseparable processes in practice. On one hand, the auditor may already have a view as to those areas of the entity's financial statements that are subject to greater-than-average risk of material misstatement due to fraud, and this view may lead the auditor to seek specific information and analysis or to intensify information-gathering efforts in a particular area. On the other hand, the information obtained may lead to the identification of fraud risk factors not previously identified. Given the iterative nature of the process, the distinction between the information-gathering phase and the identification of fraud risk factors becomes somewhat artificial. The auditor's objective, by all available means, is to identify any fraud risk factors within the body of information available, much of which the auditor will probably gather for other audit-related purposes.

◆ ANALYTIC PROCEDURES

Analytic procedures represent one of the most important detection techniques.[20] SAS 56 (AU sec. 329.02) defines these procedures as "evaluations of financial information made by a study of plausible relationships among both financial and non-financial data. . . . A basic premise underlying the application of analytic procedures is that plausible relationships among data may reasonably be expected to exist and continue in the absence of conditions to the contrary." Analytic procedures identify changes in amounts, ratios, trends, or relationships. They may also identify unusual transactions or events.

Analytic procedures are used throughout the audit process for three primary purposes:

- *Preliminary analytic procedures* are used to develop an understanding of the company and to direct attention to high-risk areas in determining the nature, timing, and extent of audit procedures.

- *Substantive analytic procedures* are used to obtain audit evidence to evaluate account balances.

- *Final analytic procedures are used to assess the propriety of audit conclusions in an overall assessment of the presentation of the financial statement.*

SAS 99, *Consideration of Fraud in a Financial Statement Audit*, provides for "considering the results of analytic procedures performed in planning the audit." In addition, analytic procedures that are performed as substantive tests may indicate a previously unrecognized risk of fraud. The SAS recommends specific ana-

---

20. In addition to the discussion that follows, analytic procedures are discussed in detail in Chapter 19, covering financial statement analysis.

lytic procedures relating to revenue recognition, a high-risk financial statement item. SAS 99 also introduces the concept of using disaggregated analytics to further address the risk of fraud, especially in the area of revenue recognition. In large, complex companies, even a knowledgeable company executive would be hard-pressed to explain at the consolidated line item level why the numbers are what they are without a more detailed review. Asking the chief financial officer of a global manufacturer why sales increased by 6 percent but cost of sales remained flat, causing an increase in margins over the previous year, may be a question well worth asking—but it would be virtually impossible to sort out all of the causes and effects at the consolidated level.

The more detailed the level of comparison, the more likely that unexpected relationships will surface. Whenever possible, data could be disaggregated and comparisons of the disaggregated data performed. For example, data should be compared by division, by product, by location, by employee, and so on. The smaller the set of data, the less likely that unexpected changes will be minimized, masked, or offset by opposite changes. Additionally, for analytic procedures to be relevant and useful, consideration should be given to the accuracy and completeness of the underlying sources of the data being utilized. Such consideration may extend not only to the company's data but also to external data used to generate expectations, though it is not usually necessary to formally test such external data.

Once an auditor has identified the changes in amounts, ratios, trends, or relationships, the next step is to determine whether the changes were expected and, similarly, to determine whether certain changes were expected but did not occur. The need for the auditor to understand the company and its business is evident: The key factors that influence the client's business may be expected to affect the client's financial information. Changes in amounts, ratios, trends, or relationships can be accurately interpreted only in that context. Changes may be due to accounting changes, industry changes such as regulatory changes and changes in the competitive landscape, changes in general economic conditions, strategic changes such as the introduction of a new product or new pricing structure, and other issues such as changes in personnel. Unexpected changes, or no change when a change was expected, may be due to error, fraud, and sometimes simply to random occurrences.

The passage from SAS 56 cited earlier incorporates several key concepts:

- *Evaluations of financial information* is an expression that suggests that analytic procedures will be used for understanding or for testing financial statement relationships or balances.
- *Study of plausible relationships* implies an understanding of what can reasonably be expected and involves a comparison of the recorded book values with an auditor's expectations.
- *Relationships among both financial and nonfinancial data* suggests that both types of data can be useful in interpreting the financial information and, therefore, in forming an expectation.

The Auditing Standards Board has concluded that analytic procedures are so important that they are required on all audits. SAS 56 requires that analytic procedures be used in audit planning and in the overall review stage of the audit.

In addition to assisting the auditor in detecting fraud, analytic procedures confer other benefits:

- *Assessment of the entity's ability to continue as a going concern.* Conducting analytic procedures may assist an auditor in determining a company's current financial condition, its condition relative to competitors, whether the company is experiencing or may experience financial difficulty, and whether it is able to continue as a going concern.

- *Indication of the possible presence of errors in financial statements.* When analytic procedures reveal differences between a company's actual and expected performance, such differences could represent either accounting errors or irregularities.

- *Implications for audit testing and procedures.* When analytic procedures are performed during an audit and do not reveal differences or inconsistencies compared with expectations, material error or irregularity is less likely to be present. In these cases, it may be possible to perform fewer detailed tests of relevant accounts because the analytic procedures constitute substantive evidence supporting the fair statement of the related account balances. If analytic procedures do reveal differences, additional testing may be required during the audit.

Effective analytic procedures can reasonably be anticipated to identify surprising relationships. Using such procedures, auditors develop expectations for actual financial amounts, ratios, trends, and relationships based on their prior experience of the company (modified to reflect any known factors expected to change the outcome), experience of the relevant industry or of similar companies in the industry, expectations of management at the outset of the reporting period, and the actual operational activities of the company. Therefore, the following comparisons are typical aspects of analytic procedures:

- Current company data versus company data from prior period(s)
- Company data versus company budgets, forecasts, or projections
- Company data versus industry data and/or comparable company data
- Company financial data versus company operational data such as production levels, number of employees, and square footage
- Subset of company data versus other subset of company data: comparison of data on a disaggregated basis such as by division, product, location, or employee
- Company data versus auditor-determined expected results

These comparisons are discussed in more detail in later pages. However, it is important to consider items that are not truly comparable—such as a competitor that uses a different accounting method, a prior period that does not reflect a new product introduction, or a location with demographics that require lower pricing.

CURRENT COMPANY DATA VERSUS COMPANY DATA FROM PRIOR PERIODS

This procedure includes not only comparing the current period's balance with that of prior periods but also comparing ratios and percentage relationships over time. Comparing only the balances between the two periods would not take into account such factors as growth or the relationship between the financial data. Making comparisons on as small a unit of data as possible—monthly, for instance—and for more than just two years will provide additional relevant information. Trend analyses could be performed with monthly data. For example, using analytic procedures to identify fictitious sales entries posted at each quarter's end to meet the quarterly revenue or earnings goals is possible only if data is viewed by periods shorter than a quarter. Graphically depicting these trends may better enable the auditor to determine what needs to be investigated further.

COMPANY DATA VERSUS COMPANY BUDGETS, FORECASTS, OR PROJECTIONS

Most companies prepare budgets that reflect their financial performance goals. Often, these budgets are prepared for various areas within the company—such as departments, plants, and other subunits—and for various activities the organization conducts, such as sales, production, and research. Since budgets represent the client's expectations for the period, differences between actual results and the budget should be analyzed.

Tracking actual to budget from prior periods could be included in the current-year analysis as well. If the company has always had trouble staying within budget, this could be considered. The budget could be evaluated to determine whether it was realistic when prepared. Determining whether the budget was modified during the period to conform to the company's actual financials is also a consideration. The fact that actual amounts approximate budgeted amounts does not necessarily indicate the absence of impropriety. A common fraudulent scheme is to "manage the budget" to the benefit of either the company or the individual fraudster.

Comparing actual results with analysts' expectations may also provide relevant information.

COMPANY DATA VERSUS INDUSTRY DATA AND/OR COMPARABLE COMPANY DATA

Company financial data—both balances and relationship data—is compared with data from the whole industry or with that of a competitor or comparable peer. Company performance that differs significantly from industry performance may warrant further scrutiny. Performance measures to be compared with industry measures could include, among others, sales growth, gross profit, net income, bad debt expense, and various ratios.

COMPANY FINANCIAL DATA VERSUS COMPANY OPERATIONAL DATA

Auditors may consider making comparisons between certain operational activities and the areas of the financial statements that they would expect to be affected as a result. For example, it would normally be expected that increased production levels might appear in the financial statements as increased revenue or increased inventory. Similarly, revenues within units should not exceed total production after adjusting for changes in inventory levels. Other operational data that might be compared with financial data includes number of employees, square footage, number of locations, shipping volumes versus volumes invoiced, and other examples relevant to the specific industry.

COMPANY DATA VERSUS AUDITOR-DETERMINED EXPECTED RESULTS

The auditor may have certain expectations for results—such as certain amounts, ratios, relationships, or trends—based on the auditor's understanding of the client and of the industry in which the company operates. A difference between the recorded outcome and the auditor's expectations might indicate a misstatement and require further investigation and corroboration. This analysis is highly dependent on the precision of the auditor's expectation. Generally, the more precise the expectation—that is, the closer the expectation is to the correct balance or relationship, as opposed to the recorded balance—the more effective the procedure will be at identifying potential misstatements.

◆ ANALYTIC TECHNIQUES

As stated earlier, comparisons are made not only on account balances but also on financial relationships. The most common techniques for analyzing relationships are discussed as follows. An explanation of using these techniques as part of a forensic accounting investigation can be found in Chapter 19.

1. *Horizontal analysis—that is, comparison of the current period's balances with those of prior periods.* This technique calculates the percentage of change between the current-period balance, as well as prior-period balances, and a base period. Accounts that are increasing or decreasing at rates significantly higher or lower than the majority of the account balances—and especially compared with related accounts—might be subject to further scrutiny. For example, if sales increased 22 percent during the base period but if cost of goods sold increased only 9 percent, further analysis of both accounts might be warranted. See Chapter 19 for a hypothetical example of horizontal analysis.

2. *Vertical, or common-size, analysis.* This technique calculates each line item on a financial statement as a percentage of another line item. An income statement is common sized by showing each line item as a percentage of revenues. This is informative because many expenses, such as commissions or cost of goods sold, are directly dependent on the level of revenues. A balance sheet is common sized by showing each line item as

a percentage of total assets—or total liabilities plus equity. These percentages are then compared against prior-period percentages or against industry or comparable company percentages. See Chapter 19 for a hypothetical example of vertical analysis.

3. *Comparison of the detail of a total balance with similar detail for the preceding year(s).* This technique is based on analysis of the detail of a specific balance over time or at a point in time and comparison of it to similar detail from prior periods. If no significant changes in the client's operations have occurred in the current period, then much of the detail making up the totals in the financial statements might also remain unchanged. It is often possible to use this method to isolate information that needs further examination. An example might be a detailed analysis of the trade receivables account. Such an analysis could reveal that a significant increase in the number of customers occurred from one period to the next, with most of the new customers having balances below the typical materiality level for performing written confirmations. This might warrant further analysis.

4. *Ratios and other financial relationships.* Ratios reflect relevant information about a business by quantifying the relationship among selected items on financial statements. A company's ratios can be compared with ratios from a different period or periods, with a competitor's ratios, and with an industry's ratios. Anomalies in the form of erratic or unexplained changes or differences from the industry may be investigated further. It is instructive to calculate liquidity, activity, leverage, and profitability ratios and figures. Commonly used ratios and related calculations are listed later and defined in Chapter 19. Chapter 19 also identifies possible reasons why a calculated ratio may differ from the expected ratio. The list of ratios in Chapter 19 is not exhaustive, and the ratios used in any analysis should be determined on the basis of the facts and circumstances of the specific situation. Generally speaking, the ratios that may be affected by the four primary fraudulent financial statement schemes:

   ○ Current ratio
     • Working capital balance
     • Accounts receivable turnover
     • Inventory turnover
     • Asset turnover
     • Debt or debt to equity
     • Gross margin
     • Operating margin
     • Profit margin

In addition to those standard ratios, it is also relevant to analyze other relationships involving the high-risk areas of revenue recognition and inventory balances. Relationships that can be analyzed in these categories might include the following:

- Sales versus sales commissions
- Sales versus returns, allowances, and discounts
- Sales versus advertising or promotion budget
- Sales versus outbound freight costs
- Sales versus cost of sales
- Sales versus accounts payable
- Sales versus gross profit
- Sales versus inventory
- Sales versus production levels/capacity
- Sales versus measure of total market size
- Sales versus accounts receivable
- Sales versus interest expense
- Inventory versus cost of sales
- Inventory versus current or total assets
- Inventory versus production levels

Finally, analysis of relationships that involve cash or cash flow can reveal areas requiring further review. The cash account is rarely misstated because of the ease with which cash balances can be confirmed. Therefore, examining the relationship between cash—which is likely to be stated properly—and other account balances that might be misstated can identify anomalies. Some relationships involving cash or cash flow that might be analyzed include the following:

- Cash versus current or total assets
- Cash from operations over time
- Cash from operations versus sales
- Cash from operations versus net income
- Free cash flow (operating cash flow less capital expenditures and dividends)

It is generally appropriate to use more than one of these comparisons and/or relational techniques because different techniques may reveal different information. Unexpected relationships should be considered for further analysis. For example, if operations are financed with a working capital line and production and sales are up but interest expense is down—assuming no decline in interest rates—further analysis may be warranted. It may be that other efficiencies facilitated cash flow from operations to be used for financing the increased production and sales, or it may be that fictitious sales were booked.

◆ ASSESSING THE POTENTIAL IMPACT OF FRAUD RISK FACTORS

SAS 99 makes clear that the auditor must apply professional judgment not simply in determining that there is a theoretical risk of material misstatement due to fraud but also in "the consideration of the attributes of the risk, including:

- The *type* of risk that may exist: whether it involves fraudulent financial reporting or misappropriation of assets
- The *significance* of the risk: whether it is of a magnitude that could result in a possible material misstatement of the financial statements
- The *likelihood* of the risk: the likelihood that it will result in a material misstatement in the financial statements
- The *pervasiveness* of the risk: whether the potential risk is pervasive to the financial statements as a whole or specifically related to a particular assertion, account, or class of transactions"[21]

All of the above attributes will influence both the extent to which the auditor needs to take specific steps to respond to a particular risk factor and the nature of those steps.

The range of possible responses is considerable. At one end of the spectrum, the auditor may reasonably conclude, after proper consideration of the foregoing attributes, that no specific steps need be taken. At the other end, the auditor may have such grave concerns and therefore may feel unable to form an opinion. The auditor may even consider resigning the appointment.

All but one of the foregoing attributes are simply more sophisticated statements of the common, intuitive risk formula: probability multiplied by downside. The exception is *type*, which has no direct bearing on either the probability or extent of a potential misstatement but has significant impact on the nature of the response to a particular risk. For example, the auditor's approach to addressing the risk of material misstatement resulting from intentional overestimation of the value of an asset in a highly judgmental area may be quite different from the approach taken to the risk of material misstatement arising through the concealment of theft of physical inventory.

The likelihood or probability of a material misstatement due to fraud cannot be precisely quantified. An auditor's assessment of this attribute may be influenced by a personal assessment of the entity's internal controls (including the existence of an effective audit committee or other supervision of management)—in particular, the effectiveness of internal controls designed to deter or mitigate the risk in question. In any event, in keeping with the need to apply professional skepticism at all times, the auditor should not base an assessment of likelihood solely on a general belief in the integrity of management or others or on the fact that material misstatements due to fraud occur relatively rarely.

The attributes *significance* and *pervasiveness* are closely related; both address the potential scale of the misstatement that might arise. A risk is significant if it could potentially lead to a material misstatement in the financial statements. The pervasiveness of a fraud risk factor has to do with whether that risk threatens the accuracy of the financial statements as a whole or threatens only specific assertions, balances, or transactions. It is not necessary for both attributes to be

---

21. American Institute of Certified Public Accountants, Statement on Auditing Standards (SAS) No. 99, pars. 35–40.

present for there to be a risk of material misstatement. Naturally, in assessing whether a material misstatement could arise, the auditor should consider the impact on both the balance sheet and the profit-and-loss account. A deliberate overstatement of inventories may not be material in balance sheet terms but could nonetheless be material with regard to profit.

◆ EVALUATING CONTROLS

SAS 99—in conjunction with SAS 55,[22]—requires the consideration of internal controls as the final ingredient in the assessment of identified risks of material misstatement due to fraud.[23] On one hand, effective controls may mitigate a particular risk of material misstatement due to fraud. On the other hand, deficiencies in control may have the opposite effect, actually exacerbating the risk.

The potential benefit of this step is that the identification of effective controls, which genuinely mitigate a particular fraud risk, may provide the auditor with a reasonable basis for concluding that the likelihood of that kind of fraud is low. Such an assessment will be taken consistent with SAS 55 and any other relevant standards and only once the auditor is comfortable relying on the relevant controls.

Reliance on controls in specific instances does not obviate the need to consider the possibility of management override. SAS 99 suggests a number of procedures that "should be performed to further address the risk of management override of controls."[24]

- Examining journal entries and other adjustments for evidence of possible material misstatement due to fraud
- Reviewing accounting estimates for biases that could result in material misstatement due to fraud
- Evaluating the business rationale for significant unusual transactions

Using the fraud triangle (incentive/pressure, opportunity, and rationalization/attitude) as a framework, the auditor considers whether there is evidence of other fraud risk factors. The auditor also considers the possibility that collusion, which might lead to the circumvention of controls, is occurring at other levels of the organization. For example, a control over purchases involving segregation of duties between the member of staff responsible for opening supplier accounts and the member of staff responsible for processing invoices may be overridden if the two individuals collude in order to establish an account and process invoices for a fictitious supplier.

---

22. American Institute of Certified Public Accountants, Statement on Auditing Standards (SAS) No. 55, *Consideration of Internal Control in a Financial Statement Audit* (codified in AICPA Professional Standards—U.S. Auditing Standards—AU § 319).
23. American Institute of Certified Public Accountants, Statement on Auditing Standards (SAS) No. 99, pars. 43–45.
24. Id., par. 57.

In addition to SAS 99, the PCAOB's AS2 specifically requires that the auditor consider antifraud programs and controls. Common elements of an antifraud program to be assessed include:

- Code of conduct
- Ethics hotline/whistle-blower programs and activities
- Hiring and promotion
- Audit committee oversight
- Investigation and remediation
- Fraud risk assessment

While some of these common elements may be evaluated for the effectiveness of internal controls as part of the five key components of COSO (see Chapter 9), this requirement is separate from that internal control evaluation because it focuses on the risk of fraud.

ADDRESSING THE IDENTIFIED FRAUD RISKS

The identification and evaluation of fraud risk factors, discussed at some length here, constitute only the beginning. On the basis of their evaluations, auditors determine how best to address identified fraud risks to obtain reasonable assurance as to whether there is, in fact, any material misstatement due to fraud in the financial statements that are the focus of the audit. The auditor's actions may include:

- Considering the level of supervision of personnel to ensure that it is "commensurate with the auditor's assessment of the risks of material misstatement due to fraud"[25]
- Reviewing management's selection of accounting policies: When a heightened fraud risk is evident, the auditor should review the accounting policies and procedures adopted by management—especially in areas subject to significant uncertainty or judgment—and consider whether these might be applied or misapplied in such a way as to result in material misstatement.
- Incorporating an element of unpredictability into the audit approach—for example, (1) including within the scope of audit testing certain balances or transactions that are not normally included, (2) visiting locations without advance warning, or (3) changing the timing or scope of audit tests
- Considering more generally the nature, timing, and extent of audit procedures with regard to their effectiveness in addressing the risk of material misstatement due to fraud

25. Id., par. 50.

♦ UNPREDICTABLE AUDIT TESTS

Opportunity is one side of the fraud triangle. Predictability of the audit approach may create opportunity and undermine detection. Unpredictability may be adopted as a strategy on two levels. At a high level, the auditor may decide to visit locations or to audit areas of the business or components of the financial statements that are not normally audited in detail or at all. If all areas are normally subject to audit by rotation, the auditor might deviate from the expected sequence. At a more detailed level, the auditor should be wary of being too predictable in the selection of individual transactions for detailed testing and avoid situations in which the client might have the opportunity to influence the selection or manipulate audit evidence.

In one case, auditors in a company failed to detect material misstatements in the financial statements for a six-year period because all of the fictitious transactions—and there were many—were either below scope or with business partners who consistently failed to respond to confirmation requests. The perpetrators were armed with the knowledge of what scope the auditors consistently used and which entities consistently failed to respond to confirmation. The perpetrators were able to deceive the auditors and all other third-party users for an extended period of time. In another case, it was alleged that the company knew that its external auditors examined fixed-asset additions at any given facility only if those additions exceeded a certain value. In manipulating fixed-asset additions—an integral part of the alleged financial reporting fraud—the company was careful not to exceed that dollar threshold at any single facility, thereby circumventing the audit process. These examples speak to the importance of modifying the audit approach over time.

Paragraph 50 of SAS 99 specifically states that "the auditor should incorporate an element of unpredictability in the selection from year to year of auditing procedures to be performed." Modifications, either selected randomly or focused on the higher-risk areas, might include:

- Testing areas or accounts that might not normally be tested by the auditors
- Performing substantive tests in areas that have been sampled previously
- Changing sampling methods or increasing sample size
- Obtaining confirmations when historically, none have been obtained
- Obtaining oral confirmations when historically, only written confirmations have been obtained
- Performing physical observations in areas in which historically, only documentary evidence has been reviewed
- Performing procedures at different locations
- Conducting unannounced observations or tests
- Changing the timing of test work
- Modifying the materiality level for certain accounts, testing selected items that are under the materiality level, or testing selected items that are not normally tested because they are considered to be low in risk
- Making inquiries of individuals not approached in previous audits

- Incorporating unpredictable procedures in the testing of journal entries, such as randomly selecting immaterial entries for testing

The point is neither to adopt new overall procedures—such as switching from written to oral confirmations—nor to make a onetime change in procedures. The point is to continually modify the approach so as to make it unpredictable. Not only could this aid in detecting fraud, but it also may serve as a fraud deterrent.

◆ OBSERVATION AND INSPECTION

As mentioned earlier, indications of fraud risk can emerge at any stage of the audit, and the auditor should be alert to events or circumstances that may call for revisions in the previous assessment of fraud risk. There is no substitute for physically and manually reviewing documents, data, and assets. Observation and inspection are standard parts of any audit work program, including vouching and tracing and performing or observing physical counts. Substantive anomalies may come to light through these testing procedures, such as implausible transactions or financial ratios and relationships, or what might be called evidential risk factors may come to the auditor's attention. SAS 99 cites the following examples[26]:

- Discrepancies in the accounting records, including:
  - Transactions that are not recorded in a complete or timely manner or are improperly recorded as to amount, accounting period, classification, or entity policy
  - Unsupported or unauthorized balances or transactions
  - Last-minute adjustments that significantly affect financial results
  - Evidence of employee access to systems and records inconsistent with the access necessary to perform authorized duties
  - Significant unreconciled differences between control accounts and subsidiary records—or between physical count and the related account balance—that were not appropriately investigated and corrected on a timely basis
  - Tips or complaints to the auditor about alleged fraud
- Conflicting or missing evidential matter, including:
  - Missing documents
  - Unavailability of other than photocopied or electronically transmitted documents when documents in original form are expected to exist
  - Significant unexplained items on reconciliations
  - Unusual documentary evidence such as handwritten alterations to documentation or handwritten documentation that is ordinarily electronically printed

---

26. Id., par. 68, examples cited in full.

- Inconsistent, vague, or implausible responses from management or employees arising from inquiries or analytic procedures
- Unusual discrepancies between the entity's records and confirmation replies
- Missing inventory or physical assets of significant magnitude
- Unavailable or missing electronic evidence inconsistent with the entity's record retention practices or policies
- Inability to produce evidence of key systems development and program-change testing and implementation activities for current-year system changes and deployments

- Problematic or unusual events between the auditor and the client, including:
  - Denial of access to records, facilities, certain employees, customers, vendors, or others from whom audit evidence might be sought
  - Undue time pressures imposed by management to resolve complex or contentious issues
  - Complaints by management about the conduct of the audit or management intimidation of audit team members, particularly in connection with auditors' critical assessment of audit evidence or in the resolution of potential disagreements with management
  - Unusual delays by the entity in providing requested information
  - Unwillingness to facilitate auditor access to key electronic files for testing by means of computer-assisted audit techniques
  - Denial of access to key information technology operations staff and facilities, including security, operations, and systems development personnel
  - Unwillingness to add or revise disclosures in the financial statements to make them more complete and transparent

When comparing sources of audit evidence, such as comparing invoices with the accounts payable ledger or comparing bills of lading with inventory entries, the auditor does not simply locate the amount either on the document or in the books and records but reviews the source document with a critical eye for issues such as the following:

- Is the booked amount the correct amount? For example, are shipping and freight also included?
- Does the date of the document reflect the posted date of the transaction, and does it make sense given other dates such as the order-placed date?
- Do the terms—discounts, returns, and so on—reflect actual events?
- Does the document look legitimate?

Other questions may also apply.

Fake or altered documents often have certain characteristics, depending, of course, on the perpetrator's level of sophistication. Here are some examples:

- Font sizes or types may not be consistent.

- No address is shown for the vendor or customer: this is especially suspicious if a vendor has not identified an address to which a check can be sent.
- The address shown is a post office box rather than a physical address.
- The document has no identifying numbers such as invoice number, purchase order number, or customer number.
- All invoice numbers—on invoices from vendors—are numbered sequentially, with no numbers skipped.
- No tax is shown for taxable items.
- No shipping or freight is shown for items that would have been shipped at the purchaser's expense.
- No detail is provided on the invoice.

The presence of these or similar characteristics may suggest the need for further analysis.

As indicators of the possible existence of fraud—whether fraudulent financial reporting or misappropriation of assets—such evidential potential red flags may be considered to have a different status from the general fraud risk factors that have been the topic of most of this chapter. While evidential potential red flags are, like general fraud risk factors, not in themselves conclusive evidence of fraud, they do indicate the existence of a specific gap, anomaly, or other problem in the available audit evidence. As such, they require follow-up.

◆ FINANCIAL STATEMENT FRAUD: DETECTION TECHNIQUES

Knowing where to look for fraud is a key component in detecting fraud.[27] While any line item on the income statement or balance sheet is subject to manipulation, in certain areas this happens more regularly. The auditor should be most alert to potential schemes affecting these line items. Thinking about potential schemes can assist with risk identification. Most often, the goal of fraudulent financial reporting is to overstate net income or net worth—although the opposite may be true when individuals are engaged in earnings management and in building the stockpile of reserves during profitable years to be used later, during periods of lower financial performance. For net income to be overstated, revenues typically are overstated and/or expenses typically are understated. For net worth to be overstated, assets must also be overstated and/or liabilities must be understated. In the system of double-entry bookkeeping, any inappropriate entry will appear in two or more line items. The auditor should understand the client's risk identification program; not having such a program raises a potential red flag.

◆ REVENUE RECOGNITION

Fraudulent financial reporting by means of improper revenue recognition is one of the most prevalent forms of material misstatement due to fraud. For this reason, SAS 99 stipulates that the auditor "should ordinarily presume that there is a

---

27. Part of knowing where to look lies in understanding how a fraudster thinks. This is discussed in Chapter 3, Psychology of the Fraudster.

risk of material misstatement due to fraud relating to revenue recognition."[28] SAS 99 goes on to discuss examples of procedures for addressing the risks related to revenue recognition.[29]

The auditor considers the nature of the entity's business and how it generates and accounts for revenues and then identifies ways in which revenues might be misstated and how such misstatement might be concealed. Examples of the specific risks the auditor might consider, depending on the nature of the business, include the following:

- Fictitious sales of tangible goods might be created and concealed by the falsification of inventory records, shipping documents, and invoices.
- Sales might be inflated by the shipping of goods not ordered, by treating consignment shipments as revenues, or by otherwise ignoring shipping terms that deal with ownership transfer.
- Fictitious sales may be booked for product that has been packaged but not shipped to the customer—and that never will be. The sale may be written off later or re-aged in order not to affect ratios and metrics adversely.
- Sales might be subject to side agreements giving customers the right to return goods not used or to other arrangements that have the effect of partially or wholly reversing sales.
- Sales cutoff might be manipulated by holding the books open for a period after the year-end.
- Fictitious or inflated revenues from long-term projects in progress might arise as a result of aggressive estimates as to degree of completion. This risk will tend to be increased when significant judgment is required in measuring the value of work done or the state of completion—for example, in relation to large-scale capital projects or the development of intangible products such as custom software.

Indicators of such manipulation might include but are not limited to unusual sales patterns or ratios emerging from analytic procedures, discrepancies in documentation, recognition of revenues not in accordance with contract, large credit notes after the year-end, long-outstanding debtors, unreconciled debit entries on intercompany accounts, or irregularities in inventory counts. It is important to obtain a thorough understanding of significant revenue sources and related revenue recognition policies, as well as of any recent changes.

◆ CORRUPTION

Detection of bribes and kickbacks is difficult at best because these are typically buried in otherwise legitimate transactions. That is, the company usually overpays for goods and services, whereupon the perpetrator receives a kickback from

---

28. American Institute of Certified Public Accountants, Statement on Auditing Standards (SAS) No. 99, par. 41.
29. Id., par. 54.

the vendor representative. As such, bribes and kickbacks generally involve the purchasing function of the organization. Potential targets of such schemes include anyone with authority to award contracts or to purchase products—such as inventory, supplies, raw materials, fixed assets, and software. Potential targets may also include individuals whose sign-off is needed for acceptance of a contract, such as engineers, quality personnel, and other technical experts.

Since corruption frauds are so difficult to detect, the focus is weighted heavily toward deterrence. Controls need to be exceptionally good in this area to mitigate the risk that these transactions will occur in the first place. Deterrence may begin by assessment of the areas in which control weaknesses exist. (See Chapter 25.) Some excellent control mechanisms are as follows:

- Integrity in the asset procurement bidding process
- Rotation of employees through various vendor assignments
- As a way of deterring the perpetrator from informing a partner about lower-bidding competitors, the use of private fax machines whereby bids are required to be submitted to persons other than those soliciting the bids
- Establishment of a hotline and ensuring that vendors are aware of the hotline and encouraged to use it if any employee approaches them, seeking a bribe
- A strong, enforced policy on disclosure of conflicts of interest, including receipt of gifts and gratuities by buyers

As with the other types of frauds, analytic procedures and data mining may assist in detection. The typical result of a corruption scheme is that the victim company overpays for a product or service. Trending expenditures and then analyzing the reason for any increases or failures to decrease when a declining trend was expected may identify the purchase of unneeded items or of necessary items at inflated prices. Trending asset balances may also reveal the purchase of unneeded assets, including inventory. Excess inventory write-offs may be the result of a fraudster's attempt to make room for additional purchases. Other potential red flags that may indicate a possible corruption scheme include[30]:

- Orders consistently placed with the same vendor
- Cost of materials or other purchases out of line when compared with related activities
- Buyers whose lifestyles appear to exceed their income levels
- Procurement decisions—in favor of key suppliers—that are heavily influenced or made by managers outside the purchasing department
- Restrictions in solicitation documents that tend to restrict competition
- A very short time frame for responding to bids

---

30. Association of Certified Fraud Examiners, *Fraud Examiners Manual*, 3rd ed. (Austin, Tex.: Association of Certified Fraud Examiners, 1998).

♦ SUMMARY

SAS 99 lays out an iterative and holistic approach to the consideration of fraud in a financial statement audit, the foundation for which is a proper attitude of professional skepticism. The planning, testing, and evaluation of audit evidence for indicia of fraud are unlikely to be successful without that attitude, particularly because fraud is a crime of deceit and because the popularly labeled potential red flags, which may appear by hindsight as bright-red flags, are more like mere threads in their true contemporaneous context. Nevertheless, armed with attitude, analytic techniques, an appreciation of the interpretive challenges presented by fraud risk factors, and the benefit of experience, auditors will continually improve the detection of fraud that materially misstates financial statements.

CHAPTER 9

INTERNAL AUDIT:
THE SECOND LINE OF DEFENSE

Dennis D. Bartolucci

Therese M. Bobek

James A. LaTorre

Our chapter title is a deliberate provocation: if internal auditors are only the second line of defense against the occurrence of fraud in an organization, what is the first line of defense? The answer is clear: management. Management is pre-eminently responsible for fraud deterrence in two respects. First, through the example it sets—the tone at the top—management is first to deter and defend against corporate wrongdoing of all kinds. The ethical tone of the entire organization depends to a significant degree on how top management is perceived both day to day and in its handling of crises. And second, management is responsible for the system of internal controls that should be implemented throughout the entire organization to control, monitor, and document higher-risk areas such as revenue recognition, cash management, purchasing, and inventory.

Management must base its assessment of the effectiveness of the company's internal control over financial reporting on a suitable, recognized control framework established by a body of experts. As outlined in detail in Chapter 1, the Committee of Sponsoring Organizations of the Treadway Commission (COSO) has published *Internal Control: Integrated Framework,* which has emerged as the framework that management and auditors use to evaluate internal controls. The five components of the COSO internal control framework are the following:

1. The control environment
2. Risk assessment
3. Control activities
4. Information and communication
5. Monitoring[1]

---

1. PricewaterhouseCoopers, *Key Elements of Antifraud Programs and Controls: A White Paper* (2003), 26–27.

Although antifraud programs and controls must include all five components of the COSO framework, special emphasis is placed on the control environment: the tone set at the top of an organization that influences the control consciousness of its people. This environment includes management accountability and oversight of antifraud programs and controls. Since 90 percent of all financial statement fraud involves senior executives, the establishment of strong antifraud programs and controls is an essential component of a healthy control environment.[2]

This said, there can be no doubt that the internal audit unit of a company is, indeed, the second line of defense.

◆ WHAT DO INTERNAL AUDITORS DO?

The common misunderstanding is that internal auditors do what external, independent auditors do but they do it earlier—that is, they focus on financial accounts, financial accounting systems, and financial risk controls so that the house is in good order when the external auditors arrive. This is a partial truth. In reality, the internal audit function can be remarkably diverse. While some internal audit units do focus predominantly on financial accounting and the financial control environment, others have much more elaborate agendas requiring a broad mix of skills and experience.

Such a diversity of missions and skills is captured in a chart we informally call the "football" (Exhibit 9.1). Reading from left to right, the chart identifies at the left the traditional missions and skill sets of the internal audit function. Progressively to the right are more diverse and more sophisticated functions, matched to skill sets, which have become the mission of internal auditors in companies and industries that expect more from their internal auditors. The range, then, is from a strict focus on financial auditing, dedicated very largely to value protection, to an elaborate role as a multiskilled consulting entity within the organization, dedicated to value enhancement. No place on the football—no particular mix of tasks and skills—is better than any other. What matters is the alignment of the internal audit unit with the level and type of risk monitoring that management and the board view as internal audit's mission. Because that view is almost sure to change over time in response to a company's needs and to regulatory requirements, the spot the unit falls on the continuum will also change over time.

In a company that chooses not to make aggressive use of the internal audit function but that nonetheless looks to it for specific and critically important services, internal auditors are likely to be responsible for the first three functions named in the upper arc of the chart:

1. Transaction auditing
2. Internal controls evaluation
3. Business process improvement

---

2. Id., 3.

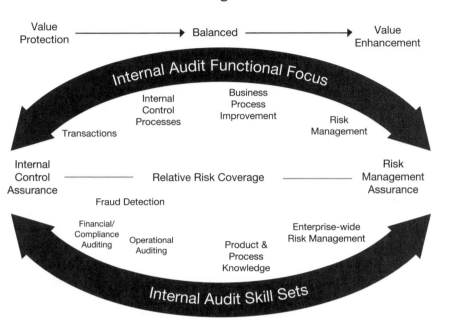

EXHIBIT 9.1   THE "FOOTBALL": INTERNAL AUDIT MIGRATION MODEL

Internal auditors examine accounts and transactions together with the under-lying infrastructure of accounting systems and built-in risk controls. To clear up discrepancies or clarify the exact nature of a problem, they will "ask the next question"—an action of real importance to their work—of those responsible for the accounts and systems. If they identify a control deficiency, they recommend to management certain appropriate solutions. With respect to business processes, they're constantly on the lookout for inefficiencies and better ways to work, again making recommendations to management. Such process reviews and rec-ommendations as to best operational practices may and should make a huge cumulative difference in productivity, profitability, and employee morale—this last in the sense that most people prefer to do things as efficiently and effectively as possible.

Further to the right around the arcs in Exhibit 9.1, the internal audit function becomes an increasingly diverse consulting unit, expert in many types of risk and the management of those risks and charged with the holistic mission of enterprise risk management. The model for internal auditing at this level of sophistication is often thought to be that of General Electric Co. (GE), whose internal auditors have historically been business process reengineers, best-practice implementers, and cost cutters. Out of some 300 to 400 internal auditors at GE, many have MBAs, and a third or more are Six Sigma trained. While the left side of the chart indicates that they remain responsible for traditional internal audit skills and services such as financial auditing, they cover the full spectrum from left to right. To address GE's diverse businesses, the company's internal audit group includes financial auditors with specialized knowledge of the plastics industry, the chemicals industry, life sciences, and other fields.

Returning to the left side of Exhibit 9.1, you will notice that *fraud detection* is positioned among the traditional, financially focused internal audit missions. This both is and is not an innovation—and the ambiguity bears discussion. *Fraud deterrence* has always been a function of internal auditors. The periodic presence of capable internal auditors visibly at work in geographically separated business units or at headquarters is in and of itself a deterrent. *Fraud detection* also represents a traditional task of the internal auditor, but recognition of the need for fraud detection has vastly increased in recent years. The internal audit function often is well placed to offer this service—provided that members of the team have acquired training in fraud detection, which encompasses everything from attitudes and methods to knowing when the red flags of possible fraud are vivid enough to call in forensic accounting specialists. Responding to the increased emphasis on fraud detection, internal auditors are—and should be— seeking the specialized training that truly makes them the second line of defense after management. In fulfilling their mission in the area of fraud detection, they function much like external auditors. And like external auditors, they need to be clear about the dividing line between the audit role and a forensic investigation. (See later in this chapter and also Chapter 7.)

Movement from left to right within Exhibit 9.1 does not mean that the basic missions of the internal audit function get de-emphasized as more sophisticated agendas get added. The movement is accretive, adding skills and functions while retaining the fundamental focus on transactions and controls. However, the percentage of time allocated to one function or another along the continuum varies according to the priorities of management and the board.

◆ INTERNAL AUDIT SCOPE OF SERVICES

Management and the board set the scope of internal audit services, typically on an annual basis. In most companies, the director of internal auditing still reports administratively to the chief financial officer (CFO) or controller, who controls the budget and periodically reviews the activities of the function. Functionally, however, in the post-Sarbanes-Oxley Act of 2002 environment, in many companies internal audit reports to the audit committee. (Later in this chapter is a discussion of the impact of reporting relationships on the internal audit.)

Through the decade or so prior to the collapse of Enron and other major firms amid allegations of massive fraud, the agenda of many internal audit groups tended to move toward the right in Exhibit 9.1. Internal auditors were increasingly asked to function as multiskilled risk consultants, thus allocating a larger share of their budget to consulting tasks than to the narrower set of functions named at the left of the chart. For the most part, this has now changed, owing primarily to two factors. In the first place, during difficult economic times, companies are less willing to field a multiskilled, high-cost internal audit team to address enterprise risk management in the style of consultants. Under those conditions, companies tend to refocus on value protection, reduce internal audit budgets, and put the emphasis on financial and operational efficiency auditing. Internal audit is a cost center, not a profit center; as such, it is susceptible to budget cuts during economic downswings and sometimes has to fight for its fair share against competing management priorities.

Second, as we just implied earlier, the catastrophic accounting frauds at major U.S. companies and the stringent new legislation and regulation to which they gave rise have forcibly turned the attention of management and boards toward the need to ensure the integrity of financial accounting and reporting. This, too, has swung the pendulum back to the left, toward the basics of internal auditing and with greater emphasis on fraud detection.

The pendulum will continue to swing, responding not only to large-scale external circumstances such as the economy, major business events, and regulatory change but also to internally recognized needs. For example, if a company whose internal audit unit is focused on enterprise risk management makes a large acquisition, internal audit may well resume the traditional focus on finance and operational efficiency. An internal audit group focused on internal controls and process improvement can tell management a great deal about the operations of a new acquisition and then make scores of useful recommendations. Similarly, as companies expand around the globe, management is likely to rely on the internal audit function to provide assurance concerning the integrity and appropriateness of financial accounting and controls in geographically separated units.

There is another issue of scope that influences the fraud detection capability of internal audit units. In their business lives, some people who do not typically interact with internal auditors often believe that internal auditors visit all parts of even the largest enterprise at least annually—that they act as the cop on the beat, never far from the neighborhood. However, in large, geographically decentralized organizations, this is rarely true. The annual risk assessment and definition of the internal audit agenda—for which senior finance executives and the directors of internal audit units are typically responsible, subject to audit committee review—determine which units of a company are to be audited in that particular year. The issue is quantifiable: "We have 40,000 hours of internal audit time to spend this year. Where should we spend them?" If the external auditors are known to be emphasizing contracts in a given year, the CFO may decide not to focus the attention of internal auditors in that area, because the time may be better spent elsewhere. Similarly, the CFO may schedule visits to business units in which there is either a suspicion of difficulty or likely opportunities for operational improvement. At any given unit, several years may pass between one internal audit visit and the next. This illustrates all the more clearly that management, which institutes the controls embedded in financial systems and business processes and which owns those controls on a day-to-day basis, is the first line of defense in deterring fraud.

◆ THE HANDOFF TO FORENSIC ACCOUNTING INVESTIGATORS AND LEGAL COUNSEL

Internal auditors operate in a network with other key players: management, the board, external auditors, forensic accounting investigators, legal counsel, and security personnel of various kinds. For purposes of fraud detection and the proper conduct of a fraud investigation, knowledgeable cooperation among internal auditors, forensic accounting investigators, and in-house legal counsel is essential. While cooperation with information technology security managers and (in industries such as retail) loss prevention specialists is also critical to a company's welfare, the renewed emphasis on fraud detection as a role for internal auditors puts the spotlight on how internal auditors interact with forensic and legal investigators.

When should internal auditors alert management and legal counsel that a fraud is suspected and call in forensic accounting investigators to investigate? The answer depends on many factors: management's policy, the skill sets and experience of the internal audit team, legal counsel's policy, and the emerging set of best practices to which this book is a contribution. These factors interact to create, in effect, a bell-curve chart.

In Exhibit 9.2 the far left shows companies whose management considers that any sign of fraud should be considered the tip of an iceberg until proved otherwise;

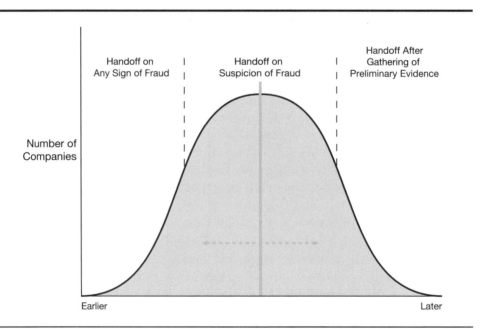

EXHIBIT 9.2 TIMING OF HANDOFF TO FORENSIC ACCOUNTING INVESTIGATORS

therefore, forensic accounting investigators and legal counsel are brought into the picture at the earliest stage. In the midsection of the bell curve fall companies— arguably, a growing majority—that require internal audit to call in forensic accounting investigators as soon as a suspicion of fraud has been detected. Because it knows the company best, the internal audit team is likely to contribute members to the forensic accounting team that sets to work, but responsibility for the investigation rests with the forensic accounting investigators. At the far right in Exhibit 9.2 are companies that authorize their internal audit units to independently gather preliminary evidence concerning a possible fraud. When they uncover evidence indicating that forensic investigation and preservation of the chain of custody over information would be prudent, they refer the matter forward.

There is, or should be, a bright yellow line separating deterrence and detection from investigation. Internal auditors need to continually improve their abilities to uncover indicia of fraud. Internal audit should be fully capable of probing the scope and character of a suspicious situation—yet also willing, if not required, by policy to bring in forensic accounting investigators and legal advisers when suspicions arise. Some internal auditors may say that until they're certain of the fraud, they should investigate a suspicion of fraud and not bring in forensic accounting investigators. This can be a mistake. The advantage of calling on forensic accounting investigators at the first suspicion of fraud is that such investigators are trained in the art of determining the next steps: the specific investigative procedures required to determine whether a suspicious circumstance is, in fact, a defalcation.

The investigation begins when routine audit procedures end. Any other deployment strategy runs a high risk of missing the fraud during the sniffing-around period that follows a suspicion of fraud and precedes the discovery of a defalcation. No matter what the internal auditors' level of training or certification—such as certified fraud examiner (CFE)—the moment comes when they must say, "At this point, we're handing it off to forensic accounting investigation professionals."

◆ PERCEPTION PROBLEM

Generally speaking, internal auditors have invested much time and care into building cooperative relationships with other company personnel. In the early days of internal auditing, their reputation within companies often had some of the flavor of their being internal police—the inspectors who are determined to find fault and discomfit the executives and staff of audited units. Internal auditors soon enough understood that that reputation tended to cut them off from the very people—managers, staff at all levels—with whom they had to interact in order to understand the quality of internal controls and to uncover opportunities for greater operational efficiency. Accordingly, they learned to emphasize the positive impact of internal audit inquiries, tests, and recommendations: "We're here to help you, not hurt you." In addition, in companies whose internal auditors function as a multiskilled consulting unit with a value enhancement agenda (the right side of Exhibit 9.1), those internal auditors enjoy considerable prestige.

Given this background, the stronger emphasis on fraud detection in the post-Enron era must be handled with sensitivity. On one hand, internal auditors do not wish to turn back the clock to the early days of fear and wariness. On the other hand, they cannot and should not disguise their mandate from management and the audit committee to dive deeper, to look for suspicious signs, and to deter and detect fraud. Now, more than ever, communication often constitutes 50 to 70 percent of an internal audit. If internal auditors cannot gather information from managers and staff in an atmosphere of collegial cooperation, their work is severely hampered. Value-added recommendations about improving controls or business processes depend in good measure on information freely offered. Internal auditors can look at huge amounts of data—and they certainly do that—but it is likely to be much more difficult to validate findings in the data and understand the implications of those findings unless managers and staff help out willingly.

We refer repeatedly in this book to the point of transition—the point at which auditors (internal or external) should consider calling in forensic accounting investigators to address a possible fraud. Because over the long term they must preserve cooperative relations with the vast majority of managers and staff in their company, internal auditors have good reason to call in forensic accounting investigators once they've uncovered a suspicion that a fraud may exist—beyond their original risk assessments. The forensic accounting investigation is likely to be conducted discreetly during its earlier stages, but ultimately, it may give rise to forceful, disturbing events. The internal audit team may assist with the investigation, but it is in their interest for the forensic team to lead the investigative effort and shape whatever communications about the outcome must eventually be disseminated within the unit or the company.

Statement on Auditing Standards (SAS) No. 99 instructs external auditors to take a neutral attitude with respect to management's integrity and to exercise professional skepticism in the conduct of their procedures. In addition, the standard instructs the auditor to assume that a risk of fraud does in fact exist. Both of these provisions are counter to many of the internal auditor's objectives. It is mission critical for internal auditors to gain the trust and confidence of those with whom they work. They are virtually certain to have developed close working relationships with the very people who may have committed a fraud. For this reason, they are not well placed to conduct a formal fraud investigation, and the appearance if not the reality of a lack of objectivity toward company personnel could be viewed as a departure from the Standards of Professional Conduct of the Association of Certified Fraud Examiners.

◆ COMPLEX CORPORATE FRAUD AND THE INTERNAL AUDIT

The recent wave of high-profile, complex frauds involving billions of dollars, wayward accounting, and catastrophic corporate failures raised many questions, including this one: Where were the auditors? The question could be asked about both the external *and* the internal auditors.

Two common reasons that have surfaced in recent cases for failure to discover fraud are:

1. Deference to senior management regarding complex financial transactions and instruments
2. Limitations on the information and scope that are being provided for internal auditors

♦ WORLDCOM AND THE THORNBURGH REPORT

The bankruptcy proceeding in the aftermath of the exposure of WorldCom's monumental accounting misdeeds included a document known as the Thornburgh report, which highlights several potential considerations, pitfalls, and lessons learned that internal auditors may confront in the course of their work.[3] Another document of interest is the report issued by the Special Investigative Committee of the board of directors of WorldCom.[4] In what follows, we draw first from the Thornburgh report:

- Maintain increased skepticism; this may contribute to discovering potential red flags of fraud in earlier periods.
- Be wary of certain limitations that may hinder internal auditors' abilities, such as management's direction to focus on operational issues rather than financial matters.
- Real support from senior management, the board, and the audit committee[5] is crucial to being effective.
- Evaluate the actual financial statement fraud risk, especially in organizations that may have an increased risk "due to the complexity and dispersed nature of the company's organization and financial operations."[6]
- Strive for adequate annual internal audit planning, if the annual plan is not followed, and determine whether this is the appropriate course of action.
- Strive for actual and active contact with the audit committee rather than relying on others. A warning may be observed from the Thornburg report: "There is no evidence that the Audit Committee requested from the Internal Audit Department updates on the status of internal control weaknesses."[7]

---

3. Dick Thornburgh, Bankruptcy Court Examiner, *First Interim Report of Dick Thornburgh*, Bankruptcy Court Examiner, United States Bankruptcy Court, Southern District of New York. In re: WorldCom, Inc., et al., Debtors. Chapter 11, Case No. 02-15533 (AJG) Jointly Administered, November 4, 2002.
4. Dennis R. Beresford, Nicholas deB. Katzenbach, and C. B. Rogers Jr., *Report of Investigation by the Special Investigative Committee of the Board of Directors of WorldCom, Inc.*, March 31, 2003, http://news.findlaw.com/hdocs/docs/worldcom/bdspcomm60903rpt.pdf.
5. Thornburgh, *First Interim Report*, chap. V, § E-3, "The Company's Internal Audit Function," 52.
6. Id., 55.
7. Id., 56.

The report of the Special Investigative Committee adds a further insight and potential lessons:

- Strive for open communication between employees and the internal audit personnel.[8]
- Focus on substantive interaction between the internal audit personnel and the external auditor.

Courage may be required to continue to probe in certain areas, especially in an environment that is not transparent or when facing objections from management. Open communication with the audit committee as well as external auditors and advisers may be able to offer assistance to internal auditors when faced with these situations.

With proper training, knowledge, and experience, internal audit can have a central role in directing the compass for fraud detection. Qualities such as professional skepticism and personal courage may be needed to establish the truth. However, in some environments, it is also possible that internal audit can be deflected from its primary mission: the auditing of what its risk assessment indicates are key areas requiring audit. What should have been an essentially routine activity took extraordinary courage to accomplish.

◆ CASE STUDIES: THE INTERNAL AUDITOR ADDRESSES FRAUD

The following brief case studies are varied examples of fraud and its detection, ranging from complex fraud by a master fraudster to many types of common fraud that can create, over time, a damaging drain on company assets. Perhaps more effectively than any theoretical explanation, these cases demonstrate the value of professional skepticism, the almost-sixth-sense awareness that arouses the suspicion of an able internal auditor, and the cooperation that is needed with upper management, forensic accounting investigators, and others to expose and eliminate the more serious types of fraud. Several of the cases also demonstrate the real-world constraints within which internal auditors must sometimes operate. The following mottoes, which we propose as a preface to these cases, represent the folk wisdom of two senior internal auditors who contributed several of the cases:

- Liars can figure, and figures can lie.
- Every good internal auditor is from Missouri, the Show Me state.

NO SEGREGATION OF DUTIES—AND A VERY NICE CAR

While visiting an outlying plant in the American Southwest, a finance executive from headquarters made a mental note when he saw that an accounts payable supervisor (the AP) was driving a Seven Series BMW—quite a car for an indi-

---

8. Beresford et al., *Report of Investigation*, 18.

vidual earning something on the order of $60,000 annually. Asked to respond to this potential red flag, the internal audit unit observed that segregation of duties had not been properly built into the accounts payable system, so that the AP was able to manipulate all parts of the system. In addition, a certain number of checks—how many was not yet clear—were being mailed to post office boxes rather than to normal vendor addresses. These preliminary indications of fraud were reason enough to call in a forensic accounting team.

Working with the internal auditors, the investigating team soon discovered that the AP had created fictitious vendors and routinely cut checks to them. The checks were showing up in private mailboxes, from which he would harvest them periodically. The team downloaded data on vendors in the preceding 24 months and discovered that fully 90 percent of them were fictitious. In that 24-month period, the AP had misappropriated $600,000.

The division of labor between the internal audit group and the forensic accounting experts was classic. The internal auditors were able to pull the financial picture together without alerting the target individual, while the forensic team did a full financial check on him: house, cars, and much more. The forensic team also interrogated data extracted from servers and hard drives and used this information to build a case. Convinced of the AP's culpability, the forensic team conducted the admission-seeking interview, which, on the basis of overwhelming evidence, achieved its purpose. A report to the company's audit committee was drawn up jointly by the leaders of the two teams at the conclusion of the effort.

Case closed? Not yet—the internal audit team had further work not just at the plant but also across the company. The company's enterprise-wide financial system was compatible with a software tool that enabled the team to run a segregation-of-duties test for everyone in the company. Did any employees have access levels that were incompatible with their duties? If an employee did have incompatible access rights, was there a valid reason? Were mitigating controls in place? On the basis of this analysis, internal audit went on to redesign the pattern of authorities and accountabilities, and it closed many loopholes, including the one through which the dishonest AP had driven his fraud.

ODD TRANSPORTATION SYSTEM

A company with several new plant locations was spending $3 million a year on van service to transport employees from one plant to another and back again. From an external audit point of view, there were only a few questions to ask about this arrangement: "You say it's a $3-million service? Fine. Vouch that amount and make sure that you have $3 million accounted for, with checks written to the van lines." There is no operational question or critique in the external auditor's approach. On the other hand, the internal auditor thinks differently. "Hmm, you're using 10 van lines. What if we narrow it down to 2 van lines and insist that they compete—promise them bulk business if they offer better rates. We could easily save $2 million."

Brilliant! But in actual fact, the internal auditor still is not exercising enough professional skepticism and should ask the next question: "Why, in the first place, were there 10 van lines, when anyone could see that two competing lines would make better business sense, and did someone's brother-in-law own one of those van lines?" Probably not—probably the whole arrangement just grew without critical oversight, but questions of that type need to be kept in mind. The new mind-set of the internal auditor is to be ceaselessly aware of the possibility of fraud. The new agenda should be to dive more deeply than in the past. It may cost more to investigate in depth some minor common fraud than to close it off and move on, but it is always worthwhile to ask the next question.

A TRAGIC CIRCUMSTANCE

Recall from earlier chapters that corporate fraud occurs—if it is going to occur at all—when the three factors of the fraud triangle coincide: need, opportunity, and rationalization. This case represents a tragic example of the compelling factor of need.

The internal audit team was executing a routine match of employee payroll records to benefits enrollment lists as a way of checking whether the benefits administration was deleting terminated employees in a timely manner from enrollment in the benefits plan. If there was any lag, the company would be losing a few hundred dollars per month. The team identified an individual enrolled in the plan whose name did not match any employee records. Naturally, they went to the benefits administrator, an older woman long with the company, to inquire. "That person doesn't work here," she said.

Something in her attitude and in the facts themselves prompted the internal audit team to dig deeper. As there was clearly a suspicion of fraud, forensic accounting investigators were brought into the engagement. Here is what they discovered—initially, through discussion with the controller, and later, through an investigation conducted by the forensic accounting team. The nonemployee enrolled in the plan was in fact the administrator's son. In the time frame under review, he was 22, had been suffering from cancer and needed extensive treatment, and had no medical coverage of his own. With no one to turn to, the administrator had signed him up as a member of the self-insured plan. Some months earlier, he had passed away, and the company had incurred $150,000 of self-insured medical expenses prior to his death.

How could the administrator bend the system to her purpose? Because she was trusted and well-known to the insurance company's own administrators, she had called them up, explained that she had forgotten to enroll an employee, and asked them to backdate his enrollment to the beginning of the year. Having no reason to doubt her word, the insurance company's people complied with her request and sent the enrollment forms and all change notifications directly to her. Information about the plan enrollment would go periodically to corporate headquarters, where no one knew Bill from Steve from Harry, and so no one was the wiser.

In this case, a routine check to save the company unnecessary expense led to a tragic instance of fraud. The company terminated the administrator but under the circumstances took no further action.

HOW MANY LUNCHES CAN YOU BUY?

Not every fraud is theft for personal benefit. Some fall into a gray zone of clearly unethical conduct but no greed or malice. An internal audit team was conducting a routine review of petty cash accounts. The average balance was $800, as expected, but the volume of money going through these accounts was $8,000 to $10,000 a month. Why? The team looked more closely. The company had imposed a strict limit on capital spending that year: "Times are tough." "Cut your capital budget." "Don't spend." But this particular unit of the company had a towering need for new computer equipment. With the capital appropriation request process basically at a standstill, the unit's information technology people had decided to buy computers and related items such as office furniture by using petty cash. They did not report the acquisitions, and they kept the petty cash accounts at about the right level at any point in time.

It was not a dramatic fraud, but it was certainly a circumvention. The managers further up, who understood why capital spending had to be curtailed, were not pleased to learn about this concealed activity at the unit. From the internal auditors' perspective, the key thing was to notice the potential red flag. How many lunches can you buy?

Forensic accounting investigators were called in to review the work of the internal auditors, who had uncovered the fraud rather quickly via only one procedure. The forensic accounting investigators knew how to search for other indications of fraud by way of ensuring that the fraud was confined to this small group and only this scheme.

MAKING THE NUMBERS LOOK RIGHT

An internal audit team at a major company was carrying out inventory audit procedures. One of the standard tests is to look at the reconciliation between booked inventory and actual physical inventory, which naturally requires the team to go out on the floor to quantify inventory on hand and then compare that measure with inventory recognized in the system. The team started on this laborious process and quickly came up with differences that nobody was able to explain. Looking more deeply into the total reconciliation process, the team realized that nothing made sense. It was time to talk with the controller, who was responsible for inventory accounting.

The internal audit team leader had hardly begun the discussion, when the controller became tremendously upset and offered what amounted to a confession, as if this purely exploratory meeting were an admission-seeking interview. The auditor accepted the circumstance and listened carefully. The controller said he had been hiding variances by means of multiple journal entries in balance sheet accounts, thereby moving the numbers around to come up with an inventory that actually seemed to be accurate.

After he started trying to make the numbers look right, he said, he found himself caught in his own game and continued to hide one erroneous entry with another—until the whole process had spiraled out of control.

The internal auditors called on inventory experts from elsewhere in their organization to untangle the mess the controller had created. Meanwhile, a forensic team probed the accounts and the surrounding circumstances—including the individual's lifestyle and financial condition—to ascertain whether a defalcation had actually occurred. Nothing remarkable was found. The scheme proved to be a matter of abysmally bad judgment, unrelated to any personal gain other than making the numbers look right in the eyes of upper management. The individual was fired, and the damage he caused was kept within bounds.

It was entirely appropriate for the internal audit leader to meet with the controller to inquire about the reconciliation. Prior to this meeting, all he had was a number of questions to better understand the reconciliation process; there had been no indicia of fraud. In that meeting, the controller voluntarily confessed and the internal audit leader realized he would want to bring in forensic accounting investigators to clarify matters, but meanwhile, he was in the middle of hearing a confession. He did the right thing by continuing the interview. It would have been foolish on his part to say something like, "Can you hold that thought until I can conference in a forensic accounting investigator?"

There might not have been a second chance; now was the time to listen. When the perpetrator of a scheme decides to confess, take notes, be consoling and appreciative, and get through it as best as you can. You can call on the forensic accounting investigator later, who is likely to arrange another interview.

HOW NOT TO EARN A BONUS

Fraud is sometimes the bad result of a problem that could have been solved by better management. An internal audit team was performing a normal test of inventory at a major facility in the tourism industry when it discovered two to three times as much inventory on the balance sheet as could actually be found in inventory. The inventory balance had grown to approximately $1.2 billion, while the physical, at-hand quantity on the books was on the order of $500,000. They knew this was not right and persistently asked the next question.

Soon they discovered a rather complicated scenario involving greed and pressure tactics. It turned out that the head of food and beverage, an extremely aggressive individual, had been pressuring the controller to keep cost of sales no higher than a certain level. He had managed to convince the controller that the fairly high cost of sales was an accounts payable problem—that the accounts payable unit had double paid and triple paid invoices in some cases, thereby causing cost of sales to appear higher than it actually was and throwing off the inventory balance. Caving in to the pressure and the spurious argument, the controller transferred the entire excess inventory into a prepaid account to hide it. This was done literally at 11 P.M. on the night before the books were to close for the year.

When the internal auditors sought out the controller to shed light on the inventory problem, he stalled them: "We'll investigate next month." That was not a good enough answer. The head of internal audit informed senior management of the problem, and his group pressed forward with an investigation, conducted by forensic accounting investigators. Soon things began falling into place. The bonus of the food and beverage director had been dependent that year on keeping cost of sales below a certain level.

The situation was corrected in cooperation with management and the external auditor. On one hand, an inventory write-down had caused the company to fall short of its revenue goals for awarding bonuses that year. On the other hand, the head of internal audit had been awarded a handsome bonus for detecting the potential red flag and courageously reporting up the line to senior management—for all he knew, at the risk of his own bonus. The food and beverage director, the controller, and several others were terminated.

In the course of the investigation, a curious fact came to light: an accounting supervisor in the food and beverage area had been aware of the manipulations, knew they were wrong, and had been trying to get people's attention. In response to his efforts, he had heard nothing but "It will be taken care of." True, he could have tried harder. For example, he could have spoken with the internal auditors. But he had nonetheless demonstrated integrity, judgment, and a measure of courage. He was promoted to the position of food and beverage controller. The company also installed a hotline facility and began an education program throughout the company so as to avoid any future problems regarding employee attempts to communicate suspicions of fraud.

In the months following the inventory write-down and dismissals, some relatively straightforward and wholly legitimate business and accounting changes were made, and the cost-of-sales problem was solved. Had the food and beverage director managed more effectively, he would have been able to drive the cost of sales down to his bonus target through legitimate means.

A CLASSIC PURCHASING FRAUD

The distinction between common fraud and complex fraud is worth keeping in mind. The internal auditor is charged with making a best effort to detect both. One of the most common types of fraud is illustrated in this case. Though common, it can cause considerable harm if it goes undetected.

An internal audit team was performing a review of a company's payables department. As part of that activity, the team was performing routine tests on a sample of purchases to verify whether they had been properly authorized. In the sample there was a vendor called United Tech—a name very like United Technologies, a major enterprise from which the company actually did make purchases. The auditors felt uneasy about the abbreviated account name. Why would this vendor name track so closely with the name of a major company? They decided to look more closely.

Suspicious signs soon turned up. The paid-to address of United Tech was a post office box, and other features of the vendor records seemed atypical. The audit director talked the matter through with the CFO at that business unit, who agreed there was reason for suspicion. More digging disclosed that United Tech was not, in fact, a legitimate vendor. With the help of a forensic accounting team, it was time to piece together the nature of the fraud.

Here are the facts that emerged. A former employee in the information technology department of the company who had access to all of its software had recorded that vendor in the company's master file. Circumventing all normal procedures, he then created transactions in the name of United Tech.

In reality, United Tech was not a legitimate business but an off-site mailbox to which company checks for fictitious goods and services were delivered. The fraudster would stop by from time to time to gather up his latest haul of checks.

Once these facts of mail fraud had been established, management called in the U.S. Federal Bureau of Investigation, which staked out the mailbox and observed the former employee picking up his mail. A strange feature of the case—and a useful warning to internal auditors and forensic accounting investigators—is that this individual was able to continue the fraud for six months after leaving the company because he continued to have access, from a remote location, to the company's computer systems.

This individual was prosecuted and served jail time.

THE LONELINESS OF THE INTERNAL AUDITOR

This case, concerning domestic pressures to overlook fraud, relates closely to the preceding international case. An internal audit team and, ultimately, the internal audit director became aware that the sales manager of a business unit was defrauding the company through his expense reporting. This fellow did not have much talent for fraud: using tear-off restaurant tabs to submit charges as though they were business meals, he overlooked the fact that the tabs were consecutively numbered. His expense reports showed food expenses sequentially numbered—13101, 13102, and so on—from report to report. This potential red flag had shown up in a routine audit of expense reporting in his department. It was obvious that he was cheating on his expense report, and forensic accounting investigators soon discovered that in his private life, he was buying gifts in the range of $75 to $200, roughly the price of meals with customers. He had converted his expense report into a small but reliable cash cow.

That is the dull part of the story. The interesting part of the story is that the sales manager's brother was a powerful executive in the company. When this issue came to light, something happened behind the scenes along the lines of a heart-to-heart conversation between the controller, to whom internal audit reported, and the influential brother. The words of that conversation are not on record, but they must have been of this kind: "There is some misunderstanding here. My brother was not trying to steal from the company." When the internal audit director again discussed the matter with his boss, the controller, he heard a different tune. The controller told the auditor he had misconstrued the evidence, making more of it than he should. The right solution was simply to tell this sales manager to be more careful with expense reporting. And the controller warned the auditor: "We don't want you to make these kinds of mistakes in the future."

End of story? The auditor knew that there was still an issue and put it on the audit committee's agenda. Sitting down with the committee, he did not realize that the controller had prereported the issue and altered the facts to make them seem innocuous. "Why would you even bring this up with us?" a committee member asked. "We're not interested." The result was just what his adversaries had expected: the internal audit director came off as seeming to have poor judgment.

What options remained for this embattled director of internal audit? Choosing not to endanger his job by stepping completely around the chain of command, he preferred to live to fight another day—to fight some other issue, not this one.

Are scenarios of this kind rare in the professional lives of internal auditors who take their fraud detection responsibility seriously? Unfortunately, they probably are not rare, and they point out a measure of the challenge of integrity and skill facing internal auditors.

HITTING THE JACKPOT IN THE GAMING INDUSTRY

It does not take much intuition to recognize that the gaming industry needs an especially strong internal audit function. Like financial services, the gaming industry is all about money, but it is also about hospitality, entertainment, transportation, and the unobtrusive policing of large numbers of pumped-up, excited people having a good time.

A senior internal auditor was invited to a meeting of casino executives to discuss the controls that would be needed around a new marketing program, initiated by the vice president of marketing, who was present at the meeting. This entrepreneurial executive was widely admired at the casino as the largest revenue producer in the managerial ranks. His reach extended far. In fact, he had a second business of his own, in partnership with the casino: a junket business that transported tourists and games players by bus and air to the casino for a day or more of enjoyment. Now he was proposing a new tour and travel program to increase traffic to the casino—and incidentally, generate a third stream of income for himself personally.

While the internal auditor participating in the meeting had been summoned on a narrow agenda—to recommend controls for the proposed business—he found himself feeling uneasy about the whole picture. Something did not seem right. With senior management's authorization, he teamed with forensic accounting investigators, and together they launched a discreet investigation that probed the accounts for which the vice president was responsible, both in the core casino business and in the related junket business.

The result was astonishing. The executive was stealing from the company in some 15 to 20 different ways. Some of the schemes were primitive. For example, by using inflated foreign exchange rates, he cheated to the tune of tens of thousands of dollars in his expense reports. In that particular scheme, he made a mistake that should have been detected much earlier: the exchange rates he reported were preprinted on the forms he used, but foreign exchange rates vary over time. Other schemes were sophisticated. Because he had significant influence over casino credit-granting and credit write-off decisions, he was able to put credit in the hands of people who were in reality not creditworthy and then authorize the write-offs, which amounted over time to many millions of dollars. The investigation did not prove whether he had profited directly from that process, but all indications were that he had. In the junket business, he also had a lucrative scheme under way, which involved buying airline tickets for his customers at the highest possible price, collecting the 10 percent travel agency commission, and then billing through to the casino company the full value of the ticket. This pattern, like much else, was undisclosed.

There was much more. This individual was a true maestro of fraud. For example, he had fraudulently arranged for the casino to pay the salary and benefits of the personnel working in his travel agency. He was billing the casino for housekeeping services at his own business offices and leasing for $12,000 a year—again, at the casino's expense—a desktop computer system that could have been purchased for $2,000. The lease was held by his outside accountant, who was also his landlord. And on and on—nearly everything he touched proved on investigation to have some element of fraud. The company's losses were at the level of many millions of dollars.

What became of him? He was not immediately terminated, because the state division of gaming enforcement had been conducting its own covert investigation and wanted to follow his movements while imperceptibly restricting his ability to perpetrate further fraud. For this reason, the state authorities chose the time of his dismissal. He actually went on to enjoy 15 minutes of notoriety when he was called to testify before a Senate committee investigating infiltration by foreign mafias into the U.S. gaming industry. The internal auditors at the company wound up their work by calculating that for every dollar of revenue this man had brought to the casino door through legitimate marketing activities, he had cost the company $1.07 million. It is worth noting that this consummate fraudster fit the profile of the white-collar criminal described in Chapter 3. He resembled any number of executives you might see walking down the streets of any major financial district. It could have taken many more years to expose him if the senior internal auditor called in to discuss controls had not felt uneasy as he listened. This was a victory for professional skepticism and experience.

◆ REPORTING RELATIONSHIPS: A KEY TO EMPOWERING FRAUD DETECTION

Fraud detection as a task for internal audit comprises both a mission and a skill set, supported by an attitude of professional skepticism and the cumulative experience of the practitioner. However, it does not exist in a vacuum: it needs the right organizational support to be fully effective. For this reason, the issue of reporting relationships is more important than one might think.

As a general rule, internal audit reports to the audit committee, with an administrative or dotted-line report to the CFO. In a recent paper, the Institute of Internal Auditors (IIA) endorsed two reporting relations, the first described as functional (to the audit committee), and the second as administrative (to the CFO, controller, in-house legal counsel, or, in a few instances, the CEO).[9] In

---

9. Institute of Internal Auditors Research Foundation, *Internal Audit Reporting Relationships: Serving Two Masters* (Altamonte Springs, Fla.: Institute of Internal Auditors, 2003), 8.

actual practice, the CFO and the CFO's immediate reports are often the dominant report. A recent study indicates that 51 percent of internal audit units report administratively to the CFO or controller.[10] In certain industries, notably banking and casinos, regulators now explicitly require internal audit to report to the audit committee in order to ensure the independence and integrity of the function. In the post-Enron, post-WorldCom era, a number of powerful federal agencies, including the Federal Reserve Board and the Office of the Comptroller of the Currency, have stated, "Internal audit should report to the audit committee—and if not, we're going to criticize you." But a forceful statement from a powerful agency is not a binding law. Except in a handful of industries, the reporting relation of internal audit remains a management decision.

Even if, as in the majority of cases, the director of internal audit reports functionally to the audit committee, that director will meet with the committee some four times annually and with the CFO much more frequently in the normal course of business. The CFO will naturally exercise a great deal of authority over the scope of internal audit projects and monitor the results and recommendations that flow from them. Although there is nothing improper in this, experience shows that in order to help ensure that internal audit gets taken seriously across the organization and can make itself heard at the right levels when it wishes to call attention to a problem, it usually is best that internal audit report administratively to a level no lower than executive vice president.

With assured and unencumbered access to both the CFO and the audit committee—and even though given human nature, such difficulties can never be eliminated entirely—some of the difficulties internal auditors experience and that we have explored through case studies likely would be reduced, but that will ensue only if all stakeholders in the internal audit process reach for a new level of excellence.

Let us be clear about what we mean. Internal auditors should improve their fraud detection skills and should program fraud detection explicitly into their work plans. Internal auditors also should be ready to exercise integrity and courage when the situation calls for it. Dual reporting lines, if they are active and reliable, can support their willingness, when necessary, to tell truth to power. The needed truth may be as simple as these words to the CFO: "I think we should still audit X this year. The risks merit it. Let's leave it in the annual work plan." Audit committees must step up to their oversight responsibilities as defined and expanded by Sarbanes-Oxley, which includes oversight of internal controls. The inclusion, per Sarbanes-Oxley, of one financial expert on the audit committee is designed to make the committee fully capable of understanding the financial structure and performance of the company, including any complex transactions proposed by management. The audit committee has, in principle, no better ally than a capable, confident, empowered internal audit team. Many audit committees have not yet understood that their control of the external and internal

---

10. Id., 9. According to this report, "The next highest is . . . 33 percent reporting to the CEO or president."

auditors is a key asset that should help them effectively fulfill their responsibility as shareholders' representatives.

Should new standards be developed around the internal audit function, now that its importance in fraud detection and in the preservation of corporate integrity has been amply demonstrated by recent events? Is it enough to leave most decisions to management regarding the scope and emphasis of internal audit projects, subject only to guidelines proposed but not enforced by the IIA? These are open questions as this book goes to press. Meanwhile, it is not too much to say that internal auditors face both pressure to disregard areas in which they conscientiously know that work is needed and pressure to overlook, minimize, or reinterpret suspicious facts they have uncovered. The internal audit function can be only as good as the audit committee and senior management want it to be.

◆ TOMORROW'S INTERNAL AUDITOR, TOMORROW'S MANAGEMENT AND BOARD

The most promising change in the professional profile of the internal auditor, now and in the future, is a shift toward greater acumen and focus where fraud is concerned. This is already occurring. In light of Sarbanes Oxley and follow-on regulations, management and boards are demanding it. And the audit profession, wounded by the negligence and wrongdoing of the few involved in the corporate scandals of recent years, is asking more of itself. Some internal auditors will seek formal training and become accredited as certified fraud examiners—not necessarily to become specialized forensic accounting investigators but, rather, to be optimally effective from within the internal audit team. All internal auditors will be expected to exercise a higher degree of professional skepticism, to ask the next question and the next, and to corroborate audit evidence rather than accept a single informant's word. The internal auditor's focus on fraud detection should be explicit and methodical.

The case studies in this chapter make clear that professional skepticism and training in fraud detection are not enough. Internal auditors will on occasion need courage and unshakable integrity to challenge others and their assertions. These can be difficult situations. This observation brings to light the need for management and the audit committee also to play their roles effectively, proactively, and with integrity.

Management must be willing to invest in fraud detection through the internal audit team and to feel that the money is well spent even if the internal audit director reports as follows: "Mr./Ms. CFO, I'm delighted to tell you that we spent 500 hours this year specifically testing for fraud in major risk areas, and we found *nothing.* To the best of our knowledge, this company is free of significant fraud." Management must come to view this as good news rather than as a pretext for cutting back on internal audit's budget in the next fiscal year.

The audit committee, now and in the future, needs to view itself as the ultimate boss and beneficiary of internal audit's activity. Its members must be sensitive to management's agenda for the internal audit and recommend modifications when they perceive the possibility of insufficiently monitored risk to the company's finances and operations. The audit committee must position itself as independent of management whenever there is any doubt about matters of integrity, accountability, and transparency—and as enthusiastically support- ive of management when management is doing its job well.

Genuine cooperation across this network of participants—internal auditors, senior executives, and the audit committee—goes a long way toward ensuring that when external auditors examine a company's internal controls and financial reporting, they will be better able to do their job.

CHAPTER 10

FINANCIAL STATEMENT FRAUD: REVENUE AND RECEIVABLES

Jonny J. Frank

David Jansen

Jamal Ahmad

Daniel V. Dooley

Overstating revenue is the most common of all financial statement fraud schemes. As a result, Statement on Auditing Standards (SAS) 99, *Consideration of Fraud in a Financial Statement Audit*, includes a presumption that improper revenue recognition is a fraud risk.[1] According to the 1999 report by the Committee of Sponsoring Organizations of the Treadway Commission (COSO), the recording of fictitious revenues was the most common revenue fraud, followed by premature recognition of revenues.[2] More broadly speaking, many fraudulent financial-reporting schemes involve earnings management, which the U.S. Securities and Exchange Commission (SEC) has defined as "the use of various forms of gimmickry to distort a company's true financial performance in order to achieve a desired result."[3]

Earnings management does not always involve outright violations of generally accepted accounting principles (GAAP). Companies often manage earnings by choosing accounting policies that bend GAAP to attain earnings targets. There is a difference between aggressive earnings management techniques that GAAP permits and those that clearly violate GAAP. At the same time, it should

---

1. American Institute of Certified Public Accountants, Statement on Auditing Standards (SAS) No. 99, *Consideration of Fraud in a Financial Statement Audit* (codified in AICPA Professional Standards—U.S. Auditing Standards—AU § 316), par. 41.
2. Committee of Sponsoring Organizations of the Treadway Commission, *Fraudulent Financial Reporting: 1987–1997, an Analysis of U.S. Public Companies* (New York: COSO, 1999), 24. In the sampling of 204 companies involved in fraud, 26 percent recorded fictitious revenues, while 24 percent recorded revenues prematurely. An additional 16 percent overstated revenues, though it was not clear exactly how.
3. U.S. Securities and Exchange Commission, *Annual Report* (SEC, 1999), 84.

be noted that the SEC has cautioned that compliance with GAAP is not a protection against an enforcement action if financial performance is distorted.[4]

There are many aspects of GAAP that require management to make a judgment, which makes the application of GAAP more an art than a science. As a simple example, GAAP allows any depreciation method so long as it systematically and rationally allocates the cost of an asset over its useful life. GAAP also allows various methods of inventory valuation, including last in, first out; first in, first out; and specific identification.[5] Other instances in which management must make judgments include:

- Changing depreciation methods from an accelerated method to the more conservative, straight-line method or vice versa
- Changing the useful lives or estimates of the salvage value of assets
- Determining the appropriate allowance required for uncollectible accounts receivable
- Determining whether and when assets have become impaired and are required to be reserved against or written off
- Determining whether a decline in the market value of an investment is temporary or permanent
- Estimating the write-downs required for investments

It is not unfair to say that GAAP allows a company to manage earnings within certain boundaries of integrity through applying their judgment to the application of accounting principles. The SEC has noted that accounting principles are not meant to be straitjackets, and a degree of accounting flexibility is essential to innovation.[6] As former SEC chairman Arthur Levitt noted in 1998, accounting and reporting abuses occur only when this flexibility is exploited to distort the true picture of the corporation.[7]

Companies have a host of reasons for exercising their judgment in applying those principles that will paint the rosiest financial picture, but typically, the most powerful reason is that the market is looking for positive results. That expectation is reflected in the stock price punishment often endured by companies if their reported earnings fall short of estimates, sometimes even by a penny. Yet market pressure to meet earnings estimates is in direct conflict with market pressure for transparency in financial reporting.

---

4. The SEC's enforcement action against Edison Schools ("Edison") is illustrative; *Securities Exchange Act of 1934* (SEA) Rel. No. 45925, *Accounting and Auditing Enforcement* (AAE) Rel. No. 1555 (May 14, 2002). Edison operates public schools on behalf of local governments, which paid directly certain school expenses. Edison Schools recognized these payments as revenue, even though the payments did not flow through its accounts. The SEC launched an enforcement action notwithstanding that the accounting technically complied with GAAP.

5. See Financial Accounting Standards Board, Accounting Research Bulletin (ARB) No. 43, *Inventory Pricing* (1953), chap. 9; see also *Accounting Technology Bulletin* No. 1.

6. Arthur Levitt, "The 'Numbers Game,'" Speech, New York University Center for Law and Business, September 28, 1998, www.sec.gov/news/speech/speecharchive/1998/spch220.txt.

7. Id.

It can be a difficult challenge for auditors to distinguish between aggressive but allowable accounting and accounting that is abusive and prohibited. The key determinant is management's intent. Fraud rarely occurs if management's intent is transparent and clearly understandable, but what if management selects a policy it knows will have both a positive and a negative effect on the financial picture—and refuses to recognize the negative effect? Does that demonstrate fraud in the selection of the policy? A difficult question, to be sure. Auditors who encounter such a situation in actual practice may counsel with others and gather facts before drawing any conclusions.

Beyond those areas of legitimate managerial judgments lie frauds that are clearly outside the parameters of GAAP. These techniques may inflate earnings, create an improved financial picture, or mask a deteriorating trend.

Financial statement fraud is based on deceptively altering the accounting records of a company so as to improperly reflect one or more of the records' basic elements: assets, liabilities and equity, revenues, and expenses. In many schemes, the requirements of double-entry bookkeeping result in two or more of these basic categories' being misstated. Some frauds, such as recognition of inventory but not the payable for it, are based on one-sided accounting entries, often accomplished through a subsidiary ledger or record that is incompletely reconciled to the general ledger. The fraud schemes that are the focuses of this chapter—revenue and receivable schemes—are generally accomplished by increasing both revenue and receivable accounts.

♦ IMPROPER REVENUE RECOGNITION

A number of reports have found that from 1981 to 2002, one-half to two-thirds of SEC enforcement actions and shareholder actions involved improper revenue recognition. Improper recognition can take two forms: either premature recognition of revenue generated through legitimate means or recognition of fictitious revenue from false sales or to false customers. Overstated revenue can come about by means of:

- Accelerating shipments or holding the books open for sales made subsequent to the end of the accounting period
- Recognizing revenue for transactions that do not actually qualify as sales, such as consignment sales not yet sold to the end user, sales with special conditions, certain bill-and-hold transactions, products shipped for trial or evaluation purposes
- Executing sham sales transacted for the purpose of increasing sales volume, such as swaps or round-trip trades and related party transactions
- Overstating percentage-of-completion sales
- Failing to reduce gross sales for all appropriate adjustments from gross to net—that is, understatement of returns, allowances or discounts including prompt payment discounts, and product markdowns
- Recording fictitious sales

Inquiries into suspected improper revenue recognition usually begin with a review of revenue recognition policies and customer contracts. The auditor may consider the reasonableness of the company's normal practices and whether the company has done everything necessary to comply with them. For example, if a company customarily obtains a written sale agreement, the absence of a written agreement may be a red flag. The review may begin with a detailed reading of the contract terms and provisions. Particular attention may be focused on terms governing payment and shipment, delivery and acceptance, risk of loss, terms requiring future performance on the part of the seller before payment, payment of upfront fees, and other contingencies. A review for these issues as well as others is designed to focus on the general requirements for revenue recognition set forth in GAAP.

- The SEC has interpreted GAAP requirements in Staff Accounting Bulletin (SAB) 101, *Revenue Recognition in Financial Statements*,[8] as amended by SAB 104, which spells out four basic criteria that must be met before a public company may recognize revenue:
  - Persuasive evidence that an arrangement exists
  - Evidence that delivery has occurred or that services have been rendered
  - A showing that the seller's price to the buyer is fixed or determinable
  - Reasonable assurance of the ability to collect payment

SAB 104 echoes the recognition requirements originally listed in American Institute of Certified Public Accountants (AICPA) Statement of Position 97-2, *Software Revenue Recognition*,[9] which governs the software industry. SAB 104 states that whenever industry-specific authority exists, companies may comply with that authority rather than follow SAB 104.

TIMING

The auditor may also consider timing, particularly as it relates to the company's quarterly and year-end periods. In which periods were the sales agreements obtained? When was the product or equipment delivered? When did the buyer become obligated to pay? What additional services were required of the seller?

---

8. U.S. Securities and Exchange Commission, Staff Accounting Bulletin (SAB) 101, *Revenue Recognition in Financial Statements*, 17 CFR Part 211 (December 3, 1999), was updated by SAB 104: *Revenue Recognition, Corrected Copy*, 17 CFR Part 211 (December 17, 2003). SAB 104 revises or rescinds portions of the interpretative guidance included in Topic 13 of the codification of staff accounting bulletins in order to make this interpretive guidance consistent with current authoritative accounting and auditing guidance and SEC rules and regulations. The principal revisions relate to the rescission of material no longer necessary because of private-sector developments in U.S. generally accepted accounting principles. It also rescinds the document *Revenue Recognition in Financial Statements: Frequently Asked Questions and Answers*, issued in conjunction with Topic 13. Selected portions of that document have been incorporated into Topic 13. While we recognize that many in the accounting profession refer to SAB 101 as the source of SEC guidance on revenue recognition, throughout this book we will refer to SAB 104 because it incorporates and amends SAB 101 for recent developments in the profession. The codified text of SABs 101 and 104 are available on the SEC Web site at http://www.sec.gov/interps/account/sabcodet13.htm, *SEC Staff Accounting Bulletin: Codification of Staff Accounting Bulletins, Topic 13: Revenue Recognition*.

9. American Institute of Certified Public Accountants, Statement of Position (SOP) 97-2, October 27, 1997.

As these questions suggest, the timing of transactions can be manipulated to accelerate revenue recognition. When the timing of recognition is manipulated, the offending company may be facing:

- Pressure to meet revenue targets as the accounting period—that is, the quarter—comes to a close
- A known or expected shortfall of sales transactions actually consummated through period end
- The potential existence of sales that are expected to be consummated shortly after period end
- Opportunity either unilaterally or in collusion with customers—that is, counterparties—to alter the dating of these postperiod end transactions in order to make such transactions appear to have been consummated prior to the period-end close of business

Red flags in this area may include:

- Falsification or alteration of documents, including backdating of delivery or shipping documents
- Backdating or alteration of the dates of invoices
- Alteration or falsification of other dating evidence that might reveal the true date(s)—post–period end—of the arrangement or of delivery of the products sold or services rendered

Some examples of other dating evidence that may require alteration include:

- Facsimile dates such as on copies of signed contracts or other documents
- Management information system transaction record dating
- Sales registers or sales journals transaction dates
- Purchase order dates: it could be incongruent and difficult to explain that the date of a purchase order was later—that is, after period end—than the purported dates falsely entered on contracts, invoices, and delivery documents.
- Dating of correspondence associated with negotiation and consummation of the transaction

A necessary result of any timing irregularity in accounting is that the current accounting period "borrows" revenues from the next period or periods, thus starting off these subsequent periods in the hole. If the next periods also have flat or declining actual sales—thereby exacerbating the revenue shortfall already created by the timing irregularity—even more premature revenue recognition accounting irregularities will be needed at the affected period ends to:

- Make up the shortfall caused by "lending" revenues to the prior period
- Cover the effects of any real decline in sales
- Achieve the expected level of sales growth

At a time when real sales are declining and such timing irregularity accounting is taking place, each period may require more and more fraudulent premature revenue recognition in order to keep up the appearance—and the fiction—that revenues are growing.

◆ REVENUE RECOGNITION DETECTION TECHNIQUES

Auditors have a variety of detection tools and techniques to use in the revenue recognition area, ranging from inquiry of relevant managers and substantive analytical tests of account balances to calling in forensic accounting investigators to investigate suspected improprieties. General detection techniques specific to revenue recognition may include the following:

- Discuss with both sales and marketing and financial personnel whether, how, and during which time period revenue targets were achieved; discuss, as well, sales that occurred near the end of the accounting period.
- Perform cutoff testing to determine whether sales were accelerated or decelerated:
  - Examine purchase orders, invoices, and shipping documents.
  - Compare shipping volumes with volumes billed.
  - Examine ending inventory.
  - Look for document pre- or postdating.
  - Make inquiries of employees in the shipping area; topics may include large shipments near period end, large returns, bill-and-hold transactions, and the like.
- Analyze large sales transactions, especially those occurring:
  - Near the end of the accounting period
  - With a new customer
  - With a related party
- Physically observe goods being shipped.
- Analyze new customers making large purchases:
  - Confirm physical location (rather than a post office box).
  - Consider comparing entity address with employee addresses.
  - Consider confirming existence through public records search.
  - Review postclosing transactions for evidence of invoicing and payment of invoice or, alternatively, cancellations or returns.
- Look for unrecorded and unprocessed returns, whether physically returned or shipped to an off-site warehouse, and those the company has made a commitment to accept.
- Inquire about side agreements—such as return rights, cancellation provisions, and other guarantees—and inquire of those outside the financial or accounting function as well as of large customers or customers placing so-called purchases late in the reporting period.
- Analyze sales returns or contract cancellations recorded subsequent to the end of the period.
- Send confirmations to customers covering quantities, dollar amounts, dates, and side agreements.
  - Consider oral confirmations in addition to written confirmations.
  - Follow up on unreturned confirmations or confirmations returned with discrepancies.

- Review non-system-generated—that is, manual—sales journal entries.
- Independently verify estimates for percentage of completion.
- Identify customers or employees and other related parties that are also vendors, and analyze transactions with those entities.
- Perform analytical procedures on relationships with sales, including disaggregated sales data. (See discussion later in this chapter.)

The auditor may consider substantive testing as a starting point and comb through materials to see if evidence supports the existence of a fraudulent scheme—for example, by requesting and reviewing contracts and support for invoices and deliveries and going on to confirm with customers the existence of accounts receivable and the amount of consigned goods. The auditor may also consider examining public records, when available, and performing background checks on or making site visits to customers, vendors, and other third parties to verify their existence.

In examining specific accounts, the auditor may consider supporting documentation, focusing in particular on round-dollar entries at the end of periods. An auditor who finds entries that are accruals may seek supporting evidence for material reversals and confirm the proper timing of the entries.

Absent a written agreement, auditors may consider other evidence of transactions, such as purchase orders, shipping documents, and payment records. They may also consider SAB 104 as well as the accounting literature for specific industries. Companies engaged in business over the Internet, for example, face unique revenue recognition issues. Emerging Issues Task Force (EITF) Abstract 99-19, *Reporting Revenue Gross as a Principal versus Net as an Agent*,[10] attempts to solve this problem by listing factors the SEC considers in determining whether revenue should be reported on a gross or net basis. Similarly, EITF 01-9, *Accounting for Consideration Given by a Vendor to a Customer (Including a Reseller of the Vendor's Products)*,[11] addresses such sales incentives as discounts, coupons, rebates, and free products or services offered by manufacturers to customers of retailers or other distributors. Being aware of the applicable authority may assist the auditor in recognizing violations.

When suspicions of improper revenue recognition exist, auditors may turn to forensic accounting techniques to dig more deeply. Those techniques may range from analytical procedures to analyzing round-dollar period-end journal entries by means of data mining. A forensic accounting investigator can assist the financial auditor in determining next steps to perform and the advisable sequence of steps.

While the aforementioned procedures focus primarily on the income statement and the sales side of the revenue recognition issue, the balance sheet side of the equation is an additional consideration. Overstatement of accounts receivable balances can be due to improper valuation and the booking of fictitious sales. Only the anticipated collectible value of accounts receivable should be

---

10. Financial Accounting Standards Board, EITF Abstract 99-19, issued 1999.
11. Issued February 2, 2002.

ANALYTICAL PROCEDURES TO IDENTIFY OR EXPLORE POTENTIAL REVENUE RED FLAGS

Analytical procedures, especially those performed on a disaggregated basis, often are useful audit tools in identifying potential revenue recognition red flags, and they can help the auditor assess fraud risk factors related to revenue recognition. However, analytics and tests are no substitutes for a good understanding of the client's business. Even seasoned auditors have been misled into believing revenue to be appropriate because they did not fully understand the business. A good question for auditors to ask themselves is, "Do this information and the results obtained make sense in light of the client's industry and business?" Comparing the client's performance against competitors' is a good way to start answering that question along the following dimensions depending upon the circumstance:

- Reviewing balances in revenue-related accounts for unusual changes
- Calculating the percentage of sales and receivables to the total balance sheet in the current period, comparing it with prior periods, and inquiring about any unusual changes
- Reviewing cash flows to determine if cash collected is in proportion to reported revenues
- Reviewing sales activity for the period and noting unusual trends or increases, particularly near the end of the period

    Significant, unusual, or unexplained changes in certain ratios may also signify areas for further pursuit:

- Increases in net profit margin (net income/total sales)
- Increases in gross profit margin (gross profit/net sales)
- Increases in the current ratio (current assets/current liabilities)
- Increases in the quick ratio (cash and receivables and marketable securities/current liabilities)
- Increases in the accounts receivable turnover (net sales/accounts receivable)
- Increases to days sales outstanding (accounts receivable turnover/365)
- Increases in sales return percentages (sales returns/total sales)
- Increase in asset turnover (total sales/average total assets)
- Increases in working capital turnover (sales/average working capital)
- Decreases in accounts receivable allowance as a percentage of accounts receivable (allowance/total accounts receivable)
- Decreases in the bad debt expense or allowance accounts

reflected on the balance sheet, and receivables should be written down for uncollectible accounts. Additionally, inflating accounts receivable with fictitious entries is a common scheme to overstate an entity's financial condition. Most frequently, when the fictitious receivables are booked, the corresponding credit is to sales. Falsified sales invoices are normally created to support the fictitious sale and receivable, often by creating phantom customers or hiding fake transactions in the records of large legitimate customers with voluminous activity. Because receivables have to be collected, written off, or disguised in some manner, such as re-aging, they are often the small but visible loose thread that unravels a revenue recognition fraud.

Detection techniques specific to receivables include the following:

- Making oral inquiries of customers regarding receivable balances
- Researching all discrepancies between the company's records and confirmation replies
- Reviewing subsequent collections
- Examining credit agency/analyst reports on key customers
- Researching all discrepancies between the subsidiary accounts receivable ledger and the general ledger
- Testing the aging of accounts receivable and, in particular, considering whether accounts can be re-aged
- Examining any manual or nonsystem journal entries affecting the receivables or sales accounts: Journal entries of this type are relatively uncommon means of recording sales.
- Investigating consistent or excessive patterns of partial payments, which may indicate kiting
- In the case of fictitious accounts receivable, techniques related to identifying fictitious sales would be applicable
- Performing analytical procedures on receivables (see Chapter 8)
- Testing receivables and inventory as a percentage of current assets—the higher the percentage, the higher the risk—and performing other analytical procedures on inventory, including the examination of data on a disaggregated basis (discussed later in this chapter and in Chapter 19)

SIDE AGREEMENTS

SAB 104 requires a definitive sales or service agreement. However, customer–vendor relationships are often complex and ever changing, and this can make it difficult for businesses to reach definitive agreements. Problems may arise when a company enters into an arrangement but later makes changes by means of a further written or oral agreement, sometimes executed outside normal control and reporting channels. In fact, managements have so often made modifications to basic or original agreements as a way of boosting sales figures that such modifications have become pejoratively known as side letters or side agreements. Side agreements created outside normal channels can be used to perpetrate a number of the schemes discussed in this chapter.

Depending on the business, the existence of numerous side agreements may be a red flag and might lead the auditor to conduct a detailed inquiry covering how, when, and why the agreements were entered into. If side agreements exist, determine whether they were prepared outside normal reporting channels. If so, that could be a potential red flag. Among the fraud schemes associated with side agreements are granting customers certain liberal or unconditional rights of return, allowing customers to cancel orders at any time, extending payment terms, and misappropriation schemes perpetrated by sales staff to inflate their commissions.

The case of Informix Corp. illustrates the improper use of side agreements.[12] Informix sold licensed software to companies, which in turn would resell the licenses to third parties. Consistent with then current GAAP for revenue recognition for software,[13] the company's written policy was to recognize revenue from the sale of licenses only upon receipt of a signed and dated license agreement. However, according to the SEC complaint, to meet its earnings expectations and those of financial analysts, management entered into numerous written and oral side agreements containing various provisions that violated GAAP. These agreements included allowing resellers to return and receive a refund or credit for unsold licenses, committing the company to use its own sales force to find customers for resellers, offering to assign future end-user orders to resellers, extending payment dates beyond 12 months, committing the company to purchase hardware or services from customers under terms that effectively refunded all or a substantial portion of the license fees paid by the customer, offering to pay for customer storage costs, diverting the company's future service revenues to customers as a means of refunding their license fees, and paying fictitious consulting or other fees to customers that would be repaid to the company as license fees.[14] These examples illustrate, in a single company, the broad spectrum of possible side agreements, though by no means do they exhaust the possibilities.

Detection of side agreements is a potentially difficult audit issue because the files and knowledge of them may not be resident in the centralized accounting departments that auditors most frequently deal with. Inquiry across a fairly broad range of company personnel may be the most important audit step. Auditors may inquire of management, accounting, salespeople, sales support staff, customer service representatives, and distribution managers as to the existence and treatment of side agreements that modify sales in any way. The auditor may also ask salespeople whether they are allowed or encouraged to use side letters or agreements to complete a sale and whether these agreements are made transparently in keeping with established reporting channels.

In addition to inquiring directly, auditors may review the company's return policies and seek to understand their rationale. In addition, they may choose to review a sample of contracts for side agreements and confirm with a sample of customers the terms of their contracts, including the existence or absence of side agreements.

LIBERAL RETURN, REFUND, OR EXCHANGE RIGHTS

Most industries allow customers to return products for any number of reasons. *Rights of return* refers to circumstances, whether as a matter of contract or of existing practice, under which a product may be returned after its sale either in exchange

---

12. *Securities Act of 1933* (SA) Rel. No. 7788; Securities Exchange Act of 1934 (SEA) Rel. No. 42326; *Accounting and Auditing Enforcement* (AAE) Rel. No. 1215 (January 11, 2000).

13. American Institute of Certified Public Accountants, Statement of Position (SOP) 91-1, *Software Revenue Recognition*, issued 1991. SOP 91-1 has since been superseded by SOP 97-2, *Software Revenue Recognition*, issued 1997, which retains the basic recognition criteria of SOP 91-1.

14. SA Rel. No. 7788; SEA Rel. No.42326; AAE Rel. No. 1215 (January 11, 2000).

for a cash refund, or for a credit applied to amounts owed or to be owed for other products, or in exchange for other products. GAAP allows companies to recognize revenue in certain cases, even though the customer may have a right of return. Statement of Financial Accounting Standards (SFAS) No. 48, *Revenue Recognition Where Right of Return Exists,*[15] issued June 1981, provides that when customers are given a right of return, revenue may be recognized at the time of sale if the sales price is substantially fixed or determinable at the date of sale, the buyer has paid or is obligated to pay the seller, the obligation to pay is not contingent on resale of the product, the buyer's obligation to the seller does not change in the event of theft or physical destruction or damage of the product, the buyer acquiring the product for resale is economically separate from the seller, the seller does not have significant obligations for future performance or to bring about resale of the product by the buyer, and the amount of future returns can be reasonably estimated.[16]

Sales revenue not recognizable at the time of sale is recognized either once the return privilege has substantially expired or if the aforementioned conditions have been subsequently met. Companies sometimes stray from the requirements of SFAS 48 by establishing accounting policies or sales agreements that grant customers vague or liberal rights of returns, refunds, or exchanges; that fail to fix the sales price; or that make payment contingent upon resale of the product, receipt of funding from a lender, or some other future event.

Payment terms that extend over a substantial portion of the period in which the customer is expected to use or market the purchased products may also create problems. These terms effectively create consignment arrangements, because no economic risk has been transferred to the purchaser. As noted at greater length later in this chapter, consignment sales cannot be recorded as revenue.

Frauds in connection with rights of return typically involve concealment of the existence of the right—either by contract or arising from accepted practice—and/or departure from the conditions of SFAS 48. Concealment usually takes one or more of the following forms:

- Use of side letters—created and maintained separate and apart from the sales contract—that provide the buyer with a right of return
- Obligations by oral promise or some other form of understanding between seller and buyer that is honored as a customary practice but arranged covertly and hidden
- Misrepresentations designed to mischaracterize the nature of arrangements, particularly in respect of:
  - Consignment arrangements made to appear to be final sales
  - Concealment of contingencies—under which the buyer can return the products—including failure to resell the products, trial periods, and product performance conditions

---

15. Financial Accounting Standards Board, Statement of Financial Accounting Standards No. 48, *Revenue Recognition Where Right of Return Exists.*

16. Id. par. 6.

- ○ Failure to disclose the existence—or extent—of stock rotation rights, price protection concessions, or annual returned-goods limitations
- ○ Arrangement of transactions—with straw counterparties, agents, related parties, or other special purpose entities—in which the true nature of the arrangements is concealed or obscured, but, ultimately, the counterparty does not actually have any significant economic risk in the "sale"

Sometimes the purchaser is complicit in the act of concealment—for example, by negotiating a side letter—and this makes detection of the fraud even more difficult. Further, such frauds often involve collusion among a number of individuals within an organization, such as salespersons, their supervisors, and possibly both marketing and financial managers.

In 1996, the SEC charged Midisoft Corp. with overstating revenue in the amount of $458,000 on transactions for which products had been shipped, but for which, at the time of shipment, the company had no reasonable expectation that the customer would accept and pay for the products.[17] The company eventually accepted back most of the product as sales returns during the following quarter.

The SEC noted that Midisoft's written distribution agreements generally allowed the distributor wide latitude to return product to Midisoft for credit whenever the product was, in the distributor's opinion, damaged, obsolete, or otherwise unable to be sold. According to the SEC, in preparing Midisoft's financial statements for fiscal 1994, company personnel submitted a proposed allowance for future product returns that was unreasonably low in light of the high level of returns Midisoft had received in the first several months of 1995.

The SEC determined that various officers and employees in the accounting and sales departments knew the exact amount of returns the company had received before March 1995, when the company's independent auditors finished their fieldwork on the 1994 audit. Had Midisoft revised the allowance for sales returns to reflect the returns information, the SEC concluded it would have had to reduce the net revenue reported for fiscal 1994. Instead, the SEC found that several Midisoft officers and employees devised schemes to prevent the auditors from discovering the true amount of the returns, including keeping the auditors away from the area at Midisoft headquarters where the returned goods were stored, and Midisoft accounting personnel altered records in the computer system to reduce the level of returns. After all the facts were assembled, the SEC took disciplinary action against a number of the company's executives.[18]

As with side agreements, a broad base of inquiry into company practices may be one of the best assessment techniques the auditor has regarding returns and exchanges. In addition to inquiries of this kind, auditors may use these analytics:

---

17. SEA Rel. No. 37847; AAE Rel. No. 846 (October 22, 1996).
18. See http://www.sec.gov/litigation/admin/3437879.txt and http://www.sec.gov/litigation/admin/3438876.txt for a significant part of the public record on this case.

- Compare returns in the current period with prior periods and ask about unusual increases.
- Because companies may slow the return process to avoid reducing sales in the current period, determine whether returns are processed in timely fashion. (This may require a visit with warehouse personnel.) The facts can also be double-checked with customers.
- Calculate the sales return percentage (sales returns divided by total sales) and ask about any unusual increase.
- Compare returns subsequent to a reporting period with both the return reserve and the monthly returns to determine if they appear reasonable.
- Determine whether sales commissions are paid at the time of sale or at the time of collection. Sales commissions paid at the time of sale provide incentives to inflate sales artificially to meet internal and external market pressures.
- Determine whether product returns are adjusted from sales commissions. Sales returns processed through the so-called house account may provide a hidden mechanism to inflate sales to phony customers, collect undue commissions, and return the product to the vendor without being penalized by having commissions adjusted for the returned goods.

CHANNEL STUFFING

Channel stuffing is the practice of offering deep discounts, extended payment terms, or other concessions to customers to induce the sale of products in the current period when they would not otherwise have been sold until later. The scheme has been widely used by companies that sell goods through mass-market outlets, such as department stores, home centers, or grocery stores. In some industries, the practice is known as loading and occurs at the end of virtually every quarter. The practice can have legitimate competitive purposes, such as blocking competitors' products, ensuring adequate supply of seasonal items, reintroducing products, or repositioning brands. However, the likely impact of the practice on current and future sales levels should be adequately disclosed to avoid presenting a misleading picture of company sales.

In December 1997, the Sunbeam Corp. established a program offering discounts, favorable payment terms, guaranteed markups, and the right of return or exchange on unsold products to any distributor willing to accept its products before year-end. According to the SEC, the company failed to disclose this practice in its form 10-Q. The SEC subsequently charged that the 10-Q was misleading and that the company had eroded future sales and profit margins by pulling them into the current period.[19]

One potential red flag that may point to channel stuffing is an increase in shipments—usually accompanied by an increase in shipping costs—either at or near the end of period. In such an instance, auditors may ask whether the goods

---

19. SA Rel. No. 44305; AAE Rel. No. 1393 (May 15, 2001).

were sold at steep discounts and then review customer contracts and side agreements for unusual discounts in exchange for sales and right-of-return provisions. They may also ask sales and shipping personnel about management's influence over normal sales channel requirements.

Customers offered deep discounts often purchase excess inventory, only to return it after the close of the period. The auditor may consider the amount of returns shortly after the close of a period compared with prior periods, as well as the margins on sales recorded immediately before the end of a reporting period.

Another potential red flag for channel stuffing may be signaled by increased commitments for off-site storage and subsequent increases in inventory reserves or inventory write-offs. Keep in mind that those inventory reserves may not be recorded until subsequent quarters or years.

BILL-AND-HOLD TRANSACTIONS

These schemes represent another common method of bypassing the delivery requirement. As its name implies, a legitimate sales order is received, gets processed, and is made ready for shipment. However, the customer may not be ready, willing, or able to accept delivery of the product at that time. The seller holds the goods or ships them to a different location, such as a third-party warehouse, until the customer is ready to accept shipment. The seller, however, recognizes revenue immediately upon shipment. The auditor may consider whether the seller has met—or is seeking to circumvent—certain SEC criteria[20]:

- The risk of ownership has passed to the buyer.
- The buyer has made a fixed commitment in writing to purchase the goods.
- The buyer has requested the transaction on a bill-and-hold basis and has a substantial business purpose for doing so.
- Delivery must be fixed and on a schedule reasonable and consistent with the buyer's business purpose.
- The seller must not retain any specific obligations under the agreement.
- Ordered goods must be segregated from the seller's inventory and cannot be used to fill other orders.
- The product must be complete and ready for shipment.

In addition to these criteria, the SEC recommends that preparers of financial statements consider the date by which the seller expects payment and whether the seller has modified its normal billing and credit terms for this buyer, the seller's past experiences with and pattern of bill-and-hold transactions, whether the buyer takes the loss if the goods decline in market value, whether the seller's custodial risks are insured, and whether there are any exceptions to the buyer's

---

20. See U.S. Securities and Exchange Commission, *In the Matter of Stewart Parness*, AAE Rel. No. 108 (August 5, 1986); see also Financial Accounting Standards Board, *Statement of Financial Accounting Concepts*, No. 5, par. 84(a); see also SOP 97-2, par. 22.

commitment to accept and pay for the goods sold—that is, whether any contingencies have been introduced.[21]

Agreements that do not meet the aforementioned criteria may be considered potential bill-and-hold schemes, and auditors may take a close look at whether:

- Bills of lading are signed by a company employee rather than a shipping company.
- Shipping documents indicate excessive shipments made to warehouses rather than to a customer's regular address.
- Shipping information is missing on invoices.
- High shipping costs are incurred near the end of the accounting period.
- Large, numerous, or unusual sales transactions occur shortly before the end of the period.
- Current-year monthly sales have decreased from the prior year, possibly indicating the reversal of fraudulent bill-and-hold transactions in a previous period.

Confronted with those potential red flags, the auditor may inquire with management about bill-and-hold policies and interview any customers with bill-and-hold arrangements. The auditor may also inquire with warehouse personnel about so-called customer inventory's being held on the premises or in a third-party warehouse or shipped to another company facility. Finally, the auditor may ask shipping department or finance personnel if they've ever been asked to falsify or alter shipping documents.

If additional investigation is warranted, the auditor may review customer contracts to determine whether they comply with SAB 104. The auditor may also review underlying shipping documents for accuracy and verify the existence of transactions; compare shipping costs with those of prior periods for reasonableness; review warehouse costs and understand the business purpose of all warehouses or off-site storage owned or used by the company; confirm special bill-and-hold terms with customers, including transfer of risk and liability to pay for the bill-and-hold goods; and test reconciliation of goods shipped to goods billed.

The auditor may select a sample of sales transactions from the sales journal; obtain the supporting documentation and inspect the sales order for approved credit terms; compare the details among the sales orders, shipping documents, and sales invoices for inconsistencies; compare the prices on sales invoices against published prices; recompute any extensions on sales invoices; and tour the facility or warehouse and inquire of warehouse personnel about any held customer products.

In early 2003, the SEC charged Anika Therapeutics with improperly recognizing approximately $1.5 million in revenue from a bill-and-hold transaction. A distributor had placed orders with Anika for approximately 15,000 units of a product in April and July 1998. As part of the agreement, Anika invoiced the

---

21. Id.

distributor for the 15,000 units in September 1998—at a price of more than $500,000—but continued to hold the product at Anika's refrigerated facility until the distributor requested the product in March 1999. However, Anika recorded the revenue for this sale in the quarter ended September 30, 1998.[22] Under the SEC's ruling, the company had to restate its financial statements, and the SEC reached settlements with the company's CEO and chief financial officer, who are no longer with the company.

EARLY DELIVERY OF PRODUCT

Companies may circumvent the SAB 104 delivery requirement in a variety of ways, including shipping unfinished or incomplete products to customers; shipping before customers are ready to accept products; shipping products to customers who have not agreed to purchase them, often called soft sales; recognizing the full amount of revenue on contracts whose services are still due; and recognizing the full amount of revenue on fees collected up front. Under SAB 104, income may not be recognized under these circumstances because delivery has not actually occurred. On the receiving end, customers often return the unfinished product or demand more work (or rework) before payment is rendered.

Auditors may seek evidence of such circumventions by comparing returns in the current period and prior periods, comparing shipping costs in the current period and prior periods, and comparing shipping costs as a percentage of revenue in the current period and prior periods. They may also scrutinize the sales contract: In relation to delivery, when must payment be made? Which party bears the risk of loss on shipment? The audit or investigative team may then compare these contract terms with the requirements of SAB 104 and other accounting literature.

To extend the inquiry beyond the financial area, the auditor may make broad inquiries among personnel in shipping, in sales, and in the warehouse, seeking answers to the following questions:

In shipping:

- Were shipments made earlier than normal?
- Is any inventory in the warehouse documented as shipped?
- Was inventory shipped to addresses other than customer sites?
- Is there inventory being held for certain customers?
- Is inventory ever sent to off-site storage facilities?
- Were there any adjustments to shipping dates?
- Are there any consigned goods, and if so, where are they?

In sales:

- Are any shipments planned for arrival ahead of the customer's required delivery date?

---

22. SEA Rel. No. 47167; AAE Rel. No. 1699 (January 13, 2003).

- How often do sales personnel pick up product and deliver it to customers?
- Are there sales personnel with excessive amounts of "samples"?
- Do sales personnel have warehouse access?

In the warehouse:

- Are there any misstatements in the amount of merchandise the company ships or receives?
- Has there been destruction, concealment, predating, or postdating of shipping or inventory documents?
- Has there been an acceleration of shipments prior to the end of the month or year?
- Have there been shipments to a temporary site or to holding warehouses prior to final shipment to customers' premises?
- Are there any other unusual, questionable, or improper practices?

But the auditors' work does not necessarily end there. To investigate further any suspicions of early delivery, auditors might compare the purchase order date with the shipment date and determine whether sales personnel are paid commissions based upon the sale of product or upon collection. They might inspect shipping documents for missing, altered, or incorrect information and review customer logs or e-mail correspondence for complaints that goods were shipped before the customer was prepared to accept them.

When auditors narrow the focus to certain personnel they suspect of participating in an improper revenue recognition scheme, they may look into whether these people have outside related business interests. To pursue this line of inquiry, auditors can search public records on certain entities and individuals to determine whether shipments have been made to these outside business interests or their addresses.

PARTIAL SHIPMENTS

Many companies recognize 100 percent of revenue on an order, even if their shipments are partial or incomplete. The delivery requirement has not been met, however, if the unshipped amount is a substantial portion of the total order.

Consider the SEC's enforcement action against FastComm Communications Corp. in 1999.[23] As part of a financial-reporting-fraud sweep that generated 30 enforcement actions, the SEC charged FastComm with recognizing revenue on the sale of products that had been neither fully assembled nor functional and that had been shipped after midnight of the end of a quarter. The case resulted in enforcement actions against the company and its three top executives.

Auditing for partial shipments is similar to auditing for early product delivery. Auditors may look for numerous returns of incomplete products after the close of the period or for large, numerous, or unusual transactions occurring shortly before the end of the period. They may also consider examining invoices to

---

23. AAE Rel. No. 1187 (September 28, 1999).

determine whether all products ordered are listed and whether shipped or not. In the case of drop shipments, if such a shipment is partial, is the invoice to the customer also partial? Auditors may need to determine how the client ensures that all drop-shipped products are properly accounted for in the sales invoice process and also in payments received. Auditors may also consider reviewing customer complaints regarding incomplete shipments.

The auditor may inquire with management and sales personnel about policies and processes for billing partially filled orders. A review of shipping documents and a comparison to the sales journal may reveal what was booked as sales and what was actually shipped. And the auditor may want to talk to customers or review correspondence from them to determine whether there are complaints about partial shipments.

CONTRACTS WITH MULTIPLE DELIVERABLES

Another common scheme is to ship product or equipment to customers that are not obligated to pay until the goods are accepted. Common customer-acceptance provisions include the seller's obligation to install and activate products after delivery, to conduct product testing, or to train personnel in product use. Acceptance typically requires a seller to fulfill such terms substantially before delivery is deemed to have occurred. If a contract requires the seller to provide such multiple deliverables, the delivery is not deemed complete unless substantially all elements have been delivered, and the sales revenue may be recognized only then.

In an assessment of whether revenue can be recognized prior to delivery of all required elements, the criterion under GAAP is whether the undelivered portion is "essential to the functionality" of the total deliverable.[24] SAB 104 enumerates several factors that may be considered in determining whether remaining performance obligations are substantial or inconsequential.[25]

The SEC action against Advanced Medical Products focused on improper revenue recognition in connection with contracts that had multiple deliverables.[26] According to the SEC complaint, rather than shipping the product to the customer, Advanced Medical Products shipped products to its field representatives, who were responsible for installing the product and training the customer's employees. The SEC charged that the company incorrectly recognized revenue upon shipment to the field representatives. According to the SEC, this policy contravened GAAP because there was no economic exchange and because risk of loss had not passed to the customer. The software industry has been particularly susceptible to this scheme.

In addition to the general indicators listed earlier, auditors may consider confirming with major customers whether all services have been performed with respect to products purchased and received. For companies that use distributors

---

24. U.S. Securities and Exchange Commission, SAB 104 § II. Topic 13.A.3—*Substantial Performance and Acceptance*, Question 3.
25. Id.
26. SA Rel. No. 7327; SEA Rel. No. 37649; AAE Rel. No. 812 (September 5, 1996).

for their products, auditors may seek to determine whether the company forces a predetermined listing of SKUs (stock-keeping units) on its distributors—even without an order. In such cases, there may be a culture of forcing product out to distributors to make the numbers. One of the symptoms of this condition is a rash of returns from the distributors in subsequent months. Auditors can ask whether such returns get processed in timely fashion.

◆ IMPROPER ALLOCATION OF VALUE IN MULTIPLE-ELEMENT REVENUE ARRANGEMENTS

Multiple-element revenue arrangements are common in the software industry and in other industries in which sales of products are combined with sales of services. For example, a multiple-element arrangement might include the sale of computer software along with the sale of a software maintenance agreement and of services related to the installation and integration of the software products. Accounting rules may call for different revenue recognition treatments for each of these elements, as follows.

- Revenues allocated to the software product might be recognizable upon delivery, assuming the seller had no significant product-related continuing obligations.
- Revenues allocated to the maintenance agreement usually would be recognizable ratably over the term of the maintenance contract.
- Revenues allocated to services may be recognized as such services get provided. Thus, the timing and amounts of revenues recognizable depend on identifying the respective elements and understanding their accounting implications, and they thereafter depend on properly allocating the total sales price of the arrangement to such elements.

Both AICPA SOP 97-2, *Software Revenue Recognition*, and SAB 104 set forth rules for the allocation of revenues among the elements of a multiple-element arrangement. Essentially, such allocations must be based on the respective fair values of the elements, and these fair value estimates must be supported by verifiable objective evidence (VOE). The accounting rules do not permit mere reliance on stated—that is, list—prices, or on the prices agreed to by the parties to the multiple-element arrangement. The SEC's concern is that prices listed in a multiple-element arrangement with a customer may not be representative of fair value of those elements because the prices of the different components of the arrangement could be altered in negotiations and still result in the same aggregate consideration. The issue was dealt with in EITF 00-21, *Accounting for Revenue Arrangements with Multiple Deliverables*, par. 4.[27]

Fraud can be introduced into the process of allocating fair values among elements within multiple-element arrangements in one or more of the following ways:

---

27. U.S. Securities and Exchange Commission, SAB 104 § II. Topic 13.A.3., Question 4, Answer 2.

- Fabricating, altering, or otherwise manipulating VOE data
- Mischaracterizing the terms or nature of the elements that require deferred or ratable recognition of their allocated revenues—usually, by attempting to minimize the significance and related values of such elements and thereby increasing the value assigned to elements for which revenues can be recognized immediately
- Bifurcating the arrangement to make it seem as if the maintenance and/or services components were sold separately, at arm's-length negotiated prices stated in their bifurcated transactions, when in fact all of the subject elements were negotiated as a single deal and are interdependent
- Misstating the prices at which the elements were planned to be sold—in the case of new products for which VOE is not yet available
- Concealment or mischaracterization of the nature of up-front fees associated with deals. Under GAAP, many such fees are required to be recognized ratably over the term of the arrangement.

UP-FRONT FEES

Some companies collect payment in full up front for services provided over an extended period, such as in maintenance contracts. SAB 104 provides that up-front fees should generally be recognized over the life of the contract or the expected period of performance.

◆ IMPROPER ACCOUNTING FOR CONSTRUCTION CONTRACTS

GAAP provides for contract revenue to be recognized by using either the percentage-of-completion or completed-contract method. The percentage-of-completion method applies only if management can reliably estimate progress toward completion of a contract.[28] When management cannot provide such estimates, GAAP calls for the completed-contract method, which requires the company to postpone recognition of revenue until the contractual obligations have been met.[29]

The percentage-of-completion method is often subject to abuse. Some companies use this method even if they do not qualify for it. Companies can artificially inflate revenue by increasing the costs incurred toward completion, underestimating the costs of completion, or overestimating the percentage completed. Accounting irregularities in this area involve:

- Misstatement of the percentage of completion either by intentionally mismeasuring such or by falsifying or manipulating engineering and/or cost accounting records

---

28. See American Institute of Certified Public Accountants, Statement of Position (SOP) 81-1, par. 23.
29. Id., par. 30.

- Hiding cost overruns, which might require accrual as contingent losses and thus reduce profits related to the contract
- Misrepresenting the nature and collectibility of cost overruns by falsely stating that such are add-ons, or contract amendments, that will be realized as additional revenue when in fact either they are not or they are subject to dispute with the customer

The auditor may start by selecting a sample of contracts and confirming their original contract price; total approved change orders; total billings and payments; details of claims, back charges, or disputes; and estimated completion date. Next, the auditor may determine whether all incurred costs are supported with adequate documentation detailing the nature and amount of expense, examining closely the estimated costs to complete. Do they seem reasonable after a review of estimates and a comparison with actual costs incurred after the balance sheet date? Are the underlying assumptions about estimated costs reasonable?

As further steps, the auditor may:

- Ensure that all contracts have been approved by appropriate personnel.
- Review unapproved change orders.
- Identify unique contracts and retest the estimates of cost and progress on the contract.
- Test contract costs to verify that costs have been matched with appropriate contracts and that costs have not been shifted from unprofitable contracts to profitable ones.
- Verify that losses get recorded as incurred.
- Review all disputes and claims.
- Visit the construction contract site to view the progress of a contract.
- Interview project managers, subcontractors, engineers, and technical personnel to get additional information on the progress of an engagement and the assumptions behind the contract.

In 1996, the SEC charged 3Net Systems with improperly recognizing more than $1 million of revenue in both 1991 and 1992 by misrepresenting to its outside auditors the degree to which certain work had been completed under certain contracts with existing customers when in fact 3Net had not completed any of the contracts and had not determined its costs to complete them. According to the SEC complaint, the company had no means of reliably estimating progress toward completion, because it lacked the systems necessary to estimate and track progress on their development. The SEC charged that had 3Net used the completed-contract method for the contracts, the company would not have reported revenue in fiscal 1991, because it had completed none of these contracts by the end of fiscal 1991.[30]

---

30. SA Rel. No. 7344; SEA Rel. No. 37746; AAE Rel. No. 833 (September 30, 1996).

◆ RELATED-PARTY TRANSACTIONS

We noted earlier that related-party transactions bear a higher risk of including sham transactions. Transactions between related parties are often difficult to audit because they are not always accounted for in a manner that communicates their substance and effect with transparency. The possibility of collusion always exists, given that the parties are, by definition, related. Internal controls, moreover, might not identify the transactions as involving related parties. While related-party transactions may involve improper revenue recognition, they may also involve other parts of the balance sheet or income statement.

An auditor may encounter related parties that are known to some members of the company, even if the relationships are not properly disclosed in the books and records. The auditor may inquire about an individual's outside business interests—and then try to determine whether they are properly disclosed—and the volume of transactions, if any, occurring between the entities. If certain entities are under scrutiny, the auditor may consider requesting a public records check of the entity to see whether there are indicators of undisclosed ties to particular individuals.

Auditors may also focus on the relationship and identity of the other party to the transaction and on whether the transaction emphasizes form over substance. Common indicators of such related-party sham transactions include:

- Borrowing or lending either interest free or significantly above or below market rates
- Selling real estate at prices that differ significantly from appraised value
- Exchanging property for similar property in a nonmonetary transaction
- Loans with no scheduled terms for when or how the funds will be repaid[31]
- Loans with accruing interest that differs significantly from market rates
- Loans to parties lacking the capacity to repay
- Loans advanced for valid business purposes and later written off as uncollectible[32]
- Nonrecourse loans to shareholders
- Agreements requiring one party to pay expenses on the other's behalf
- Round-tripping sales arrangements
- Business arrangements whereby the entity makes or receives payments of amounts at other than market values

---

31. American Institute of Certified Public Accountants, Statement on Auditing Standards (SAS) No. 45, *Related Parties* (codified in AICPA Professional Standards—U.S. Auditing Standards—AU § 334), par. 3.
32. American Institute of Certified Public Accountants, Practice Alert No. 95-3, *Auditing Related Parties and Related Party Transactions*, issued November 1995 (updated through July 1, 1999), par. 3, bullet 8.

- Failure to disclose adequately the nature and amounts of related-party relationships and transactions as required by GAAP[33]
- Consulting arrangements with directors, officers, or other members of management
- Land sales and other transactions with buyers that are marginal credit risks
- Monies transferred to or from the company from or to a related party for goods or services that were never rendered
- Goods purchased or sent to another party at less than cost
- Material receivables or payables to or from related parties such as officers, directors, and other employees[34]
- Discovery of a previously undisclosed related party
- Large, unusual transactions with one party or a few other parties at period end
- Sales to high-risk jurisdictions or jurisdictions where the entity would not be expected to conduct business

When related-party transactions are detected or suspected, auditors have several places to start. They may search public records and conduct background investigations on customers, suppliers, other third parties, and other individuals to identify related parties and confirm the legitimacy of their businesses (see Chapter 17). They may do some data mining to determine whether transactions appear on computerized files (see Chapter 20). They may review documents of identified transactions to obtain additional information for further inquiry. And they may go on to any of the following steps and procedures.

- Search for unusual or complex transactions occurring close to the end of a reporting period.
- Search for significant bank accounting or operations for which there is no apparent business purpose.
- Review the nature and extent of business transacted with major suppliers, customers, borrowers, and lenders to look for previously undisclosed relationships.
- Review confirmations of loans receivable and payable for indications of guarantees.
- Review material cash disbursements, advances, and investments to determine whether the company is funding a related entity.
- Test supporting documentation for contracts and sales orders to ensure that they have been appropriately recorded.

---

33. See Financial Accounting Standards Board, Statement No. 57, *Related Party Disclosures*, issued March 1982.
34. See American Institute of Certified Public Accountants, *Accounting and Auditing for Related Parties and Related Party Transactions, A Toolkit for Accountants and Auditors* (December 2001).

- Discuss with counsel, prior auditors, and other service providers—to the extent confidentiality permits—the extent of their knowledge of parties to material transactions.
- Inquire whether management, owners, or certain individuals conduct business with related parties.
- Inquire about side agreements with related parties for right of return or contract cancellation without recourse.

Undisclosed related-party transactions are common. In some nations and industries, doing business with friends and relatives is commonplace. For global entities, even though there may be a requirement to disclose related-party transactions and business interests, there is no guarantee that that practice is being followed or even communicated at remote locations. Understand your client's industry and businesses. What may be sound policy in the handbook may not be practiced in some parts of the world.

◆ REVENUE AND RECEIVABLE MISAPPROPRIATION

Of course, it is not the revenue or receivable that is misappropriated; it is the cash that businesses ultimately collect. While virtually any asset can be misappropriated, more than 90 percent of asset misappropriation schemes involve the taking of cash.[35] Cash is misappropriated both as it gets paid to the company—generally, sales receipts or receivables collections—and as it gets paid out by the company in fraudulent disbursements involving primarily payables, payroll, and employee expense reimbursement. Here we focus on the taking of cash receipts in the revenue cycle.

While many frauds begin on the balance sheet, many educated fraudsters attempt to move that fraud to the income statement for two reasons. First, balance sheet accounts are currently subject to more scrutiny by auditors than are income statement accounts. Second, after at most 12 months, the income statement accounts will be closed out to one of the largest numbers on the balance sheet—retained earnings—never to be reviewed again. Fraudsters often attempt to hide the theft in either a large expense line item in which the amount stolen will be immaterial or by dispersing the theft among many expense line items so that it will not be material to any single line item.

Most frauds perpetrated in this manner are not the subjects of audit programs because there is little risk of material misstatement. While money was stolen, it was expensed, and the only risk of financial statement misstatement is misclassification on the income statement. Strange as it may sound, the financial statements are likely to be presented fairly and in accordance with accounting

---

35. Association of Certified Fraud Examiners, *2002 Report to the Nation on Occupational Fraud and Abuse* (Austin, Tex.: Association of Certified Fraud Examiners, 2002). Based on survey responses from 663 certified fraud examiners: approximately 90 percent of asset misappropriation schemes involve the theft of cash, and approximately 10 percent involve theft of noncash assets. The median size of a cash theft, however, was less than half that of a noncash theft.

standards. It is only when misappropriations like these get hidden on the balance sheet that they become problematic from the standpoint of financial statement materiality. In such cases, they need to be written off, which is exactly what the fraudster may have done to disguise the activity rather than to correctly account for the transactions. Whatever the motive, an uncollectible receivable write-off *is* the correct accounting.

REVENUES

Defalcation involving revenues has to do with cash, not credit, sales. These could be retail sales or purchase orders accompanied by payment. Payment could be in the form of either cash or check. When the incoming payment is in the form of a check, the perpetrator will need to alter the check (see the following discussion on check tampering) so that it becomes payable to himself or for his benefit, or he will need to endorse the check secondarily.

Revenues can be misappropriated through skimming or larceny. *Skimming* is the term used when cash receipts are taken before they are recorded in the accounting system; therefore, the sale never gets reflected in the company's books and records. In 2003, at least eight Southwest Airlines employees were accused of misappropriating more than $1.1 million by a variety of skimming techniques. In one method, a ticket counter worker saved an old ticket that may have been voided. The unmarked ticket was then sold to a cash-paying customer, and the employee pocketed the money.

Larceny is the term used when the cash receipts are taken after being recorded in the accounting system; therefore, the sale is reflected in the company's books and records. In the case of larceny, if the debit entry to the sales entry is cash, cash will not balance. More often, the debit entry will be to receivables so that cash remains in balance.

Analytical procedures represent one of the most effective detection techniques for asset misappropriation schemes, and the more disaggregated the review, the better. The analytical relationship that will reveal such a defalcation depends, of course, on the way the defalcation was perpetrated and recorded. Analytics related to possible revenue schemes include:

- Trend revenue on a monthly basis over time for evidence of a downward or flat trend when an upward trend was expected
- Cash that is decreasing in relation to total current assets
- Cash that is decreasing in relation to credit sales
- A decrease in sales accompanied by an increase in cost of sales
- A current ratio that has decreased significantly from prior periods
- Cash collections that are significantly less than reported revenues
- Trend revenue by employee over time if multiple individuals handle revenue payments
- Trend gross profit: if the sale is made but not booked, gross profit will be reduced

- Trend payments on accounts receivable: a decreasing trend in payments indicates receivables will grow and age
- Significant write-offs in the current period compared with the previous period
- Trend accounts receivable write-offs: if the sale is made and booked as a receivable, it may be written off rather than allowed to age and included in collection efforts
- Analysis of credit memos

Customer complaints may also be potential red flags for a hidden-revenue misappropriation scheme. If a customer payment is converted but the sale is made and recorded as a receivable, customer complaints will occur if the company attempts to collect a receivable when the customer paid at the time of order. Lapping receivables, as described later, are attempts by the fraudster to conceal these thefts. A gap in issued invoice numbers is another possible red flag. In one example involving a cash-intensive business, customer tickets— essentially, invoices—were not included in submitted paperwork, and the associated cash receipts from these customers were neither reported nor submitted. This resulted in gaps in customer ticket numbers, and these gaps were noticed and made part of the detection process. Other risk factors pointing to possible point-of-sale or point-of-cash-collection misappropriation schemes are:

- Lack of segregation of duties among the sales, receipts, and recording functions
- Poor controls over the completeness of the recording of sales
- A sharp increase in the average length of time that customer cash receipts are maintained in an account before being applied to customer's outstanding balance
- Periodic, large, or numerous debits or other write-offs to aged accounts
- Recorded customer complaints regarding misapplication of payments to customer accounts
- Forced account balances, such as overstatements of cash balances, that are made to match the accounts receivable balance
- Numerous or significant reversing entries or other adjustments that have caused the books or the register to reconcile to the amount of cash on hand
- Large or numerous debit adjustments to aged receivable accounts
- Finally, journal entries made to cash, which are extremely rare and would suggest the need for deliberate scrutiny

RECEIVABLES

As with revenues, cash remittances related to accounts receivable may be taken both through skimming and through larceny. A larceny of receivables—that is, receivables taken after the collection of the receivables has been booked— results in cash that doesn't balance. As a result, receivables larceny schemes are less common than receivables skimming schemes. A receivables skimming scheme, however, ultimately results in customer complaints when the company tries to collect a receivable that has already been paid. Many fraudsters use a lapping scheme to avoid or delay detection of the fraud. A lapping scheme starts with a skimmed receivable, whereby the cash paid to relieve the receivable is stolen and not recorded. To prevent the receivable from continuing to age, a subsequent cash payment from a different customer is recorded as a payment in place of the one converted. This crediting of one account with payment by another account must continue on an ongoing basis to avoid detection of the scheme. Each additional receivable stolen or used for covering another customer's account must be covered by subsequent receipts from other customers for the scheme to continue.

If a receivables scheme is suspected, confirmations of receivables balances will have heightened importance. It may be appropriate also to confirm balances orally and to request copies of canceled checks, front and back, from certain customers. The reverse side of a canceled check may show secondary endorsements from the company to the perpetrator, or to a shell company incorporated by the perpetrator, or to an accomplice. While many banks will not accept at the teller window such checks with secondary endorsements, if such checks are deposited through the use of an ATM or night deposit, they are not typically reviewed for secondary endorsements. A review of customer checks may also reveal that the checks—typically, the payee information—were altered, thereby allowing the perpetrator to negotiate the check.

FICTITIOUS SALES

A common technique is to create fictitious orders for either existing or fictitious customers. Recording a fictitious sale in a company's books and records is as simple as posting a credit to the general ledger. False supporting documentation is created to support the nonexisting sales or services never rendered. However, the fictitious account receivable that must be created in this scheme will never be collected. Eventually, this uncollected account receivable will age; that is, it will grow older and become 30, then 60, then 90, and eventually, 120 days—and more—past due. Long-past-due receivables attract attention; therefore, they need to be concealed.

One means of doing so is simply to write off the receivable in some future period. This method is based on the fraudster's expectation that future revenues and profits will be sufficient to permit such a write-off; thus, it is a form of timing irregularity. However, evidence of the original, fictitious transaction, as well as of the subsequent write-off, still remains in the books and records, and the reason for the write-off may be questioned. Another way to conceal the fraudulent transaction is to charge it to the account called Sales Returns and Allowances, with the explanation that the customer returned the products for some plausible reason. However, this concealment approach requires that:

- The allowance balance be sufficiently large enough to absorb such a charge, permitting reprovision of the allowance over future periods.
- The effect of the charge does not raise questions about the adequacy of the allowance and sales returns provisions recorded in prior periods.
- No one challenges the circumstances of the transaction or the subsequent product return.

POSSIBLE RED FLAGS FOR FICTITIOUS RECEIVABLES

- Unexpected increases in sales and corresponding receivables by month at period end
- Large discounts, allowances, credits, or returns after the close of the accounting period
- Large receivable balances from related parties or from customers with unfamiliar names or addresses or that have no apparent business relation to the business
- Receivable balances that increase faster than sales
- Organizations that pay commissions based on sales rather than the collection of the receivable
- Increased receivable balances accompanied by stable or decreasing cost of sales and corresponding improvement in gross margins
- Lengthening of aging of receivables or granting of extended credit terms
- Excessive write-offs of customer receivable balances after period end
- Re-aging of receivables
- Excessive use of an account called either Miscellaneous or Unidentified Customer
- A large unapplied cash balance
- An increased trend of past-due receivables
- Lack of adequate controls in the sales and billing functions

---

LAPPING

Yet another way to conceal the transaction is a form of kiting, or lapping, wherein collections from a legitimate customer transaction are diverted and misapplied to pay off the fictitious receivable balance. For example, the perpetrator steals the payment intended for customer A's account. When a payment is received from customer B, the thief credits it to A's account. And when customer C pays, that money is credited to B. Of course, this exposes the legitimate receivable to noncollection because it is unlikely that the legitimate customer will pay twice for the same purchase. Therefore, subsequent diversions and misapplications of collections must be done over and over again. Lapping tends to increase at exponential rates and is often revealed because the employee is unable to keep track of or obtain additional payments to cover up the prior skimming.[36]

Lapping, like all forms of kiting, is plagued by complexity and usually requires the notorious so-called second set of books to track all of the diversions

---

36. Joseph T. Wells, "Lapping It Up: A Skimming Method Doomed to Failure over Time," *Journal of Accountancy* (February 2002), 73-75.

and misapplications and keep a record of which legitimate receivables need to be covered by which misapplied collections. Unless a future reckoning is made by eventually writing off some receivable balance(s) in the amount of the original fictitious receivable, this type of scheme becomes a perpetual motion device, which at some point must grind to a halt. Compounding this obvious problem is the tendency of these kinds of frauds to grow through more and more fictitious entries requiring more and more deceptions to conceal their existence.

REDATING

There is yet another type of scheme wherein the receivable is redated to a more current date. This keeps the amount from being captured in the bad debt reserve. However, the receivable is still at risk of being selected by the auditors for confirmation.

Such schemes can often be detected by the same methods used in detecting premature-revenue-recognition schemes. Auditors may look closely at significant revenue adjustments at the end of the reporting period, unexpected increases in sales by month at period end, customers with unfamiliar names or addresses or with no apparent business relationship with the company, increased sales accompanied by stagnant or decreasing cost of sales and corresponding improvement in gross margins, evidence of the re-aging of receivables to keep fictitious amounts from attracting attention as they age, unusual charges to Sales Returns and Allowances, improvement in bad debts as a percentage of sales, and a decrease in shipping costs compared with sales.

Fictitious-revenue schemes tend to be relatively easy to investigate, once detected. The audit team may focus on accounting personnel to determine whether revenues are being recorded outside the normal invoicing process or standard monthly journal entries, whether journal entries have adequate and genuine supporting documents, and whether accounting personnel have been pressured to make or adjust journal entries or to create false invoices for existing or fictitious customers.

The auditor may also ask sales or shipping personnel whether they have noted with no reasonable explanation any unusually high levels of sales or shipments to customers or have noted any significant sales or shipments to unfamiliar new customers.

♦ INFLATING THE VALUE OF RECEIVABLES

Inflating the value of legitimate receivables has the same impact as creating fictitious ones. GAAP requires accounts receivable to be reported at net realizable value—the gross value less an estimated allowance for uncollectible accounts.[37] GAAP also requires companies to estimate the uncollectible portion of a receivable, and the preferred method is either to record periodically the estimate of

---

37. Financial Accounting Standards Board, Statement of Financial Accounting Standards No. 5, *Accounting for Contingencies* (March 1975), Appendix A, par. 22.

uncollectible receivables as a percentage of sales or of outstanding receivables or to use a calculation based on the aging of outstanding receivables.

Under the allowance method, bad debt provisions are recorded on the income statement as a debit to bad debt expense and as a credit to allowance for doubtful accounts on the balance sheet contrareceivable account. When all or a portion of the receivable becomes uncollectible, the uncollectible amount is charged against the allowance account. When receivables are recorded at their true net realizable value, the recording of a bad debt provision decreases accounts receivable, current assets, working capital, and, most important, net income.

Companies circumvent these rules by underestimating the uncollectible portion of a receivable. This artificially inflates the value of the receivable and records it at an amount higher than net realizable value. The overvaluing of receivables also serves to understate the allowance account, such that the provision is insufficient to accommodate receivables that in fact become uncollectible.

A related scheme involves not writing off or the delaying of the write-off of receivables that have, in fact, become uncollectible. These schemes usually are relatively easy to execute, given the subjectivity involved in estimating bad debt provisions. To investigate these possibilities, auditors review and understand the provision and determine its reasonableness by asking management and accounting personnel to explain the reasoning behind the amount.

Among the potential red flags that may surface are minimum bad debt provisions or reserves that appear to be inadequate in relation to prior periods, a history of extending payment terms to customers with limited ability to repay, a history of inadequate reserves for uncollectible receivables, deteriorating economic conditions or declining sales, deteriorating accounts receivable days outstanding, untimely or irregular reconciliations, net receivables (net of the allowance for a doubtful account) that are increasing faster than revenues, uncollectible accounts that have been on the books for extended periods but have not been written off, and recorded disputes with a customer that may potentially threaten the company's ability to collect. If auditors do identify some red flags, they may consider using some or all of the extended audit procedures discussed below.

♦ EXTENDED PROCEDURES

Their suspicions aroused, auditors may consider a number of extended procedures, which include but need not be limited to the following:

- Send confirmations to and/or inquire with customers that may be associated with suspicious transactions.
- Perform alternative procedures for confirmations not returned or returned with material exceptions, such as including a blank line on which the customer must list the amount of pending returns and/or consigned inventory.
- Review journal entries and supporting documentation and verify their accuracy.

- Identify amount of returns in subsequent periods.
- Identify sales that got reversed in the subsequent period.
- Inquire of sales and credit department personnel about changes in credit policies, reserve rates, or bad debt expense policies.
- Inquire about any pressure to grant credit to customers of questionable credit quality or to extend payment terms.
- Research publicly available information to verify the existence and legitimacy of customers. Follow-up visits to listed sites may also be prudent.

Consider the case of medical device supplier Boston Scientific Japan, which in fiscal years 1997–1998 recognized more than $75 million of revenue from allegedly fraudulent sales.[38] According to the SEC, sales managers leased commercial warehouses, recorded false sales to distributors, and shipped the goods to the leased warehouses. The distributors never paid for the goods, but according to the SEC complaint, Boston Scientific Japan masked this by issuing credits to them and then recording false sales of the same goods to other distributors without ever moving the goods out of the leased warehouses.[39]

The SEC also found that company employees even recorded sales to distributors that were not involved in the medical device business but had agreed to collude in the fraud. Some false sales were made to distributors that never resold any of the goods and never paid Boston Japan for any purported sales. Also, according to the SEC, the sales managers and the cooperating distributors further colluded to cover up false sales by falsely confirming to the company's auditors the legitimacy of the sales. The SEC record of this case shows that the commission reached a settlement with the company.[40]

In situations in which fraudsters attempt to tamper with and corrupt the receivables confirmation process, fraudsters may try to cover their tracks in one or more of the following ways:

- Talking the auditors out of confirming receivables by arguing:
  - The response rate is too low. So why not just review subsequent collections? Or perform some kind of overall analysis of receivables' aged balances? Or just review documentation of sales transactions, such as invoices and purchase orders?
  - Confirmations bother our customers.
  - Customer ABC Corp. is unable to confirm overall balances; they can confirm only individual invoices, and it is difficult or impossible for us to match our invoices to their invoice references, so let's call the whole thing off.
- Falsifying the population records—such as the accounts receivable subsidiary ledger—to exclude the fictitious balances, thus preventing them

---

38. SEA Rel. No. 43183; AAE Rel. No. 1295 (August 21, 2000).
39. Id.
40. Id.

from being confirmed. This approach also requires manipulating the data file so that totals include the amounts of the balances that were excluded, which in turn must depend on the auditor's not footing, or totaling, the subsidiary ledger's individual line items either manually or by use of an automated test program.

- Intercepting either the confirmations or the responses—and, in the latter case, altering the response. This in turn requires any one or more of the following:
  - Collusion with someone at the party being confirmed
  - Theft of or tampering with the mail—outgoing or incoming
- Deceiving the party being confirmed, such as by contacting such party, alerting the party to the confirmation request being sent, and telling a lie, like: "The balance was inadvertently stated as $X, when in fact it should have been $Y. Just ignore the confirmation and don't respond to it or any subsequent inquiries. And if you have any questions, don't call the auditors; call me."
- Lying to the auditors after the fact by misrepresentations along these lines:
  - The customer is wrong. Here is all of our documentation of the transaction; the customer obviously made a mistake.
  - The customer is right. The customer did pay that balance, and we inadvertently posted the collection to the wrong account. (This requires undoing some other misapplication of collections and hoping the auditors do not follow up, by confirmation, that customer balance.)
  - The customer is right. We improperly posted the original sales transaction, which should have been recorded to customer XYZ Corp. and not ABC Corp. (This also depends on the auditor's not following up by confirming that balance with XYZ Corp.)

Obviously, the least problematic way to corrupt the confirmation process is to alter the population from which any confirmation audit sample is to be drawn. Just as obviously, maintaining the fiction surrounding the original falsified revenue and receivable entries recorded in the general ledger also requires the creation of accompanying fraudulent documents and records, including:

- A fictitious invoice, purchase order, and delivery receipt
- Fictitious shipping documents and fictitious correspondence such as documentation of negotiation of the fictitious arrangement
- Fictitious entries to the general and subsidiary ledgers, to any applicable sales journal, to any inventory stock ledger if applicable, and to any shipping record
- Fictitious collections records
- If necessary, fictitious aged accounts receivables schedules and reports

Carrying out this scheme could be hard work for just one person. For that reason, any serious fraud scheme of this type usually requires collusion by others such as revenue accountants, the manager in charge of revenue accounting, the general ledger, accounts receivable subsidiary ledger accountants, or the accountant responsible for cash collections and their application to receivables balances.

◆ ROUND-TRIPPING

Round-tripping is another approach. It consists of the recording of transactions between companies and from which transactions there are no economic benefits to either company. For example, a company provides a loan for a customer so the customer can purchase product with no expectation that the customer will repay the loan. Such transactions are deemed completed for the sole purpose of inflating revenue and creating the appearance of strong sales.

Recently, round-tripping has occurred extensively in the telecommunications and oil and gas industries. In a practice known as capacity swapping, numerous telecommunications companies boosted sales volume by exchanging the rights of use of their fiber-optic networks with other telecommunications companies. The transactions were sometimes booked as income, although the swaps generated no net cash for either company.

Indications of round-trip-revenue frauds are:

- Complexity in the structure and rationale of the transaction
- Concealment of the true sources and uses of funds exchanged in the arrangement
- Attempts to disassociate the subject transaction(s) from other transactions on which the subject transaction(s) actually is (are) dependent
- Mischaracterization of the true relationships and rights and obligations among the parties

In 2002, the SEC began investigating the way in which Qwest Communications International and certain competitors, including Global Crossing, accounted for sales of fiber-optic capacity and whether it was proper for the company to recognize the revenue immediately.[41] Qwest sold capacity on its fiber-optic network to carriers and also purchased capacity from them. In each deal, both companies recognized revenue from capacity swaps and also what are known as indefeasible rights of use (IRUs), which allow another carrier or company unfettered use of the capacity over a long period of time. In some cases, the amounts of the sale and purchase were almost identical. According to the SEC, Qwest booked the revenue from these sales all at one time instead of deferring part of it over many years, although GAAP requires companies to record the revenue generated by an IRU over the time of the contract. The SEC concluded that

---

41. SA Rel. No. 8295; SEA Rel. No. 48559; AAE Rel. No. 1879 (September 29, 2003).

the effect was to boost Qwest's revenue by $1 billion in 2001 and $465 million in 2000.[42]

Since most round-tripping transactions involve companies in the same line of business, an auditor may want to review a list of the company's significant customers. If a customer is in the same line of business, the auditor may want to scrutinize the transactions for evidence of round-tripping. The auditor may also want to review the vendor list and compare it with the customer list. A company whose name appears on both lists might also be a sign of round-tripping. Intermediaries are sometimes used in such transactions as a way of masking the activity. For this reason, the auditor would do well to beware of companies named on both lists that do not appear to be customers or vendors. Round-tripping often occurs between related parties, and so the auditor might want to also scrutinize related-party transactions.

Clearly, companies determined to recognize revenue improperly have a wide range of techniques. Always keep in mind that reasonable assurance of payment is basic to revenue recognition. Some companies circumvent this by recognizing the full amount of revenue even though the customer has for some reason disputed payment. Auditors may determine which receivables are in dispute and if necessary, confer with the company's legal counsel to assess whether collection of the revenue is sufficiently certain to be able to be properly recognized.

◆ IMPROPERLY HOLDING OPEN THE BOOKS

Improperly holding open the books beyond the end of an accounting period can enable companies to record additional end-of-period sales that have been otherwise invoiced and shipped after the end of a reporting period. Standard cutoff testing often discloses such schemes, but auditors must be skilled in detecting manipulation of information systems. Direct inquiry of accounting personnel, billing clerks, and warehouse personnel may assist in determining whether the books have been held open past the end of the period. Computer forensics can also be used to ferret out the schemes.

According to the SEC, in 1993, the management of Platinum Software Corp. was concerned about the company's days sales outstanding (DSO)—the measure of the time a company takes to collect its receivables. DSO had apparently increased throughout 1993, in part because the company had improperly recognized revenue on contingent or canceled license agreements.[43] As a "cure," the SEC found that the company decided to record improperly the cash received after period end. On the company's balance sheet, management recorded as an increase in cash and a reduction in receivables as of June 30 some checks received in July 1993. Similarly, for the quarter ended September 1993, management included cash that the company received for about a week into October, resulting in a cash overstatement and accounts receivable understatement of

---

42. Id.
43. SEA Rel. No. 37185; AAE Rel. No.781 (May 9, 1996).

$724,000. The same pattern continued through December 1993, resulting in a cash overstatement and accounts receivable understatement of $3,463,000. The company was ultimately ordered by the SEC to cease and desist in this practice.

Companies may also hold open the books to capture additional shipments and thus recognize revenue prematurely. In a recent matter, forensic accounting investigators obtained the electronic daily sales summary used to report flash results to headquarters at the end of each month and quarter. While nothing untoward was evident from the printed version of the schedule, the entry for the last day of each accounting period could be seen in the electronic version to be composed of a sum of individual entries. When asked about these entries, the division controller's secretary promptly explained that each item in the sum represented the shipments on an additional day included in the accounting period. She explained that she needed this record of how many days the quarter had been held open because the company would never condone mistakenly reporting the same sale twice! She went on to say that she had to start the next month with the "correct" date.

◆ CONSIGNMENTS AND DEMONSTRATION GOODS

As noted previously, SAB 101 prohibits revenue recognition from consignment arrangements until completion of actual sale. The same criterion applies to products delivered for demonstration purposes.[44] In a typical consignment arrangement, neither title nor the risks and rewards of ownership pass from the seller to the buyer. Consignment sales and products shipped for trial or evaluation are examples of contingent events that must be converted into actual sales before revenue can be recognized.

Careful consideration is recommended regarding the terms, facts, and circumstances of any agreement in which the buyer has the right to return the product, in order to determine whether:

- The buyer does not pay the seller at the time of sale, and the buyer is not obligated to pay the seller at a specified date or dates.
- The buyer does not pay the seller at the time of sale but rather is obligated to pay at a specified date or dates, and the buyer's obligation to pay is contractually or implicitly excused until the buyer resells the product or subsequently consumes or uses the product.
- The buyer does or does not have an obligation in the event of theft or physical destruction or damage of the product; in other words, there is no transfer of risk.
- The seller provides all economic substance for the sale transaction through credit and right-of-return transaction terms.

---

44. U.S. Securities and Exchange Commission, SAB 101 § II. Topic 13.A.2., Question 2.

- The seller has significant obligations for future performance to bring about repurchase of the product by the buyer.
- The product is delivered for demonstration purposes.[45]

◆ SUMMARY

Financial reporting fraud involves revenue and receivable accounts more often than any other type of fraudulent scheme. This is unsurprising given the revenue and growth focus of modern securities markets. Theft of cash, often during the collection process from customers, is the most common form of asset misappropriation. This, too, is unsurprising given that cash is an easily converted asset. Based on these factors, SAS 99 recognizes that:

> Material misstatements due to fraudulent financial reporting often result from an overstatement of revenues (for example, through premature revenue recognition or recording fictitious revenues) or an understatement of revenues (for example, through improperly shifting revenues to a later period). Therefore, the auditor should ordinarily presume that there is a risk of material misstatement due to fraud relating to revenue recognition.[46]

45. Id.
46. American Institute of Certified Public Accountants, Statement on Auditing Standards (SAS) No. 99, *Consideration of Fraud in a Financial Statement Audit* (codified in AICPA Professional Standards—U.S. Auditing Standards—AU § 316), par. 41.

CHAPTER 11

FINANCIAL STATEMENT FRAUD: OTHER SCHEMES AND MISAPPROPRIATIONS

Jonny J. Frank

David Jansen

Jamal Ahmad

Alongside the well-populated universe of improper revenue recognition schemes is a parallel universe of asset overstatement and liability understatement, in which fraudulent schemes also abound. A direct relationship exists between overstatement of assets and understatement of liabilities and expenses, as many recent financial frauds have demonstrated. Among the most common financial statement frauds in these areas are the following: creating fictitious assets; manipulating the balances of legitimate assets with the intent to overstate value; understating liabilities or expenses; failing to record or deliberately underestimating accrued expenses, environmental or litigation liabilities, or restructuring reserves; misstating intercompany expenses; and manipulating foreign exchange transactions.

◆ ASSET MISSTATEMENTS

Aside from accounts receivable, discussed in Chapter 10, inventory is the most misstated asset, and cash is the most often misappropriated. Among the other types of assets commonly misstated are investments, fixed assets, leased assets, research and development costs, software development costs, advertising costs, and interest costs.

INVENTORY SCHEMES

The first report by the Committee of Sponsoring Organizations of the Treadway Commission (COSO) found that fraudulent asset valuations accounted for nearly half of the cases of financial statement fraud,[1] while misstatements of inventory accounted for more than half of asset valuation frauds. Generally, when inventory is sold, the amounts are transferred to cost of goods sold and included in the income statement as a direct reduction of sales. An overvaluation of ending inventory understates cost of goods sold and in turn overstates net income. Inventory schemes generally fall into three categories:

- Artificial inflation of the quantity of inventory on hand
- Inflation of the value of inventory by postponing write-downs for obsolescence, manipulating the unit of measurement to inflate value, underreporting reserves for obsolete inventory (especially in industries whose products are being updated or have a short shelf life), and changing between inventory reporting methods
- Fraudulent or improper inventory capitalization

Among the indicators of such schemes are a gross profit margin higher than expected, inventory that increases faster than sales, inventory turnover that decreases from one period to the next, shipping costs that decrease as a percentage of inventory, inventory as a percentage of total assets that rise faster than expected, decreasing cost of sales as a percentage of sales, cost of goods sold per the books that does not agree with the company's tax return, falling shipping costs while total inventory or cost of sales has increased, and monthly trend analyses that indicate spikes in inventory balances near year-end.

Inflation of Inventory Quantity

The simplest way to overstate inventory is to add fictitious items. Companies can create fake or fictitious journal entries, shipping and receiving reports, purchase orders, and quantities on cycle counts or physical counts. Some companies go so far as to maintain empty boxes in a warehouse. In one inventory scheme, the extra boxes were filled with bricks that matched the company's product in size and weight so that the fraud would not be discovered during the physical inventory count observation if an auditor happened to pick up, move, or weigh individual boxes or pallets.

The most effective way for the auditor to confirm inventory quantities and identify valuation issues is to observe the client's physical inventory, particularly when an inventory count is being performed. Generally accepted auditing standards say, "It is ordinarily necessary for the independent auditor to be present at the time of count and, by suitable observation, tests, and inquiries, satisfy himself respecting the effectiveness of the methods of inventory-taking and the measure of reliance which may be placed upon the client's representations about the quantities and physical condition of the inventories."[2] When auditors

---

1. Committee of Sponsoring Organizations of the Treadway Commission (COSO), *Report of the National Commission on Fraudulent Financial Reporting* (1987), 103.
2. American Institute of Certified Public Accountants, Statement on Auditing Standards (SAS) No. 1 § 331 (codified in AICPA Professional Standards—U.S. Auditing Standards—AU § 331), par. 11.

are not satisfied with the client's inventory procedures and methods, they must physically count the inventory themselves and test the transactions.[3] When inventory is stored outside the company site, such as in public warehouses, auditors may conduct additional procedures to confirm balance. Those additional procedures may include surprise visits to the off-site locations as well as inquiries to identify all off-site storage locations.

Among companies that have been found to have engaged in fictitious inventory schemes are Crazy Eddie, McKesson & Robbins, and ZZZZBest, but perhaps the best-known inventory fraud was the salad oil swindle of the 1960s.[4] An entrepreneur named Anthony DeAngelis rented petroleum tanks in New Jersey and filled them with seawater, with the exception of just one smaller tank, nested inside a larger tank, which he filled with salad oil. He was able to persuade auditors and lenders, including American Express, that the tanks contained more than $100 million in vegetable oil because the opening for the dipstick went into the little oil tank. DeAngelis used warehouse receipts confirming the existence of the huge inventory of vegetable oil as collateral for $175 million in loans. Using the borrowed funds to speculate on vegetable oil futures in the commodities market, DeAngelis was doing nicely until vegetable oil prices took a dive and he lost everything. The embarrassed lenders soon discovered the truth: they now owned tanks of seawater. The equally embarrassed auditors realized that DeAngelis and his accomplices had successfully misled them.

An auditor may consider operational factors to investigate suspicions of fictitious inventory. As in the salad oil case, this includes inventory that cannot be easily inspected physically or that is stored in unusual locations. It includes, as well, the following:

- Unsupported inventory, cost-of-sales, or accounts payable journal entries
- Unusual or suspicious shipping and receiving reports
- Unusual or suspicious purchase orders
- Large test count differences
- Inventory that does not appear to have been used for some time
- Large quantities of high-cost items in summarized inventory
- Unclear or ineffective cutoff procedures or inclusion in inventory of merchandise already sold or for which purchases have not been recorded
- Adjustment of entries that have increased inventory over time
- Material reversing entries to the inventory account after the close of the accounting period
- Inventory that is not subject to a physical count at year-end
- Sales that are reversed and included in inventory but not counted in the physical observation: For example, a company "accidentally" delivers a

3. Id.
4. See Norman C. Miller, *The Great Salad Oil Swindle* (New York: Howard McCann, 1965).

product to a customer, tells the customer it was a mistake, and requests that the customer send the product back.

- Excessive intercompany and interplant movement of inventory with little or no related controls or documentation

Keeping that salad oil dipstick in mind, we can see that even physical observation is not foolproof. A company can perpetrate fraud by:

- Following the auditor during the count and adding fictitious inventory to the items not tested by modifying the count sheets
- Obtaining advance notice of the timing and location of inventory counts so that it can conceal shortages by shifting inventory from locations not visited
- Entering on count sheets, cards, or scanners additional quantities that do not exist—even adding a digit in front of the actual count
- Falsifying shipping documents to show that inventory is in transit from one company location to another
- Falsifying documents to show that inventory is located at a public warehouse not controlled by the company
- Including as part of the inventory count certain consigned items or items held for customers

What can an auditor do in the face of such determined inventory fraud? Auditors may consider company policy on both frequency of and procedures for inventory counts, compare any dollar adjustments on the books with physical counts and explore the reasons for significant differences, ask whether all inventory shrinkages have been reported, observe inventory at third-party locations, conduct physical inventories at multiple locations on the same day, and make tests counts *from* the count sheets *to* the physical inventory.

Inflation of Inventory Value

Generally accepted accounting principles (GAAP) require that inventory be reported at cost or market value, whichever is lower.[5] Companies inflate inventory value for a variety of reasons, including the use of inventory as collateral for financing. Inflating inventory value achieves the same impact on earnings as does manipulating the physical count. Management can accomplish this simply by creating false journal entries designed to increase the balance in the inventory account. Another common way to inflate inventory value is to delay the write-down of obsolete or slow-moving inventory because a write-down would require a charge against earnings.

In response, auditors may gain an understanding of the items in inventory and their life cycles, particularly in the context of the relevant industry. During physical observation of the inventory, the auditor may look for and ask about older

---

5. Financial Accounting Standards Board, Accounting Research Bulletin (ARB) No. 43, *Inventory Pricing* (1953), chap. 4, statement 5.

items that might be obsolete. In industries with changes in product lines or technology or with rapid declines in sales or markets, few or no write-downs to market or no provisions for obsolescence may be possible red flags.

When an inventory valuation problem is suspected, the auditor may ask accounting personnel about inventory pricing policy and how they identify net realizable value markdowns. The auditor may ask management, accounting, and finance personnel about the company's historical patterns and whether there has been overvaluation. The auditor may determine whether accounting personnel have been asked to delay inventory write-downs because of obsolescence or other factors. In addition to looking for old or obsolete merchandise in the warehouse, the auditor may ask whether any stock is slow moving or damaged. The auditor may inquire about whether any stock is being sold below cost. And the auditor may step back, look broadly at the industry, and ask industry experts whether the products are salable and at what cost.

Fraudulent or Improper Inventory Capitalization

Companies sometimes seek to inflate inventory by capitalizing certain expenditures associated with inventory, such as sales expenses or general and administrative overhead. Amounts that are actually expenses are improperly reported as additions to the asset balance, thus artificially increasing inventory value.

Auditors and forensic accounting investigators may need to be familiar with both the company's capitalization policies and industry practice. If past accounting policies have been aggressive on capitalization, the auditor may have reason to investigate further. Finally, the auditor may look for changes to standardized cost amounts that increase the amounts capitalized to inventory.

Overstating ending inventory in order to understate costs of goods sold for the period has one main drawback: that period's ending inventory becomes the next period's beginning inventory balance. Thus, any such overstatement will cause the next period's cost of sales to increase by that amount. This usually means that inventory frauds must be recurring and must grow in size, unless their purpose is just to shift costs from one accounting period to the next.

IRREGULARITIES IN THE INVENTORY/COST OF SALES EQUATION

Cost of sales is computed as:		Irregularity
Purchases	XX	Decrease
+ Direct Labor	XX	Decrease
+ Overhead Costs	XX	Decrease
	XX	
+ Beginning Inventory	XX	Decrease
– Ending Inventory	(XX)	Increase*
Cost of Sales	XX	Net Decrease

---

* Increased ending inventory is achieved by overstating the count of goods on hand, by overstating the value assigned to such goods, or by understating the amount of reserves or write-downs.

INVESTMENT SCHEMES

Fraudulent investment schemes provide another method for a company to over-state assets by creating fictitious investments or deliberately overvaluing existing ones.

Auditors may gain an understanding of and familiarity with all of a company's investments and understand their classifications in order to spot possible red flags that may signal potential fraudulent practices. The auditor may be aware of the current market status of all investments and confirm that the books and records reflect all increases or decreases in such status. In addition, the auditor may question all classifications of securities to ensure that they are classified in a consistent manner rather than solely to recognize gain or to forgo recognizing loss. The auditor may also be wary of losses on securities held as available for sale that are accumulating in the other comprehensive income account. The company must eventually take a charge for these losses—either through a sale or through a permanent write-down. Evidence of accumulating losses may lead the auditor to conclude that management is intentionally delaying the recognition of such a loss.

Fictitious Investments

Similar to the creation of other fictitious assets, fictitious investments can often be spotted by missing support documentation, missing brokerage statements, or investments that are unusual (gold bullion, for example) or held in remote locations or with obscure third parties. Among the steps an auditor who has a concern regarding the validity of investments might take are to confirm the existence of the investment by physical inspection or by confirmation with the issuer or custodian and to confirm any unsettled transactions with the broker/dealer. Auditors may also review the minutes of board of directors' meetings and the company's treasury policies to ensure that all investments were authorized by the board and that company policy was followed in the trading of and investment in securities. In addition, they may review internal controls to ensure that the duties of purchasing, recording, and custody are adequately segregated.

Manipulating the Value of Investments

Companies can manipulate their financial statements by inflating the value of investments, misclassifying them, or failing to record unrealized declines in market value for those investments. GAAP requires that investments of debt securities—that is, bonds and other corporate paper—be classified as either trading, held to maturity, or available for sale.[6] Investments may be classified as held to maturity only if the holder has the positive intent and ability to hold those securities to maturity. Held-to-maturity securities are reported at amortized cost with no adjustment made for unrealized holdings gains or losses unless the value

---

6. See Financial Accounting Standards Board, Statement of Financial Accounting Standards No. 115, *Accounting for Certain Investments in Debt and Equity Securities* (May 1993), par. 6.

has declined below cost and is not expected to recover. In the latter instance, the security is written down to fair value, and a loss is recorded in earnings.[7] GAAP requires that investments be classified as trading if they are bought and held principally for sale in the near term. Investments not classified as trading or as held to maturity are classified as available-for-sale securities.[8]

Trading and available-for-sale securities are reported at fair market value and must be adjusted periodically for unrealized gains and losses to bring them to fair market value. Unrealized gains or losses from trading securities are included in income for the period. Unrealized gains or losses from securities held as available for sale are reported as a component of other comprehensive income.[9]

In contrast, equity securities can be classified only as trading or available for sale. Unrealized gains or losses from changes in fair market value are reported in earnings for trading securities and as a component of other comprehensive income for securities held as available for sale.

When a security is transferred from one category of investment to another, it must be accounted for at fair value. Securities transferred from the trading category will already have had any unrealized holding gain or loss reflected in earnings. For securities transferred into the trading category, the unrealized holding gain or loss at the date of the transfer must be recognized in earnings immediately. For a debt security transferred into the available-for-sale category from the held-to-maturity category, the unrealized holding gain or loss at the date of the transfer must be reported in other comprehensive income. The unrealized holding gain or loss at the date of the transfer that results from securities' being transferred from available-for-sale to held to maturity is reported as a separate component of other comprehensive income and is amortized to interest income over the remaining life of the security.[10]

Generally, auditors looking into investments may consider asking management about company policies regarding the recording of unrealized gains or losses on trading and available-for-sale securities. The auditors may also ask accounting personnel whether they have been asked either to record held-to-maturity securities at anything but amortized cost, or to not record all unrealized gains and losses in available-for-sale and trading securities, or to postpone a write-down of a debt security.

Misclassification of Investments

Companies can manipulate financial statements by intentionally misclassifying securities or transferring securities to a class that would trigger the recognition of gain or, conversely, postpone recognition of a loss. A company might, for example, misclassify a debt security as held to maturity to avoid recognizing a

---

7. Id., par. 7.
8. Id., par. 12 (a) and (b).
9. *Other comprehensive income* is generally defined as the change in equity of a business enterprise during a period from all transactions and events except those resulting from investments by owners and distributions to owners.
10. Financial Accounting Standards Board, Statement of Financial Accounting Standards No. 115, par. 15.

decline of value in the current period. Similarly, transferring a security from held to maturity to either trading or available for sale would permit the recognition of gains that had not previously been recognized. The treasury function commonly decides the classification at the time the security is acquired. Auditors may review any changes in classification for possible abuse.

RECORDING UNREALIZED DECLINES IN FAIR MARKET VALUE

Deciding whether to write down a security because of a permanent decline in value is highly subjective and ordinarily left to the discretion of management. Accepting a write-down results in a charge against net income. The auditor may consider whether management has inappropriately failed to record or has delayed the write-down of an impaired security in order to inflate income.

RECORDING FICTITIOUS FIXED ASSETS

Similar to the concept of recording fictitious sales or receivables, companies can record fictitious assets to improve the balance sheet, thus also inflating earnings. Among the possible red flags associated with this scheme are:

- Fixed assets on the books and records that do not have an apparent relation to the business
- Lack of a subsidiary ledger to record additions and retirements
- Lack of adequate policies and procedures to determine whether property and equipment have been received and properly recorded
- Lack of procedures to account for fixed assets that may have been moved from one facility to another
- Existence of a secondhand storage facility for fixed assets that may still have useful life but for some reason are not being used
- Lack of adequate written policies and procedures concerning the recording, retirement, and disposition of fixed assets
- Subledgers that do not reconcile to the general ledger

If auditors find any of the foregoing, they may:

- Tour the client's facility to review fixed assets and select certain fixed assets from the fixed-asset listing—especially new, significant additions—to physically confirm that they exist. The assets' serial numbers may be inspected, if possible.
- Determine that retired assets are no longer included in financial statements.
- Review internal controls to ensure that written policies cover retirement procedures, which may include sequentially numbered retirement work orders, reasons for retirement, and all necessary approvals.

DEPRECIATION AND AMORTIZATION

An easy way to inflate the value of an asset and correspondingly reduce period expenses is to extend the asset's depreciable/amortizable life. Depreciation is another area in which management is given leeway to choose any method, so long as that method allocates the costs to accounting periods over the useful life of the asset in a "rational and systematic manner."

Detection of such schemes begins with a review of depreciation policy. Most companies have written policies for depreciating assets, and the lack of a written policy heightens the potential for abuse. Similarly, recent changes to the depreciation policy may be scrutinized for both their purpose and the effect on assets.

Auditors who have suspicions may:

- Review the records of depreciable assets for unusually slow depreciation or lengthy amortization periods.
- Compare prior years' depreciation charges with the current year for reasonableness.
- Identify changes in policy that may affect the rate of depreciation and appear to boost earnings.
- Inquire into historical depreciation policies to determine the extent of their aggressiveness.
- Review a detailed list of fixed assets as well as the assigned lives of the assets—and then randomly select certain fixed assets and recalculate the net book value at reporting date based on the recorded life of the asset.

HANGING THE DEBIT

As every accountant knows, for every credit there must be a debit. When companies spend money or incur costs, they recognize the event by posting a credit to cash, accounts payable, or accrued expenses. The offsetting debit will recognize that either an asset has been acquired or an expense has been incurred. A favorite tactic of financial statement fraudsters is to record expenses as assets—that is, to hang the debit up in the balance sheet. The WorldCom case is perhaps the starkest example of how a company can inflate earnings through improper capitalization of expenses. According to the Breeden Report, the company's internal audit department discovered that management had categorized as capital expenditures in 2001 billions of dollars that were, in fact, ordinary expenses paid to local telephone companies to complete calls. The scheme enabled WorldCom to turn a $662-million loss into a $2.4-billion profit. Experience has shown that certain categories of costs are the likely targets of such schemes.[11]

SOFTWARE DEVELOPMENT COSTS

GAAP requires that companies treat as expenses those costs associated with developing software—up to the point of technological feasibility. Technological feasibility is established upon completion of a detail program design or, in its absence, completion of a working model. At that point, all software production

---

11. Richard C. Breeden, *Restoring Trust: Report to the Hon. Jed S. Rakoff, the United States District Court for the Southern District of New York on Corporate Governance for the Future of MCI, Inc.* (August 2003).

costs must be capitalized and subsequently reported at the lower of unamortized cost or net realizable value.[12]

Whether technological feasibility has been reached is a subjective decision and thus subject to abuse. Arbitrarily determining technological feasibility, management can manipulate income by increasing or decreasing the amount capitalized or expensed. Auditors may consult with company engineers, programmers, and other technical personnel in reviewing management's assertions that technological feasibility has been achieved.

RESEARCH AND DEVELOPMENT COSTS

On one hand, GAAP generally requires that R&D costs be expensed because of the uncertainty of the amount and timing of economic benefits to be gained from R&D. On the other hand, a company may capitalize materials, equipment, intangibles, or facilities that have alternative future uses.[13] The U.S. Securities and Exchange Commission (SEC) has expressed particular concern about mergers in which the acquirers classify a large part of the acquisition price as in-process research and development, thus allowing the acquirer to expense the costs immediately.[14] This practice also involves the creation of liabilities for future operating expenses.

The SEC took action against Pinnacle Holdings Inc.—arising from the latter's acquisition of certain assets from Motorola—after it found that Pinnacle had improperly established more than $24 million of liabilities that did not represent liabilities at the time of the acquisition.[15] The company entered into a settlement with the commission as a result of the enforcement action.

START-UP COSTS

As with R&D, GAAP requires all start-up costs to be expensed in the year incurred.[16] It is not uncommon for companies to label start-up activities as other costs in order to capitalize them.

INTEREST COSTS

One potential scheme in this area involves a company's continuing to capitalize interest after construction has been completed. Statement of Financial Accounting

---

12. See Financial Accounting Standards Board, Statement of Financial Accounting Standards No. 86, *Accounting for the Costs of Computer Software to Be Sold, Leased, or Otherwise Marketed* (August 1985).
13. See Financial Accounting Standards Board, Statement of Financial Accounting Standards No. 2, *Accounting for Research and Development Costs* (October 1974).
14. Arthur Levitt, "The 'Numbers Game'" (speech, New York University Center for Law and Business, September 28, 1998), www.sec.gov/news/speech/speecharchive/1998/spch220.txt.
15. See *In the Matter of Pinnacle Holdings, Inc., Securities Exchange Act of 1934* (SEA) Rel. No. 45135; *Accounting and Auditing Enforcement* (AAE) Rel. No. 1476 (December 6, 2001).
16. American Institute of Certified Public Accountants, Accounting Standards Executing Committee (AcSEC), Statement of Position (SOP) No. 98-5, *Reporting on the Costs of Start-Up Activities* (April 1998).

Standards (SFAS) 34, *Capitalization of Interest Costs*,[17] requires the capitalization of interest costs incurred during the acquisition and construction of an asset. The interest cost capitalized is added to the cost of acquiring the asset and then amortized over the useful life of the asset. The total interest cost capitalized in a period may not exceed the interest cost incurred during that period. Capitalization is no longer allowed when the cost of the asset exceeds its net realizable value.

ADVERTISING COSTS

In SOP 93-7, *Reporting on Advertising Costs*,[18] the American Institute of Certified Public Accountants provides that all advertising expenses must be expensed as incurred unless there is persuasive historical evidence that allows the entity to make a reliable estimate of future revenue to be obtained as a result of the advertising. In that case, the expenditures may be capitalized.

In 2000, the SEC charged America Online (AOL) with incorrectly amortizing for fiscal years 1995 and 1996 the subscriber acquisition costs associated with the manufacture and distribution of computer discs containing AOL software. The SEC asserted that the volatile, unstable nature of Internet businesses had made it impossible for AOL to predict reliably its future net revenues. Thus, the SEC concluded, the subscriber costs were more like advertising costs and required expensing in accordance with SOP 93-7. According to the SEC, AOL had reported profits for six of the eight quarters in 1995–96 instead of the losses it would have reported had these costs been expensed. The costs improperly capitalized amounted to approximately $385 million by September 30, 1996, when AOL decided to write them off. In November 2004, Time Warner proposed a settlement to the SEC regarding its investigation of AOL's accounting for these costs.[19] According to the SEC, in March 2005, Time Warner agreed to a $300 million dollar penalty, an antifraud injunction and an order to comply with a prior cease-and-desist order, and Time Warner will restate its financial results to reduce its reported online advertising revenues by approximately $500 million (in addition to the $190 million already restated) for the fourth quarter of 2000 through 2002 and to properly reflect the consolidation of AOL Europe in the company's 2000 and 2001 financial statements. Additionally, Time Warner will engage an independent examiner to determine whether the company's historical accounting for certain transactions was in conformity with generally accepted accounting principles (GAAP).

◆ UNDERSTATEMENT OF LIABILITIES AND EXPENSES

Understatement of liabilities and expenses is the mirror image of overstatement of assets, and auditors can use various analytical indicators to search for such schemes. Among them are:

---

17. Financial Accounting Standards Board, SFAS 34, Issued October 1979.
18. Issued December 29, 1993.
19. James Bandler and Michael Schroeder, "Time Warner, SEC Are Moving to Settle AOL Accounting Probe," *The Wall Street Journal*, November 24, 2004.

- An increasing current ratio (current assets divided by current liabilities) or quick ratio (cash plus marketable securities plus net receivables divided by current liabilities) from one period to the next
- Unexpected improvements in gross margins from one period to the next
- Change in inventory with no simultaneous increase in accounts payable or accrued expenses between periods
- A percentage of change in the accrued expense account that shows revenue to be increasing faster than accrued expenses

The auditor may also ask accounting personnel whether they have ever been asked to postpone expenses until a subsequent period. In addition, the auditor may:

- Review the expense ledger and perform a cutoff test to ensure that expenses have been recorded in the proper period and not postponed until a subsequent period.
- Review prior years' expenses and liabilities and look for unusual trends.
- Perform current or quick-ratio analysis, which may indicate the concealment of liabilities.
- Examine account detail, looking for unusual debits to liabilities that would have the effect of reclassifying an expense to the balance sheet and also of improving the current ratio. (Certain levels of current ratio may be required for debt covenant compliance.)
- Consider data mining to identify significant payments for further review and then determine whether the payment may have been capitalized.
- Review internal controls regarding recognition of expenses in the proper period.
- Review capitalized expenditures to determine whether they are more appropriately classified as expenses.

♦ OFF-BALANCE-SHEET TRANSACTIONS

A legacy of Enron's collapse has been to make the term *off-balance-sheet transactions* part of everyday business vocabulary. In off-balance-sheet transactions, a company retains the benefits of assets in a corporate vehicle not consolidated for financial accounting purposes. Such investments can typically appear in the asset section of the balance sheet as a single net line item, titled either Investment in Affiliate, or Retained Interest in Securitization, or some such term. Off-balance-sheet transactions enable the company to avoid showing the individual asset of the off-balance-sheet vehicle in the balance sheet and more important, the associated debt used for acquiring its assets. In other words, the company executing the transaction reports only its proportion of the *net* assets of the off-balance-sheet vehicle as an asset rather than the *gross* assets of the vehicle, including the vehicle's total debt and outside interests held by other parties. While this form of reporting technically would not change the *net* equity of the company executing the transaction, the consolidated balance sheet would show greater total assets and greater total debt. Thus, in executing an off-balance-sheet transaction, the company looks more financially attractive. Balance-sheet-dependent financial ratios are also affected. Debt-to-equity ratios will be higher, for example, and thus less favorable, under consolidation treatment than under nonconsolidation.

Historically, off-balance-sheet treatment has been used:

- For securitization transactions, in which financial assets such as receivables are sold to an off-balance-sheet vehicle, while the seller retains a subordinated interest in that entity
- For leasing transactions in which long-lived assets are acquired by an off-balance-sheet entity and the use of the assets is then conveyed to a third party through an operating lease
- In noncontrolling investments, in which assets or businesses are held by an entity that does not convey control back to the investors: One simple example is a jointly controlled joint venture; the assets and debt of that venture remain off balance sheet for at least one of the partner/investors involved.

◆ TWO BASIC ACCOUNTING MODELS

Before Enron's collapse, accounting rules relied on two basic models to determine whether consolidation treatment was proper. The first focused on voting control and required consolidation if one entity controlled another. This model was relied on heavily in situations in which the subject of the analysis was a business rather than a pool of assets and debt.

The second model was the special-purpose-entity (SPE) model. Factors typically indicating that a vehicle is an SPE are limited powers in the vehicle's charter or the housing of assets—not a business—for which there was a limited purpose and about which few decisions needed to be made. The potential for abuse generally occurred through:

- Manipulation in the determination of whether to apply the voting control or the SPE mode
- Manipulation in the application of the correct accounting model
- Overaggressive use of the wrong accounting model

After Enron's collapse, the Financial Accounting Standards Board expanded on the accounting guidance that governs when a company may include in its own financial statements the assets and liabilities of another entity. Financial Interpretation No. (FIN) 46, *Consolidation of Variable Interest Entities*, applies consolidation requirements to applicable entities created after January 31, 2003. The technical rules are complex but can be summarized briefly. The underlying principle is that if a business enterprise has the majority financial interest in an entity (defined as a variable interest entity, VIE), then the assets, liabilities, and results of the activities of the VIE should be included in consolidated financial statements with those of the business enterprise. Previously, one company has generally included another in its consolidated statements only if it controlled the entity through voting interests. The new rule changed that by requiring that a VIE be consolidated by a company if that company is subject to a majority of the risk of loss from the VIE's activities, or is entitled to receive a majority of the VIE's residual returns, or both. A company that consolidates a VIE is called the primary beneficiary of that entity.

In general, a VIE is a corporation, partnership, trust, or any other legal structure used for business purposes that does not have sufficient equity investment at risk to permit it to finance its activities without additional subordinated financial support. The interpretation is also applicable to an entity whose equity holders have neither the direct or indirect right to make decisions about its activities through voting rights or similar rights, nor the obligation to absorb the expected losses of the entity if they occur, nor the right to receive the expected residual returns of the entity. A VIE often holds financial assets—including loans or receivables, real estate, or other property.

FIN 46 places much emphasis on a risk-and-reward model of consolidation and contains a new scope test that serves to determine whether an off-balance-sheet entity is a VIE and thus whether the provisions of FIN 46 govern and require consolidation of the off-balance-sheet entity.

The test is composed of two key questions. The first asks whether there is sufficient equity in the entity. The second asks whether the equity has the proper characteristics. A no answer to either question means the entity is a VIE that must apply the new model and consolidate. To demonstrate whether an entity has enough residual equity among the equity holders to absorb expected losses—as defined by FIN 46—in most cases requires a demonstration that equity exceeds the expected losses, if any. If this is not so, then the entity is a VIE requiring consolidation under FIN 46. The second question asks whether the equity of the entity has certain characteristics that make it act like true residual common equity.

The scope test has a high degree of subjectivity. What is sufficient equity, as required by the rule? The rule creates a rebuttable presumption that an equity investment of less than 10 percent of an entity's total assets is not sufficient to permit an entity to finance its activities without additional subordinated financial support. One can rebut that presumption by demonstrating that the entity is currently financing or intends to finance its activities without additional subordinated financial support, that the entity has at least as much equity invested as other entities holding only assets similar in quantity and quality that operate without additional subordinated financial support, or that the amount of equity invested in the entity is greater than a reasonably reliable estimate of the entity's expected losses.[20]

If an entity is a VIE and thus within the scope of FIN 46, the rule focuses on which party to the transaction has a majority of the risks and rewards. In order to

---

20. Financial Accounting Standards Board, FASB Interpretation No. 46, par. 9.

determine who bears that majority, a projection of cash flow may be required. Such projections provide the occasion for a high degree of subjectivity—and manipulation.

These rules are too new to have resulted in any reported fraud cases. Obviously, hiding or disguising information from the auditor or the investing public is the easiest way for a company to keep assets and liabilities off its books or to inflate income. Another possibility, as mentioned earlier, is manipulation of the amount of equity reported in the entity to avoid coming under the provisions of FIN 46. Management might also manipulate the estimate of expected losses in its cash flow projections in order to obtain off-balance-sheet treatment. Manipulation can take many forms, such as failing to recognize impairments that would decrease expected cash flows. Auditors will need to consider the potential of these new schemes on a case-by-case basis.

◆ COOKIE JAR RESERVES

A variation on these overstatement and understatement schemes occurs when companies overstate the amount of provisions to cover the expected costs of liabilities such as taxes, litigation, bad debts, job cuts, and acquisitions. This may be done in years when a company is extremely profitable, so that it can afford to incur larger expenses. These so-called cookie jar reserves are then tucked away for management to reach into and reverse in future years when profits may slip and a boost to earnings is judged necessary.

Intentional underestimation of loss contingencies and loss accruals is another subjective area ripe for abuse. This can affect items such as allowance for doubtful accounts, litigation reserves, inventory reserves and/or lower-of-cost-or-market write-downs, warranty reserves, and impairments of long-lived assets.

Company managers estimate reserves, and the outside auditor judges whether the reserves are reasonable. Because there are no clear accounting guidelines, it is difficult for auditors to challenge company estimates. This creates the potential for abuse.

Be mindful of account descriptions. A title such as Miscellaneous Provision may be an indicator of a cookie jar reserve account. In a recent investigation, the external auditor asked the internal auditor to identify which account the company used when it needed to make the numbers. Without hesitation, the internal auditor cited the number of an account named Miscellaneous Provision. Through account analysis and collaboration with company employees, the external auditor determined that more than $7 million was in this account for use on a rainy day. The explanation provided by the company was that it had already met its goals of paying bonuses for the end of the period, and this account represented a reserve if needed for future periods.

In June 2004, the SEC charged Symbol Technologies, Inc., with a variety of offenses. The commission's complaint alleged that from 1998 through 2002, Symbol and certain former executives had engaged in numerous fraudulent accounting practices and other misconduct that had a cumulative net impact of over \$230 million on Symbol's reported revenue and over \$530 million on its pretax earnings.[21]

The SEC complaint alleged that executives engaged in a fraudulent scheme to inflate revenue, earnings, and other measures of financial performance in order to create the false appearance that Symbol had met or exceeded its financial projections. Among other fraudulent accounting practices, the former executives were charged with the fabrication and misuse of restructuring and nonrestructuring charges to artificially reduce operating expenses, create cookie jar reserves, and manage earnings. According to the SEC, the release of the cookie jar reserves into earnings improperly boosted earnings and were not disclosed to the public at the time.[22]

◆ IMPROPER AND INADEQUATE DISCLOSURES

To this point in the chapter, we have focused on financial statement fraud involving numbers, but a company can also misrepresent its financial condition through misstatements and omissions of the facts and circumstances behind the numbers. These might include descriptions of the company or its products in news reports, interviews, and annual reports; on Web sites; and in management discussions and other nonfinancial-statement sections of annual reports, form 10-Ks, form 10-Qs, other documents, other reports, and footnotes to the financial statements.

In these instances, management has perpetrated a fraud by not providing sufficient information to make an informed decision regarding the financial position of the company.

The Sarbanes-Oxley Act of 2002[23] attempts to correct many of the shortcomings of nonfinancial disclosures. Sarbanes-Oxley requires that CEOs and chief financial officers (CFOs) acknowledge their duty to establish and maintain "disclosure controls and procedures" (DC&P) and to confirm their effectiveness. *DC&P* is a new term that expands traditional notions of internal controls to include both financial and nonfinancial information. DC&P encompasses all of the information in the company's public filings, including market share, information on the competitive environment, the regulatory environment, business goals, objectives and strategy, governance matters, planned acquisitions, customers, supply chain, and contracts. The law also requires prompt disclosure in plain English of all material changes in financial condition and of other significant company news, as well as disclosure of off-balance-sheet transactions as defined under the statute.[24] Realistically speaking, Sarbanes-Oxley is likely to

---

21. SEC Litigation Rel. No. 18734 (June 3, 2004).
22. Id.
23. 17 CFR Parts 228, 229, 232, 240, 249, 270 and 274 (August 29, 2002), § 302.17.
24. The statute requires companies to "disclose all material off-balance sheet transactions, arrangements, obligations (including contingent obligations), and other relationships of the issuer with unconsolidated entities or other persons that may have a material current or future effect on the issuer's financial condition, results of operations, liquidity, capital expenditures, capital resources or significant components of revenues or expenses."

lead to an array of new fraud schemes, as unscrupulous companies and individuals seek to circumvent the disclosure requirements and other reforms.

◆ MATERIALITY

No discussion of financial statement fraud is complete without taking up the issue of materiality. Companies—and sometimes auditors—have dismissed possible mistakes by concluding that they are not material to the financial statements. The issue of materiality draws on both legal and accounting principles. Guidance can be found from the U.S. Supreme Court, the SEC, the FASB, and academic literature. The Supreme Court has defined something as material if "there is substantial likelihood that the disclosure of the omitted fact would have been viewed by the reasonable investor as having significantly altered the 'total mix' of information made available."[25] The SEC, in Regulation S-X, defines *material items* as "those matters about which an average prudent investor ought reasonably to be informed" before purchasing the registered security.[26] The FASB has defined *materiality* to be "the magnitude of an omission or misstatement of accounting information that, in the light of surrounding circumstances, makes it probable that the judgment of a reasonable person relying on the information would have been changed or influenced by the omission or misstatement."[27]

Over time, companies and auditors had developed certain rules of thumb to assist them in determining when a matter might be material. One is that a misstatement or omission that represents less than 5 percent of some factor (such as net income or net assets) is not material. The SEC sought to settle the issue of materiality and remedy the potential for earnings management abuse with the 1999 release of Staff Accounting Bulletin (SAB) No. 99, *Materiality*.[28] SAB 99 provides guidance for preparers and auditors on evaluating the materiality of misstatements in the financial reporting and auditing process by summarizing and analyzing GAAP and federal securities laws and offering examples of what is and is not acceptable.

While the SEC does not object to the use of the 5 percent threshold for a preliminary assessment of materiality, it emphasizes that the final determination must be based on an analysis that considers qualitative factors rather than relying exclusively on a quantitative benchmark. SAB 99 notes specifically that certain qualitative factors can cause even quantitatively small misstatements to become material. It suggests that auditors must determine whether the misstatements:

- Arise from imprecise estimates

---

25. *TSC Industries, Inc. v. Northway, Inc.*, 426 U.S. 438, 449 (1976).

26. 17 CFR Part 210, Reg. § 210.1-02. Rule 1-02: " . . . (o) *Material.* The term 'material,' when used to qualify a requirement for the furnishing of information as to any subject, limits the information required to those matters about which an average prudent investor ought reasonably to be informed."

27. Financial Accounting Standards Board, Statement of Financial Accounting Concepts (SFAC) No. 2 (1980), 10.

28. Issued August 1999.

- Mask changes in earnings trends
- Cause financial statements to meet analysts' expectations
- Would change a loss to income or income to a loss
- Affect compliance with regulations or contracts
- Affect management compensation
- Arise from illegal acts

Auditors question the facts and circumstances of suspicious transactions. Auditors may, for example, make document requests that give the client information about materiality and scope, such as "Provide documentation for all transactions in account XX over $5,000." As a result of this communication, a fraudster on staff may decide to embezzle funds at transaction amounts of less than $5,000. While an individual transaction of less than $5,000 may fall below the auditor's scope, the amount of the embezzlement may be material as it relates to the financial statements. When there is any suspicion of this kind, the auditor may consider consultation with a forensic accounting investigator, who can offer assistance and guidance in the selection of additional procedures and in the performance of those procedures.

◆ DISBURSEMENT SCHEMES

A fraudulent disbursement is a payment of an entity's funds for a purpose that is not performed to benefit the entity. That is, the payment satisfies no obligation and serves no need of the entity. In contrast to schemes that steal cash at point of entry, fraudulent disbursement schemes involve theft of funds already entered into the books and records.

The audit objective with respect to cash is to verify the actual cash balance. As the actual cash balance gets reduced by fraudulent disbursements, typical audit procedures related to cash will detect only that the cash has been used and will not detect that the cash has been used inappropriately. Bank control procedures—such as positive pay, dual-signature requirements, and rejection of items with secondary endorsements—are not foolproof barriers to the creative fraudster. Positive pay systems, for example, do not prevent payments to a bogus vendor the fraudster has set up—payments the fraudster will convert.

Fraudulent disbursements, in order of frequency, are accomplished primarily through invoice schemes, check tampering, expense reimbursement schemes, and payroll schemes. Occasionally, such schemes are used in combination. Following is a discussion of detection techniques related to these schemes.

◆ INVOICE SCHEMES

In invoice schemes, which account for almost half of fraudulent disbursement schemes, fraudulent invoices are submitted to the company for payment. The invoices can be submitted either by a third party or by an employee. In many of these schemes, an employee creates a shell company and then submits fictitious invoices from the shell company to his employer for payment. Often the invoice is for consulting or other services, since there is no way to physically verify receipt of the invoiced item—as there would be for inventory or supplies. The employee perpetrator must have the ability to add vendors to the approved-vendor list, to approve vendor invoices, or to obtain the approval of a vendor invoice through altered or fictitious documents or through a supervisor who performs only a cursory review of documents requiring approval.

In one case, a public relations and investor relations officer used a false-invoice scheme to take from his employer $1 million per year for 10 years. He did this by having business associates of his wife fax him "invoices" for public relations services in Europe. As one of the five top officers in the company, he would approve the invoices and issue payment instructions via the company's regular disbursement process. Because of his seniority, no one ever questioned the fax copy of the invoice or the meager description of services. Since he was careful to budget the amount he would steal each year, he was never over budget and he escaped detection by budgetary controls. In fact, the payments were going to a series of antiques dealers throughout Europe to pay for inventory purchases by his wife's antiques shop. The court reduced his jail term to only a few years because of the substantial restitution he made from selling off the antiques.

While less common, another invoice scheme is one that also involves personal purchases with company funds. In cases of this kind, the invoices are legitimate in that they're from real vendors that actually provide goods and services on a recurring basis. The goods and services, however, are not provided for the benefit of the company but for the benefit of the employee.

The primary detection methods for invoice schemes are statistical sampling, data mining, and analytical procedures. Samples of source documents supporting purchases—usually the voucher file—may be selected and examined for irregularities. Possible red flags might include:

- No address given for the vendor or no physical address shown: only a post office box
- No invoice number
- Invoice numbers from the vendor that are sequential and with no gaps, thereby implying that the vendor issued invoices to no one other than the victim company
- No reference to a purchase order number, an order date, or the name of the individual placing the order
- No engagement letter or other documentation reflecting authorization for services
- No detail given about the goods or services provided
- No information available regarding a contact person or phone number for the vendor
- Numerous purchases at approximately the same dollar amount, especially if that amount is just below a particular authority approval level

- No indication of payment terms—or payment terms not in line with industry norms

For files containing irregularities, it may be appropriate to:

- Call listed phone numbers to see whether anyone answers the phone or whether an answering service responds.
- Check for directory assistance listings.
- Check for listings with the secretary of state and obtain information about the incorporators.
- Confirm the existence of the physical address.
- Check for credit reports with Dun & Bradstreet or a similar credit-reporting agency.
- Perform related procedures, such as data mining along the following lines:
  - Vendors with only a post office box for an address
  - Identical addresses in vendor files and in employee files
  - Vendors with similar names
  - Transactions for amounts invoiced just below an approval level
  - Recently added data

Analytical procedures may consist of performing trend analyses on various expense line items to identify any unexpected increases in spending categories, as well as trend analyses on vendors. Manual journal entries to expenses may be examined.

One scheme involving vendors with similar names was accomplished by an ad agency account executive whose agency processed about $500 million in media purchases and commercial production payments for a major consumer goods company. He opened a bank account in the name of William Morris, mimicking the name of the well-known talent agency William Morris Agency. The invoices supporting the payments were typed by his secretary and always returned to him because they required prompt processing so as not to delay the production schedule. The fraudulent disbursements were hidden in the large volume of payments processed for the client—until the client's account developed a permanent out-of-balance condition of several million dollars. Internal auditors were assigned to investigate. The scheme was discovered one day when the head of internal audit, on the point of entering the executive's office, was asked in the hallway by the CFO how the analysis of the William Morris invoices was going. The fraudster's secretary, overhearing the question, helpfully interjected that she could no doubt answer any questions because, after all, she had prepared them!

Another invoice scheme was perpetrated by employees of a retail operation. The employees at a store location submitted false invoices to corporate headquarters, generally for maintenance work performed on the store. The employees convinced corporate to send the checks back to the employees rather than directly to the vendors. The employees then deposited into the local bank account for the store the checks written to the vendors. The same amount of cash was then stolen. Both of these schemes might have been prevented if checks had been sent directly to vendors instead of being returned to the requesters.

A good deterrence technique is to continually purge inactive vendors. The easiest way to set up a vendor-based scheme is to take an inactive vendor from the approved listing and change the address to one controlled by the perpetrator. It is then easy enough to submit bogus invoices from this "approved vendor." Approvers may recognize a vendor they have not seen in a while, but they will almost never recognize the vendor's address. Thus, a change of address rarely draws the attention of those responsible for approving such payments. A former controller of a well-known hotel misappropriated more than $15 million in cash by setting up a dummy corporation and issuing phony invoices for services never rendered. The controller was able to get away with the scheme for more than six years because he maintained sole control over the hotel bank account and was able to submit phony invoices and issue checks or wire funds to the dummy corporation he controlled.

♦ CHECK TAMPERING

In check-tampering schemes, the perpetrator takes physical control of a check and makes it payable either to himself, to a shell corporation he controls, to an accomplice, or to cash. The scheme can include obtaining blank check stock or taking checks after they've been made payable to other parties and altering them so that they're payable to or for the benefit of the fraudster. In the case of preparing a check from blank check stock, the fraudster has to forge a signature or obtain a signature from a supervisor who performs only a cursory review of documents presented for signature. It is less common for the perpetrator to be the person with signature authority for the bank account. Altering checks that have already been prepared and signed generally occurs before the check is delivered to the intended recipient. It may also occur with returned checks—that is, checks returned due to undeliverable addresses or because there was an error in the check.

In one such scheme, the perpetrator intentionally double-paid vendors, then called the vendors and asked them to return the duplicate payment. Upon return of the check, the fraudster would alter it to be payable for his benefit. In a similar scheme, the controller of a lumber company wrote two checks for every tax payment. He added his own Social Security number to one of them before sending both of them to the U.S. Internal Revenue Service and would recover the money by claiming a tax refund on the one that showed his ID. He was detected by an audit inquiry directed to his accounting clerk as to why two checks to the same party on the same date would be necessary. When she replied that she had no idea but had always thought it odd, closer examination ensued and the scheme unraveled. These instances highlight the reasons to deface invoices so that they may not be used again; to reinforce a policy of paying only from original invoices, not copies; and to adequately segregate duties.

Check-tampering schemes may be difficult to detect through analytical procedures or data mining. Generally, the books and records reflect the intended and legitimate cash outflow. Complaints of nonpayment from suppliers whose payments were diverted by the fraudster are obvious red flags. Yet to detect check tampering, there is no substitute for visual inspection of the relevant documents:

- In the book balance for cash, be alert to voided or missing checks.
- Examine bank statements to make sure that voided checks did not clear the bank.
- In reviewing bank statements, carefully review the presented checks for possible alterations, forgeries, inappropriate payments, or other anomalies.
- Do not assume that a check with two signatures is unlikely to be part of a fraud scheme. It is not uncommon for both parties signing a dual-signature check to assume that the other party has carefully examined the veracity of the payment and underlying documentation, and, as a result, they each sign without review.
- Bank reconciliations may also be examined and all reconciling items analyzed.
- It may also be appropriate to request cutoff statements from the bank and perform an independent reconciliation as of that date.

One check-tampering scheme involving a private company was perpetrated through a variety of methods. The perpetrator, a financial officer of the company, had signing authority up to a maximum dollar limit and simply wrote checks for his benefit up to that limit. He also forged signatures on checks written for his benefit and altered the payee on checks with authorized signatures. In addition, the perpetrator set up a bank account in the name of the company, on which he was the only signatory. He could then deposit company checks into this account. Unwinding this fraud took a detailed manual review of all checks and supporting documents. Frauds such as these can drain millions from a company and go undetected for years, if not forever—or until the company files for bankruptcy.

◆ EXPENSE REIMBURSEMENT SCHEMES

Expense reimbursement schemes may seem like small change when compared with millions of dollars in fraudulently overstated inventory. Our experience is that if an employee is submitting false expenses, that scheme may be a potential red flag signaling other areas that may be subject to abuse. The same process applies for travel and expense reports as it does for purchase cards. Typically, purchase cards are used for smaller-dollar items; however, fraud may occur when no one examines the details of statements from purchasers.

When suspicions of false expenses arise, consider the following approaches:

- Select employees by focusing on those with high-dollar reimbursements. The 80-20 rule may apply here: 20 percent of the employees may account for 80 percent of the travel and related reimbursements.

- Rather than randomly selecting a few expense reports for one individual over the course of a year, consider reviewing a span of expense reports consecutively. In the course of examining a span of expense reports, you may consider exporting the expense detail to a computerized tool for sorting. Using this technique is also helpful when examining a group of employees. Doing so will enable you to identify:
  - Duplicate amounts: Is the same amount reimbursed more than once? Is it possible to submit an airline itinerary for reimbursement on one report, and then two weeks later submit the boarding pass for the same itinerary, and two weeks after that submit the proof of payment from the credit card statement? If you randomly selected expense reports over the course of a year, you would miss the duplicate submissions.
  - Pay attention to currency exchange. Does it make sense that someone traveling to Mexico would submit a restaurant receipt in U.S. dollars? The answer is no.
  - Do people in the company normally entertain on weekends? Sort and identify weekend travel and ask whether the pattern of entertainment makes sense.

- Compare hotel bills across the selection. In one investigation, a forensic accounting team noticed hotel bills that were generic and similar. Upon closer inspection, the local telephone number proved to be the same on a hotel receipt in Washington state as for a hotel in Washington D.C. The fraudster had created a hotel template and fabricated complete phony trips. In addition to the hotel phone bills, the fraudster booked airline tickets, submitted the itineraries, and later credited the airline ticket. When in doubt, call the hotel. You may discover that room 1304 does not exist at that location.

- Do the trips make sense? Is a salesperson traveling 800 miles while submitting meal charges for less than $25? Often, items of less than $25 do not require receipts. A salesperson can submit mileage and claim the remaining expenses as small cash items when the trip did not in fact occur.

- Are there tear-off receipts included in the documentation? If so, examine the receipts for consecutive numbering. The fraudster may have a pack of receipts, purchased from an office supply store, which he uses to document false expenses.

- Are expenses submitted with the top torn off, so that the name of the establishment is not on the receipt? Ask to see the credit card statement for the payee. If the telephone number still appears on the receipt, call to get the name of the establishment. One fraudster submitted many receipts with the establishments' names torn off; however, the telephone numbers remained. Rather than for a hotel or a meal, the purchases proved to be for shoes and jewelry.

- Does the company reimburse credit card expenses without first examining and approving the detail? If so, take a closer look at the details of credit card purchases.

- Are gifts for clients or expenses paid to clients appearing on the expense reports? Maintain a watchful eye for potential Foreign Corrupt Practices Act (FCPA) violations. In some instances, investigation has shown that an employee will pay a gift or bribe, such as digital cameras or airline tickets, through the expense report.

◆ PAYROLL SCHEMES

Payroll schemes represent the payment of wages or other forms of compensation in excess of that earned by the employee. This is most often accomplished through the use of phantom employees and the falsification of time cards. Analytical review of and reasonableness tests related to payroll expense could reveal irregularities. Data mining, an effective detection technique for payroll schemes, can include data interrogation queries to identify:

- Employees who have no payroll deductions to be distributed to taxing authorities: deducting taxes for bogus employees causes reconciling items to appear in form 941

- Employees without Social Security numbers—and to possibly take the step of verifying the accuracy of reported Social Security numbers as a way of identifying ones that may be bogus

- Common data between different employees, including addresses and electronic deposit information: one of them may be bogus

- Matching of payroll lists to employee lists maintained by the human resources department

- Names appearing on payroll records after their termination date

CHAPTER 12

WHEN AND WHY TO CALL IN FORENSIC ACCOUNTING INVESTIGATORS

Darren J. Tapp

W. McKay (Mac) Henderson

Chapter 7 discusses the many differences between the work of the forensic accounting investigator and the work of the financial statement auditor. A key question in any audit that identifies indicia of possible fraud is: When should the auditor, external or internal, consider reaching out for the forensic accounting investigator? Determining that *when* is the focus of this chapter.

Many forensic accounting investigators would take the position that the typical financial statement auditor may wait too long before calling in the forensic accounting investigator. But no savvy auditor reading these words will fail to notice the possibility of bias in the statement; after all, this book is written by a team of forensic accounting investigators. And so, part of the aim of this chapter is to demonstrate that the decision regarding when to call in the forensic accounting investigator can and must be viewed in an objective light. Before proceeding further, readers might find it helpful to review Chapter 1, where we introduce the concept of using forensic accounting investigators on audits when suspicions arise.

The thoughtful and efficient use of forensic accounting investigators often offers the right balance between conducting routine audits and investigating for possible fraud. A predicate must exist before an investigation is undertaken. A predicate is the totality of circumstances that would lead a reasonable, professionally trained, and prudent individual to believe a fraud has occurred, is occurring, and/or will occur. Predication is the basis for undertaking a fraud investigation.[1] It would be inappropriate—and a violation of the Association of Certified Fraud Examiners (ACFE) standards of professional conduct—to begin an investigation without sufficient predication.

---

1. Association of Certified Fraud Examiners, *CFE Code of Professional Standards*, § A.2: "Members shall establish predication and scope priorities at the outset of a fraud examination and continuously reevaluate them as the examination proceeds . . . "

Some auditors may call in forensic accounting investigators at the slightest suspicion of fraud. Year after year, they may bring in these forensic accounting investigators at the same client; their mind-set is to consult early and often—not only with forensic accounting investigators but also with industry experts and the risk-and-quality auditors who typically provide, from the center of major accounting firms, an internal consulting service for audit teams in the field. Auditors who rely on forensic accounting investigators at the first sign of possible fraud usually recognize that the skill set of fraud accountants differs from their own. Just like the actuary called in to evaluate the pension benefit accrual or the tax specialist who reviews the tax accrual, the forensic accounting investigator brings the experience and training required to properly evaluate suspicions of fraud. In our perhaps biased view, at the very first sign of fraud, consideration should be given to bringing in the forensic accounting investigator to evaluate.

At the other extreme are auditors who believe they possess the know-how to conduct forensic investigations but they may not have trained, or trained sufficiently in the field, and certainly lack sufficient experience to meet the circumstances that may arise as an investigation develops. When they grow suspicious of fraud, they often test, they often inquire, they often engage in extended procedures, they often inquire further—but they perhaps reach erroneous conclusions.

◆ TODAY'S AUDITORS ARE NOT FORENSIC ACCOUNTING INVESTIGATORS

Many outside the profession believe auditors have received extensive training in the skills of forensic accounting investigation. This is not so for most auditors. Undergraduate accounting programs do not, to the best of our knowledge, require courses in forensic accounting investigation, although some offer elective courses. The authors of this book are not suggesting that auditors be trained as forensic accounting investigators for all the reasons we have addressed, but principally because the discipline of forensic accounting investigation is an art requiring a different set of skills, training, education, and experience. What we expect to evolve in the education of future accountants is a curriculum that increases students' awareness of detection techniques as well as instruction that enables them to have an appreciation for the capabilities of forensic accounting investigators. In this way these accounting graduates—whether they find their place in the business world in operations, management, or internal audit or as independent auditors—will better know the footprints of fraud and when to call upon the forensic accounting investigators as illustrated in Exhibit 12.1.

◆ AUDITORS ARE NOT AUTHENTICATORS

Auditors are not responsible for detecting counterfeit documents. Any respectable fraudster with access to a color printer or copier can create a false paper trail that would deceive even an experienced auditor. We've seen situations in which entire sets of documents had been created—in some cases, overnight—to deceive

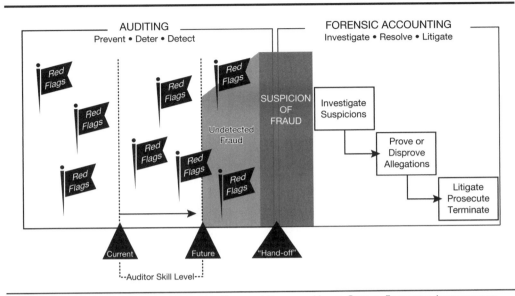

EXHIBIT 12.1   THE RED FLAGS OF POSSIBLE FRAUD: WHEN TO HAND OFF TO FORENSIC ACCOUNTING INVESTIGATORS

auditors. Audits involve the review of tens of thousands of documents by auditors who are not routinely trained or necessarily experienced in spotting altered or forged documents. The auditor's professional standards do not hold auditors responsible for detection if a fraud is concealed by fraudulent documents. However, auditors armed with a healthy dose of skepticism will question the source from which they obtain information, recognizing that that information could be fraudulent.

◆ AUDITORS HAVE LIMITED EXPOSURE TO FRAUD

Nothing short of repeated exposure to fraud can prepare one for effectively investigating frauds. Those who go on to become specialized forensic accounting investigators develop a keen sixth sense that supports the set of skills required for the resolution of complex fraud schemes.

When forensic accounting investigators launch a fraud investigation in an environment in which the perpetrator is unknown, they usually begin with interviews numerous enough to identify possible targets. During that process, they often hear such comments as: "Oh, it can't be Kathy. Kathy is one of our most loyal, long-term employees. She rarely takes time off, always works late, and helps others with their jobs. She's friendly, religious . . . " and so on. Such a commentary on Kathy's work ethic and personality has no impact on the forensic accounting investigator's attitude, which must remain one of professional skepticism. The great majority of friendly, hardworking employees are honest; they are what they seem. However, most fraudsters also seem to be honest. The word *con* is a shortened form of the word *confidence*. Fraudsters seek to gain one's confidence, and the best of them are very good at it.

No book or school can adequately teach these realities to anyone. However, conceptual studies, missing from current college curricula, could provide a foundation for on-the-job learning and effectiveness. No standard requiring professional skepticism can substitute for actual experience with deceit. Providing training to surface more indicia of fraud and having forensic accounting investigators to call upon when such evidence surfaces are the best solutions to the problem. However, not all frauds will be detected or investigated to their ultimate resolution.

◆ AUDITORS ARE NOT GUARANTORS

For most of the past century, many participants in business—as well as some courts that adjudicated business disputes—believed that the auditor "certified" a company's financial statements, thereby becoming the guarantor of those statements' accuracy and reliability. However, in the mid 1980s that understanding of the auditor's responsibility changed dramatically with the Treadway Commission report.[2] The commission found that responsibility for reliable financial reporting resides "first and foremost at the corporate level." The commission defined the auditors' role as "crucial but secondary" and explicitly stated that the outside auditors' role was not that of "guarantors of the accuracy or the reliability of financial statements."

Later, in accountant liability litigation, the courts began to reshape their view of the auditor's role. Notably, in *Bily v. Arthur Young & Co.*—a decision cited earlier in this book—the judge wrote as follows:

> An auditor is a watchdog, not a bloodhound. . . . As a matter of commercial reality, audits are performed in a client-controlled environment. The client typically prepares its own financial statements; it has direct control over and assumes primary responsibility for their contents. . . . The client engages the auditor, pays for the audit, and communicates with audit personnel throughout the engagement. Because the auditor cannot, in the time available, become an expert in the client's business and record-keeping systems, the client necessarily furnishes the information base for the audit. Thus, regardless of the efforts of the auditor, the client retains effective primary control of the financial reporting process.[3]

No doubt the investing public and others who rely on financial statements have been frustrated over the issue of fraud detection. Who can blame them? However, those who rely on financial statements cannot get what they want by

---

2. Commonly referred to as the Treadway Commission, since it was chaired by James C. Treadway Jr., a former commissioner of the U.S. Securities and Exchange Commission, the body's actual name was the National Commission on Fraudulent Financial Reporting. Its task was to investigate the underlying cause of fraudulent financial reporting, analyze the role of the outside auditor, and focus on the corporate structure and its possible effect on fraudulent financial reporting.

3. *Bily v. Arthur Young & Co.*, 3 Cal. 4th 370, 11 Cal. Rptr. 2d 51, 834 P.2d 745 (1992).

asking auditors to defy "commercial reality," as the judge brilliantly explains. As the public has clearly shown an interest in influencing all of those involved in the corporate reporting chain to improve accountability and performance, there must be greater appreciation for the skills of forensic accounting investigators.

◆ HISTORICALLY, AUDITS MAY HAVE BEEN PREDICTABLE

Many have suggested that the reason auditors did not detect in a timely manner the fraudulent schemes leading to some of the more significant corporate scandals was simply that the auditors' audit procedures had become predictable. There is no secret about what well-trained auditors examine in the course of an audit performed in accordance with generally accepted auditing standards (GAAS). Once the audit leader has identified the risk areas in a financial statement prepared by company management, the focus and scope of the planned audit are defined easily enough. However, the relatively routine, predictable character of audit planning creates opportunities for fraud. When it is easy to determine the scope of an audit, it is often easy to plan a fraud around it.

> *Predictability of auditing procedures.* The auditor should incorporate an element of unpredictability in the selection from year to year of auditing procedures to be performed—for example, performing substantive tests of selected account balances and assertions not otherwise tested due to their materiality or risk, adjusting the timing of testing from that otherwise expected, using differing sampling methods, and performing procedures at different locations or at locations on an unannounced basis.[4]

The landscape has changed rapidly for financial statement auditors. Arthur Andersen collapsed in the aftermath of the Enron scandal; a major health care provider has been accused of fabricating documents to deceive its auditors as part of a scheme to increase revenues; and other instances of accounting and audit abuse continue to emerge.

Auditors allegedly have been placed on the front line in the battle against fraud. They face the public and regulatory expectation that they will play a key and continuing role in restoring the integrity of financial reporting. This message is embedded not only in the language of Sarbanes-Oxley, but also in the new Public Company Accounting Oversight Board (PCAOB) modifications of the standards governing quality control and the independence standards and the rules that provide the framework for the audit, which are in process. These are discussed in Chapter 6.

As noted in earlier chapters, American Institute of Certified Public Accountants Statement on Auditing Standards (SAS) No. 99 outlines procedures the auditor must follow in assessing the potential risk of fraud and the impact on

---

4. American Institute of Certified Public Accountants, Statement on Auditing Standards (SAS) No. 99, *Consideration of Fraud in a Financial Statement Audit* (codified in AICPA Professional Standards—U.S. Auditing Standards—AU § 316), par. 50.

financial statement reporting. The new standard became effective for audits of financial statements for periods beginning on or after December 15, 2002. Among its many topics, SAS 99 highlights the need to bring in subject matter experts (SMEs)[5] to assist the audit team or to investigate allegations or indications of fraud. To forensic accounting investigators, the environment newly defined by SAS 99 is just the latest chapter in a lifetime's work of ferreting out fraud schemes and corporate misconduct via the use of tried-and-true techniques. Forensic accounting investigators can bring such skills and experience to any stage of the audit, and many firms are considering how best to effectively leverage these skills.

◆ POTENTIAL TRIGGER POINTS OF FRAUD

- *Anonymous allegations of fraud, whether by letter, e-mail, hotline, or anonymous call.* Whistle-blowers should be treated with utmost care. While seeking to take the allegations seriously, companies may wait too long to respond to whistle-blowers, who then believe they're not being taken seriously and who make a phone call to a third party such as the U.S. Securities and Exchange Commission (SEC) or the media. Every effort should be taken to respond to whistle-blowers immediately. Whistle-blowers should be encouraged to talk with a forensic accounting investigator who is trained in working with whistle-blowers. In such an interview, the forensic accounting investigator can form an opinion as to the probable validity of the allegations and can search for the reasons the individual has decided to come forward. The forensic accounting investigator knows there are occasions when people want revenge or attention and use the cover of whistle-blowing to satisfy their own needs. Although all whistle-blowers require immediate and thoughtful attention as required by Sarbanes-Oxley, there should be an attempt to test the allegations for validity—preferably, by face-to-face interview—before the decision is made to launch a full-scale investigation.

- *Discovery that a high-ranking official resigned due to known or possible illegal activities.* Unless there is evidence indicating an irregularity it is not usual that a forensic accounting investigator will be called in to perform an investigation. Although such an irregularity may emerge as an issue, the primary initial concern is that the executive may have acted improperly in other respects. A forensic accounting investigator may perform procedures—including interview and document examination and, very possibly, e-mail searches—to ascertain the likelihood of the allegations. If it is proved that the executive did in fact participate knowingly in

---

5. *SMEs* refers to professionals who occupy the top rung in the chain of expertise at many public accounting firms. Other terms in this book, such as *forensic accountant*, refer to professionals focused full-time on issues involving fraudulent scheme identification. Such professionals typically work under the direction of an SME whose expertise is forensic accounting investigation.

illegal activities, the forensic accounting investigator usually recommends that the audit team review its audit programs to determine areas in
which reliance was placed on the subject executive in the conduct of the
audit. Further, the audit committee should be advised that while the investigation is under way, another executive should step in to review relevant
prior-year representations so that current-year representations, including
Section 302 certifications, are appropriate.

If there is doubt about the integrity of the executive, especially about
the CEO or chief financial officer (CFO) who signs the management representation letter, the forensic accounting investigator is likely to search
for instances in which such executives worked *below* their level of authority and their expected management scope. For example, while interviewing an information technology director, a forensic accounting investigator
might learn that the company's CFO was oddly concerned about programming issues and, in fact, would come into the office on Saturdays and do a
little programming. Or the CFO had the habit of bypassing accounting
supervisors and going directly to the accounts payable clerk to order the
clerk to cut a check to a certain vendor. Facts such as these—should they
emerge—coupled with concerns that the executive has doubtful integrity,
could have a substantial effect on the audit program. Early consultation
with a forensic accounting investigator may avert problems later, when
the company's filing deadline is looming.

- *A client identified as the target of an investigation by a law enforcement
  agency.* Were the auditor to wait until the investigation is resolved before
  considering its implications for the audit, that would be a mistake. The
  length of time to complete an investigation is usually counted in months
  rather than weeks. In many instances, the company may not even know
  that the enforcement agency that launched the investigation has concluded it. Consider bringing in a forensic accounting investigator upon
  first learning of the investigation to discuss its implications.

- *A client who receives a subpoena from a law enforcement or regulatory
  agency.* A subpoena raises similar concerns as in the previous scenario. In
  this case, the forensic accounting investigator usually requests a copy of
  everything that is turned over to the agency. It would be a mistake to
  assume that the auditors have previously reviewed all of the subpoenaed
  documents, even if the auditors specifically requested and did in fact
  review what they believed to be the full selection of documents. The company may have withheld critical information. For example, the equipment
  sales contract the auditors reviewed may not have included a key rider
  allowing the customer to return the equipment under different terms than
  originally provided for in the contract, thereby disqualifying the sale for
  treatment as a sale under Statement of Financial Accounting Standards
  No. 13, *Accounting for Sales-Type Leases.* Obtaining another copy at the
  time of the agency's subpoena gives the auditor and forensic accounting

investigator a second bite at the apple. The previously missing rider or other documents may show up.

- *An auditor who believes that intentionally misleading verbal information has been provided by the client, or that requested documents have been altered, or that documents are being withheld intentionally.* Auditors may wish to confront the company personnel who they believe to be involved in the deception. If confronted, an individual may apologize profusely for creating such a misunderstanding and weave an explanation of some kind around the facts. The audit then continues, but the auditors may be left with the uneasy feeling that they have not received an honest response. Forensic accounting investigators use different techniques. For example, they may make use of indisputable facts about the suspected deception to see whether the individual lies or tells the truth in response to certain strategic questions.

- *Discovery that the client has suffered embezzlement—even of a small amount and even if the suspect is no longer on staff.* SAS 99, paragraph 76, specifically states: "If the auditor believes that misstatements are or may be the result of fraud, but the effect of the misstatements is not material to the financial statements, the auditor nevertheless should evaluate the implications, especially those dealing with the organizational position of the person(s) involved."

  Forensic accounting investigators, honed by years of experience, know that frauds often occur in the most unlikely situations and often are committed by the most unlikely individuals. Any misstatement that suggests the possibility of fraud should be investigated regardless of materiality. The cause may be innocent error. On the other hand, an accounting clerk may have perpetrated a small fraud, or the corporate controller may have a hand in it, and the seemingly small fraud may be only the tip of an iceberg. Suspicions of fraud, regardless of their materiality, require some level of investigation to resolve their implications.

- *Indications that a vendor may be fictitious.* Fictitious *anything* should be a concern. One fictitious vendor may not seem all that important—and it may not be; it may represent a small, unintentional error. But it may also be the footprint of a fraud perpetrated by top management and concealed for years. It is advisable to call in forensic accountant investigators when suspicions about possible fictitious vendors arise—for the simple reason that the range of possibility stretches from an innocent recording error to a very large fraud. If an event does indeed indicate that a fraud may have occurred, both GAAS and SEC regulations have specific requirements as to how to proceed when there is evidence of a suspicious act.

- *Indications of improper accounting for revenue or expenses such as sales recorded before completed and final, goods shipped before a sale is final, revenue recorded while the customer is still owed future service or goods, or apparently false revenues recorded.* The acceleration or outright fabrication of revenue and/or the deferral of expenses are among the most common financial statement frauds. While these issues may be investigated by auditors themselves, consultation with forensic accounting investigators may be helpful.

Other indications of fraud that may warrant consultation with a forensic accounting investigator include the following:

- Supplier refunds recorded as revenue
- Unbilled revenues or other accounts receivable being re-aged
- Bill-and-hold issues
- Recording vendor discounts as income
- Revenue recorded from self-dealing or asset exchanges
- Current expenses shifted into later periods
- Expenses improperly capitalized
- Liabilities concealed and not accrued
- Delayed asset write-offs
- Shifting expenses to a later period or advancing revenues

There are a number of other observable events that, while not necessarily indications of fraud, warrant appropriate warnings to the audit staff. The following conditions, either independently or in concert with other conditions, can be red flags of possible fraud. Where all of these conditions are concerned, auditors should proceed with a heightened level of professional skepticism in performing their planned audit procedures. Should indicia of fraud become evident, consultation with a forensic accounting specialist should be considered before proceeding beyond the scope of the audit plan.

Some of the observable events are as follows:

- Transactions that are not recorded in a complete or timely manner or that are recorded improperly as to amount, accounting period, classification, or entity policy
- Managers working below their level of authority
- Unsupported or unauthorized balances or transactions
- Last-minute adjustments that significantly affect financial results
- Evidence of employee access to systems and records inconsistent with the access necessary to perform authorized duties
- Significant unreconciled differences between control accounts and subsidiary records or between physical count and the related account balance that were not investigated and corrected on a timely basis
- Unusual transactions, by virtue of their nature, volume, or complexity, especially if such transactions occurred close to year-end
- Transactions not recorded in accordance with management's general or specific authorization

- Identification of important matters previously undisclosed by management
- Long outstanding accounts receivable balances
- High volumes of sales reimbursements and/or returns after year-end
- Suppliers' accounts with a high volume of debit and credit entries

Conflicting or missing evidential matter may also be a possible red flag suggesting fraud. These conditions include the following:

- Missing documents
- Unavailability of other than photocopied or electronically transmitted documents when documents in original form are expected to exist
- Significant unexplained items on reconciliations
- Unusual documentary evidence such as handwritten alterations to documentation or handwritten documentation that is ordinarily electronically printed
- Inconsistent, vague, or implausible responses by management or employees arising from inquiries or analytic procedures
- Unusual discrepancies between the entity's records and confirmation replies
- Missing inventory or physical assets of significant magnitude
- Unavailable or missing electronic evidence, inconsistent with the entity's record retention practices or policies
- Inability to produce evidence of key systems development and program change testing and implementation activities for current-year system changes and deployments
- Seriously incomplete or inadequate accounting records
- Contractual arrangements without apparent business purpose
- Unusual transactions with related parties
- Payments for services that appear excessive in relation to the services provided

Problematic or unusual occurrences between the auditor and the client may also be red flags of possible fraud. Such events include the following:

- Denial of access to records, facilities, certain employees, customers, vendors, or others from whom audit evidence may be sought
- Undue time pressures imposed by management to resolve complex or contentious issues
- Complaints by management about the conduct of the audit or management intimidation of audit team members, particularly in connection with auditors' critical assessment of audit evidence or in the resolution of potential disagreements with management
- Unusual delays by the entity in providing requested information
- Tips or complaints to auditors about alleged fraud
- Unwillingness to facilitate auditor access to key electronic files for testing by means of computer-assisted audit techniques

- Denial of access to key information technology operations staff and facilities, including security, operations, and systems development personnel
- Frequent disputes with the current or predecessor auditors on accounting, auditing, or reporting matters
- Unreasonable demands on auditors, such as unreasonable time constraints regarding completion of the audit or issuance of the auditors' report— sometimes accompanied by warnings about the audit fee structure and expected duration
- Formal or informal restrictions on auditors that inappropriately limit access to people or information or that curtail the auditors' ability to communicate effectively with the board of directors or audit committee
- Domineering management behavior in dealing with auditors, especially when there are attempts to influence the scope of auditors' work or the selection or continuance of personnel assigned to or consulted on the audit engagement
- Client personnel displaying a hostile or unreasonable attitude toward audit personnel
- Client engaging in opinion shopping
- Managers' lying to auditors or evasion in response to audit inquiries to the point that dishonesty seems a likely diagnosis

The ability of auditors to collaborate with forensic accounting investigators varies widely. Some do so comfortably and well, and some do not. Consider this case: An audit manager at a client happens to say to a forensic accounting investigator: "We were doing an audit at a plant in Mexico, and while we were down there, they got an anonymous letter about kickbacks and an outside business interest of the general manager. The client was concerned about costs and didn't want to bring in a forensic accounting investigator, but we were asked to make some inquiries. We didn't turn up anything, so in the end there was nothing to call you about."

Forensic accounting investigators know that many anonymous letters have some degree of merit. (See Chapter 16.) Even if preliminary inquiries "didn't turn up anything," it might have been safer and been better procedure to presume that something was going on at the plant in Mexico. Failing to bring in a forensic accounting investigation professional to dig deeper, the client now might have had a false sense of security because the auditors had made some inquiries. By letting the client influence their response, the auditors may have served it poorly and also put their own firm at risk.

Would calling in a forensic accounting investigator have cost more? Most likely, yes. If an auditor had been replaced with an experienced forensic accounting investigator, the resulting cost might have been $10,000 more. Is that too much to pay? If the preliminary inquiries uncovered further cause for suspicion, additional investigative procedures might have been necessary—at more cost. But weigh that cost against the magnitude of the direct loss to a company and the damage to reputation resulting from a fraud, especially if the fraud goes undetected for a significant period of time.

Consider the contrast between how a questionable situation might be handled—first without and then with a forensic accounting investigator. The two scenarios are hypothetical, but they run close parallels to plausible events: An accounting firm has audited the financial statements of a client company—a publicly held manufacturer and distributor—since 1990. During that time, the company experienced significant revenue growth while many of its competitors stagnated. In auditing the company's 1999 financial statements, the accounting firm found a large, rounded journal entry that materially increased revenue. The firm determined that the entry had been recorded manually, while most of the revenue entries were posted electronically from the client's billing system. The manual entry was recorded after the close of the field audit, one day before the company's earnings release.

The auditors questioned the client's controller, who said he had no support for this entry and referred them to the CFO. Both officers had previously worked at the auditing firm and were good friends who socialized with the engagement partner and the senior manager on the account. Questioned about the entry, the CFO said the entry had been made to match revenue with costs in light of entering into a large contract with a new customer after the billing system had been closed. The auditors documented that explanation in their working papers and requested additional support. Later that day, the controller provided a facsimile copy of a customer contract that supported the revenue entry, and he said the original contract had not yet been forwarded from the field to the corporate offices. The auditors documented this in their working papers, along with the facsimile copy of the contract.

Several years later, the SEC received an anonymous letter that accused the company of fabricating revenue. The company's board of directors reached out to the audit firm to investigate, and the auditors found the following:

- Revenues had been materially overstated each quarter through large, manual, and rounded journal entries entered after the close of the field audit.
- No original supporting documentation for these entries existed.
- The clerk who recorded the entries said the controller had provided on a self-stick note the amounts and accounts to record—with no supporting documentation.

While the auditing firm was looking into these matters, the controller and the CFO resigned. When the board of directors learned of the findings and the resulting restatements that followed, it asked, "Where were the auditors?" The audit firm was eventually fired and later sued in a shareholder class action for malpractice. During the ensuing litigation, it was alleged that the auditors could have uncovered the fraud in its infancy had they investigated the questionable transaction they identified during the 1999 audit. The suit also asserted that the audit firm's investigation had been compromised both by the social relationship between its partners and the corporate officers and by the $10-million fee the firm received from the client for consulting services. Ultimately, the audit firm paid a large sum to settle the lawsuit.

How might forensic accounting investigators have acted in this case? Imagine that after hearing the CFO's explanation of the large, rounded journal entry, the audit firm called in forensic accounting investigators, who suggested that the client's audit committee be notified of the transaction, the lack of documentation to support it, and the CFO's explanation. The audit committee then hired the forensic accounting investigators to investigate, including performing a review of general ledger transactions and the electronic files of the controller and the CFO. The investigative team obtained all general ledger activity from 1997 through 1999 and after consulting with the client's attorney on privacy issues, was able to obtain images of the personal computer files of the controller and CFO.

The forensic accounting investigators found similar large, rounded journal entries recorded late in the closing process for each quarter in 1999, a period when the industry was contracting. Unlike other journal entries made at corporate headquarters, no documentation was maintained in the central files to support these entries. A spreadsheet schedule on the controller's computer showed that the large, rounded entries matched the difference between system revenues and analysts' expectations. This document was also found to be attached to several e-mail messages between the two corporate officers.

Presented with these findings, the audit committee authorized additional investigative procedures. The forensic accounting investigators interviewed the two officials. The controller said he had been pressured by the CFO to record these entries and acknowledged that they were inappropriate. The CFO stood by his previous explanation and denied wrongdoing. Both men were placed on temporary leave and escorted from the building.

Subsequent interviews with employees of the accounting and finance departments produced invoices for payments made to certain vendors that had been authorized by the CFO. The forensic accounting investigators examined the company's vendor master file and found more than 10 vendors with the same post office box number. A review of the canceled checks to these vendors found that all of the checks had been deposited into the same bank account and that they totaled more than $1 million.

The audit committee notified the authorities and its insurer. An investigation led to criminal charges against the two officers. The successful investigation cemented the audit firm's relationship with the client.

◆ RELIANCE ON OTHERS

When concerns arise that require a company to undertake a 10A investigation, consider the possible advantages of early involvement in working with the company's audit committee and its 10A counsel to determine the possible financial statement impact.[6] While it is true that it is the company's responsibility to conduct the investigation, early involvement on the part of the auditor could be advantageous to the company's goals of resolving the allegations and concerns so that regulatory filings can be timely made and the company can get back to normal operations. Additionally, in order to fulfill their own 10A responsibilities, auditors may consider calling upon forensic accounting investigators to advise on the conduct of the investigation and whether or not its scope and procedures are adequate for the auditor's needs. This is usually done by shadowing the lawyers and forensic accounting investigators engaged by the audit committee. The practice of shadowing can provide greater comfort that there will be no surprises at the conclusion of the company's investigation.

In one such investigation, forensic accounting investigators received a call from an auditor, informing them of a recently concluded 10A investigation on one of his audit clients. The 10-K was due to be filed the following week. The auditor disclosed the nature of the investigation to forensic accounting investigators from his own firm. The investigation had been conducted by outside counsel, who had been retained by the audit committee. Outside counsel had chosen to conduct the entire investigation without the use of forensic accounting investigators. As the auditor recounted the allegations and the procedures performed by the law firm, the forensic accounting investigators on the call knew instantly that there were gaping holes in the investigation. The allegation was that the CFO had instructed divisional controllers to create false entries that inflated revenues. The CFO had contended in an interview that it was all a misunderstanding and that the error was already corrected. First of all, was an e-mail review performed? Yes. However, the law firm had accumulated the e-mail data by requesting the company's information technology department manager to "copy" e-mail folders. Experienced forensic accounting investigators know consideration should be given to collecting e-mail on servers and hard drives through forensic imaging, thereby capturing all deleted files. Merely copying the drives will not capture deleted files. Second, the law firm performed no assessment of the likelihood of involvement in the alleged scheme by anyone in the information technology department. The forensic accounting investigators told the auditor that due to these and other deficiencies in the conduct of the investigation, he should not rely on its results. "Then what am I to do?" asked the audi-

---

6. A 10A investigation refers to an outside investigation, that is, one conducted by individuals independent of management or the board of directors; from Section 10A, "Audit Requirements," of the *Securities Exchange Act of 1934* [Public Law 73-291, 73rd Cong., 2d sess., 13 (1934), sess. (January 23, 2002)] as amended by Section 301—"Public Company Audit Committees" of the *Sarbanes-Oxley Act of 2002* [Public Law 107-204, 107th Cong., 2d sess. (January 23, 2002)]. "Section 10A of the *Securities Exchange Act of 1934* (15 U.S.C. 78f) is amended by adding at the end the following:

(m) Standards Relating to Audit Committees—

... (5) Authority to Engage Advisers

Each audit committee shall have the authority to engage independent counsel and other advisers, as it determines necessary to carry out its duties . . . "

tor. The forensic accounting investigators suggested he contact his risk management group within the firm for further consultation on the various options to consider for possible resolution of the potential issues.

With proper planning, problems such as these may be avoided. The audit firm's own forensic accounting investigators can be called in under the scope of the existing audit engagement letter and set to work immediately. While it is certainly true that conducting an investigation into possible illegal acts is the responsibility of the audit committee, the auditor also has to be satisfied that the investigation is conducted in an appropriate way by competent people who know the requirements of 10A.

◆ CONCLUSION

The decision as to whether to bring in forensic accounting investigators is a judgment call. There is certainly no requirement in the professional standards of GAAS to do so. The benefits of consulting with forensic accounting investigators are just recently being evaluated and becoming better appreciated by auditing firms as well as the companies that use their services. If you were to ask investors and other stakeholders, they would be likely to say, "The more accountants sniffing around, the better." But even forensic accounting investigators would tell you this is not necessarily true. The profession should strike a balance between auditing to obtain "reasonable assurance" that the financial statements are free of material error and doing so in a cost-effective manner. It makes little sense to impose a tremendous cost burden on society to pay for "fraud audits" at every company. Since most companies' managements consist of honest people working for the good of the company and its stakeholders while complying with laws and regulations, conducting overly extensive and invasive audits does not make sound business sense. Yet the more that can be done to reduce the likelihood that a material fraud will occur and go undetected by the company or its auditors the better.

CHAPTER 13

TEAMING WITH FORENSIC ACCOUNTING INVESTIGATORS

Erik Skramstad

Forensic accounting investigators can make significant contributions to a financial crime investigation, provided that they can work effectively with the company's internal and external auditors, as well as with other constituents involved in resolving allegations or suspicions of fraud. In addition to a thorough knowledge of accounting and auditing, the forensic accounting investigator brings to bear a variety of skills, including interviewing, data mining, and analysis. Some auditors assume that auditing more transactions, with the use of standard procedures, increases the likelihood that fraud will be found. While this can prove to be true in some cases, when there is suspicion of fraud the introduction of competent forensic accounting investigators may be more likely to resolve the issue. This chapter explores how forensic accounting investigators can work effectively with internal and external auditors and considers the interests of other parties to an investigation.

Forensic accounting investigators work in a highly charged atmosphere and often present their findings in forums ranging from the boardroom and the courtroom to hearings before government agencies such as the U.S. Securities and Exchange Commission (SEC). Within the boundaries of an investigation, they typically deal with numerous constituencies, each with a different interest and each viewing the situation from a different perspective. These parties to the investigation may well attempt to influence the investigative process, favor their individual concerns, and react to events and findings in terms of individual biases. Forensic accounting investigators thus often have the task of conveying to all constituencies that the results of the investigation will be more reliable if all participants and interested parties work together and contribute their specific expertise or insight with truth-seeking objectivity. In the highly charged environment created by a financial crime investigation, the forensic accounting investigator usually bears much responsibility for displaying and encouraging level headedness.

All parties with a stake in the process—management, audit committee, auditors, and legal counsel—should consider including forensic accounting investigators in the process of decision making about the investigation. One of the key decisions, usually, is the degree to which the forensic accounting investigators can work with and rely on the work of others—specifically, the internal and external auditors. Another common decision is whether forensic accounting investigators—with their knowledge of accounting systems, controls, and typical fraud schemes—may be added to the team that evaluates the organization's business processes to strengthen the controls that allowed the fraud to occur.

Management may at first be inclined to push for a quick result because it feels the company will be further damaged if it continues to operate under a shadow. Senior executives may be unable or in some cases unwilling to see the full scope of issues and may attempt to limit the investigation—sometimes as a matter of self-protection—or they may seek to persuade the forensic accounting investigators that the issues at hand are immaterial. Whatever happened, it happened on their watch, and they may understandably be very sensitive to the forensic accounting investigators' intrusion into their domain. Any defensiveness on the part of management should be defused as quickly and as thoroughly as possible, usually through empathy and consideration on the part of the forensic accounting investigators. The party or entity engaging the forensic accounting investigators—for example, audit committee, management, or counsel—may be committed to a thorough investigation of all issues and is ultimately responsible for the investigation. The committee may engage forensic accounting investigators directly and look to them for guidance, or it may ask outside counsel to engage forensic accounting investigators, who usually will work at counsel's direction in fulfilling counsel's responsibilities to the audit committee. In some cases, the audit committee may need to work with two forensic accounting teams. One team, deployed by the external audit firm, gets charged with assisting the external auditors to meet their 10A responsibilities and provide advice on the adequacy of the investigation conducted by the company.[1] The other team, engaged by 10A counsel, is responsible for an investigation that assists counsel and the audit committee in determining whether there was an illegal act and, if so, what remedial action is needed. Many audit committees recognize that simply reauditing the suspect areas is unlikely to resolve the issues. They are also likely to realize that an overzealous witch hunt may alienate management and employees by implying loss of confidence in their competence or integrity. And deadlines—either self-imposed or imposed by a third party—such as a looming earnings release or regulatory filing may place significant pressure on the investigation. Amid all of these pressures, forensic accounting investigators should keep in mind the goals of all constituents yet conduct a dispassionate, objective, balanced investigation that is, to the best of their ability, on time and on target.

Internal auditors are enjoying a resurgence of respect in response to recent regulatory requirements and the public outcry for better governance (see Chapter 9 for a discussion of the internal audit function). Many companies are strengthening their internal audit functions, which vary in size, scope, focus,

---

1. See footnote 6 in Chapter 12 regarding 10A and its reference to the independence of the external auditors.

and effectiveness from one organization to another. Internal audit functions may be large or small, compliance based or consultative, executive or operational. Some internal audit units are powerful, with fully functioning administrations and a key voice at high levels, while others are less so. The practice of internal auditing recently experienced significant change—in light of the Sarbanes-Oxley Act of 2002 and the enactment of new, voluntary standards by the Institute of Internal Auditors (IIA). For forensic accounting investigators, cooperating with internal auditors should be planned in a way that reflects the role of internal audit within the organization.

◆ FORENSIC ACCOUNTING INVESTIGATORS' COOPERATION WITH INTERNAL AUDITORS

As we discuss at greater length in Chapter 9, internal auditors bring a great deal to the table when there are concerns about financial fraud. However, for reasons explained in Chapter 9, most internal audit groups do not have a subgroup of forensic investigators. As such, outside forensic investigators are typically hired to assist internal audit conduct investigations. We have found in the majority of our experiences that teaming with internal audit enhances both the efficiency and effectiveness of the investigation: internal audit knows the company and its personnel and systems better than outside forensic investigators, which causes the investigation to be more targeted.

While it is ideal to work with internal audit in conducting investigations, it is important that a number of factors (explored later) be considered by those assigned the responsibility of conducting an internal investigation—usually the audit committee.

INTERNAL AUDIT'S POSITION AND FUNCTION

Note the group's position in the company's organizational chart and its actual, day-to-day role—which due to any number of factors may differ from the role implied by the organizational chart. For example, internal audit's function and reporting relationship may have, by necessity, been diverted in the period following enactment of the Sarbanes-Oxley Act, wherein companies were working to document and assess financial-reporting internal control structures as required by the Act. Begin this assessment with a look at the mission and charter of the internal audit unit. If possible, consider the way in which the internal auditor is measured by the company with respect to coverage, number of locations visited, types of issues raised, financial savings, and improvements to operating metrics. Among the considerations are the following:

- Is the internal audit unit focused on controls assurance—typically evidenced by location-based or compliance auditing—or on controls consulting, typically evidenced by forward-looking projects, early involvement in system deployments, and so on?

- Does the internal audit plan comply with IIA standards for a risk-based approach—usually in the form of a risk assessment?[2] A coverage-based metric, such as a site visit to every location every three years, is evidence that risk is not the primary driver.
- Are any internal auditors trained in forensic investigative accounting? How experienced are they? Do they provide for a separate and distinct group of investigators? When fraud is suspected, do the internal auditors conduct investigations by means of this specialized group of forensic accounting investigators, or do they use auditors already assigned to the particular project?
- Is there consensus about the role of the internal audit unit within the organization?
- Are internal audit's recommendations implemented, and if not, why not?

All internal audit units must grapple with the issues of independence and conflict of interest. The auditors cannot fulfill their obligations without independence of mind and action, but the types of work they perform call for coordination with operational management. This is a balancing act, and it can often generate tension. How much of the internal audit budget is available to auditors at their own discretion? Are the audit strategic plan and budget developed by the auditors themselves, or are they heavily influenced by the chief financial officer? Has the internal audit unit aided in forensic investigations in the past? Experienced auditors are likely to understand the imperatives and the required mind-set, while inexperienced auditors, however skilled in other elements of internal auditing, may require a strong lead throughout the investigation. A high degree of correlation usually exists between the level of empowerment granted to the individual and the independence and effectiveness of that individual's performance. Many internal audit units are oriented toward compliance or operational efficiency and not financial crime investigation. Internal reporting relationships and organizational tone may either enhance or severely limit the effectiveness of the internal audit unit. Most often, the formal report is made to the audit committee, but there may be an administrative reporting relationship with the finance function. Further considerations: How is the auditor evaluated and by whom? What degree of interaction exists between the internal audit group and the audit committee? Do the two meet frequently and discuss matters in depth, or do they meet only at several formal meetings a year?

RESOURCE MODELS

The internal audit unit's mission also usually drives operational issues such as the resource model, annual budget, and auditing plan. Among the questions and issues that normally need to be considered in an evaluation of the resource model are the following.

---

2. Institute of Internal Auditors, *Standards for the Professional Practice of Internal Auditing*, § 2010, "Planning": "The chief audit executive should establish risk-based plans to determine the priorities of the internal audit activity, consistent with the organization's goals."

- Whom does the internal audit group principally hire: accounting and controls specialists, certified fraud examiners, certified public accountants (CPAs), MBAs, new or experienced people, internal recruits?[3]
- How are the internal auditors trained? Is their career path restricted to accounting and controls, or does it enter into operational areas of the company? Do internal auditors rotate through internal auditing and then move to other positions in the company? While benefiting the rest of the organization, such a practice may be counterproductive to building a deep skill set of forensic investigation abilities within the internal audit group.
- Whether the internal audit draws entirely on in-house resources or is cosourced is not a significant issue unless the views of the cosourcing partner differ on methodology, tools, and approach. These issues should be considered in a determination of what support is available, together with the contractual arrangements with the co-sourcing partner. Cosourcing is usually done for one of two reasons: to fill gaps or to build a function. The company may have an internal audit unit but lack specialized information technology resources and look to a cosource provider. Building a function involves obtaining a capability quickly while providing knowledge transfer from outside forensic accounting investigators to company employees. On one hand, when the cosource partner is filling gaps, the mission, direction, and sometimes the supervision of day-to-day work are in most cases controlled predominantly by the company. On the other hand, when the cosource partner has been hired to build or reengineer the function, the company normally sets the mission and overall direction, but the cosource provider usually exercises tactical leadership.

WORKING TOGETHER

After gaining a thorough understanding of the factors discussed earlier, consider ways in which the investigative team can best work with the internal auditor and be prepared to make recommendations to the audit committee. Each group brings different skills to the task, and the best solution is usually one that incorporates both working together. The internal auditors usually bring:

- *Core skills in auditing.* Collecting and corroborating documentation, sampling, interviewing, and testing and analyzing data
- *Core skills in project management.* Planning, scheduling, document management, creating audit steps (including follow-up), managing issue resolution, and recording and communicating results
- *Knowledge of the company and systems.* Organizational structure, how transactions take place, how errors are likely to evidence themselves, and the strengths of the company's people, systems, and processes

---

3. When staffing an internal audit unit whose mission emphasizes consulting activities, the human resources department of a company may bring MBAs rather than CPAs on board. However, the MBA skill set may not be as valuable to a forensic accounting investigation as fundamental auditing experience and the ability to understand how financial transactions are recorded.

With these competencies, the internal auditor is very well positioned to obtain background information on people, systems, and processes. Past audits may provide insight. The auditor is also a valuable team member in collecting data or serving as an adviser to the forensic investigators on matters of approach, specific issues that come to light, and potential follow-up actions.

At the same time, all parties should acknowledge that normal auditing protocols do not apply. Sending out announcements of visits and advance requests for documentation may not be consistent with the objectives of a forensic accounting investigation. The internal auditors' cumulative knowledge of the company can be a powerful frontline force in detection and deterrence. Bear in mind, however, that knowledge of the entity can cut both ways: as an efficient jump start or as a set of assumptions that may hinder objective investigation.

The audit committee or whoever carries ultimate responsibility for the investigation might choose to have it conducted without input from or reliance upon internal resources. The forensic accounting investigator may be asked for input into this decision and should be prepared to respond appropriately. The foregoing discussion of factors to consider may be helpful for all parties involved in conducting investigations.

◆ FORENSIC ACCOUNTING INVESTIGATORS' COOPERATION WITH EXTERNAL AUDITORS

The external auditors of a company are commonly engaged to perform an audit under generally accepted auditing standards, and the primary focus of those external auditors is on auditing the financial statements in compliance with professional standards. How well forensic accounting investigators interact with external auditors typically depends on several factors, including the following.

CLIENT HISTORY

The external auditor may be a trusted adviser or may have a strained relationship with the company owing to previous events. Because the forensic accounting investigator is often placed between the company and its external auditor during an investigation, understanding their current relationship is likely to be critical to successful communication during an investigation.

Because external auditors likely know the company better than a newly appointed team of attorneys and forensic accounting investigators, selected in part because of their limited prior experience with the company, they may be very useful sources of information. The audit firm's knowledge about a company's areas of risk, business processes, documentation, systems, and personnel can get the investigative team off to a fast start. The forensic accounting team will also be able to use the auditor's working papers and audit staff to assist in gaining an understanding of the client's systems, culture, and personnel, as well as other important data. Gaining access to information contained in the working papers of the external auditors may require formal access letters, the terms of which should be carefully considered by counsel. Also, the process of obtaining access letters may often take time away from getting the investigation started promptly.

There are situations permitted by law and professional standards wherein an audit committee may retain a forensic accounting team from the external auditor's firm. Considerations in choosing this option include timing, knowledge of the company's accounts, systems, personnel, and industry specifics. Relying on a forensic team from the external auditors has an added benefit: the audit firm and hence its forensic accounting team are independent, whereas the other immediately available resources such as the internal audit team or the company's general counsels' office is not. A discussion of the rules allowing these services is found in Chapter 6 (see discussion surrounding our commentary regarding Rule 2-01(c)(4)(x) of Regulation S-X and Exchange Act Rule 10A-2).

Note, however, that the nature of the allegations or certain external events such as the commencement of a lawsuit or a regulatory investigation may require the audit committee to insist on several degrees of separation between the external auditors and the investigative team—especially if the cry "Where were the auditors?" has already been raised.

THE EXTERNAL AUDITOR IN TODAY'S ENVIRONMENT

To meet capital markets' expectations that financial statements must not be tainted with material fraud and in compliance with the new regulatory requirements of Sarbanes-Oxley, the external auditor will be involved to some extent in most investigations. This is particularly so in situations involving allegations that the financial statements may have been affected by an illegal act. Any investigation to assess this concern will likely be conducted by the audit committee, the process and results of which will be closely monitored by the auditors in accordance with their responsibilities under professional standards and 10A of the Exchange Act. Many external auditors will not complete their audit fieldwork until the investigation is complete and they have access to the findings and the company's remedial action plan.

Recognizing the responsibilities of the auditor, the investigation team (counsel and forensic accounting investigator) may consider asking for input from the external auditor early on in the investigation. If there is a disagreement with the external auditor on scope, approach, or procedure, the forensic accounting investigator should find that out earlier rather than later and work through the issues raised. The work and findings of the 10A counsel team cannot be kept entirely from review by the external auditors. While 10A counsel and their forensic team may draw certain boundaries around work relating to legal advice and other matters of privilege, it is generally best to include the external auditors in significant aspects of the investigation with periodic reports. Without this level of cooperation, time to complete the financial statement audit once the investigation is completed may be extended while the audit partner digests the findings, establishes the scope of and carries out related audit work, and evaluates the remedial actions, control implications, and financial statement disclosures.

Invariably, the question of the attorney work product and attorney–client privileges arises when the question of sharing the findings of the investigation gets discussed. This is a complex question and the subject of evolving law. Accordingly, audit committees, auditors, and forensic accounting investigators should be prepared to evaluate the specific circumstances of each situation with counsel before reaching a conclusion. It must be recognized, however, that the external auditor has a legitimate need for fully comprehending the scope, findings, and remedial actions taken as a result of the investigation, which may, under certain circumstances, implicate the privileged nature of certain aspects of the investigation. Auditors are generally well advised to inquire at both the beginning and the end of an investigation as to whether any material either will be or has been withheld from them because of privilege issues. It may be simplest for the auditors to tell the audit committee, with its 10A counsel present, that they need to be informed at any point in the investigation when the privilege is being asserted.

◆ OBJECTIVES OF ALL INTERESTED PARTIES

The forensic accounting investigator must bring independence and objectivity to the investigation and recognize the objectives of each of the interested parties to the investigation.

FORENSIC ACCOUNTING INVESTIGATORS' OBJECTIVES

Forensic accounting investigators' objectives are determined by the scope of work and the desire to meet the goals of whoever retained their services. Regardless of the differing interests of the various constituencies, forensic accounting investigators must typically answer the following questions:

- Who is involved?
- Could there be coconspirators?
- Was the perpetrator instructed by a higher supervisor not currently a target of the investigation?
- How much is at issue or what is the total impact on the financial statements?
- Over what period of time did this occur?
- Have we identified all material schemes?
- How did this happen?
- How was it identified, and could it have been detected earlier?
- What can be done to deter a recurrence?

Forensic accounting investigators should always keep in mind that they are primarily fact finders and not typically engaged to reach or provide conclusions—or, more formally, opinions.[4] This differs from the financial auditor's role, as often

---

4. The exception is that in civil litigation, a forensic accountant may be asked to opine on the existence of fraud under the civil evidence standards, wherein the existence of a tort is based on a preponderance of the evidence, as opposed to the stricter, criminal evidence standard of "beyond a reasonable doubt." A forensic accountant who is asked for an opinion takes on elements of the role of auditor and must determine whether the nature, scope, and timing of the procedures were or are sufficient.

noted in previous chapters. The financial auditor is presented with the books and records to be audited and determines the nature, extent, and timing of audit procedures. On one hand, the financial statements are management's responsibility, and an auditor confirms they have been prepared in accordance with generally accepted accounting principles after completing these procedures and assessing the results. The forensic accounting investigator, on the other hand, commands a different set of skills and works at the direction of an employer that may be management, the audit committee, counsel, or the auditing firm itself.

The selection of audit procedures is judgmental and an integral part of the audit team's responsibilities. Not surprisingly, when auditors choose to enlist the services of subject matter experts such as forensic accounting investigators they expect the investigators to offer suggestions on appropriate procedures to be performed as well as related costs, risks, and expected outcomes. The investigators should be careful not to execute such procedures unless specifically asked to do so by the audit team (or whoever is directing the investigators). This approach can lead to frustration on the part of the investigators if, during an investigation, forensic accounting investigators are ordered to stop and in effect put down their pencils. Should that situation occur, it may be entirely appropriate to discuss their concerns with the audit team. But keep in mind that the audit team is generally more knowledgeable about the client's business as well as other audit procedures that may mitigate the forensic investigator's concerns. In extreme cases, it may be appropriate to resign in protest, an eventuality discussed in more detail later. But the forensic accounting investigators should take direction from those who engage them, as requested, be they auditors, directors, or counsel.

OBJECTIVES OF OTHER PARTIES TO THE INVESTIGATION

During an investigation, each interested party may view the same facts differently. For this reason, it is important to understand the likely biases and goals of all stakeholders and to view, in a broad context of expected and quite naturally differing points of view, any conflicts that may emerge.

Management understandably may be eager to bring the investigation to a quick conclusion. The chief financial officer may be defensive over the fact that his or her organization "allowed this to happen." The CEO may be concerned about the investigation's impact on share price, company reputation and liability, and employee morale. Perhaps citing cost or scope issues—but likely more concerned about staying as close as possible to events as they unfold in the interest of no surprises—management's overall reaction may be to tightly manage the investigation.

The *board of directors,* through the independent members of its audit committee, is likely to focus on conducting a thorough and complete investigation, but its members may lack the experience needed to assess the effort. In addition, they may be concerned about their personal reputations and liability. The board is likely to look to legal counsel and in some cases, to forensic accounting investigators to define the parameters of the project.

Regulatory agencies, including the SEC and law enforcement agencies such as the U.S. Department of Justice (DOJ), have enforcement and prosecutorial objectives beyond the scope of the investigative team's objectives.

Counsel will act in the best legal interests of its client, which could be the management team, the audit committee, or other directors, with the exception of counsel engaged to conduct a 10A investigation. Such 10A counsel must conduct an independent investigation free of the advocacy role required of counsel engaged to prepare a defense of the company in a pending civil litigation, or DOJ or SEC, or other regulatory agency investigation. The role required of forensic accounting investigators by the legal team may vary depending on the team's needs. As such, the forensic accountants should not expect to participate in all activities typical of financial crime investigations. For example, the legal team may or may not see a need to include the forensic accountants in all interviews, favoring instead to have them attend only those interviews in which the legal team expects accounting issues to surface. In most investigations in which counsel is involved, they are responsible for the conduct of the investigations and will assign and allocate resources accordingly.

The *internal auditor* may have a variety of objectives, including not alienating management, staying on schedule to complete the annual audit plan, and not opening the internal audit team to criticism. The internal audit team may also feel embarrassed, angry, and defensive that it did not detect the wrongdoing.

The *external auditor* may have several concerns, including whether the investigation team will conduct an investigation of adequate scope, whether the situation suggests retaining forensic accountants from the auditors' firm, whether forensic accountants should be added to the audit team, and even whether the investigation will implicate the quality of past audits.[5] The concerns on this front are complex.

Registered independent accounting and auditing firms are good places to look for forensic accounting investigators. However, in light of the requirements of the Sarbanes-Oxley Act, in some circumstances the external auditors may not be engaged and additionally, when they can be engaged, some audit committees are nevertheless averse to engaging forensic professionals from their external auditing firm. This may be the correct decision, although not in every case. (For further discussion, see Chapter 6.)

Additionally, there will likely be situations in which auditors may elect to consult with a forensic accounting investigator from their own firm regarding the proposed scope or method of an investigation being conducted at an audit client.[6] For example, the law firm conducting a 10A investigation may decide not to conduct an e-mail review as part of its investigation. This decision may or may not be appropriate. Consultation with a forensic accounting investigator may assist the audit partner and the partner's team in assessing the scope of

---

5. See Chapter 12 regarding specific requirements of the auditor under Section 10A of the Exchange Act.
6. Id.

investigation either proposed or performed. As an example of a detailed issue pertaining to scope, in some investigations e-mail is obtained by "copying" the relevant server files. The audit firm's forensic team might suggest that hard drives found on personal computers, portable mass storage devices like pen drives, personal digital assistants, and the like be imaged instead of simply copied, so that files not retained on the servers as well as deleted files are captured.

Audit partners may use their firm's forensic accounting investigators to assist in a variety of ways, including:

- Receiving detailed reports of questions and facts discovered by 10A counsel: Attending selected interviews with 10A counsel and/or counsel's forensic accounting advisers may be appropriate in some situations as well.
- Additional document review—which may include e-mail review—or expanding the audit tests of certain accounts
- Attending update meetings called by 10A counsel to advise on the progress of an investigation

If the forensic accounting investigators are from the audit firm, the firm may expect to be involved in the procedures and findings at every stage. Some counsel and boards view this as a barrier to hiring the audit firm's forensic accounting investigator to conduct the investigation; however, no matter who completes the investigation, critical information must still be communicated to the auditors.

Stockholders may become concerned once suggestions of financial impropriety surface. They may file a class-action lawsuit with the objective of extracting the largest possible settlement from the company and other parties, including the external auditors.

The company's *lenders* are likely to be concerned about their exposure to losses. The investigation may take place during a period of financing negotiations and may therefore need to address the lenders' objectives.

The *public at large* may feel some degree of vested interest in the investigation, particularly if the entity is a public, quasi-public, or charitable organization or if it is a significant regional employer. These concerns are often reflected in and fed by media attention, and they create pressure to "get to the bottom quickly."

◆ HOW SHOULD THE INVESTIGATION OBJECTIVES BE DEFINED?

Forensic accounting investigators should develop a plan that offers the client investigative alternatives. The investigation should obviously focus on the facts that cause concern, with the ultimate objective of determining if an illegal act has been committed. In their quest to achieve the objectives of the investigation, forensic accounting investigators must be mindful that they are governed by the ethical principles and other guidelines of the authoritative professional organization(s) to which they belong—be it the American Institute of Certified Public Accountants, the Association of Certified Fraud Examiners, or both.

The forensic accounting investigator should recognize that auditors may be apprehensive when confronted with issues of fraud—and appropriately so. Sensitivity to auditors' concerns will go a long way toward easing their natural disquiet when it is determined that the company has begun an investigation to evaluate allegations of fraud. Keeping auditors informed in an appropriate manner, agreed to by the client, will help ensure the efficiency of the financial statement audit.

In earlier chapters of this book, the issue of financial statement materiality has been raised more than once. In the course of an audit, numerous immaterial variances and adjustments are identified, documented in the working papers, and never adjusted on the books and records of the company.[7] This is appropriate and consistent with auditing standards. Materiality is a filter that allows the auditors to work efficiently and effectively. In the course of a financial investigation, however, a small fact, immaterial under normal circumstances, may have a critical bearing on the overall investigation.

◆ WHO SHOULD DIRECT THE INVESTIGATION AND WHY?

A ship has but one captain and, generally, a company's audit committee must proactively lead the investigation. Forensic accounting investigators follow the evidence wherever it leads and communicate their findings to the audit committee or to the committee's designee, such as counsel, whose decisions direct the conduct of the investigation. While the external auditors must be satisfied that the audit committee has directed a proper investigation, they neither direct the investigation nor decide what remedial actions are required by the circumstances. Financial crime investigations are fraught with uncertainty, and a wrong move can produce harmful results. Audit committees recognize the value of consulting with a competent team of advisers, including counsel and forensic accounting investigators. A forensic accounting investigator working for an audit committee that does not seek advice or that interferes with the investigation would be well advised to resign the assignment.

In the course of an investigation, a time may come when the forensic accounting investigator is alone in advocating a certain course of action or series of procedures. Suppose the audit committee interprets whistle-blower allegations as implicating the revenue recognition practices of the company but not policies involving the deferral and amortization of related marketing costs, and the forensic accounting investigator disagrees? What is the forensic accounting investigator to do? The evidence should be the driving force in determining the scope and course of the investigation. On one hand, in situations of this kind, be insistent

---

7. Historically, materiality has been evaluated primarily by using quantitative measurement standards such as X percent of total assets or net income. In 1999, however, the SEC released Staff Accounting Bulletin 99 (SAB 99), which reemphasized the view that materiality should be evaluated from a qualitative as well as a quantitative standpoint. View at http://www.sec.gov/interps/account/sab99.htm.

while following the standards, methodologies, and practices that experience suggests are most appropriate in the circumstances. On the other hand, unlike decisions about the scope of the audit procedures—which rest solely with the auditors—decisions about the adequacy of an investigation's scope rest with the audit committee. Typically, the best and most practical use of a forensic accounting investigator is to conduct sufficient procedures to unambiguously resolve the allegations. This is the clearest outcome of an investigation. There is, of course, another outcome: "We conducted our investigative procedures and noted no evidence of fraud." This may or may not be acceptable, depending upon whether the investigation was robust and thorough. A no-fraud-found result could amount to a comfort level consistent with the objective of the investigation at its outset: that of resolving the allegations. Or, if those who evaluate the outcome of the investigation—such as the auditors or the SEC—conclude that procedures were not robust and thorough, it will be difficult for them to arrive at a satisfactory comfort level with a finding of no fraud. In situations in which a no-fraud finding is the investigative result, the adequacy of the scope is often a key element in justifying the conclusion.

Ideally, the forensic accounting investigator should have significant influence over procedures pertaining to the financial aspects of the investigation. Counsel should obviously take responsibility for the legal aspects of the matter and support the efforts of the forensic accounting investigator by providing appropriate guidance. The audit committee should rely on these and other professionals, but in the end *it is the audit committee's investigation*. The committee must take ownership, albeit with the advice of other parties in the core team that influences the direction of investigation. These may include forensic accounting investigators, legal counsel, internal and external auditors, and possibly others such as a public relations firm. Conferring early and often is routine in these matters and should be strongly encouraged by the forensic accounting investigator.

◆ READY WHEN NEEDED

While fraud is not an everyday occurrence at most companies, boards and auditing firms should anticipate the need to conduct a financial fraud investigation at some time in the future. To this end, they may establish protocols that ensure that if fraud exists, there is a high probability that it will be identified completely and dealt with in a timely and correct manner.

Companies and auditors alike may gain benefit from considering (1) whether heightened risk of fraud exists and (2) when there is heightened risk of fraud, what would be an appropriate audit response to the heightened risk. Once indicators of fraud have been identified, a protocol may be put in place for conducting an investigation. If this planning takes place long before the need for an investigation, the procedures can be vetted by all relevant personnel, including the audit committee, management, the legal department, human resources, risk management, and internal auditors.

The external auditing firm may also want to develop a protocol for handling possible red flags and suspicions of fraud. An auditing firm's basic vision as to how to deploy resources for addressing these concerns would typically address many of the points covered in the sidebar entitled Fraud Response Protocol, which follows.

◆ WHERE TO FIND SKILLED FORENSIC ACCOUNTING INVESTIGATORS

INTERNAL AUDIT

When the need arises for an investigation within a company, management or in-house counsel might naturally first look for a forensic accounting investigator in the company's internal audit group. Owing to a number of constraints, however, companies and their lawyers often find themselves sooner or later having to look to outside resources. The first and foremost constraint may be a lack of experienced forensic accounting investigators in the internal audit unit. Many companies have the practice of rotating accountants and auditors (as well as other operational disciplines) through their internal audit groups for a variety of reasons. However, rotation makes it difficult to cultivate the deep skill sets of forensic accounting investigation—for example, interviewing skills.

When an investigation is needed, it is best to deploy the most experienced fraud detection experts available. In actual practice, there is often a strong desire to use the internal auditors: they are already on site or nearby, and it would appear to be most cost-effective to engage this internal resource in the investigation. This strategy can be most effective if companies develop groups of forensic accounting investigators within internal audit. In the absence of experienced, in-house forensic accounting investigators, our advice is to look outside the company when the need arises.

Internal auditors need access to the same fraud detection and deterrence skills as outside auditors. They may have robust audit programs to deploy on the traditional preventative, cyclic, or rotational basis, absent any specific concerns about possible fraud. Should someone in the organization express specific concerns, even in a general way, consideration should be given to deploying forensic accounting experts. Because audit committees look to internal auditors as the primary group focused on fraud detection and deterrence, a certain number of internal audit professionals should consider attaining the certified fraud examiner (CFE) designation. When testing identifies any situation in which a suspicion of fraud arises, company policy should provide for consultation with professionals from the organization's risk management and forensic accounting groups.

Building the right investigative team is part of the challenge facing audit committees. The combination of internal and external resources can greatly enhance the investigative effort if undertaken with eyes wide open, with experience as a guide, and with a deliberate approach.

ENGAGING EXTERNAL FORENSIC ACCOUNTING INVESTIGATORS

If forensic accounting investigators are unavailable within the company, a variety of professional services firms can provide them. Those firms include:

- The external auditing firm
- Registered independent accounting and auditing firms
- Consulting firms (nonauditing and unregistered)

What are the criteria for choosing among these service providers? Care is, of course, needed. Unfortunately, people sometimes identify themselves as forensic accounting investigators even though they do not have sufficient training and experience. No formal requirements in terms of education, specialized training, or experience help the buyer of these services gain some initial sense of the service provider's real capabilities. The area of forensic accounting investigation has become popular of late, and some firms have added the specialty to their service offerings despite a lack of strongly credentialed, thoroughly experienced professionals. Companies and their lawyers should, therefore, consider quite a range of factors in deciding what type of individual to engage to direct an investigation. The requisite skills and experience appear in the following, by no means exhaustive, list:

- Technical qualifications, including certifications such as CPA and CFE
- Experience in forensic accounting investigation, with a track record of successfully and unambiguously resolving allegations
- Global resources
- Forensic technology tools and the experience to deploy them
- The ability to understand complex business transactions and their effects on financial statements
- Knowledge of criminology and the workings of the white-collar criminal's mind and methods
- Testimony experience before regulators such as the SEC and DOJ and at deposition or trial
- Forensic interviewing experience
- Ability to work effectively in an unstructured and dynamic environment
- Patience and listening skills
- The ability to approach situations objectively and without bias
- Persistence and the will to ask tough questions and deal with difficult, high-stress situations
- Integrity

ACCOUNTING AND AUDITING FIRMS

The largest accounting firms have gone through tremendous change in the past decade, and even more change in very recent years. The majority of these firms now concentrate on audit, internal audit, tax, and selected special services such as forensic accounting.

Larger firms have a pool of auditors that may be trained to become forensic accounting investigators. As well, they have large client bases and employ individuals who have conducted investigations in virtually every industry. The majority of the larger firms have both national and international operations, with global resources that can be quickly mobilized to put an engagement team in place. Such firms are efficient; they do this type of work day after day.

While the larger firms' assets, resources, and tools are valuable to clients, cost is the biggest drawback to hiring a large firm to design and execute an investigation. However, because of the larger firms' resources, vast industry experience, networking abilities, and well-recognized expertise, some companies find it prudent, despite the higher cost, to access that richer pool of expertise.

Many smaller firms have professionals who may have worked previously in larger firms and who may hold both the CPA and CFE credentials. They may or may not support a core group of people who concentrate exclusively on forensic accounting investigation, but they may nonetheless field professionals with backgrounds similar to those possessed by forensic accounting investigators at larger firms. Although many small forensic accounting firms are judged to be less expensive than the larger firms, they also have a smaller presence across the United States and may have limited or nonexistent access to international resources. These issues are, of course, factors in the selection process. A Midwestern company recently had a problem in Indonesia and needed investigative resources there without delay. The board first turned to the company's auditor, a large, regional Midwestern firm at which a few individuals performed forensic work. However, U.S. practitioners with the necessary skill set were not available from that firm to travel to Indonesia, and the firm had no Asian offices at all. Under the circumstances, the company decided to engage a Big Four firm, and within 48 hours an Asian investigative team was on-site at the company's Indonesian subsidiary.

Other factors in the selection process may include:

- How the outcome of the investigation may be used—for example, to initiate a legal proceeding, arbitration, or response to the inquiry of a regulatory or law enforcement agency
- Whether the investigation assignment is initiated in response to significant matters, including:
  - Whistle-blower allegations in potential *qui tam* matters
  - Regulatory inquiries
  - Federal subpoenas
  - 10A investigations
  - Foreign Corrupt Practices Act violations
  - Breach of physical security or data security measures

The decision as to whom to engage in a financial crimes investigation is difficult. It should be considered with the thoughtful advice of the board, both inside and outside counsel, and management, internal audit, and risk management directors.

FRAUD RESPONSE PROTOCOL: AUDIT FIRM DEPLOYMENT CONSIDERATIONS

- *Deployment.* Deploying an organization's most experienced fraud detection experts when there is greatest risk to the organization—for example, when a heightened suspicion of fraud has surfaced—ensures that the best resources attack the problem. When suspicions of fraud arise, forensic accounting investigators should be among the professionals considered for deployment.
- *Clarity of roles.* Clarity should be promoted within the organization. Those who deploy the firm's resources in matters in which suspicions of fraud arise should be aware of who in their firm possesses the necessary training and experience to deal with such issues. The distribution of services performed by the firm should be determined by its business unit leaders, which should cover the deployment of those resources charged with forensic accounting investigation. When audit testing, control reviews, or other attestation services identify a situation in which suspicions of fraud arise, it may well be advisable for firms to consider requiring consultation with their risk management group. This group may suggest further consultation with a forensic accounting investigator from the firm's forensic accounting practice. The organization should have a clear policy as to who must be involved when there is a suspicion of fraud (see Chapter 12).
- *Resources.* Alignment of resources having similar skills aids in addressing such issues as training, industry specialization, and accreditation programs. Accordingly, forensic accounting investigators should be aligned within a single business unit just as a firm might recognize other specialists, such as tax specialists, actuaries, and pension specialists. This strategy ensures that all financial crime investigations are performed by a relatively small and specialized group of professionals.
- *Audit team readiness.* Audit team readiness may be enhanced by cultivation of fraud detection skills. While financial statement auditors need not become fully prepared forensic accounting investigators, they will likely have as part of their audit methods certain practices aimed at surfacing suspicious transactions, should they exist, as suggested by SAS 99.

When an investigation into significant allegations is going to be conducted, a variety of parties must team up to ensure the most efficient possible result. These include the board, audit committee, general counsel, management, internal auditors, external auditors, special counsel, and the forensic accounting investigator. Whether or not the forensic accounting investigator is working with independent counsel or is supporting audit colleagues, communication and cooperation generally create substantial efficiencies in the process and help ensure that the expectations of all concerned with the outcome are met.

CHAPTER 14

POTENTIAL MISSTEPS: CONSIDERATIONS WHEN FRAUD IS SUSPECTED

Thomas W. Golden

Kevin D. Kreb

This chapter explores some of the unintended consequences that may arise when well-intentioned, competent auditors and company executives detect the possibility of fraud and understandably want to reach an immediate resolution. A good knowledge of the more significant potential missteps should help both auditors and their clients in the proper conduct of an investigation. As discussed in earlier chapters, when there is a suspicion of fraud, the surest path is to employ appropriate experts and to do so early. Most of the missteps put the natural desire to shed immediate light on the problem ahead of the painstaking professional approach that is far more likely to uncover the truth, expose the issues to the fullest possible extent, obtain desired legal outcomes, improve control remediation efforts, and increase recoveries.

◆ CONFRONTING SUSPECTS

One step commonly taken by executives or auditors untrained in fraud investigation is to confront a suspect with certain facts immediately after discovery. Such executives or auditors are understandably eager to resolve the apparent discrepancy and take what they believe to be the quickest path to resolution, but they may unknowingly complicate future investigation and actually increase the cost of resolving the allegations. By way of illustration, consider the following. A corporate controller is reviewing quarter-end journal entries and notices several large entries that do not make sense. He retrieves the supporting documents and notices not only that his signature has been forged but also that the documents bear no relation to the entry. He believes the assistant controller made the entries to cover up a defalcation. The controller is naturally upset. He discusses the matter with the chief financial officer, a human resources representative, and an attorney from the general counsel's office. All agree the entries look bad, and the decision is made to confront the assistant controller with the facts to "get to the bottom of this matter." Consulting with a forensic accounting investigator does not occur to them.

The controller summons his assistant to his office and confronts him with the facts and evidence. The assistant controller is by and large silent, taking it all in and periodically asking questions to clarify details. In fact, while the assistant controller remains calm, his superior is visibly upset. The controller continues laying out the facts for about 10 minutes while the assistant quietly follows along. Finally, the controller reaches the end of his recitation of facts and suspicions and asks: "What's going on here? What's being hidden?"

The assistant controller has at least two choices: first, he can say to his boss: "I'm really sorry about this confusion. I understand why you're upset. Let me take this back to my desk. I'll figure it out and get right back to you. It will be my top priority today." The assistant controller exits with an armful of the "evidence" that his boss has laboriously assembled and will soon be doing who knows what with it. The controller meanwhile is relieved; he feels he has handled the situation like a good manager. He returns to his work and awaits a response. Later confrontations yield little more—until a week later, when the assistant controller resigns via e-mail.

Under the second scenario, the assistant controller says nothing. Thinking this strange, the boss prompts him for a response, receiving a mumbled, "I'm not feeling well." The assistant controller tells his boss he is going home sick and will address the issue in the morning. The controller is very unhappy with this response, berates his subordinate for creating the situation, and demands that he make some statement about it then and there. The assistant simply reiterates that he is not feeling well and walks out. The next morning, the controller listens to a voice mail from his assistant saying he is still under the weather, is taking a sick day, and has a doctor's appointment later. On the following day, no assistant controller, no voice mail, and the formerly trustworthy assistant is not even answering his home telephone.

By directly confronting the miscreant, the controller believed he was doing the right thing. However, never having confronted someone skilled at deceit and cover, as the assistant controller apparently was, the controller was soon out of his depth. In such a situation, he may have been better off to have consulted with a forensic accounting investigator. Unknowingly, the controller had conducted an admission-seeking interview (see Chapter 18). A trained forensic accounting investigator knows that this type of interview is often most effective *after* a thorough investigation has been performed, when the interview or series of interviews can be carefully scripted and always conducted with a prover[1] in attendance. Without intending to do so, the controller alerted the miscreant to the fact that he would be exposed, thus making further investigation both difficult and costly. In addition, the assistant controller's unresponsiveness on the day after the interview signaled that he had probably fled. That in itself significantly reduced the likelihood of recovery.

---

1. As explained more fully in Chapter 18, it is best to include a colleague in the interviews who can vouch for what was said, by whom, and when. Without this prover, the suspect can later recant an admission, and then it is your word against his.

The moral of the story, as in any situation in which evidence is found indicating a suspicion of fraud, is to consider consulting with a forensic accounting investigator early on. Suspicion is sufficient reason to do so. We all are naturally curious, and managers often are proud and intelligent individuals, unlikely to feel that a situation cannot be directly addressed and resolved. But reliance on forensic expertise may be critical in achieving the desired result: identification of all of the perpetrators, determination of the extent of fraud, analysis of the pattern of fraud and the faulty controls that permitted it, and recommendations for deterring such fraud in the future.

Here is another case that illustrates the inadvisability of immediate confrontation. A forensic accounting team recently completed an investigation in the Middle East. The company, a U.S. multinational manufacturer of heavy equipment, had received an anonymous letter alleging that certain employees in the purchasing department—two in particular—were soliciting bribes and accepting kickbacks from vendors. This practice was alleged to have been occurring for a number of years. The forensic accounting investigators were asked to uncover the truth.

Kickbacks are often the most difficult of allegations to prove. The most compelling proof is an admission by the recipient or the vendor. However, both parties are profiting from the corrupt action and have no incentive to tell the truth. Further, kickbacks are not usually paid in front of witnesses; there is little, if any, documentation to establish that they have occurred; and they're usually paid in cash. For these reasons, they're difficult to trace. Kickbacks may greatly increase costs over a period of time, and those costs are often not at all obvious in the records.

In this particular investigation, a confession was not forthcoming. However, after conducting a number of interviews and performing procedures focused on detail, including document examination, the forensic accounting team did identify suspicious e-mails, purchase order violations, and evident lies. They also received two additional anonymous allegations by e-mail. Essentially, they had smoke but no smoking gun—at least none they would describe as solid proof of a kickback. Nevertheless, they had learned enough to believe that most of the allegations in the anonymous letter were true. They just could not prove it yet.

Everyone with whom the forensic accounting investigators talked believed that the two targets were accepting kickbacks, but the targets did a good job of hiding the trail. In the end, the forensic accounting investigators identified several key witnesses who provided enough facts and documents for the team to confront one of the suspects. He in turn incriminated the purchasing supervisor. In an admission-seeking interview, the purchasing supervisor confessed. He lost his job and identified all of the vendors paying bribes. The company has pursued recovery from those vendors.

The investigation took seven weeks to complete and cost the client about $250,000 in fees and expenses. Senior management recognized the value of using forensic accounting investigators. However, the division manager of procurement in the Middle East disagreed with the forensic accounting team's approach and spoke with the members after they had been on-site for about two weeks. He suggested that if he were conducting the investigation, he would simply have confronted the targets with the anonymous letter on the first day of investigation to see whether they would admit to the allegations and thus save the time and money allocated to the investigation. He also floated the idea that the forensic accounting investigators could have confronted the alleged wrong-doers by telephone—in this way saving the money that had been spent on travel to the Middle East. Were they to have made no admission, he argued, the team should then have conducted an investigation on-site.

The forensic accounting investigators agreed with him that investigations should be conducted in the least time-consuming and most inexpensive manner, provided that the desired result was consistent with the methodology used. Here, senior management had explicitly asked for all reasonable efforts to produce the clearest possible outcome—a positive and knowledgeable disposition of the allegations—and any ambiguity in resolving the allegations was deemed in advance to be unacceptable. The result of the investigation that actually took place was to identify two individuals who had been working together for the previous 10 years to solicit and accept kickbacks.

Had the forensic accounting investigators confronted the targets early on as suggested by the division manager, it is unlikely that either would have confessed to the scheme. The strategic disadvantage of confronting the targets before substantive investigative work had been completed would have been too great a cost to pay for an unlikely event: their immediate confession. Admission-seeking interviews conducted in circumstances like these, without the benefit of facts discovered in a preliminary investigation often put interviewers essentially in the weak position of simply taking notes. As to the division manager's suggestion that the forensic accounting investigators should have conducted an interview by telephone, the suggestion is easily dismissed as the least desirable alternative: forensic accounting investigation is a field in which you should definitely not "let your fingers do the walking."

Often, confrontation is the first thought that comes to mind upon encountering disturbing facts. Most people want to resolve matters immediately to allay their discomfort and get on with their own work. Unsettled and unresolved situations often cause disruption in organizations—never a good thing. Yet it is often better to go against natural impulse. An executive with suspicions should be advised to move carefully. There is often a tremendous strategic advantage when only one party—honest management—knows that an investigation is under way.

To sum up, admission-seeking interviews are often best conducted after learning certain facts through investigation. Facts are extremely useful in achieving investigative objectives; they are the friends of the honest person and the enemies of the fraudster. We recommend performing at least a preliminary investigation before interviewing the target. You may then be ready, at a relatively early stage of investigation, to test the veracity of a key individual. Should the individual admit wrongdoing or provide clear and persuasive evidence of honesty, procedures from that point forward may be brief and inexpensive. Do not confront the target until the appropriate preparatory work is completed. Sometimes a company employee begins to unexpectedly confess to wrongdoings to an executive or auditor. In such situations, it usually makes sense for the executive to continue talking with the individual. It would not be prudent to say to the subject, "Please hold that thought until I go get a forensic accounting investigator." These situations are rare, but they do occur. When the situation permits consideration of alternative approaches, enlisting the assistance of a forensic accounting investigator is often beneficial. Admission-seeking interviews are explored in Chapter 18, The Art of the Interview.

◆ DISMISSING THE TARGET

From the standpoint of a forensic investigation, an unfortunate fact that one might hear during the first call from an executive who believes that a fraud has been perpetrated on the company resembles the following: "We believe the controller has been recording bogus journal entries to inflate revenue. The evidence we have is quite solid, and we have just terminated him. Not surprisingly, he denied the allegations, but his denials carried no weight in light of the evidence we have on him. He's gone. Now we want to hire you to perform an investigation." From an investigative point of view, such a termination will often hamper an investigation.

Whenever there is a suspected defalcation, management and the board want answers to the following questions:

- Who is involved?
- Could there be coconspirators?
- How much was stolen or what is the total impact on the financial statements?
- Over what period of time did this occur?
- Have we identified all material schemes?
- How did this happen?
- How was it identified, and could it have been detected earlier?
- What can be done to deter a recurrence?

Paid administrative leave may be less disruptive to an investigation than termination. The concerned executives are, naturally, angry over what they have found, but it is best to set anger aside for the duration of the investigation.

◆ ASSUMPTIONS

Most auditors and their clients are intelligent people who have risen to positions of responsibility. Yet one of the features of high intelligence can be a detriment to investigation: Many smart people do not like to ask stupid questions. They prefer to think they can understand almost any set of circumstances by extrapolating intelligently on the basis of limited information. It follows that most intelligent people *assume* certain facts based on learned facts. Their assumptions may actually prove to be correct, but sound investigative conclusions cannot be based on assumptions. Whoever wrote the scripts for the long-running television shows *Columbo* and *Monk* understood a great deal about the conduct of a real investigation. Both characters appear to be bumbling, preoccupied, and confused. "Just one more question, ma'am: I'm really sorry to trouble you, but I forgot something that may be important." Now, most intelligent people are not like Columbo or Monk. Rather than ask an embarrassingly dumb question, they just assume a fact. This is unwise. It is far better to ask the simple question than to assume.

A good forensic accounting investigator is not an opiner but a fact finder. To do the job well does not mean the fact finder will make no assumptions whatsoever; rather, the fact finder will be strict about avoiding *needless* assumptions. Some assumptions are almost always necessary, but they should be made only when additional fact-finding is impractical.

Facts are so valuable to the forensic accounting investigator—and ultimately, to the trier of fact—because they provoke admissions and remove defenses the target could later use. Admissions include more than simply the target's direct admission of guilt. They encompass varied elements of evidence that can build toward concluding on the matter at hand. In well-structured target interviews, those interviewed will make helpful admissions along the way, although they're unaware they're providing damaging information. Failing to see the whole picture, they realize they must cooperate with the investigation because lack of cooperation could suggest fraud—the last thing perpetrators want to suggest. For that reason, they're likely to give the forensic accounting investigator bits and pieces of information, some of which could fit into a pattern that will eventually lead to clear and certain facts.

An illustrative example will help. Suppose it is important to a case to establish that the target knew the policy related to the authorization of certain expenses. It is also important to the forensic accounting investigator to understand exactly what the target has done with respect to approving and generating payments. The line of questioning proceeds as follows:

Q: How long have you been with the company and in this department?

A: Ten years with the company, three of them as director of accounts payable.

Q: What are the job responsibilities of the director of accounts payable?

A: [He explains all of his job responsibilities and indicates that he and he alone has primary approval authority for the validity of vendors and all payments to them.]

Q: What is your understanding regarding the required documentation for purchases of IT [information technology] consulting services?

A: I understand that any such services must be approved first by the IT department head and then by me.

Q: Is that for all services, or is there some dollar limitation?

A: It is for all purchases greater than $5,000.

Q: So then, purchases of $5,000 or less do not need approval by the IT department head—only your approval. Do I have that right?

A: Yes.

Q: I just want to be certain I know what your sign-off or initials look like. Is this it? [The interviewer places in front of the target a copy of the initials reproduced from some of the fraudulent approval documents. The target is not aware that his initials were copied from such documents.]

A: Yes, that's my sign-off.

Q: Besides you, are there any others in your department or another department who could approve such transactions without your knowledge?

A: No.

Q: Are you certain?

A: Yes.

Q: And if you're on a business trip or taking a vacation?

A: We're a small shop. They wait for me to return. I travel infrequently, and my vacations never extend longer than a week. The vendor can wait.

Q: Have there been instances in the past three years when this practice has not been followed?

A: No.

Q: You seem sure of this.

A: I know my department and company policy, and I run a tight ship.

Let's review the circumstances and then look at what we have learned through this interview. First, the premise for the interview: although the target does not know it, forensic accounting investigators have found 28 checks of less than $5,000 each that were written during the past three years to a legitimate vendor of the company. They have established that an individual at the vendor company is a coconspirator and that the invoices issued by the coconspirator were for nonexistent services. They also have a number of checks significantly higher than the $5,000 limit, which they suspect are for nonexistent services, but they're not yet sure of their facts. Their best strategy is to induce the target to admit the fraud involving checks of less than $5,000 and then work their way toward finding out that others are involved in a scheme to defraud the company on much larger purchases of IT consulting services.

One of the target's defenses may be that he was unaware of a fraud and simply approved payment of the invoices in accordance with company policy. In actuality, as the forensic accounting team later discovered, there was a trio of conspirators, including the company director of accounts payable—our target interviewee—a company department head, and an individual at the vendor company. All of the suspicious checks, when received by the vendor, were endorsed with just a checking account number and no company name and were deposited into an account other than the target's primary checking account, known from his payroll direct deposit.

Prior to the interview with the target, the forensic accounting team strongly suspected he had stolen money; they were not blindly confronting the accounts payable manager, he had not been fired, and they were keeping their assumptions to a strict minimum. However, there was much they did not know: they did not know quite how the target did it, how long he had been doing it, whether there were coconspirators, and whether this was the only scheme he used. Because the accounts payable manager knew the forensic accounting team was investigating, he was unlikely to perpetrate additional thefts until they left the scene.

Let us now examine what the investigative team knows because it did not assume facts but instead chose to ask a great many seemingly dull, repetitive, and unnecessary questions. The team is certain of the following:

- From investigation prior to the interview, the team knows that through this scheme alone—there may be others as yet undiscovered—the target stole about $625,000 in the past three years.
- By his own admission, he is the sole approver on transactions of $5,000 or less.
- By his own admission, no one else could have generated the checks without his knowledge. He either knew or should have known.

As you will learn from the later admission-seeking interview of this target in Chapter 18, he admitted to the theft and disclosed important facts of which the investigative team had been unaware. All of this occurred because the forensic accounting team structured the interviews in such a way that the target was left with no escape hatch.

Had they *assumed* facts and had they then been wrong in their assumptions, here is how the target could have evaded the truth when confronted. Assume that the line of questioning proceeded in roughly the following way.

Q: How long have you been with the company and in this department?

A: Ten years with the company, three of them as director of accounts payable.

Note: The interviewer assumes he knows what a director of accounts payable does and therefore does not seek clarification from the target. This is an error. We record in this box, and in boxes to follow, the critical gaps in the interview.

Q: What are the job responsibilities of the director of accounts payable?

Q: What is your understanding regarding the required documentation for purchases of IT consulting services?

A: I understand that any such services must be approved first by the IT department head and then by me.

Q: Is that for all services, or is there some dollar limitation?

A: It is for all purchases greater than $5,000.

Q: So then, purchases of $5,000 or less do not need approval by the IT department head—only your approval. Do I have that right?

A: Yes.

> *Note:* The interviewer feels he does not need to confirm the target's sign-off. He's seen it many times and therefore takes a pass on this question—a decision he will come to regret.
>   Q: I just want to be certain I know what your sign-off or initials look like. Is this it? [The interviewer places in front of the target a copy of the initials on some of the fraudulent checks. The target is not aware that his initials were copied from such documents.]

Q: Besides you, are there any others in your department or another department who could approve such transactions without your knowledge?

A: No.

Later, the interviewer calls on the target for what he believes will be an admission-seeking interview. The interviewer lays out some of the fraudulent canceled checks and invoices with the target's initials signifying approval. The interviewer tells the target that he believes the target knew these invoices were for services not performed and that the target benefited from the scheme. The target looks at the interviewer in shock and amazement and immediately denies the allegations. Undeterred, the interviewer then confidently discloses more evidence.

Q: You told me previously that you are the director of accounts payable. You should have known about this.

A: Sure, that's my title, but our controls are not as tight as they should be around here. Others could have put my initials on that invoice.

Q: Are you telling me that is not your sign-off on this invoice?

A: That's exactly what I'm telling you.

> *Note:* Now he has the interviewer on the defensive. The interviewer assumed that as director of accounts payable, the target controlled everything in his department. He also assumed that the invoice contained the target's sign-off.
>   Q: You told me that you and you alone approved transactions of this type.

A: That's not true; I must have misunderstood your question. When I'm not here, others can approve these types of transactions. We're pretty loose around here because we're a small shop. All I can tell you is that those are not my initials.

> *Note:* Now the interviewer is frustrated, while the target is doing a fine job of wiggling out of the accusations. The interviewer's case theory and proof are disappearing. Taking a closer look at the invoices and comparing the target's initials with the initials on the invoice, the interviewer sees that they arguably show some degree of dissimilarity. Beginning to doubt his own case, the interviewer decides on the spot not to move on to the matter of conspiracy with others to falsify even larger payments. The initial confrontation with the target has failed. It has failed because of too many assumptions and too few verified facts.

◆ THE SMALL STUFF COULD BE IMPORTANT

For the most part, auditors devote much of their time to auditing material trans-actions and account balances, and many such tests are directed at balance sheet items and accounts. With the exception of revenue and certain expenses with unique risk, a fair portion of time allocated to the auditing of accounts such as selling, general, and administrative expenses (SG&A) on the income statement focuses on the adequacy of controls as opposed to individual transactions. That focus is for many reasons, not least among them what the profession calls detec-tion risk: the risk that a material misstatement will occur and not be detected by planned audit procedures is generally greater in respect of material transactions and account balances than in respect of individually small expense payments. Further, keep in mind that if a significant amount of money gets embezzled but the theft is run through the income statement instead of being hidden on the bal-ance sheet, the fraudster is taking advantage of general perceptions of detection risk to more effectively hide the scheme. This is a technical point, but a simple example can clarify it.

The theft of $2 million is a substantial loss, but in the context of detection of material misstatements at a company with $30 billion in total assets and $18 bil-lion in SG&A (assume that the fraud is buried under this caption), $2 million is likely to be quantitatively immaterial to the financial statement taken as a whole. Even if pretax net income is only $1 million (net of the fraud for purposes of this example), it is included in SG&A and therefore in the determination of net income. Of course, qualitatively the financial statements contain a misstatement in that funds that were actually stolen have been characterized and reported as a productive expenditure of the company. Both qualitative and quantitative mate-riality have to be evaluated according to relevant professional standards before determining whether the financial statements taken as a whole are, or are not, materially misstated, but regardless of that conclusion, because the theft is already recognized in the determination of net income—along with many other individually small transactions—it is more difficult to detect.

The difficulty in detecting such embezzlement schemes is somewhat different if the $2 million were recorded on the balance sheet as a hanging debit[2] in accrued expenses or accounts payable. Quantitatively, however, the $2-million theft (presumably recorded as some sort of asset or as a reduction to a liability) would be material when detected and written off in comparison to the company's pretax net income. Continuing with the example, because it does not flow through the income statement, the $2-million write-off would now be con-sidered relative to $3 million in pretax net income and by most quantitative assessments would be material to net income. Since management, internal audi-

---

2. A hanging debit is a charge that should have been recorded on the income statement but is placed on the balance sheet instead. Whether recorded in error or with the intent to deceive, the charge is inappropriate. A hanging debit is similar to a suspense account, with the key difference being that a hanging debit is hidden in a standard balance sheet account, such as accounts payable—usually with the intent to hide it from discovery.

tors, and external auditors all give substantial consideration to balance sheet errors that could be material to reported net income, the chance that this $2-million hanging debit will be detected and dealt with is increased. There have been several recent examples in which a fraudster took advantage of knowledge of the auditor's detection risk and quantitative materiality assessments to hide a theft by running it through the income statement, including breaking up the transactions among a few hundred expense accounts.

In both scenarios, the fraud is hidden until discovered, but in one the fraudster uses knowledge of risk and quantitative materiality assessments to more effectively shield the scheme from discovery. If the theft is concealed in SG&A, detection is more difficult for the company and its auditing firm in part because of the quantitative aspects of detection risk and materiality judgments—even though both would very much like to know about such a defalcation. A company needs to determine whether a theft of this amount represents an acceptable detection risk. If not, it can design appropriate controls to mitigate the risk. Even frauds that do not rise to a quantitative level of financial statement materiality could prove to be embarrassing. Defalcations, whether material or not by the standards of generally accepted accounting principles, reduce a company's value. Accordingly, some companies, through their internal audit group, design audit tests to mitigate the risk that such frauds can occur and go undetected. Such tests involve procedures that go beyond the audit procedures commonly selected by internal and external auditors alike. Among the more advanced and more thorough techniques, data mining can be particularly helpful in detecting such frauds (see Chapter 20).

◆ MATERIALITY: MORE ON A KEY TOPIC

Auditors live in a world in which materiality matters. While auditors, management, investors, and other constituents and members of the corporate-reporting supply chain would prefer that all frauds be exposed, that is not a realistic objective, because most fraud is immaterial to the financial statements taken as a whole. On one hand, the financial burden of audits designed to uncover all frauds of any size would be unimaginably onerous. On the other hand, the public and the capital markets want independent and searching checks of the books and records of public companies. Not surprisingly, the audits of today fall somewhere between the two extremes. Herein lie the questions: how much auditing is enough? And when is it prudent to pursue a matter even if it is immaterial?

Prior to Statement on Auditing Standards No. 99, *Consideration of Fraud in a Financial Statement Audit* (SAS 99), many "errors" in record keeping were dismissed because they fell below the materiality threshold established by the auditing firm at the outset of the audit. *Pass* or *waive due to immateriality* were and remain legitimate expressions in the auditor's working papers, signifying either a transaction, groups of transactions, or balances that had been noted but that fell below the predetermined threshold. Subsequent to SAS 99, though, specifically as required by paragraphs 75 and 76, the auditor can no longer dismiss all such immaterial occurrences at first sight without further consideration. The two paragraphs read, in part:

> **75.** *Responding to misstatements that may be the result of fraud.* When audit test results identify misstatements in the financial statements, the auditor should consider whether such misstatements may be indicative of fraud. That determination affects the auditor's evaluation of materiality and the related responses necessary as a result of that evaluation.
>
> **76.** If the auditor believes that misstatements are or may be the result of fraud, *but the effect of the misstatements is not material* to the financial statements, the auditor nevertheless should evaluate the implications, especially those dealing with the organizational position of the person(s) involved [*emphasis added*]. For example, fraud involving misappropriations of cash from a small petty cash fund normally would be of little significance to the auditor in assessing the risk of material misstatement due to fraud because both the manner of operating the fund and its size would tend to establish a limit on the amount of potential loss, and the custodianship of such funds normally is entrusted to a nonmanagement employee. Conversely, if the matter involves higher-level management, even though the amount itself is not material to the financial statements, it may be indicative of a more pervasive problem, for example, implications about the integrity of management.

While to some these requirements may seem in many respects exercises in chasing rainbows, they actually often represent excellent fraud detection practices. The loose-thread theory, discussed in Chapter 6, suggests that most fraud is very difficult to detect and that, once indicators are found, it is risky to ignore loose threads. The loose thread could be an indicator of a large fraud. Under the new auditing guidance, the auditor is instructed to "evaluate the implications" of the transaction, especially with regard to the position of the culpable party. If an accounts payable clerk wrote a check to himself for $30,000, it may be an immaterial event. However, if the culpable party was the divisional controller, you have quite a different matter on your hands. If the controller did this much, what else could that controller have done? Here is where the forensic accounting investigator could provide useful assistance by, for example, looking at everything the controller touched. This may assist an assessment as to the overall possible effect on the financial statements.

◆ ADDRESSING ALLEGATIONS

Even though the False Claims Act, which gave birth to the modern-day whistleblower, has its roots in the legislation of the Civil War, society has historically frowned upon snitches. With the increase in corporate ethics programs, training, and education, that historically-held negative attitude has given way to a broadly-shared employee awareness of corporate responsibility to come forward and "do the right thing." In fact, three whistle-blowers were selected for person-of-the-year honors by *Time* magazine in 2003. Employees are now held to a higher standard of integrity in the workplace, a standard that approaches military values and discipline. For example, the Honor Code at Virginia Military Institute in Lexington, Virginia, is inscribed on the front wall of every classroom. It reads, "A Cadet will not lie, cheat or steal, nor tolerate those who do." The refusal to accept others who do has moved a long way toward becoming an expected element in the code of conduct in many corporations.

There is always some initial skepticism as to the credibility of a whistle-blower allegation. Thoughts of grudges against the company or against certain individuals or a failure to understand the legitimacy of an unusual business transaction may come to mind as the person responsible for the hotline or whistle-blower communications takes a first look at allegations. It is actually quite natural to discount calls or letters that offer sketchy details, at best, about an alleged illegal or unethical act. However, the best advice is to investigate all such letters and calls. The extent of the investigation is a matter of professional judgment, with all appropriate parties weighing in on that decision. It is important to be mindful of the reporting requirements regarding such letters and calls under the Sarbanes-Oxley Act.

Apply the loose-thread theory to these types of allegations. On one hand, if anonymous allegations are not properly investigated, no harm may be done and the communication may be no more than a shot in the dark from someone with a grudge. On the other hand, there are two more possibilities. First, the allegation could be true. If you ignore it, the fraud may continue and the whistle-blower may return to daily duties with the conviction that the company does not care even about its own assets, let alone its employees. Or, the whistle-blower may persist in seeing that justice is done—for example, by making contact with the U.S. Securities and Exchange Commission (SEC) or the U.S. Department of Justice, expecting to find a more receptive ear. No one wants to begin the day with a call from an assistant U.S. attorney announcing that both the company and the chief financial officer are targets of investigation.

◆ THE CASE OF THE CENTRAL AMERICAN GENERAL MANAGER

Many of the potential missteps discussed above are addressed in the following case study. As fully as any narrative in this book, the case illustrates that a forensic accounting investigation is a complex process, thoroughly distinct from financial auditing, although using some of the auditor's methodologies.

The divisional controller of a $500-million Central American food-processing unit of a Fortune 500 company received an anonymous letter alleging several important but relatively minor offenses. The letter alleged that the general manager (GM), whom we'll call John, was cheating on his expense reports, using company property for personal use, and having an affair with his secretary. The controller—let's call him Paul—could have been inclined to discount the allegations, as John had been honored at the most recent global meeting as a role model for other GMs. An expatriate from Michigan with a Ph.D. in chemical engineering, John had been with the company for 22 years.

On the few occasions when Paul had met John, he was impressed in every way. Why should he be overly concerned, even with this anonymous letter in front of him? It could be from a disgruntled employee. However, Paul had learned long ago that things are not always what they seem. The letter was a potential red flag, and he preferred not to dismiss it until properly investigated. Some years earlier, Paul had encountered another "John" and elected to ignore certain trouble signs, only to learn later that the suspect in that instance was defrauding the company. Since then, Paul had learned to take all such indicators seriously. Trust but verify.

Paul first dispatched three internal auditors to interview John and several other executives and to poke around to see whether anything surfaced. The team spent a week on the task and reported that all seemed to be in order. Nonetheless, Paul decided to wait until the external auditors finished their statutory audit, due to begin in a few weeks. In the course of that audit, the auditors showed the letter of allegations to John and recorded his responses. John flatly denied the allegations and invited what he called a full audit to clear his name. When asked why someone would be motivated to send such a letter, he said that recent, necessary changes in overtime policy might have angered an employee.

Chapter 18 addresses the art of interviewing and surveys the most effective means of obtaining answers to sensitive and critical questions without asking the obvious questions for which the target will almost certainly have well-prepared answers. In this case, if the auditors felt compelled by the statutory requirements of their profession to question John about the allegations, they might have been more effective had they used some of these strategic techniques.

It might have been strategically wiser to approach him in something like the following manner: "John, as a part of our review, we'll be questioning employees, including your secretary, about their comfort level with the integrity of management at this plant. Can you forecast what their responses might be?" If John has been acting with integrity, he would likely answer without hesitation, "All is appropriate, and I don't know why anyone would think otherwise." However, if he has been engaging in inappropriate activities, he might pause before responding and may have a troubled look on his face. He'll have to construct a story that allows for the possibility of someone's coming forward to reveal his illicit deeds—perhaps his secretary. If he is in fact guilty of wrongdoing, he may go so far as to provide the auditors with anticipatory reasons why some may attempt to implicate him. On the forensic accounting investigator's part, at this point, silence is golden. It may cause the target to feel uncomfortable or offer a rambling response that points in a certain direction. Remain silent, wait for the subject to answer as completely as he wishes, be attentive, take good notes.

The auditors completed their statutory audit and reported to Paul that the allegations seemed without basis. They had found nothing to indicate wrongdoing, although they had even confronted John with the letter. Paul, however, remained unsure. He decided to contact the engagement partner from the external audit firm, who until now knew nothing of the possible problem. "Do you have a forensic accounting group? I'd like to talk to them." Acting quickly, the audit partner called in forensic accounting investigators.

The forensic accounting investigators now engaged in this investigation knew that they should not immediately confront John with the allegations put forth in the letter. The lead forensic accounting investigator chose to interview him in an attempt to determine whether he was an honorable person or had something to hide. Such an interview needs a factual basis to be effective, and so the forensic accounting investigator hired a private investigator to perform a weeklong investigation in John's hometown. Certain facts emerged. John owned a small office building in which he housed two businesses, the nature of which was not readily apparent. He also had a passion for classic boats. He owned 12 classic boats and was president of a local boating club with about 40 members and a lavishly appointed clubhouse. The forensic investigator wondered who had paid for the clubhouse. In any event, he now had an array of facts that could serve as a litmus test of John's truthfulness, and it was time to pay him a visit.

The forensic investigator received a very warm welcome from John in his office, which was surprisingly well appointed. Prominently placed on his desk was a framed advertisement of a well-known gun manufacturer displaying a variety of shotguns and automatic weapons. This was the first thing that caught the forensic accounting investigator's eye as he sat down, and he wondered whether this unusual "office art" was deliberately intended to send a subliminal message.

John began the substantive part of the meeting by informing his visitor that there had been a break-in at his offices just the night before. He inquired whether his guest was aware of local reports of civil unrest. Replying, no, he was not familiar with local matters, he redirected the discussion back to the break-in. John then reported that people who were believed to be disgruntled workers had stolen the window air conditioner in the accounting department and also "stolen all the accounting documents." He pointed out that further examination of accounts by the external auditor would be impossible from a historical perspective due to this wholly unfortunate turn of events.

The forensic accounting investigator remarked that he had noticed disarray and confusion in the accounting department as he was escorted to John's office. He added that the computers had not been stolen and were apparently undamaged. He offered to send in IT professionals to assist John's group in rebuilding the accounting documents and expressed his willingness to return at a later date to review the accounting records. Surprisingly, John had not foreseen this set of possibilities. He paused for what seemed a long time, head down, until he reached what he felt would be an adequate response.

Here is an application of the use of silence in an interview. After the forensic accountant commented that his firm's IT team could assist in restoring the accounting records, he became silent. He did not care if John sat there, head down, pondering his response, for hours. He was not going to let him off the hook by offering any further options. He wanted to let John come up with his own story and was prepared to wait patiently for it. Silence and inactivity at the right moment also represent a good technique for assessing the veracity of a target's responses. How long does the individual pause? What are his facial expressions and physical movements during this period of doubt and stress?

After a minute or so had passed—an eternity in a free-flowing conversation—John responded: "That would not be possible. They also stole the computer hard drives." Now, the first reaction to this news might be a hearty laugh. "Sure," thought the forensic accounting investigator, "the individuals involved in the rumored civil unrest had brought along their Phillips screwdrivers, had stolen the hard drives, and at this very moment were installing them in their home office computers." In reality, most of the city was not equipped with either the electrical or communications infrastructure necessary to support widespread personal computer usage, but, playing along, the forensic accounting investigator quietly remarked that this recent turn of events did indeed present problems. He said he would be leaving the country the next day and would inform both his audit partners and the company's corporate headquarters that examination of the local accounting records was impossible at this time and that he would await their further counsel.

John and his guest then went to lunch. Believing he had completely fooled the forensic accounting investigator, John became relaxed and casual and the forensic accounting investigator found in this setting an opportunity to explore further John's truthfulness.

The treatment John received at the restaurant was impressive. He was obviously a regular—private room, an exclusive server, attention worthy of a dignitary. All of these were indications that John was an influential individual. As the forensic accounting investigator was later to learn, John had paid plenty for this kind of treatment. The lunch moved leisurely into its second hour, when the forensic accounting investigator felt that the time was right to pose certain questions to test John's integrity. "John, you're obviously a very successful businessman, and the company holds you in high regard. What do you do when you're not working so hard?" He was reaching out to see whether John would mention his side businesses and his passion for classic boats. John replied that he was devoted to the company and had no time for pleasures apart from an occasional trip to the United States or his native city. The forensic accounting investigator pushed the question in another form—in order to give John one more opportunity to be honest. He did not bite. He insisted that he had no time for simple pleasures. His job demanded his full and complete attention.

At the end of lunch, the forensic accounting investigator thanked John for his hospitality and expressed the hope that they would get together again soon. John left, thinking he had successfully concealed his deceitful operations and believing the forensic accounting investigator would convey the message to corporate that John was an able manager, although certain unfortunate events had occurred owing to the break-in and would soon be rectified. In other words, John was relieved and confident, not suspicious, and thus unlikely to take any further steps to hide his fraud while the next phase of the investigation was being planned.

The forensic accounting investigator met two days later in the United States with the corporate management committee. He reported that although the size of the problem was unknown, he believed there was a problem.

Now let's dissect some of the features of this case that explain why the forensic accounting investigator came away with a different opinion from both the company's internal auditors and the external audit team. The internal and external auditors knew more about the target and the operations of his plant than the forensic investigator would ever know. However, the forensic accounting investigator applied the lessons of a long career in practical forensic investigation.

◆ EXERCISING SKEPTICISM

Trust but verify; this was the guiding principle during the initial meeting with John. The forensic investigator knew he could not properly evaluate the interview or the evidence from the accounts, had there been any, if he allowed bias of any kind to affect his judgment. The forensic investigator's mind was completely open—free of assumptions about the individual's character or acts. However, after the initial interview, including the telling conversation at lunch, the forensic accounting investigator had collected enough facts to shift rapidly toward suspicion. The forensic accounting investigator walked away from John with the concern that if John had lied about the theft of accounting records and refused to disclose his passion for classic boats and his other business operations, he was perhaps concealing other matters of greater importance. There was, as yet, no evidence of fraud—but there was compelling basis for believing the investigation should continue.

This forensic accounting investigator understood how to conduct the investigation, including the nature, extent, and timing of investigative procedures and who should perform them. Performing the correct procedures at every turn, the forensic accounting investigator was methodical in the application of those procedures and in the evaluation of evidence. The result or conclusion from such an investigation is simply a culmination of all of the facts uncovered, together with a minimum of assumptions when facts are still missing. If all the facts fit a pattern of fraud—either a fraud known from prior investigations or a new twist on an old theme—the forensic accounting investigator can be *reasonably certain* that the target with or without coconspirators has perpetrated a fraud.

This is not to apply the familiar criminal standard of guilt beyond a reasonable doubt. As discussed in Chapter 24 and elsewhere, proving fraud to the beyond-a-reasonable-doubt criminal standard may ask too much of a company before it moves to cut its losses by suspending or firing the alleged fraudster or turning over evidence to the appropriate law enforcement agency. A judge or jury as the trier of fact may ultimately make a determination that the evidence, both circumstantial and testimonial, meets the standards for criminal conviction. This is not the forensic accounting investigator's assignment. Forensic accounting investigators are fact finders.

◆ CASE OUTCOMES

In this chapter of potential missteps, the case study investigating John's deceptions has illustrated sound practices. What happened to John? There is good and bad news. The ensuing investigation, covering a span of 12 weeks, was arduous due to John's tactics of intimidating employees and refusing to provide requested documents. It did not take long for him to realize he was the central target of investigation, and he played every angle to dissuade the forensic accounting team from doing its job and to prevent his employees from talking. In the end, the investigation determined that he had embezzled $35 million over a period of two years. Most of it was hidden on the balance sheet in the intercompany account and had hanging debits in accounts payable. The approximately $2 million that did flow through the income statement was buried in the foreign currency translation account to take advantage of the country's high currency fluctuations. That explanation was given to the audit firm and recorded in its "reasonableness" test working papers for this expense account.

The company terminated John, 15 of his managers and supervisors, and the president of that division in the U.S. Within the next two years, the company also closed the plant for which John had been responsible.

CHAPTER 15

INVESTIGATIVE TECHNIQUES

Mona M. Clayton

This chapter is a toolbox. While many preceding chapters have discussed investigative techniques in the context of other topics (see in particular Chapter 8), we have not yet opened a number of trays in the toolbox. The chapter also looks at the administrative issues surrounding forensic accounting investigations, which require knowledgeable management. In any specific circumstance, some tools will be more useful than others in the effort to generate investigative results that can withstand scrutiny by the client, legal counsel, and regulatory and judicial authorities, not to mention quality and risk management reviewers in the forensic accounting investigator's own firm. All of the tools have their place and purpose. We begin with the administrative issues and then go on to specific techniques.

♦ TIMING

While audits are usually predictable in their timing and fieldwork, most investigations are not. On one hand, with few exceptions auditors know their client commitments 6 to 12 months in advance, and clients know what to expect of their auditors over the same time horizon. On the other hand, forensic accounting investigators often enough cannot anticipate their client commitments even two weeks in advance, let alone six months in advance. It is not unusual for them to receive a call on a Friday afternoon and, in response, over the weekend deploy a team to a distant location in time for the opening of business on Monday.

Pending filing deadlines may affect the timing, priority, and sequence of investigative procedures. Investigating can be a lengthy process due to the volume of data requiring review. Transaction review takes time, document review takes time, e-mail review takes time. Investigative leads may take the team into areas not contemplated at the outset of an investigation. Yet all of this is normal. Discuss these issues with the client, audit committee, or counsel to determine the priority and sequence in which existing and new issues should be addressed.

Having a plan and working to that plan structures the engagement. A looming deadline is rarely a good reason to trim procedures and back away from a thorough investigation as initially planned. Stand firm on quality. Communicate timing proposed scope changes, and proposed fees early and often to avoid surprises for the client and investigative team.

◆ COMMUNICATION

While communication sounds as if it is a basic and well-understood aspect of conducting an investigation, it should not be taken lightly. Effective communication, including setting clear expectations, is an essential skill of the investigative team. Working for and with various parties, ranging from audit committees to outside regulatory bodies, the forensic accounting investigator's communications are, in fact, critical. More than one master may be needed for those communications, including the risk management group and legal counsel at the forensic accounting investigator's own firm, audit partners, consulting partners, other accounting firms, outside legal counsel, prosecutors, the U.S. Federal Bureau of Investigation (FBI), management, and internal auditors—and this roster is not necessarily complete for any given circumstance.

Clear, frequent, and timely communications are necessary. Unanticipated complications can often occur when communicating with international, multicultural teams and across multiple time zones. Whether you're dealing with language barriers, cultural assumptions, or the simple mechanics of a conference call, leave nothing to chance. This cannot be stressed enough. The absence of clear, frequent, and timely communications can result in misunderstood time lines and deadlines, missed conference calls, dissatisfaction, even fee disputes. If in doubt, communicate. Even if not in doubt, communicate.

◆ EARLY ADMINISTRATIVE MATTERS

The following administrative concerns usually come up early in the process of setting an investigation in motion and remain important throughout:

- *Relationship review and conflict check.* This process identifies the entity and party names to be compared with outstanding engagements. Potential conflicts should be cleared, calls made, and responses documented prior to accepting the engagement. Usually, the names of the parties are obtained from the person, such as an attorney, who requests your services. For some potential clients, additional research or vetting may be needed—for example, by obtaining a Dun & Bradstreet report, calling a foreign office, or reviewing public records to determine the viability of the entity. Retainers may be obtained and applied to the final billing to offset potential risks that may show up through this qualification process.

- *Engagement letter.* The engagement letter is likely to vary by firm and to include various elements. At a minimum, it would normally include the name of the client, the scope of services, fee arrangements (which may include a retainer), and, perhaps, indemnification and reference to legal matters. On engagement letters, consider obtaining signatures from legal counsel as well as the ultimate client who is paying the fees. Note that for existing external audit or internal audit clients, an addendum to the existing engagement letter, outlining additional scope and fees, may be sufficient. The process may vary, depending on the firm's risk management protocol.

- *Billings/fees.* Strive to keep the client aware of fees incurred and outcomes. You do not need to wait until a bill is sent on your firm's normal billing cycle to inform the client of a fee estimate or fees incurred. Some clients do not balk at fees, while others do. You may prefer to communicate fees in phases or in terms of fees per week/day/professional. The level of detail depends on your own firm's business practices and the preferences of the client. Based on priorities, the client may opt to delay some tasks or perform them through in-house resources, once the time and expense associated with the tasks have been communicated.

◆ PREDICATION

The investigation may begin with a telephone call from a concerned client or audit committee chair. There may be allegations in an anonymous letter or a suspicion of fraud uncovered by an audit team. From whatever source, there are allegations, and the party contacting you has decided that it would be an error to ignore the allegations.

All valid reasons to contemplate launching an investigation can be categorized as predication. According to a trusted resource, the *Fraud Examiner's Manual,* predication is "the totality of circumstances that would lead a reasonable, professionally trained, and prudent individual to believe a fraud has occurred, is occurring, or will occur. Predication is the basis upon which an examination is commenced. Fraud examinations should not be conducted without proper predication."[1] Anonymous tips, complaints, and audit inquiries may surface predication meriting further inquiry. Further, predication can be identified by a number of sources, including but not limited to external auditors, internal auditors, management, employees, third parties, and regulators.

The following examples of predication should not be viewed as a comprehensive listing, but they suggest the various forms that predication may take.

Responding to Regulatory Action

- The SEC has initiated, or a knowledgeable party anticipates that it will initiate, an informal inquiry into certain issues, and our company wants to be able to respond effectively.
- The company is under a 10A investigation.[2] What must it do next?
- If the foregoing question is raised by the company's external auditors, the next questions may well be: What procedures do we need to perform? What fraud risks do we need to consider?

Difficulties in Financial Reporting/Information/Disclosure

- We cannot seem to get timely and accurate reports from [a person, department, location, division, subsidiary].

---

1. Association of Certified Fraud Examiners, *Fraud Examiners Manual* (Austin, Tex.: Association of Certified Fraud Examiners, 1998).
2. See fn. 6 in Chapter 12 regarding 10A and its reference to the independence of the external auditors.

- We made an investment in [location/product], and the early performance reports are troubling despite our up-front due diligence efforts.
- Our internal audit/operations team has just returned from a visit to [location] and reports serious discrepancies.
- There may be a problem with the accounting for [issue]. We want you to take a look at the accounting process and treatment in certain locations and give us your assessment. We are unsure of the impact on the financial statements and the possible need for a restatement.

Issues Involving Customers or Vendors

- Our [department/location] manager seems to insist that we use a certain vendor. That strikes us as a red flag.
- We noticed that a new customer made a $300,000 purchase this month, but we cannot reach anyone at the entity. Could you conduct a public records search and tell us what you find?

Matters Relating to the Foreign Corrupt Practices Act

- We are doing business in [location], and we are concerned that bribes, kickbacks, or unwarranted commissions are being paid to conduct business there.
- We have just completed an investigation in [location], which surfaced some FCPA issues, and we would like you to perform similar procedures in [location].

Lifestyle

- Our [title of individual] just left for a vacation in [super luxury location] and has been acquiring possessions that exceed his expected lifestyle.

Anonymous Tips

- Our [division, location] always hits the numbers, but we have received an anonymous tip that something is wrong there.
- Our [high-level executive] just resigned/died unexpectedly. We have heard rumors and want you to come in and talk with some of our employees.

Conflicts of Interest

- One of our employees was watching late-night television and saw a commercial for a new restaurant in town. The restaurant owner is one of our plant general managers.
- We've heard rumors that our operations manager is an officer of a temporary services company that provides employees for our warehouse. We have paid this entity $1.5 million in the past nine months. Our employees are required to disclose potential conflicts of interest, but we do not have a disclosure from this operations manager. We would like to take a look at all areas for which this person is responsible, and we want to know about the person's real or potential undisclosed conflicts of interest.

Obviously, the list could continue. The intent is to illustrate that predication takes many forms.

◆ WHAT SHOULD YOU KNOW BEFORE YOU START?

Assuming that you are in a position to accept the engagement to which you have been alerted, you will need answers to many questions. A basic understanding of the issues is key to planning and gathering the right resources in order to execute whatever procedures you select from the toolbox. The questions below may not generate direct and immediate answers, and not all of them will be suitable to the circumstance. As well, there may be other questions of importance not listed here. However, consider the following partial list of typical areas of inquiry, and remember that some of them may be brought up again after the fieldwork begins.

GAINING AN UNDERSTANDING

1. *What is the time frame under review?* The client may elect to start with a certain time period and then progress the investigation forward or backward depending on the results of the initial assessment.

2. *What is the nature of the concerns or allegations?* Obtain a complete understanding in order to identify individuals to interview and documents to secure or obtain.

3. *Where is the site, and what are the logistical demands to work there effectively? Do we have the necessary linguistic skills if the site is in a foreign country? Who is our contact at the location?* Obtain details of the locations and names of liaisons at the locations. In remote or foreign locations, the names of hotels and landmarks can be helpful.

4. *Who are the targets?* Based on the predication, determine the potential targets of the investigation. The client may have taken disciplinary action prior to engaging you, perhaps by terminating personnel or putting them on administrative leave. Obtain information about any employment disputes and other relevant history, as well as security concerns.

5. *What type of deadlines, reporting requirements, audit committee meetings, and the like are pertinent to the investigation?* These milestones may affect the timing and scope of the investigation and the sequencing of tasks.

6. *Have other investigations of the focus issues been conducted at this location?* If so, obtain the reports or an understanding of the findings.

7. *What other entities, regions, or sites may be involved?* When asking this question, you may discover, for example, that the general manager under scrutiny also recently managed a different geographic area for the company. The question may identify other at-risk locations to include in the investigation.

8. *Are background checks of employees conducted as a precondition of employment?* If so, request the information and/or consider updating the

information. If not, consider performing public records searches for entities and/or individuals pertinent to the investigation. (See Chapter 17.)

9. *How long has the problem apparently existed? Does it predate any of the key current players?* Depending on whom you ask, you may receive different answers to this question. It may be within the scope of the investigation to resolve the discrepancies in responses to this question. Persistence and attention to detail are key.

10. *Is there an employee, vendor, or customer with a personal or family problem or an addiction (drugs, alcohol, gambling), who might seek additional financial resources at any potential cost and risk?*

11. *Is this an industry or location that has a history or culture of corruption?* If so, gaining an understanding of common industry or culturally tolerated schemes and scams may enhance your ability to evaluate risk and scope.

12. *Has the entity been in compliance with reporting and regulatory requirements?* Regulatory requirements may be at multiple levels with various government entities and regulators.

13. *What is the profitability of the entity? Has it hit its targets? Has it been adversely or positively affected by industry trends or the general economy? If the entity is meeting or exceeding expectations, does that make sense in light of industry trends and the economy?*

14. *What level of growth or decline has the company had, and how does that compare with the growth or decline of its industry and peers?* Ask yourself, "Does this make sense?"

15. *If there has been a recent acquisition, is former management still in place? If yes, is there an earn-out provision in effect?* If so, management may have a large incentive for achieving certain financial measures. Such measures can be achieved honestly—or by fraudulently manipulating a few journal entries or postponing updating estimates.

16. *Does the company have a fraud policy? An annual conflict-of-interest policy or attestation?* If so, consider obtaining the attestations of certain individuals if these issues are part of your investigation.

GATHERING AND SECURING INFORMATION

It is imperative to maintain control of documents requested and received. Documents may be obtained in many forms, ranging from paper to electronic. Requesting, obtaining, and maintaining document control usually are important aspects of any investigation. This task should not be taken lightly, especially in cases in which there are thousands if not millions of documents, and binders and boxes may be in the hundreds.

- *What information can I obtain before the field visit?* The information may include organizational charts, alleged smoking-gun documents, electronic files, personnel listings for potential interviews, financial statements, operational statements, public filings, press releases, and Internet postings (stock chat rooms). If there were anonymous tips, complaints, or letters, now would be the time to obtain them.

- *Is there information that should be secured in advance of the field visit?* The client may need to secure or obtain backup tapes, computers, or network data to avoid destruction of data after your arrival. Now is the time to involve the forensic technology professionals to ensure that the correct information is obtained in the right way the first time around. Doing so probably will prevent rework and incomplete data sets. A visit may also be scheduled to review the offices and files of certain employees.

- *Are the audited and statutory financial statements available for review?* Obtain the financial statements and management letter comments. For off-site locations, confirm whether the corporate office ever received its financial statements, management letter comments, and/or internal control observations and recommendations.

- *Are the auditor's working papers available for review?* Usually, the client assumes that the work papers will not be made available for review or access. However, the request is worth making, and you may be pleasantly surprised by the cooperation you obtain. Releases may need to be signed prior to reviewing the work papers of other firms. Coordinate with your office of general counsel to ensure that the correct protocol is followed in these situations. Scheduling discussions with the outside auditors can sometimes be arranged without difficulty when the proper protocol is followed. Remember here also that clear communication is your friend.

- *Are there internal audit reports available for review? What about reports from compliance, security, legal, due diligence, risk management, or ethics personnel?* Sometimes investigations may be conducted by departments other than internal audit. In addition, there may be preliminary reports or findings that have been made available to the audit committee, special committee, ethics committee, compliance office, and so on. Ask for all reporting—formal or informal—to/from these groups.

- *Is e-mail available for review?* If e-mail is in the scope of the investigation, the files may need to be secured prior to the arrival of the team in the field. A specialist may be needed to obtain and copy or image network files, backup tapes archives, and files on PCs or desktop computers and to prepare them for analysis.

- *Are there PCs or laptops that need to be secured?* Identify the particular computers, and consider when to sequence the imaging of the machines in the investigative plan. Some clients may opt to delay this process until after initial scoping is completed, so as to determine whether copying the computers is warranted. Note that there is a difference between copying a hard drive and imaging a hard drive. A forensic image of a hard drive is more complete than a copy. Without imaging technology, deleted and encrypted files may be ignored. A recent investigation found deleted files and 18,000 deleted e-mails that had been deleted just hours after the suspect learned that his computer was to be obtained as part of an investigation. Without imaging, this information would never have been found. (See Chapter 20 for more information on this topic.)

- *What public records searches should be conducted?* It may be useful to obtain the names of entities (customers, vendors, etc.) and to conduct public records searches prior to the field visit, if those names appear in the predication or allegations. Performing a public records search prior to the field visit may yield valuable information, such as knowing whether any employees are undisclosed officers of key suppliers. Keep in mind that public records searches in some countries may take longer than you expect. The legality of conducting searches and the ability to do so are likely to differ across geographies. Obtaining permission from the company's general counsel before proceeding is always recommended.

- *Where are documents and computerized records?* The client location may be in Idaho, while disbursements may be processed in India. You may encounter different locations for different records depending on what you are seeking. Voucher packages for prior years may be in off-site storage, and a service provider may be used to archive e-mails and computer files. Request computerized information to conduct data mining and analysis. Obtaining and analyzing certain information in these categories may be useful prior to the field visit. If the client site has been recently purchased or sold, the records for prior years may exist at another entity.

- *Was there a computer system change during the period under review?* Determining this item may answer your questions on the time period under review. However, obtaining information from predecessor systems and/or prior owners may be difficult. (See Chapter 20.)

- *What third parties should be considered for interview, contact, or confirmation purposes?* This category may include former employees, vendors, customers, or competitors. There may be some pressure from the company not to extend inquiries out to third parties, owing to a concern that the external inquiries will be disruptive. However, forensic accounting investigators should not retreat from planned and relevant inquiries, even if the inquiries raise initial concerns of this kind. They need to communicate effectively the importance of the external inquiries. After consideration, many companies often are willing to experience some level of uncertainty along the path to resolving allegations. Obviously, if your client does not agree to such contacts, you should not perform them.

- *Have the authorities been contacted? Do you know how to handle the media?* Local police, regulators, prosecutors, the FBI, banking officials, and news media all may play some role in the inquiry. At some point in your career, you may find yourself investigating a high-profile situation with daily if not weekly coverage in the business press. If the press contacts you, consult with your office of general counsel, as well as a public relations professional, to determine whether making a statement is appropriate. Remember that nothing is really off the record, reporters' assurances notwithstanding.

COORDINATION

How often should the investigative team communicate internally? The desirable frequency of teamwide communication depends on the situation. For fast-moving assignments with large teams, you may need to coordinate frequent conference calls among the team members. The team may include internal as well as external members. If in doubt, communicate.

OTHER

- *What reports, written or oral, does the client expect?* Reports take time and cost money, and they may be discoverable. Caution should be exercised if you are requested by the client to quote fixed fees for investigations and written reports. You can perform procedures in phases and keep the client informed and involved in the process to avoid surprises.
- *What is the integrity of management?* This question may be assessed periodically during the engagement.
- *Are you in a situation in which you are shadowing another team of forensic accounting investigators*? Ensure appropriate communications with all parties, ranging from the special committee to your internal legal counsel. In such situations, consider having initial and ongoing input to the scope of the work plan that the other investigative team is using as the basis for their procedures.
- *What is the timing? When do we start?* The quick answer is usually "yesterday." The practical answer may be "sometime soon," especially if the client wants you to review information and conduct public records searches before you gather additional data and conduct interviews. Deadlines may dictate when you start, when you stop, and to whom you report. Obtain dates of upcoming earnings releases and audit committee meetings; the client may assume that you know these dates and expect you to be there and report the findings to date.
- *Do you have insurance coverage?* Please see the following section, A Word about Insurance.
- *What is the budget?* Depending on the client, budget restraints may or may not be significant considerations. Consider working in phases to manage budgets and fees. Communication often is key in this area in order to manage the client's expectations in a courteous and open manner.
- *Is outside security warranted? Are there safety concerns?* This is primarily a consideration for global assignments, especially in developing countries and countries undergoing volatile political or social unrest.
- *What else should I know at this time?* This open-ended question may yield pertinent information. A group of forensic accounting investigators poised to launch an investigation once asked this question—and learned

that during a prior visit by internal audit, security guards had shot at the auditors' vehicle. Their investigation still went forward, but with the aid of bodyguards.

◆ A WORD ABOUT INSURANCE

Can your client recover insurance monies against a fraud? To determine the answer to this question, examine these issues with the client's risk manager.

- *Do you have an insurance policy that covers employee dishonesty, errors and omissions, or fidelity claims?*
- *Does the policy have a provision for paying investigative costs?* If so, all or a portion of investigative fees could be covered by the policy.
- *Who is the carrier?* You may already know people at the insurance carrier through prior claims.
- *What is the deductible?*
- *What types of events are covered?*
- *What types of events are excluded? What are the policy limitations, if any?* For example, if the deductible is $100,000 and the policy covers losses up to $500,000, the client may decide not to pursue losses much in excess of the policy limits. The risk of doing so is that the insurance carrier may not honor some of the transactions. By limiting the transaction review, you may also limit the amount of other potential claims in addition to the insurance claim—a lawsuit against the perpetrator, for example.
- *To what time frame does the coverage apply? Months? Years?* If the time period under review is extensive, there may be multiple carriers and claims to consider and prepare.
- *What is the notification requirement after an event has been discovered?* (Example: the policy may require that the insurance company be notified within 30 days of acquiring knowledge of an event.)
- *What is the timing for providing a detailed claim for the insurance company after having knowledge of an event?* You may be able to obtain an extension if you request one, usually in multiples of 30 days. Make the request for extension early in the process to avoid surprises.
- *Is the client required to pursue prosecution to obtain payment under the policy?*
- *Regarding an insurance claim, the forensic accounting investigator can usually assist the client in areas including but not limited to the following:*
  - Identify the pertinent time period for review
  - Assist in identifying schemes
  - Quantify and document the impact of the schemes
  - Conduct background research on companies and individuals that may be parts of the claim
  - Conduct interviews with key personnel to understand the schemes and to identify certain weaknesses in the internal controls that allowed the

unauthorized transactions to occur (the insurance carrier will ask about these matters)

- ○ Accompany the client to meet with the insurance company to explain key components of the claim
- ○ Assist the client in preparing the claim
- ○ Answer questions of the accounting firm hired by the insurance company to review the client's claim.

◆ EXCEPTIONS AND OTHER CONSIDERATIONS

As previously noted, while financial audits focus largely on materiality thresholds, investigative techniques may well focus on identifying exceptions below the auditor's materiality threshold and also on areas, such as employee morale, which are intangible though observable. For example, the fraud examiner may focus on any of the following.

- • Transactions that appear unusual as to:
  - ○ Time (of day, week, month, year, or season)
  - ○ Frequency (too many, too few)
  - ○ Places (too far, too near, unexpected)
  - ○ Amount (too high, too low, too consistent, too alike, too different)
  - ○ Parties or personalities (related parties, oddball personalities, strange or estranged relationships between parties, management performing clerical functions)
- • Internal controls that are unenforced or often compromised by higher authorities
- • Employee motivation, morale, and job satisfaction levels that are chronically low
- • A corporate culture and reward system that tends to support unethical behavior toward employees, customers, competitors, lenders, or shareholders.

Consider the following examples, some of which may not be considered material by financial statement audit standards and others of which look not at recorded amounts but at the circumstances surrounding amounts. Any or all may warrant review in the course of an investigation.

- • *Time.* Does it make sense that the transactions under review were recorded on weekends or after hours? This skeptical view can also be applied when reviewing the timing and recording of journal entries as part of an investigation into whether entries are being forced to make the numbers.
- • *Frequency.* Does it make sense that Mr. X is paid $4,000 every week? While the individual transactions or total amount may not be material to a financial statement audit, it may be significant that Mr. X works in the mailroom and is receiving large round-dollar payments with little or no documentation.

- *Place.* Does it make sense that a company located in El Paso, Texas, supports a charity located in San Diego to the tune of $300,000 per year?
- *Amount.* Does it make sense that large round-dollar amounts are paid each quarter with no supporting documentation in the files?
- *Parties.* Does it make sense that one of the highest-paid suppliers has an address that upon investigation, turns out to be a post office box in a residential suburb?
- *Petty cash.* Does it make sense that hundreds of thousands, if not millions, of dollars of transactions were recorded through petty cash? While the financial statement auditor may not blink at petty cash because the account balance on the financial statements is a mere $1,000, the forensic accounting investigator will focus on the activity in the account rather than the balance. The activity can be summarized through the data-mining routines discussed in Chapter 20.
- *Salary levels.* Does it make sense that an office manager for a small subsidiary in rural Illinois makes a salary significantly above the market conditions for that area?
- *Perks.* Does it make sense that the vice president used the company jet to attend a World Series game, when the company had no event sponsorship or business guests to entertain? Probing into salary and perk issues may pinpoint undisclosed payments related to executive compensation. It may also be instructive to see an executive push the limits of rationalization, thereby begging the question, "Where else could he have exercised poor judgment?"

Answers to these types of questions will probably assist the client and forensic accounting investigator in determining next steps. Do everything you can to corroborate verbal responses with related documents. What statements can be substantiated through documents, further inquiry, or third-party sources, including public records searches? The tangible evidence you are looking for includes documents, third-party written confirmations, original bank statements, canceled checks, and the like. Consult with others: does what you are observing make sense? Probe for the underlying facts.

◆ DOCUMENT REVIEW

Document review can be critical to a case. Relatively inexperienced people may overlook a feature of a document, while an experienced forensic accounting investigator will view that feature as a potential red flag. Consider the following illustrations.

COMQUEST

Exhibit 15.1 reproduces an invoice from what proved, through investigation, to be a phony company. This invoice was approved, submitted for payment, and subsequently paid. While the document deceived the accounts payable clerk and the check signer, close examination reveals a series of red flags.

ComQuest

5837 Karrie Square, Suite 130
Dublin, OH 43016

Phone: 801-555-3617
Fax: 801-555-1234

Invoice

Invoice #:   476463
Invoice Date: 03/24/2000
Customer ID: BP-486

RECEIVED BY OPERATIONS ON

APR 2 1 2000

Bill to:
ABC Manufacturing
1234 Walnut Drive
Columbus, Ohio

Ship To:
Same as bill to

Date	Your Order #	Our Order #	Sales Rep	OR	Ship Via	Terms	Tax ID
March 24, 2000		576463	Ken Quinn			Net 30	31-236452

Quantity	Item	Units	Description	Ordrment N.	Taxable	Unit Price	Total
1	PBX-4638	EA	Comdial 6730 Telex Switch	13	N	$17,236.00	$17,236.00
2	ST-798T	EA	Comdial 6810 CSU/DSU	10	N	$3,635.00	$3,625.00
76	LBR-05	HR	Labor	0	N	$85.00	$6,460.00

Subtotal	$27,321.00
Tax	
Rate paid.	
Other charges	
Balance Due	$27,321.00

REMITTANCE

Customer ID: BP-486
Date: 03/24/2000
Amount Due: $27,321.00
Amount Enclosed: _____

Communications for the next millennium

EXHIBIT 15.1   COMQUEST INVOICE

Invoices typically have an address, telephone number, contact name, reference number, and description of parts and services along with amounts, taxes, etc. While this invoice does show an Ohio address, the 801 area code is in Utah! Note the icon on the right—a woman speaking on the telephone. In style, it is straight from the 1950s. Compare this icon with the tagline at bottom right: "Communications for the Next Millennium." The icon is probably so-called clip art downloaded from a cost-free online image bank.

Note the invoice's columns for Quantity, Unit Price, and Total. We would expect these numeric amounts to be right justified with decimal points aligned, not left justified. Focus on the second line item, indicating that two items, identified as Comdial 6810 CSU/DSU, were purchased. The unit price is the same as the total. If this were produced on a bona fide electronic invoicing system rather than with a word processing program, one would expect the system to calculate correctly.

Here is a finer point: the tax ID number (see right column in the middle of the document) is an eight-digit number. It should be a nine-digit number. Additionally, while there is an address on the invoice, it was easily proved to be a mailbox drop business. Last, the invoice had no folds, strongly suggesting that it was produced in-house and not actually mailed as would be expected from a valid vendor.

CPA SERVICES

The second invoice, Exhibit 15.2, appears to be for CPA services. Note that there is no telephone number, fax number, or contact name. The invoice is allegedly a retainer for professional services, but not the round-number amount you would normally expect to see. A directory investigation would in time show that *CPA Services* is actually an acronym for *Columbus Preferred Apartments.* An inquiry with that entity would then show that the payment was for an apartment rental rather than professional services.

Note there is a *Ship to* section on the invoice. One would not expect *Ship to* on an invoice for professional services (or, for that matter, for rent on an apartment). The dates in the upper right and lower left are different from each other and in inconsistent formats. The invoice amount is left-justified. Finally, be mindful of generic vendor names as potential red flags.

HOW TO READ A CHECK

Exhibit 15.3 illustrates the information found on a typical check. Forensic accounting investigators with knowledge of the codes for the Federal Reserve districts, offices, state, and bank identification numbers may be able to easily identify a forgery. Additionally, another key number on the check is the magnetic ink character recognition (MICR). The MICR includes the paying bank's ABA (American Banking Association) routing number, the account number of the writer of the check, and usually the sequential check number. If the check number in the MICR does not match the check number at the top of the check, that may be an indication of a forged check.

The endorsement of the payee is located on the back of the check. Other important information found on the back of the check is the date and name of the bank where the check was deposited and the date and location of the Federal Reserve office through which it was routed. By following the endorsements, a forensic accounting investigator can follow the path from the point at which a check was deposited to the point at which it was cleared. When reviewing checks that are hand signed rather than electronically signed, a forensic account-

CPA CPA Services
80 E. State Street
Westorville, OH 43081

INVOICE

Invoice #:   R07412-05-00-A
Date: 02/24/2000
Customer ID: ABC-200

Bill To:
ABC Manufacturing
1234 Walnut Drive
Columbus, Ohio

Ship To:
Same as Bill to

Our #
R07412-05-00-A

Description	Total
90 day Retainer - Professional services March 1 to May 31, 2000	$6, 097.00
Bal Due	$6,097.00

Remittance

Customer ID: ABC-200
Statement #:   R07412-05-00-A
Date: 02-23/2000
Vendor ID:
Amount Due: $6,097.00
Amount Enclosed:

EXHIBIT 15.2   INVOICE FOR CPA SERVICES

ing investigator should compare the signature on the front of the check with the signed endorsement and look for similarities. Although forensic accounting investigators are not necessarily handwriting experts, they should be able to notice whether or not certain letters look similar.[3]

3. Jack C. Robertson, *Fraud Examination for Managers and Auditors* (Austin, Tex.: Viesca Books, updated annually).

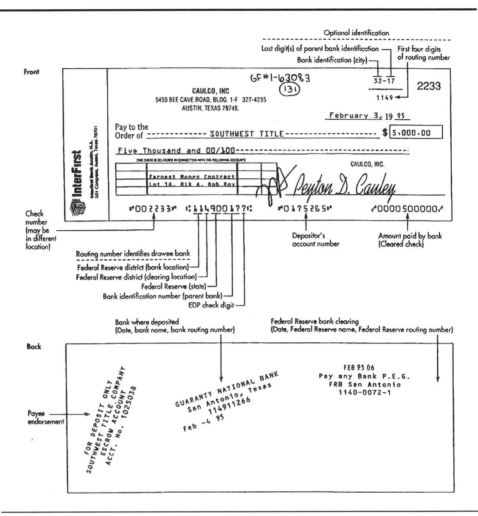

EXHIBIT 15.3   HOW TO READ A CHECK

AIRLINE TICKETS

While we have not included an airline ticket exhibit, some basic information on this topic may be helpful for expense report reviews. Many tickets issued as e-tickets may contain sparse information. However, e-tickets may still contain the passenger's name, travel destinations, ticket price, travel dates, and class. An important aspect of a paper ticket is the form of payment. Usually, a credit card number is masked, with the exception of the last four digits, for security purposes. The last four digits can be matched to an employee's credit card number to trace the payment to the passenger.

Another fraud that forensic accounting investigators should look for is duplicate payment. Duplicate payments (collusion) can occur when another person charges the ticket and the passenger then submits the ticket for reimbursement as well. Duplicate payment can also occur if an itinerary is accepted as proper documentation for reimbursement. Companies should refrain from accepting itineraries as acceptable documentation, since an itinerary can be obtained and then canceled without the employee actually making the trip.

Obtaining details of expense reimbursements in an electronic file can assist in identifying duplicate payments. With some basic sorting and analysis, transactions may come to your attention that could be missed if total reliance is placed on sampling or hard-copy review.

◆ CONCLUSION

This chapter has provided a taste of what a forensic accounting investigation is like and how it differs from a financial statement audit. Although the educational backgrounds of the financial auditor and the forensic accounting investigator may be similar, the mind-set and work processes are drastically different. No two investigations are alike, and "last year's work papers" do not exist in these situations. Further, materiality has little meaning to the forensic accounting investigator.

We have also illustrated various reasons why an investigation can become necessary and the considerations that must be weighed by the forensic accounting investigator in planning the investigative approach. The next chapters will guide you through the investigative process even further and explore in greater detail many of the investigative techniques mentioned in this chapter. Applied effectively, these techniques can crack the case—although the usual caveat applies: there will usually be some degree of corporate fraud, and some portion of it cannot help but go undetected or unresolved.

CHAPTER 16

ANONYMOUS COMMUNICATIONS

W. McKay (Mac) Henderson

Peter J. Greaves

An increasingly frequent occurrence in the corporate world is receipt of an anonymous communication[1] that suggests the existence of issues within or affecting an organization and usually relaying a broad range of allegations. Anonymous communications, often called "tips," may take various forms, including a posted letter, telephone call, fax, or e-mail. In years past, some recipients may have felt comfortable disregarding communications of this type. However, in today's environment such communications are usually taken seriously, and an effort is made to resolve the allegations. By their very nature, such investigations are triggered suddenly and generally require a prompt and decisive response—even if only to establish that the allegations are unfounded or purely mischievous. The allegations may be general statements or they may be very specific, identifying names, documents, situations, transactions, or issues. The initiators of such tips are motivated by a variety of factors, ranging from monetary recovery (substantial monetary recovery is available to whistle-blowers under the U.S. False Claims Act, discussed in later pages), moral outrage, and genuine concern over an issue to the desire of a disgruntled employee to air an issue or undermine a colleague.

While anonymous tips are by no means new phenomena, legislation such as the Sarbanes-Oxley Act of 2002, corporate scandals such as Enron and WorldCom, and the increased scrutiny of health care providers and defense contractors through suits under the False Claims Act have served to raise the awareness of whistle-blowers[2] and the importance of anonymous reporting mechanisms. This awareness, coupled with the dismay of some employees and members of the

---

1. For this chapter, the term *anonymous communication* or *tip* refers to anonymous information received through various media.
2. In this chapter, we use the term *whistle-blower* generically to refer to any individual providing or submitting an anonymous communication. The term *whistle-blower* denotes a person who informs against another or reveals something covert. No negative connotation is implied; the individuals involved are often concerned employees raising genuine issues, and in many cases, the entity appreciates their initiatives.

public that there has been a violation of public trust by some large businesses, has led to an increase in the number of anonymous tips received by organizations.

Faced with the sudden receipt of a tip, often one that makes far-reaching allegations, auditors and executives should rapidly plan and implement an investigation based on a reasoned, tried and tested, and fully case-specific approach to ensure that the interests of all parties are protected. Management should resist the urge not to conduct an investigation because the allegations appear to be groundless. Such an approach may expose the company to unnecessary risk. The allegations should be investigated promptly and effectively. One has only to look at certain terms in the False Claims Act, such as *willful blindness* and *reckless disregard,* to begin to understand the exposures, not the least of which could include having to explain to a corporate board or regulatory body why the company chose to take no action. The failure to act may lead to fines and penalties that may not have been levied if the underlying situation had been addressed appropriately at the outset.

◆ TYPICAL CHARACTERISTICS OF ANONYMOUS TIPS

Anonymous tips come in a wide variety of forms and, as we have said, through quite a number of channels and are addressed to various individuals and groups within the company or to outside entities, government agencies, and even outside news agencies. Recipients within the company may range from legal counsel, audit committee members, senior management, and department supervisors to human resources managers and the compliance or ethics officer. A tip may take the form of a typical business letter addressed to the company,[3] an e-mail (usually from a nontraceable account), or an official internal complaint. It may also duplicate tips submitted to news agencies, competitors, Internet Web site postings, chat rooms, or government agencies. Or it may also be a message to an internal ethics hotline number. Whatever form it takes, a tip may contain allegations that are factually correct at its core, although it also may include embellishments or inaccurate information, wildly emotional allegations, or poor grammar. Further, it may be disorganized, repetitive, and display unprioritized thoughts, and in many cases, key issues will be mixed with irrelevant matters and unsupported personal opinions. However, while the tip's information about specific issues may not be absolutely correct, it may contain a grain of truth or may identify elements of several unrelated but potentially troubling issues.

In one notable case, an accounting department employee alerted the board of directors regarding his concern that the finance director was ignoring demands from the tax authorities and allowing penalties to accrue. Upon investigation, this proved to be so, but the reasons behind the finance director's actions proved to be of greater concern and indeed led to the bankruptcy of the company: the finance director, in collusion with others, had been inflating the company's performance for a number of years, and this had led to a material overstatement of

---

3. In such instances, the letter's postmark is typically nondescript and useless in investigations.

asset values. The scheme had been perpetuated by borrowing against the fictitious assets, and it unraveled when the level of borrowing failed to cover the funds needed to settle taxes levied on fictitious profits.

In some situations, the allegations aired in an anonymous tip may be known within the company and labeled as rumors or gossip. Some whistle-blowers are neither gossip hounds nor disgruntled employees but, rather, frustrated employees who have tried to inform management about a problem and have gone unheard. Only then do they file a complaint by sending a letter or an e-mail or making a phone call.

While one should never leap to conclusions upon receipt of an anonymous communication, inaction is not a recommended option. One of the dangers of ignoring an anonymous tip is that a situation that can be satisfactorily addressed with prompt action at lower levels or locally within the company may become elevated to higher levels or to third parties and regulatory bodies outside the company because the whistle-blower believes the communication has been shunted aside. This can have damaging consequences for an organization's reputation and brands if the allegations become public or attract media attention and a cover-up appears to have occurred, however well intentioned the organization may have been. Ignoring an anonymous tip also may negatively impact staff morale and motivation, if suspicions of impropriety are widespread among staff and it appears that the employer is uninterested or doing nothing to rectify the situation. Ultimately, management may leave itself open to criticism or perhaps the danger of regulatory censure or legal action by stakeholders or authorities if it cannot demonstrate that it has given due consideration to the issues raised in an anonymous communication.

◆ FEDERAL STATUTES RELATED TO ANONYMOUS REPORTING AND WHISTLE-BLOWER PROTECTIONS

The False Claims Act (FCA),[4] dating from the American Civil War, provides that a private citizen may bring an action against a person or company believed to have violated the law in the performance of a contract with the government. Such actions are brought for "the government as well as the plaintiff" and are referred to as *qui tam* actions[5] or whistle-blower lawsuits. In such cases, the individual plaintiff is known as a relator. The relator can file a lawsuit under seal with the court, to be reviewed by the U.S. Department of Justice (DOJ). If the government, after reviewing the complaint, decides to intervene or join the suit, the complaint may stay under seal for a significant period of time while the government investigates. The government has the right to conduct an investigation with or without notice to the subject entity and may choose not to inform the

---

4. False Claims Act, 31 U.S.C. § 3729 et seq.
5. In a *qui tam* action, the plaintiff sues for the state as well as for himself. *Black's Law Dictionary* provides the Latin original and translation: "*qui tam pro domino rege quam pro sic ipso in hoc parte sequitur,*" meaning, "who as well for the king as for himself sues in this matter."

WHO DID IT?

Often, the initial impulse of a company is to speculate on who did it. While such brain-storming can have real benefits in terms of identifying individuals who may have knowledge of the situation and should be interviewed, auditors and executives should be cautioned not to jump to conclusions or speculate to excess, because they may soon be imagining problems everywhere or reading more into statements than the circumstances actually merit. The most important issues at this early stage are not to fasten onto unverified theories or conclusions that may jeopardize the investigation and not to take retaliatory actions against individuals who are suspected whistle-blowers.

After a company received an attention-getting anonymous letter, the forensic accounting investigators assigned to the investigation planned a series of interviews to obtain a basic understanding of the company's operations, processes, controls, and structure. At the early stage of the investigation, the company decided not to disclose the existence of the letter in the course of its interviews. This was out of respect for the confidentiality of the whistle-blower, whose identity was unknown.

In the course of an interview, one individual seemed unusually knowledgeable about many of the accounting, customer information, and record-keeping systems. His position in the company did not call for such extensive knowledge. Probing more with curiosity than with investigative purpose, the interviewer asked how he came to have this knowledge. Could he shed light on other areas? The gentleman immediately became very nervous and from then on, provided cautious answers. The interviewer decided to depart from the interview plan and asked him whether he was aware of allegations recently raised in a whistle-blower complaint received by the company. He said, "Yes, in a way. I am the whistle-blower."

In situations in which the identity of the whistle-blower becomes known, direct exploration of the whistle-blower's information and perspective may assist the forensic accounting investigator to expedite resolution of the allegations. However, the forensic accounting investigator should proceed with caution in these situations and consult with others. We have encountered situations in which whistle-blowers revealed themselves but thereafter wanted to control the investigation by attempting to insert themselves in the process and evaluate the progress of the forensic accounting investigators.

---

subject entity until the complaint is unsealed, thereby becoming public information. The FCA provides for payment to whistle-blowers up to a certain percentage of the recovery, ranging from 15 to 25 percent.[6] The FCA also provides for certain protections against retaliatory action against the relator by an entity or individuals. While the FCA focuses primarily on complaints related to violations of government regulations or contracts, it illustrates that private persons can expose events that result in significant liabilities.

DOJ used this statute very effectively in the mid-1990s as part of its health care fraud initiative. The number of whistle-blower suits filed that were related to this initiative was in the thousands. *Qui tam* actions sometimes involve current or former employees who become frustrated that a corporation has failed to address their concerns over certain issues. The employees' response is to formalize their complaints and file them under the FCA. All the more reason to take such complaints very seriously.

---

6. 31 U.S.C., § 3730 (d).

Another statute that contains mechanisms for anonymous reporting and protections is the Sarbanes-Oxley Act of 2002. As is well-known, Sarbanes-Oxley was introduced in response to concerns over corporate governance after the devastating capital markets impact of a series of corporate scandals, including Enron and WorldCom, which resulted in public outcry and calls for increased supervision of public companies. Section 301 of Sarbanes-Oxley requires corporations to have a process in place that encourages, receives, and investigates issues of concern raised by employees. Section 301(4) of Sarbanes-Oxley reads verbatim as follows.

Each audit committee shall establish procedures for—

(A) The receipt, retention, and treatment of complaints received by the issuer regarding accounting, internal accounting controls, or auditing matters; and

(B) The confidential, anonymous submission by employees of the issuer of concerns regarding questionable accounting or auditing matters.

In our view, this mechanism is intended to encourage employees to come forward with concerns or to raise their concerns anonymously to the audit committee, which oversees the financial-reporting process. Since passage of Sarbanes-Oxley, there has been a steady increase in the number of anonymous tips sent directly to audit committees and independent audit firms. Such tips typically raise several issues and request that the issues be investigated for the good of the company and its stakeholders, including shareholders, employees, and creditors.

Employers are looking for effective ways to receive employee complaints and concerns. While they may have communicated a hotline number that rings to a telephone in the general counsel's office, some employees may perceive that hotline number as not entirely anonymous and may question its effectiveness. While each company may adopt various means to gather the information, ranging from contracting with outside hotline providers to establishing fax numbers to receive complaints, the key is to provide mechanisms that are free from reprisal and to communicate with and educate employees concerning the means available. We have encountered large organizations that established hotlines but never communicated the existence of those lines to their employees in developing countries and markets—the very places where there is thought to be a higher risk of unauthorized transactions and questionable business practices.

Section 806 of Sarbanes-Oxley (Protection for Employees of Publicly Traded Companies Who Provide Evidence of Fraud[7]) is intended, we believe, to encourage the reporting of potential fraudulent behavior. The section provides a variety of protections and relief for the whistle-blower in the event of retaliatory action by the whistle-blower's employer. Namely, a whistle-blower employee

---

7. *Sarbanes-Oxley Act of 2002*, Public Law 107-204, 107th Cong. 2d sess. (January 23, 2002), § 806: "(a) In General. – Chapter 73 of title 18, United States Code, is amended by inserting after section 1514 the following: '§ 1514 A. Civil action to protect against retaliation in fraud cases.'"

may not be fired or discriminated against. The employee can seek remedies for such treatment, including reinstatement, back pay, and compensation for special damages. Section 806 may increase the number of reports of suspected impropriety to audit committees. It remains to be seen to what extent disgruntled employees will use these new powers for leverage by raising baseless accusations against their employers. As discussed later in this chapter, most anonymous tips result in some level of investigation and analysis of information to determine whether the issues raised are genuine or groundless.

The external auditor's considerations when encountering anonymous tips are addressed in AS 2 and SAS 99. Additionally, as noted earlier, Sarbanes-Oxley requires audit committees to develop mechanisms to track, investigate, and resolve all allegations of misconduct.

External auditors need to understand the audit committee's complaint-handling process. Whistle-blower communications are likely to arrive through a wide variety of channels. In some cases, these communications may be directed to the external auditor, but in many cases, management, counsel, or the audit committee initially receives them. External auditors may consider such matters as the committee's ability to monitor the completeness of the population of the complaints, with particular emphasis on those relating to financial statement information.

Depending on the nature of the complaints, the external auditor may conduct inquiries in other areas of the company such as risk management, human resources, or divisional management in addition to the audit committee and the company's in-house counsel. Obviously, a cookie-cutter approach cannot be applied for each allegation. The external auditor's response depends on the particular circumstances encountered. In all cases, it would be prudent for external auditors to seek advice of counsel and their own firm's risk management office. If allegations are meritorious and could potentially have a material impact on the company's financial statements, an investigation of some type may be necessary. At that point, the company may decide to retain the services of a forensic accounting investigator to conduct the investigation. If an investigation has already been conducted or is in process, the auditor may want to gain an understanding of the procedures performed to evaluate risk and any potential impact on the financial statements.

The remainder of this chapter addresses the forensic accounting investigator's investigative approach when dealing with an anonymous tip.

◆ RECEIPT OF AN ANONYMOUS COMMUNICATION

Once notified by a client of the receipt of an anonymous tip, the forensic accounting investigator should obtain an understanding of all of the circumstances of that receipt. While the circumstances may appear unremarkable and trivial, that information is often a key factor in determining the best approach to dealing with a tip and, more broadly, often provides clues that are helpful in other areas. Initial facts and circumstances to be established include:

- *How?* This refers to how the information was conveyed—for example, whether it was in a letter, phone call, or e-mail and whether the letter was handwritten or typed. Additionally, the forensic accounting investigator seeks to determine whether the message includes copies of corporate documents or references to specific documents and whether the tip is anonymous, refers to individuals, or is signed.
- *When?* This includes establishing the date on which the message was received by the entity, the date of the tip, and in the case of a letter, the postmark date and postmark location.[8]
- *Where?* This involves establishing where the tip was sent from, be it a post office, overseas, a private residence, within the office, a sender's fax number, or an e-mail account.
- *Who?* To whom was the tip sent? Was it a general reference such as "To whom it may concern"? A specific individual? A department such as the head office or internal audit? The president's office? The press? A competitor? Sometimes an anonymous notification will indicate that another entity has been copied on the document; this requires verification.[9] Always consider the possibility that the tip may have been sent to the auditor and/or the U.S. Securities and Exchange Commission.
- *What?* This refers to understanding the allegations and organizing them by issue. Often, a tip will contain a number of allegations that are variations on the same issue or that link to a common issue. For this reason, it is often helpful to summarize the tip by issues and related subissues. Does the information in the tip contain information that may be known only to a certain location or department? If so, that may point to a group of individuals or former employees as the source of the tip.
- *Why?* What is the possible motivation for the tip? Issues with misreporting financial information? Ethical decisions? Disgruntled employee? Former employee airing grievances?

Assuming that the anonymous tip comes to the attention of the external auditor, a best practice for the external auditor may be to consult with risk management and a forensic accounting investigator to determine whether additional procedures should be performed.

---

8. This type of background information should be obtained for any communication channel the whistle-blower uses such as e-mail, fax, or voice mail. Computer forensic techniques may assist in analyzing electronic transmission media.
9. Whistle-blower letters often indicate that they have been copied to various enforcement agencies such as the Department of Justice, the Federal Bureau of Investigation, the Securities and Exchange Commission, or the Department of Defense; to the press, such as newspapers or TV; or to competitors. However, it is often the case that either the letters were not in fact sent to those agencies or the agencies will not confirm receipt of a letter except in the case of a formal notification related to an enforcement action. If the press does receive a letter, the entity is generally able to confirm the same based on queries from reporters.

♦ INITIAL UNDERSTANDING OF ALLEGATIONS

The forensic accounting investigator should initially take enough time to understand the allegations. All allegations should be taken seriously but viewed
objectively and without preconceptions. The allegations may be close to the truth
but not absolutely correct, perhaps owing to the likelihood that the statements are
clouded by emotion or limited by the individual's somewhat incomplete grasp of
the facts. It is also usually a helpful exercise to consider the possible motivation
for the tip (see earlier, Why?) and to think through how the alleged activities,
actions, or incidents could have occurred. It may be helpful to discuss with the
client the nature of business processes in the area of alleged wrongdoing to assess
the credibility of the allegations.

♦ DETERMINE WHETHER ANY ALLEGATION REQUIRES IMMEDIATE REMEDIAL ACTION

The initial assessment of the tip should focus on whether or not any aspect of the
allegations poses an immediate threat to the safety of employees or property. In
a great many whistle-blower situations, this assessment will indicate that the
entity must move quickly. The question as to whether the alleged activity may
involve criminal or civil liability will also affect the forensic accounting investigators' approach and should be considered carefully in consultation with legal
counsel. The investigation should be planned in such a way that if circumstances
warrant, immediate actions may be taken to protect the individuals and assets
involved and to safeguard the integrity of evidence and information that may be
exposed to destruction, alteration, or removal.

In each particular set of circumstances, consideration must be given to the
need to protect the identity of the whistle-blower if known or to take steps to
ensure the safety and welfare of individuals identified in the tip or otherwise
thought to be at risk based on the allegations. Employee welfare issues can range
from minor inconveniences and unpleasantness to verbal abuse or, in extreme
cases, physical danger. Reducing the physical proximity of those involved is
often sufficient—for example, placing individuals on administrative leave or
moving them to a different location. In some situations, it may be necessary to
consider personal protection by private security providers or even law enforcement agencies. These considerations will differ with circumstances and jurisdiction, and personal safety is a much greater factor in certain territories.

While forensic accounting investigators are not typically expert on personal
security matters, they can assist client executives by making them aware of the
issues and working with them to obtain advice and assistance from qualified
legal, risk management, human resources, and security personnel. Depending on
the nature of the allegations, the forensic accounting investigator should advise
the client of the potential need to eliminate access to or limit access to buildings/
areas and to computer systems in order to eliminate or reduce the loss, damage,
or destruction of assets and information. There may be other issues and materials

that need to be protected and secured such as documents, backup tapes, credit card access, bank account access (signature cards, wire transfer authority, check stock, etc.), off-site storage access, combinations to safes, and passwords to bank accounts and credit cards. To assist with the investigation, obtaining access and securing access to relevant information sources—including but not limited to certain employee files, accounting records, calendars, electronic records, security tapes, phone logs, and expense reports—should be considered in order to ensure the physical security of the client's assets. In addition, existing security, access to assets by suspected individuals, the nature and portability of assets, and assessment by internal personnel as to the accuracy of the whistle-blower's allegations all determine the extent of the physical security needed in a particular situation. Even after precautionary measures have been taken, if the target has alliances with employees still on-site, something could slip through the cracks.

Finally, consideration should be given to locating the investigative team in a secured site such as an office with reliable security and to controlling access to documents obtained during the investigation.

◆ DEVELOPMENT AND IMPLEMENTATION OF THE INVESTIGATIVE STRATEGY

THE INVESTIGATION TEAM

Upon initial receipt and evaluation of the tip and after decisions on employee safety and asset preservation have been taken, the client, independent counsel,[10] and forensic accounting investigator should discuss the organization and structure of the investigation team and then develop a strategy to address the allegations in the tip. Discretion, speed, and effectiveness are the key considerations in the assembling of a team to respond to the issues created by receipt of an anonymous tip. The team needs to be large enough to address the various issues, but at the outset a small team of experienced professionals is most effective. The team can be expanded as appropriate in the course of assembling a better understanding of the situation.

The use of forensic accounting investigators may not be suitable in some circumstances—for example, harassment matters—but when the allegations suggest financial improprieties, accounting issues, or misappropriation of assets, forensic accounting investigators become critical members of the investigative team. The forensic accounting investigator also may bring interviewing experience, technical skills, and industry expertise to a particular issue or industry sector. The forensic accounting investigator typically works closely with computer forensic specialists to download and analyze electronic information, whether

---

10. In engagements of this type, upon receipt of a letter the client often hires independent legal counsel. The independent counsel is usually actively involved because significant legal issues tend to arise (see Chapter 24).

easily available, backed up, or in some cases, deleted. The team may also include individuals from the client company with sufficient authority, corporate knowledge, and independence from the issues and individuals in question to ensure a timely and well-directed approach to the allegations and developments.

A further consideration is control of the team. A typical engagement structure appropriate to many situations is for the audit committee or a special committee of the board to engage an independent counsel. Counsel then engages forensic accounting investigators and other professionals and oversees the assembled team (see Chapter 24).

In most instances, knowledge of the investigation and its progress may be restricted until completion of the investigation or attainment of some other appropriate milestone determined by the investigative team or client. At that stage, a report—preliminary or final, depending on circumstances—can be made to the board, external authorities, shareholders, or other stakeholders.

◆ DISCLOSURE DECISIONS

An early decision facing the investigative team concerns whether there are any required external or internal disclosures. Addressing the timing and approach for disclosure is a very difficult process. The client should consider obtaining professional risk and crisis management advice, attorney advice regarding legal requirements, and public relations counsel. Forensic accounting investigators are typically aware of the issues surrounding disclosure and can provide valuable insight into the process, but they should refer the client to appropriate professionals for conclusive advice outside of their specific expertise. When the investigation concludes, the issue of disclosure needs to be addressed. Disclosure must be consistent with legal and accounting requirements, regulatory guidance, and any accurate information that investors may already have obtained from other sources. Disclosure can be used on occasion to assist the investigation as a means of gathering information—for example, by tactically inviting media attention or soliciting information from employees on a broad scale. Disclosure is also a signal to regulatory authorities that the company and the board are taking prompt, appropriate, and thorough action, and it is often appropriate to meet with the relevant members of the regulatory community and brief them on the scope and progress of the investigation.

Regardless of the decision on disclosure, the appropriate structure, timing, and format of any notice to employees should be considered and a strategy implemented to minimize rumors on the corporate grapevine due to the presence of external investigators. On one hand, it may be necessary to reveal basic information and confirm the existence of an investigation, although just what is communicated depends on the extent to which it is clear at the time that further investigation is merited. After the first day of interviews, the corporate grapevine typically comes alive. In many situations, the corporate client has a legitimate interest in balancing the natural desire of its employees to understand the details of the investigation against the predictable distraction that the information will cause as employees digest its meaning. On the other hand, that is not the only balancing act: the company will need to protect the privacy of the whistle-blower and its own economic interests while minimizing the adverse effects of the rumor mill. A proactive notice to employees can be very helpful in halting the rumor mill and notifying those with pertinent information to come forward.

Disclosure to the public, including regulators, about the investigation may also be warranted or required. The advice of counsel should be sought in this regard. Consideration also should be given to engaging the company's corporate communications department at an early stage to prepare suitable responses to any unexpected press interest or if public disclosure should become necessary. In significant matters, outside public relations assistance should be sought. Depending on the investigation findings, the company may also need to respond to press inquiries or stories at a later stage.

◆ PRIORITIZE THE ALLEGATIONS

Anonymous tips often include a number of allegations and information presented in a random order, with overlapping issues and issues that initially appear to be unique but later prove to be parts of a larger pattern. The allegations must be carefully sifted to establish those that are potentially genuine and to set priorities for investigation—that is, where the greatest potential problems are in terms of financial loss, physical danger to persons or assets, legal implications, and so on. The forensic accounting investigators need to cut through the verbiage in the tip and separate any personal or judgmental comments from the basic allegations. This should be done systematically, paragraph by paragraph, to map out and agree among the investigating parties as to the principal allegations. The goals of the forensic accounting investigator are to arrange a structure that addresses each issue, to devise a road map to the relevant information, and to consider evidence that will enable the investigation to confirm or refute the allegations.

Once the core allegations have been identified, each one must be understood in the context of the specifics of the business in question, and a plan should be developed to conclude on each allegation. For example, if the first allegation is that an individual has falsified a document, steps should be taken to locate and analyze that document. If the allegation concerns vendor kickbacks, a plan must be developed to investigate, by legal means, any flows of money or gifts between the parties in question, any relationships between the vendor company and the subject company's employees, and those who may be involved at the vendor company.

A key to planning the investigation of each allegation is to grasp how—within the framework of the existing systems, structures, and practices of the organization—the alleged activities could have been carried out. Loopholes and weaknesses in systems help identify switch points at which there were opportunities for impropriety. The forensic accounting investigator should also consider how the alleged wrongdoing could have been concealed. In essence, if the alleged activity did occur, the forensic accounting investigator should be asking:

- How could it have happened?
- Were system controls overridden?
- How would I hide it in the system?
- What were the controls?
- How did cash get out the door?[11]
- How were accounting records adjusted and balanced?
- How were assets diverted?
- Who would have had to be involved?
- Were third parties such as vendors or customers involved?

It has been our experience that most anonymous tips usually merit further investigation because many contain a kernel of truth. In one case, an anonymous tip pointed to financial-reporting issues involving a long-standing financial manager. The forensic accounting investigators immediately focused on internal controls related to check disbursements. After investigating the controls in this area, conducting interviews, and performing data mining, they discovered weaknesses that enabled the suspicious transactions to occur. Among the weaknesses was a practice of presigning blank dual-signature checks, which could then be signed and cashed by the perpetrator. Further investigation revealed that the finance manager had covered up the fraud by faking annual auditors' reports and signing off on them himself. The embezzlement had started many years before and increased in frequency and amounts as the years went by.

In such matters, the forensic accounting investigator will often have to address the question, How can we fill a documentary gap? Proving that a document has been falsified is usually easier than collecting evidence to demonstrate that an omission has been covered up, a document trail has been destroyed, or individuals have colluded. It is typically necessary that forensic accounting investigators piece together information to surround an issue in such a way that even though a specific document has not been found or no one has confessed to wrongdoing, the facts build on each other sufficiently to allow sound conclusions to be drawn.

Consideration also needs to be given to the time period of the impropriety, as suggested by the allegations. If it is alleged that a specific event happened at a single point in time, the issue of time period is less relevant. However, if it is alleged, for example, that an individual has been stealing inventory and falsifying records for an extended period, then consideration must be given, at least in the early stages of an investigation, to the necessity and cost-effectiveness of investigating every incident. In some cases, it may be essential to gain a complete picture of the economic loss in order to make the necessary adjustments to the financial statements. In other circumstances, it may be necessary only to find evidence of one incident rather than every occurrence. For

---

11. A simple technique is to determine how the cash or asset got out the door of the corporation and then work backward to the original source of the funds or the location of the asset.

example, if the allegation involves kickbacks from suppliers to the head of purchasing, evidence of one instance may be sufficient to conclude on the matter and take remedial action.

Finally, on one hand, the forensic accounting investigator should approach the allegations with an open mind; no allegation can be dismissed without due investigation. On the other hand, the forensic accounting investigator should avoid the trap of believing allegations without supporting evidence. A common scenario involves allegations founded in truth but embellished or clouded with emotional rhetoric. The forensic accounting investigators may find themselves repeatedly coming back to an allegation, asking the same questions, and determining whether any new pieces of information support or dismiss the allegation. Proving the negative—filling information gaps with sound evidence—can be a very difficult task.

◆ INTERVIEWING EMPLOYEES

Documentary evidence is key to the investigation and establishment of the facts, but the complete story rarely can be established without structured interviews.[12] In light of the allegations and an understanding of relevant business processes, the forensic accounting investigator and investigative team need to draw up a list of employees who may be able to provide initial insights on systems, processes, procedures, department structures, and documents.

If it is possible to establish the identity of the source of the anonymous communication or if the individual self-identifies,[13] an early interview will often add key information and enable the investigative team to assess the credibility of the allegations. Whenever possible, the investigative team should conduct its interview after sufficient review of facts and evidence has been performed to test the veracity of the allegations. It will often be necessary and appropriate to reinterview the individual after the accuracy of the information provided has been corroborated.

Identifying the source of the tip may create a dilemma for the investigation team depending on the facts and circumstances. The company should use care in dealing with the individual so as to avoid allegations of harassment and to avoid providing a basis for the individual to allege retaliation. However, the company may need to take action to protect other employees and assets. Further, the individual may have uncovered a serious corporate misdeed and may need to be protected from harassment by other employees. Often, the treatment of the

---

12. Consideration must be given to various issues when interviewing employees, including attorney-client privilege, advice to employees, the company's obligations to employees, provision of separate counsel, and the potential for an employee to refuse to cooperate. These topics are covered in Chapter 24; the present chapter addresses issues unique to the response to an anonymous letter.

13. Whistle-blowers often reach out for help by leaving obvious clues to their identity in the hope that the investigators will identify them and make the first approach. When investigators request information, whistle-blowers can experience the lifting of the burden and in some cases, the feeling of guilt associated with proactively disclosing the issues.

individual in question needs to be managed carefully because the person has key knowledge and occupies a reasonably responsible position in the business, which may suffer commercially without that person on the job.

A decision needs to be taken as to whether to tell employees of the tip, to show them a copy of the tip, or to refer only to the fact that allegations have been made. Once employees become aware of the issues, they will naturally speculate as to who may be the whistle-blower or who would have had access to the information. The interview process, while creating speculation, is essential to the investigation by helping the team determine and evaluate:

- Which individuals (employees, former employees, customers, suppliers, and others) may have the most relevant information about the allegations
- Which additional individuals should be interviewed
- Which documents should be secured and obtained, including e-mail

This relatively open search for truth may generate new lies and could reveal the identity of the whistle-blower. Employees who participated in the improprieties, or others with knowledge of them, may craft stories so as not to expose their participation and/or knowledge, and after the interview they may warn coconspirators. Interviewing is, therefore, a calculated risk in any investigation.

Concerning possible targets of the investigation, the forensic accounting investigators should consider the personal circumstances of the individual involved—for example, whether the person is in debt, is living in what seems excessive luxury, or is involved with unsavory elements. And the person may also have assets that can be traced back as acquisitions from the proceeds of fraud. The forensic accounting investigators should factor these issues into evaluating the motivation of the individual, the validity of the person's statements, and whether there may be alternative motives. A final point—whether or not the source has been identified—concerns the potential involvement of third parties. For example, is it one person in one department? Is it people across several departments? Is it an external fraud? Or is the perpetrator in collusion with an external party such as a customer or supplier?

On occasion, the forensic accounting investigator may use modified audit procedures to assist in resolving the allegations. In some instances, the forensic accounting investigator may opt to request transaction confirmations from certain suppliers or customers or simply telephone them to verify transactions. One recent investigation involved allegations that salespeople were inflating revenues by billing consigned goods to customers. As part of the receivable confirmation process, the forensic accounting investigators included additional line items such as the amount of consigned goods. When the confirmations were received, it was easy to determine which companies and salespeople to investigate further by taking note of discrepancies in the confirmations related to consigned goods.

In many instances, the anonymous tip may allege kickbacks or phony invoices with a certain supplier or customer. To determine whether the allegation has merit, the forensic accounting investigator may first conduct a public records search to determine the existence and location of a company. Consider these facts from an anonymous tip:

- Operations manager dictates to purchasing department which packaging supplier to use.
- No bids are obtained from other suppliers.
- In the past six months, packaging suppliers that had enjoyed long-term business relationships with the company have been discontinued.
- An employee believes the operations manager is creating the invoices that are being approved by one of his buddies.
- Packaging supplies are being received, but customers are complaining about quality.

Before visiting the premises of the company, forensic accounting investigators determined that the address of the supplier was five minutes from the client company's site and that the company had paid this packaging supplier approximately $500,000 over the past six months. On the way to the client company's site, the forensic accounting investigators drove by the address and took a photograph (Exhibit 16.1). The picture showed an ordinary house in an economically deprived area of the city. There was no signage for a packaging business. The company's legal counsel took the view that this photograph was sufficient predication to continue the investigation, and in time many of the original allegations were confirmed.

The interview process should consider the impact of an investigation on the operations of a business. Because operations must continue, the investigation should be designed to disrupt the business as little as possible—although here,

EXHIBIT 16.1   A REVEALING FORENSIC PHOTOGRAPH

too, there are calculated risks. In situations involving customers and suppliers, the company is often reluctant to approach those parties for fear of damaging ongoing business relationships. Disruption may also occur when individuals are interviewed, and that needs to be considered. The investigative team should weigh the benefits of quickly determining whether there is any basis for the allegations against the potential for some degree of disruption in normal operations.

A common situation in investigations of anonymous tips is the identification of a former employee, perhaps one who had been with the company for some time but who recently departed the area of the company under investigation. This former employee may be the whistle-blower or know the whistle-blower. Employees in this category often provide a wealth of information. For that reason, the forensic accounting investigator should always have an inquiring mind as to who else should be interviewed or may have knowledge of the issue. There may be situations in which knowing the whistle-blower or being reasonably certain of the identity of the whistle-blower can be helpful in evaluating the veracity of the allegations. Identifying such knowledgeable persons early in the process may bring efficiencies to the investigation and can assist the investigative team in focusing on important details easily overlooked if former employees are not considered on the list of possible interviewees.

The forensic accounting investigator and investigative team need to combine the information gained through interviews, public records searches, data mining, hard-copy document review, e-mail review, and electronic discovery to piece the puzzle together. To confirm the facts, they may find it necessary to reinterview individuals several times, comparing their notes with other documentary evidence as well as other interviews. The forensic accounting investigator may have to interview very junior members of a department or organization to identify potential discrepancies in statements gained through interviews.

In this chapter we have only briefly covered issues related to the identification, collection, and control of documents obtained in the course of investigation. Those topics are addressed in detail in Chapter 21. However, a few thoughts may be helpful here. In investigations of the type now under discussion, preserving a record of who provided documents and computer files and precisely when they provided them often is critical to developing sound conclusions. The record makes it possible to compare the responses of an individual (or source of information, if not an employee) over time and evaluate whether there is an indication of that person's involvement or guilt. Depending on the size of the case and the nature and volume of the information, consideration should be given to using an evidence management system. Such systems are often helpful in graphically presenting trails of evidence and relationships. Regardless of the sophistication of the evidence management system, it is necessary to keep strict control of all evidence to maintain integrity and ensure that all available evidence is brought to bear in the investigation.[14]

---

14. If there is the potential for criminal violations, extreme care must be used to document the chain of custody of the evidence and the integrity of the original documents.

The majority of the information flow in a modern office is in electronic format; for that reason, it is often necessary to consider evidence in electronic format and to use computer forensic techniques.[15] Electronic discovery can also uncover key documents—for example, a prior draft of a document that was modified to cover up the issues or an e-mail that was deleted by both sender and all recipients. Once identified by the forensic accounting investigators, such documents can be used to confront individuals on the inconsistency of their statements. When a blatantly inconsistent document or statement is identified, individuals will often admit additional facts.

◆ FOLLOW-UP TIP

Just when the forensic accounting investigator has exhausted all areas of inquiry, has reviewed all documentation, has interviewed all relevant individuals, and believes it is time to pack up, sometimes a follow-up tip arrives. Such tips usually follow the same themes as the initial tip, covering the same issues and urging the company to keep looking. Sometimes the relator indicates that the forensic accounting investigators are not on the right path and so provides additional details. A tip of this nature can indicate that the relator is still employed by or has access to current employees of the company. In one case, the relator was identified as a former employee and—given the nature of the matter—the investigative team was concerned that there were active communications between current employees and the relator. After analyzing the phone logs of certain suspected employees, the team identified a clear pattern of communication between an employee and the whistle-blower, his former colleague.[16] Knowing this information helped the team craft its inquiries and interviews and build trust with these employees. The team was able in this way to obtain the facts that validated the allegations.

Given that whistle-blowers are typically fearful for their own positions and wish to avoid any reprisal or stigma, every effort should be made to make it simple and safe for them to contact the investigation team discreetly and in confidence. Once an investigation is under way and especially after receipt of a follow-up tip, the investigative team should consider setting up a hotline or central contact. There is value in a tactic as simple as having the investigative team members give out their business cards and in making sure that the corporate grapevine knows where to contact the team during and after business hours. In one investigation, the team members let it be known that they would be staying at a certain hotel for a week. At 11 o'clock one night, the relator called and provided additional details on the issues, including who specifically was involved.

---

15. Computer forensics and electronic discovery can often provide the critical information in a format that allows for effective data mining. Specific recommendations in this area can be found in Chapter 20.
16. In this case, the employee would call the relator within minutes of completing the interview.

◆ CONCLUSION

Whistle-blower communications are increasingly frequent phenomena. In the wake of corporate scandals, lawmakers are responding to public concern by encouraging employee monitoring of corporate ethics and affording statutory protection for whistle-blowers.

Dealing with an unexpected anonymous tip can be a challenging matter, even to the most seasoned forensic accounting investigator. Objective analysis and the strategic approach taken by professionals skilled in corporate investigations can assist clients in successfully addressing issues that may have serious legal and financial implications. Protection of employees from retaliatory action and the company's need to decide whether or not and to whom to disclose information are among the many issues created by the receipt of an anonymous tip. While the typical initial impulse of the company is simply to hunt down the whistle-blower, the key to resolving cases of anonymous tips usually involves a detailed examination of large amounts of data obtained from many different sources such as interviews, public records searches, data mining, hard-copy document review, and electronic discovery.

A careful, experience-based investigative strategy is imperative in order to address the circumstances surrounding the transmittal and receipt of an anonymous tip and to tackle the allegations prudently and thoroughly.

CHAPTER **17**

BACKGROUND INVESTIGATIONS

Jonny J. Frank

Gregory Schaffer

While some companies handle investigations in-house, background investigations have grown into a multibillion-dollar industry, with providers ranging from sole practitioners to multinational companies. This chapter examines the broad range of information available, covers how much of it is available online, and discusses some of the pitfalls faced by forensic accounting investigators. Auditors and forensic accounting investigators use background investigations for a variety of purposes. Sometimes a background investigation is used to seek direct evidence of a fraud, digging deeply into related-party transactions. At other times, a background investigation can identify investigative leads, locate interviewees, and perform asset searches.

The enormous growth in information resources available on the Internet and through commercial online services has revolutionized the investigative process. Virtually every business investigation now begins with some form of online research. In a matter of hours, a skilled forensic accounting investigator can develop critical leads and make connections that may never be found through traditional field investigation. Knowing when to use commercial databases and the Internet is part of developing a comprehensive investigative strategy. The forensic accounting investigator should identify which databases or Internet sites are most likely to contain information relevant to the target of the investigation. As more information becomes available on the Internet, forensic accounting investigators should keep current with the various tools and their content.

Relying on information found on the Internet without consideration of the source is never advisable. While some laws regulate what can be posted in certain commercial contexts, for the most part the public is able to post virtually anything it likes, though it may subsequently be called to account for libel, defamation, misappropriation, unfair dealing, and more. In some cases, it may be necessary to conduct two investigations: one investigation of the subject and one investigation into the sources providing information about the subject.

The Internet provides links to information vendors that can provide private records such as credit card statements, bank statements, telephone records, utility bills, academic transcripts, and tax returns. However, these records are generally private information, and if the vendor obtained them in an unlawful manner, customers may incur potential liability as an accomplice or abettor of criminal activity.

An important first step in any investigation is to identify the subject accurately. This information should include properly spelled first, middle, and last names; additional names used by the subject—for instance, Theodore J. Jones may also be known as Theo Jones, Ted Jones, Teddy Jones, or even TJ Jones; date of birth; Social Security or other national identification number; addresses; and telephone numbers. Much of this information can be found in audit documents, business cards and stationery, personnel records, and conversations with people who know the subject.

When comprehensive identification information is not available, the initial research should focus on its development, especially when a subject's name is a common one. Without this basic information, it is hard to separate public records about the subject from those that refer to an individual with a similar name—for example, "the other Michael Jordan." In addition, some state and local governments require a date of birth to conduct a check of criminal records.

◆ COMMERCIAL MEDIA DATABASES

The most valuable sources of information fall into two main categories: (1) news and media coverage and (2) the public record. Media can provide historical and background information regarding entities and individuals. These sources include local, national, and international newspapers; magazines; trade publications; and television and radio broadcast transcripts. A high-profile subject's legal, financial, or business troubles are often written about in news media in well-researched and thoughtful articles. The media can also be helpful in identifying a subject's employment history and personal history, as well as charitable and philanthropic relationships.

Among the commercial media databases, four provide the most extensive news and media coverage:

- *Dialog* (www.dialogweb.com), similar to Nexis in scope, is noted for its strong full-text coverage of regional newspapers such as the *Philadelphia Inquirer* and the *Detroit Free Press,* as well as its extensive collection of industry-specific newsletters. In conjunction with Dow Jones and Financial Times Information, Dialog also offers a vast collection of international news sources.

- *LexisNexis* (www.lexis.com) provides access to a massive collection of news sources, including extensive archives of national newspapers and business and industry news sources. It has the largest archive of *New York Times* articles, as well as a growing number of local newspapers. It also offers access to Bloomberg News, a fast-growing provider of business news. Strong content, as well as software that simplifies searching for and reviewing documents, makes it a good starting place in any investigation.

- *DataStar* (www.datastarweb.com) is particularly strong in international news sources, primarily from Europe. Although DataStar is an affiliate of Dialog, many of DataStar's European news sources are not included in the Dialog database. These sources include newspapers, newswires, and business magazines from Germany; Italy; Switzerland; the Baltic states of Latvia, Lithuania, and Estonia; and other countries. DataStar's search language is challenging and requires much practice to master.
- *Dow Jones* (www.dowjones.com/index_directory.htm) is the only database that provides full-text access to the *Wall Street Journal,* the *Dow Jones Newswire,* and *Barron's.* It also has an extensive collection of local newspapers, industry publications, and international news sources.

These databases are constantly adding sources and removing underused ones. For this reason, researchers should stay alert to changes and adapt their search strategies accordingly.

Beyond media coverage is the vast compilation of abstracted public records information. Online public records, perhaps the fastest-growing area of online information, are routinely included in any business investigation. However, their availability varies from state to state and covers variable time periods. For this reason, the extent of coverage in a particular jurisdiction should be carefully considered. Forensic accounting investigators routinely encounter situations in which a manual search of the public record reveals significant litigation matters that were not identified online despite the fact that court records were supposedly online for that particular jurisdiction and time period. Many online records, moreover, contain only select portions of the original document, because the online provider may provide only abstracts. A combination of online searching and on-site searching at relevant courthouses or agencies is usually the best approach.

Following is a list of some of the many useful public records that are also available online. Note that some commercial providers compile various public records in one search.

- *Credit header files* contain only the header section of a credit bureau file, which includes name, address history, telephone numbers, and vital information such as date of birth and Social Security number. Header information is part of public record and readily accessible through online commercial sources. In contrast, full credit bureau reports include employment history, credit history, and inquiry history; by law, this is restricted, private information and accessible only with a release from the subject of the investigation.
- *Incorporation records and fictitious business name (or doing-business-as [d/b/a]) filings* are filed on the state level at the secretary of state's office or, in some states, at the county level in the county clerk's office. Each state maintains basic information about businesses that register to make their business names public and protect the uniqueness of their names. These records can confirm the business affiliations of a subject and identify when a business was incorporated, whether it is in good standing with

tax authorities, who its officers and directors are, and whether it is operating under any trade names. All 50 states offer this information online.

- *U.S. Securities and Exchange Commission (SEC) filings* are required of all public companies with at least $3 million in assets and at least 500 shareholders of one or more classes. The filings provide general and specific information about business and financial conditions, including legal proceedings; acquisitions, mergers, and tender offers; major activities; and key personnel information.

  Readers of this book will be well aware that private companies are not required to disclose financial information to the SEC. However, media publications, analysts' reports, company Web sites, and the Forbes 500 listings are helpful in developing financial information about private companies. So, too, are government agency Web sites, which may reveal a private company's records regarding labor and environmental issues. Government Web sites, a rich information source, are discussed in detail later in this chapter.

- *Significant stock ownership* is listed on SEC Forms 3 and 4 and identifies stockholders with a 5 percent or larger interest in any publicly traded company in the United States. These records are easily accessible online.

- *U.S. Tax Court and Internal Revenue Service (IRS)*—when the IRS files a Notice of Deficiency against a taxpayer, the taxpayer has three options: pay the taxes, do not pay the taxes and become delinquent, or sue the IRS in U.S. Tax Court to seek to overturn the tax bill. When people take the IRS to Tax Court, they put their once-private financial affairs into the public realm. Most Tax Court cases include the tax returns of the filing party. However, there are some restrictions that could be applied from certain sections of the tax law.

  The U.S. Tax Court Web site, www.ustaxcourt.gov, offers free docket inquiries for corporate and individual tax cases. Once you locate the court case you are interested in, you can visit the court and request this public information. Docket records are available for cases filed on or after May 1, 1986.

- *Bankruptcy* petitions for all 50 states and the District of Columbia, both personal and business, are available online. These include Chapter 7 liquidation filings, Chapter 11 reorganization filings, Chapter 12 adjustments of debt of a family farmer with a regular income, and Chapter 13 adjustments of debt of an individual with a regular income, as well as dismissal or discharge information. The information in a bankruptcy filing can be used to gather background data on parties and judgment debtors, to track business and consumer bankruptcies, and to determine the collectibility of potential judgments.

- *Uniform Commercial Code filings,* documenting a loan or lease with secured assets, are called UCC (Uniform Commercial Code) financial reports. Filing a UCC financial report protects the note holder by helping ensure that the debt is paid. A UCC financial report contains the debtor's and creditor's names and addresses and the asset used to secure the loan. Information about UCC filings is widely available online and can be found at the office of the county recorder of deeds or the secretary of state's office. UCC statements can be used to document who is doing business with whom, the address of a borrower unlisted in telephone directories, the name of a borrower's spouse or business partner, property owned by a borrower, and transaction dates that reflect changes in a subject's financial condition.

UCC documents may provide other valuable investigative leads. A UCC listing an airplane or yacht as the debtor's collateral may lead the forensic accounting investigator to previously undiscovered assets. If the collateral is a painting, that suggests a line of inquiry among art dealers. When a UCC filing reveals that a subject borrowed from a marginal finance company, it may suggest that the subject has a poor credit rating. Borrowers sometimes end up with liens placed against their property by the IRS or a state agency because of unpaid taxes. The lien is generally filed at the recorder's office in the borrower's home county. In some states, federal tax liens are filed in one office and state tax liens in another.

OTHER PUBLIC RECORDS

Other useful public records exist. Depending on geography, some information may be available online, while other information is not. Some records can be obtained by mail, while others require a visit to the repository.

- *Vital records* include birth, death, marriage, and divorce certificates, and online access to them is rare. They are helpful in locating sources, as well as providing information about the subjects under investigation. Most states have central repositories that need to be searched manually for each type of vital record. State regulations vary on which vital records are public and which are subject to restrictions.

- *Social Security numbers* are often used as identifiers that tie together multiple records, but access to Social Security numbers is highly restricted by various privacy laws and regulations. In 1997, leading information industry companies created self-regulatory principles to govern the dissemination and use of personal data. Under these regulations, Social Security numbers obtained from nonpublic sources could not be displayed to the public on the Internet, and the companies agreed to restrict access to Social Security numbers to commercial and professional subscribers. The Financial Modernization Act of 1999 includes provisions to protect consumers' personal financial information held by financial institutions and applies to other companies that receive such information. More information about consumer privacy and access to Social Security numbers is available from the Federal Trade Commission at Web site www.ftc.gov/privacy/glbact/index.html.

Social Security numbers can also be used to verify whether a subject is alive. This information is especially helpful when trying to confirm the validity of a client's pension payments or when evaluating ghost employees. Among the Social Security number death indexes that can be searched without charge is one at Ancestry.com (www.ancestry.com/search/). There are also services available for a fee that can evaluate the validity of Social Security numbers; this is useful for large data sets. An example of one such service is Pension Benefit Information (www.pbinfo.com).

- *Education records* of attendance, completion, and degree or certificate granted are maintained by individual academic institutions. Some consider this public information and make it accessible online, by telephone, or by written request. Many institutions require approval from the student before releasing records. Private data of this kind become public when subjects disclose their academic history to a biographical directory such as *Who's Who*. Because the subject usually provides the biographical material, it should be verified.

- *Voter registration records* are effective means of locating a missing person, although online availability varies from state to state. A voter registration application may show the state of birth, thereby helping the forensic accounting investigator narrow the search for a birth certificate; age; previous place of residence; length of residence at current address; and occupation.

- *Driving history* is available from each state through whatever department oversees the licensing and oversight of drivers and in some cases is available online. This department maintains records of all traffic violations and driving-related offenses, as well as of license suspensions or revocations. Every state has an efficient mail-in, mail-back method for processing requests. These reports detail basic information about an individual and can supply surprisingly helpful information, including ownership and value of vehicles, addresses, and potential substance abuse problems.

- *Company credit and information reports* reveal information about the background and financial health of a business, uncover relationships between companies, and provide information about key individuals in an organization and potential conflicts of interest.

- *Professional licensing boards* provide information on the status of a license and whether any disciplinary action has been taken against a licensee. Each state sets its own regulations and requirements for continuing education. How much of this information is made public varies widely from state to state and profession to profession. Licensing authorities include bar associations for attorneys; accountancy boards for certified public accountants; medical licenses for physicians, nurses, and home health care agencies; and education departments for teachers' certifications. To be licensed, a professional must meet certain standards, including age, citizenship, residency, type and level of education, examination scores, field experience, and moral character. State or federal statutes or municipal ordinances set out the standards. Professionals must adhere to performance standards or face losing the license through suspension or revocation. Grounds for revocation or suspension include felony conviction, obtaining fees by misrepresentation, drug or alcohol abuse, mental incompetence (as judged by a court), physical abuse of patients, or other dishonorable or unethical conduct that harms the public. A complaint filed by a fellow professional or a member of the public usually initiates an investigation. In some states, licensing boards have the power to start an investigation on their own initiative. Many licensing boards can release complaint files, but only after the case has reached an advanced stage.

Many licensing boards and professional associations maintain Web sites that allow searches for licensing information and disciplinary histories. A good starting point is the site maintained by the Council on Licensure, Enforcement, and Regulation, which provides links to most boards of professional and occupational licensure in the United States and Canada (www.clearhq.org/boards.htm).

The American Medical Association's Web site can be searched by physician name, location, or medical specialty (www.ama-assn.org).

The National Association of Securities Dealers' Public Disclosure System enables researchers to access data about the qualifications, employment histories, and disciplinary histories of more than 850,000 current and former brokers and industry representatives.

Many states provide their own online license verification searches. These include the New York State Education Department's Office of the Professions (www.op.nysed.gov/opsearches.htm#nme), the Florida Department of Business Regulation (www.myfloridalicense.com), and the New Jersey Office of the Attorney General, Department of Law & Public Safety, Division of Consumer Affairs (www.state.nj.us/cgi-bin/consumeraffairs/search/searchentry.pl).

Searches for other licenses and permits may be useful depending on the specifics of the investigation. Such licenses and permits could include marriage licenses, gun permits, concealed weapons permits, liquor licenses, notary licenses, and building permits, to name a few. These sources could provide personal information as well as information on a subject's previously unknown businesses. Depending on the state, you may find them online.

- *Criminal history records* can be found in state databases and at county courthouses. In most states, criminal court information is openly accessible from the local court where the arraignments, preliminary hearings, and trials took place, but little of this information is available online. To be thorough, each county that may have had jurisdiction over an individual should be searched. An incomplete history of the locations with which the individual has had contact raises the danger of gaps in the record. It is also possible that an individual has been convicted of a criminal offense in a county or a state without having resided there. One category of criminal records that is widely accessible online is sex offense convictions. Government Web sites listing sex offenders typically include photos of the offender and a current or last-known address, as well as a list of sexual offense convictions, but no other criminal convictions. The only truly national criminal database is the U.S. Federal Bureau of Investigation's National Crime Information Center file, which is not open to the public. Some states, however, do have criminal records available, and inmate information is available at www.bop.gov.

- *Civil court records* are available online in only a few states and local court systems. Civil suits are generally divided between higher and lower courts, based on the monetary amount of the claim. Actions under state laws are found within the state court system at the county level. In Michigan, for example, claims for $10,000 or more are filed in the appropriate circuit court, and claims for less than $10,000 in district court. Actions under federal law are found at U.S. district courts. Generally, whatever occurs in a courtroom is a matter of public record, but some proceedings, such as juvenile cases, are closed, and judges may close or seal any portion of any case record at their discretion. Litigation and judgment information is often collected by commercial database vendors. A review of court records may provide insights into the litigation history of the parties involved in the lawsuit, pending suits, relationships among parties and witnesses, business affiliations, and patterns and practices of individuals and institutions.

- *Divorce court records* are often-overlooked sources of financial information about private companies. Divorce court records may contain detailed financial data about one or both litigants, revealing otherwise unobtainable financial information concerning the companies of which each litigant is an officer.

- *Tax liens* are involuntary liens filed against a person or business that owes a debt, which would otherwise be unsecured. The federal and state governments file tax liens against the assets of a subject who fails to pay income or withholding taxes. These reports will state which type of tax has gone unpaid, the tax period involved, the Social Security number of the subject, the date the lien was assessed, the last day for refiling, and the balance due on the unpaid tax. Such liens may indicate financial instability, poor judgment, or disregard of the law.

- *Civil judgments* are filed at the county clerk's office of each state in the U.S. These records profile encumbrances against parties and uncover debtor/creditor business and banking relationships. In some areas, these judgments are available online.

- *Environmental regulation reports* on issues such as disposal of hazardous materials and soil composition inspection are public records, but finding online access is difficult. Civil actions filed by the Department of Justice on behalf of the Environmental Protection Agency may be searched by defendant name through the Right-to-Know Network at www.rtknet.org/doc/def.php. As the scope of information provided by this database is limited, researchers should also check records made available by the Environmental Protection Agency (www.epa.gov) and the Department of Justice (www.usdoj.gov). Searches of federal litigation filings should also be conducted.

- *Property ownership* can be determined by searching tax assessor, deed transfer, and mortgage records available online for certain states and counties. This information has many uses, such as discovering the ownership and value of a particular property, assessing the collectibility of judgments, finding a mailing address for service of process, finding elusive parties and witnesses, finding property for judgment and lien attachment, or researching the subject's financial interests.

- *Automobiles, aircraft, and watercraft records* identify all motor vehicles registered with departments of transportation to a particular titleholder or address; civil aircraft registered with the Federal Aviation Administration; and all merchant vessels documented under the laws of the United States and registered with the U.S. Coast Guard. Pleasure boats are generally not required to be documented with the U.S. Coast Guard unless over a certain size; however, many lenders require such documentation as better protection over their collateral. If not documented, they will be registered in the state of their port of call.

- *Bibliographies and directories* cover a wide range of information, from listings of America's wealthiest individuals and genealogy indexes to directories of trade groups and professional associations, to congressional directories. There are even directories of directories. The delivery medium for these items varies. Some may be available online at no charge, others could require a subscription service with updates delivered via CD-ROM, and still others may be available only for purchase in print format. There are far too many titles to include here, but some examples are the Marquis *Who's Who* publications, the *Directory of Corporate Affiliations,* and the *Martindale-Hubbell Law Directory.*

◆ COMMERCIAL DATABASE PROVIDERS

A number of commercial database providers offer broad coverage of public records, and forensic accounting investigators should be familiar with each and its strengths. These databases overlap substantially in content, and, conversely, one of them might have a document not included in another's database. An experienced forensic accounting investigator may choose which service to use based on cost and search features, which differ widely across the public record databases. Numerous services, including ChoicePoint and AutoTrack, also provide manual records retrieval services, should forensic accounting investigators require more information than is available online.

- Noted earlier but now in more detail, LexisNexis (www.lexis.com) contains bankruptcy filings, state and federal civil lawsuits, tax liens, judgments, UCC filings, corporate records, and property records in most jurisdictions. Many consider its greatest strength in searching public records is its full-text-search feature. A post office box number—for example, P.O. Box 12345—used by a subject could be searched in secretary of state records to identify other companies or fictitious business names (d/b/a's) associated with the subject, which might *not* turn up through a search of the subject's name. Not all information providers offer full-text searches.

  LexisNexis also offers reported legal decisions at the federal and state levels. The published opinions often contain extensive factual information that may not have been reported in the media. LexisNexis has a finder feature, which can be used to locate and identify individuals from more than 300 million credit header and telephone records nationwide. Other features include a military locator feature for checking on an individual's reported military service; driver's license information for about half of the states; and the Social Security Death Master File, which can help determine if a subject is using a retired Social Security number.

  Disciplinary actions and sanctions from various federal and state agencies and regulatory groups, including the NASD, the SEC, the Department of Housing and Urban Development, state real estate regulators, and other agencies are covered in various libraries. The FEDSEC library in LexisNexis contains civil lawsuits and administrative proceedings initiated by the SEC.

  Real property ownership, transfer, tax assessor, and mortgage records can be reviewed in a global search that covers the District of Columbia and the majority of counties in every state except Maine. These records can be searched by name or address and often allow a forensic accounting investigator to identify assets involved in a bankruptcy or fraudulent transfer.

- *ChoicePoint* (www.choicepoint.net) contains bankruptcy filings, civil lawsuits, limited criminal case information, liens, judgments, property records, UCC filings, professional licenses, corporate records, voter registration information, and aircraft and vessel ownership records. ChoicePoint has records from most states in the country and is particularly strong in California, where it covers criminal cases and municipal court civil cases in numerous counties. ChoicePoint's Discovery Plus feature can locate individuals nationwide with only a name or Social Security number.

- *AutoTrack* (www.atxp.com) is one of the best online resources for locating individuals. Its national report feature provides a subject's Social Security number, date of birth, business and residential addresses associated with the subject for the past 8 to 10 years, telephone numbers listed in the subject's or spouse's name, possible business affiliations, UCC filings, and a list of all individuals associated with the addresses reported for the subject.

Running a national profile report by using AutoTrack usually is a good first step in developing personal identifiers for the subject, including a list of jurisdictions in which the subject has worked, resided, or attended school. In these jurisdictions the forensic accounting investigator can then probe more deeply for assets, litigation, criminal records, businesses, and other public information.

Using individual or business names, AutoTrack can identify property ownership information, boat and aircraft registration, Drug Enforcement Administration controlled-substance licenses, firearms and explosives licenses, professional licensing information, motor vehicle records, business affiliations, bankruptcies, liens, judgments, driving records, phone listings, secretary of state filings, and other useful records.

- *PACER* (www.pacer.psc.uscourts.gov) provides access to most U.S. district (criminal and civil), bankruptcy, and appellate courts, including those in the District of Columbia, Puerto Rico, and the U.S. Virgin Islands. While most databases provide only limited federal case abstracts, PACER provides complete docket sheets for most cases. It has a federal court index that permits nationwide searching, and through its Web version provides links to the docket sheets. Its ability to search the majority of federal court indexes across the country in just a few minutes makes it an extremely powerful search tool. Note, however, that each court has a different archiving policy. Careful attention should be paid to the coverage dates of each district. The PACER Web site's list called Non-Participating Courts should be checked to verify that all courts relevant to your research are covered (www.pacer.psc.uscourts.gov/cgi-bin/miss-court.pl).

- *CourtLink* (www.courtlink.com), a division of LexisNexis, provides access to U.S. district court and bankruptcy court cases and, like PACER, provides full docket sheets. CourtLink's advantage is its proprietary software, which allows the researcher to navigate the PACER system more easily. CourtLink allows the user to search combinations of disparate courts simultaneously, a feature not available on PACER. CourtLink also provides comprehensive access to state-level criminal cases and civil lawsuits in Oregon, Texas, and Washington (in some instances back to the 1970s). See CourtLink for updated information about availability and access of records by state and by jurisdiction.

- *CourtExpress* (www.courtexpress.com) provides access to the U.S. Supreme Court, U.S. courts of appeals, U.S. district courts, U.S. bankruptcy courts, and selected state courts. CourtExpress's proprietary software allows the researcher to more easily navigate the PACER system and provides access to state-level criminal cases and civil lawsuits in a number of states, although at this writing information is not available for all 50 states. See CourtExpress for updated information about access and availability by state and by jurisdiction.

- *Superior Information Services* (www.superiorinfo.com) is the most comprehensive source for civil litigation records, judgments, tax liens, bankruptcies, corporate records, and foreclosures for the Mid-Atlantic region, including Delaware, the District of Columbia, Maryland, New Jersey, New York, Pennsylvania, and parts of New England. Because the database gathers its information from primary sources, it has a high degree of reliability. LexisNexis buys much of its civil litigation information from Superior. Superior's powerful search engine, more intuitive than many in design, returns records featuring names similar to the one entered by the researcher, including common misspellings and name variations such as Tom/Thomas, Maggie/Meg.

All of the commercial database providers offer some form of global search capability, which allows the user to search millions of records simultaneously.

OTHER SOURCES

In addition to commercial database vendors, forensic accounting investigators should consider Dun & Bradstreet, which provides self-reported business and credit information on public and private domestic and international companies. Its people locator services, like those provided by LexisNexis and ChoicePoint, can be critical in locating key witnesses. Many state and federal agencies make records available without cost on the Internet. A number of sites also index and provide links to searches of freely available public records—for example, www.brbpub.com/pubrecsites.asp and www.crimetime.com.

Industry Benchmark Information

Industry benchmark information can be used to compare the target company's financial information and common financial ratios with those of its industry as a whole. Significant variances from industry norms might trigger the forensic accounting investigator to determine whether the company possesses unique characteristics that could cause these variances or whether the variances could be potential red flags of fraud. Sources for such industry information include ValueLine Investment Survey, Hoover's Online, EdgarScan's Benchmarking Assistant, S&P NetAdvantage Industry Surveys, DJI Company Profiles, One-Source, and Profound.

♦ UNIQUE INTERNET SOURCES

While the availability of public information on the Internet is increasing at a fast pace, freely available public records offerings on the Internet remain insignificant in comparison to the offerings of commercial services. In tandem with commercial databases, however, the Internet can provide valuable leads and critical information about individuals and entities and should not be underestimated. The Internet has also spawned a number of unique research resources:

- *Message boards* and *chat rooms* are sites where people discuss various topics. Many such sites are topic specific. Forensic accounting investigators can monitor continuing discussions or search the vast pool of archived postings. These sites can provide a wealth of information, particularly in the context of information about pending litigation. The message boards maintained by Raging Bull (http://ragingbull.lycos.com/mboard/viewclub.cgi) are frequented by people in the financial and investment communities. In addition, Yahoo! maintains numerous message boards that address various issues (http://messages.yahoo.com/index.html). Other industry-specific message boards may be identified through Internet search engines.

- *Home pages* of companies can provide a wealth of information. A company site may list sales information, geographic territory, the biographical information of corporate officers, joint venture partners, and product information. A private company may provide on its home page a more detailed history or corporate structure than it provides for a commercial credit-reporting service. It may also inadvertently leave outdated but perhaps useful information on its Web site, which a commercial vendor deletes once the information is updated. A broad range of old and discontinued Web pages is available at www.archive.org. Many individuals have home pages that may reveal how individuals present themselves and suggest potential avenues of inquiry about the individual.

  Web tools are available that can help forensic accounting investigators determine who the registered owner of an Internet site is, what company hosts the site, where the site is hosted, and what other sites are owned or operated by those entities. This may reveal relationships among entities that otherwise appear to be distinct operations. Among the Web sites that maintain such information are www.internic.com/whois.html and www.namedroppers.com. Web services are also available, for a nominal fee, that will verify academic degrees and professional certifications—for example, National Student Clearinghouse, www.nslc.com.

  The Internet is a useful tool for locating consulting and testifying experts whose credentials and other information can be found online at http://expertpages.com/, http://national-experts.com/Members2/search.html and www.expertlaw.com/.

- *Private records* can be investigative gold mines, but they are frequently unavailable to forensic accounting investigators.

- *Credit reports,* as noted earlier, contain an individual's Social Security number, date of birth, current and previous addresses, telephone numbers (including unlisted numbers), credit payment status, employment, assets, ownership interests, and sometimes information about lawsuits and other legal information, but they are not available to the public. The Fair Credit Reporting Act spells out the responsibilities and liabilities of businesses

---

FREEDOM OF INFORMATION ACT

The Freedom of Information Act (FOIA), passed by Congress and signed by Pres. Lyndon Johnson in 1966, provides many, including forensic accounting investigators, with a tool for obtaining a wide range of public records. Federal agencies are required to disclose records requested in writing by any person, and the FOIA places the burden on federal agencies to show why information ought to be withheld. Yet obtaining information is not always a simple task and the act is not a right of access. FOIA requests must be worded very specifically and contain the descriptions and filing dates of the documents requested. FOIA requests must be addressed to the correct government agency; they will not be automatically forwarded. If a forensic accounting investigator is unsure of which of several agencies possesses a document, a separate request should be submitted to each. If more than one type of document is needed, the forensic accounting investigator should submit separate requests for each category of information.

To assist the public in navigating the FOIA highway, the Department of Justice makes available the online FOIA Reference Guide, which details the information available, how to submit a request, the appeals process, contact information for all federal agencies, and other information (www.usdoj.gov/04foia/04_3.html). The nine exemptions written into the law are national security, confidential business information, law enforcement records, banking documents, oil and gas data, records protected by other statutes, some internal memoranda, personnel-related documents, and invasion of privacy.

Most states and some cities in the U.S. have FOIA laws similar to the federal FOIA legislation.

---

that provide information for, and access data from, credit reporting agencies. Under certain circumstances, credit reports may be available to entities and individuals who are considering granting credit—for example, landlords, insurance companies, employers, loan companies, and credit cards, only if the individual consents and signs a release.

The company ordering a background check may have a credit report in its files along with appropriate consents that allow the use of the report in the course of an investigation. In other cases, consent may have been obtained as a condition of employment, thus allowing a credit report to be pulled by the employer under specific circumstances. To allow the broadest flexibility, some employers obtain employee consent at the time of initial employment, giving the employer permission to obtain credit reports and background checks at any time during the course of the subject's employment. It is the forensic accounting investigators' responsibility to verify that they have a legal right to review a particular credit report and that privacy laws are not violated by this review. As evidenced in some cases, one of the risks is that the forensic accounting firm may be classified as a reporting agency, subjecting it to additional restrictions. It is always best to seek the advice of your client's counsel for all credit and background checks.

- *Medical records* contain information that may be useful to a forensic accounting investigator, such as individual medical history, family medical history, lab test results, prescribed medications, and details of the patient's lifestyle, which might include smoking, high-risk sports, or alcohol or drug use. Medical and patient records are generally considered to be private and confidential. Most medical providers will not release these records unless ordered to do so by a court or by consent of the subject.

A new federal law protecting the privacy of medical records went into effect in April 2003. The Health Insurance Portability and Accountability Act of 1996 includes provisions that promote electronic record keeping and transmission, but the act also requires that safeguards be put in place to protect the security and confidentiality of medical information that is shared electronically. The law covers all written, oral, and electronic medical records and other personally identifiable health information. All health and life insurance plans and health care providers—including physicians, dentists, medical groups, hospitals, clinics, and pharmacies, as well as business associates who use protected health information, such as lawyers, forensic accounting investigators, and data processing and billing firms—must comply with the law or face civil or criminal penalties (see www.hhs.gov).

The Americans with Disabilities Act provides additional protection of medical records. The law forbids employers from asking job applicants for medical information or requiring a physical examination prior to offering them a job. Existing employees may be asked to submit to a physical exam if it is a blanket requirement for all employees with similar jobs in the company. Some state laws protect medical records privacy, but they vary widely. A state-by-state listing of medical privacy laws is available at www.healthprivacy.org.

OTHER GOVERNMENT AGENCIES

As mentioned earlier in this chapter, government agency Web sites are useful for researching both public and private companies' records with regard to labor and environmental issues and sanctions. These sites include the Equal Employment Opportunity Commission (www.eeoc.gov), the National Labor Relations Board (www.nlrb.gov), the Occupational Safety and Health Administration (www.osha.gov), and, as mentioned previously, the Environmental Protection Agency (www.epa.gov).

Other government agencies can provide additional background information on individuals. The U.S. Department of Defense (DOD) maintains records on all active military personnel. The DOD Web site (www.defenselink.mil) provides information on how to request personnel information for the various branches of the military. The National Archives and Records Administration maintains records of inactive military personnel (www.archives.gov/facilities/mo/st_louis.html). The U.S. Bureau of Prisons (www.bop.gov) maintains records on individuals who have been incarcerated in federal prisons; this information is also available at the state level from each state's bureau of prisons (www.corrections.com/links/viewlinks.asp?Cat=30). In addition, state gaming commissions maintain records of the owners of gaming establishments, the financial information of gaming establishments, and names of individuals banned from gaming establishments. One example of this is the Nevada Gaming Commission's Excluded Person List that can be found at http://gaming.nv.gov/loep_main.htm. Links to many information sources such as these can also be found at the Crime Time Publishing Company Web site at www.crimetime.com.

INTERNATIONAL INVESTIGATIONS

International investigations generally follow the same protocols as domestic ones, but information publicly available in the United States is often not available in other countries. In a few cases, information that is not public in the United States can be found lawfully abroad. While online information from abroad is limited, more is becoming available each day. LexisNexis has added limited court case abstracts from Australia, the United Kingdom, New Zealand, and parts of Canada. Dun & Bradstreet features international company reports. Several online information vendors feature media coverage in the English language from publications around the world. Foreign companies that sell shares in the United States must comply with SEC filing requirements, and Form 6-K, filed annually, lists officers, directors, and wholly owned business entities.

When truly comprehensive information about an individual is required from a foreign country, it is usually advisable to retain the services of a local vendor with experience and local contacts who can be expected to navigate with ease that country's laws and practices. The scope of what is publicly available to a local forensic accounting investigator and the means of accessing that information vary considerably. In the United Kingdom and Germany, for example, criminal litigation filings are not considered public information, and the only public information of a subject's involvement in a serious criminal matter may be through media reports. In Mexico, public records may be maintained in remote locations, and accessing them may require a visit to each location and time-consuming manual searches. In Brazil, litigation records are filed on the state level and may be accessed only by licensed attorneys. In China, no corporate or individual computerized information has been made available.

Forensic accounting investigators should take specific note of the Foreign Corrupt Practices Act (FCPA), which prohibits payments to foreign officials for purposes of obtaining or maintaining business. In many countries, it is a matter of common knowledge that legal and regulatory officials provide information in exchange for payments. Such payments may violate both local law and the FCPA. The Transparency International Corruption Perceptions Index annually reports an index for more than 150 countries. See www.transparency.org for more information.

◆ CONCLUSION

The ability to perform an Internet search obviously does not qualify an individual as a professional investigator. The skills and savvy required to conduct comprehensive, timely, and cost-effective online searches develop over time. An effective online investigator must be familiar with the dozens of domestic and international online databases and Internet sources currently available and must stay abreast of innovations and new services appearing in wave after wave, not always with publicity that would quickly call one's attention to them. Investigators should be adept at navigating and exploiting each online research tool to its fullest potential in the most cost-effective way, learning and using more than a dozen different search languages and syntaxes. They should be able to swiftly analyze and cross-reference all of the raw data, identify leads and suspicious omissions, and integrate new findings into the larger investigative tableau.

Although the skill set is large and demanding, the return on investment can be immense. New information resources as well as resources newly delivered online can break a difficult case wide open.

FURTHER HELPFUL WEB SITES

In addition to sites mentioned in the text, the following additional sites—and further comments on sites already noted—may be helpful:

- The *SEC* (www.sec.gov) provides access to quarterly, annual, and other reports filed by public companies, as well as the adjudication of any disciplinary matters related to individuals or public entities. Some commercial databases—such as LIVEDGAR (www.gsionline.com) and 10-K Wizard (www.10kwizard.com)—allow searches of thousands of SEC filings, through which the forensic accounting investigator may be able to establish an association between the subject of investigation and companies or transactions previously unnoticed.

- The *NASD* (www.nasd.com) allows researchers to check the licensing status of any individual or firm broker/dealer, including any disciplinary history. Reports about an individual or firm broker/dealer can be ordered online and received by e-mail.

- The *Better Business Bureau* (www.bbb.org) provides access to business and consumer alerts and can help the forensic accounting investigator identify a pattern of complaints against a company.

- The *Federal Trade Commission* (www.ftc.gov) maintains a compilation of news briefs and warnings on illegal business practices. Perusing this site can save the forensic accounting investigator hours on the telephone with government regulatory agencies.

- The *Occupational Safety and Health Administration* (www.osha.gov) lists workers' compensation claims and other information.

- The *Federal Election Commission* (www.fec.gov) records contributions to presidential, House of Representatives, and Senate campaigns; political parties; and political action committees.

CHAPTER 18

THE ART OF THE INTERVIEW

Thomas W. Golden

Michael T. Dyer

An interview is a conversation with a purpose. The purpose is to obtain information and, in some cases, an admission. Experienced forensic accounting investigators know that the great majority of white-collar crimes are solved by a skilled interviewer, not by other forensic means. Arguably, there is no more compelling proof of a crime than a perpetrator's voluntary admission.

Effective interviewing is an art to be studied, a skill to be honed. In the later twentieth century, interviewing also emerged as a science, drawing on decades of psychological and sociological research, including a great deal that had been learned from wartime interrogation. Volumes of scholarly research exist, and more are published each year. Yet whatever scientific techniques are brought to bear—Gudjonsson's cognitive-behavioral model of admission, for example, or Reik's psychoanalytic model of admission[1]—in the end, the interview process itself is a subtle art that draws on the experience and skill of the practitioner.

The interviewer must plan effectively beforehand, approach the session with a variety of tools and tactics to choose among, follow a line of questioning, evaluate its effectiveness as the interview proceeds, and, if necessary, move seamlessly to a new approach. Effective interviewing is more than a well-executed analytical exercise; it requires great sensitivity to the subject's feelings and thoughts.

Interviewing skills must be developed. The best way to develop them is to sit in with or observe experienced interviewers at work. Some courses provide excellent training in conducting interviews, but just as learning to drive a vehicle requires considerable road time, so interviewing requires conducting interviews with an experienced mentor close at hand. After the interview, interviewers should critique how it went, summarize what was learned, focus on what could have been learned more quickly, review where the questions flowed smoothly and where they disrupted the flow, take note of what leads were developed, and discuss any key questions that went unanswered or, even worse, unasked. Interviewers must learn to hear and see what works and what does not and must learn from successes and failures.

---

1. David E. Zulawski and Douglas E. Wicklander, *Practical Aspects of Interview and Interrogation*, 2nd ed. (New York: CRC Press, 2002), 12–13.

There is no one right way to conduct an interview. Inducing someone to make an admission is a difficult task indeed. The interviewer must be prepared to assume a variety of stances, moods, or roles. Interviewers can be sympathetic, logical, confrontational, accusatory, or intimidating. Generally, in dealing with white-collar criminals, intimidation is less successful than the softer, sympathetic approaches, but that does not mean that a hard line is never appropriate.

♦ DIFFICULTY AND VALUE OF OBTAINING AN ADMISSION

Later, we will describe the different types of interviews that a forensic accounting investigator will encounter; however, note that the admission-seeking interview is the most challenging of interviews and requires substantial skill on the part of the interviewer. The interviewer must quickly evaluate the success of the line of questioning and be prepared to move seamlessly, if necessary, to a new strategy and another line of questioning. The interviewer must evaluate what may persuade the witness to provide information that the witness has no intention to disclose. The success of an interviewer is often more dependent on the ability to craft a persuasive argument than the ability to craft precise questions. Remember the opening sentence to this chapter: an interview is a conversation with a purpose. The good interviewer constructs a line of questioning interspersed with selected commentary and documents in an attempt to induce the subject to confess. Simply crafting a line of questioning without regard to building a persuasive argument quickly turns into a note-taking assignment unlikely to benefit the purpose of the investigation.

Even highly experienced interviewers know that it is extremely difficult to get someone to admit to a crime. Go back to your early years as an adolescent, or recall instances with your own children. The car has a mysterious dent in it. The window is broken. You were caught cheating on an exam. You know you did something wrong, you feel guilty about it, and the last thing you want is to be discovered. Your dad comes to you asking about the dent in the car, and your first reaction is, "What dent?" You do not want to lie; you just want to deflect the question. You want to keep deflecting until he drops the issue. If he does not let go but keeps coming at you, he slowly decreases your desire to continue lying. If Dad is good at getting to the truth, he says things that increase your desire to tell the truth. "Son, I know you didn't mean to do it because you are a good kid. If you caused the dent, now is the time to discuss it."

In most investigations, obtaining an admission can be of significant benefit to the overall objectives of conducting an investigation, especially when the client wishes to refer the matter to a prosecutor (see Chapter 22). There is no one successful strategy—hence, the title of this chapter, The Art of the Interview. Keep in mind that we are usually not dealing with a hardened criminal but, rather, with someone who fits the profile of a typical white-collar criminal (see Chapter 3).

Incorporating a sequence of interviews into an investigation can be a costly strategy, but the value of obtaining an admission cannot be underestimated. An admission can go a long way toward ensuring a successful prosecution should a referral be made to a prosecutor.[2]

♦ PLANNING FOR THE INTERVIEW

In preparing for the interview, a number of important issues must be considered. A good starting point is the question of what the interview subject is likely to know. Solid investigative work and previous interviews can help the forensic accounting investigator focus on the subject at hand, develop a line of questioning designed either to carry the investigation forward or to elicit an admission, and contemplate what approach is likely to be the most effective. Among the issues to consider are the following.

- *Timing.* The forensic accounting investigator must ensure that there is adequate time for a thorough interview. If the subject says, "I can drop by from 4 to 4:30, but then I have to pick up my kids," the interviewer should schedule another time. The interviewer must insist on adequate time and resist any suggestion that the interview be spread out over several sessions.
- *Location.* Ultimately, the forensic accounting investigator must conduct the interview at whatever location the subject insists on, but whenever possible the interview should be conducted in a business environment that can be controlled. The ideal setting is a room with few distractions: no windows to look out, no clock, no photos, books, or model airplanes. The goal is to create an environment in which the subject has nothing to look at except the interviewer and that makes clear to the subject, not so subtly, just who is in control. The forensic accounting investigator should plan to seat the subject facing the interviewer or interviewers, with a plain wall behind the interviewer. When possible, the interviewer should sit between the subject and the door. Of course, the subject cannot be held against his will, but if the subject wants to walk out, the layout of the room should make that act as uncomfortable as possible for the subject.

  On the other hand, the forensic accounting investigator must be flexible. If the client no longer employs the person being interviewed, the interview is likely to take place outside the office. The forensic accounting investigator should offer to go to the subject's residence or place of employment but be prepared to conduct the interview even in a car or at the mall. The forensic accounting investigator should not let a disagreement over location become an obstacle to gaining information.
- *Legal issues.* Interviews, and especially admission-seeking interviews, may raise certain legal issues and may expose the company and the forensic accounting investigator to certain risks, one of which is a defamation lawsuit. The forensic accounting investigator should proceed only after consulting with counsel. A lone, zealous forensic accounting investigator

---

2. As discussed in Chapter 22, the prosecutor will determine if a matter is worthy of prosecuting. Such actions are not made for the benefit of an individual or corporation.

should not go off on his own. The forensic accounting investigator should seek and obtain team decisions.

- *Recording.* Whether to electronically record interviews is a matter of some debate. Recording an interview works against the goal of lowering the subject's defenses. While federal law does not preclude such recordings, you may be in violation of state law if you decide to record an interview covertly (if only *one* party is aware that the conversation is being recorded—in other words, if the forensic accounting investigator records without the interview subject's consent). Some states permit covert recording of an interview, and others do not. Many states require that both parties consent to the recording. A recorded interview can be a powerful negotiating tool in settlement talks. Many factors must be considered before deciding whether or not to record an interview, including state law, the forensic accounting investigator's experience and the advice of counsel. If you are working at the direction of law enforcement or under a 6(e) order, you may be subject to different restrictions.

- *Polygraph.* The Employee Polygraph Protection Act, passed by Congress in 1988, does not allow private employers or their representatives to require employees to take a polygraph, with few exceptions. It also prohibits employers from disciplining or discharging employees who refuse to take the test.[3] Many commentators have suggested that the law should be interpreted to forbid forensic accounting investigators from asking employees if they are willing to take a polygraph. Whatever the appropriate interpretation of the act, forensic accounting investigators should leave this tool to law enforcement and other government authorities.

- *Participants.* Two people should conduct most interviews. The interview will proceed more smoothly and with fewer gaps if one interviewer asks questions while the other takes notes. Of course, the interviewers can switch roles, but the second interviewer should primarily observe the behavior of the interviewee and consider what questions that behavior suggests. When interviewers work together over a period of time, they learn each other's pattern of interviewing. The second interviewer might step in to fill a pause in the interview while the primary interviewer gathers next thoughts. The second interviewer also provides a witness for any admission that emerges, as well as for any disputes about the conduct of the interview.

  In some cases it quickly becomes clear that the primary interviewer and the subject have a personality clash. Switching interviewers may ease the tension and lead the subject to open up. This has been termed the good cop/bad cop scenario, with the good cop providing a more sympathetic ear and reducing the tension created by the hard-nosed approach of the

---

3. "Admissibility of Confession as Affected by Its Inducement through Artifice, Deception, Trickery or Fraud," *American Law Reports* 2d, 772 (Rochester, N.Y.: The Lawyers Cooperative Publishing Company, 1965), 69–70.

bad cop. For this approach to work effectively, the two interviewers need to coordinate beforehand their goals and tactics.

A forensic accounting investigator must be cautious when working with an unfamiliar partner. What one person perceives as a gap in the interview might be a deliberate silence created by the first interviewer. Or the second interviewer may believe that the primary interviewer missed a question, when in fact he was holding it in reserve. Let your partner know that at a certain point in the interview, you will turn it over to him to cover the possibility that you missed an important question. You will now have a second chance to pose that question through your partner. A good exchange would be to simply turn to your partner and ask, "Do you have any questions?" It is a good practice for interviewers to excuse themselves from the room at certain times or just prior to concluding the interview in order to compare notes privately and thus ensure that all relevant topics have been addressed.

- *Multiple interview subjects.* Forensic accounting investigators should never interview more than one person at a time. Even with two employees from the same department, forensic accounting investigators should interview them separately, and at best consecutively, so that one cannot tell the other anything about the interview. Separate interviews provide the best opportunity to draw out a subject and to ensure that one person's statements are not influencing the other's.

- *Concurrent interviewing.* When more than one person must be interviewed, it is sometimes useful to conduct the interviews simultaneously and use information obtained in each interview in the other. The interviewers need to be in touch with each other, perhaps through a phone call, email or instant message suggesting a quick meeting in the hall.

◆ TYPES OF INTERVIEWS

Interview planning must reflect the type of interview that is anticipated. For purposes of this chapter, all interviews are divided into two categories: information seeking and admission seeking.

THE INFORMATION-SEEKING INTERVIEW

Not everyone interviewed in an investigation is a suspect. Some individuals will be interviewed because they have information about the company, the industry, or the accounting at issue. Such interviews are necessary parts of the investigation, providing knowledge that will sustain further inquiry. In most investigations, the forensic accounting investigator starts interviewing at the periphery of all possible interview candidates and moves toward the witnesses appearing more involved in the allegation that is the subject of the investigation. (One useful technique is to interview people on the periphery and then watch to see if anyone comes along to inquire of them about what questions were asked.

Individuals who are particularly curious about the goings-on of the investigation should receive attention.) The more pertinent the information obtained during information-seeking interviews, the more likely it is that the admission-seeking interview will be successful.

The information-seeking interview is usually nonconfrontational and not particularly stressful, but the interviewer should never assume that such interviews are unimportant. In some cases, the interview subject may provide the only evidence available.

The interviewer must prepare for witness interviews by forming and assessing various theories about what has occurred, yet the interviewer must always be open to new possibilities. Remember, too, that while forensic accounting investigators are trained at asking questions, the various witnesses are most likely *not* trained in providing answers. Even if they are cooperative, they may not be efficient and may not be aware of what information is important. The forensic accounting investigator's challenge is to draw them out with the right questions. It is rare for a witness to provide all of the information sought without the help of probing questions. A common tactic of fraudsters is to give honest but incomplete answers, and innocent witnesses may also have difficulty assembling full sets of information for the interviewer. For this reason, forensic accounting investigators must be very good listeners.

The interviewer must also beware of making assumptions (see Chapter 14, where this is identified as a common misstep). Most intelligent people prefer not to ask dumb questions. Instead, they make assumptions, but this is not a good idea during an investigation. The interviewer should not be afraid to ask many questions, even when the answers may be obvious. And the interviewer should not be afraid of sounding dumb. Ask for whatever information is needed, more than once, of the same person, of different people, and take good notes.

THE ADMISSION-SEEKING INTERVIEW

This is the most challenging of interviews. It requires substantial skill to complete successfully. In planning the interview, the forensic accounting investigator should be confident that the witness has committed the crime under investigation or has knowledge of the illegal act. The interviewer must consider what may persuade the subject to provide information the subject has no intention of relinquishing. As noted earlier, a successful interview more often depends on the interviewer's ability to craft a persuasive argument than the ability to craft precise questions. Some experts defines this characteristic as the ability to be a "confident negotiator."[4]

Even in cases in which guilt can be established through evidence and testimony from others, an admission is extremely useful because the suspect may admit to acts previously unknown to the forensic accounting investigator and is likely to be more cooperative in any subsequent civil, criminal, or administrative action. An admission may also make a trial unnecessary.

---

4. Id., 38.

To extract an admission of guilt, interviewers may need to make clear that they know the suspect is lying. People react to this accusation in different ways: some become emotional, break down, and confess everything; some respond aggressively; others grow silent. Experienced interviewers know they must first find ways to obtain an initial admission of wrongdoing and then continue questioning to expand that admission into all pertinent areas. To be successful, the interviewer must be well versed in and comfortable with a variety of approaches, including the following:

- *The logical approach.* This direct approach begins by laying out the evidence of guilt that has been found and explains the futility of not confessing. "If I committed a crime and there was no evidence," the forensic accounting investigator might say to the suspect, "I would not make any statement. But here, because we have adequate evidence of your guilt in the accounting records, it is to your advantage to appear to be cooperative, and this statement will demonstrate a willingness to cooperate. Tell us your side of the story. It will be difficult to maintain in the future that you were cooperative in resolving this matter if you are not cooperative now. Maybe someone else who knows what you know will come forward and cooperate with us. Then, what information you may decide to disclose to us at a later time becomes much less important. The value of the information you have about these transactions has a short half-life. Disclosing now what you know may be your best course of action."

  This logical approach may start the suspect talking, which is always a good sign. Major admissions often start with small admissions. Sometimes the witness grows so comfortable talking that the ultimate admission includes admissions of additional improprieties of which forensic accounting investigators were unaware.

- *The do-the-right-thing approach.* During preparation for the interview, if the forensic accounting investigator learns that the interview subject had a history of doing the right thing, that information can be used to appeal to the subject's feelings. As we discussed in Chapter 3, the profile of most white-collar criminals fits that of people who, but for a situational experience or misguided rationalizations, by and large have lived normal lives in which doing the right thing has been a way of life. Reminding them of this commonly held belief oftentimes evokes a willingness to revert to that behavior.

  o "I know your family raised you to do the right thing."
  o "You were a Marine. You know how to accept the responsibility of citizenship. You know what honor means."
  o "Your dad was in law enforcement, and he taught you to do the right thing."

- *The silent approach.* When two people are engaged in conversation, silence almost always makes one of the individuals uncomfortable. To relieve the uncomfortable feeling, someone usually begins to talk. Silence often makes interviewers uncomfortable to the point that they even suggest answers to the suspect! Do not fall into this trap. Make silence work for, not against you. Here is an example:

Interviewer: I am here to ask you if anyone that you report to has asked you to make journal entries or other accounting entries that made you uncomfortable.

Witness: No response.

This is a question that forensic accounting investigators may suggest to auditors to include in the risk assessment stage of their audits. This question could cause the subject to pause and ponder over a response, especially if the subject actually is aware of an event that may be an indicator of fraud.

No matter how long it takes to get an answer, wait. After a period of time, perhaps two minutes of silence, you may repeat the question. Whatever you do, do not let the silence prompt you to relieve it by saying something like the following:

Interviewer: If that's not the case, then just say so and we'll move on. I don't mean to imply that there's anything going on here [*and on and on . . .*].

Silence is a powerful tool. Use it well and use it often. After you ask a question, stop talking and wait for a response.

- *The rationalization approach.* The interviewer's effort in this approach is to give the subject a moral or psychological excuse. Helping the witness place the crime into a rational context—one implying that others similarly situated would do the same thing—can unlock the needed admission.

  In Chapter 3 we discussed the three ingredients that enable someone to commit a financial crime: need, opportunity, and rationalization. The third ingredient, rationalization, offers the basis for an effective interviewing tactic. Let's say that the suspect is withholding information. By identifying with the suspect, the forensic accounting investigator may prompt the suspect to talk. Many white-collar criminals are truly sorry that their fraud and cover-up have caused trouble internally or harmed investors. Because they believe that they are good people at heart, they rationalize what they have done. The forensic accounting investigator should be sympathetic and help the suspect recreate and articulate the rationalization.

  "I'm sure you were angry when Bill got the bonus you should have received," the interviewer might say. "I know you're one of the major reasons this business became successful, and you were grossly underpaid. I understand why you felt they owed you money." A suspect who is feeling guilty may want to get it off his chest by telling someone empathetic why he committed the crime. Helping someone arrive at what might appear to be a rationale for his or her actions allows the subject to save face. "Anyone in your situation would have done this; everybody makes mistakes," the interviewer might say. The interviewer's mission here is to give the subject an acceptable reason to come clean.

In one example, the interview witness was an individual who had created a series of falsified journal entries having the effect of increasing financial statement income. The forensic accounting investigators believed that at least part of the motivation for the falsification was to meet the requirement for an annual bonus: were the individual to achieve division sales of $20 million, a bonus equal to his annual salary would be paid to him. One dollar less and there would be no bonus. Various interview techniques had failed. The perpetrator avoided making any admissions until it was proposed by the interviewer that perhaps part of the reason for the falsification was to protect other employees at the company from possible loss of their jobs should the division fail to meet budget. Apparently, the witness turned out to have been hankering for a noble motive to rationalize his illegal and selfish act. He admitted to falsification of the financial statements because he could now justify the act as an effort to protect fellow employees. The rationalization approach is often successful because it allows the subject to save face during the interview.

- *Asking questions to which you know the answers.* This approach is best to determine a subject's credibility. Its effective use early in the investigation could save countless hours in blind alleys. If you can determine the validity of what someone says at the moment the person says it, the investigation can be structured much more efficiently and is likely to yield a much better result.

  Lying about an important matter is not easily rationalized. If you come across someone who has the ability to rationalize lying to you, then you may have found someone who quite possibly has been lying for quite some time. If you are interviewing someone whom you have just caught in a lie, regardless of the context, as soon as you practically can, focus on the allegations that triggered the investigation.

  Alternatively, you can review documents and conduct a host of other interviews in search of something to support the initial allegations. However, asking the right questions of the right person at the right time in the investigation could save your client time and money. Remember: liars lie. Find a liar, and you may be well on your way to finding criminal activity.

Forensic accounting investigators must always bear in mind that a method successful with one subject may be ineffective with another. The interviewers must be nimble enough to evaluate whether a strategy is working and to abandon it for another when it is not. They must remain flexible, acknowledge mistakes and false starts, and never lose sight of the objective: to obtain information and ultimately, an admission.

One approach we did not discuss earlier is to bluff. Bluffing almost always fails, and our advice is never to bluff. It is also important to note that interviewers are *not* permitted to use coercion or duress. Consult counsel for definitions, but here is an example of coercion: "I know you stole the money, and if you don't admit it, I will tell your employer and you'll get fired." And here is an example of duress: "If you don't confess, you could have an unfortunate accident on your way home tonight." Both coercion and duress are illegal.

◆ OTHERS MAY WISH TO ATTEND INTERVIEWS

In the course of forensic accounting investigations, a number of parties are interested in what witnesses have to say. Officers and managers from the victimized entity often want to participate in the interview of a subject. They are angry and impatient to know the truth. However, it is not at all productive to have highly emotional individuals attend. They may insist on sitting in, on the grounds that they have the facts to prevent the witness from lying; however, victims make poor interviewers. The interviewer should take the necessary time to learn the facts of the case, and on this basis be ready to determine if the witness is lying. The interviewer can deal with lying in a professional and advantageous manner. The less emotionally involved the interviewer, the more likely the interviewer will achieve the objective of the interview.

It is preferable to have no more than two interviewers conduct the interview in most situations. Others may wish to simply sit in on the interview as silent onlookers; however, that may distract the witness and create difficulties in establishing rapport and getting the witness to speak openly. There are situations, however, particularly when both counsel and forensic investigators are participating in an investigation, in which there will be more people who may need to attend certain interviews.

Forensic accounting investigators nearly always prefer to perform some level of document examination prior to beginning the interview process. Only after obtaining a reasonable knowledge of the company's processes and of relevant transactions do they typically begin the interviewing process, usually in a selective and strategic manner. This well-prepared approach is, we believe, critical to achieving desired outcomes. The most important leads and breaks in investigations often come from testimonial rather than circumstantial evidence; that is, facts learned in an interview are often more beneficial to achieving the desired result than documents are, which serve well to corroborate testimony. But to conduct good interviews, you still need good documents.

The interview process is clearly all-important to the forensic accounting investigator. Do the interview too early, and you could tip your hand and lose a critical advantage. Do it without adequate factual knowledge to ascertain the honesty of interview answers, and the interview could become just a note-taking exercise that fails to advance the investigation.

◆ INTERVIEW PROCESS

Your objective is to obtain information. You are a fact finder. Therefore do not hesitate to cover the basics with the interviewee: who, what, where, when, and how. In forensic accounting matters, you should always consider asking the interviewee what documents exist to support his or her information. In order to obtain additional witnesses, ask the interviewee if anyone else is aware of the information provided in the course of the interview. "Who else do you think I should talk to?" People are different; one approach will not work with everyone. Be prepared to try different approaches. If you are unsuccessful with one approach, back off and try another. Just do not lose the interviewee's attention. Keep it focused on you and on the issues at hand. The interviewee needs to know that you are in control. This is *your* interview. The interviewee can end the interview at any time, but if properly conducted, the interview may well proceed along the desired lines. If an employee offers undue resistance to the interview, his employer may consider mandating cooperation as a condition of continued employment.

With these varied interview approaches in mind, let's walk through an interview step by step.

Step 1. Bonding. As a first step, the interviewers try to bond and build rapport with the witness. They advise the interviewee generally of the reason for the interview, the point being to put the subject at ease. In some cases, the interviewee knows why you are there and so may be reluctant or uncooperative. Management should consider, on advice of counsel, various methods to ensure the employee's cooperation with the investigation, including the investigator's saying to the employee, "The company expects your full cooperation with this investigation."

At all times, be courteous toward interviewees. Remember, you are attempting to obtain information. Be friendly, sympathetic, polite, professional, and interested in what the interviewee has to offer. A condescending or bullying attitude will be ineffective. It is very important to establish rapport at the outset, especially in interviews that seek an admission, and for this reason it is usually a mistake to jump right into the questioning.

Why not begin questioning at once? Assume that you have been working with this person during the investigation. If you have been doing your job correctly, you have been friendly and cordial to the subject throughout. At the stage of the investigation where you have a reasonable certainty that the witness either has committed a crime or has knowledge that one has been committed, you want the witness's defenses to be low. You want the individual to continue to be comfortable around you. Keep in mind that most white-collar criminals would be very embarrassed if someone knew of their crime. In most of these types of interviews, you will likely come to a point where you let the witness know that you know he is lying. The reactions you expect are shame and disappointment. You also expect that the witness will be eager to win back your approval. That wish could convert into an admission if the witness feels he simply cannot go on lying and hurting people.

Does this approach work all the time? Of course not, but keep in mind that you are likely to be interviewing a person who is otherwise good,[5] although he has done something—which in hindsight he would recognize as ill-advised—and now regrets his actions. He has a tremendous sense of guilt and wishes relief from it, as if it were a physical pain. If you push the right buttons and say the right things in a sympathetic and understanding manner, you may provide just the right environment to elicit an admission. That is exactly why you want to establish rapport or confirm an existing rapport early in the interview. You will need it later on.

Step 2. Baselining. Interviewers learn from experience, and in-depth research in interviewing techniques supports the observation that putting the witness at ease with small talk about sports, the weather, where they are from, and so on achieves two aims. The first aim is to lower the subject's anxiety level and get him talking in a comfortable manner (as discussed in the preceding section). The second aim is to enable the interviewer to get a feel for the subject's body language, eye movements, facial expressions, and voice inflections under various stress levels. The value of observing body language, a technique used by some interviewers to draw conclusions about a witness's veracity, is supported by an enormous amount of scientific research. For example, crossing the arms or scratching the nose could be indications of lying; there is sound evidence to this effect.[6] Later, when you ask the tough questions, you may notice differences in these behaviors and others, which could be instructive as to the witness's culpability.

On one hand, the consensus among researchers is that one-half to two-thirds of all communications that take place between individuals are nonverbal, involving movements, gestures, facial expressions, and posture.[7] On the other hand, experts agree that no one behavior is a reliable indicator of truthfulness, even for a specific individual. One researcher, Paul Ekman, in *Telling Lies* (New York: Holt, Rinehart and Winston, 1981), pointed out that even when hand and arm gestures are reliable signs that an interview subject is upset, they are not reliable indicators that the subject is being untruthful.

The interviewer, however experienced, must proceed very carefully in both observing behavior and interpreting what it may mean. A body of research suggests, for example, that an interview subject with something to hide will adopt a posture that appears to protect the abdomen—leaning forward, perhaps with elbows on knees or crossing an ankle onto the opposing knee. A person with nothing to hide is

---

5. See Chapter 3 for a discussion on the profile of white-collar criminals.

6. The medical explanation for why someone who is lying may scratch his nose is as follows: under stress (as when someone is lying), the body's defense mechanism causes the blood to retreat toward the organs and away from the capillaries, which are near the surface of the skin. The retreat causes a tingling sensation.

7. An extensive discussion of the wide range of verbal and nonverbal behavior can be found in *American Legal Review* (see ALR 2d 38, 106ff.).

more likely to sit up, with feet flat on the floor and arms and shoulders relaxed. But if a subject suddenly crosses his arms during an interview, does it mean he feels insecure and is lying? Or does it mean that he feels a draft? If someone starts sweating, does it mean he is lying? Or does it mean that he wishes the air-conditioning were on?

Experienced interviewers, as noted earlier, begin the interview with easy questions to set the subject at ease and to register the subject's posture, expressions, and tone of voice. Then they ask a tough question and observe whether the body language changes. But this approach should never be more than a supportive technique—used to probe for more information or an admission. The science of body language is far from precise, and so anything learned by observation has to be viewed as anecdotal rather than as a sure finding. Note, too, that an experienced con man may be confident, manipulative, and in control of his nonverbal indicators.

Step 3. Admissions and Defenses. Forensic accounting investigators want to develop a line of questioning that will cause their subjects to admit to knowledge about certain facts, procedures, policy, practices, and any deviations from them, thereby eliminating possible defenses when the time comes to state accusations. If the forensic accounting investigator knows where he wants to end up, he can lay the groundwork through a series of questions that lock the subject into a story that is wiggle free. Time spent in planning will serve well during the interview. A good rule of thumb is that the planning stage will be three times the duration of the expected interview. Before the interview, the interviewers should prepare a list of questions, consider the possible responses to each, and then determine what the follow-up questions would be for each response. Do not hesitate to ask open-ended questions such as the following. These are among the best questions to ask:

- While you were working at the organization, were you ever asked to do anything that made you feel uncomfortable?
- Did you suspect illegal activities were occurring that you could not prove?
- Did you ever speak to anyone else regarding this information?
- Who do you believe would have information that would help us?
- If you could change something about this organization, what would it be?
- Is there anything else that we should have explored or that you want to tell us?

The interviewers must also consider how the witness might respond to accusations, when the interview reaches that point. Interviewers want to avoid, for example, a situation in which the witness can say, "It's true that our policies preclude unauthorized journal entries, but anyone could have made those entries without my knowledge." To anticipate this defense, the interviewers should ask questions that result in a dialogue somewhat like the following:

Q: Is it possible that someone could create journal entries to these accounts without your knowledge?

A: That would not be possible.

Q: Why?

A: Because I review an edit listing of all JEs every Friday. I would have seen it.

Q: What if you're on vacation? What happens then? Could someone make an entry that you simply wouldn't catch?

A: No way. If that happened, I wouldn't be doing my job, and I do my job. I review that edit listing every Friday and if I am away, I always see it on Monday. It's an important control mechanism, and I make sure it gets done.

This line of questioning has now trapped the subject and precluded him from using possible defenses later, when you may become accusatory. The interviewers have eliminated a possible exculpatory response to the allegation that he made unsupported journal entries to inflate revenue. They have established that no one else could have done it and escaped attention in the review process.

Step 4. Confrontation. The interviewer lays the groundwork, then brings the accusation. The goal is to make the witness feel the burden of guilt while also perceiving the interviewer as a sympathetic person in whom one can confide. The interviewer wants the subject to feel that further lying is fruitless.

"Kathy, I'm very troubled by your last comment," the interviewer says. "Actually, I'm troubled by several of your comments here today. You have been telling me that you control the deposit of all donations and that you make them all in timely fashion. Yet the minister of the Houston First Presbyterian Church told me that he gave you a $10,000 check on June 15. It never showed up in the foundation's checking account. The endorsement on the check shows that it was deposited in your personal bank account." Kathy is likely to lower her head, a shocked expression on her face. She has been found out. Her guilt is huge. That is just where you want her. You have confronted her with the fact that you know she has been lying. This will take a moment for the witness to grasp, and the immediate reaction may be total silence. Allow her to stew about her situation. This is not the time to coach her through what you believe has happened. Be silent. Do not teach the witness that you will provide explanations, when in fact you may not yet know the whole story.

Alternatively, the witness could respond aggressively to the accusation and express adamant denial. The interviewer should remain calm and retrace his steps. He should review some of the previous questions and answers. The subject's aggressive behavior may merely be a test to see what else the interviewer knows and how certain he is that the subject has done something improper. In this situation, the interviewer should stick to his plan. Repetition is his ally. Silence will work well, too. Stay on the offensive and keep the pressure on. Should the denial shift from an emphatic "no" to an explanation, an admission of guilt may be close at hand.

When the timing appears appropriate, the interviewer can help the suspect rationalize the crime. "Look, I know you to be a good person at heart," the interviewer might say. "Not one person here thinks ill of you. Everyone knows of the financial hardship you have endured lately. In similar circumstances, most people would react the way you did. You saw an opportunity to borrow some money, fully intending to pay it back. That's what you did, isn't it?" Then let silence weigh on the subject.

"I'm ashamed," Kathy may respond. "It's true that I only borrowed the money and had every intention of paying it back."

Now the interviewer responds, "I believe you. You're an honest person, and I know what a burden this has been for you. I guarantee you, though, that if you work with me on this, you will feel better."

The interviewers have achieved their goal of getting the suspect to talk.

Step 5. The Admission. Now the interviewers should walk the subject through the facts and specific instances of the crimes. They should bring out documents and ask questions that will solidify her involvement, knowledge, and intent. They should nail down the details, although always remaining sympathetic and compassionate. They should comfort and encourage the subject. And all the while, they should take good notes and close the remaining gaps in knowledge.

When the interview is coming to a close, the interviewers should stay in character. They should not burn any bridges through inflammatory comments. They may need additional information in the future and so should advise the interviewee that they may be in touch later with more questions. The subject may recall additional facts that might help the investigation, or circumstances may change to make the interviewee more cooperative. The interviewers should ensure that the subject knows how to contact them.

During the conduct of an investigation, it is important to segregate and control all evidence until it can be examined forensically. This is a standard procedure when considering physical documents and electronic evidence, but it certainly applies to what people know, by their own experiences and actions, at the time of the start of an investigation. As such, it is important to do two things during an interview. At the end of each interview, tell the subject not to discuss with anyone the topics covered in the interview. In addition, a question that should be asked of every subject is, "Have you discussed this matter or any previous interview you have had during the course of this investigation, or has anyone approached you regarding such?" People can still talk behind the scenes, but you will stop most such discussions by incorporating these two steps into your investigation.

◆ DOCUMENTING THE INTERVIEW

In most cases, the interview should be documented contemporaneously. Between the two participating interviewers, there may be some differences of perspective. This is not uncommon. They should review their notes, and if there are material differences they should attempt to clarify with the witness when possible. They should then create a single master version of the interview and follow their document retention policy as well as any applicable laws and regulations. If direct quotations from the interviewee are included, they should be identified as such. Documenting the interviewee's own language, particularly key portions of the admission, may be helpful to those evaluating the import of the facts disclosed in the interview.

USE OF SUBTERFUGE

Subterfuge is the use of pretext or deception about who you are in order to obtain information that may not otherwise be forthcoming. An example of subterfuge is a forensic investigator's claiming to be a bank employee. The use of subterfuge has many legal implications and should not be undertaken unless you have clear direction from counsel and confirmation about its consistency with the client's internal policies and its legality in the particular circumstances. For our part, we do not engage in this practice because we believe the detriments far outweigh any potential benefits except possibly in situations when the forensic investigator is being hired by a government body and the practice has been specifically sanctioned by the client.

More specifically, in considering whether to use subterfuge in an investigation, one should recognize that the practice may very well backfire. What happens when the forensic investigator takes the stand and is asked, "At any time during the course of your investigation did you lie?" What would the jury's reaction be to a yes answer? And what impact would the answer have on the overall credibility of the forensic witness?

An otherwise well-executed investigation could be for naught because of this plausible scenario. And so we repeat: extreme care and caution should be used in considering whether to use subterfuge.

◆ SUMMARY

The full scope of these techniques is to be used by forensic accounting investigators experienced in conducting admission-seeking interviews. Further, on one hand, some of these interviewing techniques are broadly useful in the regular conduct of financial statement audits—for example, preparing well, questioning and listening intently, using silence to make sure you get an adequate response, and being persistent if you do not. Forensic accounting investigators, on the other hand, will frequently deal with individuals who either know of a crime or who committed one, and they need to be thoroughly familiar with the full range of interviewing techniques and capable of using them effectively.

CHAPTER 19

ANALYZING FINANCIAL STATEMENTS

Martha N. Corbett

Mona M. Clayton

Analytic procedures have long been useful investigative techniques when the subject matter of the investigation is likely to be reflected in company accounting records and financial statements. This is true of most types of economic crime, and, accordingly, the forensic accounting investigator will frequently encounter investigations in which analytic procedures are needed. Analytic techniques have the overall objective of identifying the unexpected—relationships that do not make sense. Because of this attribute, they may be useful at the start of an investigation to aid in developing a logical scope. As an investigation progresses and more becomes known about schemes and perpetrators, analytic procedures can also be used to identify areas for further review and inquiry. Due to the volume of transactions processed by a company every day, it is not possible for management, the auditor, or the forensic accounting investigator to examine every transaction. Therefore, analytic procedures may be used to focus the scope of investigation on certain elements of the financial statements that may have been affected by the fraud. Combining analytic methodology with the intuitive processes and judgments of forensic accounting creates a logical basis for identifying indications of fraud and focusing the initial steps of an investigation.

The use of analytic techniques based on financial statement information is fairly pervasive in business. Managers use analyses to monitor performance and to communicate with external investors. Securities analysts use them to rate and value companies. Bankers use them to determine whether to grant a loan or to monitor business results that may lead to the identification of troubled loans. Auditors may use these techniques to identify areas of fraud risk and to determine whether financial statements are stated fairly; however, it is up to the auditors to use their appropriate firm audit methodology in assessing and identifying such risk.

While an explanation of analytic procedures can be found in this chapter, each company or engagement is different, and therefore the selection of analytic procedures must be appropriate to the circumstances. It is also likely that no matter what the particular situation may be, a variety of analyses in combination will be needed to corroborate the overall results. For example, in an investigation into whether an executive misreported revenue, performing a sales trend analysis without a corresponding accounts receivable analysis could lead to the wrong conclusion about revenue growth if a deteriorating trend in customer collections is overlooked.

◆ DEVELOPING EFFECTIVE ANALYTIC PROCEDURES

In the development of effective analytic procedures, the forensic accounting investigator should do the following four things: develop an expectation, define what result constitutes a significant difference from the expectation, compute the difference, and investigate the difference in order to draw appropriate conclusions.

Step 1. To *develop an expectation,* the practitioner must consider available information, including historical results, forecast amounts, industry trends, and general economic conditions. Simply expecting an account balance to be similar to historical results may be faulty logic. In light of this varied background information, ask yourself, "Does this make sense?" Realize, as well, that there may be still other environmental factors, which could help explain why consistency with prior years is not a reasonable expectation. Experience also shows that when management's only expectation is the achievement of budgeted income statement results, the pressure to meet that expectation can lead to fraudulent financial reporting that goes unnoticed precisely because the expectation is being met.

Step 2. To *define what result constitutes a significant difference from the expectation,* the forensic accounting investigator may consider the materiality of the account balance being analyzed, the risk of misstatement associated with that account balance, and even the controls surrounding that account balance. Each of these factors may have an impact on defining the significant difference. When considering the definition of a significant difference, the forensic accounting investigator should also consider the overall materiality of the financial statements, because a small fraudulent change in a large balance sheet item could have a material impact on the overall financial statements.

Step 3. To *compute the difference,* the forensic accounting investigator will prepare the actual mathematical analysis or analytic procedure. In the creation of the mathematical analysis, it is critical to consider the validity and completeness of the underlying information on which the analysis is based. Fraudulent transactions quite typically do not go through the normal checks-and-balances system. They are often included in or improperly excluded from "other" accounts, or they are on the corporate balance sheet as opposed to a division's. The inclusion or exclusion of a reconciling item between the subledgers and the general ledger is a common technique for concealment. The same can be said of reconciling items to outside sources such as between the general ledger and bank statements.

Step 4. To *investigate the difference in order to draw appropriate conclusions,* the forensic accounting investigator should consider seeking explanations from management concerning the differences noted. When possible, explanations from management should be corroborated by other evidence or corroborated by other company personnel not in the financial-reporting chain. For example, under a scenario of alleged inflation of revenue from transactions with certain new customers, if a significant increase in sales is explained by the fact that the company obtained a new customer during the period, the practitioner may request to see the customer contract and correspondence. The forensic accounting investigator may also consider speaking to the salesperson or customer service representative responsible for the new customer so as to better understand the relationship and verify the reality of the sale or sales and associated revenue. As you can see, a variety of approaches and techniques can be used depending on the situation.

Similarly, analytics may show that there is little fluctuation from prior years and that the company, subsidiary, or division is meeting or beating its budget or forecast. In situations in which management receives incentives based on achieving budgeted or forecast results, an analysis of annual changes may not be helpful. Analyzing quarterly or monthly changes may be more revealing as to whether financial information has been falsely presented and dressed up to meet expectations.

Applying disaggregated analytics when analysis is performed at the subsidiary or acquisition level can be a source of direct insight into allegations of wrongdoing and also identify areas for further review.

Analytics have revealed manipulations of financial data on a quarterly basis not only when management receives bonuses or incentives to meet and beat budget but also when there is an earnout agreement in place. For instance, the former management of recent acquisitions may be eligible to receive considerable payments if they meet a certain metric associated with earnings before interest and taxes or associated with earnings before interest, taxes, depreciation, and amortization, otherwise known as an earnout payment. In an actual case of this kind, analytics revealed that management was not meeting expectations to receive the earnout payment during the first two quarters. During the third quarter, the results were almost at expectation to receive the payment. In the fourth quarter, the results were achieved and management was paid millions based on the earnout-agreement provisions.

The auditors examined the calculation and found it to be calculated correctly. However, millions of dollars of false entries had escaped their attention during the audit because the debits were posted to accounts such as Intercompany, Fixed Assets, and Accounts Payable. In each instance, the entries were below the auditors' materiality threshold of $250,000. By the time of the audit, former management had resigned, their pockets lined with multimillion-dollar earnout payments.

Obviously, those earnout payments had not been earned in the spirit of the agreement. While the financial statement auditors may have applied analytics to the division in question, they did so annually and did not notice large, unexplained fluctuations. Analytics performed quarterly might have raised questions for review. Forensic accounting investigators applied this technique, and it led them to several bogus and unsupported general ledger entries posted at the end of the quarter, that had overstated the results by a material amount. With further probing, the forensic accounting investigators also learned that the financial statements for the acquisition had also been inflated, and thus the parent company had paid more for the subsidiary than it should have. The former owners and management profited by falsifying the financials on two occasions: once preacquisition, once postacquisition.

Where was the due diligence team at the time of the acquisition? The parent company sent an internal team that was gung ho to do the acquisition. The team was so gung ho that due diligence was limited to a few top-level interviews and little analysis. Moral: it pays to do your homework and dive into the details. Analytic techniques, applied correctly, can often point the forensic accounting investigator in the right direction.

The issue of when to apply the techniques depends on the facts and circumstances of an engagement. Some situations may dictate applying the techniques early and often, while in other situations, it may be more useful to apply the techniques at a disaggregated level, when more detailed financial information has been received and available.

Financial statement analysis generally falls into five categories: vertical trend analysis, horizontal trend analysis, ratio analysis, reasonableness testing, and analysis through data mining. For a discussion about using analytic techniques as an audit procedure, see Chapter 8.

VERTICAL ANALYSIS

Vertical analysis (also referred to as common size analysis) compares elements of the financial statements with a common base item. For example, all elements of the income statement are expressed as a percentage of sales. These relationships are compared within each accounting period, and then the period under analysis can be compared with historical periods or industry information for context.[1] Performing the same analysis on a disaggregated basis by business unit or by geography often gives the forensic accounting investigator a deeper insight into which business unit is driving an unusual relationship or whether one partic-

---

1. For useful comparisons, industry information may be retrieved from EdgarScan Benchmarking Assistant (http://edgarscan.pwcglobal.com/cgi-bin/EdgarScan/edgarscan_java), Standard & Poor's NetAdvantage Industry Surveys (http://www.netadvantage.standardpoor.com), and Factiva (http://www.factiva.com).

ular business unit is an outlier. The analysis can be further disaggregated through analysis of a particular financial statement line item by component. For example, cost of goods sold can be analyzed by business unit and by component: materials, labor, overhead, and variances. Again, this analysis may uncover an unusual trend in material costs, which would have been masked by opposite trends in other components of cost of goods sold.

Vertical analysis can also be effective when a practitioner is performing analysis of the balance sheet. For example, comparing percentage of accounts receivable aging categories across business units may indicate cash collection deterioration in a particular business unit.

HORIZONTAL ANALYSIS

Horizontal analysis is used to understand the percentage of change in individual financial statement items over a period of time. A base period, say, last year, is selected, and a percentage of change is calculated for other periods, say, this year, compared with the base period. Changes in certain line items, such as sales, should be the drivers for expected changes in cost of sales or selling expenses, for example. Looking at trends on a quarterly, monthly, or even weekly basis can also assist in identification of areas to be pursued. Disaggregating this monthly analysis further by business unit, geography, or customer may enable the practitioner to identify periods when revenue or expense trends are unusual. For example, monthly or weekly trends may indicate that a significant amount of the quarterly revenue is generated in the last week or month of the quarter with a particular customer. Exhibits 19.1 and 19.2 are discussed later in the chapter and illustrate hypothetical examples of vertical and horizontal analysis.

RATIO ANALYSIS

Ratio analysis assesses and measures the relationships among differing financial statement items and between these items and nonfinancial data. These ratios can be compared either on a historical basis, or on an industry basis, or against a benchmark. When unexpected changes occur, source documents and related accounts can be researched and examined in more detail. For example, in the retail industry, analyzing sales based on the square footage of each store location and comparing that information with other stores in the chain or with industry norms can be helpful in identifying stores that may not be performing as expected.

Literally thousands of ratios can be calculated, but more is not necessarily better. The nine key ratios most useful in analysis, risk assessment, and determination of the existence of fraud will be explored later in this chapter.

REASONABLENESS TESTING

Reasonableness testing is used to benchmark the results recorded in the financial statements against an independent expectation. For example, the forensic accounting investigator may calculate expected interest expense for a given period by multiplying the average outstanding debt balance by the average published index upon which the interest is based. Any unusual fluctuations identified when comparing this independent view with the amount recorded in the financial statements should be investigated. Another example of reasonableness testing is to calculate expected depreciation expense for a whole category of fixed assets by dividing the average outstanding fixed-asset balance by the useful life and comparing that amount with the recorded depreciation expense. Again, reasonableness testing is usually more effective if the underlying information is disaggregated (by analyzing each loan individually rather than analyzing a group of loans).

Reasonableness testing can make good use of regression analysis, which will yield an explicit prediction based on solid inputs to establish the prediction on which to make a comparison. Sales, for example, could be estimated through regression analysis based on budgets, forecasts, or commission expense and then compared with actual sales.

DATA-MINING ANALYSIS

Data-mining analysis (see Chapter 20) might include all of the following:

- Scanning transaction listings
- Identifying gaps in check runs or shipping documents
- Identifying duplicate invoice numbers, payments, or payroll transactions to the same payee
- Matching return dates and credit memos to test for proper cutoff
- Comparing recent invoice prices with costs on the perpetual inventory records
- Filtering to identify all new suppliers, nonstandard journal entries, accounts under dispute, and the like
- Stratifying or grouping customer accounts by balance size or employees by overtime pay

Data-mining analytics are different from the other types of analytic procedures in that they are queries or searches performed within accounts or other client data to identify anomalous individual items, while the other types use aggregated financial information. What can be expected of data mining depends on the purpose of the procedure. For example, scanning a numerical sequence may bring to light certain gaps that merit investigation, while scanning payment amounts may yield evidence of duplicate payments. The expectation in searching for large and unusual items is based on the forensic accounting investigator's assessment of what constitutes normal. While some analytics such as a scan of closing or adjusting entries may be performed manually, others such as filters, duplicates, gaps, and sorts may require computer-assisted audit techniques using software packages like Audit Command Language, Access, or Excel. You may also opt to build your own tool for large data sets. See Chapter 20 for a more detailed explanation of this technique.

◆ USING FINANCIAL RATIOS AS MEASURES OF RISK OR INDICATIONS OF FRAUD

Knowledge of the company and the industry in which it operates is critical to a thorough analysis. A company's business operations, segments, plant, and geography need to be understood fully before comparisons with an industry benchmark or another company can be made. Be particularly wary of using industry or other information that is not comparable. For example, while ratio analysis is intended to facilitate comparisons by eliminating size differences across different businesses, the resulting ratios may not always be to the point.

Identifying issues or responding to a specific allegation usually dictates the level of financial data analyzed, and the required analysis may need to go more deeply than an overall financial statement analysis. Operational indexes that drive the financial information used by management in analyzing business performance can also be helpful in the identification of fraud. Management will often use detailed metrics to pinpoint and remedy a problem, and those metrics may not be subject to manipulation. Key management metrics focus on measures of revenue, profitability, and return on investment as well as on debt level and liquidity.

At the outset, most analytic investigative processes involve the use of vertical, horizontal, and ratio analyses, and the trending of those analyses over a period of time. See Exhibits 19.2 and 19.3 for simple examples based on summary financial data. Both financial and nonfinancial data can be useful in understanding a financial statement relationship. The first step in the forensic process is to develop expectations and identify inconsistencies, if any, in the following dimensions of the company's strategy, operating environment, and performance:

- Knowledge of the company and its strategic objectives
- Industry performance and economic factors
- Expected budgeted performance
- Historical performance
- Competitive benchmarking
- Operational metrics, including nonfinancial data

Establishing a point of view about the expectations in each area is an important part of the homework that should precede an investigation or occur during the planning stages of an investigation or audit.

As previously indicated, more ratio analysis is not necessarily better. The Association of Certified Fraud Examiners *Fraud Examiners Manual* points to nine key ratios that may lead to the discovery of fraud.[2] Just as with a horizontal or vertical analysis, these ratios should be studied on a time series basis, so that trends can be evaluated in comparison to the period analysis. The forensic accounting investigator should also consider performing the ratio analyses discussed below at a disaggregated level. For example, comparing current ratios at

---

2. Association of Certified Fraud Examiners, *Fraud Examiners Manual*, 3rd ed. (Austin, Tex.: Association of Certified Fraud Examiners, 2002).

the business unit level is likely to provide better insight than analyzing the current ratio on an overall basis. The interpretive results of those ratios are discussed next:[3]

$$\text{Current Ratio} = \frac{\text{Current Assets}}{\text{Current Liabilities}}$$

The *current ratio* measures the ability of a business to meet its current obligations from its current assets, such as cash, inventories, and receivables. The current ratio, like the quick ratio, described below, is a liquidity ratio. A current ratio higher than 1 indicates that current liabilities can be covered with existing current assets.

Poor receivables, fictitious or low inventory turns, or fictitious inventory limit the usefulness of the current ratio. For that reason, this ratio must be reviewed in conjunction with ratios of those activities. Embezzlement will generally reduce the current ratio as cash declines, while unreported liabilities will result in a more favorable ratio. In some instances, embezzlers may hide their theft by reducing liabilities with a debit to accounts payable, which would improve the current ratio.

$$\text{Quick Ratio} = \frac{\text{Cash} + \text{Marketable Securities} + \text{Accounts Receivable}}{\text{Current Liabilities}}$$

The *quick ratio* compares the most liquid assets of the business with liabilities. Because inventories are typically the least liquid of a company's current assets, the quick ratio is the measure of a firm's ability to pay off short-term obligations without relying on the sale of inventories. The quick ratio thus represents a more conservative measure of liquidity than the current ratio. A dramatic decline in the quick ratio may require a closer review of accounts receivable or accounts payable.

$$\text{Inventory Turnover Ratio} = \frac{\text{Cost of Goods Sold}}{\text{Average Inventory}}$$

The *inventory turnover ratio* measures the number of times inventory is turned over in a year. A higher ratio is considered a favorable indicator of greater efficiency in generating sales. However, inventory theft or diversion will lower ending inventory (less inventory on hand) and increase cost of goods sold (from writing off stolen inventory), thereby causing this ratio to be abnormally high. Substantial changes in this ratio from one period to the next should be analyzed to determine whether they are being caused by inventory fraud.

$$\text{Average-Number-of-Days-in-Inventory Ratio} = \frac{365}{\text{Inventory Turnover}}$$

---

3. The ratios presented here do not represent an exhaustive list of potentially useful ratios. Circumstances might dictate the use of other ratios, although in many cases the ratios here may be sufficient. The interpretive results focus on the identification of fraud or the needs of related follow-up inquiries rather than on changes resulting from other causes.

The *average-number-of-days-in-inventory ratio* is the inventory turnover ratio expressed in number of days. This ratio is important because days in stock increase the risks of obsolescence, price reductions, and additional expenses for storage. Significant changes or increases in the ratio can be indicators of inventory or purchasing schemes that result in fictitious inventory.

$$\text{Receivable Turnover Ratio} = \frac{\text{Net Sales on Account}}{\text{Average Net Receivables}}$$

The *receivable turnover ratio* measures the time between on-account sales and the collection of those sales. Receivable turnover will increase in a fictitious sales scheme, because the fictitious sales will not be collected. Changes in the ratio may also be the results of failing to record bad debt reserves.

$$\text{Collection Ratio} = \frac{365}{\text{Receivable Turnover}}$$

The *collection ratio*, or days sales outstanding, measures the average number of days it takes a company to collect its receivables. A lower ratio generally indicates faster receivables collection. Significant fluctuation in this ratio could result from changes in billing policies or collection efforts or could result from inflated or fictitious sales. If sales are inflated or fictitious, the ratio will rise. It is possible for sales to be inflated or fictitious if the receivables are consistently re-aged, because the ratio would not be adversely affected.

$$\text{Debt to Equity Ratio} = \frac{\text{Total Liabilities}}{\text{Total Equity}}$$

The *debt-to-equity ratio* is frequently used by creditors to manage the level of business risk assumed, because it measures the degree of ownership resources invested in the business, as compared with debt. It is sometimes referred to as a leverage ratio, because it shows the relative use of borrowed funds as compared with resources invested by owners. Unexpected increases in the ratio that correspond to an increase in accounts payable should be investigated further. Conversely, unexpected decreases in this ratio, perhaps to meet debt covenants and typically a decrease to accounts payable, should be investigated further. Debits to accounts payable may be indications that unauthorized expenses are being moved from the income statement to the balance sheet.

$$\text{Profit Margin Ratio} = \frac{\text{Net Income}}{\text{Net Sales}}$$

The *profit margin ratio* measures the profit margin achieved by selling the company's products. The profit margin assists in understanding the company's pricing structure, overhead structure, and profit level. Obviously, the goal of most businesses is to manage costs and prices in order to achieve a higher level of gross profit and, ultimately, net profit. The expectation is that this ratio should be fairly consistent over time. Analyzing this ratio is important for the detection of various inventory-related schemes or possible fictitious sales or cut-off issues.

$$\text{Asset Turnover Ratio} = \frac{\text{Net Sales}}{\text{Average Assets}}$$

The *asset turnover ratio* measures how effectively a company uses its assets. The higher the ratio, the more efficient the company in utilizing its assets. If the asset turnover ratio is increasing due to increases in sales, that could be the result of fictitious sales transactions.

Exhibit 19.1 offers the opportunity to examine these nine ratios for a hypothetical company utilizing the financial data in Exhibit 19.2. Beneath the exhibit is a set of observations based on the numbers.

	2000	2001	2002
Current Ratio	1.05	0.93	0.73
Quick Ratio	0.82	0.66	0.50
Inventory Turnover	10.46 [1]	11.51	9.60
Average Number of Days in Inventory	34.89	31.71	38.02
Days Sales Outstanding/Collection Ratio	82.77	61.04	65.30
Receivable Turnover	4.41 [2]	5.98	5.59
Debt to Equity	10.40	31.88	(130.50)
Profit Margin	0.01	(0.03)	(0.03)
Asset Turnover	0.95 [3]	1.21	1.10

[1] Beginning inventories for year 2000 are unavailable; ending inventories are used rather than average inventories.
[2] Receivables for year 2000 are unavailable; ending receivables are used rather than average receivables.
[3] Beginning assets for year 2000 are unavailable; ending assets are used rather than average assets. Results are rounded.

EXHIBIT 19.1   RATIOS

Examining the ratios in Exhibit 19.1, the forensic accounting investigator might frame the following questions for further investigation.

- The current and quick ratios have declined steadily over the past two years. That is likely to have resulted from higher inventory levels, given the decline in inventory turnover and the increase in days in inventory. If the inconsistency is unexpected, inventory valuation issues may be worth a second look, particularly in light of the decline in profit margins.

- From 2001 to 2002, receivable turnover has decreased slightly, consistent with the increased collection ratio. Given the aforementioned inventory issues, that could signal a problem with returned product.

- The negative debt-to-equity ratio is explained by cumulative losses that have resulted in negative equity. Debt is also increasing at a rapid rate. With the decline in the quick ratio, cash flow problems are likely to be on the horizon.

- The decline in profitability has obviously contributed to the problems noted earlier. A more detailed review, breaking down the data on a geographic, divisional, or even product basis, is necessary as a step toward pinpointing specific problem areas.

While the ratios in Exhibit 19.1 may not as a whole indicate a fraudulent inventory scheme or a scheme to increase liabilities, they may indicate higher risk factors facing the company, which in turn may generate increased pressure to manipulate earnings.

◆ IDENTIFYING OTHER RELATIONSHIPS THAT MIGHT INDICATE FRAUD

Time series analysis or trend analysis often is useful in the evaluation of overall changes in company operations. As shown in Exhibits 19.2 and 19.3, a vertical and horizontal analysis of the income statement, in conjunction with an analysis

	2000	%	2001	%	2002	%
Income Statement						
Net Sales	$158,718	100	$249,821	100	$291,175	100
Cost of Sales	136,163	86	218,803	88	259,444	89
Gross Profit Margin	22,555	14	31,018	12	31,731	11
Selling, and Administrative Expenses	15,835	10	21,960	9	22,675	8
EBIT	6,720	4	9,058	4	9,056	3
Interest	4,599	3	12,293	5	15,676	5
Taxes	1,325	1	3,911	2	3,045	1
Net Income (loss)	$ 796	1	$ (7,146)	(3)	$ (9,665)	(3)
Balance Sheet						
Cash	$ 10,326	6	$ 14,206	6	$ 6,518	2
Inventories	13,019	8	25,003	10	29,061	10
Accounts Receivable	36,021	22	47,580	19	56,527	20
Total Current Assets	59,366	36	86,789	35	92,106	32
Total Non-Current Assets	107,128	64	158,364	65	194,094	68
Total Assets	$166,494	100	$245,153	100	$286,200	100
Accounts Payable	$ 17,814	11	$ 33,333	14	$ 46,495	16
Other Current Liabilities	38,772	23	59,723	24	79,592	28
Total Current Liabilities	56,586	34	93,056	38	126,087	44
Total Debt	95,307	57	144,642	59	162,323	57
Total Liabilities	151,893	91	237,698	97	288,410	101
Shareholder's Equity	14,601	9	7,455	3	(2,210)	(1)
Total Liabilities and Shareholder's Equity	$166,494	100	$245,153	100	$286,200	100

Note: Only selected financial statement items are presented for analysis. Percentages are rounded.

Exhibit 19.2   ABC Holding Company Division Vertical Analysis

	2000	2001	% Change	2002	% Change
Income Statement					
Net Sales	$158,718	$ 249,821	57	$291,175	17
Cost of Sales	136,163	218,803	61	259,444	19
Gross Profit Margin	22,555	31,018	38	31,731	2
Selling and Administrative Expenses	15,835	21,960	39	22,675	3
EBIT	6,720	9,058	35	9,056	(0)
Interest	4,599	12,293	167	15,676	28
Taxes	1,325	3,911	195	3,045	(22)
Net Income (loss)	$ 796	$ (7,146)	(998)	$ (9,665)	35
Balance Sheet					
Cash	$ 10,326	$ 14,206	38	$6,518	(54)
Inventories	13,019	25,003	92	29,061	16
Accounts Receivable	36,021	47,580	32	56,527	19
Total Current Assets	59,366	86,789	46	92,106	6
Total Non-Current Assets	107,127	158,364	48	194,094	23
Total Assets	$166,494	$245,153	47	$286,200	17
Accounts Payable	$ 17,814	$ 33,333	87	$46,495	39
Other Current Liabilities	38,772	59,723	54	79,592	33
Total Current Liabilities	56,585	93,056	64	126,087	35
Total Debt	95,307	144,642	52	162,323	12
Total Liabilities	151,893	237,698	56	288,410	21
Shareholder's Equity	14,601	7,455	(49)	(2,210)	(130)
Total Liabilities and Shareholder's Equity	$166,494	$245,153	47	$286,200	17

Note: Only selected financial statement items are presented for analysis. Percentages are rounded.

EXHIBIT 19.3   ABC HOLDING COMPANY DIVISION HORIZONTAL ANALYSIS

of the balance sheet over a period of time, may be a useful step in identifying relationships that warrant further inquiry and in differentiating problems between the two documents. Such analysis can help identify certain line items on the financial statements that need further review. Is the level of sales growth reasonable, for example, in light of measures of sales to profit, operating income, certain expense levels, and related balance sheet accounts such as inventory and receivable balances?

The results of vertical and horizontal analyses may require further investigation to help identify asset misappropriation or financial statement misrepresentation. The investigation could focus on the following areas.

MARGIN ANALYSIS

Does the gross profit margin (sales minus costs of goods sold) make sense over time? How does it compare with other company locations? Further analysis might reveal that the cost of goods sold is increasing at a rate higher than that of sales, a possible indicator of inventory theft or an embezzlement scheme. Additional analysis into the components of costs of goods sold will be required in order to understand fully the deviation from the expected relationship. Are unexplained or nonoperating transactions boosting profits? Analysis of gains on sales of assets or gains from other transactions may indicate false transactions. Do inventory levels make sense relative to sales increases? Fully analyze the components of inventory to determine whether there has been an unexpected buildup, given the increases in sales.

FOCUS ON DISPARITY OF NET INCOME TO CASH BALANCES

While in some industries earnings and operating cash flow may be different, they should bear some relationship to one another in a time-based or trend analysis. Follow-up procedures could include a cash flow and collection analysis. Changes in cash and net income relationships may also indicate issues with accrual estimates.

Do warranty expenses display a consistent relationship over time? As sales increase, warranty expenses and other expenses tied to volume should increase in a consistent manner.

In performing horizontal and vertical analyses of the income statement on an interim basis, do revenues and expense trends make sense on an interim reporting basis when compared with year-end results?

EVALUATE INCREASES IN ACCOUNTS RECEIVABLE IN RELATION TO SALES INCREASES

Unusual increases in accounts receivable can be indicators of fictitious sales or of sales being forced through the distribution system, such as manufacturers sending and billing product to their distribution network without a specific order from the distributor. If sales are overstated, certain accounts receivable may not be collectible.

EVALUATE INTERIM RESULTS AND SEASONALITY

Large fluctuations in the fourth quarter may indicate an orientation of management toward aggressive interim reporting. However, in the case of a seasonal business, there may be expected fluctuations, given the cyclical nature of the business.

COMMON ANALYTIC PITFALLS

- *Using incomplete data sets.* Ensuring that the disaggregated data add up to the expected total, as gap analysis (identifying the differences and determining whether they are significant), is often critical to the identification of journal entries or activities not reflecting normal business processes. In and of itself, understanding why disaggregated data may not agree to the totals expected on the financial statements can be a valuable analytic technique.
- *Not establishing independent expectations prior to performing the analysis.* If independent expectations are not established, there may be a tendency to accept rather than question explanations for fluctuations. This

lack of establishing independent expectations may lead to incorrect conclusions and analysis.

- *Not performing corroborative analytic procedures.* Not corroborating the results of one analytic procedure with the results of other analytics increases the risk of overlooking an unusual trend. Effective analytic procedures will enable the forensic accounting investigator to compare the results of one analysis (revenue trends by customer by month) with that of another analysis (accounts receivable aging or days sales outstanding by month) to corroborate explanations.

- *Not corroborating management's explanations with other evidence.* Accepting management's explanations without corroborating with other evidence is a common problem when fraud is subsequently uncovered. Here is a ripe area for application of the practice of "trust but verify," which was discussed in Chapter 6.

- *Using industry or other information that is not comparable.* As noted earlier in this chapter, larger firms may have proportionately higher investments in fixed costs, and assuming a linear relationship to a smaller firm may be incorrect. Industry benchmarks can be misleading in industries undergoing difficulty. Further, companies often account for revenues and costs in different ways based on their unique situations. Direct comparisons may not be meaningful—or they may be. Care is required.

◆ IDENTIFYING SIGNS OF EARNINGS MANAGEMENT

For purposes of performance measurement, management's use of industry norms or other benchmarks in ratio analysis can have the effect of leading management to view those numbers as targets, which they hope to hit through the normal growth of the company. However, if the company's ratios fall somewhat short of the mark, management may then at least look at improving them through changes in their accounting methods. Incentives and bonus programs based on metrics can have effects similar to those created by analysts' expectations.

The quality of a company's earnings is often defined as the degree to which earnings reflect the actual economic reality of the business. Earnings management rises to the level of fraud when companies intentionally misstate information. Understanding key performance-based targets and the components of financial information that drive them can assist the forensic accounting investigator in understanding the risks associated with pressure to hit those targets. Exploring and monitoring the reasons behind changes in the key ratios and why they occur are helpful techniques in ensuring the validity of reported information.

THE BENEISH RESEARCH

Are analyses available that may predict the likelihood of financial statement manipulation? Prof. Messod D. Beneish of Indiana University has researched the quantitative differences between public companies identified through restatements, enforcement actions by the U.S. Securities and Exchange Commission, or other means as having manipulated financial statements and those that have not been so identified.[4] The indexes he calculated are based on changes in account balances between the year in which the first reporting violation was uncovered (denoted as *cy*, for *current year*) and the prior year (denoted as *cy – 1*). His study found that on average, those identified as manipulators had significantly larger increases in days sales in receivables, greater deterioration of gross margins and asset quality, higher growth, and larger accruals than nonmanipulators. The table in Exhibit 19.4 summarizes the mean indexes for manipulators compared with nonmanipulators that resulted from Beneish's sample population, which was restricted to public companies.[5] In addition to the data from Beneish's research, we have included the calculated indexes for Global Crossing, Ltd., a telecommunications company that filed for bankruptcy in January 2002. JPMorgan Chase and a group of major banks, which loaned the company more than $2 billion, filed suit against Global Crossing, alleging that company executives initiated fraudulent transactions prior to the bankruptcy filing to inflate earnings and conceal the company's true financial position. As of August 2005, 23 former Global Crossing executives had been named in the $1.7-billion suit. The Global Crossing data illustrates how Beneish's work can provide a useful comparative or benchmarking tool for the forensic accounting investigator.

Beneish's study indicated with the exception of the Total-Accruals-to-Total-Assets calculation, an index of 1 is the neutral result, meaning that the underlying components of the index have remained unchanged relative to one another from the previous year. Generally speaking, Beneish's study states that any index greater than 1.08 *could* be worth a closer look. We recognize that this is a general statement and does not align with the Sales Growth Index, which has a nonmanipulator index of 1.134, greater than the 1.08 generalization. Beneish notes that in order for this model to be effective, the first year under comparison must be known to be nonmanipulated because comparison of two manipulated years will produce invalid results. In reality, it may be difficult to determine initially whether the first year of the comparison has not been manipulated. As with the use of any technique, there may be drawbacks and limitations. If the result is less than 1, the research suggests that there has been no manipulation of financial information.

Index Type	Nonmanipulators	Manipulators	Global Crossing
Days Sales in Receivables Index	1.031	1.465	3.436
Gross Margin Index	1.014	1.193	1.177
Asset Quality Index	1.039	1.254	1.170
Sales Growth Index	1.134	1.607	3.964
Total Accruals to Total Assets	0.018	0.031	−0.069

EXHIBIT 19.4   FROM THE BENEISH RESEARCH: GLOBAL CROSSING RESULTS

4. Messod D. Beneish, "The Detection of Earnings Manipulation," *Financial Analysts Journal* 55, No. 5 (September–October 1999), 24–36.
5. Joseph T. Wells, "Irrational Ratios," *Journal of Accountancy* (August 2001), 80–83.

The Total-Accruals-to-Total-Assets calculation is the only calculation that Beneish does not refer to as an index. For this calculation, an amount greater than 2.0 percent (0.02) may generally warrant further review.

These indexes may be calculated using any two consecutive years of financial statement data from a public company. But a word of caution is in order: the indexes may function or be used only as a screening technique to "evaluate the likelihood of manipulation"[6] in a company's financial statements. Beneish stresses that the indexes are not foolproof and have frequently produced erroneous results. They merely provide an indicator of manipulation that may trigger further investigation. If any or all of the indexes for a particular company exceed the defined thresholds, a forensic accounting investigator may need to evaluate the underlying components of those indexes: perhaps the unexpected result is due to a change in the company's credit policies, a strategic acquisition, or the disappearance of a competitor from the market. Perhaps when compared with comparable measures for several others in the industry, the initial result appears more typical. The likelihood that fraud is occurring may typically become greater when there appears to be no plausible explanation for the results.

In the calculations shown in Exhibits 19.5–19.9, and summarized in Exhibit 19.4, we chose to use information from Global Crossing. We realize that Global Crossing had very large year-over-year sales growth at the end—a potential red flag in itself. However, we chose the example to illustrate how some calculations may trigger further review and some may not—even in situations of alleged financial statement manipulation. In light of the Global Crossing results in Exhibit 19.4, the forensic accounting investigator might initially choose to focus efforts in sales and accounts receivable, since the indexes for both Days Sales in Receivables (3.436) and Sales Growth (3.964) are much greater than the manipulators index of 1.465 and 1.607, respectively.

(A) Days Sales in Receivables Index Formula

$$\frac{(\text{Accounts Receivable} / \text{Sales})}{(\text{Accounts Receivable} / \text{Sales})} \quad \frac{(cy)}{(cy-1)}$$

(B) Days Sales in Receivables Data and Index: Global Crossing Data

	1998	1999
Sales	$420,000,000	$1,665,000,000
Accounts Receivable	$71,000,000	$967,000,000

(C) 1998–1999 Days Sales in Receivables / Beneish Index

$$\frac{(\$967,000,000 / \$1,665,000,000)}{(\$71,000,000 / \$420,000,000)} = 3.436$$

EXHIBIT 19.5   DAYS SALES IN RECEIVABLES INDEX

---

6. Beneish, "The Detection of Earnings Manipulation."

The Days Sales in Receivables Index shown in Exhibit 19.5 measures the relationship between receivables and revenues in two consecutive reporting periods and indicates whether they are out of balance.

Utilizing actual data from Global Crossing in Exhibit 19.5, the Days Sales in Receivables Index of 3.436 may trigger further investigation because it is greater than the 1.465 mean index of manipulators in Beneish's study.

Further investigation may be warranted, because an inflated ratio may reflect either fictitious sales/receivables or a more liberal credit policy. Disproportionate increases in receivables relative to sales volumes may be strong indicators that revenue is overstated. (See Exhibit 19.4.)

The Gross Margin Index shown in Exhibit 19.6 offers a measure of the risk of earnings manipulation. As gross margins decline, management may be more likely to commit fraud to create artificial profits or to decrease losses. While the mean index of manipulators was 1.193, Global Crossing's result of 1.177 is slightly less than the mean index of 1.193; however, it is greater than the 1.08 generalization noted above. Review in this area may be warranted, perhaps at a lower priority than the indexes for Days Sales in Receivables and Sales Growth.

(A) Gross Margin Index Formula

$$\frac{(Sales - Cost\ of\ Sales)\ /\ Sales}{(Sales - Cost\ of\ Sales)\ /\ Sales} \quad \frac{(cy - 1)}{(cy)}$$

(B) Gross Margin Index: Global Crossing Data

	1998	1999
Sales	$420,000,000	$1,665,000,000
Cost of Sales	$178,000,000	$ 850,000,000

(C) 1998–1999 Gross Margin / Beneish Index

$$\frac{(\$420,000,000 - \$178,000,000)\ /\ \$420,000,000}{(\$1,665,000,000 - \$850,000,000)\ /\ \$1,665,000,000} = 1.177$$

EXHIBIT 19.6   GROSS MARGIN INDEX

A red flag associated with this index may indicate an increasing risk of false profits. However, if the company was already engaging in fraud in prior years, then gross margins will be higher than normal and cause a lower index.

The Asset Quality Index shown in Exhibit 19.7 is intended to measure or to be a determinant of the risk propensity of a company to capitalize costs. It measures the proportion of total assets for which future benefits may be less certain. With Global Crossing, the result of 1.170 is greater than the nonmanipulator of 1.039 and the 1.08 generalization. However, it is less than the manipulator index of 1.254. (See Exhibit 19.4.)

A more focused investigation into the increase in the index may be warranted, because a high asset quality index may indicate an inappropriate deferral of costs.

The Sales Growth Index shown in Exhibit 19.8 measures sales that have increased and may not be legitimate. Growth companies are often viewed as

---

(A) Asset Quality Index Formula

$$\frac{1 - (\text{Current Assets} + \text{Net Fixed Assets}) / \text{Total Assets}}{1 - (\text{Current Assets} + \text{Net Fixed Assets}) / \text{Total Assets}} \quad \frac{(cy)}{(cy - 1)}$$

(B) Asset Quality Index: Global Crossing Data

	1998	1999
Current Assets	$ 977,000,000	$ 2,947,000,000
Net Fixed Assets	$ 434,000,000	$ 6,026,000,000
Total Assets	$ 2,639,000,000	$ 19,706,000,000

(C) 1998–1999 Asset Quality / Beneish Index

$$\frac{1 - (\$2,947,000,000 + \$6,026,000,000) / \$19,706,000,000}{1 - (\$977,000,000 + \$434,000,000) / \$2,639,000,000} = 1.170$$

EXHIBIT 19.7   ASSET QUALITY INDEX

(A) Sales Growth Index Formula

$$\frac{\text{Sales}}{\text{Sales}} \quad \frac{(cy)}{(cy - 1)}$$

(B) Sales Growth Index: Global Crossing Data

	1998	1999
Sales	$420,000,000	$1,665,000,000

(C) 1998–1999 Sales Growth / Beneish Index

$$\frac{\$1,665,000,000}{\$420,000,000} \quad 3.964$$

EXHIBIT 19.8   SALES GROWTH INDEX

more likely to commit financial statement fraud, given the pressure to meet earnings targets. Global Crossing's result appears much greater at 3.964 than the mean index of manipulators of 1.607. Further investigation in sales and revenue areas may be warranted, based on the result of this index.

A higher index means a higher-than-normal increase in sales. Note that if fictitious sales were recorded to stay even with previous-year results, the impact of those fictitious sales is not isolated in this analysis.

The Total Accruals to Total Assets calculation shown in Exhibit 19.9 measures the risk related to accrual policies, which in actuality are financing mechanisms for losses. The mean index of nonmanipulators was 0.018, while the mean index of manipulators was 0.031, or 72 percent higher. As noted previously, an amount greater than 0.02 may warrant further review.

A high ratio may indicate that a company is financing its losses. Other legitimate forces, however, may have caused the index to be high. In this instance, the Global Crossing data do not exceed the red flag threshold; therefore, the forensic accounting investigator may choose to focus attention elsewhere. An important

(A) Total Accruals to Total Assets Formula

$$\frac{(\Delta \text{Current Assets} - \Delta \text{Cash}) - (\Delta \text{Current Liabilities} - \Delta \text{Current Portion LTD} - \Delta \text{Taxes Payable}) - \text{Depr. \& Amort.} \quad (cy)}{\text{Total Assets} \quad (cy)}$$

(B) Total Accruals to Total Assets: Global Crossing Data

	1998	1999
Current Assets	$ 977,000,000	$ 2,947,000,000
Current Liabilities	$ 256,000,000	$ 1,853,000,000
Cash	$ 806,000,000	$ 1,633,000,000
Current Taxes Payable	$ 16,000,000	$ 140,000,000
Current Portion LTD	$ 6,393,000,000	$ 5,496,000,000
Depreciation and amortization	$ 1,000,000	$ 124,000,000
Total Assets	$ 2,639,000,000	$ 19,706,000,000

(C) 1998–1999 Accruals to Assets / Beneish Calculation

$$\frac{(\$2,947 - \$977) - (\$1,633 - \$806) - ((\$1,853 - \$256) - (\$5,496 - \$6,393) - (\$140 - \$16)) - \$124}{\$19,706} = -0.069$$

EXHIBIT 19.9   TOTAL ACCRUALS TO TOTAL ASSETS

point to note: each of these calculations is unique. Depending on the underlying scheme, some of the calculations will represent a potential red flag, while others will not.

Overall, Professor Beneish's indexes represent calculation techniques based on readily available financial data, and they are potentially powerful indicators. Like other analytic techniques discussed in this chapter, they may assist in focusing the investigation of unexpected results in a company's financial statements.

CHAPTER 20

DATA MINING: COMPUTER-AIDED FORENSIC ACCOUNTING INVESTIGATION TECHNIQUES

Mona M. Clayton

John C. Moorman

John Wilkinson

Malcolm Shackell

Gregory Schaffer

Data mining uses software[1] to assist the forensic accounting investigator in identifying and reviewing unusual data trends, patterns, and anomalies. Regardless of size, many of today's organizations maintain the majority of business transaction data in electronic formats. That is also true for many of the other primary sources of data potentially relevant to a forensic accounting investigator: customer and supplier information, product and price documentation, telephone logs, building security and access details, and employee data, to name but a few sources. The likelihood is high that most of the data the forensic accounting investigator is engaged to review will exist electronically, although previous chapters have made clear that forensic accounting investigators collate many different types of information, not all of which initially exists electronically. Studies have shown that as much as 93 percent of a modern society's intellectual output is stored digitally.

As a result of the use of small-business management programs such as Quick-Books in smaller firms and enterprise-wide accounting packages in national or global firms, today's computer systems are vast warehouses containing data from finance, operations, marketing, and personnel. While small companies engage in hundreds or thousands of transactions, large-company transactions

---

1. See software appendix at the end of the chapter.

number in the tens or hundreds of millions, even billions. Given such volume, relying exclusively on manual investigation skills (without using computer-aided techniques) to uncover suspect transactions is too expensive and likely to overlook key data. Within those thousands or millions of records could be fraudulent activity that may remain hidden unless the right tools and know-how are applied to bring the issues to light.

Data analysis is often the fastest and most effective tool at the forensic accounting investigator's disposal for gathering much of the evidential material needed to support findings. Much of the data, particularly the nonaccounting data, is never used directly by the organization in question, but any of it may hold the key to an investigation. In cases in which the forensic accounting investigator has been engaged on the basis of a suspicion or an as yet unsubstantiated allegation, the results of data mining may provide the forensic accounting team with that all-important place to start.

Auditors too often use software tools—some of them generic or homegrown—to query accounting systems, gain assurance with respect to data integrity, and in some instances, identify so-called unusual transactions.[2] American Institute of Certified Public Accountants Statement on Auditing Standards (SAS) 99, *Consideration of Fraud in a Financial Statement Audit,* refers to such measures as computer-assisted audit techniques. These tools form part of the forensic accounting software tool set. The tools can uncover anomalies and patterns that might go undetected by an approach that relies on testing samples.

Data mining is the process of looking for trends, patterns, and anomalies within a data set. These trends, patterns, and anomalies—or exceptions to them—may be completely innocuous and can be verified as such. However, unusual transactions—those falling outside expected norms—may signal the need for an investigation by forensic accounting investigators who will apply their experience in data mining and in investigative techniques to the overall situation that appears to be emerging.

The technical process by which data mining is carried out is often complex. The analyst must be a competent user of the relevant tools. While a full description of the complexities of the data-mining process is beyond the scope of this book, this chapter can usefully focus on the ways in which the forensic accounting investigator can utilize data mining to maximize its contribution to an investigation. The chapter also discusses, with plenty of examples, how a range of data analysis techniques—including data mining, targeted querying, and data matching—can assist the investigative team.

◆ BENEFITS AND PITFALLS

Using software applications and understanding their capabilities from basic to advanced can bring rapid and powerful results to the successive phases of an investigation. However, to be most efficient, users must know how and why to

---

2. That is, those that exist outside a predefined norm.

employ such tools. One cannot assume that all forensic accounting investigators, experienced or otherwise, are skilled users of software as an investigatory tool. In lieu of using software, many experienced forensic accounting investigators continue to rely on interview techniques and document review. However, once forensic accounting investigators have been introduced to advanced software tools, they often find that depending on the situation, they are likely to bring added value to clients through increased efficiency.

Many types of software applications and an ever-increasing array of new products and versions are available. The vast range of software offerings argues against any attempt to provide a comprehensive listing of such tools. It is possible, however, to describe both the benefits and the pitfalls of requesting, obtaining, and analyzing computerized information. The benefits will make clear why data mining should be viewed as an integral part of the investigation process. The pitfalls will help steer the reader away from the more common mistakes.

BENEFITS

- The forensic accounting investigator is able to analyze a large number of transactions, identify trends, spot documents that need further review, and gain initial insights without waiting for the cumbersome process of collecting documents by traditional means.
- Data mining is often a more cost-effective and more comprehensive approach than hard-copy document review.
- Computerized information can assist in providing reasonableness checks of findings based on documents, especially in situations in which document sets may be incomplete. It also enables the investigating team to check 100 percent of an entity's transactions for certain characteristics such as date, time, dollar amount, approvals, and payee depending on the nature of the computer record.
- With data analysis linked to presentation software, findings can be more clearly summarized for board, audit committee, or management presentations.

OTHER CONSIDERATIONS

- Data mining is only one part of the forensic accounting investigation process. The investigation cannot be conducted from the computer screen alone. The computer is not a substitute for the forensic accounting investigator's good judgment and experience. It cannot replace document reviews, interviews, and follow-up steps.
- If possible, data should be gathered at the outset of an engagement and prior to the initial field visit. Doing so reduces the risk of the data being compromised.
- An incorrect and incomplete data set may contribute to premature and incorrect conclusions. Data obtained should be checked for accuracy and completeness.

- Certain data-mining tools may not be appropriate to certain tasks. The complexity of the tools used should be commensurate with the size and complexity of the engagement.

- Some forensic accounting investigators may place too much reliance on the tool itself. Absent the needed blend of skilled technical use of the tools and sound analysis and judgment, many of the operational and financial benefits of data mining may be lost.

- Legal issues must be carefully considered. Not all legal environments are the same. Care must be taken and advice considered—before commencing data collection or analysis—to ensure that planned procedures are allowed from a legal perspective and that any evidence gathered may be used for legal purposes if required.

- Data collection across national boundaries must be done with proper legal advice about the export of data—for example, about Swiss bank secrecy laws—or about the type of data being collected—for example, prohibitions about reading e-mail, pursuant to European Union privacy regulations.

- Because copying a computer file can alter certain elements of the file if not executed correctly, proper computer forensic techniques must be used to avoid inadvertently altering evidence.

NEARLY EVERY INVESTIGATION CAN BENEFIT FROM FORENSIC TECHNOLOGY

Fraudsters necessarily make use of the computer systems that corporations depend on for day-to-day operations. Tech-savvy fraudsters often make use of e-mail and instant messaging, they access networks, they create and manipulate all sorts of files, and they work with databases and general ledger systems. They may also use printing, scanning, and fax technology to create all types of fictitious documents, many of which have the look and feel of the real thing.

In many cases, these traditional frauds, con games, and embezzlement schemes are also cybercrimes. Whenever an employee exceeds authorized access on the employer's computer network in order to change an accounting record or steal a trade secret, a violation of the Computer Fraud and Abuse Act (18 USC §1030) or the Economic Espionage Act (18 USC § 1832) has potentially occurred. In other cases, a fraudster may simply use computer networks just as fraudsters in the past used telephones and filing cabinets.

But there is a difference. Computer networks often provide better audit trails and information about what was done by a would-be fraudster than the paper-based record-keeping systems that have been replaced in the past 25 years. Understanding the tools and techniques of forensic technology investigations provides a wealth of information to review that would be otherwise unavailable or at least more difficult to obtain. In investigations, having more information is a key asset.

◆ EFFECTIVE DATA MINING

At the planning stage of any forensic accounting project, the project manager should consider three key questions when deciding whether and how to gather electronic evidence:

- What relevant data might be available?
- What skills are available within the team?
- How will the data analysis fit in with the wider investigation?

WHAT RELEVANT DATA MIGHT BE AVAILABLE?

Metadata is data about data.[3] Metadata is not apparent when files are printed to paper or converted to an image format such as a TIFF or PDF file.[4]

When computers store information for later retrieval, the operating systems necessarily create certain data about the stored information in order to facilitate ongoing processing. Some programs also allow users to add their own metadata to a file, such as a document title, the subject of the file, the name of the author of the document, the name of the manager responsible for the document, and the name of the company that owns the document. In addition, some programs permit a user to assign metadata to a document in order to facilitate later retrieval. This type of metadata can include assignment of the document to a particular category, inclusion of searchable keywords, or a description of the document's contents.

In addition to these types of metadata, there are other, less obvious variations. For example, spreadsheets and databases can contain complex mathematical formulas and links among fields, which play key roles in calculating the numbers that appear in various cells. Typically, the printed spreadsheet will show only the result of the calculation, not the formula used to calculate the result. Similarly, modern word processing documents can contain links and references to other types of electronic files such as pictures, charts, spreadsheets, and sound files. These linked files may be stored either in the same location as the main document or halfway around the world on another computer linked by a proprietary network or by the Internet. The printed document may show the content of the other files without revealing that those elements are not integral parts of the electronic document but are really borrowings from other electronic sources. The electronic document will necessarily contain the code needed to connect to the data in the linked files and may give a forensic accounting investigator point-

---

3. Such information, called metadata, typically includes the name of the file being stored, the date the file was created and last modified, and the file size. Many programs automatically add other metadata to the file, such as the type of file being stored, the location the file was stored to, the name of the author, the name of the person who last saved the file, and the number of revisions the file has gone through.

4. The *tagged-image file format* (TIFF) is a widely used format for storing image data. The *portable document format* (PDF) was developed by Adobe Corporation to allow efficient electronic distribution of large documents.

ers to additional sources of relevant information. This in turn may lead to additional witnesses, such as the author of a linked document in a remote location.

AUDIT TRAILS (TRAFFIC DATA)

In addition to metadata created at the file level, many computer systems generate significant amounts of traffic data when information is manipulated within a computer or across a computer network. Such traffic data, often referred to as audit trails, may be useful when trying to tie activity back to a particular user or set of users and may give clues as to its authorship. Network traffic data (if it is being stored) may indicate which user account was responsible for storing the document to that location.

Many types of traffic data may be available to the forensic accounting investigator. For example, most general ledger systems can be configured to record the user name associated with the most recent change to any value in the system. Some systems allow users to record the user names responsible for every change to a value over time. Similarly, many e-mail systems retain information about the dates and times associated with transmissions of each e-mail and attachment. Some of these systems also record the date and time of message deletions. Operating systems may maintain dates associated with accessing, moving, or deleting files. All of this information can be useful in the course of an investigation.

Yet traffic data can take an investigation only so far. It is sometimes said that the last inch in a cyber investigation is the hardest. Electronic audit trails may indeed lead a forensic accounting investigator back to a particular computer as the one responsible for a given set of activities—for example, a particular change to a general ledger system.

FASTER/BETTER/CHEAPER

A computer can search, sort, and manipulate an electronic document in a fraction of the time necessary for a human to perform the same tasks. In a case involving hundreds of thousands or millions of pages of printed materials, human review and search for specific information can be tedious, imprecise work. But computer searches across the same volume of electronic files can reliably discover—and in short order—every instance of a particular word or combination of words. Similarly, a computer can instantly sort a large volume of information by date, file name, author, storage location, or any number of other criteria, thereby highlighting key documents in what could otherwise be an extremely time-consuming manual review.

ACCESS TO RELEVANT DATA

The existence of information does not guarantee that it will be readily available to the forensic accounting investigator. There may be technical, organizational, or legal barriers that potentially prevent the forensic accounting investigator from gaining access to that data. For example, in many investigations, forensic accounting investigators find that the organization's archiving system restricts access to data they need, particularly historical data. Depending on the format and media to which data has been archived, the forensic accounting team may find that the cost of restoring the archived data is prohibitive.

In one engagement, a forensic team found that detailed transactional data were copied to microfiche six months after the transactions occurred. The original documents were then destroyed. Because of the cost involved in restoring the data to a usable format, the forensic accounting investigators had to develop an alternative approach to analyzing the transactions, which included searching for a sample of transactions on the existing microfiche—an incomplete and extremely time-consuming process.

Many organizations archive only the information they are required by law to keep. When this is so, information on historical transactions may be available only in summary or overview form. It may also be that the needs of the forensic accounting team conflict with the organization's security policy concerning access to especially sensitive information. While such factors may not ultimately prevent the forensic accounting investigator from accessing relevant data, they need to be considered, particularly when the project is subject to time or other constraints.

In recent years, difficulties have arisen because of organizations' outsourcing of their data management function. Consider this example: a forensic technology team was called in, at an outsourcing agency, to review the work of a technology team from another firm. The review team members noted that they were dealing with an accounting system that contained over 1,400 tables with multiple links among many of them. Complicating the situation even further, only one contract engineer at the outsourcing agency possessed a thorough understanding of the system. While forensic technology professionals could have spent time piecing together an understanding of the multiple links, in this particular engagement that would not have been the best use of professional time or client money. The investigation was delayed until the engineer could be released from other projects to assist the forensic team with the data extraction. Only in this way could the team be sure of performing the task correctly the first time around. Having this specialized knowledge on the team is more than likely to add value in determining the course of action.

One factor that forensic accounting investigators ignore at their peril is the potential for legal restrictions governing access to the data they need to review. Data protection legislation is often in place, particularly in Europe, where such legislation is stricter than in many other parts of the world. Forensic technologists and others who are asked to investigate or evaluate such data should familiarize themselves with the relevant legislation, which may be complex and is sometimes untested. In addition, while the team might legally be able to obtain and access certain information within a particular geography or country, restrictions may exist on transporting that information beyond country boundaries.

Ways can often be found to work within such data protection restrictions. For example, forensic accounting investigators might request data only from individuals who cannot be personally identified. Solutions can often be found that comply with the requirements of the legal environment. When an investigation requires the use of customer, staff, or other personal details, access to such data may still be possible. Each country or jurisdiction may have laws that protect privacy and even dictate whether computerized files can be removed from the premises or out of the country. A good practice is to always seek appropriate legal advice before attempting to acquire any personal data.

◆ ASSESSING DATA QUALITY AND FORMAT

Early assessment of the quality and format of available data is vital to ensure that the forensic accounting team's technological resources will be used effectively. If data is potentially unreliable or extremely difficult to extract or format, the team may be better off concentrating on other investigation methods. However, cases in which no tool can be found to deal with system output are rare, and in most instances at least some of the data is reliable.

A person experienced in data management should perform the initial assessment of data quality and format; this is important. Additionally, if the data is of a highly specific nature, it may be necessary at this stage to involve individuals with specialized industry and technical skills and knowledge. The person assessing the data sources should have good background information about both the operational activities of the client and the nature and purpose of the investigation.

Close coordination between the forensic technologists and the organization's systems administrator is highly recommended. Generally, the systems administrator should be the forensic technologist's first point of contact and often provides considerable input about the structure of the system, relevant input controls, and potential formats for extractions.

Clearly, such coordination would be inappropriate if the systems administrator is the probable focus of the investigation. As well, forensic accounting investigators should be aware that systems administrators' objectives might differ from those of the forensic accounting team. Administrators may be concerned about their own or their team's workload; or there may be a desire to make data validation controls seem tighter than they actually are; or administrators may attempt to persuade the forensic team that their team's technical competencies are more robust than they actually are. Because administrators are frequently more cooperative when dealing with other data management specialists, using such an individual to carry out the assessment will make it less likely that the team will be put off by an uncooperative systems administrator.

The initial assessment should cover:

- Scope of available data
- Quality of available data
- Time required and data requests

SCOPE OF AVAILABLE DATA

Given the breadth of data that is available, a clear understanding of the investigation is useful in guiding the forensic accounting investigator to the relevant data. Data can come from many different sources within an organization, and while financial reporting systems are frequently the main data sources, less obvious sources may exist from which supplementary information can be gathered.

In one case, management of a bank alleged that certain mortgages were being falsely attributed to an intermediate broker instead of to the customers who had directly applied for the mortgages. The purpose of the alleged fraud was to generate additional broker's commission. In gathering evidence, the forensic team matched the names of bank customers found in the branch's daily appointment diaries to details taken from the bank's mortgage portfolio. The diaries proved to be unusual but effective sources of data. Other useful data sources for forensic accounting investigation engagements might include bank statements, supplementary accounting systems, and logs from telephone networks or electronic security systems.

The integration of data from such sources can be one of the most productive investigative methods for the forensic analyst. Fraudsters rarely manage to cover all traces of their activity. The forensic accounting investigator's ability to cross-check various data sources against common key fields and to identify potential inconsistencies between sources can be a most valuable investigative tool.

In their search for data, forensic accounting investigators should not focus exclusively on digital sources. Paper records can be scanned and converted into usable files with optical character recognition tools. For example, bank statements are often scanned and then matched against the accounting system, creating, in effect, an electronic bank reconciliation. In environments in which checks are used, another option is to request that the bank provide a tape of cleared checks. By comparing this information with the client's disbursement file, the forensic accounting investigator can create a list of outstanding checks.

Every forensic accounting investigation engagement is different, and for each, the key sources of data may vary. However, the following are among the most useful and readily available records:

- Vendor master file
- Employee master file
- Customer master file
- General ledger detail
- Cash disbursements
- Customer invoices
- Other data or data sources, depending on the circumstance, including receiving and purchasing information, telephone data, voice mail, e-mail, personal digital assistants, BlackBerrys, and computer hard drives.

QUALITY OF AVAILABLE DATA

In most cases, system input controls will determine the quality of the data available within an organization. On certain systems, particularly nonfinancial systems, few such input controls may exist. Together with the systems administrator or another internal information technology (IT) professional who has detailed knowledge of the system's functions, the forensic technologist should first assess these input controls and their potential impact on data quality. In addition, forensic investigators should check their conclusions against discussions with actual system users, who may be inputting particular data items even though the system does not require them to do so.

When the system does not perform internal validation checks—such as checking a tax code against amounts input or restricting the range of values that can be input into a field—the quality of the data will in most circumstances be lower. The forensic accounting investigator should consider this important detail before requesting a data extract that can often require several days' work on the part of a systems administrator and the forensic technologist. If it is determined that no—or relatively few—controls over system input are in place, or if key fields can be left blank, the forensic technologist should assess how much value the data will add to the investigation.

TIME REQUIRED AND DATA REQUESTS

Data can be extracted from a system in a variety of formats. In descending order of convenience for the forensic accounting team, the formats include database files, delineated text files, and headed report files. While the use of software is an important aspect of any investigation, the challenge is to obtain accurate and complete data in the proper format the first time. Awareness of common pitfalls and mistakes can avoid frustration and erroneous conclusions.

The forensic technologist and systems administrator should jointly prepare an estimate of the time it would take to produce extracts in each available format and should review that estimate in light of both the risk of extraction errors and the estimated cost of cleaning the data.

At this juncture, a compromise is usually reached as to the degree of effort the systems administrator expends to extract the data and the degree of effort the forensic technologist expends to prepare the extract for analysis. For example, the systems administrator may be able to provide standard reports that with very little effort, can be made available in the form of text files. Even using powerful cleanup tools such as Monarch, the forensic analyst may spend considerable time cleaning out headers and expanding multirow data. As a general rule, whenever possible the forensic technologist prefers data in nonreport format that can be accommodated within the investigation plan.

The number of available data formats may be restricted by the technical expertise available within the organization. A significant number of smaller organizations outsource their IT function and receive very little nonstandard support from the external contractor. In situations in which little or no support is available either from the organization or from its appointed contractor and when technical expertise is lacking, requesting the data in a less convenient format is preferable to running the risk of making mistakes during the data extraction process.

Before conducting any of the data-mining techniques, forensic accounting investigators need to ensure that they are requesting the correct computer files for the assignment. The investigative team should meet with appropriate IT personnel to confirm that it has searched all potentially relevant sources. Especially with multinational companies, the team should not assume that transaction processing is maintained at the location where the transactions occur. Such transaction processing or other elements of the process may have been outsourced or may be located at a central service center. For example, the data required for an operation in Pittsburgh may actually reside at a shared services center in India. The team should document in writing the information it is requesting, speak to IT and finance personnel, and ask probing questions so that information is correct and complete the first time around. See the appendix immediately following this chapter for an example of a data request.

The team should establish a protocol for requesting specific information by combining requests and by speaking to IT and finance/accounting personnel to verify completeness. The requests should be in writing and include requirements regarding the format in which the information should be received—for example, text, tab delimited, or ASCII. Lack of clarity and precision in the request can cause additional work and problems associated with cleaning up or scrubbing data, which can be avoided by planning and clear communication at the time that files are requested.

A clear understanding before beginning any analysis can avoid false starts and erroneous preliminary conclusions. Requesting a data dictionary can be helpful to an understanding of what types of information are captured in a system or in a database of information. The data dictionary specifies which files have the data and fields required for analysis. This approach is preferable to asking for specific fields and thereby running the risk of not obtaining all required information the first time around. If in doubt, the forensic accounting investigator should err on the side of asking for more data rather than less. Even after receiving the computerized information, the investigative team should determine the completeness and accuracy of all information received.

There are two key requirements for the preparation of a comprehensive data specification: a good understanding of the structure of the data source and clarity as to the aims of the forensic accounting investigation. By way of illustration, consider a hypothetical investigation at a manufacturing plant in Matamoros, Mexico. The company's corporate headquarters is located in the Midwest. Embezzlement and kickbacks have been alleged. The investigative team's assignment is to determine where the money has gone and who is involved. In this hypothetical situation, the team must ask where payments are processed and what level of detail can be obtained from the system. The answer may be twofold: (1) Payments to vendors are processed in Mexico, sometimes in pesos and sometimes in cash, and (2) payments to vendors are processed in the United States in U.S. dollars. Both sets of data may be necessary to the investigation.

The team must not rely solely on the data from Mexico or from the United States. By obtaining both data sets, the team might determine, for example, that the same vendors are paid in pesos and in U.S. dollars for the same services, with both sets of payments approved by local Mexican management.

As noted earlier in this chapter, the cooperation of the systems administrator can be invaluable in determining and understanding the system structure. However, circumstances may exist in which systems administrators are unable or reluctant to help or in which they themselves are suspected of being complicit in the fraud. In such circumstances, the forensic technologist will need to seek out other ways to obtain this information. A helpful source in this regard often is the system documentation itself. Alternatively, if the system type is familiar to the analyst, inspection alone might yield valuable information.

The forensic technologist should spend time with the forensic accounting investigator in charge of the investigation to determine which data could be relevant to the analysis or to the collection of evidence. Close coordination between the forensic accounting investigator leading the review and the forensic technologist during the initial stages of the investigation, prior to the extraction of data from the organization's systems, can save all parties valuable time and effort.

In the design of the data specification to be submitted to the organization, it is important to build in certain flexibility in terms of the upcoming data analyses. In many cases, requesting extra data fields will require minimal additional extraction work. However, once an extraction has been prepared, requesting an extended data extraction can often be difficult. Doors should not be closed at the early stage of an investigation.

Another reason the scope of the data specification request should be as broad as possible has to do with the processing time required for extraction. For example, extracting data from an organization's systems that relates to all customers who have made more than three payments in the past month may take considerable processing time. Requesting data on all customers and all payments and, subsequently, identifying customers relevant to the analysis may actually take less time.

The investigation will rely on the data extracted by administrators. Minimizing the likelihood of errors will save time and money. The team should discuss the extraction process with the systems administrator to identify exactly what that process will entail. Taking this step not only provides a clearer idea of what will be received and how but also reduces the risk of error.

In one investigation, the systems administrator had to prepare the data extract from archived tapes that covered overlapping periods. In order to try to correct for this factor within the data extract, the administrator deleted all duplicate records. Unfortunately, no unique key had been included in the extract. As a result, many genuine records were accidentally erased.

Once the team decides which data are relevant to the investigation, it should convert that decision into a detailed written data specification. Care should be taken when drafting this document. In all likelihood, the systems administrator will provide the forensic technologist with only those fields for which the team explicitly requests data specifications. The document also should include requirements about how the information should be received—for example, as database files, as delineated text files, or as headed report files. When requesting e-mail files, the forensic technologist should consider asking the systems administrator for superuser passwords or user passwords to gain access to password-protected or encrypted files.

On one occasion, a bank prepared a data extract for an internal investigation that occurred before engaging forensic accounting investigators. As part of the internal investigation, the investigator requested information on the date, amount, currency, and narrative of all transactions. The systems administrator did not include a transaction ID—which would be useful in providing a link between debits and credits for internal transactions—because it was not requested in the data specification.

The specifics of any data request typically depend on the nature of the organization and its systems and on the nature of the potential fraud. A general checklist should include the following:

- *Primary key.* The most vital element of any data extract, the primary key is the field that uniquely identifies each record in the data set.
- *Foreign keys.* These keys are present when the data provided consists of more than one table. In a well-managed data source, they provide the link from their own table to the primary key of another table.
- *Lookup tables.* While foreign keys are often present in the main data extract, the relevant look-up table is absent. For example, branch codes may exist but not a list of the specific branch to which each code relates.
- *Row count.* Comparing the number of records received with the number of records that the client thinks it has extracted is an apparently simple but nonetheless important step.
- *Hash totals.* With large-scale data extracts, hash totals requested from the client should be compared with totals computed from the data used in the investigation. These are sums generated by totaling data items such as transaction IDs or product codes. They provide an additional check that the data has not been compromised as it passed from the client's system to the investigation database.
- *Data specification/data dictionary.* The systems administrator should provide a short description for each field within each table. This avoids the possibility of inaccurate calculations if the forensic accounting investigator must make assumptions about the contents of key fields.
- *Extraction specification.* All data requests should be submitted in writing to avoid confusion. E-mailing such requests is a perfectly acceptable method of communication. Knowing exactly what the extracted data represents and the period it covers is important. For example, if the forensic accounting investigator has requested "invoices over $100,000 from the eastern division from 200X to 20XX," then the investigator should seek written confirmation that the data has been delivered. If possible, the person who actually produced the data extracts should provide the confirmation.

◆ DATA CLEANING

This process involves removing page headers and footers from files, expanding data with more than one row per record, stripping out nonnumeric characters from number fields, and a host of other procedures aimed at standardizing the data to make it suitable for use with the analysis tool selected as most appropriate for the data analysis exercise.

The data-cleaning stage is critical to the data analysis process. It is the only point at which alterations are intentionally made to the extracted data, and it is imperative that amendments made at this stage not affect the accuracy of the information. A documentation log should be maintained of all alterations undertaken. The log may be needed at a later date to prove the integrity of the analyzed data and its relation to the information extracted directly from the organization's systems. We strongly advise that only forensic technologists with relevant and up-to-date experience undertake complex data-cleaning exercises.

Data cleaning can also involve the standardizing of common abbreviations within a data set and removing extraneous information. These steps make useful information available to the forensic accounting investigator. Not all software programs may be capable of this type of cleaning, and special programming may be necessary. In the long run, particularly for matches that are performed frequently, the cleaning procedure can increase efficiencies and improve consistency.

In Exhibit 20.1 on the next page, all directional components of addresses—that is, north, east, south, and west—and extraneous words and characters such as *street* and *suite* are removed. Additionally, spaces for characters such as periods, commas, and apostrophes are deleted. For example, compare the address from the vendor file, column D, with the cleaned address in column F. If the cleaning process were not performed in this way, lines 4 and 8 would result in a potential match because each address is "123 W. Main St." When the cleaning process is applied, the addresses do not match because the comparison is then between "123MainIL" and "123MainOK." In practical terms, designating long strings of characters to obtain matches does not make sense—for example, to identify multiple entities or individuals at the same address. Instructing the software program to match on the street number, the street name, and the state would yield results far different from instructing it to match only on the street number and street name. Similarly, matching street addresses based on the first few characters plus the state will yield results far different from matching street addresses based on the street number, street name, and state.

Exhibit 20.1, an excerpt from vendor and employee addresses, indicates when data has been cleaned and when it has not. With proper data cleaning, all line items would be street-address matched; however, line 8 would be an exception because the state was OK, not IL.

Using this data helps the forensic accounting investigator focus on which data to request for additional review; otherwise, some may resort to manual techniques to identify matches. The latter is a time-intensive and potentially inefficient process.

A Order	B Vendor #	C Name	D Address	E State	F Cleaned Address
1	0123	ABC Company	123 W. Main	IL	123mainIL
2	0125	ABC Company, Inc.	123 West Main	IL	123mainIL
3	0127	ABC Enterprises, Inc.	123 W. Main Street	IL	123mainIL
4	0226	Best Enterprises, Inc.	123 W. Main St	IL	123mainIL
5	0229	A Best Enterprises	123 West Main Street	IL	123mainIL
6	0129	Ahab Best Company, Inc.	123 W. Main	IL	123mainIL
7	0128	XYZ Company	123 W. Main St., Suite 200	IL	123mainIL
8	0330	Consultants, Inc.	123 W. Main St	OK	123mainOK
9	0337	Mark Hunt (Employee)	123 W. Main St., Suite 400	IL	123mainIL

Exhibit 20.1   Vendor/Employee Addresses

Often, an address match is only similar rather than exactly the same. In the aforementioned instance, a forensic accounting investigator should be suspicious when the only difference between an employee's address and a vendor's address is the suite number. A common scheme is to set up a vendor with a fictitious suite number at the same street address as a residence. Just because an address is listed with a suite number does not rule out the possibility that the address actually corresponds to an apartment number or post office box number.

In this example taken from an actual case, "123 W. Main" was factually the same as "123 W. Main Street." Without proper data cleaning, the forensic accounting investigator may not gain the information needed to conclude that multiple vendor names exist at the same address in Illinois—and that the address is that of a particular employee. Proper data cleaning enables the forensic accounting investigator to identify and focus on the types of transactions that require further review.

◆ ELIMINATING DUPLICATE INFORMATION

One of the problems forensic technologists encounter is that multiple copies of various materials may be recovered as part of the investigative process. Because of the expense involved in reviewing such duplicative materials, elimination of duplicates (deduplication, or deduping) in the recovered data sets is often the first order of business after the data has been acquired and the documentation has been completed.

One might suspect that deduplication would be a straightforward process; however, several variations of the process need to be considered before work can begin. First, the examiner must decide what qualifies as a duplicate. Do all of the fields of data need to match exactly, or should two e-mail messages be considered duplicates if the subject and body are identical without regard to the date and routing information? If you require all of the data to match exactly, then any message with a *bcc* will appear at least twice because the bcc field will show up only in the bcc recipient's mailbox and not in any other recipient's. Similarly, if the time stamp is off by a second, the message will appear more than once in the review data.

Second, the practitioner must decide which universe of documents should be subjected to deduping. Consider an investigation involving the e-mail of 25 employees, one e-mail server, and four sets of backup tapes. There are likely to be at least six sets of data available for each employee—four sets of mail from the backup tapes, one set from each individual's office computer, and one from the active server—and there could be many more depending on a variety of variables such as data from one or more additional laptop or desktop computers, BlackBerry devices, pagers, e-mail-enabled cell phones, and home PCs. Deduplication of this data could proceed on (1) the basis of the entire universe of data, so that each message would be reviewed by forensic accounting investigators only once, or (2) across the data related to each user, so that each message would appear only once in each user's mailbox but might be reviewed up to 25 times by forensic accounting investigators if all 25 targets received a copy of the same message; or (3) across a subset of the entire universe, such as all employees in a certain department.

Each of these choices has advantages and disadvantages. Deduplication across the entire universe of messages may be the most efficient process in terms of limiting the amount of time it will take to review the data, but it also poses challenges. For instance, if the reviewers are divided into teams, with each team focusing on the activities of one of the targets (a typical arrangement) and only one copy of a message sent to seven people will appear in the review data, then which team will see the message? Should one target be considered the prime suspect such that all messages sent to that target and other targets will appear only in that target's data? And if so, won't that make the review of the other targets' data nonsensical because many of the messages will appear out of context, with all duplicated messages not appearing in the secondary subjects' data set? As a practical matter, these issues require the examiner and the entire investigative team to map out their approach in advance and choose a process that is consistent with the particular project's needs.[5]

Deduplication can dramatically reduce the cost of reviewing a large data set. In one recent investigation, 5 terabytes (nearly 21 million files) of e-mail and user file data recovered from backup tapes was reduced to less than 900 gigabytes of data (less than 5 million files) through the deduplication process, thereby cutting the review time by over 75 percent.

◆ TESTING THE DATA FOR COMPLETENESS AND ACCURACY

How does one ascertain the completeness and accuracy of the information? The files requested determine the approach. Sometimes the situation is complicated by incomplete, inaccurate, inconsistent, and incorrect information. In

---

5. Some of these concerns can be obviated if all of the reviewers have access to the same centralized and duplicated database, but that is not always possible or practical.

such instances, ascertaining completeness and accuracy can be very difficult, if not impossible, and supplementary reasonableness checks may need to be performed.

The completeness checks can include confirming that the totals and rows extracted from the system are the same ones that the forensic accounting investigator received from the company. Other tests for reasonableness include the following:

- Comparing total payments, payroll, and profits with annual revenues

- Comparing total payments with debits on the bank statements: this may be done initially at a high level and then at lower levels of detail. Multiple accounts and/or numerous transfers that are not accounted for on the check register make this procedure more difficult.

- Comparing subledger and/or general ledger postings

- Testing selected transactions to determine whether they have been posted to the general ledger

- Discussing potential exceptions with management to confirm appropriate inclusion or exclusion of known problem cases

Forensic accounting investigators who are dealing with multiple currencies and multiple years may have to deal with more than one currency within the same payment information file. The data analyst will need to test to confirm that the currency conversion is functioning properly. Some currencies have undergone large fluctuations in value relative to others. For example, prior to 2002, Argentina's currency tracked with the U.S. dollar; however, this is no longer the case due to dramatic fluctuations in the Argentine peso that occurred in 2002. A 50,000-Argentine-peso payment in 2001 may be equivalent to $50,000, while the same payment in 2003 may be equivalent to less than $20,000.

During a recent investigation in the Middle East, a forensic team requested check disbursement data in U.S. dollars for the branch office under investigation to facilitate comparison to data from other branches worldwide. Upon receiving the data, the team tested the currency conversion and found errors totaling as much as $70 million in a data set of $270 million—more than 25 percent of the total payment amount.

Discussed below are some additional false starts commonly encountered when an investigative team attempts to obtain data. They serve to illustrate the point that even when experienced investigators obtain computer files, miscommunications can occur.

UNDERSTATED AMOUNTS

After receiving payments data from a location in Mexico City, the investigative team quickly determined that the payments file was significantly understated. The vendor payments file had been requested numerous times both verbally and in written form and in both English and Spanish. The request specifically highlighted the importance of providing complete data. The team attempted to work together with the controller to determine the cause of the understatement. However, the controller said he did not realize the request also included payments for inventory suppliers. In his mind, he did not consider an inventory supplier to be in the same category as a vendor. The complete file was obtained after the second attempt, and in the course of its analysis, the investigating team was able to identify several payments as possible bribes and kickbacks.

OVERSTATED AMOUNTS

On another cross-border assignment, a member of the investigative team observed that Ms. X had received 10 million pesos in a recent year—a significant sum for that person. The payment register files had totals that were a multiple of the annual revenues, a sign that data was probably incorrect. Upon closer examination, each line item had had two zeros added to the end of every payment that occurred during the data conversion. While Ms. X had received substantial payments, the magnitude was far less than originally surmised. This reinforces the fact that verifying the completeness and accuracy of the data is an important step before undertaking any analysis.

INCOMPLETE RESPONSES

When requesting a payroll file from a government entity, the investigative team noticed that the payments amounted to only a fraction of the payroll expense when compared with the general ledger. Upon inquiry, the IT department staff member responsible for fulfilling the team's request commented that the request was for "payments," which he interpreted to mean a physical check. All payroll direct deposits—those not paid with a physical check—were not included in the data file he had provided.

INCOMPLETE DATA SETS

While reviewing files to ascertain completeness, an investigative team may discover heretofore unknown or undisclosed transfers to other bank accounts. The team may use these transfers to uncover additional bank accounts and check registers, thus revealing many suspect transactions that could have gone unnoticed had the completeness and accuracy test not been performed.

◆ SKILLS OF THE FORENSIC TECHNOLOGIST

Investigative data analysts should possess strong technical skills and a good understanding of the relevant tools. However, beyond the tools, the analysis process usually involves many other skills, such as accounting skills and an understanding of investigative methods. The process also requires communication between the analyst investigating the data and other members of the team.

TECHNICAL SKILLS

Most obviously, a forensic technologist should possess technical IT skills, which are fundamental to the performance of data cleaning and analysis and the presentation of results. Many data-cleaning and data analysis tools are available. While some are noticeably more powerful than others, all require that users possess a good understanding of how they work. Many such tools require that users be able to write code in one language or another, and a simple mistake such as putting a bracket in the wrong place could lead to distortion in the results. Forensic technologists will often not perform all of the analysis or presentation of results themselves. Rather, they will prepare the information in a format that the forensic accounting team can use to perform additional analysis. Nonetheless, the forensic technologist should continuously support the forensic accounting team throughout this process in an overview or advisory function by providing needed IT technical expertise.

Data analysis is an explorative technique. As with any non-IT-based investigation, approaches to investigating a particular set of facts or circumstances can vary. The process is iterative, and both accounting and investigative skills may be necessary to respond to results and to design the next investigative steps to be taken—or, in the case of data analysis, the next set of data queries to be run. Forensic technologists who have knowledge of accounting mechanisms usually are able to highlight unusual items and recognize the various ways in which a transaction might be reflected in the system. Such knowledge is clearly useful. Anyone undertaking a forensic accounting exercise is likely to need specialist technical support from an experienced forensic technologist. Coordination is essential to avoiding misunderstandings with regard either to the analysis requirements or to the results produced.

COMMUNICATION SKILLS

Forensic technologists should possess good communication skills, both verbal and listening. During the investigative process, the forensic technologist should liaise with the systems administrator and share information with the investigation team. The forensic technologist is also frequently called upon to explain the data analysis process to in-house or external counsel.

Throughout the forensic data analysis process, decisions must be made about which data to acquire, what tools to use, and which data queries to run. To make these decisions, the forensic technologist should have up-to-date knowledge of all significant factors relevant to the investigation. Only if analysts are thoroughly aware of the results or evidence identified in the manual investigation can they best respond to the interim results of the data analysis process. In cases in which the forensic technologist does not possess the accounting and investigative experience necessary to make such decisions, members of the forensic accounting team should be fully informed about all stages of the data analysis results so that the team's requirements can be fed into the next stage of the process. Close coordination will lead to a process of efficiently integrating the technologist's work product into the forensic accounting team's work and vice versa.

When sorts and queries recur, supplying the forensic technologist with a listing or script indicating which queries to perform may be more efficient.

Results presented to the forensic accounting team must be fully understood. At the very least, data given to the forensic accounting team might well be accompanied by a narrative explaining what that data represents. Even if the forensic accounting investigators believe the team understands the information they have presented to the team, the team may benefit from this explanatory paragraph. Mistakes should be identified before incorrect data becomes the basis for further investigative procedures. This technique may be useful in cross-cultural teams.

◆ EFFECTIVE USE OF DATA ANALYSIS RESULTS

A powerful method of gathering evidence, data analysis becomes most effective when it is integrated into the wider forensic accounting project. If the end results must cohere with findings from other sources, forensic data analysis should not be performed as a separate investigation. This section looks at the role of forensic data analysis methods in a forensic accounting project, including typical data analysis tests, typical data analysis tools, and methods of presenting results.

ROLE OF DATA ANALYSIS IN THE INVESTIGATION

Data analysis can serve many functions within a forensic accounting project. On some occasions, it is the main engine of an engagement. When such is the case, data analysis is used for highlighting potentially unusual items and trends. More often, however, data analysis is a complementary part of a wider forensic accounting investigation that involves several other methods of information analysis or evidence gathering, including document review, physical inspection, and investigative interviews.

The timing of the data analysis work depends on the extent to which the forensic accounting team needs to work with the results. In some cases—for example, once the method of a fraud has been established—data analysis is conducted to estimate the amount of damages. If the team knows that several branches of an organization were affected by a fraud scheme, that team may be able to compare these results with those derived from analyses of unaffected branches and after adjusting for other relevant factors, provide management with a broad estimate of the total effect on the financial statements. When such an approach is used, the comparison should be performed after the investigation has determined the characteristics of the fraud scheme. However, in most cases, the purpose of data analysis in an investigation is to identify suspicious activity on which the forensic accounting team can take action.

Suspicious transactions can be identified in a number of ways: comparing different sources of evidence, such as accounting records and bank statements, to find discrepancies between them; searching for duplicate transactions; or identifying sudden changes in the size, volume, or nature of transactions, which need to be explained. While data analysis often is a fast and effective way of highlighting potential areas of fraud, it will never capture every detail that a forensic accounting investigator can glean from reviewing an original document. If data analysis is performed to identify suspicious activity, it should be performed before any manual review is carried out. This will help ensure that investigative resources are targeting suspicious areas and are concentrating on confirming fraudulent activity rather than concentrating on a search for such activity within a sea of legitimate transactions.

On one occasion, forensic accounting investigators spent two weeks creating a list of suspicious payments from source documentation before any data analysis was carried out. Within an hour of importing the data into its system, the investigative team had created a list that contained over 90 percent of the transactions that appeared on the manually prepared list, plus a few additional transactions that had been overlooked. Having this list at the start of the investigation would have been more efficient.

However, the role of the analyst goes beyond manual inquiries. Frequently, the results of manual inquiries need to be fed back into and incorporated in the analysis process. For example, if inquiries show that the fraud is limited to one or two suppliers, further analysis can concentrate on transactions in those accounts. While data analysis alone can be the focus of some investigations, most projects require an iterative analysis, alternating between input from the investigation team and feedback from analysis results. When this is the case, the infrastructure used in performing the analysis and communicating results to the team should support that level of interaction.

◆ DATA MINING IN ACTION

The forensic team can use data mining in many situations. Whether conducting proactive procedures as part of an internal or external audit or performing reactive procedures to resolve allegations, the team likely will find that data-mining techniques are efficient and valuable. For instance, in cases concerning the location of "lost" money, examples of sample queries and procedures could include but would not be limited to the following.

CHECK DISBURSEMENT FILE

Sort Payments in Alphabetical Order

As illustrated in Exhibit 20.2, an alphabetic sort of the check disbursement file at a client identified the following look-alikes.

Vendor #	Vendor Name	Amount Paid
362862	STRATIGIC BUSINESS SOLUTIONS	$48,445
362866	STRATEGIC BUSINESS SOLUTIONS	$52,788
370535	STRETIGIC BUSINESS SOLUTIONS	$43,547

EXHIBIT 20.2 LOOK-ALIKES

Payments on the first and third lines were fraudulent. The key to identifying the phony company was the deliberate misspelling of the word *strategic*. This was not detected by the entity's manual monitoring process because to the untrained eye, all three payments presented at different points in time appear to have been made to the same valid payee. In a comparable instance, a check for a payment for monthly phone charges seemed routine and innocuous. A closer look revealed that the payee was *A&TT* and not *AT&T,* the telecommunications giant—and the possibility of fraud immediately became apparent. What appears to be a keystroke error may be the hiding place to record a false transaction.

Identify the Frequency of Payments to Vendors

Frequency measures the number of times a vendor receives payments over a given period of time. During an investigation, a forensic team noted that an employee received over 100 payments per year, exceeding a total of $400,000— many of them in large, round amounts. During inquiries, the team discovered that the employee was a courier and errand person. The high frequency of payments resulted from the fact that when the general manager needed money, a check was made payable to the courier. The courier went to the bank, cashed the check, and gave the money to the general manager. While all of the items were recorded as expenses, corporate headquarters was surprised to learn that the company was paying bills for the general manager's house, cleaning service, landscaping, and other personal expenses. The transactions were identified within 24 hours of the team's acquisition of the data file. Without the query on frequency, it is likely that the situation would not have been discovered so quickly, if at all.

Sort Payments in Descending-Dollar Order

This test allows the forensic accounting investigator to focus on major payments to commonly named or controlled enterprises. Exhibit 20.3 illustrates a data-mining excerpt for an investigation in Mexico that revealed that *Juan Carlos Rodriguez* was paid $1,590,000, whereas *Juan Rodriguez,* the same person, was paid $991,730. While the controller maintained that the payments were for maintenance services, the forensic accounting investigators later determined that the maintenance services were performed at another entity owned by the general manager and undisclosed to the parent company. Additional observations for further review were transfers made (*traspasos*) and payments to individuals who were not employees. In the following example, 3.64 million pesos was paid to Juanita Sanchez (in bold). After reviewing the employee master file, forensic accounting investigators discovered that Ms. Sanchez was not an employee of the company. Through discussions with employees, it became clear that she was an official for the government, and the money paid to her was a bribe to keep the plant operating in a residential neighborhood. This raised Foreign Corrupt Practices Act (FCPA) concerns for the client and triggered additional review for FCPA transactions. It should be noted that payments to individuals do not neces-

Payee per Disbursement Records	Total
Supermercado de Dos Hermanos	$102,347,555
Ucb de Mexico S.A. de C.V.	$6,225,555
Juanita Sanchez	$3,640,000
XGM, Inc.	$3,400,929
Juan Carlos Rodriguez	$1,590,000
Elena Ma. Clatona	$1,262,901
TRASPASO 116-123	$1,140,000
Canal Vanessa Marcales	$1,138,353
TRASPASO 113-18	$1,100,000
Borchemex S.A.	$1,069,119
Domingo Luis Ramirez	$1,018,885
Juan Rodriguez	$991,730
111-20 COMPRA DE 100,000 DLLS	$952,000
Alexiant Mexico, S.A. de C.V.	$923,042

EXHIBIT 20.3   SORT BY DESCENDING-DOLLAR ORDER

sarily mean either that those individuals work at the company or that the payments are improper. However, identification of certain individuals receiving large aggregate payments usually raises a potential red flag for the forensic accounting investigator. Subsequent procedures would be to flag these payments for further review, conduct inquiries regarding the nature of the payments, and possibly set in motion a detailed document review.

Search for Common Payment Amounts or Duplicate Check Numbers

Data mining can identify duplicate payments. Exhibit 20.4 offers the example of an invoice that was paid twice. The individual was able to perpetrate this fraud by inserting a blank space in the *Invoice #* field and truncating a leading zero, so that the two invoices would not appear to be duplicates. Duplicate payment may simply be a system or processing issue. However, it is also a common embezzlement scheme.

Check #	Amount	Date	Vendor #	Vendor Name	Invoice #
17353	$647,615.60	7/9/2002	644033	NEW HORIZON SYSTEM SOLUTIONS	REF# 80815-21
21655	$647,615.60	1/10/2003	722345	NEW HORIZON SYSTEM SOLUTIONS	REF# 080815-21

EXHIBIT 20.4   DUPLICATE PAYMENTS

Identify Gaps, Voids, and Canceled Checks

Gaps in a series of check numbers, other than numbers corresponding to voided checks, may be red flags, especially if those checks are clearing the bank statements. Such gaps could imply that manual checks are being issued without actually being recorded in the general ledger.

Exhibit 20.5 shows an example of voided checks that appeared in the disbursement data of a company in South America. Voided checks generally have no dollar amounts associated with them unless a separate reversing entry is recorded. In this instance, certain checks with the payee "Cancelado" had, in fact, cleared the bank account but had not been recorded on the books. Such discrepancies may explain large reconciling items[6] on the bank reconciliation that are later written off. However, by the time the bank reconciliation is performed, the write-offs may already have been recorded on the books in a later period under a valid vendor name, thus hiding the fact that voided checks actually cleared the bank. Exhibit 20.5 shows that a voided (*cancelado*) check for $152,225.04 cleared the bank. The description for this payment (*varias facturas*) means *various invoices*. When the investigative team realized there were general ledger descriptions for voided checks, it examined a copy of the check provided by the bank and noted that it was made payable to the general manager. The payee "cancelado" was then queried on the check register and several instances were identified. Once the issue was identified, the team focused its attention on voided checks in large amounts.

Date	Payee per Check Register	Description on GL	Ck #	Amount
29-Jul-98	CANCELADO	VARIAS FACTURAS	2896	2,239.53
4/AGO/98	CANCELADO	CANCELADO	2924	0
6/AGO/98	CANCELADO	PAGO DE NOMINA	2936	0
6/AGO/98	CANCELADO	VARIAS FACTURAS	2962	152,255.04
14/AGO/98	CANCELADO		784	0
14/AGO/98	CANCELADO		786	0
14/AGO/98	CANCELADO	PAGO DE FACT.	802	14,894.00
14/AGO/98	CANCELADO	CANCELADO	819	2,759.30

EXHIBIT 20.5 VOIDED CHECKS

Identify Round-Dollar Payments

This query is useful for identifying payments for further review. Payments ending in *00* and *000* dollar amounts (not cents) are obtained and sorted by descending-dollar order and by vendor. Exhibit 20.6 shows a series of round-dollar payments. After inquiries, an investigative team determined that the

---

6. In this case, the reconciliation hid the defalcation with a corresponding deposit-in-transit for an amount equal to the defalcation (bank balance was below the book balance).

ACCOUNT	CHECK NUMBER	DATE	BENEFICIARY	AMOUNT
156	7252	9-Mar-01	Mr. X	50,000.00
156	7253	9-Mar-01	Mr. X	50,000.00
156	7315	19-Mar-01	Mr. X	50,000.00
156	7316	19-Mar-01	Mr. X	50,000.00
156	7317	19-Mar-01	Mr. X	50,000.00
156	7318	19-Mar-01	Mr. X	15,000.00
156	7440	6-Apr-01	Mr. X	3,100.00
156	7663	16-May-01	Mr. X	8,000.00

EXHIBIT 20.6   ROUND-DOLLAR AMOUNTS

amounts were bribes paid to government officials to keep an industrial plant open in a residential neighborhood. (The names of actual payees have been deleted from this exhibit.)

Sequential Vendor Invoice Numbers

Exhibit 20.7 offers an example of payments made to a particular vendor. The invoice numbers from that vendor are in sequential order without gaps—as noted by sorting the invoice register by vendor, by invoice number. When sequential invoices are observed, the question must be asked: is the client company the vendor's only customer? Does that make sense? Further investigation revealed that these invoices were from a vendor established by the purchasing manager, who was the focus of the whistle-blower allegations. Even though the vendor was providing packaging materials, the goods were inferior and over-priced. The purchasing manager was behind the scheme and had not disclosed any conflict of interest. Note, as well, that the person ordering the goods, R.M., also approves the invoice for payment. R.M.'s associate in the warehouse, J.D., indicated that the goods were received. It would appear that J.D. and R.M. were perhaps collaborating on the scheme. If someone else had received the goods, that person might have noted the inferior quality and higher price.

Ck #	Ck Amt	Inv #	Inv Date	Inv Amt	Ordered	Rec'd	App'd
2065	53,686.60	317	11/02/1999	30,905.60	R.M.	J.D.	R.M.
2065	53,686.60	318	11/22/1999	2,101.00	R.M.	J.D.	R.M.
2065	53,686.60	319	11/22/1999	20,680.00	R.M.	J.D.	R.M.
2478	160,668.20	320	01/17/2000	25,124.00	R.M.	J.D.	R.M.
2478	160,668.20	321	01/17/2000	51,177.50	R.M.	J.D.	R.M.
2478	160,668.20	322	01/17/2000	84,366.70	R.M.	J.D.	R.M.

EXHIBIT 20.7   INVOICE NUMBERS IN SEQUENTIAL ORDER

EXAMINING THE VENDOR MASTER FILE AND PAYMENTS HISTORY

Identify Vendors with the Same Address and Different Names

Exhibit 20.8 illustrates two vendors that have the same address. Further investigation revealed that the vendors were related parties.

VENDOR NAME	ADDRESS 1	ADDRESS 2	AMOUNT
TXA SERVICES LTD	123 MADISON AVE	COLLINSVILLE, IN	$247,744.00
GREG SPORTING GOODS LTD	123 MADISON AVE	COLLINSVILLE, IN	$327,725.00

EXHIBIT 20.8   MULTIPLE VENDORS WITH THE SAME ADDRESSES

Identify Vendors with the Same Name, Different Addresses

Exhibit 20.9 is an example of two vendors with the same name but different addresses. Further investigation revealed that one was a fictitious vendor using the address of an employee's accomplice. Vendors with the same telephone numbers and the same tax identification numbers should also be identified.

Vendor Name	Vendor Number	Vendor Address	Amount
Slater Trading	P1411	P.O. BOX 1762, DUBAI, U.A.E.	$24,724.00
Slater Trading	P0222	P.O. BOX 8490, SS LOOTAH BLDG, DUBAI	$52,027.00

EXHIBIT 20.9   VENDORS—SAME NAME, DIFFERENT ADDRESSES

Compare the Vendor Master List with the High-Risk-Address Databases

Exhibit 20.10 illustrates vendor addresses that match mailbox drop and other high-risk addresses throughout the United States. Note the similar names and multiple vendors at the same address (*Central Ohio Resource* and *ComQuest*). Using the actual address of a business that rents mailboxes, rather than using an address showing just the P.O. box number and no street address, does not draw suspicion to the address. Accounting staff may be deceived into thinking that 5837 Karric Place is an office complex because multiple suites exist at the address. In reality, Suite 130 and Suite 197 proved to be just mailbox numbers inside the mailbox drop, not physical offices in a sprawling office complex.

In addition to utilizing the information extracted from the client company's IT systems related to payment, customer, vendor, employee, and general ledger data, forensic technology investigations are also likely to include imaging of individuals' hard drives and e-mail repositories. The process of gathering this evidence is discussed in detail in Chapter 21. The sections that follow discuss investigative techniques that can be applied to this data.

Vendor Name	Vendor Address
ComQuest	5837 Karric Place, Suite 197 Dublin, OH 43017
SBS	4719 Reed Road, Suite 137 Columbus, OHIO 43220
Stratigic Business Solutions	130 E. Wilson Bridge Road Worthington, Ohio 43085
Stretigic Business Solutions	544 Wilson Bridge Road Worthington, Ohio 43047

Commercial Mailbox Drops

EXHIBIT 20.10   MAILBOX DROP/HIGH-RISK ADDRESSES

Exhibit 20.11 illustrates an employee and a vendor at the same address. If undisclosed conflicts of interest are a concern, matching the vendor file with the employee file may be useful.

Address	ID	SSN	Payee	Telephone Number
617 SHERIDAN AVE NEW ORLEANS LOUISIANA 70265	70328	390627191	DAVIS, SANDY J.	256-555-1872
617 SHERIDAN AVE NEW ORLEANS LOUISIANA 70265	70198	625480632	E & S Transportation	256-555-1872

EXHIBIT 20.11   EMPLOYEE AND VENDOR WITH SAME ADDRESS

GENERAL LEDGER SEARCHES

A search on the general ledger is very similar to the disbursements queries discussed earlier. General ledger queries are typically engagement dependent. For instance, in one engagement forensic accounting investigators may be interested in manual journal entries recorded at the end of a quarter, while in another engagement they may be interested in round-dollar entries recorded postclosing that debited balance sheet accounts and credited an income statement account. General ledger queries are not limited to only amounts, dates, and accounts. Depending on the situation, forensic accounting investigators may be interested in seeking journal entries recorded from a certain workstation or entered by a certain individual. This tool is helpful in an investigation of financial statement fraud, such as revenue recognition schemes. The tool can also be helpful in an investigation of allegations about increasing profits to attain earnout thresholds associated with acquisitions.

An investigative team examined the general ledger. Focusing on account 22400—shown in Exhibit 20.12—the team identified entries containing search terms pertinent to the investigation, such as *bill backs, reclass, reconcile,* and *adjust.* There were also entries identified as *adjust to budget amt.* By targeting certain line items using those search terms in this account, the team identified

Journal ID	Journal Date	Posted Date	Operator ID	Description	Account	Monetary Amount
0000334927	1/15/2003	2/4/2003	Mary Johnson	Bill Backs	22400	(277,684.64)
0000339402	1/15/2003	2/6/2003	Mary Johnson	Reclass	22400	(15,567.82)
0000349075	2/15/2003	3/4/2003	Mary Johnson	Reclass	22400	(1,830.59)
0000351686	2/15/2003	3/4/2003	Mary Johnson	Reconcile	22400	(405,681.73)
0000368088	3/15/2003	4/2/2003	Mary Johnson	Adjust to budget	22400	2,644.70
0000380900	4/15/2003	5/6/2003	Mary Johnson	Reconcile	22400	(405,881.30)
0000394780	5/15/2003	6/3/2003	Mary Johnson	Adjust to budget	22400	(503,504.56)
0000408303	6/15/2003	6/28/2003	Mary Johnson	Bill Backs	22400	(322,627.58)
0000447562	9/15/2003	9/27/2003	Mary Johnson	Bill Backs	22400	(571,101.60)
						(2,501,235.12)

EXHIBIT 20.12 A GENERAL LEDGER WITH POTENTIAL RED FLAGS

the individual who processed the entry, interviewed the individual to find out additional information about the entries, and eventually discovered a series of unsupported and falsified entries.

KEYWORD SEARCHES

Keyword searching is the most basic type of search that can be conducted across a set of electronic data. It involves simply asking the computer to look for a string of characters appearing in a certain order. Some programs index all of the data on a particular piece of media in order to expedite the search process and allow the forensic accounting investigator to perform complex Boolean[7] searches based on multiple keywords, word proximity, and other criteria. Other tools allow searches based on various wild cards and variations.

There are two key things to keep in mind when conducting keyword searches. First, and as noted in other contexts in the course of this book, computers are precise. They will find only exactly what you tell them to look for within the data set. A search for *Robert P. Smith* will not find *Robert Smith, Bob P. Smith,* or *Robert.P.Smith@aol.com.* You can fashion searches that will find these vari-

---

7. English mathematician George Boole developed a logical combinatorial system—now known as Boolean algebra—that symbolically represents relationships between entities, such as those implied by the logical operators *and, or,* and *not.*

ants, but doing so requires precision and a clear understanding of the search syntax of the particular program used by the forensic accounting investigator.

Another point to keep in mind is that certain terms are nearly useless as keywords. Virtually any search term of four characters or less will result in massive false-positive[8] results. This does not mean that such searches should never be run if you have the human resources necessary to separate the wheat from the chaff, but longer, more complex search terms are likely to be more fruitful.

For example, *SEC* may be one of your search terms; however, a poorly executed search may yield all words that contain the letters *sec,* such as *consecutive* and *second.* To avoid such false positives, *SEC* can be a search term with limitations that it not be preceded or followed by any alpha or numeric character. Framing the search in this way should help yield results that limit the number of false positives.

It is also useful to limit keyword searches to certain data sets, where possible. In an investigation for a large distributor, more than four terabytes of e-mail and user files from personal computers, file servers, and e-mail servers were collected and had to be searched for relevant documents. Users did not use private or home directories on the corporate network but had instead saved the majority of their files in common or group directories accessible to a large number of people. For this reason, it was necessary to search several million files. The use of complex search terms instead of single keywords helped identify quickly the most relevant documents. For example, the single keyword that was searched was *reinvoice.* This search brought back a tremendous number of hits. However, the investigative team knew that John had instructed Sue on numerous occasions to reinvoice customers to lower the daily sales outstanding. In light of this information, a complex search was conducted of all e-mail from John to Sue containing the word *reinvoice.* Out of several million initial files, 200,000 files were identified as relevant in a 10-week span.

Prior to instructing searches to be performed, the forensic accounting investigator should have a complete understanding of the data that is being searched and any limitations of the search tool. Do not assume that any and every component of an e-mail or file on the subject's computer is being searched. Understand the procedures being performed and the time required to do the search. For instance, when searching e-mail, will the search tool identify hits only on the subject line in the e-mail or only in the e-mail text? If there are e-mail attachments, will the search tool also search the e-mail attachments, or is that another procedure? Similarly, if a file or e-mail has been password protected or even encrypted, a separate identification of those files and follow-up searches may need to be performed after the password has been identified or broken. Such files should be identified by the e-mail search tool used.

Known File Searches: Hash Values

In some cases it may be possible to search large sets of data very efficiently without using keywords at all. If a forensic accounting investigator is looking for a known

---

8. Unintended matches returned from a search.

electronic file within a set of data—such as a memo that an executive claims never to have received—a hash-value search may be the best way to proceed.

Hash values are unique numbers calculated by performing a fixed mathematical formula or algorithm against all of the data in a file. The resulting hash of the file is a very long, unique value that identifies the file and can be used to search for additional copies of the file within a large data set.

Hashing every file in a large data set will enable a forensic accounting investigator to identify a known file by searching for its hash value. Once the hash values have been calculated, this type of search goes much faster than searching through the file data itself.

For example, consider a list of names:

- Michael Smith
- Sarah Finch
- Roger Radley

To create an index, called a hash table, for these records, one would apply a mathematical formula or algorithm to each name to produce a unique numeric value like the following:

- 1348573—Michael Smith
- 3097309—Sarah Finch
- 4872345—Roger Radley

Then, to search for any records containing *Roger Radley,* one needs to search only for the value 4872345, which would yield the correct record(s). Often, there is the difficulty of determining whether a file has changed and the question of how to determine that fact if the file names are the same. On one hand, reading through both files in search of differences is impractical. On the other hand, using hash values to compare an original file with a modified file can provide the answer quickly because the odds of two files with different contents having the same hash value are approximately 10 raised to the 38th power, or 1 followed by 38 zeros.

Hash values are also useful for identifying identical files within a data set. A forensic accounting investigator merely needs to sort the data by hash value to find files that are identical, even though the file names may be different. (Hash values are generally calculated on the file data only, not on the associated metadata such as file names and dates.) This approach often is particularly useful for identifying all copies of an incriminating file, even if a user has changed the file name.

One caveat about hash values is that they will identify two files as identical only if the contents of the file are absolutely the same. If one comma, space, or letter is changed in the file, the hash value will also change.

◆ DELETED/SLACK/UNALLOCATED SPACE

Up to this point, our discussion has centered on active files stored on a computer system, backup tape, server, or other electronic media. One of the beauties of computer forensics is that a forensic accounting investigator is not limited to examining these so-called active files. When files are "deleted" from a computer hard drive, the operating system typically just removes references to the data in the file system. The actual file data is typically not removed from the drive until the operating system needs the space to store other data. Although this unallocated space generally cannot be seen by normal operating system tools—such as Windows Explorer—it can be seen, searched, and sorted by computer forensic tools. Some data in unallocated space will be fully recoverable as if it had never been "deleted." Other data may consist of file fragments that have been partially overwritten. While such data may not be fully recoverable, it may still provide clues about the computer user's activities.

Such tools can also search through the space at the end of files between the end-of-file marker and the end of the cluster in which the active file data resides. This slack space, not being used by any active file, may contain bits of data from files long ago marked for deletion from the hard drive. Forensic tools can search and find data stored in these spaces that might otherwise go undetected if drives are simply copied rather than imaged.

There are several potential limitations on the use of data discovered in slack and unallocated space. First, it may not always be possible to attribute dates accurately to such information because the normal operating system dates will not typically be available. Second, highly fragmented data found in slack or unallocated space may be hard to place in context. For this reason, drawing conclusions about the data may be difficult in some cases. Third, it may be hard to attribute data found in slack or unallocated space to a particular user, especially if the computer under investigation was used by more than one person.

Notwithstanding these potential limitations, the ability to review data that has been marked for deletion by a user is one of the key advantages of a forensic approach to the review of electronic data.

DATA SORTING

Although the ability to sort investigative data is mundane, it may also be essential to the project goal, especially when millions of e-mail messages or pages of file documents must be reviewed. Data sorting enables the forensic accounting investigator to separate the data into more manageable subsets for review and analysis. As mentioned previously in the chapter, attributes such as date/time are examples of metadata, which, depending on the matter at hand, can be useful information to the forensic accounting investigator. For example, in a Word document, having a date accessed prior to a creation date is not possible. Examining this item of metadata may raise a red flag for the forensic accounting investigator.

Date/Time

Date and time sorts are common criteria in the sorting of data as part of an investigation. In such sorting of computer data, many dates may be associated with a single document or data point. It is important to understand exactly what a particular date means before drawing conclusions about the data. For instance, in a typical Windows environment, one may find up to five dates associated with each file: file created, last accessed, last written, deleted, entry modified. All of these dates will not necessarily be available for each file. And each date has a different meaning. Following are the general meanings of these date references.

FILE-CREATED DATE

This is a record of when a particular file was created at the particular location where it is found. Thus, a file actually created before the end of December may have a file-created date in January of the following year if it is found by forensic accounting investigators on the desktop hard drive to which it was copied in the new year.

LAST-ACCESSED DATE

This date refers to the most recent time the file was accessed—by either viewing, dragging, or even right mouse clicking. A file does not have to be changed for the last-accessed date to change. It is important to note that certain automated processes, such as backup routines and virus-checking software, can change last-accessed dates.

LAST-WRITTEN DATE

This date refers to the most recent time a file was opened, changed, and saved. Merely accessing the file without making changes will not change the last-written date.

ENTRY-MODIFIED DATE

Some file systems (notably NTFS [New Technology File System] and Linux) can store the date when the size of a file last changed. Changes to the file that do not affect its size will not change the entry-modified date.

Different programs may use different criteria when assigning dates of various types. It may therefore be necessary to research the particulars of a given set of dates if timing is important to an investigation. The above-mentioned dates are created independently of each other and can be quite useful in a review of documents. For example, Sarah Finch creates a document on July 27 and saves it on her computer. The system automatically ascribes the date saved: July 27. Two days later, on July 29, Sarah decides to make changes to the document, but she wants to backdate the changes made on July 29 to July 25, two days prior to the actual date of the primary document. With this in mind, on July 29 she changes the system date to July 25. She opens the document, reviews it, and closes it without making any changes. The following values will show for the four date fields:

Created:	July 27, XXXX (to designate year)
Modified:	« Blank »
Accessed:	July 25, XXXX
Printed:	« Blank »

With forensic technology, it is possible to review the metadata and identify anomalies. In this case, the anomaly would be an *accessed* date prior to a *created* date. Logically, a creation date would be prior to dates such as modified, accessed, and printed. If Sarah Finch was suspected of backdating a document, this technique would be useful in identifying such instances.

The metadata for common Microsoft Word/Excel documents can be reviewed by using the menu option File, Properties, but a forensic tool should be used to conduct similar reviews to preserve this metadata, which can easily be changed if normal review techniques are used. An overview of common types of metadata was offered earlier in this chapter.

Owner/Author

As noted earlier, many programs either automatically insert author information or allow users to input author information into the metadata associated with files. While sorting by author be mindful to search for documents pertinent to the investigation. It is important to understand the limitations of reliance on author data. First, if the data are input automatically every time a document is created, then every document produced on a certain person's computer will indicate that that person is the author. But what if another person was for some reason using that computer? What if a computer initially issued to one employee was later assigned to another, without changing the default author setting? Then again, sometimes a document created by one user becomes a form for documents created by many other users. In this circumstance, the author information for all of the documents created from the form will reflect the original author of the form. And, finally, if author information is input manually, there is an opportunity for manipulation.

File Types/Extensions

It may be useful to sort by file type or extension the data found on a computer. This approach enables the forensic accounting investigator to segregate all of the word processing documents, spreadsheets, presentation slides, and other user-created files from program files, from dynamic link libraries, and from system files. Understand, however, that users can attempt to hide documents by adding false extensions to make a spreadsheet look like an executable program—or any other file type.

Forensic practitioners can get around this situation by performing on the files what is called a signature analysis. Most programs require that certain specific programming codes be placed in the initial bytes of data in files used by the program. These codes are sometimes referred to as file signatures. Forensic tools can search for these bits of code and compare them with the file extensions used in the file name. If the code does not match the file extension, the software can report a file signature mismatch. Moreover, if the file signature is of a known file type, the software may be able to report what the file actually is, as opposed to what the file extension falsely suggests.

While file signature analysis cannot guarantee that all relevant materials will be reviewed by forensic accounting investigators, it will increase the likelihood that user-created files are found and reviewed.

◆ CHOICE OF TOOLS

Many tools are available to help forensic accounting investigators mine and analyze data. Each has a different standard for the user interface, its own method of connecting to data, and different possibilities for presenting the results. The choice of tool will very much depend on the skills available within the team and on how data analysis fits into the wider investigation. The level of the analyst's technical skill will determine the necessity of a graphical front end. Systems without graphical interfaces tend to be more flexible and to allow for a wider range of analysis procedures. However, these systems typically require a higher level of knowledge.

Systems with user interfaces range from standard auditing tools to complex data-mining packages with built-in graphical results displays. The latter are best suited to investigations that aim to uncover trends and patterns within the data rather than to investigate fraudulent transactions.

Visual analysis packages provide a comprehensive graphical overview of data trends and patterns. These software tools are useful at early stages of investigation, when the analyst needs to quickly gain an understanding of potentially suspicious areas of activity.

Some auditing tools can be attached to the data, thereby eliminating the need to import the data separately.

In many visual analysis packages, icons are used to depict objects such as people or bank accounts. In addition, boxes can be drawn around these icons, and links between items—such as relationships or cash flows—are depicted as lines or arrows, which may be solid, barred, or dotted depending on the certainty and reliability of the underlying information.

In situations in which data analysis underlies a large part of the investigation, database systems provide a more flexible, integrated approach to data management. Customized front ends can be built relatively quickly, which allow the investigative team to query the underlying data and work directly with the results of the analysis without affecting data integrity.

Such investigation support systems increase the speed and efficiency of the investigative process. They also ensure that an audit trail exists for all items of evidence, and they eliminate potential problems with version control, which can occur when results are passed to forensic accounting investigators as separate files.

In addition, investigative findings can be input alongside the underlying data. For example, bar codes or document references can be attached to the original data record they support rather than being recorded in a separate file. As additional information gets linked to the original data, subsequent changes to the analysis results will be reflected automatically—together with all earlier findings—in the data set with which the investigative team works.

When it is not possible to implement an investigation support system—for example, because the relevant teams are at disparate locations—results should be provided for the forensic accounting investigators in electronic tables that include the primary key of each record. In this way, any additional information can be automatically imported into the analysis system.

In cases in which specialized techniques are required, cost can be a constraining factor. Matching unfielded name information—for example, matching *Mr. John Smith* with *Smyth, John R*—has long been an issue for the forensic accounting community. Software packages exist that can identify matching names from within a whole range of impossible formats regardless of order or spelling, but these packages are extremely expensive because of their technical complexity. While such packages often can be rented rather than bought, even the rental cost can be prohibitive for smaller investigations.

Alternatives will be determined by the skills available within the team. For most data sets, procedures can be designed that will place unfielded information into fields and then identify the majority of potential matches. However, this requires complex technical procedures and should ideally be carried out by people experienced in this area and knowledgeable about naming conventions in the relevant language.

The client's infrastructure may be another factor that determines tool choice. If the work will be carried out on client networks—as may sometimes be the case when forensic accounting investigators must deal with particularly cumbersome or sensitive data—consideration should be given to the compatibility of the software used with the client's operating systems.

One final factor of importance in the choice of tools concerns how and to whom the results will be presented. Output should be produced in a format that clients, lawyers, and other interested parties are able to use. Most tools can produce tables, charts, and other standard data-presentation formats. Keep in mind, however, that some tools designed directly for the investigation community are able to produce storyboards, time lines, transaction maps, and other illustration formats that can help a wide range of audiences understand the results.

◆ PRESENTING RESULTS

The art of presenting results resides in one's ability to communicate a message effectively to a specific audience. This is not always easy, particularly when information will be passed on to several different groups with different information needs and different levels of financial knowledge.

Lawyers and forensic accounting investigators are likely to need to see the full detail of all relevant transactions. Such data is most easily communicated in electronic tables, which can be queried and sorted as necessary. Any such tables must include the relevant primary keys to facilitate accurate referencing of transactions in subsequent communications. Files containing analysis results should be write-protected to prevent accidental alteration.

For planning purposes, a high-level overview is likely to be more appropriate. The investigation leader should discuss his or her requirements with the analyst and decide on suitable grouping levels and on the types of aggregate figures required. The reports can then be designed to order and can include tables, graphs, and charts as necessary. Such summaries may also be appropriately given to clients or to prosecutors. Any official report should include an appendix, detailing the source of the data and summarizing the data analysis process from extraction to reporting. The appendix should be referenced on all tables and charts.

Visual analysis programs usually work very well when they are incorporated into investigation support systems. In this way, the results of data analysis can be charted automatically, together with related findings from other investigative methods.

◆ REVIEWING THE ESSENTIALS

In many data investigations, the principal forensic accounting investigator will manage the forensic technologist and ensure that the data analysis work gets integrated into the wider investigation. While playing this role does not necessarily require knowledge of technical procedures, the forensic accounting investigator should possess a good understanding of factors that affect the analysis: availability of data, specification of data extracts, skills required to prepare and analyze the data, and possible formats for the output of results.

One key factor to be determined at the planning stage is how the results should be incorporated into the investigation. To ensure a full and consistent audit trail through the evidence gathered, forensic accounting investigators should not work on stand-alone copies of results that must be updated every time an amendment is made to the analysis criteria. At the very least, primary keys should be retained so that any necessary updates do not have to be executed manually.

However the results are disseminated, communication is the key to successful use of data analysis in a forensic project. The skill sets of both forensic technologists and forensic accounting investigators are necessary to make the most of the available data. In a timely way, both parties should share new data as it becomes identified so that each group can adjust its procedures accordingly. Data analysis should be considered a complementary, rather than a separate, line of inquiry.

◆ CONCLUSION

Many of the forensic technology techniques described in this chapter were considered exotic just a few years ago, but today they have become routine practices in major investigations of all types, from pure cybercrime investigations that track hackers through compromised networks to the more common, but equally complex, forensic accounting investigations designed to identify fraud in the books and records of large corporations. Given society's dependence on computers, it is reasonable to anticipate that five years from now, these procedures will be routinely performed in most investigations. We can also anticipate that new and better tools and techniques will be brought to bear over time. The only constant in forensic technology is rapid change. By making use of the most up-to-date practices and procedures, forensic accounting investigators can hope to stay one or two steps ahead of tech-savvy fraudsters.

APPENDIX: A SAMPLE DATA REQUEST

DATA REQUEST

1. *Overall Request*
   a. All data tables as listed below, preferably a data dump for each of the data files from the accounting system without any modification (e.g., linking tables to manipulate data into the standard data request format). Please provide all lookup tables related to the requested data tables.
   b. Preferable format of the data files is Pipe Delimited Text files.
   c. Data schema/dictionary along with the data provided for each of the data files requested.
   d. Data-mapping cross-reference that highlights all fields that match to the data specification provided in this request, including all code values to eliminate any guessing or confusion while retrieving information from the data file.
   e. Please include relevant IT personnel's contact information (e.g., phone number) in order to provide a direct point of contact if there are any systems-related questions.

   The data tables that we need are listed below, along with the required fields. Please note that we would like to receive the complete data files as mentioned in (a) that have all, but are not limited to, the fields listed for each table.

2. *Check Register (detailed information on invoices and checks)*
   Check Number
   Check Amount
   Check Date
   Check Type
   Vendor Number associated with Check
   Vendor Name associated with Check
   Description of Check
   Invoice Number associated with Check (if any)
   Invoice Amount associated with Check (If any)
   Invoice Date associated with Check (If any)
   General Account Number associated with Check

3. *Check Header (distinct line of data for each check number)*
   Check Number
   Check Amount
   Check Date
   Check Type
   Vendor Number associated with Check
   Vendor Name associated with Check
   Total of Invoice Amount

(continues)

DATA REQUEST *(CONTINUED)*

4. *Vendor Master (general vendor information)*

> Vendor Number
> Vendor Name
> Vendor Attention
> Vendor Address 1
> Vendor Address 2
> Vendor Address 3
> Vendor Address 4
> Vendor City
> Vendor State
> Vendor ZIP Code
> Vendor Country
> Vendor Telephone Number
> Vendor Tax ID
> Vendor Comments

5. *Employee Master (general employee information)*

> Employee ID
> Employee Social Security Number
> Employee Last Name
> Employee First Name
> Employee Middle Initial
> Employee Address 1
> Employee Address 2
> Employee Address 3
> Employee Address 4
> Employee City
> Employee State
> Employee ZIP Code
> Employee Country
> Employee Telephone Number
> Employee Date of Birth
> Employee Banking Account Number (for direct deposit)
> Employee Hire Date
> Employee Termination Date (empty for currently employed employees)
> Employee Comments

CHAPTER 21

BUILDING A CASE: GATHERING AND DOCUMENTING EVIDENCE

Frederic R. Miller

David L. Marston

Gathering, documenting, and retaining evidence are crucial steps in any investigation and critical to forensic accounting investigations. Decisions taken with respect to the gathering of evidence are intertwined with judgments about the scope and manner of investigation, and the value of the conclusions of an investigation ultimately rests on the credibility of the evidence discovered. Thus, care must be taken at all times to properly gather, preserve, store, and use evidentiary materials. Performed correctly, the means and manner of evidence gathering create a clear, straightforward, and convincing trail to the ultimate conclusions of the investigation. Conversely, laxity or error in the handling of evidentiary material may obscure the logic of an investigation and undercut its conclusions.

One should always begin an investigation as if the matter may end up in a criminal court and for this reason take all appropriate steps to gather and preserve the evidence. Even if it is believed at the outset that it is unlikely the matter will be referred for prosecution, it is best to maintain that option. After all, one never knows where investigations may lead, and there may be no choice in the matter if an enforcement agency decides that the investigation is of interest.

In forensic accounting investigations, several types of evidence are normally relevant, and most of them are documentary in nature. Documents generally can be divided into broad categories: those that exist in electronic form or media and those that are physical in nature, such as paper documents. The two categories often overlap in that a document available in electronic form may have been printed and perhaps modified by notations placed on it by a recipient. Another type of evidence commonly encountered, indeed often critical to the success of forensic accounting investigations, is testimonial evidence of people who were involved in the matter. This generally takes the form of oral explanations offered to the investigative team and is reflective of either people's memory of events or their interpretation of documents containing information about the events under investigation. Gathering such evidence presents issues that differ from the collection of either electronic or physical documentary evidence.

Finally, in addition to business records created contemporaneously with the issues, transactions, or matters under investigation, the forensic accounting investigators themselves may create documents that ultimately become evidence of the scope and findings of the investigation. Those documents may be presented as evidence to regulators, arbitrators, or courts charged with adjudicating or regulating the matters under investigation. Like the business records of the company, these materials must also be the subjects of proper preservation and control.

♦ CRITICAL STEPS IN GATHERING EVIDENCE

CONSIDERATIONS AT THE TIME OF RETENTION

While each investigation has unique requirements, in most cases the proper gathering and preserving of evidence call for similar considerations and steps. Those considerations begin at the outset of the engagement by consideration of the conditions under which the forensic accounting team has been engaged and the setting forth of basic expectations about the handling of evidentiary material in the engagement letter. The two key points at this stage are (1) Will any portion of the evidence be subject to privilege—either the attorney work product privilege or the attorney-client privilege? (2) Who will be responsible for preserving the evidence and for what period of time?

Whether any evidence gathered or created in the course of an investigation is subject to privilege is a legal issue that cannot often be predicted with certainty. If you are retained by in-house counsel or outside counsel, your work product may, in fact, be privileged, and as such it is best to treat all work product as though it were privileged. If, down the road, the client wishes to assert privilege through its counsel, you will at least have done everything in your power not to have waived the privilege in the course of your work. The expectation of privilege is often set out in the forensic accounting investigators' retention letter. If the privilege is contemplated, prudent practice makes make clear in the letter that (1) counsel will direct and supervise the forensic accounting investigators' work and (2) materials created for analyzing or summarizing the findings of the investigation are executed at the direction of counsel for counsel's use in giving legal advice to the client. And there is a third key point: have both counsel and the client sign the retention letter.

To the extent it is contemplated that the privilege will apply, among other things, the forensic accounting team members should not disclose information to others who have no role in the engagement, should not discuss the matter with client personnel without the permission of counsel, and should formalize their expectation that the material is privileged by recording an appropriate legend on each document at the time of its creation. Thus, for example, an analysis of an accounting issue in the form of a schedule should bear the legend *Privileged and Confidential: Attorney Work Product* or *Privileged and Confidential: Prepared at Counsel's Request in Contemplation of Litigation*, as appropriate. Because analyses are prepared throughout an investigation, they change as new information is discovered or old information is understood in a new light. In response to the circumstance, it is customary practice also to use a legend such as *Draft: Subject to Change* on work product, where appropriate. Forensic investigators should consult with counsel regarding these and other practices that should be followed to protect privileged communications.

DOCUMENT RETENTION CONSIDERATIONS

Document retention and preservation are especially significant in forensic accounting investigations of financial statement issues. This is a complex area and should be discussed with counsel, but following are some considerations.

In the ordinary course of business, transactions are executed; divisions are acquired or sold; accounting systems are modified, updated, or replaced; and estimates are changed as new information becomes available. All of those things may be relevant to preserving the electronic evidence resident in a corporate accounting system. At the beginning of the engagement, it may be appropriate to consider whether the forensic accounting investigator will be responsible for retaining records as the records exist at a given date—for the benefit of the company and the investigation team—and, if so, exactly what documents and for how long the documents should be retained. Document retention practices represent a complex area, and counsel should be consulted in this regard to ensure compliance with firm policies and all applicable laws and regulations. There are usually massive amounts of paper and computer files that get created or reviewed during the course of an investigation, and it may be burdensome to retain every document and electronic file. However, there may be situations in which that may be exactly what is required under the circumstances. One such situation would be when subpoenas call for such information.

In some matters, the forensic accounting investigator may be asked to review evidence collected pursuant to grand jury proceedings. Such evidence is confidential and may be shared only with those who have signed the required confidentiality statement pursuant to Rule 6(e) of the Federal Rules of Criminal Procedure, commonly referred to as a 6(e) statement. The obligations undertaken in the 6(e) statement are personal, and the forensic accounting investigators should be aware that it is a crime to disclose federal grand jury materials to unauthorized parties. Separate filing and other document-handling procedures within the office may need to be established so that only those authorized to view the material have access to it.

PLANNING CONSIDERATIONS

Depending on the issue under investigation, it is often necessary to meet with the client to discuss the types of evidence you may require and to locate that evidence for the time periods under review. This is especially true of financial accounting records, owing to the constantly changing business structure of many entities and of those entities' data processing operations. If, for example, you plan to perform an e-mail review of six people at the company for the past two years, you may be sadly disappointed when you show up with your information technology (IT) and investigative staff at company headquarters, only to learn that off-site backup tapes cannot be located and the e-mail server rewrites over files every 60 days. Best to plan for these issues ahead of time. Such planning considerations should include the following:

- Review of client's record retention policies and whether there is compliance
- Storage locations for paper records, both on- and offsite
- Imaging technology used for transaction documents, such as customer invoices, vendor invoices, and contracts
- Existence and storage of employee files
- Existence of files at employees' homes, including home computers
- File retention practices at different corporate locations, which may vary substantially
- Organizational chart and reporting hierarchy
- Storage medium for computerized records, both on- and offsite
- Backup procedures used for employee computers and e-mail, including when backups occur and what information is lost or retained and what is contained on servers versus individual hard drives
- Retention of records kept by or about former employees of the company
- System changes in relation to corporate accounting systems or e-mail systems
- Existence of documents related to outsourced corporate functions such as payroll and internal audit

Creation of a written plan for the collection of documents is frequently an excellent tool for focusing the efforts of the investigation team on material most likely to be relevant. At the end of the investigation, this plan will serve to show that the scope of investigation in terms of documents sought was appropriate for the issue at hand. This methodical approach also helps avoid the scorched-earth approach that results in accumulation of an excessively broad collections of records or of different types of records at different locations from different witnesses. In some circumstances the forensic accounting investigator may legitimately take this approach but should consider a more focused approach at the outset.

Creating a written plan also helps reduce the confusion of terminology that often arises with accounting and financial records. Most forensic accounting investigators have had the experience of receiving documents or materials that fail to fulfill the requirements of a detailed and carefully planned request. The undiscovered fraudster may be behind certain difficulties that come up—for example, conflicting terminology or nomenclature intended to confuse forensic accounting investigators. In one instance, a request for a customary accounting document, an Aged Trial Balance of Accounts Receivable, resulted in the surprising response that no such document existed. In fact, the company personnel kept such a record, but it was called the Listing of Open Receivables. Later, when the facts became known as to who the likely culpable party was, that individual told the forensic accounting investigators that he had not deliberately withheld the document; he simply had not recognized the term used by the forensic accounting investigators. Obtaining a listing of all user reports—identifying the exact report name, users' names, and when the reports are prepared and distributed—often will help avoid this potential conflict. It is also possible that some parties from whom documents are sought may be motivated to deflect the requests by their own legal positions or other concerns. Having a clearly spelled out plan and well-worded requests helps make it possible to expose such behavior in later proceedings.

CREATING A CHAIN OF CUSTODY

The chain of custody has the purpose of establishing from the time the evidence is collected to the time of its presentation to a court or perhaps to a regulatory body that it has been properly preserved from alteration or damage and thus retains its probative value. Before gathering any evidence, the forensic accounting investigator should consider with counsel and the client the level of detailed record keeping necessary to establish the chain of custody over the evidence. For the most part, establishing the chain of custody is merely a record-keeping procedure not very different from physical inventory procedures with which many accountants are familiar. The procedure is used for establishing where the evidence came from and that it has been properly secured, principally against alteration, since it was acquired.

Consider the forensic investigation of an inventory theft disguised by the falsification of physical inventory records by a company executive. It may be important to demonstrate what records the executive was aware of and perhaps had under direct control. In this circumstance, creating a record that indicates the location in the executive's office from which each file was gathered will be important. Files taken from the executive's locked desk drawer for which only the executive has the key may be properly viewed in a different light from records taken from a stack on the conference table in the executive's office used for team meetings on a daily basis. Because the different levels of precision require different amounts of time and effort to create and maintain, the establishment of such procedures at the beginning of the evidence-gathering effort is an important cost and efficiency issue. Generally, the more care required to document the chain of custody, the higher the cost to your client for the investigation. For this reason, it is important (1) to agree at the outset of the engagement on the measures that your client requires on this issue and (2) to incorporate the client's instructions in the retention letter, if at all possible.

Creating a written record that identifies the item of evidence, tells where it was found, shows its quantity (for example, the number of pages in a document), and assigns it a control number is an important procedure in establishing the chain of custody. Almost all evidence physically collected by forensic accounting investigators is in the form of documents rather than other physical evidence such as a fingerprint. Properly numbered through a process often referred to as Bates numbering[1] and detailed as to their nature and source, copies of documents can generally be made and used during the analytical phase of the investigation. This approach preserves the originals and secures them from loss, damage, or alteration. If that cannot be done and the evidence must be transferred between geographic locations or team members, the written custody record should be updated to reflect the date and time of transfer. The signature of both the delivering and the receiving parties will evidence the fact that each item was in fact transferred. If material is packed in boxes, each box should also bear a unique identifying number and should be tracked through each step in the exchange. Each piece of evidence must be coded such that its location of discovery by the forensic accounting investigator can be determined.

The condition of the evidence should be noted and documented as it is gathered. With respect to documentary evidence, it is important to be alert to indications that the documents may not be complete or authentic. Erasures, use of correction fluid, incomplete printing, and missing pages or attachments all may be red flags alerting the forensic accounting investigators to alterations. Noting such issues at the time the documents are collected creates a record that may be useful later in establishing that the documents were not altered nor sections lost subsequent to their collection. One of the means of recording the collection of physical evidence or of securing devices containing electronic files is to use evidence bags. Although clear-plastic evidence bags are not recommended for most document collections, for notes or other records found in the desks of suspect employees they may be useful.

On global assignments or in situations in which documents are identified and transferred from remote locations, consider augmenting the chain of custody procedures with photographs. The pictures shown in Exhibits 21.1 and 21.2 were parts of an investigation in a developing country. The first photograph, sent by 'e-mail, quickly demonstrated to counsel why some documents were illegible and could not be transported.

Later, when evidence that could be transported was ready for shipment, a photograph of the materials en route supplemented the written chain-of-custody records, consisting of the document and box log, air freight bills, and signatures of receipt once delivered.

In today's world, much of the information pertinent to an investigation may be stored electronically. The following devices often contain relevant data:

---

1. The Bates Company was long the source of a mechanical ink-pad number stamp that advanced a counter to the next digit each time the stamp was used. This process became known as Bates numbering, and the numbers themselves were referred to as the Bates numbers of a document. The numbers provide a convenient shorthand for identifying documents exchanged in litigation or collected in an investigation. The process serves to eliminate confusion over which document is being referred to, especially in situations in which the same or similar documents may have been collected from different sources, such as the same memorandum from several different people. Today, many alternatives to the Bates stamp are available, ranging from copy machines to software programs that add numbers to documents.

EXHIBIT 21.1   PHOTOGRAPH DOCUMENTING THE CONDITION OF EVIDENCE

- Personal computers
- Network servers
- Wireless and cordless telephones
- PDAs and BlackBerry devices
- Answering machines
- Paging devices
- Caller ID devices
- Digital cameras
- Facsimile machines
- Printers
- Scanners
- ID card printers
- Copiers

EXHIBIT 21.2   EVIDENTIARY MATERIALS EN ROUTE

- Compact disc duplicators
- Smart cards/magnetic stripe cards
- Security systems
- Global positioning systems
- Electronic game devices
- Vehicle computer devices
- Storage media

The best practices for gathering electronic information are constantly changing as technology evolves, and staying up-to-date requires expert help. The investigative team must have access to the specific IT skills needed to identify and gather all relevant information—and particularly to be able to assess and affirm the integrity of the electronic data. The practitioners who gather and identify the information may differ from the professionals who read and analyze the results. For this reason, make sure that the information gathered during the electronic search includes the make, model, and type of computer(s); internal and external disk drive capacity; operating systems used; applications used; design of the network; and the computer literacy of the users. All of these points would be carefully noted by forensic technologists.

As with documentary evidence, handling electronic evidence requires establishment of a chain of custody. The information contained on the subject computer is considered evidence and must be handled and stored in a manner that ensures the integrity of the data. That is accomplished in a number of ways: by keeping documentation on all procedures and/or applications performed on the electronic evidence, by storing the electronic media in a secure location (a locked file cabinet or safe), by making a bit-by-bit image copy of the hard drive rather than a file system copy, by analyzing the copy rather than the original, and by using forensic software to prove the integrity of the original contents.

◆ WHOSE EVIDENCE IS IT?

In gathering both physical and electronic documents, the investigative team may encounter privacy or other issues limiting its right of access to the data and/or its right to transport data across geographic borders. For example, in collecting desk files or computer files from employees, documents of an obviously personal nature, such as bank account records, may be encountered. In general, obviously personal material should be viewed as outside the scope of investigation and set aside until counsel's advice can be sought as to the appropriate disposition. The laws of foreign countries also vary considerably with respect to privacy and may set limits on both the collection and transportation of data across borders. It may be improper to collect or transport to other jurisdictions employment data such as home address or national identity numbers such as social security numbers. Some countries—as a basis for permitting transport of data—have laws that look to whether the receiving nation's laws offer privacy protections equal to their own. For example, some countries, notably Switzerland, have special laws related to banking data. The Swiss bank secrecy laws make it illegal to transport bank account data or documents out of the country.

One significant and far-reaching example of privacy legislation is the Data Protection Act (DPA) enacted by the European Union. The DPA provides that anyone processing personal data must comply with DPA principles. The principles provide that data must be:

- Processed fairly and lawfully
- Processed for limited purposes and not in any manner incompatible with those purposes
- Adequate, relevant, and not excessive
- Accurate
- Not kept for longer than necessary
- Processed in line with the subject's rights
- Secure
- Not transferred to countries without adequate protection

Corporate ownership of data and files related to employees' personal information, or documents created by employees—e-mail, for example—may be protected by one or more privacy regulations. HIPAA[2] regulations in the United States offer an example of such privacy regulations. The forensic accounting investigator should be generally familiar with such regulations, which provide, among other things, that under no circumstances should you avail yourself of medical information of any kind. Where you must be especially careful is in requesting personnel files: always ask the employer to remove any medical information before giving you a file. As a general rule, it is prudent to obtain clearance from counsel before attempting to gather any such evidence.

◆ EVIDENCE CREATED BY THE FORENSIC ACCOUNTING INVESTIGATOR

WORKING PAPERS

During the course of an investigation, the forensic accounting team is more than likely to produce analyses and summaries of the factual material discovered. Such analyses and summaries are likely to form the basis of testimony if litigation to recover losses is commenced, if litigation is brought against the enterprise as in shareholder class-action lawsuits, or if you are instructed or compelled by law to produce them for regulatory or other authorities. Accordingly, care should be taken to include all appropriate materials in the files of the engagement. The practice of cross-referencing analyses to sources of information is critically important

---

2. The Health Insurance Portability and Accountability Act of 1996 (HIPAA) requires any entity that maintains health records for others (such as its employees) to keep such records private. HIPAA has forced many companies, especially hospitals and HMOs, to overhaul their records storage and retrieval systems and information security standards and policies.

and often conveniently accomplished by noting the Bates number of the document from which the data was taken subject to the document retention requirements set forth earlier. The unique subject matter of each investigation will dictate what should be maintained in the working papers, but some types of documents that would typically be included in addition to the report of findings, are the following.

- *Accounting records and other documents.* General ledger, subledgers, financial management reports, reconciliations, journal entries, internal audit reports, purchase orders, vendor information, accounting journals, management reports, contracts, telephone, computer system and security system records, desk files, e-mail files, Web sites—and still other types of records and documents in this category.
- *Public record searches.* Reports from third-party investigations, such as related-party evidence, Dun & Bradstreet reports, and investigative reports and information from Internet sites (see Chapter 17): the information may be as varied as newspaper articles, chat room discussions, links to hobbies, and philanthropic and other outside interests and investments. Sources of this material may include filings with the U.S. Securities and Exchange Commission (SEC), accessed through EDGAR.[3]
- *Electronic computer files.* E-mail (copies of To, From, cc, and bcc), computer files or imaged records of entire drives (see Chapter 20), and data stored in handheld personal digital assistants.
- *Photographs or digital photos, preferably with a date/time stamp.*
- *Chain-of-custody documentation.*
- *Interview notes and audio recordings.* Interview notes taken by you and your staff professionals during the investigation of witnesses—both targets and company personnel.
- *Third-party information.* Provided by legal counsel or other interested third parties, this material might include external audit reports, management letters and reports, records of nonaudit services, bank statements (canceled checks, bank advices, and other supporting documentation), and documents obtained by subpoena or search warrants.
- *Court pleadings and deposition transcripts.*

REPORTS

Providing written reports is not invariably required in investigations. Adding substantial time and cost, written reports may or may not be needed, depending on circumstances (see Chapter 23). As a general practice, retaining evidence and

---

3. EDGAR, the Electronic Data Gathering, Analysis, and Retrieval system, performs automated collection, validation, indexing, acceptance, and forwarding of submissions by companies and others required by law to file forms with the U.S. Securities and Exchange Commission. Use of EDGAR serves to benefit investors, corporations, and the economy by accelerating the receipt, acceptance, dissemination, and analysis of time-sensitive corporate information filed with the commission.

analyses as if a report will be prepared and issued is an appropriate efficiency measure, although the decision as to whether or not that will actually occur can usually be deferred until late in the investigation. In some cases, it is true that you will be informed at the outset of the investigation that a report is required. For example, if conducting a 10A investigation, you may be asked to provide a report for the counsel who retained you to assist in performing the investigation.

The topic of reports is well covered in Chapter 23, but we do wish to address one important issue here. If a report is undertaken, the question arises as to the treatment and distribution of report drafts. The question of drafts may also pertain to analyses or summaries created in the course of the investigation. On these matters, the forensic accounting investigator should have a clearly stated policy (see earlier discussion—Document Retention Considerations—this chapter) with which all staff are familiar. Counsel should be consulted as to counsel's obligation to retain and produce drafts of reports.

Your firm or company will no doubt have policies and practices regarding what to do if you receive or reasonably anticipate receiving a subpoena for materials collected or created in the course of an investigation or if you reasonably anticipate litigation regarding the subject matter of the investigation. Such policies may cover the handling of all documents, files, notes, and records of any type—even if not considered to be officially part of the working papers—with regard to their preservation and retention.

You should consult your firm/company counsel and, as well, your client's counsel immediately upon receipt of a subpoena. These consultations provide both sets of attorneys the opportunity to evaluate any means of quashing the subpoena if they conclude that it is desirable to do so and will also permit counsel an opportunity to advise on any document retention issues arising as a result of the subpoena. A forensic accounting investigator retained as an expert witness in a state court matter was once served just after giving a deposition. The subpoena was later quashed because the party was not permitted by law to subpoena an out-of-state expert witness. The subpoena could still be served in the expert's state of residence, but in this case it was not. Point is, do not assume. Consult with your client's counsel.

◆ WHAT EVIDENCE SHOULD BE GATHERED?

As noted earlier, no hard-and-fast rules exist as to the selection of documents for retention (subject to document retention requirements set forth earlier). The following discussions highlight the types of documents that should be retained in a variety of investigations.

INVESTIGATIONS OF VENDORS

Investigations of vendors should focus on where the money went and for what purpose. All relevant disbursement information should be collected. That would normally include:

- Vendor information setup in the company's master file data for the accounts payable system
- Contracts, purchase orders, invoices, and documents used to accumulate payment approvals, receiving documents, correspondence concerning credits, billing errors, or other matters
- Internal reviews of vendor quality and the results of public record searches performed to qualify the vendor

Collection of these materials is likely to be facilitated by computer forensic techniques such as data mining for duplicate addresses, similar names, or duplicate payments, invoices, or purchase orders, among other queries. Interviews may be required, as will additional public records searches about the vendors' current situations.

INVESTIGATIONS OF FOREIGN CORRUPT PRACTICES ACT VIOLATIONS

Investigations of Foreign Corrupt Practices Act violations typically require disbursement review and interviewing. In one illustrative case, certain large payments related to the award of government contracts were made through a middleman identified in the company's record keeping as a consultant. The investigation team sought to identify the services rendered but could find no fair value exchange for the payment. As in investigations of vendor fraud, thorough payment documentation should be gathered, and interviews focused on the purpose of each payment may be needed.

INVESTIGATIONS OF IMPROPER RELATED-PARTY ACTIVITY

Investigations of improper related-party activity usually require all information regarding the nature of the relationship, interview notes, relevant internal control policies, e-mail streams, and public record searches, as well as any documents that would support analysis of economic exchange at fair value in an arms-length transaction.

INVESTIGATIONS OF EMPLOYEE MISAPPROPRIATIONS

Investigations of employee misappropriations most often center on the documents and records kept by the employee and may include desk files, computer files, e-mails, records of access to and use of corporate computer systems, records of access to company facilities, security camera tapes, employment records, payroll records, and material obtained in interviews with coworkers. Outside information related to lifestyle and property ownership may also be relevant. PDAs, BlackBerrys, and cell phones in particular should not be overlooked, because they may contain information about people assisting the employee in the scheme.

INVESTIGATIONS OF SPECIFIC ALLEGATIONS

Investigations of specific allegations vary widely, arising from whistle-blower letters, hotlines, anonymous tips, and exit interviews. Depending on the nature of the allegations, the investigative team must develop an appropriate plan for accumulating evidence most likely to be relevant. As a general rule, your evidence-gathering plan should begin broadly. Even though some of the allegations could be unfounded or overblown by disgruntled employees, it may be unwise to ignore them. The breadth of the initial response helps demonstrate to any interested third parties such as regulators or external auditors that the allegations were taken seriously and addressed in a complete manner. This degree of thoroughness is a key element in sustaining the conclusions of the investigative team.

INVESTIGATIONS OF FINANCIAL STATEMENT ERRORS

Investigations of financial statement errors are likely to require access to just about every element of a company's financial accounting and business records, as well as the files of many employees and the e-mail files of all involved in the subject transactions. Such investigations may also require interviews and the collection of transaction evidence from outside parties such as banks, customers, vendors, and former employees. In major investigations, it may be worthwhile to copy the general ledger system and e-mail servers to another data center location, so that when the investigation team is ready to review the material, the material has been properly preserved.

◆ IMPORTANT CONSIDERATIONS REGARDING DOCUMENTS AND WORKING PAPERS

- Originals should be marked as evidence and filed separately. Obtain permission to remove original documents from a client site.
- Advise staff that most of the working papers are essentially copies of documents and electronic spreadsheets gathered as part of the investigation and that have tick marks, notes, and other descriptors written on them to document our work. Consider that working papers may need to be produced to a third party. As such, separate copies should be maintained apart from the working papers so that the original document can be replicated or copied as it existed before it was written on as part of the normal course of testing by the forensic accounting investigator.
- Whenever responding to a request by a third party for some or all of your working papers, make a completely separate copy of the documents you send, and create an index of those documents—to be maintained in a separate binder or box. In this way, you will always know exactly what you have given to a third party. Do not simply place a sticky note on a document that reads, "Sent copy to SEC Enforcement." Counsel should be consulted and may even manage this production process.

- Each working paper should stand on its own. You should be able to understand just how the document (working paper) supports a report or findings. This is usually indicated by the tick marks indicating where a particular number may be coming from, i.e., its source from another working paper, and where it is going to, i.e., its use on another working paper. Tick marks should be explained in a legend proximate to the working paper being reviewed (see Exhibit 21.3). If the purpose or source of the working paper is not clear, then a note written on the working paper should provide such clarity. It is important that each working paper stand on its own so that it can be viewed in the larger context that clarifies its significance.

- Working-paper binders should flow from the report, all the way down to the lowest form of support (see Exhibit 21.4). This means that a clear road map from summary results and conclusions through all summarizations and calculations down to the most detailed item should be included. Such

XYZ COMPANY

Summary of Accounts Receivable Write-Offs by Quarter

Q4 Fiscal 2000 - Q3 Fiscal 2001

		Q4 00		Q1 01		Q2 01		Q3 01		Subtotal Q4 00 - Q3 01	
Income Statement Impact											
Acquisition Expense	1.1	$30,000,001	2.1	$1,000,000	3.1	$26,647,535	4.1	$ -	5.1	$57,647,551	✔✔
Bad Debt Expense		-		-		-		13,411,931		13,411,931	
Miscellaneous Expense		56,931		68,050		116,457		177,025		418,462	
Total Income Statement Impact		30,056,932		1,068,050		26,763,992		13,588,956		71,477,930	A
Balance Sheet Impact											
Accrued Liabilities	1.2	3,339,867	2.2	2,375,414	3.2	6,466,414	4.2	3,451,862	5.2	15,633,572	
Acquisition Accrual		-		-		16,930,463		-		16,930,463	
Allowance for Doubtful Accounts		2,302,580		570,097		1,131,206		2,891,325		6,895,208	
Miscellaneous Other		-		24,339		2,680		956,741		983,761	
Total Balance Sheet Impact		5,642,447		2,969,850		24,530,764		7,299,928		40,442,989	B
Total A/R Write-Offs		$35,699,379		$4,037,900		$51,294,756		$20,888,884		$111,920,919	C
		✔		✔		✔		✔		✔	

Draft - Subject to Change

Attorney Work Product
Privileged & Confidential

Legend:

✔ Foot
✔✔ Cross foot
1.1 - 5.2 Source Document Reference

A+B=C

Prepared by: Edna Everage
Date: 12/31/01

fn: XYZ_Q3_2001

EXHIBIT 21.3   WORKING PAPER WITH TICK MARKS

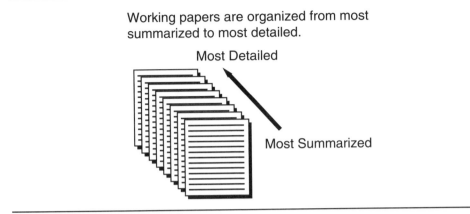

Working papers are organized from most summarized to most detailed.

Most Detailed

Most Summarized

EXHIBIT 21.4   WORKING-PAPER ORGANIZATION

an approach permits a quick and easy determination of how each part of the evidence was used, how each data element was included, or why data elements were not included in calculations.

- There is no requirement that working papers must be neat, but they should be readable and organized. If you are at a restaurant and you write down some important information or do an analysis on a napkin while at lunch, that can become a working paper. If it is readable and understandable, simply tape it to a sheet of paper when you return to your office, and file it in your working-paper binder. Your clients will appreciate your efficiency.

- While reviewing a working paper, if you find a deficiency that can be corrected or clarified with the stroke of a pen, do it then and there. There is no requirement to correct it on your computer and then reprint and refile. If it is possible to be efficient without sacrificing quality or understanding, do it.

- Most investigations are document intensive, and even the simplest of engagements can generate a mass of working papers. Consider preparing a binder that can be used for client meetings when you present updates on the investigation. The binder contains the report or a listing of findings to date, cross-referenced to a tabular index of relevant support (but not all the support). Documents in the binder are just enough of a reminder to indicate to your client exactly what document supports your findings. For example, if a specific contract provision is an important point of reference, include only the first page to identify the contract and to identify the page with the key provision. The balance of the longer document can be produced at a later time; it is filed in the complete set of working papers maintained by your staff.

- At the end of an engagement, take time to organize your working papers before sending them to storage consistent with your firm/company's document retention policies.

♦ CONCLUSION

Gathering evidence and keeping proper control of it from the time it is first collected until its ultimate use in legal proceedings or other forms of reporting are highly significant aspects of a properly conducted forensic accounting investigation. Rigorously controlled evidence gathering is the infrastructure on which the credibility of the evidence rests and, consequently, the credibility of conclusions resulting from the investigation. Like all inventory control systems, keeping appropriate records of the chain of custody requires consistency and discipline. Ideally, evidence created by the work of the forensic accounting team should be properly filed, indexed, and controlled.

CHAPTER 22

SUPPORTING A CRIMINAL PROSECUTION

Albert A. Vondra

Thomas W. Golden

John Gallo

Isabel M. Cumming

*T*his chapter addresses the issues your client and your client's counsel confront in evaluating when and how to refer a matter to a prosecutor for investigation of those believed to be involved in criminal acts.[1] Recent U.S. Department of Justice (DOJ) guidelines lay out in unambiguous language the DOJ's desire for vigorous enforcement of criminal laws against corporate wrongdoers, including the corporation itself. The government's view is that indictment of corporations for wrongdoing in appropriate circumstances enables the government to be a positive force in changing the corporate culture in favor of a new paradigm of deterring, detecting, and punishing white-collar crime. The environment has changed such that corporate cooperation with government prosecutions of illegal activity is becoming commonplace. The question of whether or not to report the crimes of individual employees when the corporation is the victim is an extremely important decision, and this chapter explores considerations related to it.

Our experience shows that many corporations find the decision to refer an errant employee for prosecution a difficult one because of the reality that prosecution can have long-lasting, widespread effects on the company. The decision as to whether or not to refer a matter generally rests with senior management and counsel, including the company's general counsel and in some cases, the board of directors. In light of the many considerations, discussed in this chapter and inherent in the decision to make a criminal referral, a very careful and sophisticated assessment should be made by senior management and counsel, aided and

---

1. Throughout this chapter, we refer to *prosecution* as the right of a company or individual to inform a government law enforcement agency of a violation of the law. However, only the government can determine whether or not to prosecute a case. Our reference to *prosecution* by a company implies a referral to a governmental representative legally empowered with this responsibility.

informed by the forensic accounting investigator as well as other experts as needed. Once a decision has been thoughtfully made, the company should act with conviction and see the decision through to the end.

◆ KEY CONSIDERATIONS

The decision confronting management and counsel as to whether or not to move forward with a referral for prosecution often depends on many circumstances.

DETERRENT EFFECT OF APPROPRIATE RESPONSE

Many companies have the view that violators should be prosecuted—in the belief that culpable parties need to be held accountable for their actions and punished "to the full extent of the law," and doing so will deter comparable acts by others in the future. This view continues along these lines: if an employee who perpetrates a significant fraud is simply demoted or terminated without being held criminally liable in court, the wrong message may be sent to the rest of the organization. In our experience, rigorously pursuing that well-chosen remedy is the true deterrent. The best practice is to communicate throughout the organization that if employees do something inappropriate, they will be caught and their punishment will be swift and commensurate with the crime. If a criminal referral is the appropriate remedy, the company should not hesitate to elect that option— and doing so will send a powerful message throughout the entire organization.

It is our experience that few things are more damaging to employee morale than to see that a company does not walk the talk. In recent years, many companies have gone to great lengths to promote ethical governance and conduct by all directors, officers, and employees of the company. For the most part, they have done an excellent job of formulating and communicating the importance of ethical behavior. However, employees are aware of whether and how the company walks the talk when actually responding to violations.

U.S. SENTENCING COMMISSION GUIDELINES

As noted earlier, in our experience the rigorous pursuit of a well-chosen remedy is the most successful deterrent to future instances of fraud. The U.S. Sentencing Commission in 1991 established organizational federal sentencing guidelines (FSG) that apply to corporations, partnerships, labor unions, pension funds, trusts, nonprofit entities, and government units (virtually all types of organizations). The guidelines set out criteria for corporate compliance programs, which are consistent with the rigorous pursuit of fraud. They require consistent punishment of individual wrongdoers, and can hold an entire organization criminally liable for illegal acts committed by the organization's employees.

Although no corporate compliance program can prevent all types and occurrences of fraud and wrongdoing, such programs must be well designed and vigorously implemented to maximize their effectiveness in deterring and detecting wrongdoing by employees. They cannot be just paper programs. The seven key criteria for establishing an effective compliance program, as outlined by the guidelines, are as follows:

1. Compliance standards and procedures reasonably capable of reducing the prospect of criminal activity
2. Oversight by high-level personnel
3. Due care in delegating substantial discretionary authority
4. Effective communication to employees at all levels
5. Reasonable steps to achieve compliance
6. Consistent enforcement of standards, including disciplinary mechanisms
7. Reasonable steps to respond to and prevent further similar offenses upon detection of a violation[2]

In 2004 the guidelines were amended to include 10 modifications known as FSG II. Each item is intended to eliminate ambiguities from the original seven components of an "effective program to prevent and detect violations of law." FSG II was intended to synchronize the guidelines with both Sarbanes-Oxley and "emerging public and private regulatory requirements." The 10 recommended modifications are:

1. *Tone at the Top*—Emphasize within the guidelines the importance of an organizational culture that encourages a commitment to compliance with the law.
2. *Conduct and Internal Control*—Provide a better description of *compliance standards and procedures*—namely, "standards of conduct and internal control systems that are reasonably capable of reducing the likelihood of violations of law."
3. *Leadership Accountability*—Specify the responsibilities of an organization's governing authority and organizational leadership for compliance.
4. *Resources and Authority*—Emphasize the importance of adequate resources and authority for individuals with responsibility for implementation of the program.
5. *History of Violations*—Replace the current terminology—"propensity to engage in violations of law"—with the more objective requirement of determining whether there has been a "history of engaging in violations of law."
6. *Conduct Training*—Include training and the dissemination of training materials and information within the definition of *effective program.*
7. *Evaluate Programs*—Add "periodic evaluation of the effectiveness of a program" to the requirement for monitoring and auditing systems.

---

2. Paula Desio (Deputy General Counsel U.S. Sentencing Commission), *An Overview of the Organizational Guidelines*, http://www.ussc.gov/TRAINING/corpover.pdf.

8. *Whistle-blower System*—Require a mechanism for anonymous reporting.
9. *Encourage Employees*—Establish a system whereby employees can both report actual violations and seek guidance about potential violations in order to more specifically encourage prevention and deterrence of violations.
10. *Risk Assessment*—Provide for the conduct of ongoing risk assessments as part of the implementation of an "effective program."[3]

EXPENSE AND POSSIBLE OUTCOMES

It is important to understand the time and financial commitment required, once management and counsel decide to refer a matter for prosecution. The most appealing case for any prosecutor is one that involves clear and simple facts. Because of limited resources, prosecutors at every level of government typically have no staff forensic accounting investigators and may not have the resources to pursue all of the cases presented to them. They must choose their cases wisely and select those most likely to yield a successful prosecution that furthers their primary responsibility of protecting the public interest. Because white-collar crimes often are complex, they are sometimes perceived as having less jury appeal. As well, experience shows that jurors often sympathize with white-collar criminals, believing that through loss of a job and reputational damage, the defendant has been punished enough. However, recent business catastrophes bringing to the spotlight certain deceitful financial reporting practices have likely made the public much less sympathetic toward white-collar criminals.

Forensic accounting investigators can assist the prosecutor in white-collar cases. The forensic accounting investigator should be able to explain complex scams in simple, straightforward terms so that the great majority of jurors—even those without significant experience in corporate life—can understand the facts and how they should be interpreted. Even with the assistance of a forensic accounting investigator, there is, of course, no guarantee of a successful prosecution.

REFERRALS FOR PROSECUTION MAY ATTRACT PUBLIC ATTENTION

If the decision to refer a matter for prosecution is taken, it is our experience that the organization should be prepared for public inquiry as a possible consequence. Consider the following experience.

The director of a national charitable foundation stole $10 million from the organization before being apprehended and prosecuted. The entire matter unfolded before the public eye. Ultimately, nearly 80 percent of the stolen funds were recovered, but many news commentators and the public criticized the charity for hiring a bad apple in the first place, claiming the charity should have known better. The public was indignant: "How dare they play with the money of tens of thousands of contributors? I'll never again give to that organization." It happens that the organization had very strong controls—better than in many

---

3. See http://www.ussc.gov/GUIDELIN.htm.

other companies. However, as most accountants know, when a senior executive perpetrates fraud, it is difficult to prevent it, let alone recover the funds.

The charity passed through its nightmare and eventually emerged quite strong again. Asked whether, in the end, he thought it had been wise to refer the matter for prosecution and bear the public's response, one of the organization's veteran executives—a principled elder statesman—had this to say: "If he had not been prosecuted, there was a strong likelihood that this relatively young executive would have found a job at another charity and stolen again. But we paid a high price by disclosing to the public that we had been duped by one of our own. We risked the very survival of our mission, which is saving lives!"

This veteran executive teaches that the burden placed on society by a decision not to pursue prosecution may be significant. Because the overwhelming majority of employees who defraud their employers are terminated without prosecution, many remain in the workforce. Not surprisingly, some return to their devious ways. Had they been convicted of a crime at the first detected occurrence, future employers would more likely learn that this person should not be placed in a position of trust. Avoiding prosecution sends a criminal out into society to potentially prey on another victim.

◆ REFERRAL CONSIDERATIONS

When referring a matter for prosecution is the course of action selected, a series of considerations remains regarding when to do so. In our experience these are issues for management and counsel to evaluate. Each case will present different issues, but a number of issues will likely arise and are considerations in deciding the timing of contacting the authorities. Among them are:

- Whether or not the investigation is sufficiently advanced to make a reasonably informed decision about the nature of the suspected crime
- What the specific laws or regulations related to the suspected crime, or the industry in which the entity operates, require of the company
- The level of the individual nature of the offense
- Whether or not the company's insurance coverage contains any clauses that would affect the timing of the referral

As noted earlier, there are many considerations confronting counsel about the timing of a referral. More often today, companies are deciding to self-report incidents at the early stages of their investigations followed by periodic updates to government enforcement officials such as the U.S. Securities and Exchange Commission. In our experience, reasons that may suggest a prompt referral include some or all of the following.

- There is a possibility that the company has violated laws or regulations, and it is advantageous under the relevant law or regulatory rules to self-report. In that case, time may be of the essence.

- The prosecutor may separately have commenced an investigation and could bring the forensic accounting investigator into his investigation under a 6(e) procedure that gives access to some or all of the prosecutor's evidence. This is explained more fully in Chapter 24 and may greatly facilitate both the public prosecution and the internal investigation and remediation efforts within the company.

- The client is satisfied that the extent of the scheme is known and desires that the prosecutor move quickly. The company engages a forensic accounting investigator with instructions to work with the prosecutor, thereby encouraging the prosecutor to pursue the case expeditiously by taking advantage of the fact that the victim is offering and paying for expert assistance.

- The client's analysis of its fidelity bond or other insurance policies that may provide for recoveries determines that a prompt referral for prosecution is the best course of action.

REFER THE MATTER TO STATE, LOCAL, OR FEDERAL PROSECUTORS?

One of the interesting legal issues that may arise is the determination of what laws were violated. Clearly, if counsel determines that the referral should be to a federal prosecutor, a violation of federal law must be suspected. The forensic accounting investigator's findings as to the actual method by which the fraud or other type of crime was carried out may have a bearing on counsel's judgment. A case study will illustrate some of the issues.

A charitable organization was using a lockbox for the collection and processing of all of its contributions. One day a donor called to ask why a check she had mailed several months ago had not been cashed. Since the check had been for $10,000, the organization's administrators became alarmed. Soon they were receiving similar calls from other puzzled donors. After some investigation, the charity noticed a higher incidence of such occurrences at one of its lockbox locations. It notified its bank and local post office but could not determine the cause. Then a hotline tip came in that prompted the administrators to focus on a certain processing clerk at the bank. Law enforcement representatives followed the clerk home one day and, armed with a warrant, examined the clerk's property. They found a backpack and some trash that contained over 200 envelopes, complete with checks—all of them from donors.

What was going on? Overwhelmed with envelopes to process and unable to keep up, the clerk had not asked the supervisor for help but instead was taking unprocessed mail home and throwing it in the trash. A forensic accounting investigation soon estimated that over a period of nearly two years, the clerk had discarded more than $9 million in contributions! Not surprisingly, the leaders of both the charity and its bank were livid. They wanted to prosecute—especially because these amounts could never be recovered, as they had no idea whose contributions had been discarded.

The bank promised to make good on the defalcation, but its executives were anxious to prosecute and thereby send a message to all employees about ethical conduct. They took the case to the local U.S. attorney, who was interested in prosecuting the matter. The forensic accounting team had already done all the investigative work and developed an excellent evidence package. All parties prepared to move forward with federal prosecution of the clerk. But a little problem surfaced: the clerk had not violated any federal law. Because of not having cashed any of the checks and thereby gaining no financial benefit—except to have kept her job during that period—the clerk could be charged only with vandalism, which was a violation of a state, not a federal, statute.

PROSECUTORS MUST PRIORITIZE CASES

Should your client decide to go forward with a criminal referral, you should understand that while the federal government and state and local governments may differ in choosing which cases to prosecute, the principle that guides all of them is that they are duty bound to protect the public from harm. The more harm they perceive, the more likely they are to pursue prosecution. A corollary principle is that prosecutors at all levels of government are resource constrained, and accordingly, you may discover that the referral of a white-collar crime matter has to wait in line behind more pressing priorities. For example, other types of crime—say, terrorist activity, government corruption, or child pornography—or crimes of violence like rape and murder. As noted above, some citizens view white-collar crimes as being victimless, but are they? White-collar crimes can be devastating on a personal level when a company collapses and employees lose their savings, pensions, and jobs. Despite the significant personal impact, prosecutors nevertheless have many legitimate demands on their resources, and given this, focusing the attention of a prosecutor on a financial crime case may be difficult. Some forensic accounting groups include team members with experience as law enforcement agents—such as people from the U.S. Federal Bureau of Investigation—or with experience as prosecutors. These professionals can use their substantial experience to present the case in a manner that best deals with the prosecutor's concerns about resource limitations and complexity.

Regardless of the jurisdiction, however, the process may take as much as several years. If counsel is also advising a civil suit for recovery of losses, you may have to wait until the criminal matter is adjudicated before proceeding. Lastly, bear in mind that the authorities are not necessarily interested in determining your entire loss. They are not private investigators. They are looking only for sufficient evidence to satisfy the needs of a successful criminal prosecution. For example, say a controller has been stealing for several years by means of fraudulent invoices paid to bogus vendors. Further, the prosecutor identifies $500,000 in theft over a one-year period. Do not be surprised if the prosecutor's investigation is concluded and the case prosecuted on this basis alone. The company may have unanswered questions: How long did this scheme go on? How much was stolen in total? Are there coconspirators? Were there other schemes? These issues are relevant to the company, but not necessarily to the prosecution. Management may need to conduct an internal investigation to answer these questions.

FORENSIC ACCOUNTING INVESTIGATOR MAY INCREASE THE SUCCESS OF A REFERRAL

The forensic accounting investigator may become an important member of the prosecution team by helping assess evidence of financial wrongdoings and by advising the client and the prosecutor. Although not a lawyer and not in a position to offer legal advice, the forensic accounting investigator can point out weaknesses in the evidence and possibly suggest alternative investigative procedures to mitigate any risks that have been recognized. For example, if the CFO has set in motion an accounting scam, forensic accounting investigators can analyze financial statements and accounting transactions to determine what actually occurred. Many prosecutors do not have the in-house expertise to perform these steps. A forensic accounting investigator's expertise in gathering and interpreting financial evidence helps enable the prosecutor to strengthen the case and prepare to refute defenses.

Once a forensic accounting investigator is involved, it is important for that individual or team to conduct a very thorough investigation. For example, if the validity of the defenses offered by the suspect during admission-seeking interviews is not tested, that may leave a weakness. The defense could use the weakness as a basis for portraying the forensic accounting investigator as an agent of the prosecution rather than an independent and objective witness. At a trial, there is an important distinction between a testifying forensic accounting investigator and, for example, a testifying psychologist. On one hand, the psychologist is considered an expert witness by virtue of testifying under the specific Federal Rules of Evidence that govern expert-opinion testimony. On the other hand, the testifying forensic accounting investigator often is serving as a fact witness at a criminal trial: not generally offering an opinion but reporting the factual findings of the work. The forensic accounting investigator's task is to communicate the facts that that investigator has determined to be relevant to the matter at hand. While actual trial situations will differ depending on the circumstances, as a general matter it means the forensic accountant does not offer an opinion about fraud—as in, "Yes, in my opinion a fraud has been committed, and the defendant did it"—but, rather, presents evidence related to each of the elements of fraud in such a way that the trier of fact—in the form of judge or jury—may reach a conclusion based on the facts the forensic accountant has discovered.

REPUTATIONAL BENEFITS

Reputational gains may also result from a referral. The company may be praised for standing up to fraudulent criminal activity and protecting other potential victims. Such a stand ultimately may have a positive impact on the company's bottom line or its stock price. The reaction of the market to the announcement of a prosecution against white-collar crime is not wholly predictable, but taking a stand may enhance the company's reputation.

Employees are likely to be positively impressed if they see that management will not tolerate criminal activity, particularly in the managerial ranks. Further, they will understand in very practical terms that the company's code of ethics is real and binding on all, and they probably will be more willing to come forward—to blow the whistle—if they see inappropriate activity in the workplace (see Chapter 16).

Customer and vendor relationships may also be enhanced if the company is perceived as taking a stand against financial wrongdoing. Both may feel more comfortable doing business with a trusted, reputable company.

The community also will be impressed. Public officials and community leaders admire companies that proactively take a stand against white-collar crime. Note that the term *proactive* is chosen deliberately: companies that appear to be merely *reacting* to external pressures may tarnish their reputations, while companies that communicate their active concern for values and the general welfare gain in reputation.

True, there also are risks to public disclosure of a significant fraud, such as adverse publicity. And therefore, an assessment of (1) the amount and character of the publicity that may accompany a long public trial and (2) the way in which the company should address that publicity is generally recommended. A public relations firm with a strong track record in this area should be engaged to determine the best way to deal with public perceptions of the company in the event of a trial.

In our view, the risks of adversely affecting a company's reputation through going to trial are outweighed by the possibility of enhancing a company's reputation through a firm and successful prosecution. A quote from Albert Einstein may help guide a company faced with tough decisions: "In the middle of difficulty lies opportunity."

◆ PLEA AGREEMENTS

Plea agreements are very common in white-collar prosecutions and out of the control of the victim corporation. Often, the defense will realize early on that it cannot fight the documents. The defense attorney will attempt to minimize his client's possible jail time by putting the emphasis on mitigation at the time of sentencing. It is important to realize that even if a case pleads out, it does not mean the defense obtained a sweetheart deal. It usually it means that the case was just too strong and the defense knew that a trial could result in more risk to the defendant. A strong forensic accounting investigator can help the prosecution achieve this type of result.

◆ FILING A CIVIL LAWSUIT

It may be advantageous for the company to pursue a civil suit, especially in circumstances in which substantial financial recovery is possible. A company may file a civil suit at the same time as the prosecutor's pending criminal case, although discovery available under the civil statutes will often be stayed until after the criminal matter has been decided at the request of the prosecutor.

A forensic accounting investigator can be of value in a civil case, especially in the process of discovering and presenting evidence. If counsel is pursuing civil litigation, the forensic investigator may well have access to sources of evidence through the discovery process not available in an internal investigation. For example, it may be possible to obtain additional documents such as the personal banking records and tax returns of suspects or to question suspects in a deposition under oath.

CHAPTER 23

REPORT OF INVESTIGATION

Thomas W. Golden

Ryan D. Murphy

*D*ocumenting an investigation is as important as performing it. A poorly documented case file can lead to a disappointing conclusion, can result in a dissatisfied client, and can even damage the financial accounting investigator's reputation and that of the investigator's firm. Various means by which the forensic accounting investigator may report his findings are discussed in greater detail in this chapter. The form of that report—whether oral or written—is a matter to be discussed with the client and with counsel. While it is not the responsibility of the forensic accounting investigator to advise on the legal perils associated with various forms of reporting, there are certain issues of which forensic accounting investigators should be aware as their clients debate the form of reporting that will conclude the investigator's investigation. This chapter addresses both written and oral reports of investigation.

We suggest that you determine at the outset whether a written report is expected from you and, if so, its form and timing. In the common circumstance that this point cannot be decided at the inception of the engagement, you should conduct the investigation in a manner that will facilitate a comprehensive oral report, including the key documents and any exhibits necessary to illustrate the findings. Many investigations begin small, but there is no way to know with certainty where they will lead and what will be required at the conclusion. Although your client may not have requested a report at the outset of the investigation, some event in the course of the investigation may change the client's mind, and you should to be prepared to respond. For example, you may determine in the course of an investigation that an officer of the company violated a law or regulation, thereby requiring the company to consider self-reporting and possibly bringing a civil action against the officer and other third parties. Alternatively, you may be subpoenaed for your part in an investigation that has captured the attention of regulatory agencies or law enforcement. While you can testify only as to what procedures you recall performing and the attendant findings, your client—and your own reputation—will be better served if you have proper documentation. Our advice is to conduct an investigation as if you might be asked at a later time to report formally on your findings and on the procedures performed.

◆ TYPES OF REPORTS

The following types of reports are relevant.

- Written reports
  - *Report of investigation.* This form of written report is given directly to the client, which may be the company's management, board, audit committee of the board, in-house counsel or outside counsel. The report should stand on its own; that is, it should identify all of the relevant evidence that was used in concluding on the allegations under investigation. This is important because the client may rely on the report for various purposes such as corporate filings, lawsuits, employment actions, or alterations to procedures and controls.
  - *Expert report filed in a civil court proceeding.* We will touch on this topic only as it pertains to civil fraud court proceedings. The American Institute of Certified Public Accountants (AICPA) publishes an excellent practice aid on the full range of expert reports.[1]
  - *Affidavits.* These are voluntary declarations of facts and are communicated in written form and sworn to by the witness (declarant) before an officer authorized by the court.
  - *Informal reports.* These consist of memos to file, summary outlines used in delivery of an oral report, interview notes, spreadsheets listing transactions along with explanatory annotations, and other, less-formal written material prepared by the investigation team.
- Oral reports
  - Oral reports are usually given by the forensic accounting investigation engagement leader to those overseeing an investigation, such as a company's board, or to those who represent the company's interests, such as outside counsel.
  - Oral reports involve giving a deposition—as a fact witness or expert witness—during which everything that is said, by all parties to the deposition, is transcribed by a court reporter.

◆ IMPORTANCE OF ADEQUATE PREPARATION

"I could have given you a more thorough and accurate report if I had had more time to prepare." The inexperienced forensic accounting investigator will no doubt say that at least once in a career in response to an irate client who is dissatisfied with a report on the preliminary results of an investigation. In our busy and complex world and in the course of a busy and complex investigation, not everything on the task list has the same priority. Experienced forensic account-

---

1. American Institute of Certified Public Accountants, Consulting Services Practice Aid 96-3, *Communicating in Litigation Services: Reports* (New York: American Institute of Certified Public Accountants, 1997).

ing investigators know that any request for an update on an ongoing investigation is a report in the truest sense of the word *report*. One should not assume that an update delivered orally can be treated more casually than a written update. All reports deserve adequate preparation time and presentation in accordance with professional standards of practice.

Reporting is a critical responsibility of the forensic accounting investigator, and adequate preparation is necessary to present the status of the investigation in a manner that enables the decision makers to assess how to proceed. No report, oral or written, should be considered "unofficial." Regardless of what you say or write to qualify your comments, once a document leaves your hands or words leave your lips, you cannot control the further distribution of the information you have communicated. Take the time to get it right.

◆ STANDARDS OF REPORTING

Depending on your professional affiliations, you will be required to follow the reporting standards of your profession. If you are a certified fraud examiner (CFE), the applicable standards can be found in the *Fraud Examiners Manual*,[2] published for its members by the Association of Certified Fraud Examiners. If you are a certified public accountant (CPA), you should follow the reporting standards required for consulting engagements and found in the AICPA's *Statement on Standards for Consulting Services*.[3] If you are both a CFE and a CPA, you will be required to follow the standards of both associations. Because the AICPA standards are quite broad, while the standards of the Association of Certified Fraud Examiners (ACFE) are specific to fraud investigations, there is unlikely to be contradictory guidance if both professional standards are followed.

AICPA CONSULTING STANDARDS

CPAs are required to follow the AICPA Statement on Standards for Consulting Services (SSCS), formerly known as Statement on Standards for Management Advisory Services (SSMAS). The SSCS provides guidance for its members regarding certain types of consulting services. Section 100 of the AICPA Professional Standards contains the applicable guidance for CPAs who are performing consulting services, which encompasses essentially any professional service performed by members that is other than an examination, audit, review, or compilation.

The AICPA provides no specific reporting standards for consulting services per se and instructs members to look to the general standards of the profession, contained in Rule 201 of the AICPA Code of Professional Conduct. Those standards are the following.

---

2. Association of Certified Fraud Examiners, *Fraud Examiners Manual* (Austin, Tex.: Association of Certified Fraud Examiners, 2002).
3. American Institute of Certified Public Accountants, *Statement on Standards for Consulting Services* (New York: American Institute of Certified Public Accountants, 1991), codified in AICPA Professional Standards—Consulting Services: Definitions and Standards—CS § 100).

- *Professional competence.* Undertake only those professional services that the member or the member's firm can reasonably expect to complete with professional competence.

- *Due professional care.* Exercise due professional care in the performance of professional services.

- *Planning and supervision.* Adequately plan and supervise the performance of professional services.

- *Sufficient relevant data.* Obtain sufficient relevant data to afford a reasonable basis for conclusions or recommendations in relation to any professional services performed.

In addition to the general standards applicable to all members, the AICPA stipulates additional general standards for all consulting services, promulgated to address the distinctive nature of consulting services in which the understanding with the client may establish valid limitations on the practitioner's performance of services. Those standards are established under Rule 202 of the AICPA Code of Professional Conduct:

> *Client interest.* Serve the client interest by seeking to accomplish the objectives established by the understanding with the client while maintaining integrity and objectivity.[4] Integrity requires a member to be, among other things, honest and candid within the constraints of client confidentiality. Service and the public trust should not be subordinated to personal gain and advantage. . . . .[5] Objectivity is a state of mind, a quality that lends value to a member's services. It is a distinguishing feature of the profession. The principle of objectivity imposes the obligation to be impartial, intellectually honest, and free of conflicts of interest. Independence precludes relationships that may appear to impair a member's objectivity in rendering attestation services.[6]

> *Understanding with client.* Establish with the client a written or oral understanding about the responsibilities of the parties and the nature, scope, and limitations of services to be performed, and modify the understanding if circumstances require a significant change during the engagement.[7]

> *Communication with client.* Inform the client of (*a*) conflicts of interest that may occur pursuant to interpretations of Rule 102 of the Code of Professional Conduct, (*b*) significant reservations concerning the scope or benefits of the engagement, and (*c*) significant engagement findings or events.[8] A conflict of interest may occur if a member performs a professional service for a client or employer and the member or his or her firm has a significant relationship with another person, entity, product, or service that could be

---

4. *Statement on Standard for Consulting Services,* CS § 100.07.
5. Notes to CS § 100, Note 2, Article III of the Code of Professional Conduct, ET § 54, par. 2.
6. Notes to CS § 100, Note 2, Article IV of the Code of Professional Conduct.
7. CS § 100.07.
8. Id.

viewed as impairing the member's objectivity. If this significant relationship is disclosed to and consent is obtained from such client, employer, or other appropriate parties, the rule shall not operate to prohibit the performance of the professional service. . . . [9]

AICPA SSCS says the following about performing consulting services for attest clients:

The performance of consulting services for an attest client does not, in and of itself, impair independence. However, members and their firms performing attest services for a client should comply with applicable independence standards, rules and regulations issued by the AICPA, the state boards of accountancy, state CPA societies, and other regulatory agencies. [10]

The concluding caveat, warning members to comply with "other regulatory agencies," serves to direct members to, among other things, the requirements of the Sarbanes-Oxley Act, which prohibits the performance of certain consulting services for attest clients (see Chapter 6).

ACFE STANDARDS

The ACFE Reporting Standards are included in the *Fraud Examiners Manual*, a comprehensive guide designed specifically for use by members of the ACFE. (The *Fraud Examiners Manual* is also available to nonmembers.) Unlike the AICPA's rather general rules, ACFE reporting standards document a basis for reporting the results of a financial crimes investigation in a practical manner that can aid the forensic accounting investigator in preparing reports. The standards, both broad and detailed, give the forensic accounting investigator an overview of conceptual objectives as well as enough detail to guide both the novice and the experienced professional in reporting matters. The following points reflect ACFE reporting standards.

Preparation

Do not expect to generate a well-written report from a poorly performed and/or poorly documented investigation. If the investigation has been performed and documented properly, then the reporting of procedures and findings should flow as a natural extension of the investigation. Preparation is critical to the reporting process and serves as the foundation for the other reporting standards. Preparation requires organizing each stage of the investigation from the initial engagement letter and data gathering to analysis and corroboration. Deficiencies in performing the investigation are likely to be very evident in the Report of Investigation.

---

9. Notes to CS § 100, Note 3, Interpretation of 102-02.
10. CS § 100.09.

Accuracy

It goes without saying that all reporting should be accurate. Accuracy applies not only to the information conveyed in the report, no matter how incidental, but also to the mechanics of communication: grammar, spelling, and the like. Mistakes in your report, however trivial, could cast doubt on the credibility of information that you know to be decisive. Accuracy in reporting basic data, dates, events, and names is critical.

Clarity

Use clear and simple language to eliminate to the greatest degree possible any doubt about your intended communication. Written communications should be crafted in such a way that an average group of citizens selected for jury duty could understand the facts and their interpretation. Because forensic accounting investigators are fact finders, the fact pattern described in the report should make the evidence clear, thus enabling the trier of fact—the individual (judge) or group (jury) rendering a decision—to reach the proper conclusion. You are there to assist them.

Impartiality

Bias destroys credibility. The AICPA SSCS rules on integrity and objectivity, discussed earlier (see CS 100.07), parallel the impartiality requirement of the ACFE Reporting Standards. As a fact finder, the forensic accounting investigator contributes a crucially important set of findings to the trier of fact. Any perception of bias detected in reports may destroy the credibility of reported facts and thereby render the forensic accounting investigator's work less useful. Opinions as to culpability in criminal matters should not be stated. Subjective opinions and impressions often express unstated (or stated) bias and have no place in reporting, oral or written. The facts must speak for themselves.

Relevance

Every investigation uncovers information that is irrelevant to the issues at hand. The report should include only facts relevant to resolving the allegations being investigated. Not only is irrelevant information distracting to recipients, but also the forensic accounting investigator's credibility may be at risk by implying flawed judgment as to what really matters.

Timeliness

The report, as well as information gathered in support of it, should be submitted in a timely manner. This point is especially true of interviews that, if not documented and reported upon without delay, may cause decision makers to be less influenced by their contents.

THE WRITTEN REPORT OF INVESTIGATION

Needless to say, reports documenting an investigation differ considerably from audit opinions issued under generally accepted auditing standards (GAAS). The investigative report writer is not constrained by the required language of a governing standard, and investigative reports differ from one another in organization and content depending on the client's stated needs. In contrast, audit reports adhere to set formula prescribed by GAAS. The uses of written reports also differ. The client could do any of the following things with an investigative report, among others.

- Distribute the report to a select group of individuals associated with the company in various capacities.
- Voluntarily give the report to a prosecutor as a referral for prosecution.
- Enter the report as evidence in a civil fraud proceeding.
- Give the report to outside counsel for use in preparing regulatory findings, entering negotiations, or providing other legal services on behalf of the company.

Whatever the ultimate fate of the written report, its basic elements will be much like the following elements.

BASIC ELEMENTS TO CONSIDER FOR INCLUSION IN A REPORT OF INVESTIGATION[11]

- Identify your client:

[Firm] was engaged by Cutting Edge Technology Corporation (the "Company").

- In the case of a lawsuit, identify the parties:

I, [forensic accounting investigator's name], have been retained by [name of law firm] ("Counsel") to investigate certain of the claims and allegations made by Philip Hart ("Hart"), John Harrington ("Harrington"), and Robert Geller ("Geller") against Peter Langley ("Langley").

- State in broad terms what you were asked to do—for example, "to provide expert testimony or investigate certain allegations":

. . . to provide forensic accounting investigation services in order to assist in pursuing your concerns related to certain allegations made against Jane Branford ("Branford") and Phyllis Long ("Long"), General Manager and chief financial officer, respectively, of the Company's Houston office.

---

11. This excludes certain reports following established reporting requirements such as Rule 26(b) of the Federal Rules of Civil Procedure.

- Describe your scope, including the time period examined:

I was engaged to perform investigative procedures related to review of the Company's purchasing and receiving policies and practices in effect over fiscal years 2001–03. We have performed background checks of certain employees at the direction of [name of outside counsel], reviewed and analyzed certain of the Company's accounting records and other documents, performed various data mining and data interrogation of the Company's electronic files, and conducted interviews of current and former Company employees.

- Include mention of any restriction as to distribution and use of the report:

This report was prepared in connection with the aforementioned matter and is intended solely for your information. It may be used only for the purposes of this engagement and may not be used for any other purpose without our written consent.[12]

- Identify the professional standards under which the work was conducted:

We performed our work in accordance with the American Institute of Certified Public Accountants' ("AICPA") Statement on Standards for Consulting Services and the Association of Certified Fraud Examiners ("ACFE") *Fraud Examiners Manual.*

- Identify exclusions in the reliance on your report:

Our work does not constitute either an audit performed in accordance with the AICPA's generally accepted auditing standards or an attestation service. We make no representation as to the adequacy of our procedures for your purposes.

- State that your work should not be relied on to detect fraud:

Fraud and irregularities by their very nature are most often hidden, and no absolute assurance can be given that all such matters will be detected. Our engagement cannot be relied on to disclose all irregularities or illegal acts, including fraud that may exist. During the course of this engagement, we will inform you of any such matters that come to our attention unless they are clearly inconsequential.

- Include the procedures you performed, technical pronouncements relied upon, and findings:[13]

---

12. You might consider indicating that if you are presented with a subpoena, you will inform the client that you intend to comply unless the client makes court filings in an attempt to quash the subpoena.

13. If appropriate, also perhaps include the implications of your observations and findings.

Work Performed and Observations

With respect to the issues expressed above, we performed the following work:

- Considered the following accounting literature:
  - Accounting Research Bulletin (ARB) No. 43, Chapter 4, Inventory Pricing
  - Accounting Principles Board (APB) No. 20, Accounting Changes
  - Statement on Auditing Standards No. 73, Appendix C, Statement of Position 85-3, Accounting by Agricultural Producers and Agricultural Cooperatives
- Reviewed the Company's financial statements and U.S. Securities and Exchange Commission filings

Conclusions Based on Work Performed

Based upon our work and observations as described below, the utilization by the Company—either as a grower of fruit for resale or as a juice manufacturing concern—of the specific identification method approximating first in, first out (FIFO) appears reasonable. Properly performed the specific ID method matches the costs incurred to the actual physical flow of goods used in the manufacturing process. We found this to be the case in our review. We found no evidence supporting allegations that the company manipulated its inventory accounting records.

Generally accepted accounting principles (GAAP) does not require growers, bottlers, or manufacturers to apply any specific inventory costing method. Neither does GAAP mandate a change in accounting method, as the Company altered its focus from that primarily of a grower to that primarily of a juice manufacturer.

The Company has contended that in the case where different pools of inventory were utilized, applying the specific ID method more accurately matched the true physical flow of goods, as these items are costed at the actual cost of the pool being consumed. Furthermore, the inventory on hand at period end is recorded at the cost of the items remaining in inventory. To the extent that inventory was utilized in the order in which it was grown or purchased, the use of specific ID in this regard approximated FIFO. Our procedures confirm the Company's position.

Flowcharts and exhibits within the body of the report or in the form of a referenced appendix will aid understanding. Refrain from including exhibits that are not referred to in the body of the report.

SUMMARIZING YOUR FINDINGS

A summary can be helpful to the reader but may be perilous for the report writer in terms of keeping critical information and perspectives intact. Caution is advised when preparing two types of summary sections: executive summary and conclusion.

We do not recommend writing a summary conclusion. If for any reason you nonetheless do so, be careful not to offer an opinion on the factual findings unless specifically requested to do so. The facts should speak for themselves. It may be appropriate to position in a concluding section of the Report of Investigation certain recommendations for additional investigative procedures or a description of control breakdowns you have observed.

Again, while we do not recommend summary conclusions, a carefully written executive summary at the beginning of the report can be extremely helpful to the reader, especially when it precedes a long and complex report. The executive summary should offer in simple, straightforward language an accurate statement of significant findings. Each summarized finding should include a reference to the full description of findings included in the complete Report of Investigation. Exhibit 23.1 provides an illustration.

EXECUTIVE SUMMARY

As a result of our work, we have noted the following preliminary findings as summarized below. It is important to note that the evidence we have identified in this Report of Investigation suggests but in no way incriminates any individual or entity. This Executive Summary is not meant to substitute for our following Report of Investigation. A summary of the evidence we have reviewed suggests that:

- Clark and Kent skimmed at a minimum $2,500,000 in cash from the Atlanta Division from February 1999 through their termination on July 5, 2001. (See *Section A-1*.)
- Clark directed at least $1,280,000, in aggregate from the Atlanta Division, to his brother's company, Built-Right Construction, and his father's company, B&B Construction, from 1999–2001. Invoice review and interviews with personnel indicate that the services provided by these two companies may not have been performed. (See *Sections B-3 & B-4*.)
- Approximately $8,500,000 was paid from the Atlanta Division to twenty-six construction companies during 1999–2001 (see *Section B-2*); $415,000 was attributable to companies in which "cut and paste" invoices were discovered in Kent's desk. (See *Section A-4*.)
- Clark, Kent, and Clark's brother also benefited financially through transactions involving petty cash and theft of store merchandise. (See *Sections A-9 & D*.)

Our analysis has utilized Company-provided documentation and files beginning when the Company acquired a 100% interest in the Atlanta Division in 1999. Due to the schemes noted, the size of the dollars at risk, and general manager Clark's tenure of 26 years, we recommend that the Company inform the seller and expand the scope of this investigation to include the years where only a 50% interest was held.

Additionally, we recommend that further investigative procedures be conducted to resolve the allegations we present in our findings below.

EXHIBIT 23.1   SAMPLE REPORT OF INVESTIGATION—EXECUTIVE SUMMARY

◆ WRITTEN REPORT OF EXPERT WITNESS OPINING FOR THE PLAINTIFF ON A CIVIL FRAUD CLAIM

A report written for submission at trial or like proceedings, such as arbitrations, is beyond the scope of this text. Forensic accounting investigators required to author such a report should take direction from client counsel in preparing a report that meets all of the requirements of Rule 26(b) of the Federal Rules of Civil Procedure or such other rules as may be applicable to their appearance.

In most forensic accounting investigations there is no need to provide expert witness testimony. The forensic accounting investigator may, however, be asked to testify as a fact witness. As indicated earlier, the forensic accounting investigator is principally a fact finder and reports facts in a straightforward manner so that others—judge, jury, audit committee, board of creditors, or other interested party—can interpret those facts and make determinations as to their implications, including compliance with laws and regulations. There are, however, instances in which the forensic accounting investigator may be asked to prepare a formal expert report to a court in advance of a planned court appearance, at which time the investigator is expected to testify as to findings and to offer an opinion on a civil fraud claim. An example of a civil fraud claim opinion follows.

In the example, the expert witness is a forensic accounting investigator with both CPA and CFE credentials. He conducted an investigation at the request of counsel representing the buyer of a manufacturing business. In the course of the investigation, he learned that most sales under the previous owner had been effected through the payment of kickbacks and bribes. When the new owner took possession, he was unaware of the pattern of kickbacks and bribes, and he refused to pay when he was approached by customers or their agents. Not surprisingly, sales dropped off significantly. Through his lawyer he filed a civil lawsuit, including among his claims that the defendant seller had known of the kickbacks and bribes, had failed to disclose them, and had thereby materially damaged the buyer. The forensic accounting investigator was asked to opine on the civil fraud charge. Following is that section of his report:[14]

IV. OPINION

Based upon my review, it was evident to me that there were numerous disbursement transactions between BUILDIT Manufacturing (BUILDIT) and a number of its vendors prior to buyer's involvement, which misrepresented the proper business purpose of the transactions. That is, invoices were presented to BUILDIT for goods and services that had not been furnished. However, given the level of kickbacks and bribery within BUILDIT, the testimony of individuals, and other evidence, I believe that the preponderance of the evidence indicates that a fraud was perpetrated upon the buyer of BUILDIT. I base my conclusion on the following definition of fraud.

Fraud in the inducement

Fraud occurring when a misrepresentation leads another to enter into a transaction with a false impression of the risks, duties, or obligations involved; an intentional misrepresentation of a material risk or duty reasonably relied on,

---

14. The following illustration represents only a portion of the entire expert report prepared in accordance with Rule 26(b) of the Federal Rules of Civil Procedure.

thereby injuring the other party without vitiating the contract itself, esp. about a fact relating to value.

Misrepresentation

I believe that the seller made numerous misrepresentations to the buyer, which include:

- Failure to disclose that at least $2,469,910 was paid to shell companies, thereby providing cash for bribes to be paid to the owners of the companies ("Shell Companies") listed on page 3 of this report. No goods and services were provided in exchange for cash paid to these entities.
- Failure to disclose that these payments were made to companies owned by individuals that were employed by significant customers of BUILDIT
- Incorrectly classifying the payments to the Shell Companies as "direct labor" and "materials" expense
- Providing the buyer with financial statements that included misclassifications of both revenue and expense

In my opinion, transactions were created in such a way as to conceal the true nature of the expense. There may have been other misrepresentations made by the seller to the buyer. However, these examples, I believe, satisfy the above definition.

Reliance

The misclassification and recording of the payments to the Shell Companies concealed material risks that were not known by the buyer. In my opinion, had the buyer known about the existence of kickbacks and bribes, he would not have gone forward with the purchase. The fact that the buyer did go forward with the purchase demonstrates reliance.

Value/Damages

I have not been asked to calculate damages; however, it is my understanding that counsel has retained another expert to perform this task.

♦ AFFIDAVITS

An affidavit is a written statement submitted in a legal proceeding. Affidavits should receive the same level of care as that given to more extensive written reports. Typically not as long as reports of investigation, they attempt to summarize salient facts or they are submitted as sworn testimony previously submitted in the form of the forensic accounting investigator's report of investigation. The forensic accounting investigator should carefully edit the affidavit so it accurately conveys his own thoughts. The investigator should use words and phrases that are terms of art to the accounting profession, not the legal profession. A poorly drafted affidavit signed by a forensic accounting investigator can diminish that investigator's credibility. Like the report of investigation, the affidavit is the work product of the forensic accounting investigator.

◆ INFORMAL REPORTS

There are certain informal types of reports, the most common of which are memos to file and presentations. Because any communication, written or oral, may be discoverable, professional care should be taken to ensure that all communications are accurate and comply with the relevant reporting standards.

A memo to file is a standard approach to the documentation of important events and understandings at points in time. The purpose of such memos is to document certain events and facts in the working papers of the forensic accounting investigator. At times, clients may ask for copies of such memos as substitutes for formal reports. While some clients may insist on receiving the memos prepared during the course of the investigation as opposed to a written report, they should be reminded that a memo is prepared at a point in time and is not a substitute for a written report. Presentations are an informal manner of reporting the results of an investigation. Presentations have the attributes of both written and oral reports—and can be dangerous if prepared carelessly. A written report allows for the possibility of thoroughly explaining a finding and its impact. The very nature of a presentation is brevity—in the expectation that the presenter will flesh out the information summarized in the slides. When using the presentation format in lieu of a detailed written report, the financial accounting investigator should consider whether a page with a boilerplate "Statement of Responsibility" could serve to remind the audience of certain limitations (see similar material at the beginning of the earlier discussion on the written Report of Investigation). Also, consider including a statement at the bottom of each page reading, "The accompanying Statement of Responsibility is an integral part of this presentation."

While oral reports may require less effort and therefore generate less expense for the client, preparation for an oral report should be no less comprehensive than for a written report. Planning an oral report also requires both designation of a member of the team to deliver it and a decision regarding other team members who should be present. It may be wise to have staff members present or at least nearby who are most familiar with the details of certain interviews and events so the staff members can be called on in the event that the client wishes more detail.

An advantage of oral presentations is that there is ample opportunity for the forensic accounting investigator to clarify points, and those receiving the report can seek clarification by asking questions and can convey their particular concerns then and there. The interactive aspect of oral reports is probably their greatest benefit.

In the context of financial investigations, reports can take many different forms. Due to the dynamic nature of financial investigations, stakeholders involved in the oversight of investigations or relying on the results may want interim reports, which, while preliminary, represent an important responsibility of the forensic accounting investigator. Interim reports or updates are more useful if they include both a summary of the procedures performed, with related findings, and an overview of recommended procedures and expected outcomes. Additionally, an interim report should record what, if any, obstacles have hindered the forensic accounting investigators in the performance of their work. Investigations are something like a black box for those who must evaluate the results. The more factual information investigators report, the better it is for their audience, who are the decision makers.

An illustration may help here. Let us say that forensic accounting investigators have been investigating allegations that a drug company paid kickbacks to physicians for favoring the company's products. About two weeks into the investigation, the audit committee calls a hastily planned meeting with the forensic accounting investigators and asks for an update. The partner investigator indicates that his team of three professionals has been in the field for two weeks and has incurred $100,000 in fees and expenses. The partner reports that to date, the team has found no evidence of wrongdoing. The audit committee is pleased to hear this report. However, this bare-bones summary report, while correct, hardly gives either a correct impression or the comprehensive status of the investigation.

Preferably, the partner leading the forensic investigation advises the audit committee that a day of preparation to assimilate information from the team covering planned procedures performed to date, obstacles encountered, findings to date, and recommended further procedures will be beneficial. During this fact-gathering stage, the partner may reevaluate previously planned procedures and identify others he intends to suggest to the audit committee. Now he is adequately prepared. He presents orally to the audit committee and includes the same information as before regarding fees and expenses, but he is also in a position to add the following: "We learned yesterday that the electronic general ledger file is missing some journal entries made during a critical period. We have our information technology forensic team working to rectify the problem and get us complete electronic files. Additionally, we learned from several doctors whom we called randomly that they do recall being solicited by a company representative in a manner they felt was inappropriate. While we have yet to find conclusive evidence of the alleged improprieties, the preliminary evidence does suggest an expansion of the scope of our investigation to include telephone interviews of most of the doctors likely to have been called and follow-up with face-to-face interviews of those reporting that they received such calls." The partner could continue the update by citing other issues and possibly including change-of-scope recommendations.

The example here focuses on oral reports because the oral report is a form of reporting that is often treated too informally—that is, not with the same diligence of preparation and review that a written report generally receives.

◆ GIVING A DEPOSITION

The forensic accounting investigator may be called on to give a deposition, which is testimony in the presence of a court reporter and sometimes a videographer. Giving a deposition is an important activity and should not be taken lightly. Your professional reputation is at stake. Everything you have done in the course of an investigation is likely to come under close scrutiny. Your analysis, findings, and conclusions—even procedures you determined *not* to perform—all may be questioned. Expect that opposing counsel has met with another forensic accounting expert and received coaching on questions to ask you. Opposing counsel is likely to use techniques that attempt to impeach your credibility. That is opposing counsel's job, and experienced attorneys generally are very good at it. Do not underestimate their ability to dissect responses and catch the unwary forensic accounting investigator in a contradiction. Be sure to spend adequate time with counsel who will be defending your deposition, and consider all of counsel's recommendations. If you take issue with any of them, work it out before the deposition. Surprises at the deposition are unwise. While we recommend that you dedicate time to training materials such as the videotape *Preparing for a Deposition in a Business Case*,[15] the following are general guidelines to keep in mind when you've been engaged to give a deposition.

BE PREPARED

A mistake on the part of inexperienced forensic accounting investigators is to prepare inadequately. They may believe that because they have performed the investigation, merely telling someone about it will be a simple matter. Caution is the preferable attitude: take depositions seriously, and take the time to prepare well. Scrutinize each working paper just prior to the deposition, even if you have previously performed a detailed review. Question yourself on findings and procedures as a final step in preparing for a deposition.

IT'S *YOUR* DEPOSITION

The most important thing to remember is that it's *your* deposition. You are in control from the standpoint that no else knows the material of your report better than you do. Also, you can have a substantial impact on the tone and the pace of the deposition. For example, counsel may try to rush you through questions, but you are entitled to take the time required to formulate the best response to each question.

It is important to take the necessary time to prepare for your deposition. Remember that your reputation and your firm's reputation are at risk if you are ill prepared. Tell counsel approximately how much time you need to prepare, and do not waiver from this point. It is your deposition, and you should treat it according to your own and your firm's high standards.

During the deposition, if you do not understand a certain question or if opposing counsel asks compound questions that are confusing, either ask for the question to be rephrased or simply say that you do not understand. Counsel may try to make you uncomfortable by commenting that you should be capable of understanding and answering a question. Such a comment may seem intimidating.

---

15. Jeffrey A. Jannuzzo, *Preparing for a Deposition in a Business Case* (Albany, N.Y.: Matthew Bender, 1983).

Do not be intimidated; respond with professional courtesy and politeness—especially in more heated situations. If the opposing attorney fails to rephrase the question suitably, you can always say, "I apologize, and I want to be as complete in my response as I can, but I don't understand your question and cannot properly answer until I do."

OBJECTIVES OF A DEPOSITION IN CIVIL LITIGATION

A deposition is a form of discovery. The other side is permitted to "discover" what you did, what you learned, your opinions, if any, and their basis. You are required to be responsive to all questions, but you need not volunteer any information that has not been requested. You will not convert the opposing lawyer to your perspective, no matter how hard you may wish to try. You are not there to educate opposing counsel even if it is evident from the line of questioning that opposing counsel is confused. No points are scored for being witty, and witty responses may backfire. Stay true to your objective, which is to listen to the questions very carefully and to answer only those questions as honestly and succinctly as possible. Listen closely to the question and answer only the question asked.

YOU ARE BEING MEASURED

The deposition is probably the first opportunity for the other side to meet you. While you are in their presence, you are being measured. They are picturing you in front of the judge or jury, evaluating what kind of witness you will make at trial. They will notice your appearance, your demeanor, and your level of overall confidence. Introduce yourself to the other side as well as to the court reporter. Present your business card to them. As with any business meeting there is often causal discussion of various topics at the beginning: the weather, travel plans, and the like. Joining these discussions should be approached cautiously because one of them may turn into a discussion of the case and your role in it—"This must be your biggest case"—which is not an appropriate subject to discuss off the record. This advice also holds for casual encounters with opposing counsel in the elevator or hallway. Project confidence, and watch what you say at all times.

Without question you are required to be honest and not withhold information; however, it is perfectly acceptable to say, "I don't know" if in fact you don't. Granted, we have heard tales of witnesses who, when they are trying to hide some incriminating facts, say they don't recall or they don't know. This is not what we mean to suggest here. It seems that one of the toughest things for some professional advisers to say is "I don't know" to a question put to them in an area they did not investigate or should not be realistically expected to comment on. They believe that an admission of ignorance will make them look weak, so they make the mistake of speculating, which in most cases is not a good idea. Unless you are specifically asked to speculate, you should not. Opposing counsel is free to ask questions and probe—sometimes in an effort to get you to speculate—or to ask for an opinion. You may hear the following, for example, from opposing counsel: "Well, wouldn't you expect the CFO [chief financial officer] to be informed about such matters?" This question calls for your *opinion,* not a report of your *factual findings.* As with all questions, you must respond truthfully. If you had such an expectation, you must say so. If, however, you have not formed opinions about what *should have happened*—as opposed to reporting your discoveries of what *did happen*—you should say so. Counsel may try to make you feel you *should* know by following up with a comment along these lines: "You told us just a moment ago that you have been a CPA for 20 years and have done hundreds of audits. Shouldn't you know the answer to this question?" Do not be intimidated; you have no obligation to know what others were hoping you would know or were hoping would be within the scope of your work. Often, the worst thing you can do is to assume or speculate in response to a question when you really do not know the answer. You are not expected to have a photographic memory. In this regard, you may wish to consult with counsel about preparing a binder containing the most relevant materials from the investigation, precisely because you are unlikely to remember every detail of a complex case.

REVIEWING YOUR DEPOSITION TRANSCRIPT

Generally, each person deposed may review the deposition transcript for any errors made by the court reporter and then sign the deposition after noting any corrections necessary. Counsel establishes different protocols in different cases, and accordingly, you may be asked to waive signature at the conclusion of your deposition. This means that the deposition will stand as transcribed—without your review. Counsel can advise you in advance of the practice in the particular case, and if you are unsure whether or not it is acceptable to you, discuss it with counsel. Whether signature is waived or not, it is important to read your deposition transcript with several objectives in mind. First, you want to ensure that what you said was transcribed correctly. Second, you may notice an inaccurate response unknown to you at the time but now evident as you review your comments. Third, opposing counsel's questions and your testimony may identify a weakness in your investigation for which you will want to be prepared at trial. And if you gave a response that was factually inaccurate, you will want to advise counsel of the error. Even if you believe the deposition went well, take time to read it thoroughly.

OTHER CONSIDERATIONS

One of the best ways to ensure a successful deposition is to spend adequate time with the attorney who will be defending your deposition. No two depositions are alike, so even if you have given a number of them, you must still become acquainted with your counsel's strategy for the deposition. Also make sure counsel defending your deposition knows the limitations of your knowledge and expertise. Again, the deposition is not the place for surprises. Based on the experience of the authors, the following are additional considerations.

- Think before you speak. The deposition transcript bears no indication of the time it takes you to respond to a question. Once said, words cannot be deleted from the deposition transcript.

- Be cautious in responding to questions that contain absolutes such as *never* or *always.*

- Avoid clever sound bites that may be used against you at trial.

- Speak in complete sentences, using proper grammar in a lucid manner at an ordinary speed. That will enable the court reporter to record your words accurately.

- Pause before each answer, no matter how confident you are of your answer. That allows you to repeat the question silently to yourself and gives counsel defending your deposition time to enter an objection if counsel cares to do so.

- When asked to comment on an exhibit, if time to read it isn't offered, ask permission to read it before responding. Make sure you are familiar with it, and if you are not, state that for the record. You have the right to read every document presented before responding to questions about it. Opposing counsel may seem annoyed at your request to read a document, but despite that discontent it is generally advisable to make sure you know what a document says before answering questions about it.

- Be specific in your answers, and do not exaggerate. For example, if you are asked, "Have you ever audited a financial institution before?" and your answer is, "Sure, a great many," do not be surprised if opposing counsel pulls out a sheet of blank paper, gets ready to start writing a list, and says, "Please tell me the name of the first financial institution you audited, your responsibilities in that engagement, and when that occurred." If it is true that you have audited "a great many," opposing counsel would expect to write down a very long list. If your experience includes eight financial institutions, you may think eight is a great many, but others may think of eight as only a few. The better reply to the initial question may be, "Yes, I have."

If you are properly prepared, giving a deposition is somewhat similar to an oral report, although often not organized in the manner you would select. Remembering that your comments will become a written transcript and that your spoken words, once transcribed, can never be taken back, should instill in you the importance of adequate preparation.

◆ MISTAKES TO AVOID IN REPORTING

The following brief discussions highlight and review issues raised earlier in this chapter.

AVOID OVERSTATEMENT

In the memorable TV series *Dragnet*, Sgt. Joe Friday used to say, "Just the facts, ma'am." The same holds true when it comes to reports of investigation. The closer one sticks to the facts, all the facts, and just the facts, without embellishment, the better the report. The facts should speak for themselves. This is not to say that all facts are created equal: some facts are smoking-gun discoveries—for example, memos demonstrating both knowledge and intent. However, even in respect of obviously important facts, be careful not to overstate them.

AVOID OPINION

Other than the engagement to serve as an expert witness in a civil matter, the forensic accounting investigator should not offer opinions about the matter at hand. Also, opinions as to the intent or culpability (in criminal matters) of certain persons or as to whether an act was in fact a fraud should be avoided. These are matters to be decided by the trier of fact based on the factual material gathered and presented by the forensic accounting investigator. The forensic accounting investigator should not endeavor to influence the outcome beyond presenting the findings of the investigation in a clear and logical order.

IDENTIFY CONTROL ISSUES SEPARATELY FROM INVESTIGATIVE FINDINGS OF FACT

Often your client may ask you to identify control issues spotted during the course of your investigation. While appropriate to include in your report, we suggest including them in a separate section so as to focus on your primary task, which is that of a fact finder. The discovery of facts, leading to the resolution of potential criminal issues, is the forensic accounting investigator's professional calling. Identifying control breakdowns is a natural by-product of a fraud investigation, but such breakdowns should be addressed in a separate section of the report.

What does it mean in practice to give precedence to the pertinent facts? An example: A number of laptops are missing, and several of them can be traced directly to your target. If you actually wanted to give precedence to the control issue, you would write, "The control over laptop assignments is weak, and it was therefore impossible to account for all laptops acquired by the accounting department." But if you put your focus where it belongs, you would write something of the following kind: "Over the past year, 11 laptops were purchased by accounting and assigned to 10 individuals, including two to the controller. When questioned, the controller showed us one of the laptops and could not account for the other."

USE SIMPLE, STRAIGHTFORWARD LANGUAGE FOCUSED ON THE FACTS

The task of the forensic accounting investigator is to take a complex situation, properly investigate it to determine the relevant facts, and then report those facts in a simple, straightforward manner so that the reader or person hearing the report understands the facts and how they should be interpreted for resolution of the allegations. Who was involved? How much damage was caused? How did the events occur? Why did the company not catch the problem earlier? In reporting the answers to these questions, there is no room for speculation.

Again, let us reduce these observations to an example. We would not recommend writing as follows: "The CFO admitted to recording false revenue but said he didn't mean to hurt anyone. He wanted to keep the numbers up so that the division would not be closed." Text similar to the following may be preferable: "The CFO admitted to generating false revenue in an effort to achieve budgeted sales figures. He admitted to making the monthly entries with full knowledge of the fact that he was deceiving corporate officials and that his actions were improper under GAAP and company policy. His stated reason for his action was his fear that corporate headquarters would close the division and lay off a large number of employees in his division."

AVOID SUBJECTIVE COMMENTS

As a fact finder, the forensic accounting investigator must restrict comments to presentation of the facts in such a way as to resolve the allegations that occasioned the original engagement.[16] The investigator may give opinions about standard and customary business practices that relate to the observed behavior but not directly attempt to characterize the facts as discovered. The investigator should simply report them. If the finding is, for example, that the executive director of a charity has taken a number of trips, reportedly for business purposes, accompanied by family members, the investigator should not characterize such trips as "excessive" or "without business purpose" but should report only the facts. Those reading or hearing the facts can evaluate them in light of organizational policies and applicable laws and regulations.

In the written or oral report, how should the forensic accounting investigator convey an understanding of the facts? We would not recommend the following: "We noted that the executive director took *excessive* trips to New York with his family, which were *inappropriate* and *unrelated to the business of the organization,* although he expensed the trips as business related." The foregoing is replete with errors.

- *Excessive.* The word *excessive* is judgmental and appears to reflect the personal standard of the forensic accounting investigator. Synonymous words—such as *abusive, unacceptable,* and *extravagant*—are also judgmental characterizations and may not have a valid place in your report.

- *Inappropriate.* This term characterizes the observed action and should be avoided. It conveys a conclusion, not a fact. In the strictly factual realm, the report could note that such travel took place, that it required approval by the individual's supervisor, and whether or not the required approval was sought or given. The report could also reference a specific provision

16. As discussed earlier in this chapter, opinions by the forensic accountant are permitted if engaged as an expert in a civil fraud matter.

of the organizational-policy handbook to document the requirement. Each of these facts would enable readers of the report to characterize the subject's actions—and those readers are then more than likely to deem the actions inappropriate. But that is *their* role, not the forensic accounting investigator's role.

- *Unrelated to the business of the organization.* Such statements are usually made on the basis of assumptions. More likely than not, the trips were indeed unrelated to the organization's business, but it would be wrong to characterize them as such. The investigator should report either that no business purpose was discovered or that the individual admitted in interview that he knew the trips were strictly personal. Either of these statements may be a better manner of reporting. They report facts, not characterizations.

◆ WORKING PAPERS

Given the familiarity that most auditors have with working-paper-documentation techniques, many of which are applicable to forensic investigation, those techniques are not discussed at length here. However, certain techniques are especially pertinent to investigation, as the following pages demonstrate.

A forensic accounting investigator, once engaged, needs to take certain internal steps to document procedures, findings, and in some cases, recommendations. These elements of the investigation process are documented in a collection of evidence termed *working papers,* which divide into two broad categories: internal/administrative and substantive work product.[17]

Forensic accounting investigators naturally want legitimate protections over their work, such as liability limitations and work product privilege, when applicable. Here are a few important tips for achieving those goals. Judgment, as always, is needed here—these tips are not applicable in all cases—but generally speaking, we advise the following measures.

SIGNED ENGAGEMENT LETTER

It is always best to begin the engagement only after you have a signed engagement letter in hand. While there are exceptions to this rule, they should be rare. Even if the client states you will receive it on the first day of fieldwork, insist on having it faxed to you before traveling to the client site. Often, the client is not focused on engagement administration when there is a need to get the investigation going, but from your standpoint that is exactly the time to get the paperwork done. A client that knows you will not begin the investigation until the engagement letter is signed will be motivated to complete this aspect of engagement administration to set the investigation in motion.

---

17. *Merriam-Webster's Dictionary of Law 1996* defines *work product* as "the set of materials (as notes), mental impressions, conclusions, opinions, or legal theories developed by or for an attorney in anticipation of litigation or for trial." Definitions vary from jurisdiction to jurisdiction.

The engagement letter should address a variety of items. They include but are not limited to the scope of services, timing of the work, the deliverable (written or verbal report), fee structure, governing law and jurisdiction, and limitation of liability. In some situations, the engagement letter will be addressed to the law firm as the client.

Engagement letters for investigations differ in several respects from audit engagement letters, most notably in the treatment of liability protections for the forensic accounting firm, for example, as follows:

> *Liability limitation and indemnification.* In no event shall [name of forensic accounting firm] be liable to you or your client—whether a claim be in tort, contract, or otherwise—either for any amount in excess of the total professional fees paid pursuant to the engagement letter or any addendum to which the claim relates—or for any consequential, indirect, lost profit, or similar damages related to [name of forensic accounting firm]'s services provided under this letter of engagement except to the extent finally determined to have resulted from the willful misconduct or fraudulent behavior of [name of forensic accounting firm] related to such services.
>
> You and your client agree to indemnify and hold harmless [name of forensic accounting firm] and its personnel from any and all third-party claims, liabilities, costs, and expenses related to services [name of forensic accounting firm] renders under this engagement letter except to the extent finally determined to have resulted from the willful misconduct or fraudulent behavior of [name of forensic accounting firm] related to such services.

While this contract provision is not allowed by the U.S. Securities and Exchange Commission for purposes of performing an audit, it is an important provision in a financial investigation. For audit services, the auditing firm determines the scope of the engagement in keeping with regulatory and professional standards, industry norms, and its own professional judgment. The company turns over its financial statements and supporting documentation, books, and records and allows interviews of its employees, observations of assets, and inquiries of third parties by the auditor. In the event of an undue attempt by management to restrict the scope of the audit, the auditor may modify the audit report (scope limitation) or resign the engagement.

Matters differ for forensic accounting investigators. While investigators certainly make recommendations as to scope and procedures, they are essentially working at the direction of others. The client is responsible for conducting the investigation, and the forensic accounting investigator is, so to speak, a tool at the client's disposal. The provision discussed earlier is intended to protect the forensic accounting investigator from claims that an investigation was not properly performed or that individuals were harmed as a result of the investigation.

Given the sensitivity of the issues covered in the engagement letter, you may now agree more fully than at the beginning of this discussion that it is best to have a signed engagement letter before setting to work.

◆ RELATIONSHIP REVIEW

Most firms that provide forensic accounting services have their own procedures for performing a relationship review, or conflicts check, that is, identifying relationships that the firm may have had or now has with any of the parties involved. The points reviewed and documented may well include the following:

- The date on which the relationship review was cleared
- The individual who cleared it
- Notations of pertinent discussions in clearing current and prior relationships
- The date on which the assignment was accepted

In order for forensic accounting investigators to become familiar with a specific company or situation, they may perform some background research such as checking the Internet, performing a public records search, obtaining a Dun & Bradstreet report, and searching various fee-based data bases. However, no investigative work of substance should begin before the relationship check has cleared. Identifying a conflicting relationship that may preclude a firm from accepting the assignment after work has begun reflects negatively on the practitioner, the firm, and even the client, especially if court-imposed deadlines—such as deadlines for naming experts—have passed.

◆ SUBSTANTIVE WORKING PAPERS

Depending on the assignment, substantive working papers in either hard copy or electronic form may include many different items. If the work is being performed under privilege (see Chapter 24), all working papers should be clearly marked to that effect.

The practitioner should endeavor to prepare working papers as though a third party or regulatory authority may seek to review them. It is not the task of the forensic accounting investigator to assert the privilege or contest subpoenas; the forensic accounting investigator's task is to maintain its viability of privilege should counsel decide to assert it and likewise to advise counsel if subpoenas are received so counsel can decide whether to contest them. Exhibit 23.2 is an example of a working paper clearly marked with the designation "Privileged, Attorney Work Product" to help identify it as a privileged communication.

◆ EACH WORKING PAPER SHOULD STAND ON ITS OWN

Any working papers created by the engagement team should be clearly marked to indicate the name of the creator, the date, the source of information, the information's classification, and the issue addressed. Such working papers should also be secured so as to ensure that only members of the immediate engagement team have access to them. Certain matters will require the forensic accounting investigators to prove that they have used reasonable means to secure from others the working papers and other evidence. In such matters, custody can be

Check Number	Amount	Check Date	Vendor Number	Full Name
394795	$56,117.80	5/4/2000	3D SYSTEMS	Johnson Safeguarding
400341	$56,117.80	6/29/2000	3D SYSTEMS	Johnson Safeguarding
401256	$56,117.80	7/27/2000		Johnson Safeguarding
402004	$56,117.80	8/30/2000		Johnson Safeguarding
393821	$15,545.00	1/3/2000		Reed Diagnostics
394002	$15,545.00	2/6/2000		Reed Diagnostics
394211	$15,545.00	3/8/2000		Reed Diagnostics
394526	$15,545.00	4/4/2000		Reed Diagnostics
394701	$15,545.00	5/2/2000		Reed Diagnostics

Attorney Work Product
DRAFT - Tentative and Preliminary
Privileged and Confidential

EXHIBIT 23.2   PRIVILEGED WORK PRODUCT

proved by ensuring that working papers be kept in a secure room with a sign-in sheet for all who have access to the room.

If a working paper was prepared by the client, it should be so designated, usually by the initials *PBC* (for *prepared by client*). If the purpose of a working paper is not evident upon inspection, a simple note of explanation should suffice. The purpose of a complete set of working papers, as noted earlier in the chapter, is to document the forensic accounting investigator's work, which should be planned and performed in the expectation that a report will be issued at the conclusion of the engagement even if not specifically requested at the outset.

Numerical amounts or other relevant data should be cross-referenced using the to/from format. The cross-reference on the left should indicate where the number is coming from—for example, an invoice—and the right cross-reference should indicate where it is going to—for example, another schedule or the Report of Investigation. Working papers using this format will tend to have an even flow, such that an independent reviewer will have little difficulty in understanding the nature of support for the conclusions ultimately reached.

Many of the preceding observations have made clear that working papers should be prepared in such a way that they are understandable to an independent reviewer. It is important from an efficiency perspective to consider that the purpose of the working paper is to document procedures performed and conclusions reached. Neatness, while desirable, is not an end in itself; if it is understandable, then it is acceptable. The most efficient method to make corrections should be used. In many instances that method will entail simply writing on it. Redoing the entire working paper may be unnecessary. Working papers need not be typed or formal. They are intended to document your work. That is all. If the document you create is clear, accurate, and readable, it qualifies as a working paper.

◆ TESTIMONY BINDER

A forensic accounting investigator may be called upon to testify at a deposition. Depending on the complexity of the matter, you might consider preparing what is called a testimony binder to assist in your preparation for the deposition. This is a matter to be discussed with counsel prior to the deposition. Many find it helpful to refer to certain key documents when discussing their procedures and findings in the deposition.

◆ INTERVIEW MEMORANDUMS

Documenting an interview is critical. If later evidence proves that the interviewer was inaccurate even on a seemingly insignificant aspect of the interview, the credibility of the Interview Memorandum may be called into doubt. Most experts advise against recording the interview in a question-and-answer format, because the format itself suggests a greater degree of accuracy than is usually necessary. You do not want to give the impression that it is a transcript. However, it may be useful for certain key responses as a means of providing appropriate emphasis and clarity. Exhibit 23.3 samples the opening section of an Interview Memorandum.

Duration: Approximately 2 hours
Interviewers: Bill Peters and Sulaksh Godrej
Location: Conference Rm 8-F, Lab Building, Chicago

Date: October 2, 2005

David has been with [the company] for 16 years and has primarily been responsible for the Chicago operations. He started with [the company] as Vice President and Treasurer and was primarily responsible for the company's consolidated financial statements. He has a staff of six accountants reporting to him. He was the President of the Chicago Division from 1992–2002, and then the CEO from 2002–2003. At present he is the CFO and Treasurer of [the parent].

Prior to joining [the company] he was with [accounting firm] from 1978 through 1985 and left one year after promotion to manager. He focused mainly on the textile industry and served on the audit team for [the company] until he was offered to join [the company] in 1989 as controller of the Chicago Division. He is an accounting graduate of Notre Dame, having passed the CPA exam on his first sitting in 1979. He is married and has two young children. His wife is not employed outside the home.

EXHIBIT 23.3 INTERVIEW MEMORANDUM: OPENING SECTION

Interviewers' impressions of the witness's behavioral characteristics are appropriate. Exhibit 23.4 offers an example of this type of reporting and shows as well how the question-and-answer format can be used effectively for emphasis.

The sequence of the interview is best structured either by time or by topic. Exhibit 23.5 is an example of the witness's responses grouped by area of interest.

David was very defensive and adversarial throughout the interview. When he almost walked out of the interview at the very beginning of the questioning, Tom asked him:

> **Q:** Are you telling us that you are refusing to cooperate with this investigation; with the management of [the company]?
>
> **A:** All I am saying is I am not going to sit here and answer all your questions. I am a director and shareholder of this company and I will deal with the management directly. I want copies of your report and other supporting documents and I will address your concerns with the management.

He almost walked out of the interview more than once.

Throughout the entire interview, every time he was asked a question about a sticky point, before giving the answer he asked if we had an e-mail on the topic. The entire interview was a game of "Ask me the right question and I'll answer it"—which he did not. Toward the end of the interview I told him that he treated this as a deposition when all I wanted was his help. He repeatedly said he would help, but he never told me anything I did not already know. Nothing. He insisted that he did, but when asked for one example, he could not come up with anything and eventually responded by saying, "Just read his notes," and pointed to my cointerviewer.

Exhibit 23.4   Interview Memorandum: A Defensive Interviewee

- He understood the FCPA and was not aware of any payments made to government officials anywhere.
- Bribes to General in Thailand—Asked him several times about FCPA violations, specifically bribes. He denied any knowledge. After referring to the Southeast Asian business, I asked him again, and he said no. Then I showed him the e-mail. Asked if he remembered it. He reluctantly said, "Vaguely."
- Cuba—Before showing him the series of e-mails, he was emphatic that he knew nothing about any sales to Cuba. When I showed him the series of three e-mails, he still maintained that he had heard nothing about such a venture but then began to speculate about what probably happened: "Well, what I think is happening here is that Jon came up with an idea, which he often does, and then they all kicked it around." I said I did not wish to speculate about what might have happened, only tell me what he recalls. He recalled nothing about Cuba. Interestingly, he was prepared to walk out of the room until I said I had some questions about sales to Cuba. He then said, "All right, let me get some paper," whereupon he did so and returned. He took notes during the remainder of the interview.

Exhibit 23.5   Interview Memorandum: Recording by Topic

CHAPTER 24

WORKING WITH ATTORNEYS

Thomas W. Golden

Michael T. Dyer

Sonya Andreassen

When matters arise at a company that require investigation, in-house or outside counsel often participate in or direct an investigation. The forensic accounting investigator often works with such counsel. That relationship is the subject of this chapter.

◆ IN THE COMPANY OF LAWYERS

The first person to be contacted when there is a suspected fraud is typically in-house counsel. Depending on the apparent severity of the matter and its apparent location in the company, other internal resources to be alerted at an early stage, in addition to the board typically through its audit committee, may include corporate security, internal audit, risk management, the controller's office, and the public relations and investor relations groups. Investigations usually begin with extensive conversation about who should be involved, and the responsible executives may naturally wish to involve some or all of the functions just mentioned.

Depending on the circumstances, the group of internal auditors can in fact be a tremendous asset to an independent forensic investigative team. As participants in the larger team, internal auditors' knowledge of the company may improve both the efficiency with which evidence is gathered and the forensic team's effectiveness in lining up interviews and analyzing findings. Our advice to client executives and in-house counsel is to engage an external team but to consider making available to that team the company's internal auditors and other internal resources for any investigation of substantial size.

Forensic accounting investigators can expect to work with or for attorneys in a number of circumstances, including:

- Internal investigations with respect to accounting or reporting matters, generally triggered by:
  - Anonymous tips

- ○ Audit committee concerns
- ○ Internal audit concerns
- ○ External auditor findings
- ○ Media or regulatory reports or communications

- Regulatory investigations such as investigations by the U.S. Securities and Exchange Commission (SEC)

- Tax authority subpoenas or inquiries

- Civil litigation such as contract issues, shareholder lawsuits, wrongful-termination claims, and fraud recovery actions

The number and kinds of attorneys are broad and varied. The forensic accounting investigator may work with the general counsel for the company; SEC counsel; special independent (external) counsel to the board of directors or the audit committee, often referred to as 10A counsel[1]; attorneys for specific board or audit committee members; counsel for specific employees or groups of employees[2]; civil or criminal counsel; counsel for personnel who may be under suspicion or who hope to avoid that unwanted designation; and still others. The attorneys may be positioned as your client's adversary or your client's advocate, or they may be positioned as independent, as in the role of 10A counsel. It would not be at all unusual to have attorney representation of the following groups in a typical 10A investigation:

- The audit committee of the board of directors

- The company, defending against a potential SEC enforcement action or a U.S. Department of Justice (DOJ) indictment

- Officers or employees of the company, especially those named as "subjects" or "targets" enforcement actions or investigations. Each could have separate counsel.

Each attorney serving a client in this roster generally has varying interests to protect, timetables to work against, and different views as to the significance of specific documents, interviews, and theories. The forensic accounting investigator should keep in mind these varying perspectives throughout the investigation in order to avoid unintentional sharing of privileged information, loss of confidential points of strategy, and the like.[3] While lawyers must adhere to ethical and legal guidelines, it is possible to communicate information accidentally,

---

1. See fn. 6 in Chapter 12 regarding 10A and its reference to independent counsel, auditors, and other advisers.
2. This is frequently the case for individuals who are expected to be interviewed.
3. The issue of *privilege* is a matter best considered by counsel. The comments expressed in this chapter do not represent legal advice, and are based on the personal experiences of its authors, who are not attorneys. Privilege issues vary by jurisdiction and it would not be surprising to find differing views among equally competent counsel regarding what constitutes *privileged material*, or if privilege even exists. Seek competent legal counsel on this issue.

especially when working in physical proximity or with the same documents and personnel.

◆ CONFIDENTIALITY REQUIREMENTS

A potentially material overstatement of asset values or understatement of liabilities is often the focus of investigation, and there may be an urgent need to inform stakeholders and markets that previously published financial statements may be unreliable. The extent of the problem should be determined and corrective action taken. In that scenario, a multitude of questions often swirl around the company: Was the misstatement deliberate? Who knew or should have known of the misstatement? What needs to be done?

In such investigations, confidentiality is usually very important. Leaks of information to the press or competitors may be particularly damaging. If the investigation is to be successful in uncovering the facts, the number of people within the company who are aware of day-to-day developments should be properly limited to avoid such leaks. The company may, however, voluntarily disclose information to regulators during such investigations. On occasion, the forensic accounting investigator may become involved in an external investigation in support of various law enforcement or government organizations such as the SEC, the DOJ, the Federal Bureau of Investigation, the Internal Revenue Service (IRS), or even state or local prosecutors. This can come about in a variety of ways but typically occurs when the forensic accounting investigator's client has decided to refer the matter for prosecution and offers the forensic accounting investigator's assistance to the investigating agency. In such situations, attorneys for the government may find it useful to seek a 6(e) designation for the forensic accounting investigator. That designation grants the forensic accounting investigator access to grand jury or subpoenaed documents; forensic accounting investigators do not have subpoena powers, but they can review documents obtained through subpoena if working under a 6(e) order. While access to such information can be very helpful to the investigation, a 6(e) designation may require some modifications to the investigation process, which should be discussed with the investigating team, including counsel. When retained in such instances, the forensic accounting investigator should have a thorough initial discussion with counsel and the government agency to ensure that the ground rules are understood and that the forensic team is fully aware of required modifications to the investigation process or methods. Later in this chapter, we return in more detail to the topic of working with law enforcement or government organizations.

◆ FORMING THE INVESTIGATIVE TEAM

Forensic accounting investigators are frequently called upon to investigate potential financial statement manipulations or misstatements and asset misappropriations. For purposes of this discussion, we refer to such engagements as internal accounting investigations. When investigating asset misappropriation, the forensic accounting investigator may be engaged by the general counsel of a company or by the outside attorney who represents the company.

The forensic accounting investigator conducting an asset misappropriation investigation typically receives excellent cooperation from company executives, who perceive themselves and the company as the victim. Experience has shown, however, that an investigation focused on asset misappropriation may produce evidence suggesting other schemes, in which the company may have been benefiting from illegal acts. Once the forensic accounting investigator picks up on a loose thread and follows it, there often is no telling where it might lead.

When potentially material accounting irregularities—or allegations of potentially material fraud—come to its attention, the board of directors typically seeks the advice of counsel on a number of considerations that may include the following:

- Identification of an independent committee—generally a subset of the board of directors and typically the audit committee—to lead the investigation and determine the company's approach[4]
- Initial communications with stakeholders, including employees, the market, stockholders, bondholders, lenders, and regulators
- Formation of an investigative team, generally through retention of appropriate counsel and other experts such as forensic accounting investigators and other specialists
- Urgent personnel decisions such as arranging for paid leave, restriction of duties or access, and termination
- Data stabilization and security to avoid any loss of critical information
- Notification of insurance providers at the company and board levels

The investigating team often includes:

- ○ Independent counsel
- ○ Forensic accounting investigators
- ○ Forensic technology experts
- ○ External auditor partner and key staff
- Based on the specifics of the investigation, the team may include other experts or specialists such as:
- ○ Engineers
- ○ Actuaries
- ○ Tax experts
- ○ Investment bankers

---

4. It is important to recognize that it is the responsibility of the company to conduct a thorough investigation, especially in any matter that may be material to the financial statements. Whatever authority the forensic accountant has in the conduct of the investigation, it is not the forensic accountant's investigation; it is the company's. This does not, however, release forensic accountants from the ethical obligations and rules required by their professional associations, such as the American Institute of Certified Public Accountants and the Association of Certified Fraud Examiners.

- o Valuation or appraisal specialists
- o Damages experts

How involved will the attorney be in the planning and execution of the investigation? On one hand, the forensic accounting investigator may find that the attorney gives the forensic accounting investigator free rein to devise and execute a strategic investigative plan, subject to the attorney's approval. That scenario is particularly likely in cases of asset misappropriation. On the other hand, some attorneys insist on being involved in all phases of the investigation. It is the attorney's call. When engaged by counsel, forensic accounting investigators take direction from counsel. They should advise according to their best judgment, but in the end they work at counsel's direction.[5]

Forensic accounting investigators bring a special skill set, perspective, and experience to the internal accounting investigation, complementary to the skills of auditors, counsel, and other experts typically involved in these investigations. Capable forensic accounting investigators can be found within most large accounting firms as well as in boutique, or specialist, firms. Whether approached by counsel or directly by the company to participate in an internal accounting investigation, forensic accounting investigators should immediately assess their independence (see Chapter 6 and a later section of this chapter). Once independence has been determined and forensic accounting investigators have been retained, those investigators should obtain a thorough understanding of the respective roles and responsibilities of the various team members to allow for efficient and effective coordination across the team. Failure to clearly establish and fulfill roles and responsibilities may lead to wasted time and money—or worse, to gaps in the investigation process and incomplete or inaccurate results. These shortcomings may reduce the value of the investigation and may even subject the company and its officers and directors to adverse publicity or liability.

While it usually is easy enough in theory to delineate the team members' responsibilities and to set up procedures that ensure communication across the team, it often is much more difficult to accomplish those things in practice. Forensic investigations are often conducted in a crisis atmosphere that disturbs communication and allows duplication in the investigative process to slip through. In spite of deadline pressure and extensive work to be performed, time must be found to coordinate and share the information being obtained. When working with attorneys, forensic accounting investigators should specifically understand:

- Their expected role and responsibilities vis-à-vis other team members
- What other professionals are involved (current or contemplated)
- The extent and source of any external scrutiny (SEC, IRS, DOJ, and so on)

---

5. Quite obviously, forensic accountant investigators should ensure that they are performing the investigation in compliance with the discipline's own professional standards of conduct, and they should resign if placed in a compromising position.

- Any legal considerations (extent of privilege, expectation that the company intends to waive privilege, expectation of criminal charges, and so on)
- Anticipated timing issues, if any
- Expected form, timing, and audience of interim or final deliverables
- Specifics of the matters under investigation, as currently understood by counsel
- Any limitations on departments or personnel that can be involved, interviewed, or utilized in the investigation process

As noted at the beginning of this chapter, prudent forensic accounting investigators typically perform their assignment under the presumption that any deliverables, work product, or work process may become publicly available or accessed and utilized in civil or criminal litigation proceedings. That being said, when a company employs an attorney to represent it, the attorney's work product usually cannot be subpoenaed. Attorneys enjoy a number of privileges that are necessary to ensure that their client can be completely honest with them without fear of disclosure. The forensic accounting investigator who is employed directly by the attorney is considered an extension of the attorney, and the forensic accounting investigator's work product may be protected from subpoena, unless the adverse party in litigation can prove, among other things, that there has been a "waiver of the privilege." If work product or other privileged information is intentionally shared with individuals outside the privileged group, the privilege may be lost.

The forensic accounting investigator should be careful to protect the privilege and should mark each and every individual document prepared with the caption "Privileged and Confidential—Attorney Work Product" or words to that effect. This caption serves as a reminder and notice that the documents are privileged and not subject to subpoena or discovery. In practice, it is true that the privilege may be waived by the company and that the forensic accounting investigator's spreadsheets, documents, and other working papers, as well as testimony, will be volunteered or subject to subpoena. It should also be understood that privilege is a jurisdictional issue and decisions can fall either way. However, when privilege is contemplated, it is still good practice to mark all documents with the privilege disclosure, so that they can be readily identified as privileged later on. It also makes it easy to determine documents prepared by the forensic accounting investigator as opposed to ones prepared by client staff.

Independent counsel, with the help of forensic accounting investigators, often takes the lead in setting up, organizing, and managing the investigative team. This process may include the selection and retention of other parties who make up the team. Independent counsel's responsibilities typically encompass the following:

- Preparing, maintaining, and disseminating a working-group list (very helpful in sorting out which law firms or experts represent whom)
- Establishing the timetable in conjunction with the board of directors or management, disseminating the timetable to the investigating team, and tracking progress against it

- Compiling, submitting, and tracking the various document and personnel access requests that the investigating team members will generate
- Organizing client or team meetings and agendas
- Preparing the final report with or for the board or its special committee, or doing so in conjunction with other teams from which reports are forthcoming
- Establishing and maintaining communication channels with the board of directors and other interested parties, generally including internal general counsel, company management, regulatory personnel, law enforcement or tax authority personnel, and various other attorneys involved

Although the attorney may lead the investigation formally, the forensic accounting investigator frequently is the cornerstone of a successful investigating team. The forensic accounting investigator may provide the following types of assistance and support for the larger team directed by the attorney:

- Ability to plan and conduct a proper financial crime investigation
- Expertise in accounting, in regulatory (such as SEC) auditing, in internal controls, and in financial analysis
- Interviewing skills, both fact-finding from witnesses and admission seeking from targets
- Expertise in performing data mining and data interrogation of the company's books and records, including e-mail
- Experience in document authentication and knowledge of a network of subspecialists trained in highly technical authentication procedures such as typewriter/printer analysis and authentication through forensic laboratory science
- Ability to review and interpret internal accounting transactions and their compliance with various rules
- Ability to accumulate public financial and nonfinancial information, including SEC or company registry filings, if applicable
- Forensic imaging and other information technology (IT) expertise such as e-mail search tools
- Support of counsel in developing various hypotheses and investigative procedures and techniques
- Background checks on relevant personnel
- Vendor validity checks on the basis of publicly available information
- Preparation of specific sections of the draft and final reports or support of counsel for report sections that focus on accounting, reporting, or financial information
- Coordination with both internal and external auditors and the audit committee
- Review and critique of financial, accounting, or reporting analysis and advice provided by other specialists

- Among larger firms, a global network of investigators to assist in multinational investigations

Particularly when investigations include review and analysis of accounting and financial information, the forensic accounting investigator is often a critical member of the team. Some attorneys do not have extensive accounting or auditing experience, and certain accounting concepts may be foreign to them. In a recent investigation, counsel contacted the forensic accounting investigators as the final draft of the report was being prepared because counsel was uncertain about the concept of a "reserve"—its significance and how to explain it in the report. The forensic team gave an instant tutorial on how reserves can be manipulated and then helped draft the relevant section. In another instance, counsel coordinated interview schedules with the forensic accounting team to ensure that an experienced SEC accounting specialist was available to participate with counsel in the interview of the company's controller and chief financial officer (CFO). The SEC specialist's participation turned out to be critical because the interview agenda included discussion of the adoption of two new accounting rules as well as discussion of the extent to which the external auditor was familiar with the new rules.

Forensic accounting investigators are frequently conversant in areas related to financial accounting and reporting such as valuation, tax, and financial aspects of human resource management, but "conversant" does not necessarily indicate a sufficient level of knowledge to guide a complex investigation. For complex investigations or investigations that involve public companies, it is often wise for the lead forensic accounting investigator to assemble a team that includes the following skills and experience:

- Ability to conduct or assist with the investigation
- Knowledge with respect to generally accepted accounting principles relevant to the applicable time period of the investigation
- Knowledge with respect to SEC-compliant accounting, financial disclosure, and other reporting
- Familiarity with the regulatory investigative process
- Knowledge with respect to generally accepted auditing standards and procedures
- Ability to immediately access industry or specialist knowledge as required—for example, expertise in derivative financial instruments, bank regulation requirements, and long-term contract accounting
- Familiarity with the uses and abuses of offshore companies and trusts
- Ability to identify departures from customary commercial behavior and business practices
- Relevant language skills and ability to meet the challenges of a geographically diverse investigation, as required

Each of the foregoing skills represents an area in which independent counsel frequently requires guidance and support by the forensic accounting investigator.

While forensic accounting investigators often are critical components of an effective internal accounting investigation, it is important to remember that they are engaged as fact finders. Forensic accounting investigators may need to educate or remind counsel about the limitations of the forensic accounting investigator's expertise and scope of service. In particular, the forensic accounting investigator should take care to avoid:

- Providing legal advice or making legal assertions in their work or deliverables
- Providing actuarial or valuation guidance unless appropriately credentialed and trained
- Acting as a judge or jury by making judgments as to the guilt or innocence of particular people or groups
- Expressing an audit opinion on financial statements or internal control effectiveness. Note, however, that commenting on specific elements of financial statements is entirely appropriate and can be legitimately expected of forensic accounting investigators with accounting and auditing experience.[6]
- Creating legal exposure as a result of comments that may lead to claims of defamation, libel, slander, and the like

On occasion, the forensic accounting investigator may need to remind staff, other parties, and counsel of those limitations.

The board or special committee of the board, in conjunction with counsel, frequently issues a written report following an internal investigation, especially if the focus of investigation is a public company. The report may include work performed or evidence reviewed by the forensic accounting investigator, sometimes with an explicit reference to the forensic accounting investigator. For example, a report of the Special Investigative Committee of the Board of Directors of Enron Corp.,[7] prepared by counsel, exceeded 200 pages and specifically referred to a major accounting firm that had been engaged to provide accounting advice. In other instances, the various experts involved in an investigation issue separate, stand-alone reports. As previously mentioned, the forensic accounting investigator should discuss the form, timing, and audience of all final deliverables early in the process to avoid confusion, unnecessary work, or misunderstandings.

◆ DOCUMENTATION

Owing to the presumption that an internal investigation may result in or ultimately contribute to litigation, appropriate documentation practices are critical. Generally, the documents reviewed by the forensic accounting investigator in both print and electronic formats will come from the following sources.

---

6. As discussed in Chapter 7, it would be wrong to assume that all forensic accountants have accounting, auditing, and/or SEC regulatory experience. Intensive interviews of potential financial experts are critical to assembling the right investigative team.

7. Special Investigative Committee of the Board of Directors of Enron Corp. (William C. Powers Jr., chair), *Report of Investigation, February 1, 2002* (Austin, Tex.: Enron, 2002), http://www.loc.gov/law/guide/enron.html.

- Public information, including SEC filings, press releases, analyst reports, background checks, and Internet searches
- Documents provided by the company—voluntarily, for most internal investigations
- Legal documents and filings available to counsel
- Accounting records provided by the company
- Information from the external auditor

Information critical to forming conclusions that support remedial actions may also emerge from interviews with key company personnel and possibly other parties.

Document volume and complexity will be driven in large part by the scope and duration of the investigation. Regardless of the volume, it is incumbent upon the investigating team to track, organize, disseminate, and control the documents. Counsel often assumes primary responsibility for document management and gives instructions to other team members. Counsel may establish an indexing process via Bates numbers, may establish imaging or warehouse storage, and may assume primary responsibility for providing for all relevant members of the team the documents and data files obtained. It is important for the forensic accounting investigator to conform to these practices. Proper communication at the outset may prevent misunderstandings.

Although many documents and data files typically will be provided directly for counsel by company personnel, forensic accounting investigators are likely to receive many financial, accounting, or reporting documents and data files directly from company personnel. The forensic accounting investigator should establish procedures for sharing any such documents with the rest of the investigative team and for accurately cataloging and tracking them according to source, date received, investigation topic, and so forth. This approach often is especially useful when the time comes to write the report or to respond to questions after the fact. Consistent with the process used in an external audit, the forensic accounting investigator should prepare and retain sufficient documentation to support any reports, memorandums, or other deliverables issued. When documents are to be presented to third parties, duplicate copies are essential: one for distribution as requested, one for counsel, and one for the forensic accounting investigator's records. It is not enough simply to make a note as to what documents have been issued. Avoid all possible confusion by making a copy of the document supplied and filing it separately. This system is especially helpful when the investigative team is preparing for depositions or trial and has to know exactly what documents and files are in the opposing lawyer's possession. It takes extra time to follow this procedure, and it creates a much larger document cache, but the effort is well worthwhile. As noted in the previous chapter, we encourage early discussion with counsel regarding document retention.

◆ CIVIL LITIGATION

If civil litigation is ongoing, the investigating team can utilize the discovery process to gain access to various types of personal information from the charged individuals not typically available to the team in the normal course of most investigations, including:

- Financial records
- Bank statements and account information
- Tax returns
- Asset ownership details
- Purchase, sale, and investment documentation
- Travel records or other data of interest to the investigation

In many investigations it is extremely helpful to learn whether the target has sources of income that cannot be explained. How to go about this? Courteously asking the individual to produce bank statements is usually unlikely to result in the individual's compliance with the request, and from a strategic perspective, you will have tipped off the target that an investigation is under way. The target may also decide to document for you only accounts that show benign and perfectly normal transactions.

◆ INTERVIEWING

While this topic is covered extensively in Chapter 18, a few points should be summarized here about working with attorneys. It is not an uncommon practice for the investigating team to conduct a large number of interviews. Interviewing is a valuable tool in understanding an organization and individual roles, responsibilities, and perspectives. Interviews may extend beyond company personnel to include suppliers, customers, legal counsel, business partners, ex-employees, and still others.

When the investigation includes accounting issues, interviews typically encompass accounting and reporting personnel, management with responsibilities for the financial statements, the internal audit department, audit committee members and staff, external auditors, and perhaps others. The background and expertise of the forensic accounting investigator often are well suited to support counsel during these interviews. Unlike external investigations conducted by the SEC, DOJ, or IRS, internal investigations face a number of limitations, including:

- *Lack of subpoena power.* Interviews are voluntary, and the person being interviewed can walk away at any time.
- *Testimony not under oath.* The individuals being interviewed are not under oath to tell the truth, but lying to the forensic accountant may trigger liability under statutes that preclude such conduct.
- *Interviews that are more informal than depositions.* The output consists simply of interview notes taken by counsel or others participating.

- *Interviews that rely on the cooperation and availability of the interviewee.* Continuing employment is usually enough of a motivator to compel an interviewee to talk with you.

◆ EXTERNAL AUDIT FIRM

Before accepting a forensic accounting investigation engagement, the forensic accounting investigator should assess whether there are independence issues that disallow the engagement or limit its scope. Although this topic is discussed in detail in Chapter 6, it is worthwhile to summarize the general guidelines here.

While it is true that one of the goals of the Sarbanes-Oxley Act is to mitigate independence concerns by identifying services that the external auditing firm is precluded from performing for audit clients, Congress did not want to restrict audit committees from engaging those professionals whom such committees regard as fully competent to perform investigations into allegations of financial improprieties. It may be entirely appropriate to engage forensic accounting investigators from the company's external audit firm in some but not all situations. The decision to utilize or to refrain from utilizing the external auditor firm to investigate allegations of fraud usually depends on several key factors, discussed later. When an audit committee is made aware of indicia of fraud or even the slightest suspicion of fraud, it usually wants answers fast. Assembling a competent investigative team to fulfill the board's responsibilities as quickly as possible is generally a high priority. In some cases, the quickest way to find valid answers to the questions asked by the company's directors is to bring in forensic accounting specialists from the external audit firm. Are the allegations true? And if they are true:

- What are the financial implications?
- Who is involved in the alleged improper act?
- How significant and pervasive is it?
- How did it occur and go undetected until this time?
- What actions need to be taken to remediate the system of internal controls so that this does not happen again?
- Are we vulnerable in any other areas?

Those who would argue for a forensic accounting team from a firm other than the external auditors do so for reasons other than Sarbanes-Oxley, because Sarbanes-Oxley specifically allows for this. There may be a belief that the auditing firm cannot be independent; however, it has already been established that the external public auditing firm is independent: under no other circumstances could it perform the audit. There may be a belief that engaging the external audit firm would generate a conflict of interest. This may in fact be a valid concern—for reasons explored in Chapter 6. If there is a conflict, the appearance of objectivity may be impaired. When there is a concern that the allegation may lead to a potential restatement of the financial statements, a conflict of interest is entirely possible. In that case, a forensic team independent of the external auditor would need to be retained—probably by counsel.

During a 10A investigation, counsel may be assisted by an independent forensic team. It is possible that the audit firm will deploy its own group of forensic accounting investigators in a specialist role, consulting with the audit team. The group will shadow the investigation conducted by company's counsel to aid in bringing the investigation expeditiously to completion. This is not to imply that the audit team should in any way instruct the 10A investigative team on procedures that should be performed. It is the audit committee's investigation. However, close and timely communication between the investigative team and the auditors is a good way to ensure that all parties, including the auditors, are comfortable that the investigation was conducted in an appropriate fashion and that findings were communicated to the auditors timely enough for them to react to the findings appropriately. Absent this level of cooperation, the auditors would not be informed of the investigative team's findings until communicated by the investigative team to the audit committee and therefore could not begin their independent review of the support or bases for conclusions reached until subsequent to that communication. Alternatively, audit committees may retain a forensic accounting team from the company's auditing firm to investigate, provided—as prescribed by SEC rules—that no regulatory proceeding or investigation has been initiated.

Under both scenarios (the audit firm's forensic team is engaged or the audit firm shadows a forensic team engaged from another firm), the auditor is more than likely to require attorneys leading the investigation (10A counsel), on behalf of the company, to disclose the investigative findings and supporting evidence. The auditor will be well-advised to inform the audit committee and its counsel in advance that the auditor needs to be kept fully informed. Notifying in this way may avoid difficulties at the conclusion of the investigation, which could delay the timely filing of SEC reports.

If a formal proceeding is initiated or the company is notified that it is the subject or target of an investigation by an enforcement agency such as the DOJ, the company should consider engaging a forensic accounting team independent of the auditing firm. It is still likely that the audit firm's forensic accounting investigators will shadow the investigation for reasons mentioned earlier. The findings of that shadow team may be shared with the company and its counsel. Duplication of efforts may be avoided or at least somewhat mitigated in this manner. For example, e-mails can be reviewed by the forensic team from the auditing firm and findings communicated to 10A or other counsel at the company's direction. However, certain limitations would need to be well understood and respected. The auditing firm may not, for example, provide litigation support, a service specifically precluded by the Sarbanes-Oxley Act when a regulatory proceeding is under way.

Most auditing firms take the view that counsel appointed to conduct a 10A investigation must be independent of the company. This requirement does not mean that counsel is not permitted to have ever worked for the company before, but attorneys playing this role cannot be drawn from the company's law firm of choice for prior litigation. Similarly, while knowing that it will shortly act as an advocate for the company in any enforcement action, 10A counsel cannot be expected to render an objective opinion on the possibility that an illegal act has been committed. Also, a forensic accounting team selected to support the company's legal defense must likewise be independent of the forensic accounting team that assists 10A counsel. These are obviously intricate issues—with extended implications concerning who can do what while remaining strictly within regulatory guidelines.

It is possible to make available certain of the auditor's working papers to the forensic accounting investigators assisting either 10A counsel or the company's defense counsel. This may be accomplished through an access letter.

Before permitting access to the working papers, the incumbent accountant may wish to obtain a written communication from the firm providing forensic accounting investigative assistance regarding the use of the working papers. These letters are not required by professional standards but certainly make good business sense. Why give voluntary access to a party that may later use what it finds as a basis to bring a claim against you?

Even with the client's consent, access to the incumbent accountant's working papers may still be limited. Experience has shown that the incumbent accountant may be willing to grant broader access if given additional assurance concerning the use of the working papers. Accordingly, the forensic accountant might consider agreeing to the following limitations on the review of the incumbent accountant's working papers in order to obtain broader access:

> Because your review of our working papers is undertaken solely for the purpose described above and may not entail a review of all of our working papers, you agree that (1) the information obtained from the review will not be used by you for any other purpose; (2) you will not comment, orally or in writing, to anyone as a result of that review about whether our engagement was performed in accordance with Statements on Auditing Standards; (3) you will not provide expert testimony or litigation services or otherwise accept an engagement to comment on issues related to the quality of our engagement.[8]

Such letters will likely enable the recipients to review by sight only selected working papers. The access letters should restrict the use of the information and prevent both counsel and the independent forensic accounting team from assisting the company in any action against the audit firm.

---

8. American Institute of Certified Public Accountants, www.aicpa.org/download/members/div/auditstd/Illustrative_Successor_Accountant_Acknowledgment_Letter.pdf.

◆ WORKING FOR OR INTERACTING WITH LAW ENFORCEMENT OR GOVERNMENT AGENCIES

In the course of a forensic accounting investigation, the forensic accounting investigator often encounters law enforcement agents and prosecutors. Both will inevitably ask for information concerning the progress or results of the forensic accounting investigation. The forensic accounting investigator should determine from the client—and often, client's counsel—what information the client wishes to turn over voluntarily. The client may decide it is advantageous to assist the prosecutor and may wish forensic accounting investigators to assist the prosecutor by turning over the results of their investigation, sharing information, or conducting additional investigation procedures as requested by the prosecutor. However, investigation processes often become more complex if the prosecutor makes grand jury material available to forensic accounting investigators for review.

Grand jury rules vary depending on whether it is a state or federal grand jury, but there are broad similarities. The grand jury conducts an investigation to determine whether there is sufficient evidence to indict. The prosecutor drafts an indictment, and the grand jury votes as to whether the evidence reviewed is adequate to support the indictment. Grand jury materials and information are confidential, and criminal and civil penalties are imposed for grand jury secrecy violations. However, the prosecutor may turn over subpoenaed information to authorized individuals, including law enforcement. Grand jury material may be shared with other individuals in some circumstances in order to obtain information that furthers its investigation. Normally, an administrative process lists everyone who is authorized to access grand jury material. That list is detailed and precise, and only those listed are granted access.

If the prosecutor has requested that the forensic accounting investigator review documents obtained by the grand jury and if the client has agreed to such an arrangement, an interesting situation is created. The client is paying the fees of the forensic accounting investigator, but the forensic accounting investigator will in most instances be barred from giving any of the new information to the client. The client must be content that assisting the prosecutor corresponds to also assisting itself, even though that client will have no knowledge of the information to which the forensic accounting investigator now has access. When authorized to work with grand jury material, the forensic accounting investigator must make sure that the client understands the restrictions. The forensic accounting investigator must also (1) discuss in detail with the prosecutor how to ensure that there be no violation of the rules of access and (2) keep an open line of communication with the prosecutor for inquiries as to whether said accountant's actions fit within the rules.

In some instances, state and federal prosecutors have hired forensic accounting investigators to conduct entire investigations, generally in situations in which the available law enforcement officers do not have the requisite resources. In such instances, the forensic accounting investigators' involvement with the grand jury may be extensive and ongoing, and those investigators will be exposed to the full range of rules governing grand jury procedures and documents: the access rights of outsiders, the rights of subjects under interview, chain-of-evidence requirements, and the like. The forensic accounting investigators should work very closely with the prosecutor throughout the investigation and fully understand the rules and guidelines in advance.

◆ DISAGREEMENTS WITH COUNSEL

From time to time, disagreements with counsel will arise when forensic accounting investigators are shadowing a 10A investigation. They are advising the auditors as to the conduct of the investigation and likely sufficiency to satisfy the auditor's responsibilities under Section 10A of the Exchange Act. Such differences usually focus on the scope and strategy of the investigation. The authors have been fortunate to work with many bright, experienced, and informed attorneys who conduct their investigations with the expert skill and proper independent mind-set required of professionals charged with the responsibility of determining all the facts. On occasion, however, we have also found ourselves working with attorneys who are inexperienced at serving as independent 10A counsel, falling back instead on their more familiar role as client advocates playing the defense counsel role. In such situations, it is always best to try to work out your differences with counsel. Forensic accounting investigators who find they still have issues after a strenuous good-faith effort to resolve differences need to bring those differences to the attention of the directors charged with oversight of the investigation—usually, a special committee of the independent directors of the audit committee.

A recent SEC action has brought to the forefront the commission's concerns about the conduct of some investigations. SEC enforcement director Stephen Cutler said in a September 20, 2004, speech that he is "concerned" that some lawyers hired to conduct financial crime investigations might actually have helped "hide ongoing fraud, or may have taken actions to actively obstruct such investigations."

Judging by threatened enforcement actions and other communications, it appears the SEC is reviewing the quality and robustness of investigations, in which most decisions about procedures to perform and whom to interview are under the judgment of the lawyers charged with conducting the investigation. There will no doubt be more to come on this issue, but early signs from the SEC should serve as warnings to lawyers that they should conduct financial crime investigations in a rigorous and robust fashion as an expected part of doing their job. The issue of the quality of investigation will continue to evolve, as evidenced by the SEC's notification to a lawyer that he may face civil sanctions for his role in an investigation at a medical-device maker in Irvine, California. The unusual action of the SEC's suing a lawyer over allegedly mishandling a corporate probe sends the message to lawyers that they must choose between serving as defense counsel and conducting a thorough investigation as independent professionals responsible to the audit committee, which serves investors' interests.

Here are some examples to illustrate our point about selecting appropriate investigative procedures and executing them well.

- *Gathering electronic evidence:* Either electronic evidence should ideally be gathered by the forensic accounting firm's own IT specialists or those specialists should closely supervise the company's IT personnel. In addition, in some cases, forensic images should be made of hard drives and the like rather than merely copying them. And it is best to be more, rather than less, aggressive in choosing the number of personnel whose electronic data you select to examine. For example, the hard drive of a controller who has been accused by a whistle-blower of manipulating earnings is an urgent subject of forensic examination. It might be prudent to image the hard drives and examine the e-mail of some of those reporting to that controller as well as the controller's administrative assistant.

- *Interviewing:* Chapter 18 explores this complex investigative procedure in depth. The complexity of the interviewing procedure is not always understood or respected. For example, we have seen certain lawyers approach interviewing as a simple note-taking exercise: put the documents in front of the subject, and write down what the subject says in response. That is clearly the wrong way to conduct an interview in these matters. Imagine you have discovered an e-mail in which the CFO writes, "Don't tell the auditors about this transaction." Before showing this e-mail to the CFO, you would want to probe the subject through questioning: "Have you ever instructed anyone to withhold information from the auditors?" This would be just one of many questions you would ask. You want to nail this issue down *before* producing the e-mail. Yet some lawyers would begin the interview by simply handing over the e-mail and asking the CFO to explain it. That gives the CFO ample time to come up with some inane explanation for making the comment.

Consider another example. A shipping clerk says in a preliminary interview that the supervisor said to record the goods as shipped, even though the goods were still on the dock. In order to get to the bottom of the matter, the lawyer decides to interview both the clerk and the supervisor together. Not surprisingly, the shipping clerk now changes his story to agree with the supervisor's. The two should have been interviewed separately and instructed not to discuss the matter with anyone.

In situations in which you believe the lawyers are not conducting a robust enough investigation, it is wise to take your concerns directly to those charged with oversight of the investigation. It is ultimately their responsibility to ensure a thorough and proper investigation.

◆ CONCLUSION

The forensic accounting investigator can expect to work with or for attorneys in most investigations. To help ensure that the investigation progresses as smoothly as possible and reach appropriate conclusions and satisfactory resolutions, each member of the investigating team should:

- Work collaboratively within the investigative team assembled by the client: Frequent conference calls are likely to facilitate this objective.
- Communicate early and often with the team: When disagreements arise as to approach, which is not uncommon, discuss them immediately and thoroughly to reach a mutual understanding.
- Demonstrate respect and recognize the distinct expertise of the various investigative team members: Both counsel and the forensic accounting investigator have unique skill sets that may be critical to the success of the investigation. Egos should not get in the way of serving the client.
- Foster a professional, cooperative environment: "We have a job to do. Let's work together to get it done."
- Acknowledge and manage the typically high-pressure environment and the likelihood of external scrutiny.
- Understand the rules of the game in terms of documentation and reporting expectations, other parties involved, expected level of assistance from the company, 6(e) restrictions, Section 10A requirements, and so on.
- Have clearly understood roles and delineated responsibilities in an effort to minimize both duplication and gaps in the investigation process.

Generally speaking, qualified forensic accounting investigators and attorneys work well together. Many engagements end with the appreciative recognition among all team participants that cooperation and a mix of highly professional skills brought clarity and resolution.

CHAPTER 25

CONDUCTING GLOBAL INVESTIGATIONS

Frederic R. Miller

Edward J. Mizerek

Mona M. Clayton

A survey conducted by Control Risks Group, a global consulting firm, discovered that 40 percent of its respondents believe that they have lost business to competitors due to bribes.[1] The study also reported that almost 70 percent of its respondents believe that U.S. businesses use local-country middlemen to skirt the U.S. Foreign Corrupt Practices Act (FCPA).[2] If all of this is true, global business remains a good deal more hazardous than many of us would like to think. The rapidly growing volume of forensic accounting investigation engagements on an international scale testifies to the reality of the findings. Investigations of cross-border fraud schemes and other types of alleged wrongdoing have notably increased in the past five years, a trend expected to continue.

What is different and what is essentially the same when the forensic accounting team turns from domestic to global investigations? What are the opportunities and challenges? If this chapter meets its goals, it will help you understand how to hit the ground running when you are asked to participate in an investigation in a distant part of the world, and alternatively, if you are an executive or company director obliged by suspicious circumstances to engage an international forensic team, it will help you better understand how to assist that team to

---

1. Control Risks Group, *Facing up to Corruption: Survey Results* (2002), 4. Control Risks commissioned IRB Ltd. to conduct a telephone survey of business attitudes among 250 international companies based in the United Kingdom, the United States, Germany, the Netherlands, and two jurisdictions which are nonmembers of the Organization for Economic Cooperation and Development: Hong Kong and Singapore, http://www.jti.ee/en/tie/mis-on-korruptsioon/corruption_survey2002.pdf.
2. *The Foreign Corrupt Practices Act of 1977*, 15 U.S.C. 78m, 78dd-1, 78f (1988) [Public Law 95-213, 91 Stat. 1494, as amended by the Omnibus Trade and Competitiveness Act of 1988; Public Law 100-418, sections 5001-5003 (H.R. 4848); and the International Antibribery and Fair Competition Act of 1998 (S.2375)], http://www.usdoj.gov/criminal/fraud/fcpa.html.

a successful conclusion. We turn at once to a hypothetical case study that illustrates many of the key issues.

◆ ON INTERNATIONAL ASSIGNMENT

As in any good detective story, the story begins when the phone rings. A law firm and the client it represents desperately need forensic accounting investigators to participate in an internal investigation for a publicly held global entity. True to form, they need you to start *yesterday*. You meet with the lawyers later that morning, and they provide a quick overview of the situation. The company has identified a potential fraud in a foreign location. Because of the company's concerns about bribe payments, there is a threat of possible violations of the FCPA. The client is alarmed because a senior corporate officer is alleged to have been involved in bribery payments to public officials in order to help the company achieve its business objectives. The company is widely and accurately known as a high-pressure organization in a go-go industry in which making the numbers is priority number one.

The company's lawyers have just finished up a conference call with the client's overseas office, and the initial assessment is unpromising. A new managing director recently started work at the company's operations in Country X. Soon after his arrival he made some unusual and troubling observations. Not only does the local marketing director seem to be living a very high life, but also he is singularly successful in obtaining government business contracts. He spends a great deal of time socially in the company of government officials. Other employees have indicated their concerns regarding this individual; something does not feel right. Interestingly enough, the marketing director is responsible not only for sales in Country X but also for sales in the regional group of countries.

The matter needs to be resolved without delay. The company is in the middle of potential acquisition negotiations with another company. If there are any FCPA problems, they need to be recognized and rectified at once, so that regulators are more inclined to approve the acquisition transaction if and when the time comes. The suspicious situation in Country X has alerted headquarters to the need for a broader sweep of investigation: management wants every country with a potential problem to be investigated for potential FCPA violations. This will involve offices in 15 countries on three continents.

The lawyers tell you that your work product will initially be covered by the attorney work product privilege. However, the company hopes to be in a position to fully disclose the results of the investigation to the U.S. Securities and Exchange Commission (SEC) and the U.S. Department of Justice.

The lawyers then ask you several questions: Do you have experience with these types of matters? Do you have knowledgeable local personnel in all of the countries where the company has foreign offices? If not, do you have contacts with people who do business in those countries? How soon can you have teams on the ground in all locations? Do you have people with language skills in all of the countries? How do you propose to perform the investigation? How soon will you complete the investigation? How much will it cost? The lawyers know that your firm is not the external auditor for the company, but they ask whether you have any business relationships that would preclude you from performing this assignment. They reemphasize the urgency of the engagement. Can you get people started in all locations by the end of the week? While the lawyers realize it will take some time to look into everything, they want to size up the problem as soon as possible. They need to determine in how many locations the company may have similar issues—or worse issues—that have to be identified and stopped. And they need this information as soon as possible.

You head back to your office as you think about what has to be done. This is obviously a huge task, and the time frame is short. The identification and coordination of the right resources will be critical because you realize you cannot do everything with your lean core team; others will be needed. You initiate a check on your own firm's relationships for potential independence conflicts and draft a letter of agreement with the law firm and the company. You then turn your attention to deciding how to perform the engagement.

The basic skill sets and procedures for performing international forensic accounting investigations are essentially the same as for domestic investigations. You need deep forensic accounting, investigative, and electronic discovery skills for both. On one hand, the procedures performed and the methods used are also generally the same. On the other hand, language skills and cultural awareness are essential for international assignments. Coupling the technical skills with the requisite language skills can be a challenge, and it usually is not enough to field someone who investigates effectively with someone who speaks the language and knows the culture; it is often best for those assets to be combined in one and the same person. And that is not the only unusual challenge encountered in international assignments.

The remainder of this case indicates what some of those challenges are likely to be, although no single case can cover all of the potential challenges you may face.

GETTING STARTED

The time has come for you to identify and select the team to perform the engagement. Among other things, solid up-front planning is critical. While you do not have the luxury of extensive planning time, a well-executed work plan typically will prove critical to success. You need to ensure that your proposed team contains a sufficient number of people with the right skill sets not only to execute the fieldwork but also to take care of logistics—for example, moving people into and out of multiple locales on short notice. Everyone will have to remain focused on the ultimate objective and work from the same playbook, and that does not happen by itself: you will probably need to actively manage the entire process.

Large engagements typically need to be overseen by a dedicated central team of senior personnel who direct and coordinate the field teams. This core function is especially critical to the successful completion of large international engagements. It is difficult enough to investigate complex matters when everyone speaks the same language and understands the local business environment. But international assignments are by definition different from this, and the ability to work effectively across cultures is of utmost importance. Most practitioners would agree that the degree of difficulty increases by several magnitudes when you work outside your home country unless you personally are fluent in the local language and have a thorough, up-to-date understanding of the local business environment and customs.

The first step in staffing the engagement is to contact a coordinating person for forensic accounting work in each of the various countries—or at least regions—in which work must be performed. In this case study, coordinating personnel are alerted on the three continents where the client has offices outside the United States. These local coordinators are asked to identify their best multilingual people with the requisite forensic skill sets to serve as key service providers in the countries of their region. Personnel in the United States with forensic accounting *and* language skills are also identified and directed to travel at once and begin working with personnel in the local-country offices.

Generally, only a global organization with deep resources in forensic accounting can undertake this type of engagement. Experience has shown that it is most effective to use mixed field teams with personnel both from the local country and from the country where the client is headquartered—in this instance, the United States. Multinational teams have a number of advantages. In this case, the client is a U.S. company with foreign operations. On one hand, typically, U.S. personnel will be better able to communicate and understand the needs of both client corporate personnel and the law firm. They should also have a greater appreciation of issues related to the FCPA (a U.S. law) and the types of transactions that would be of particular interest to U.S. authorities. On the other hand, local-country forensic accounting investigators usually will be better able to communicate with personnel in the client's foreign offices and should have a much better understanding of how business is conducted locally. This is especially important when you are attempting to determine which transactions fall into the ordinary course of business and which do not. For these reasons, a multinational team whose members have uniformly high levels of skill should yield the best results for the client.

COORDINATING THE ENGAGEMENT

The complexities of coordinating an international engagement can be daunting: you need to pull together a team of people from various countries who must consistently work toward a common goal. As coordinator, you encourage and indeed insist on that commonality while keeping in mind that team members have different backgrounds, speak different native languages, and grew up in different business cultures. Another interesting fact of life is that the sun never sets fully on global investigations: it is always the workday in some part of the world, and as coordinator, you have something approaching a 24-hour schedule. And poor communications infrastructure in some parts of the world may interfere with your coordination efforts. Despite these challenges, multinational engagements are deeply interesting and tend to bring out the best in all participants.

LOGISTICS

The central, or core, investigative team should develop a comprehensive package of workflow or instructions and logistical information to be distributed to the field teams. While this is a normal practice on large engagements, it is even more critical on international engagements. Locating and communicating with people across the globe on a 24-hour basis is not always straightforward. Field teams may not have immediate access to e-mail in some locations, and delivery of hard-copy information may take days.

A contact list of all engagement personnel should include local office contact information, e-mail address, phone number, cell phone number, pager number, and the like. The list should also include hotel name, address, and telephone numbers; telephone numbers at the client site; and local mobile phone numbers. The same information should be included for attorneys assigned to the project and for local-office client contacts.

The logistics package should contain detailed background information on the client's operations; the contact list; known concerns; specific concerns about particular locations; detailed instructions for the reporting of information, including spreadsheet templates and report formats; a detailed work plan; and an expected timetable. All of this information should be presented in a straightforward manner, avoiding slang, buzzwords, and technical terms that might be unclear to team members for whom English is a second language.

It is typically beneficial to establish regular conference calls with the field teams, sometimes even on a daily basis and particularly when the time frame is short and the work intense. Early and frequent communications to get the team rolling are critically important. Later, the frequency of calls can typically be reduced to an as-needed basis while the engagement progresses. Calls can and should be grouped by geographic region, but you should expect to schedule late-night calls because your nighttime may well be some team's daytime. The value of regular communications cannot be overemphasized. Regular communications provide a real-time opportunity to share fast-breaking information, clarify engagement objectives, and adjust forensic accounting procedures as necessary. Factual information identified at one location often has implications for other locations, and this information can be shared immediately with other field teams.

◆ WORK PLAN

Many domestic forensic accounting investigation engagements are time sensitive and start immediately. Initial interviews are conducted, and a work plan is developed to perform the detailed work. The same is true of international engagements; however, it is essential that at least a preliminary work plan be sent to the field teams before work begins at multiple locations. The following hypothetical work plan illustrates the level of detail and the types of instructions that would typically be developed to get started immediately. Such work plans need to be specific enough to elicit the investigative information you need yet flexible enough to allow field teams to pursue locally identified issues. More detailed electronic data extraction such as e-mail or transaction-level data mining will follow in the second phase of most engagements.

PRELIMINARY WORK PLAN EXAMPLE

This work plan is intended to accomplish certain objectives in a very limited time frame. A significant portion of the detailed information we are seeking should come from a combination of employee interviews and contemporaneously prepared client records. It will also be necessary for you to prepare schedules and summary memorandums as the engagement progresses. Additional procedures may be required depending on our preliminary results. Likewise, in light of our findings or other changing circumstances, some of the procedures listed here may not be performed.

Our work product is initially being prepared under the direction of counsel, and each page of the work product we prepare should contain the same legend as in the header of the following document:

Attorney Work Product: Privileged and Confidential[3]

The initial deliverables will consist of completion of the attached spreadsheet and an explanatory memorandum that briefly describes our procedures and findings.

1. Obtain an understanding of the client's business and the issues to be addressed in the first phase of our work by reading the attached background memorandum.

2. Logistical arrangements should be made immediately for all locations to be visited. The attached contact information provides the name, address, and telephone number of your client contact person. Coordinate all questions or concerns with the engagement partner (+ xxx-xxx-xxxx) or the engagement manager (+ xxx-xxx-xxxx) in the United States.

3. Conduct interviews of selected local client personnel. For certain locations, an attorney from the law firm may be present at the interview or alternatively may participate by telephone. You will be informed if your location will have an attorney present for interviews.

   While the following information is intended to be a guide to conducting your interviews, you should use judgment in determining the nature and extent of your questions. Keep in mind that this first phase of our work is intended to determine very quickly certain information. For this reason, try to adhere as closely as possible to the suggested topics. There

---

3. Include this disclosure only if so instructed by counsel.

will be an opportunity to follow up on other areas after we have completed this first phase of our work.

We have suggested titles of the individuals you are to interview. While the exact titles of personnel may vary by location, the general duties and responsibilities should be the same. It is anticipated that you will interview the country manager or other person in charge of the location, the lead accounting/bookkeeping person, the cashier, the outside accounting person, and—if you deem it necessary—other personnel with knowledge of the transactions we are attempting to identify.

The general nature of your inquiry is to identify transactions that may be actual or potential violations of the United States Foreign Corrupt Practices Act. Such transactions typically take the form of bribes, kickbacks, and other payments of cash or in-kind services that are intended to inappropriately influence the person receiving the benefit. In this particular case, we are looking for payments to government employees and/or directly to government entities that could be construed as payments for referrals of business or for the actual provision of business. As soon as you determine there have been payments to employees of government entities and/or to government entities either in cash or in kind, please notify the U.S. engagement partner or manager immediately. This is especially important when we do not have a lawyer at the location. We do not need to determine whether the payments were appropriate or inappropriate, since the lawyers will be making the legal determination. However, we do need to make sure that we advise the lawyers that we have identified these payments so that the lawyers can make arrangements to participate in interviews by telephone.

Your questions will vary to some extent among the different interviewees but you should do and ask the following.

○ Obtain a basic description of the person's duties and responsibilities, length of time with the company, and positions held.
○ Obtain a basic overview of the company's methods of recording and processing of financial information. What systems are used? What information is available electronically and for which time periods over the past five years? What information is available in hard copy by time period?
○ Were payments made to government employees? To government agencies?
○ What was the purpose of those payments?
○ How are those payments identified in the financial records—that is, to which accounts were they posted? (*Note: Commission payments* and *referral fees* are expressions typically used to describe such payments.)
○ Obtain a general description of how the payments were determined and of the methods used to pay and record them, the name of the person or persons who received the payments, and details on how long this practice has been going on.

   ○ Determine the person or persons who authorized and made the payments.
   ○ What was the time period over which such payments were made? (*Note:* Our analysis should cover the past five years.)
   ○ How were the payments determined: A specific amount? A percentage of sales price? Some other method?
   ○ Determine the form of the payments, such as cash or some other method. How were payments made: Personal delivery? Wire transfer? Check? Some other form?
   ○ How were the payments recorded in the accounting records? What accounts were used? (*Note:* We are aware of payments' being recorded in the advertising and promotion accounts and of disbursements from petty cash accounts in addition to regular cash accounts.) Were those payments included in the financial information sent to the corporate office? If so, on what financial statement line items?
   ○ Is there a separate schedule of these payments? If not, determine how a schedule of payments could be prepared from the source documentation.
   ○ Were the payments included in the local country's tax returns and/or statutory financial statements?
   ○ Are there payments or noncash benefits to individuals, such as gifts, sponsorships of parties, and travel and entertainment expenses to attend conferences?
   ○ Determine how a schedule can be prepared that identifies the total payments made by the government entity—by year for the past five years. Determine how to obtain the amount of revenue by government entity by year for the past five years.

4. Obtain supporting documentation to prepare the schedule (attached format) described below. Obtain in hard copy—and in electronic form if possible—the following information for each of the past five years.
   ○ Year-to-date transaction histories for each general ledger account identified as containing inappropriate payments
   ○ Year-to-date cash disbursements
   ○ Client-prepared schedules, if they exist, summarizing the inappropriate payments for each payee

5. Use the attached spreadsheet format to prepare a summary schedule of revenues by government entity for the past five years. The schedule should be prepared in the local currency with a separate identical schedule prepared in U.S. dollars. The schedule distinguishes between government customers and private customers. For those government entities wherein possibly unauthorized payments have been identified, include payments made by government entities for each of the past five years. Calculate the percentage of possibly unauthorized payments compared with revenue for each of the past five years and for the total five-year period. The payments should be listed in U.S. dollars with the conversion rate stated on the schedule.

Supporting schedules should also be prepared for each general ledger account that contains potentially inappropriate payments. Examples include advertising and promotion, sponsorships, travel, and entertainment.

Refer to the attached spreadsheet with instructions to complete this step.

6. Obtain the current year-to-date general ledger, and scan the ledger for unusual account names and/or unusual account balances. (*Note:* One location identified inappropriate payments by inquiring into the reason why the advertising and promotion account had such a relatively high balance.) Review the accounts with the local-office accountant and obtain explanations for the accounts you have selected. Examine supporting documentation on a sample basis for accounts that you determine could be unusual.

7. Obtain the year-to-date cash disbursements listing, and scan the listing for payments to hospitals or doctors. Obtain explanations for the purpose of the payments. Examine supporting documentation to verify the nature of the expense.

8. Obtain the year-to-date general ledger account history for all cash accounts, including petty cash accounts. Scan the account history for unusual payments such as those in the form of large withdrawals of cash, wire transfers, purchases of money orders, and cashier's checks. Obtain supporting documentation as required.

9. Update the schedule prepared, as described above.

10. Prepare a draft memorandum describing the results of the aforementioned procedures. Include any issues or other matters you believe should be brought to our attention based on the procedures you have performed.

This concludes the model preliminary work plan. However, the following discussions should be considered required knowledge for all participants in a global forensic investigative team.

♦ FOREIGN CORRUPT PRACTICES ACT

Because international companies are subject to the FCPA, you should be familiar with its provisions when conducting forensic accounting investigations of foreign operations of U.S. companies. The Foreign Corrupt Practices Act of 1977, as amended by the Omnibus Trade and Competitiveness Act of 1988, is an amendment to the Securities Exchange Act of 1934 (the 1934 Act). Its primary purpose is to prevent the use of corporate funds for bribery of foreign governments and foreign officials in order to obtain or retain business. Its accounting standards provisions, however, have a much broader effect, reaching the record-keeping and internal-accounting-control systems of companies subject to the 1934 Act. It should also be noted that the antibribery section of the FCPA is applicable to all U.S. companies, not just those registered with the SEC. A brief summary of certain of the record-keeping and antibribery provisions follows.

INTERNAL-ACCOUNTING-CONTROL PROVISIONS

The FCPA requires every registrant to devise and maintain a system of internal accounting control sufficient to provide reasonable assurance that the following four broad objectives are being met:

- Transactions are executed in accordance with management's general or specific authorization.
- Transactions are recorded as necessary (1) to permit preparation of financial statements in conformity with generally accepted accounting principles or any other criteria applicable to such statements and (2) to maintain accountability for assets.
- Access to assets is permitted only in accordance with management's authorization.
- The recorded accountability for assets is compared with the existing assets at reasonable intervals, and appropriate action is taken with respect to any differences.

ANTIBRIBERY PROVISIONS

The antibribery provisions of the FCPA make it unlawful for (1) any issuer with securities registered pursuant to Section 12 of the 1934 Act or required to file reports under Section 15(d) of the 1934 Act; (2) domestic concerns not otherwise subject to the 1934 Act; (3) any officer, director, employee, or agent of such issuer or domestic concern; or (4) any shareholder thereof acting on behalf of the issuer or domestic concern to bribe (offer, promise, authorize the giving, or give anything of value to) any foreign official, foreign political party or official thereof, candidate for foreign political office, or any person while knowing that such thing of value will be used directly or indirectly for the purpose of influencing or inducing any official act or decision regarding obtaining or retaining business for or directing business to any person. The term *foreign official* means any officer or employee of a foreign government or any department, agency, or instrumentality thereof or any person acting in an official capacity for or on behalf of such government or department, agency, or instrumentality.[4]

The antibribery provisions of the FCPA apply to every domestic concern, whether public or private, incorporated or unincorporated, which is either organized under the laws of a state, territory, etc., of the United States or has its principal place of business in the United States.[5]

RECORD-KEEPING PROVISIONS

The record-keeping provisions of the FCPA are intended, among other things, to eliminate unrecorded assets such as slush funds and to prevent disguising the payment of bribes as otherwise legal transactions. This intention manifests itself

---

4. *Foreign Corrupt Practices Act of 1977*, http://www.usdoj.gov/criminal/fraud/fcpa.html.
5. Id.

in the requirement for SEC-registered companies "to make and keep books, records and accounts which, in reasonable detail, accurately and fairly reflect transactions and dispositions of assets." The FCPA provides a prudent-man test for defining *reasonable detail.*

Compliance with the FCPA requires, of course, a legal determination. Accountants and investigators can greatly assist with the identification of potential books and records matters and internal control issues. However, legal counsel will need to make the determination regarding whether the facts of a particular payment are or are not violations of the FCPA.

◆ ADDITIONAL CONSIDERATIONS

Depending on the situation and allegations under investigation, some or all of the additional points that follow may be useful points of reference for the global forensic team.

PLANNING THE ENGAGEMENT

Consider doing your investigation in phases with appropriate checkpoints regarding timing and fees. Obtain confirmation, in writing, of any changes in scope during the course of the engagement. Obtain an understanding in advance regarding whether a written report will be required and whether a certified translation of the report is required in the local language, regarding the degree of formality required, and regarding who will be the ultimate users of the report.

ACCOUNTING ISSUES

Confirm that the foreign location's financial statements agree with its local books and records. The point will seem basic; however, if you are working with a financial reporting package such as Hyperion, keep in mind that it may not be a system requirement to interface the general ledger with the reporting package. It is possible to report something different from the local books of records, and in some situations that difference can foreshadow millions of dollars of write-offs and/or missing funds.

Inquire about the local auditor's reputation. Obtain copies of statutory reports and other reports from local auditors. These may include reports to local management, perhaps not sent to corporate, as well as management reports that may not have been communicated to the accounting firm's lead office.

Know where the cash is going. Is the business cash intensive? If the location is a cost center, compare cash requests with cash outflows. Trace cash transfers and the destinations of unknown wires. Review statements for direct payments such as credit cards and ATM withdrawals.

Which are the highest-paid vendors? Does the pattern make sense? Focus on departmental and noninventory types of payment such as legal, information technology, marketing, promotion, travel, and commissions paid to outside parties such as individuals and sales representatives.

Check out travel reimbursements, especially for salespeople. "Gifts" may be given to vendors and customers through this channel as another form of bribe payment. "Gifts" can range from furniture to electronics such as digital cameras and computers and go even as far as a set of tires! "Gifts" may also be recorded on credit card statements and purchase cards, especially in entities that pay statement balances without much review.

Does the location use a petty cash account? Because petty cash may be a relatively small balance on the financial statements, it may be overlooked by outside auditors and internal auditors alike. The point of interest in petty cash is not the amount on the trial balance but, rather, the amount of activity flowing through the account. Petty cash is an area where suspicious transactions can occur with low probability of detection.

Know whether account reconciliations are completed on a timely basis. Obtain and review reconciliations for all accounts. If there are large write-offs to key accounts on the balance sheet,

- Obtain an understanding of the nature of the adjustment, especially if material.
- Identify the most recent time a 100 percent physical inventory was taken.
- Is inventory stored at off-site locations?
- Are commissions paid on sale rather than collection? (The facts here may relate to accounts receivable write-offs as well as revenue schemes.)

KNOWLEDGE OF CORPORATE PERSONNEL

Know about local management and key personnel. For example, are earn-out agreements in effect? If so, managers may have an incentive to misstate financial results for their own benefit. Understand the payments inuring to local management: housing, credit cards, domestic services (landscaping, cleaning, nanny), ATM withdrawals, tuition for children, vehicle/transportation, security, monthly living allowance. How long have key local managers been in place? Have any due diligence or public records searches been performed on local management? Does local management have an undisclosed interest in another entity or entities? Some of these issues may be common in developing countries due to lack of transparency.

UNDERSTAND COMPANY POLICY

Understand company policies concerning conflicts of interest and ethics. Are employees aware of company policies? Are employees required to disclose related-party interests? Is there an anonymous hotline in place with multilingual capability and access? Do employees know it exists?

UNDERSTAND THE COMPANY'S NETWORK

Obtain the names of local professionals and service providers, and understand their relationships with the company. Where banks are concerned, obtain copies of local signature cards associated with all bank accounts. Identify local legal counsel, as well as U.S. counsel when relevant. What accounting firms are used and for what services? What administrative service centers are used for invoice, check, payroll, and lease processing? Review the identity of landlords and the language of leases. Who is the computer services provider? What regulators are directly concerned with the company's conduct of business?

LOCAL LICENSES

Obtain copies of local licenses, and identify the purpose of each. While licenses vary greatly by country and industry, they may provide a road map of payments made in violation of the FCPA.

◆ SCHEMES AND OTHER MATTERS

Many of the schemes that are used to conduct inappropriate activity prove to be the same, whether they are defalcations in Paris, Texas, or Paris, France. That said, there are nonetheless important differences between countries. For example, not all countries use the same accounting and reporting standards. Certain practices that are considered inappropriate in the United States are not necessarily viewed as such in other regions of the world. The forensic accounting investigator needs to become familiar with local business practices and customs in order to know what to look for and where to look when performing international investigations.

The following illustrate some of the situations you may encounter in FCPA violations.

- *"Sometimes you just need to ask."* Believe it or not, inappropriate payments are sometimes found simply by asking the right question—for example, "Do you make payments to local public officials?" In some countries, where the local business culture is tolerant of bribery, such payments are recorded and well documented. The entity making the payments may keep detailed records to make sure that the amount of business it is obtaining reflects the amount of bribe money it is paying. Simply asking about such documents during interviews can bring them to light.

- *"If I need an invoice, I'll buy one."* It is not uncommon in some countries to purchase invoices from a third party to use as support for inappropriate payments. The third party provides no goods or services and merely sends an invoice to the perpetrator, who submits it through the company's payables system after approving it. The bogus invoice describes what appear to be ordinary business services. The third party receives a small commission for providing the invoice, and the company's files include the invoice as supporting documentation for the inappropriate payment. The forensic accounting investigator may need to identify the payee on the check register versus the actual recipient of the payment. There may also be differences between the payee on the invoice and the payee on the check register. Those differences may produce clues toward identifying possible FCPA violations.

- *"Just add it to the invoice."* Inappropriate charges are sometimes included in legitimate invoices sent to an organization. The person receiving the bribe is in a position to authorize payment of the invoice. The actual bribe is made in cash. The company receiving the services pays the bribe through the inflated invoice charges. The company making the bribe does so at no cost to it.

- *"It would be nice to attend that industry conference at the golf resort."* Do not assume that all bribes are in cash. Some in-kind bribes are given by "sponsoring" the favor-dispensing individual at an attractive event. Airfare, plush hotels or resorts, food, and entertainment are paid directly by the company to benefit the person being bribed.

- *"We don't pay bribes. Those are just gifts."* Gifts may appear as payments through disbursement records. You may need to query for the name of a customer or the word *gift* in the local language when searching descriptions in the disbursements. Such items as computers and digital cameras may get recorded to fixed assets; however, the item may have been given to the government official in the form of a gift rather than cash. Do not overlook detail on expense reports, where the bribe may take the form of payment for anything from leisure travel to a new computer.

- *"Why are they doing business in that country when there doesn't seem to be a business purpose for being there?"* Some countries have less rigid laws and regulations on what constitutes inappropriate business activity— or such activity is largely ignored. It is often important to scrutinize foreign operations in multiple countries under the common control of one manager when there seems to be no business purpose for the company to be active in that locale. Inappropriate transactions may be recorded on the books of more lenient countries where they are less likely to be detected or where penalties and extradition treaties are nonexistent or little enforced.

- *"Our company doesn't allow us to pay bribes, but it's OK if our sales reps do."* Obtain commission contracts with sales reps, and compare the commissions paid with the amounts stipulated by contract. The excess amount may be justified as an "extra commission" when in fact it is a cover for a bribe to maintain a government contract.

- *"It's a consulting study."* Payments for ill-defined "consulting work," which in reality may not have been performed, should be carefully reviewed to ensure that such work was necessary and actually performed. Bribes often take the form of payments for fictitious consulting services because there are typically fewer documents providing evidence of services performed than documents recording the purchase and delivery of goods. Be mindful of consulting service payments that appear to be inflated or unreasonable. Data mining, summarizing payments by payee, and comparing amounts over time can be the keys to identifying payees for further review (see Chapter 20 for its discussion of data mining).

- *"Why are fixed assets missing?"* Bribes can also take the form of in-kind payments for computers and other electronic equipment that is purchased, put on the books and depreciated, and then given to an individual as a bribe.
- *"Why is so much activity flowing through petty cash?"* Because cash is often the method of choice for making bribes, payments from the petty cash account should be analyzed. Even though the petty cash balance may be small and therefore not likely to be audited, the forensic accounting investigator should not overlook it. More relevant are the amounts and frequency of replenishment. Use data mining to summarize payments through petty cash. Compare those payments with disbursements through accounts payable to identify total payments to a given vendor. Knowing the total payments to the payee will assist the forensic accounting investigator in identifying payments for further review. Legitimate payments may be handled through accounts payable, while the kickback payments may be handled through petty cash.
- *"A little 'grease' might be acceptable."* Not all payments to government officials are considered bribes. With certain restrictions, "facilitating payments" are allowable under the FCPA. The purpose of such payments is to expedite or secure the performance of a routine government action, such as obtaining permits, licenses, or other government documents. Special care, under legal advice, must be exercised when navigating this particular minefield.
- *"Why are we paying commissions to people who are not on our payroll?"* Be mindful of commissions paid to customers and vendors. In some countries, a "commission" paid to an individual not on the company payroll is another word for *bribe* or *kickback* by U.S. standards.
- *"What else is going on?"* Expect to find questionable items other than those you originally expected to find. You are interviewing about one or two matters, but the actual scope of the problem is often greater. Avoidance of personnel income taxes is a favorite. In some countries, you may find managers cooperating with employees to avoid income taxes—for example, by paying only part of the salary through the payroll system and the balance as if it were a third-party invoice not recorded as salary expense.

The common point among all of these schemes and situations is that the more experienced forensic accounting investigator is more likely to see them for what they are. Like all phases of accounting and auditing, only more so, forensic accounting requires an apprenticeship through which the practitioner gradually develops not just skills but also a sixth sense for where the problem lies. The foregoing list is only a representative listing of the possibilities, but it goes a long way toward suggesting what to look for as you exercise professional skepticism in the international forensic arena.

◆ PERSONAL CONSIDERATIONS

Conducting a global investigation is a complex activity but in many respects rewarding. Your professional skills are likely to be stretched farther and exercised more thoroughly than in the past. Those skills include diplomacy. Show appreciation to everyone, from drivers and accounts payable clerks to the managing director. You never know who will ring you in your hotel with key information or provide documents that were allegedly lost, deleted, or stolen—simply because you have treated them courteously and they respect the task you have undertaken.

Performing forensic engagements in foreign places may sound like a dream come true. However, the dream can become a nightmare without sufficient preparation. As a professional, you are already aware of much that needs doing, but it is worth remembering that visas and, in some countries, work permits will be required. Pity the poor forensic accounting investigator who is asked to exit a foreign location because of a work permit violation. It may be hard to explain that one to your client. The rule is to know before you go.

Rather than engaging in comprehensive data gathering, understand the local laws governing privacy, and ensure you are in compliance. As mentioned in Chapter 21, Building a Case: Gathering and Documenting Evidence, and referenced in data mining, the most significant and far-reaching example of privacy legislation is the Data Protection Act (DPA) enacted by the European Union. The DPA requires that those who process personal data must comply with DPA principles.

Before traveling to underdeveloped countries, consult with a physician to determine whether you should obtain immunizations. Your physician will have access to up-to-date information about required immunizations and matters deserving caution. Ensure that your prescriptions are filled, and consider whether other remedies should travel with you among your personal articles.

Delays in obtaining information are normal. Expect delays and prepare yourself for a longer stay than originally scheduled.

Some regions of the world are insecure. If personal and team security is needed, arrange for it before your arrival, and never assume that local security resources at a local plant or office are necessarily on your side. At one engagement in a developing country, a local security firm secretly installed listening devices in the conference room where a forensic team was working. For several weeks, local management stayed one step ahead of the forensic accounting investigators, until the light dawned and the forensic team hired its own security.

A global forensic investigation is a remarkable blend of systematic procedure, teamwork on a sometimes vast scale, and individual skill. From individuals, more than skill is sometimes needed. Courage, perseverance, and intuitive intelligence are not parts of any job description, yet those traits can make the difference between a successful global investigation and an investigation that loses its way in the complexities of unfamiliar business cultures. It may be helpful from time to time to recall what Dorothy realizes in the classic movie *The Wizard of Oz:* "Toto, I've a feeling we're not in Kansas anymore."

CHAPTER 26

MONEY LAUNDERING

Andrew P. Clark

Will Kenyon

Alan Shel

Money laundering within the United States alone, let alone in other parts of the world, remains a serious problem. Exhibit 26.1 conveys a sense of the dimensions of the problem. In fiscal 2003, for example, the Internal Revenue Service achieved more than 1,000 indictments and close to 700 sentencings.

	FY 2004	FY 2003	FY 2002	FY 2001
Criminal Investigations Initiated	1789	1590	1448	1459
Pros. Recommendations	1515	1141	1061	1294
Indictments/Informations	1304	1041	943	1237
Sentenced*	687	667	861	897
Incarceration Rate	89.1%	89.2%	89.5%	89.4%
Average Months to Serve	63	66	70	66

*Includes confinement to federal prison, halfway house, home detention, or a combination thereof.
Source: Internal Revenue Services http://www.irs.gov/.

EXHIBIT 26.1 STATISTICAL DATA: MONEY-LAUNDERING ENFORCEMENT

This chapter introduces the range of circumstances in which money laundering may be encountered in business. It examines the relationships and distinctions between fraud and money laundering as well as the remote likelihood of indicia of money laundering showing up in the course of a financial statement audit. The chapter looks at the unique skills and perspectives necessary to successfully investigate money laundering and identifies some of the potential red flags a financial statement auditor may encounter if money-laundering transactions are taking place. For purposes of this chapter, *money laundering* refers to the crime or activity of moving funds of illicit origin, and anti–money laundering (AML) refers to formal and informal systems and controls designed (1) to prevent or frustrate attempts to launder money and (2) to report incidents of money laundering when they are suspected or detected.

While most companies or institutions could potentially be used as conduits for money laundering, AML is of particular concern for institutions in the regulated financial services sector, in which many entities are legally obliged to introduce and maintain AML systems and controls. The distinction between the regulated financial services and unregulated sectors is addressed later in the chapter.

◆ RELATIONSHIP BETWEEN FRAUD AND MONEY LAUNDERING

Although both fraud and money laundering are crimes based on deception and although the movement of funds obtained by fraud is a type of money laundering, fraud and money laundering are distinctly different and should not be confused. Money laundering has been defined in a number of ways, but essentially, it is a process undertaken by or on behalf of criminals with the object of hiding or disguising their criminal activities and the origin of their illicit proceeds. The goals are often achieved through a series of financial transactions, sometimes involving a number of countries and through a variety of financial products.

The Financial Action Task Force (FATF) of the Organization for Economic Cooperation and Development (OECD) has defined money laundering as follows:

> The goal of a large number of criminal acts is to generate a profit for the individual or group that carries out the act. Money laundering is the processing of these criminal proceeds to disguise their illegal origin. This process is of critical importance, as it enables the criminal to enjoy these profits without jeopardizing their source.[1]

The FATF is an intergovernmental body set up in conjunction with the OECD and with the mandate to develop policies for combating money laundering. It is considered to be the preeminent, global AML watchdog. Its primary role is to monitor the development of AML strategies in member countries—of which there are currently 31—although it also seeks to educate both members and nonmembers about the risks of money laundering at the national and international levels. For example, every year the FATF considers money-laundering trends and vulnerabilities and issues a report of case studies summarizing its findings.

Another important FATF program is its Non-Cooperative Countries and Territories (NCCT) initiative. The aim of this exercise is to identify nonmembers whose AML systems and controls are considered to be deficient to such an extent that they could present a risk to financial institutions that have relationships with counterparties in these jurisdictions. Informed financial institutions

---

1. Financial Action Task Force, *Basic Facts about Money Laundering*, http://www1.oecd.org/fatf.

are well aware of additional measures necessary to mitigate such risks. Ten countries and jurisdictions are currently on this list. The listed jurisdictions are also considered to be, and sanctioned as, noncooperative on the international level and generally passive about law enforcement.

The money-laundering process has been characterized as consisting of at least three distinct stages: placement, layering, and integration. These stages are often referred to as the money-laundering triad.

PLACEMENT

This initial stage is considered by many as the riskiest part for criminals to achieve as they attempt to introduce the proceeds of a crime into the financial system. Although banks have been used for facilitating this stage in the past—for example, by narcotics traffickers' making cash deposits at local branches—the banks' AML systems and controls have become and are perceived to be increasingly sophisticated, and launderers have sought alternative means of placing their illicit cash. One such method is to infiltrate cash-intensive businesses—such as restaurants and other public venues—to provide a plausible explanation for the movement of large amounts of cash. Recent proposals to regulate casinos and other gambling businesses, for example, respond to a perceived vulnerability to money laundering.[2] When this scheme succeeds, "dirty" money is commingled with income derived from the legitimate business and deposited with a bank.

Financial fraud, by contrast, may not necessarily have a placement stage in the conventional sense. The funds may already be in the financial system, particularly when a financial institution has been defrauded.

LAYERING

Once the cash has been successfully placed in the financial system, the launderer typically initiates a number of related transactions with a view to obscuring the origin of the funds by undermining any trace of an audit trail. That is often achieved by moving the funds between financial products, between institutions, and between jurisdictions.

INTEGRATION

Finally, the laundered funds need to be extracted from the financial system so that they can be used to acquire legitimate assets or finance further criminal activities. At that point, the funds or assets have a veneer of respectability within the legitimate economy. Successfully laundered funds may be integrated back into the economy in three ways: by being invested, loaned, or spent. Although investing and lending are similar, keep in mind that funds loaned to a third party enter the economy in the name of the third party and become more difficult to trace.

---

2. Financial Action Task Force, *Review of the FATF Forty Recommendations* (Paris, May 30, 2002), Chap. 5, § 5.1.1, "Casinos: Vulnerability to Money Laundering," par. 237, 81. According to the FATF, the large amounts of cash being circulated by legitimate customers provide effective covers for the launderer.

Two important characteristics of money laundering distinguish it from fraud. The first is that because of the conduit phenomenon, money laundering is far less likely to affect financial statements than the broad spectrum of frauds is. Hence, it is highly unlikely that financial statement auditing procedures will identify or even stumble onto possible indications of money laundering. The second important distinction is that fraudulent activity usually results in the loss or disappearance of assets or revenue from the business, whereas money laundering may actually create significant fee income because businesses may charge fees for the transactions that permit the illicit proceeds to be distanced from their source.

Nevertheless, many conditions and control deficiencies that may contribute to fraud vulnerability may also contribute to money-laundering vulnerability—that is, the risk of criminal activity's going undetected. Prominent among these are the following.

- Lack of a strong control environment
- Lack of a strong regulatory compliance function, in the absence of which a business is subject to high compliance risk and reputational risk
- Lack of well-defined and well-communicated enterprise-wide ethical guidance and standards and related training programs
- Lack of a robust internal audit compliance program
- Previous examiners' or auditors' reports, memorandums of understanding, and past administrative and enforcement actions citing compliance problems, control deficiencies, or concerns over management's competence and/or integrity
- Significant revenues stemming from or assets or liabilities associated with high-risk jurisdictions—notably, bank secrecy havens
- Abnormally high electronic funds transfer activity from and to high-risk jurisdictions—with insufficient controls
- Lack of background checks on new employees
- Unreasonably infrequent or nonexistent reviews of security software and systems

◆ VARYING IMPACT OF MONEY LAUNDERING ON COMPANIES

Both fraud and money laundering may result in criminal activity, but perhaps equally significant to companies and financial institutions is the reputational risk associated with those activities. The media interest in Enron, WorldCom, and other massive frauds in recent years is indicative of the public appetite for stories involving crime and big business. Whenever such a story breaks, it often is difficult for the company under siege to manage the public relations impact. Not only can share prices fall dramatically, as in the Bank of New York money-laundering case in the late 1990s, but also any investment by a company in building its brands may be at risk. These issues are addressed in greater detail later in the chapter.

The extent to which a company, its board of directors, and its senior management are focused on money laundering is guided in part by whether or not the company is regulated. The extent to which a company or institution *must* have specific AML systems and controls depends on whether its industry and/or sector is regulated for AML purposes. Today, the degree of regulation varies considerably among AML regimes around the globe. Historically, the regulated sector has been limited to the banking community; it has been widely acknowledged for some time that banks are on the front line in the fight against money laundering. However, over time and in many jurisdictions, the regulated sector has expanded to include nonbanking financial institutions—such as insurance companies, investment managers, and other participants in the financial sector—stemming in large part from the conventional wisdom that money launderers tend to move their operations into channels where they believe their illicit activities are likely to go undetected.

AML regime expansion across financial services sectors is a primary characteristic of the PATRIOT Act of 2001, unquestionably the most sweeping piece of AML legislation in U.S. history.[3] The act is applicable to U.S. institutions and to foreign entities with U.S. operations. Congress also sought to shore up perceived weaknesses in the existing AML regime through renewed attention to the regulation of offshore banking, correspondence banking relationships, and private banking services.

Allied with the conviction that the AML environment needed change was the perception that previous efforts had been impeded by inadequate legislation and enforcement powers, particularly in cases involving foreign persons, foreign banks, and foreign countries. To this end, the act widened the AML regime to incorporate the nonbanking financial sector, including investment managers and broker/dealers. The U.S. Treasury has in process, as of this writing, a consultation exercise to consider how the AML requirements should be extended to capture hedge funds. Further expansion of the regulated sector to cover nonfinancial institutions, including accountants, is addressed later in this chapter.

If a company is regulated for AML purposes, it is likely that, at a minimum, the company needs to introduce systems and controls designed to minimize and frustrate money laundering. Although the particular requirements vary by jurisdiction, there are five main areas that regulated institutions need to address to varying degrees. The purpose of underlying programs that incorporate these five concerns is to know your customer (KYC) and to monitor transactions in such a way that for more detailed inquiry, apparently unusual transactions can be pulled out of the normal processing flow either before or after they are executed.

---

3. *PATRIOT* is an acronym. The short title of the act is Uniting and Strengthening America by Providing Appropriate Tools Required to Intercept and Obstruct Terrorism (USA PATRIOT) Act of 2001. The portion of the act that relates to AML is Title III, International Money Laundering Abatement and Anti-Terrorist Financing Act of 2001.

◆ THE FIVE-POINT PROGRAM FOR AML-REGULATED BUSINESSES

WRITTEN COMPLIANCE PROGRAM

Businesses should have a regulator-approved AML policy framework, enterprise-wide guidance and standards, implementation policies, and robust operating procedures that integrate compliance into the business and into support areas of consequence. The written AML compliance program should clearly articulate mechanisms for discharging business unit and individual AML responsibilities. The institution is also expected to consider appropriate controls to authorize policy and procedural variances. Increasingly, there is an expectation that the institution should carry out and document its own risk assessment—that is, its own assessment of the vulnerability of its products and services to money laundering and the corresponding controls that have been introduced to mitigate these risks. Institutions are also expected to transform risk assessment into a continuous and sustainable process.

MINIMUM STANDARDS OF CUSTOMER DUE DILIGENCE

The AML requirements also stipulate the circumstances in which customers or counterparties need to be identified and the extent to which identity needs to be verified and documentation reviewed. The documentary requirements should vary according to the type of customer—for example, the requirements for an offshore trust are tougher than those for a private individual—and the extent to which the immediate customer is acting on behalf of another. In addition, KYC principles have come to apply to employees, vendors, agents, and other external service providers.

ACTIVITY MONITORING AND REPORTING

After accepting a customer or counterparty and opening an account, the institution is likely to have an obligation to monitor customer activity for evidence of money laundering and, depending on the AML regime, other reportable suspicious conditions. When money laundering is identified or suspected, a report should be made to an appropriate external authority. In many jurisdictions, the relevant external authority is the nominated Financial Intelligence Unit (FIU). There are now more than 50 national FIUs globally, and most of them are members of the international FIU union, the Egmont Group.[4] Although there is a common requirement to report to a nominated authority, the specific role of the FIU varies depending on a number of factors, which are in turn functions of the technical and legal framework established for the unit and the FIU infrastructure

---

4. The larger, better-funded FIUs include the Financial Crimes Enforcement Network (FinCEN) of the United States, the United Kingdom's National Criminal Intelligence Unit (NCIS), France's Traitement du renseignement et action contre les circuits financiers clandestins (Tracfin), Canada's Financial Transactions Reports Analysis Centre (FinTrac), and Australia's Australian Transactions and Reports Analysis Centre (AUSTRAC).

that has been created. While some FIUs may simply collate and analyze information received and then forward it to another authority for investigation, others play a more active regulatory role in the administration of the country's AML regime. The FIU is often responsible for undertaking compliance examinations, issuing fines and penalties, providing disclosure information, and drafting regulations. The U.S. Financial Crimes Enforcement Network (FinCEN) is both an AML policy-making and enforcement agency.

TRAINING

As well as documenting its approach to AML in its policies and procedures, the institution should ensure that AML policies and procedures are communicated to staff via training on a regular basis. Training is likely to cover obligations under the law, circumstances that could indicate that products and services are being used for money-laundering purposes, and when and to whom suspicions should be reported. AML training needs to be tailored to the needs and circumstances of the trainees and to be continually refreshed and tracked.

RECORD KEEPING

Finally, the institution should consider storage and retention policies for AML-related documents. The documents should include evidence obtained when verifying customer identity, suspicious transaction reports made internally, reports submitted externally to the FIU, and records of training.

In certain jurisdictions, AML obligations go even further. In Germany and Switzerland, for example, auditors have an obligation to monitor and report on a bank's compliance with AML legislation and regulation. In the U.S., the obligation lies primarily with the business.

Within the regulated sector, customers, products and services, channels, and service providers have their own profiles of AML risk. Banking relationships, for example, are likely to be higher risk because they facilitate regular receipts and payments to third parties without the verification of the third party. That risk is magnified when wire transfers are available, because funds can then be moved between jurisdictions. At the other end of the risk spectrum are products involving small regular payments that are repayable only to the account holder and products include certain insurance contracts and personal investment plans, among other instruments. Although no institution is immune to money laundering, its AML policies, procedures, systems, and other controls should realistically correspond to the money-laundering risks posed.

The company's regulated status will inform its general attitude toward money laundering, AML, and financial crime. Some financial institutions have appointed directors responsible for financial crime, including fraud and money laundering. In the United States, AML compliance officers are legally required at covered financial institutions.

A company's regulated status and the attitude of the board and senior management—that is, the tone at the top—have impact on the extent and quality of the control environment. At a minimum, AML compliance should respond to regulatory requirements. In more sophisticated organizations, those responsible for AML typically are informing other aspects of the business, such as acquisition strategies, introduction of new products and services, entry into new distribution channels, and development and deployment of new technologies.

All of these factors should have an impact on the ability of the financial auditor, forensic accounting investigator, and regulator to assess the impact of money laundering on a business. In the United Kingdom, for example, the company officer responsible for money-laundering matters, including compliance and reporting—the money-laundering reporting officer, or MLRO—has an obligation to annually prepare and deliver to management a report that deals with a number of matters related to money laundering and AML. This is an important document for identifying any problems the organization encountered during the period, but more significant, it is an indication of the organization's and management's attitude toward the issue.

Although a great deal of attention has been paid to money laundering through the movement of funds in the regulated sector, it is important to recognize that nonfinancial companies, too, can be used in money-laundering schemes. According to the FATF, for example, its members continue to observe situations in which the movement of goods and services is used as a front for money laundering or as an actual money-laundering mechanism.[5] For example, in one German case, an importer paid a large amount for goods that were basically worthless. The source of the payments lay in proceeds from narcotics trafficking, and the goods were junked or resold for a nominal amount. The narcotics trafficker was able to relocate the funds under the guise of payment for goods received.

It has been argued that customs officials are in a position to identify such suspicious activity by comparing the amount paid with the nature of the goods imported, but there are several barriers to the detection of this type of money laundering.[6] First, duty is often paid on the items being shipped so as to add another layer to the veneer of legitimacy around the transaction. The duty paid is viewed by the criminals as just another cost of doing business. Second, importing as a means of money laundering is not currently addressed in the training of customs officials. The focus of customs officials' training has been on uncovering contraband or attempts to avoid paying import duties.

The point here is that while the regulated sector has more obligations than any other in relation to AML, no company or institution is immune to money laundering and money launderers. The challenge for business managers is to evaluate the risk profile of the company in question and to understand where it could be exposed to money laundering—internally or externally.

---

5. Financial Action Task Force, *Report on Money Laundering Typologies 1999–2000* (Paris: February 3, 2000), 10.

6. Id.

◆ IMPACT OF MONEY LAUNDERING ON FINANCIAL STATEMENTS

The impact of money laundering on financial statements should be considered in terms of both direct and indirect consequences on fairly representing the state of a business. While the direct impact is clearly important, the indirect consequences can be just as significant—and they are often underestimated by management.

Money launderers tend to use the business entity more as a conduit than as a means of directly expropriating assets. For this reason, money laundering is far less likely to affect financial statements than is a fraud such as asset misappropriation. Consequently, it is unlikely to be detected in a financial statement audit. In addition, other forms of fraudulent activity usually result in the loss or disappearance of assets or revenue, whereas money laundering involves the manipulation of large quantities of illicit proceeds to distance them from their source quickly and without drawing attention.

Although money laundering rarely has a direct impact on financial statements, it may also have other consequences of concern. The consequences could be any of the following.

- *Law enforcement interest.* Law enforcement agencies may act on the suspicion that a business has been infiltrated by money launderers. A significant amount of time can be expended responding to requests from law enforcement agencies, ranging from discovery requests and disclosure orders to asset-freeze orders.

- *Regulatory revocation.* A financial services business could have its license and charter revoked in the event that a significant breach in its AML systems and controls is discovered.

- *Operational catastrophe.* There is also the possibility of civil seizure of assets or shareholder derivative suits when it is determined that the institution was negligent in its duties and facilitated the movement of funds.

- *Reputational damage.* Perhaps the most significant implication for an institution is the reputational risk accompanying the incidence or even the allegation of money laundering. This combination of the respectable and disrespectable, of business and crime, is an attractive proposition for the media. As well, the discovery of money laundering at an institution could undermine the trust of previously loyal savers and investors, prompting them to look elsewhere. A brand in which significant resources have been invested could be harmed if money laundering is alleged or discovered.

In sum, although money laundering may not have a direct impact on financial statements, it has the potential to expose a company or financial institution to considerable risk.

◆ AML AND FORENSIC ACCOUNTING INVESTIGATION

When money laundering is suspected or controls are considered vulnerable to abuse, a forensic accounting investigator with the requisite knowledge of AML may be engaged to undertake an investigation, a compliance diagnostic, or a controls review. In general a money-laundering investigation usually begins with the detail rather than with high-level controls and reviews transactions and documentation related to specific customers. From such a process, the forensic accounting investigator charged with executing the review generally will form a bottom-up view of the controls environment and ascertain whether it complies with the regulatory regime governing that jurisdiction. Although the scope of AML assignments is determined on a case-by-case basis, in practice all three aspects—investigation (including background checks and interviews), compliance diagnostic, and controls review—are likely to be reflected to varying degrees. The assignments themselves are likely to come from one of two sources at the request of the regulator or of the institution. These assignments are distinctly different from financial statement audits in that they focus specifically on compliance with relevant laws and regulations as well as on particular suspicious transactions and not on financial accounting processes or the entity's reported financial results.

AT THE REQUEST OF THE REGULATOR

The regulator may seek the involvement of a forensic accounting investigator for a variety of reasons: the regulator could suspect that the institution has perpetrated financial crime or been the victim of financial crime and accordingly authorizes an investigation. Alternatively, the regulator could request an AML review before it is willing to grant a financial license or authorization. The regulator could also request a review as part of a wider but more routine examination of an institution's systems and controls.

Law enforcement officials may also investigate whether an institution was aiding and abetting money laundering through systemic deficiencies or major control failures that permitted the money-laundering activity to remain undetected. Faced with a challenge of that kind, the institution may wish to engage forensic accountants with specialized AML knowledge.

AT THE REQUEST OF THE INSTITUTION

Of its own volition the institution could engage a forensic accounting investigator to undertake a money-laundering-investigation assignment. One of the more common instances is a review in advance of a regulatory visit to identify areas that may need to be addressed. However, the institution may also require a money-laundering review as part of a wider strategic-vulnerability assessment. A review also may be appropriate in conjunction with an acquisition. The assignment could involve a review of the target's systems and controls or an assessment of the risk profile of its customer base to determine whether any pricing adjustments to the proposed deal might be appropriate.

In the course of an AML review, a forensic accounting investigator should consider all five of the areas that make up the typical AML system and controls, ranging (as discussed in earlier pages) from policies and procedures and customer due diligence to monitoring and reporting, training, and record keeping. All of these areas enter into a thorough AML review, starting with a detailed examination of transactions and records and concluding with an assessment of the overall corporate culture.

REVIEW OF TRANSACTIONS AND RECORDS

Transactions are reviewed or tested for purposes of confirming a number of different aspects of the control environment.

- *Account-opening procedures.* Is the requisite documentation obtained?
- *Exception procedures.* Are departures from policies and procedures signed off by an appropriately senior member of staff? Are the reasons documented?
- *Transaction monitoring.* Is suspicious or unusual activity identified?

This stage of the review addresses aspects of the customer due diligence and record keeping requirements but may also indicate whether staff have been suitably trained and comply with the employer's policies and procedures.

DECISION MAKING

The decision-making process typically is reviewed at a number of levels, from the application of customer acceptance procedures and departures from accepted practice to the role of compliance and the role of other units of the business, such as internal audit. Investigations in this area build on the results of the review of transactions—for example, in the areas of exception procedures and feedback from management. Examination of decision making often sheds another light on customer due diligence and policies and procedures, but even more significant, perhaps, on record keeping.

THE AML REPORTING PROCESS

The reporting process can be addressed from a number of angles.

- By tracing the progress through the organization of suspicious or unusual activity reports made by staff, with the associated record of outcomes and justifications for acceptance or rejection
- Through analytical review of reports—forwarded for consideration by the relevant FIU—that compare the institution with its peer group and with national averages for companies of comparable size
- By looking at the scope of reportable conditions identified through the aforementioned benchmarking process
- By measuring the frequency of reports to and from the MLRO or other relevant compliance officers

This part of the money-laundering review is often concerned primarily with the monitoring and reporting processes but also covers record-keeping and training requirements.

CORPORATE CULTURE AND AML CORPORATE GOVERNANCE

Finally, a thorough money-laundering review should consider the corporate culture and the tone at the top—that is, the extent to which the organization takes AML seriously. The degree of commitment is often reflected in the quality of training the institution provides, and a variety of methods can be used to examine this variable. A sample of training records can be reviewed to identify evidence of attendance at training sessions covering the subject of money laundering, including the frequency and scope of training given. Review of the sample records can be supplemented by discussions with staff to confirm attendance at training sessions and question staff's evaluation of the training and its key messages. The training material itself can be reviewed for relevance. Is it part of a wider, ongoing training and awareness program for staff? Finally, the corporate culture is also indicated by the extent to which the seniormost members of the board focus on the issue of money laundering. For example, do the minutes of board meetings show that AML matters are being discussed? Has remedial action been taken to address any weaknesses? Fundamentally, senior management is responsible for raising AML matters with the board when, in management's judgment, a serious problem has arisen or may possibly arise. Many of the AML compliance failures of recent years have been attributed to a board's failure to notify and seek counsel.

◆ LEGAL ARRANGEMENTS LENDING THEMSELVES TO ANONYMITY

Corporate entities may be victims of money laundering, but as noted earlier, corporate entities may also be created and used for the sole purpose of money laundering. Falling between these two extremes are legitimate companies that are unwittingly exposed to money laundering by the activities of someone or some group of conspirators in their organization. This category includes the large multinational entity with a subsidiary infiltrated by organized crime but also includes dishonest bank clerks who accept money they know to be illegitimate, possibly in return for bribes or other perks.

Increasingly, and disturbingly, corporate entities are being used by criminals as integral components in sophisticated money-laundering operations. Corporate entities are attractive for a number of reasons—primarily, the degree of anonymity afforded by complex corporate structures and legal arrangements. That anonymity is useful in avoiding or defeating the inquiries of financial institutions into the true ownership for purposes of assessing who the customer is and the type of business conducted. The lack of transparency is driven by two things: the scarcity of shareholder information in certain jurisdictions and the characteristics of certain legal arrangements that lend themselves to anonymity—in particular, the availability of bearer shares, nominee directors, and certain so-called international business companies (IBCs).

Bearer shares facilitate transfer of ownership of a company through the physical transfer of the share certificate from one individual to another. Unlike ordinary shares, details about the owner are not registered with the company. According to the FATF, these instruments are attractive to money laundering because (1) assets can be transferred without leaving a paper trail—that is, they are highly negotiable instruments—and (2) companies can be owned and controlled without interests being declared.[7]

A nominee director is an officer of the company who is employed to act on behalf of another, either a shadow director or the beneficial owner. The nominee director may be an individual or corporation, and that name is often the only one that appears on documentation filed with the relevant registries. The problem with nominee directors is that they undermine the value of obtaining information about the company and, like bearer shares, potentially enable someone to effectively control a company without declaring an interest. It is also possible to use corporate nominee directors to lengthen the chain of corporate vehicles[8] within a corporate structure and so minimize transparency by putting additional layers between the officers and representatives of the company and the ultimate beneficial owners.

IBCs have been available primarily to nonresidents of the United States in offshore locations. The threat posed by these entities is that they are often available off-the-shelf for as little as $100,[9] they can be incorporated by using bearer shares and/or the strategy of nominee shareholders and directors, and they may attract little in the way of regulation. Offshore territories that permit the formation of IBCs often have two distinct regulatory regimes, offering greater protection to residents by stipulating that the IBC's products and services can be offered only outside the jurisdiction.

Each of these vehicles or mechanisms is related to beneficial ownership in one way or another, and financial institutions should consider how these risks are to be mitigated. If KYC is the core of AML, then these mechanisms are custom designed to defeat that. However, the matter is complicated by the fact that there are some legitimate reasons for their continued use, related mainly to concerns for personal safety in turbulent jurisdictions and legitimate tax minimization strategies.

◆ POTENTIAL RED FLAGS

The accounting and auditing profession and its authoritative organizations and regulators around the world increasingly recognize the importance and value of AML training and awareness for practitioners in a wide variety of business roles. Internal and external auditors, forensic accounting investigators, managerial

---

7. Financial Action Task Force, *Review of the FATF Forty Recommendations* (Paris: May 30, 2002), Chap. 4, § 4.2, "Bearer Shares," par. 196, 62.

8. Organization for Economic Cooperation and Development, *Behind the Corporate Veil: Using Corporate Entities for Illicit Purposes* (November 2001), 32.

9. Id., 24.

accountants, compliance officers, attorneys, business executives, and board members may find it useful to be mindful of the following potential red flags, which may indicate that the entity in question is being used for purposes other than those stated in its public documents.

- Unusual cash transactions
- Payment to or receipts from jurisdictions regarded as high risk (listed under the FATF's NCCT initiative)
- Same or excessive transfers into or out of bank accounts
- Frequent deposits or withdrawals just below reporting thresholds

As noted earlier, a trend in the development of AML regimes around the world is to expand beyond the banking sector and incorporate other types of business, including professional services firms, within the scope of regulation. If accounting and law firms, for example, were to be included within the AML regime, they would be likely to encounter some of the following:

- Specific policies and procedures addressing the money-laundering risks in their business and measures introduced to mitigate those risks
- Client identification procedures, including documentary standards and requirements
- Internal and external reporting arrangements to facilitate the reporting of any suspicious activity identified in the course of auditing a client
- Training to ensure that staff are aware of their individual responsibilities and have the necessary tools to discharge those responsibilities
- Record keeping, including length of time that client identification needs to be retained and the degree to which it needs to be accessible

◆ AUDITING AND MONEY LAUNDERING

As noted earlier, money laundering is likely to have only a limited effect on the accuracy of financial statements. However, a money-laundering scandal at a financial institution or commercial enterprise can undermine its reputation and put its future in question. The regulated status of a company and the relevant auditing standards of the jurisdiction in which it operates determine the extent to which money laundering gets addressed in the course of a financial statement audit. It is possible that in some of the circumstances discussed earlier, a company committed an illegal act. If this is the case, the various auditing standards governing the auditor's conduct when an illegal act either may have occurred or did occur are brought into play. In the United States, for example, a known or suspected incidence of money laundering may require the auditor to extend or expand audit procedures pursuant to Statement on Auditing Standards No. 99, *Consideration of Fraud in a Financial Statement Audit,* of the American Institute of Certified Public Accountants, or to report to management and—possibly, in some situations—to the U.S. Securities and Exchange Commission pursuant to the requirements of Section 10A of the Securities Exchange Act of 1934.

Accounting professionals other than external auditors are more likely than external auditors to encounter evidence of money laundering. Financial statement auditors normally test only a small sample of the actual transactions that receive or disburse cash during a fiscal year. Further, money-laundering transactions are normally disguised to look like legitimate business transactions. Because external auditors do not, in accordance with generally accepted auditing standards, specifically test the authenticity of business documents in the course of an examination,[10] they are less likely than internal accountants in various positions inside a company and in day-to-day contact with the transactions flowing through the entity to detect possible signs of money laundering. The responsibilities of managers and accountants other than external auditors are addressed in both authoritative and nonauthoritative guidance.[11] Among the varied accountancy roles are the following:

- Accountants in management positions whose duties may include recording and reporting entity transactions, such as CEOs, chief operating officers, chief financial officers, chief information officers, controllers, risk managers, compliance officers, and related staff
- In-house financial systems consultants
- Internal auditors responsible for operations and compliance auditing
- Practitioners who provide outsourced regulatory examination services
- Forensic accounting investigators
- Public practitioners who perform compliance and operational audits
- Risk management practitioners and compliance specialists
- Tax practitioners, especially in jurisdictions where filings connected with AML laws—such as reports on currency transactions and suspicious activities—are directed to tax authorities

Finally, it is worth noting that in general, internal auditors and other types of accountants who work for management, as opposed to engaging in public practice, are subject to the same AML requirements as the institutions that employ them.

♦ RELATIONSHIP BETWEEN FRAUD INVESTIGATION AND AML

This chapter opened with a discussion of the relationship between fraud and money laundering. Before bringing the chapter to a close, we should briefly consider the similarities between fraud investigation and AML investigation. There

---

10. D. Larry Crumbley and Nicholas Apostolou, "The Accounting Profession and Financial Statement Fraud," *The Forensic Examiner* (Springfield, Mo.: American College of Forensic Examiners International, January 1, 2003), http://www.acfei.com/ce-Acctg%20Prof%20and%20Fraud%20-%20Crumbley2.htm.

11. For example, *Anti-Money Laundering*, 2nd ed., an AML white paper by the International Federation of Accountants, released in March 2004, http://www.ifac.org/store/Details.tmpl?SID=101043515678981.

are clear similarities, specifically in terms of the due diligence or research undertaken in relation to companies and individuals. Both fraud investigations and
AML assignments are interested in understanding the relationship between individuals and companies. On one hand, in fraud investigations, the search is for an
individual or coconspirators, the details of the fraudulent scheme, the scheme's
impact on the company, and the control weaknesses that gave the perpetrator or
perpetrators their opportunity. AML assignments, on the other hand, often examine customer relationships to verify whether the beneficial owners of financial
assets are appropriately identified and reported, and there is as well a search for
pattern, coconspirators, and control weaknesses that should be remedied.

Both assignments employ similar techniques, such as data mining, in the
course of their investigations. Data-mining software is used in fraud investigations to identify relationships or anomalous transactions within any data under
review. Similarly, the technique is used in AML assignments to uncover suspicious transactions, suspicious relationships between accounts, and questionable
entities. Viewing both types of assignments from 30,000 feet, one could say that
both are concerned with the quality and consistency of the data reviewed.

One of the advantages of sourcing investigative services in the private sector
has been that the disclosure of a fraud can often be managed. When a company
prefers to keep findings out of the public arena altogether, it can often succeed in
doing so if it moves quickly and with the right resources. There is a risk that
information may leak to the public and cause both embarrassment and reputational damage. While it is usually best to at least begin an investigation before
alerting law enforcement, the United States requires reporting of suspicious
activity within 30 days of detection.

To return to the points made at the beginning of the chapter, in many circumstances it is conceivable that fraud could be accompanied by money laundering.
Whenever there are transactions that move the proceeds of fraud through a business, the activity could be construed as money laundering, particularly when
coconspirators are engaged to facilitate the transaction. If AML obligations are
extended to cover accounting professionals and forensic investigators, there
could be considerable impact on the profession. If in the future, requirements to
report suspicion of money laundering are added to AML regimes, the forensic
accounting investigator might receive a new duty to report the matter to external
authorities regardless of the preferences of the client. But if forensic accounting
investigators become adversarial whistle-blowers, the willingness of regulated
entities to engage in self-examination aided by knowledgeable specialists to
improve compliance may be substantially curtailed. Further, this could even
have an impact on the free and open access to books and records, which financial
statement auditors expect to receive in the conduct of audits. This is a critical
future issue, requiring dialogue within the profession and within governments.

CHAPTER 27

OTHER DIMENSIONS OF FORENSIC ACCOUNTING

Michael S. Markman

James E. Bucrek

Aron Levko

Stephen P. Lechner

Mark W. Haller

Robert W. Dennis

Mona M. Clayton

J. Christopher Dineen

Gregory Schaffer

Some believe that all forensic accountants perform financial crime investigations. This view is explained largely by the fact that in the post-Enron, post-WorldCom era, forensic accounting has for many become associated solely with fraud detection and investigation. In reality, forensic accountants offer a much wider range of services. Although this book is focused predominantly on the deterrence, detection, investigation, and resolution of corporate fraud, it makes sense to offer here a chapter-length overview of the other dimensions of forensic accounting.

In their day-to-day practice, some forensic accountants focus on commercial disputes in specific industries or practice areas. In commercial disputes, forensic accountants typically play three roles: expert witness, consultant on technical accounting or financial issues, and arbiter of facts. As an arbiter or trier of facts, sometimes referred to as special master, forensic accountants are appointed by the court to act as judge and jury. In their consulting role, forensic accountants may provide discovery assistance, prove business facts, compute damages, and assist counsel in the development of strategy. One should not assume that a forensic accountant involved in commercial dispute projects is qualified to perform financial crime investigations. For an inventory of the skills to look for in selecting a forensic accountant who focuses on financial crime investigation, see Chapter 13. Close attention should be given to the individual's qualifications—including certifications and especially experience—before deciding on the right forensic accountant for the task at hand. Assuming that all forensic accountants are interchangeably capable of executing all forensic accounting investigation engagements would be analogous to assuming that all certified public accountants are qualified to prepare tax returns.

While fraud can be sensational and garner headlines, commercial disputes as well as, say, marital disputes among high-net-worth individuals occur often, may entail billions of dollars, and may involve complex issues requiring expert analysis. The majority of forensic accounting work actually occurs outside of investigations in a wide range of specific practice areas. A glimpse of these areas, suggesting why forensic accounting expertise may be helpful, follows.

◆ CONSTRUCTION

"How does a capital project with a $100-million budget end up costing us $1 billion?" This question is heard all too often from municipal authorities as well as chief executives and board members of corporations, universities, and hospitals. Unfortunately, when the creation, development, and execution of a capital project are not the core activities of an organization, cost overruns, scheduling delays, and quality issues sometimes occur.

Good counsel during the planning stages and an active approach taken toward risk management of capital projects may head off many problems before they even start. Ultimately, however, disputes and litigation are reasonable probabilities because capital projects often are fraught with change, and many changes may have various implications for the cost, scheduling, and quality of the project. In many disputes, the contractor brings a construction claim against others involved in the project who are responsible for the added costs. The list of those against whom claims may be made often includes owners as well as other contactors involved in the project. These added costs may take several forms: additional work, forced delays, acceleration of time frames, disruption of work flow, unabsorbed overhead, and marginal cost of capital are some of the possibilities. Proving the sequence of events, facts, and circumstances that lead to these additional costs may require specialized forensic accounting that blends construction with accounting expertise.

Suppose that in the scope of a project during construction, changes arise that affect the contractor, the construction manager, and several subcontractors. Further assume that each must now revise estimates regarding time, cost, and materials. Owing to the complexity of the work and the interdependency of relationships, the costs associated with unplanned changes may have multifaceted consequences or cumulative effects that may wipe out all of the contractor's anticipated profits for the project. Unfortunately, a simple ticking and tying of invoices may not help the contractor prove its case. Forensic analysis is often helpful in proving a logical connection between changes in the project and the resulting damages. Moreover, those damages should be calculated to the standard of reasonable certainty, which has been well established by legal precedent.

Given the complexity of the accounts and sequence of events, forensic accountants are often found on both sides of such cases. While one set of forensic accountants may calculate damages and provide expert testimony in court or at arbitration on behalf of the plaintiff, others may work for the defendants by analyzing plaintiff's expert's findings and possibly additional issues not considered by plaintiff's expert, ultimately providing expert testimony intended to rebut damage claims with due force and persuasiveness. Defendant's expert may also be asked to support a counterclaim with financial analysis and expert testimony.

♦ ENVIRONMENTAL ISSUES

The shock felt across the United States when the Cuyahoga River caught fire in 1969 or when the entire community alongside Love Canal was evacuated in 1977 because of hazardous chemicals buried there has been converted into reasonably tough federal and state environmental legislation. The Comprehensive Environmental Response, Compensation and Recovery Act (Superfund Act); the Resource Conservation and Recovery Act (Hazardous Waste Act); and to a lesser extent the Clean Air and Clean Water Acts sometimes generate complex disputes in which forensic accounting expertise may be helpful.

Specifically, the cradle-to-grave provisions of the Hazardous Waste Act and the shared responsibility of successive owners in the Superfund Act mean that environmental costs and damages can occur quite suddenly and under the leadership of a management team that was not in place at the time of the event. As a result, companies seeking to limit, reduce, or eliminate the costs of cleanup may engage forensic accountants to help reconstruct and present the operations of the company during the period in question.

Suppose that the successive owner of a property that is now a Superfund site is sued for the cleanup of a certain chemical remaining there. By conducting a forensic investigation that demonstrates that it never bought, sold, made, or took possession of the chemical in question, the defendant in the litigation may be able to eliminate or significantly reduce its liability.

In the environmental arena, forensic accountants may be useful in helping to reduce fines levied by the U.S. Environmental Protection Agency under the so-called economic benefit model. While the government looks at the economic benefits that have accrued to a company for being out of compliance, forensic accountants look at and present historical expenditures that were made to achieve compliance. Such expenditures may be used to offset portions of penalties ultimately payable.

♦ INTELLECTUAL PROPERTY

In 1982 the value of intellectual assets constituted approximately 38 percent of the aggregate market capitalization of the Standard & Poor's 500 Index. By 1992 the figure had grown to 62 percent, and in 2002 the figure climbed to over 80 percent.[1] Those figures demonstrate that intellectual property—consisting of patents, trademarks, copyrights, and trade secrets—represents a significant portion of corporate value. As intellectual property grew in importance, so too did the patent and copyright activity designed to protect such assets. For many industries, patents and copyrights represent an important barrier to entry. Yet even as many companies move to protect their intellectual property, they increasingly engage in technology-sharing agreements as well.

While all of these trends contributed materially to the quality of life and productivity gains, they sometimes create fertile ground for disputes, including litigation. Because intellectual property has unique characteristics, determination of damages may require complex analysis. For instance, in an intellectual property infringement case, there may be claims of lost sales and profits. But infringement tends to have an impact on prices, competition, and quantities in the marketplace. Therefore, forensic accountants may often go beyond lost sales and find the additional losses associated with the effects of price erosion, reduced economies of scale, and the presence of competition, among other factors that might not have otherwise existed. In some disputes, forensic accountants may calculate what a reasonable royalty would have amounted to had such a royalty arrangement been in place. This calculation often considers the large number of terms and conditions that typically appear in complex royalty agreements—for example, exclusive versus nonexclusive—and their economic implications.

Many disputes arise out of licensing agreements. Licensors of intellectual property, disputing the ways in which licensees utilize their rights, may claim damages as well as lost profits. Forensic accountants may be consulted to help establish the damages sustained by the licensor, as well as the lost profits resulting from actions taken by the licensee.

In the area of patents, owners of intellectual property may seek protection not just for specific technologies but also for fundamental processes and algorithms. For example, in 1991 Kodak paid $873 million to Polaroid in a patent rights dispute involving instant cameras and films.[2] The figure that forensic accountants had to establish in this case was the amount of profit that Polaroid had lost.

---

1. These percentages were derived by a PricewaterhouseCoopers team from S&P 500 market capitalization amounts rather than actual valuations of assets represented on public company financial statements, which do not recognize the market value of most types of intellectual property unless and until there is a transaction such as a sale of the company. Needless to say, investors do factor in off-balance-sheet values, such as market capitalization, when making investment decisions. The percentages are calculated as follows: Market Value of Invested Capital < (Share Price × Shares Outstanding) + Long-Term Debt > Less Book Value ÷ Market Value of Invested Capital.

2. Intellectual Property Library, *Polaroid Corp. v. Eastman Kodak Co.* (DC Mass) 17, USPQ2d 1711 *Polaroid Corp. v. Eastman Kodak Co.*, U.S. District Court District of Massachusetts, 17 USPQ2d 1711 (Bureau of National Affairs, Inc., 2003), http://www.patents.com/apl/kodak3.pdf.

Meanwhile, forensic accountants for the defendant were given the task of rebutting the argument of lost profits.

♦ GOVERNMENT CONTRACTING

The federal government is the largest customer in the world and has unparalleled creditworthiness. Given the size of contract awards—frequently in the hundreds of millions and billions of dollars—disputes and litigation often arise in the course of government contracting that require complex financial analysis.

In some instances, the government litigates to recoup its costs. For instance, in one landmark case the termination of a contract for a U.S. Navy attack plane, the A-12, provoked a $2-billion demand from the government for the return of progress payments, which in turn resulted in several countersuits for wrongful termination. In disputes brought by the federal government, forensic accountants typically support counsel for the defense, since the government is supported by expertise from other governmental agencies such as the Defense Contract Audit Agency or Office of the Inspector General. The government will also retain external forensic accountants or experts to assist with litigation.

The vast majority of suits, however, are actions brought against the government by contractors or disputes between parties that are government contractors. Claims in these suits often revolve around two primary issues: costs and performance.

Cost disputes frequently center on allocation between direct and indirect costs and their allowability. When the government disallows costs, plaintiffs may obtain a forensic analysis to help determine the compliance of a cost with a contract or the connection of a cost to work requested.[3]

Performance-based disputes take several forms. For instance, if a government contractor is being terminated, questions may arise as to whether the termination is based on performance or simply for the convenience of the government. Forensic accountants sometimes conduct a financial analysis of costs incurred against established, time-phased budgets to help demonstrate whether performance is adequate or not. When forensic accountants can help plaintiffs establish that termination was for the convenience of the government, the plaintiff will receive better compensation than if allegations of inadequate performance had withstood scrutiny and trial. Finally, disputes related to the costs of performance often occur when the government makes so-called constructive changes to a contract. Forensic accountants assist plaintiffs by analyzing and quantifying the amounts involved.

Corporate forensic investigations can intersect with government contracting when a corporation detects fraudulent activity in the work it is doing for the government. Forensic accountants also provide investigation support for *qui tam*

---

3. The forensic accountant's testimony is not intended to provide insight on how the contract should be interpreted. Forensic accountants do not offer legal opinions. The financial accounting expert provides a financial analysis based on a specific contract interpretation communicated by counsel, who has engaged the expert.

cases brought against a company by a relator and the government, when fraudulent activity is alleged. In such cases, in addition to conducting an investigation to detect the possible existence and extent of the fraud, forensic accounting investigators may assess the financial impact of the fraud so that adequate reparations can be made to the government in an effort to ward off litigation with attendant possible criminal sanctions.

◆ INSURANCE AND BUSINESS INTERRUPTION

Many insurance policies now include a professional fees endorsement. Many believe that the existence of these endorsements represents recognition on the part of insurers that the preparation of a claim in the event of a catastrophe and the resulting interruption of business involve a complex matter that generates a risk for the policyholder. Companies often retain forensic accountants to help them prepare claims, establish damages and losses, and, in some circumstances, rebut the arguments of the insurance company's forensic accountants.

One of the primary challenges often facing the insured is to put accounting information into a format that reflects how insurance policies are written. Specifically, while corporate accounting calculates profit and loss within a production framework, losses from business interruption claims are structured quite differently. In the context of a business interruption claim, loss represents the difference between what happened to a company following a loss versus what would have happened had the loss not occurred. In other words, but for the loss, how would the company have performed? Calculating loss in this fashion is often a multifaceted challenge that, while utilizing accounting, also requires an understanding of factors such as the industry and company personnel. Forensic accountants are often able to reconstruct and estimate how a business might have performed had the insured event not occurred. This is usually compared with postevent performance, recognizing the changes in revenues and expenses that occur as a result of the disaster. Changes in the revenue and expense components can be complex because the operations of the business—from what it sells, to where and how products and services are produced—can be fundamentally changed by the disaster that befell the company.

Forensic accountants may establish and calculate the company's sustained loss and also provide expert-witness services to defend their findings. The challenge is compounded by the activities of similar expertise on the other side of the dispute. Given that reality, forensic accountants acting on behalf of the plaintiff may adopt the pragmatic goal of fighting for the best possible result rather than an overwhelming victory.

◆ MARITAL DISSOLUTION

The incidence of divorce between spouses with substantial wealth often creates several challenges in setting entitlement awards as well as the valuation and division of marital property. For example, when there is a prenuptial agreement, such contracts often specify entitlements based on the living expenses of each spouse. Thus, in a marital dispute, the calculation of the entitlement may rely on estimating these expenses. A complication: the spending patterns established during the marriage often reflect joint expenditures. Forensic accountants may help analyze and separate historical spending to provide a basis for and defense of a proposed entitlement.

Apportionment of marital assets may present a number of challenges, compounded by whether or not the divorce is occurring in a community property state or an equitable distribution state. Questions may arise as to the value of assets that were initially brought into the marriage (premarital assets), their current value, and the portion of the marital estate they now represent. The task of apportionment of assets may lead to the work of tracing assets to determine who acquired them initially and how and of ensuring that all assets are taken into account during the apportionment process. The location of assets not disclosed by a spouse may materially weaken a proposed apportionment or give rise to dispute over a proposed settlement. Forensic accountants may be helpful in bringing important facts to light.

Forensic accountants may also address the value of professional goodwill in cases of marital dissolution in community property states. There is a wide range of valuation techniques for professional goodwill. Establishing a value for this asset—or determining whether it even exists—may have a material impact on the apportionment of marital assets.

◆ SHAREHOLDER LITIGATION

Three federal securities acts create the framework in which interstate securities transactions are regulated. These are the Securities Act of 1933, the Securities Exchange Act of 1934, and the Private Securities Litigation Reform Act of 1995. Together these laws attempt to ensure that the investing public has sufficient information to enter knowledgeably into securities transactions. Although each law defines a different standard of recovery for investors, the three share a common goal: to make the plaintiff whole via reversal of inappropriate transactions or through monetary compensation of losses stemming from the violation or infraction of the law.

In general, the remedy of monetary compensation requires forensic analysis in order to estimate damages. There are several widely accepted techniques for estimating damages. One of the most widely employed is the so-called out-of-pocket measure, which is the difference between the price paid for a security and the actual value at the date of the sale. While this approach is easily understood, its application is often complex. Forensic accountants can estimate the value of the security in question, absent the alleged fraud or misrepresentation that provoked the action to begin with. The process often requires analyses that take into account macroeconomic information as well as industry and company-specific information. A more numerical, statistical approach to valuing securities uses linear regression analysis.

Shareholders sometimes file lawsuits against corporate officers and directors for violation of securities laws in addition to a wide range of other alleged offenses, including breach of fiduciary duty, personal appropriation of corporate opportunities, discrimination, self-dealing, oppression of minority shareholders, and violation of environmental laws. The majority of suits are brought against directors for the first alleged infraction in the preceding list: breach of fiduciary duty. In such suits, forensic accountants may be engaged to evaluate the causes of a business decline and assess the relationship of that decline to a board's decisions and performance.

◆ BUSINESS VALUATION

The concepts and principles of business valuation for litigation purposes are the same as those for business valuations pursuing other purposes such as a buyout, creation of an employee stock option plan, or an equity investment. Business valuation in litigation frequently may occur as a result of marital dissolutions, dissident shareholder disputes, corporate dissolution, or a taxable transaction that is subsequently challenged by the Internal Revenue Service or other taxing authorities.

Forensic accountants engaged to clarify such situations often perform intensive data gathering in terms of the financial, contractual, legal, operational, and historical dimensions of the business under review. That information may be used to develop valuations under a number of generally accepted techniques, including market comparisons, discounted cash flow, net assets, comparable transactions, and comparable sales. Because disputes can arise with shareholders of different classes, the analysis often goes beyond the aggregate determination of value. In many instances, forensic accountants take into account the rights, privileges, and restrictions on various equity securities and assign values to each class.

Forensic accountants sometimes value preferred shares as well as pure equity securities. In such instances, the focus of analysis usually shifts toward a risk-based examination, in which forensic accountants evaluate a company's ability to make preferred-share payouts based on the presence of other fixed-payment obligations and other short- and long-term debt.

◆ BUSINESS COMBINATIONS

Some business combinations provoke disputes related to antitrust laws, while others may generate disputes because of clauses in merger and acquisition contracts and the effects they have on purchase prices. In the former arena, plaintiffs establish harm from the anticompetitive effects of the defendant's antitrust violations. Forensic accountants may be engaged to help plaintiffs prove, and defendants rebut, alleged damages stemming from restraint of trade. Restraint of trade can take numerous forms, including monopolization, exclusive dealing, price discrimination, and mergers that substantially lessen competition, among others. In many cases, success may rest on testimony and analyses by forensic accountants, who may be able to demonstrate lost profits based on a competitive impact analysis, market definition analyses by product and geography, and price elasticity in the marketplace.

Of course, not all business combinations provoke antitrust claims, but merger or acquisition contracts may generate disputes between buyers and the sellers—for example, disputes that arise from irregularities discovered after closing, the application of offsets, notices of objection immediately following closing, interpretations of materiality, and earn outs. Those are just a few of the possible grounds for dispute. Forensic accountants may assist one or both parties in formulating the dispute, discovery, analysis, and calculation of damages. In litigation connected to merger and acquisition activity, there can be a high degree of subjectivity because of the personal involvement by the principals in the transaction. Forensic accountants may be helpful in such situations: they have no emotional involvement in the transaction. By providing objective, unbiased analysis, they may help move disputes toward resolution.

◆ CYBERCRIME

In the current environment, a security breach may more likely refer to the attack and penetration of a computer network than to a masked intruder on the premises after hours. When an electronic breach occurs, security specialists may be retained to determine the point of weakness in a corporation's information systems and to implement remedies that will prevent a comparable breach from occurring in the future. Forensic technologists may be called on to help determine what information or records were compromised and perhaps to look for telltale signs that could aid in identifying the attackers.

Often, however, an attack has consequences that go beyond the immediate need to repair a security breach. In such instances, forensic accountants may be called on to help quantify losses that may include costs to remedy, lost productivity, price erosion, reduction in barriers to entry, and still other factors. Quantifying these losses may also be required in support of criminal or civil litigation. During the course of litigation, forensic accountants may serve as expert witnesses to establish facts and fact patterns associated with a cybercrime. Forensic accountants may also assist in the filing of an insurance claim associated with losses from cybercrime.

When a cybercrime has occurred, forensic accountants may be asked to help support the settlement of claims between a company and its vendors. The existence of outsourced technology services often means that an attack and penetration result in liability for one or more companies providing technology services. Forensic accountants may be able to assist counsel in formulating claims specified by their technology outsourcing agreements. The formulation of such claims is often complicated by the interdependent relationships among technology vendors. As a result, counsel may desire detailed analysis to support claims it is making on vendors.

CHAPTER 28

LOOKING FORWARD: THE FUTURE OF FORENSIC ACCOUNTING INVESTIGATION

Thomas W. Golden

Paul T. Pilkington

The preceding chapters have looked at forensic accounting investigation from a multitude of different perspectives, but one further perspective remains to be explored: the future of the discipline. Compared with the well-defined professions of accounting and auditing, forensic accounting investigation is in its infancy. The largest and most recognized certifying organization in the field, the Association of Certified Fraud Examiners, was founded in Austin, Texas, only in 1988. There could be no clearer sign that the future of the forensic accounting investigation specialty, emerging out of financial auditing and criminology and developing its own repertoire of goals and methods, will be much longer than its past. What can be understood on the basis of conditions and trends today about the further development of this very young branch of accounting?

We propose to approach the intriguing topic of "where-do-we-go-from-here?" in terms of five concerns:

1. The evolution of the discipline itself, including the boundary between financial statement auditing and forensic accounting investigation

2. Education and training for a new generation of forensic accounting investigators

3. The changing regulatory and legislative environments

4. The changing corporate environment, in which the decision to investigate and the process and results of investigation encounter real-world benefits and costs

5. Changes in corporate reporting, especially with respect to nonfinancial operating data (NFOD) that may be subject to some form of assurance or formal review and may be subject to fraudulent manipulation

◆ EVOLVING DISCIPLINE

We believe that the boundary between financial statement auditing and forensic accounting investigation will become more clearly drawn as major practitioners, from the Big Four accounting firms to forensic accounting investigation consultancies, gain more experience. At the time this book went to press, that boundary appeared to be still somewhat fluid in firms that offer both audit services and forensic accounting. Statement on Auditing Standards (SAS) No. 99, *Consideration of Fraud in a Financial Statement Audit,* of the American Institute of Certified Public Accountants (AICPA) has sharpened the focus on professional skepticism by instructing auditors to design and conduct tests for detecting material fraud and to hold periodic team discussions that cover the potential for material fraud. Many of the larger audit firms have instituted increased levels of training in fraud awareness. All of these developments are needed and important, yet throughout this book we have underscored the critical importance of bringing in qualified, specialized forensic accounting investigators when the red flags of possible fraud become evident. In our view, the complexity and breadth of forensic accounting investigation—and the need for experience—make this the appropriate decision. The more thoroughly forensic accounting investigation is understood, the more quickly and prudently policy is likely to be developed in multiservice firms—and in the minds of corporate management, directors, and counsel—as to when it makes sense to engage forensic accounting investigators. Paradoxically, a clearer boundary between financial statement auditing and forensic accounting is likely to be accompanied by greater contact between the two functions—more "touch points," as some people put it. This will not arise in the normal course of auditing but, rather, only when suspicions of fraud arise on the audit.

An interesting parallel to the discipline of forensic accounting investigation can be found in the medical profession. There was a time when the general medical practitioner was the first and last doctor to see a patient. However, as medical science progressed, specialists emerged to diagnose and treat complex ailments that were becoming increasingly well understood. We believe the discipline of forensic accounting investigation will evolve in much the same way—and very rapidly. Just in the past decade—and certainly since Enron and World-Com—there has been greater appreciation of the discipline of forensic accounting investigation. Management and the board better understand the discipline's effectiveness in investigating and resolving allegations of fraud, and independent audit firms have built forensic accounting investigation teams within their organizations to be deployed when the need arises.

Like the movement from the general medical practitioner to the medical specialist, we believe that the next step, over the coming 5 to 10 years, will be forensic accounting investigation subspecialties within the broader discipline. Just as forensic accounting investigation emerged as an independent specialty from two disciplines—financial accounting and criminology—we expect subspecialties to emerge soon within the field itself. They are likely to be industry focused, offering expertise in the business practices that investigators will encounter in such industries as telecommunications and financial services (examples chosen because they are global and complex). However, before this change can occur, the numbers of those specializing in forensic accounting investigation will need to increase drastically from current levels. While there are more than 336,000 certified public accountants (CPAs) in the United States, only about 5 percent carry CFE (certified fraud examiner) certification from the Association of Certified Fraud Examiners. On a global basis, the percentage is even lower when compared with accounting certifications that are comparable to the CPA. With the increasing levels of complexity and integration in the global economy, demand for the specialized insight of forensic accounting investigators will increase, especially if regulatory regimes continue to add requirements.

A third trend is toward greater use of digital tools in aid of forensic accounting investigation. Two factors appear to be driving that trend: (1) increasingly clear technology preferences and strategies among businesses and among regulators that require business data and (2) improvement in the digital tools available to forensic accounting investigators. U.S. regulatory authorities are beginning to standardize around certain systems and to have preferred software. On their side, many companies are becoming increasingly skilled at using their digital networks to reduce costs. They use networks to limit their paper, store records, operate systems of approval, and to do much else. In many enterprise-wide accounting systems, the approval recorded in the system awaits the matching of documents, after which the transaction is automatically approved and moves through the system.

The still-growing role of digital networks has implications for the future of forensic accounting investigation. One of the subspecialties that may well appear is data gathering, which is distinct and separate from data analysis and which may evolve into a commodity-like, standardized service. We believe it is important that the two functions remain combined for the simple reason that data analysis may fall far short of its objective if data is not gathered in a forensic manner. Data gathering is too important a task to outsource to those unfamiliar with forensic accounting investigation. It would be comparable to having the police outsource evidence gathering and opt only to analyze whatever the service provider gathered and dropped off at the police station. Most of us would not think this a good idea. Data gathering is no different.

At present, collecting and interpreting data are closely linked services performed by unified teams of professionals who really understand accounting systems. They typically know where to look, how to find the critical data points in a fraud investigation, and how to interpret what comes to light. Will the increasing capabilities of digital systems drive a wedge between doing and thinking, between data collection and interpretation? We don't think so. Experience indicates that the two capabilities are complementary and equally necessary in corporate investigations. However, the challenge for the provider of these services is to manage a business based on intellectual capital while at the same time offering commodity-like services based on standardization.

◆ NEW TOOLS

There can be no doubt that the electronic tools available to forensic accounting investigators will continue to ramify and improve. As in many other fields, the Internet has created communities of interest at Web sites where participants can share information about new tools and the use of existing tools.

One of the most interesting trends is toward improving on existing software applications by developing proprietary applications of far greater capability than those offered commercially. For example, while powerful data-mining software is commercially available, it may not always be capable of extremely high-volume, data-mining exercises. Forensic accounting investigators involved in such projects may need to ask their technology coworkers to adapt existing programs to meet the demands of such large-scale projects. For projects of average scope, however, commercially available software is virtually certain to keep improving and to be up to the challenge.

◆ EDUCATION AND TRAINING: TO BETTER SUPPORT THE NEW DISCIPLINE

We see signs of a positive trend: in the future, an increasing number of undergraduate and graduate programs are likely to offer courses in forensic accounting investigation. For courses to be more than conceptual overviews, they should be taught by those who have performed hands-on work in actual investigations. This need suggests the value of crossover teaching arrangements that have, in fact, already been piloted with success at a handful of U.S. institutions. Working forensic accounting investigators often prove to be enthusiastically willing to teach, and team teaching with resident academics may be the most effective formula. Even guest appearances by experienced forensic accounting investigators would be gains in the context of ongoing courses on audit methods. Seasoned forensic accounting investigators should find a place in universities.

Firms with forensic accounting investigation capabilities may be persuaded to fund tours of duty for academics to join their forensic accounting investigation teams, so that those individuals can experience the attitudes and methods and the uncertainties and problem solving of the real world of forensic accounting. As well, we would expect—and we certainly hope for—a trend toward investment in education on the part of major firms with forensic accounting investigation capabilities either by their funding of college programs or by their funding of chairs in forensic accounting investigation.

Fraud detection is a continuing concern of regulators and auditors. The cooperation of auditors with forensic accounting investigators is an important element in restoring investor confidence. Education and training need to catch up with the new realism initiated by SAS 99 and the Sarbanes-Oxley Act. We believe this will occur in the next 5 to 10 years.

◆ REGULATION AND ENFORCEMENT

Today's environment in corporate reporting is one of increased transparency. Major U.S. corporate scandals and the 2002 enactment of the Sarbanes-Oxley Act signal what we take to be a prolonged swing toward heightened regulation and enforcement. The 302 and 404 requirements of Sarbanes-Oxley, the definition and enforcement of services prohibited to professional services firms, the reactions of audit committees to those new rules, highly publicized criminal charges against formerly influential executives, investigations and enforcement actions against entire sectors of the financial services industry and world-class financial institutions—all of this and more signal a strong swing of the pendulum toward a risk-averse operating environment for U.S. businesses and for foreign businesses operating in the United States.

Will the trend last forever? Has it become an enduring feature of the U.S. business and economic climate? Even while it has been gaining strength, there have been dissenting voices, not without reasonable points of view. It is all costing too much to no purpose, some say. It is anticompetitive. It is making our capital markets less and less attractive to foreign companies and investors. Material financial statement fraud is estimated to occur in just 2 percent of all U.S. public companies, and in any year typically less than 1 percent of all registrants are accused of making false filings. In light of these statistics, aren't the American public, legislators, and regulators overreacting by treating all companies as if they were about to enter that 2 percent category?

From our perspective, these are all reasonable points, although they too should not be taken too far. While the percentage of wrongdoing is small, the devastating effects of the catastrophic business failures of the past few years should not be minimized. One could argue, for example, that the Federal Aviation Administration imposes excessive scrutiny on the airline industry out of concern for safety. But would any of us be happier with less oversight and a markedly higher crash rate? That is highly unlikely. While it may not be fair to compare loss of wealth to loss of life, both safe aviation and the integrity of public companies are significant matters of public concern, on which the lives and welfare of many millions of people depend. We believe the trend toward risk-averse regulation and aggressive enforcement will continue for at least another five years.

By the fall of 2004, the U.S. Securities and Exchange Commission (SEC) had nearly completed building a much-enlarged staff. The SEC was deliberately hiring very experienced individuals—including partners and directors from major accounting firms. The Public Company Accounting Oversight Board, created by Sarbanes-Oxley and still very new as this book went to press, had not yet fully demonstrated how it would approach its mandate, including enforcement. But overall there could be little doubt that federal agencies charged with safeguarding the integrity of public markets and overseeing independent public accounting services would be more far-reaching and active than at any time past.

Pressure exists on the accounting profession—external auditors, internal auditors, and forensic accounting investigators—to scrutinize accounting policies and practices, and to respond quickly and thoroughly to government inquiries. Regulators have widened their focus on alleged acts of individual wrongdoing. How can or should the regulatory and enforcement environments affect the forensic accounting investigator? From a technical perspective, they have their impact: new regulation is likely to create additional zones of corporate activity in which fraud allegations show up and require investigation. The forensic accounting investigator's advisory role is likely to increase as clients decide on how to respond to new regulation imposed on corporations and on the accounting profession and how to create safeguards and systems to comply with the requirements as economically as possible. The forensic accounting investigator's role is unlikely to decrease. There is a constant need for such expertise and practical capability, and the integrity of public markets relies in part on the readiness of forensic accounting investigators working in concert with auditors, directors, and management to resolve allegations thoroughly and efficiently.

◆ CHANGING CORPORATE ENVIRONMENT

In many cases, managements and boards of directors are becoming much more aware of their obligations, new and long-standing, to deter and combat fraud within their organizations. Many audit committees are listening; they are meeting more frequently and more probingly with auditors, and they are requesting additional investigation of alleged frauds when that seems to be the prudent course. Some audit committees are adopting the loose-thread approach to evidence of possible fraud, which we have recommended in this book: where there are small indicia of fraud—small threads out of place—those audit committees are interested in looking more closely to discover whether something more important and pervasive may be underlying. The professional standards governing the work of those committees now require further inquiry when evidence of possible fraudulent behavior surfaces, even if the amounts are likely to be quantitatively immaterial.[1] The CEO and chief financial officer (CFO) are specifically charged with certifying the financial statements, and they must report to the external auditors and the audit committee any incidence of fraudulent behavior committed by those involved in the internal controls over financial reporting.[2]

Many companies are recognizing the need for codes of conduct and ethics statements that suit their particular industry and circumstances. When there are ethical benchmarks of this kind in place—and training programs to support them—companies can hold their executives and staff to certain standards: "What do you mean, you didn't know that you shouldn't do that? You signed off on the

---

1. American Institute of Certified Public Accountants, Statement on Auditing Standards (SAS) No. 99, *Consideration of Fraud in a Financial Statement Audit* (codified in AICPA Professional Standards—U.S. Auditing Standards—AU § 316), par. 76.
2. See Sarbanes-Oxley Act of 2002, Public Law 107–204, 107th Cong., 2d sess. (January 23, 2002), § 302(a)(5)(B).

code of conduct, and the code is crystal clear in this area." Companies can leverage well-constructed codes of conduct to ensure accountability from the top to the bottom of the organization.

In the coming years, more companies will be clarifying their organizational approach to fraud investigation. Often enough, still today, a business unit in a distant location may prefer to conduct its own investigation of alleged fraud rather than refer the issue to headquarters for advice and counsel. Unfortunately, when distant business units act in this way, they may prevent corporate management and the board from gaining an accurate picture of the problems of geographically remote operations. In the end, putting up a screen around local fraud investigations, so as to avoid criticism or questioning from higher-ups, can work against the larger purposes of the company. The local business unit may assert that it was only trying to do the right thing, but headquarters may have the perception that the unit has something to hide. That is hardly a productive situation for either party. There are signs that companies are becoming aware of this type of problem and addressing it.

Similarly, we see a positive tendency on the part of companies to prepare better in advance through policies and procedures that will address allegations of fraud without delay, should they arise. Companies are learning not to wait until fraud is detected to develop an operating plan. Management and/or the audit committee is more frequently asking itself such questions as, What will we do if we're subject to an investigation by SEC enforcement? and, What will we do if the president of a foreign subsidiary is accused of cooking the books? Management and the board need not adhere in every detail to the crisis management plan thus formulated, if and when a serious fraud allegation crops up, but at least they have a blueprint for response. Companies wholly unprepared for these types of events may become, at least temporarily, ineffective and slapdash in their decisions, with negative consequences both internally and in the public arena.

Thorough planning in advance of an event is becoming more common today, driven by the requirements of Sarbanes-Oxley, by SEC rules, and by evolving professional guidelines for financial statement auditors.

INTERNAL AUDIT

Are there signs of change in the fraud detection capabilities of the internal audit function in U.S. public companies? Some companies' internal audit functions are becoming more capable of fraud detection through training. It is fair to say that internal audit teams in public companies are under pressure to make a solid contribution to procedures that comply with Sarbanes-Oxley Section 404, which requires public companies "to publish information in their annual reports concerning the scope and adequacy of the internal control structure and procedures for financial reporting. This statement shall also assess the effectiveness of such internal controls and procedures." While internal audit units are quickly becoming more skilled at doing process reviews and 404-related work, few of them may be ready at this time to undertake, for example, an investigation of alleged fraud in a workers' compensation fund or suspicious accounting in an overseas subsidiary, to name two types of investigations that can be complex in scope and depth, but the trend is toward increased awareness and clearer recognition of circumstances in which it makes sense to call in forensic accounting investigators.

There are many, fully justified, barriers that prevent internal audit shops from growing their own fraud investigators—for example, staff rotation and the desire to dispel the perception that internal auditors are corporate police. This does not mean that management and the audit committee should not direct internal audit to prepare for the possibility that investigations may be needed. To touch again on the theme of advance preparation, many perspicacious managers and directors are also prearranging with outside accounting firms or other forensic service providers for the timely engagement of forensic accounting investigators. Thoughtful planning will enable a company to properly interview prospective firms and agree on terms and hourly rates ahead of time so that when the need arises, forensic accounting investigators can be deployed immediately. Having these arrangements in place can go a long way toward meeting the challenges of investigation in a timely and effective manner, and time is often of the essence.

CORPORATE JUDGMENT CALLS

We want to call attention to an issue that is more than likely to evolve as companies gain experience under the new fraud-related rules and obligations applicable to management, boards, and auditors. Management and the board face decisions when allegations of fraud are investigated and there appears to be evidence of questionable conduct or outright wrongdoing. In times past, some managements have found themselves weighing their regulatory obligations and personal ethics against their mandate to enhance shareholder value and protect their company's reputation. These companies in the past may have struggled with a decision whether to disclose the conduct that today is made much more easily. Today's environment demands greater transparency and full disclosure.

We believe that the new reality argues toward fuller disclosure and greater transparency despite the potential risks of public disclosure that corporations may fear. Sarbanes-Oxley and other regulation have put a firmer legal framework around greater transparency, and companies are learning—at least from the experience of other companies that get into trouble on issues of fraud—that it can serve long-term shareholder interests to investigate and report.

FORENSIC ACCOUNTING INVESTIGATORS SERVING INDIVIDUAL CORPORATE CLIENTS

Individual corporate leaders are likely to continue to be the targets of investigations by the U.S. Department of Justice (DOJ) and the SEC. The result may be a new deployment of forensic accounting investigation expertise directly in defense of individual executives. As this book went to press, forensic accounting investigators continued to be deployed primarily to investigate allegations within the corporation and alleged irregularities in financial statements. But it seemed clear enough that senior executives and directors under fire might find it useful to turn to forensic accounting investigators to help them sustain the assertion that, given the facts they had at the time, they made reasonable judgments about the issues subject to investigation.

The formal accounting definition of error, in APB 20, reads that you can err in making an estimate if you overlook, misuse, or misinterpret facts available to you at the time. An estimate is basically a decision. Forensic accounting investigators have long looked at estimates, as have auditors, and considered whether the decisions in question were reasonable in light of the portfolio of information available at the time. This long-established element of both forensic accounting investigation and financial statement auditing may become a core defense over the next 5 to 10 years for senior executives who are alleged by the DOJ or SEC to have broken the law.

Because actions against individuals often occur after actions against companies, attorneys defending those individuals and calling in forensic accounting investigators to help them assemble and analyze the facts will often be able to draw on records already established, such as the trial record, discovery record, deposition record, and/or SEC hearing record. It may serve these individuals well to be able to demonstrate that they did not know certain things at the time they reached certain decisions or that someone with the intent to do what they are accused of doing would have had to know certain things, entirely unknown at the time, in order to accomplish the alleged wrongdoing. The forensic accountant's command of investigation and analysis may become a central asset on both sides of these cases.

NONFINANCIAL OPERATING DATA

For the most part, this book addresses the risks to financial statements and their attendant disclosures, but an even greater challenge awaits. Beyond the financial statement numbers lies an entire universe of numbers and assertions disseminated by corporate management that influences investors and lenders alike as they decide how and where to deploy their capital resources. Financial statement numbers are not the only numbers that generate interest in companies. For example, an impressive, publicly stated number of cable subscribers or the dazzling, publicly stated market prospects of a new drug may well attract an investor's gaze more quickly than any balance sheet, income statement, or earnings forecast. While regulators and legislators are quickly implementing rules designed to restore investor confidence over financial reporting, another issue has arisen. Nonfinancial operating data (NFOD) is quickly gaining importance in the investment community, and although many investors and market analysts may not yet realize it, very little if any of this data is audited. True, management bears the responsibility, imposed by regulators, to report NFOD accurately, and the external auditor must read such data, but the external auditor provides no assurance on the accuracy, completeness, and validity of such data. Hence, the concluding topic of this book: NFOD in relation to the work of the forensic accounting investigator. Real challenges lie ahead.

To ensure success, businesses today must carefully manage a complex web of what we call value drivers, many of which can be measured and reported. And, as noted earlier, investors are increasingly looking at indicators other than historical earnings to assess the financial health of a corporation. Value drivers vary from company to company and from industry to industry, but they typically include the ability and commitment of their people to deliver on strategy, the degree to which customers trust their products and services, the competitiveness and reliability of their business models, and their capacity to share knowledge, to learn, and to adapt to changing circumstances. None of these is a financial measure, yet all are increasingly important not only as pieces of internal management information but also as measurable, reportable data. Other nonfinancial performance indicators of growing importance to investors include metrics applicable to innovation, brands, customers, people, supply chain, and reputation—the last one often divided into the triple bottom line measuring the company's environmental, social, and economic impacts.

Looking forward, we expect nonfinancial value drivers to become increasingly accepted and important components of publicly reported corporate information. While financial statements are subject to independent audit, many other disclosures (NFOD) in press releases, management discussion and analysis, and analyst briefings are not currently subject to any independent, external, critical review under recognized standards such as those promulgated by the AICPA—that is, generally accepted auditing standards (GAAS). As financial reporting moves into a new era with increasing reliance on NFOD, we expect that fraudulent reporting of this type of data will periodically require the services of forensic accounting investigators. Just as financial information can be fraudulently manipulated, so too can reported measures of nonfinancial value drivers such as the research and development pipeline at pharmaceutical and technology companies or customer churn rates at telecommunications companies. The vehicle for fraudulent reporting may be earnings statements—or it may be NFOD.

Given the legitimate appetite of the investing public and all stakeholders in public corporations for accurate, comprehensive, and timely financial and performance information and given the power of information technology to capture and format that information, we believe that there will be a need for skilled forensic accounting investigators to address concerns over possibly fraudulent NFOD, when those concerns arise.

RESPONSIBILITY FOR DISCLOSURE AND VALIDATION OF NFOD

The incentives for management to misstate NFOD are little different from the incentives to misstate financial statements—for example, to present the company's activity in the best light, to cover up underperformance, or to disguise a significant, perhaps fraudulent misapplication of resources. The SEC monitors disclosures of such information and brings enforcement action when it deems them to be false. By way of example, the 1933 Act places ultimate responsibility for all disclosures on the directors, who must exercise due care in making disclosures. The precise means by which "due care" should be exercised are not explicit.

While the financial statements are subject to full independent audit, many other disclosures in press releases, in management discussion and analysis, and in analyst briefings are not currently subject to any independent, external, critical review under recognized standards such as those promulgated by the AICPA—that is, GAAS.

The following is an excerpt from an administrative proceeding[3] of the SEC against Web Works Marketing.com, Inc.: "The Web Works home page described Web Works as the 'Internet's Fastest Growing Company.' Another section of the web site stated that 'we feel that Web Works ... will grow to become one of the great Internet based businesses of all time.' In several other places on the Web Works website, Web Works was described as a 'rapidly growing business.' The home page also included a graph which indicated that Web Works had approximately 10,000–12,000 satisfied customers. There was no basis in fact for these statements. As of early May 1999, Web Works had only 35 customers and the company had only received $26 in gross revenues. The statements that Web Works was 'the Internet's fastest growing company' was no more than a 'slogan' that was intended to 'build excitement' but which was not factually accurate."[4]

OTHER LEGAL AND STOCK EXCHANGE REQUIREMENTS

Directors' responsibilities for disclosure of material nonfinancial information are set out in legislation in the United States. For example, the U.S. Exchange Act prohibits a person from making an untrue statement of material fact or from omitting to state a material fact necessary in order to make statements not misleading. The SEC considers a fact to be material if there is a substantial likelihood that a reasonable investor would consider the information to be important. This standard includes both financial and nonfinancial information, and the SEC has prominently cited misstatements of nonfinancial information in recent proceedings against a number of well-recognized corporations. Similarly, Section 302 of the Sarbanes-Oxley Act stipulates that senior officers must certify that required material nonfinancial information, as well as financial information, is included in an issuer's quarterly and annual reports and that all such disclosures be governed by adequate internal controls.

Neither of these acts addresses independent assurance of nonfinancial information. Although it may be significant to stakeholders, it is not subject to the same requirement for independent assurance as financial information is. A recent Sarbanes-Oxley roundtable discussion—which included accounting firms and major corporations such as PespiCo, Philip Morris, Colgate Palmolive, and Newscorp—noted that some organizations have developed compliance committees and compliance programs specifically to address nonfinancial disclosures.

---

3. *In the Matter of Web Works Marketing.com, Inc. and Trace D. Cornell, Respondents,* § III. C., "Misrepresentations and Omissions of Material Fact," par. 1, http://www.sec.gov/litigation/admin/34-41632.htm.

4. Id., par. 2.

When rigorous scrutiny is applied to NFOD across all industry sectors, one result will be increased demand for forensic accounting investigators to investigate allegations of fraud specifically with reference to NFOD assertions.

◆ FUTURE OF FORENSIC ACCOUNTING INVESTIGATION: INCREASINGLY GLOBAL

Chapter 25 made clear that international forensic accounting investigation assignments can be among the most challenging, intricate, and interesting. The trend is toward more of them. As this book goes to press, complex global investigations are under way concerning several global companies and certain of their executives, accused of massive accounting and other types of fraud. Rule-making bodies in the European Union are tending to converge toward regulation in the spirit of Sarbanes-Oxley and SEC final rules. Even without the benefit of a crystal ball, it is evident that well-trained and experienced forensic accounting investigators from many parts of the world should find that their skills are needed and valued both at home and abroad.

The field of forensic accounting investigation is advancing in the United States and worldwide, with more sophisticated challenges to address and resolve and with more sophisticated tools at hand. The field will be, and deserves to be, a gathering place for outstanding auditors who have looked at the conceptual and practical challenges of forensic accounting investigation and looked also at the personal demands of the field, which are not small. In light of everything those auditors have seen, they recognize a strong affinity, and they seek the training and experience that will make them capable practitioners. They belong to the profession. The profession will repay them many times over, not only with sound careers but also with the knowledge that they are making a unique contribution to the integrity and strength of markets on which all economies depend.

However, this book is only secondarily an undeclared recruiting poster for the next generation of forensic accounting investigators. Primarily, it is just what the title proposes: a guide offering insight into the nuances of forensic accounting investigation and the underpinnings of corporate financial fraud. We trust that its many chapters and all but innumerable concepts, facts, and cases have served well to give you an appreciation for the field and that they will continue to do so in years to come. Critical to a company's success in addressing the very real threat of financial fraud are knowledgeable auditors, directors, and management working effectively with skilled and experienced forensic accounting investigators.

INDEX